IMPORTANT:

HERE IS YOUR REGISTRATION CODE TO ACCESS
YOUR PREMIUM McGRAW-HILL ONLINE RESOURCES

MCGRAW-HILL
ONLINE RESOURCES

D0083780

For key premium online resources you need THIS CODE to gain access. Once entered, you will be able to use the Web resources for the length of your course.

If your course is using **WebCT** or **Blackboard**, you'll be able to use this code to access the McGraw-Hill content within your instructor's online course.

Access is provided if you have purchased a new book. If the registration code is missing from this book, the registration screen on our Website, and within your WebCT or Blackboard course, will tell you how to obtain your new code.

Registering for McGraw-Hill Online Resources

TO gain access to your McGraw-Hill web resources simply follow the steps below:

1. USE YOUR WEB BROWSER TO GO TO: **register.dushkin.com**

2. CLICK ON **FIRST TIME USER**.

3. ENTER THE REGISTRATION CODE* PRINTED ON THE TEAR-OFF BOOKMARK ON THE RIGHT.

4. AFTER YOU HAVE ENTERED YOUR REGISTRATION CODE, CLICK **REGISTER**.

5. FOLLOW THE INSTRUCTIONS TO SET-UP YOUR PERSONAL UserID AND PASSWORD.

6. WRITE YOUR UserID AND PASSWORD DOWN FOR FUTURE REFERENCE. KEEP IT IN A SAFE PLACE.

TO GAIN ACCESS to the McGraw-Hill content in your instructor's **WebCT** or **Blackboard** course simply log in to the course with the UserID and Password provided by your instructor. Enter the registration code exactly as it appears in the box to the right when prompted by the system. You will only need to use the code the first time you click on McGraw-Hill content.

THank you, and welcome to your McGraw-Hill online Resources!

REGISTRATION CODE

denouement-20228271

* YOUR REGISTRATION CODE CAN BE USED ONLY ONCE TO ESTABLISH ACCESS. IT IS NOT TRANSFERABLE.

0-07-292166-8 T/A EDGINTON: LEISURE PROGRAMMING, 4/E

Leisure Programming

Service-Centered and Benefits Approach

Leisure Programming

Service-Centered and Benefits Approach

FOURTH EDITION

CHRISTOPHER R. EDGINTON
University of Northern Iowa

SUSAN R. HUDSON
University of Northern Iowa

RODNEY B. DIESER
University of Northern Iowa

SUSAN R. EDGINTON
University of Northern Iowa

Mc
Graw
Hill

Boston   Burr Ridge, IL   Dubuque, IA   Madison, WI   New York   San Francisco   St. Louis
Bangkok   Bogotá   Caracas   Kuala Lumpur   Lisbon   London   Madrid   Mexico City
Milan   Montreal   New Delhi   Santiago   Seoul   Singapore   Sydney   Taipei   Toronto

Higher Education

LEISURE PROGRAMMING: SERVICE-CENTERED AND BENEFITS APPROACH, THIRD
EDITION

Published by McGraw-Hill, a business unit of The McGraw-Hill Companies, Inc., 1221 Avenue of the Americas, New York, NY
10020. Copyright © 2004, 1998 by The McGraw-Hill Companies, Inc. All rights reserved. Previous editions © 1980 by Saunders
College/Holt, Reinhart and Winston, © 1989, 1992 by Wm. C. Brown Communications, Inc. No part of this publication may
be reproduced or distributed in any form or by any means, or stored in a database or retrieval system, without the prior
written consent of The McGraw-Hill Companies, Inc., including, but not limited to, in any network or other electronic storage
or transmission, or broadcast for distance learning.

Some ancillaries, including electronic and print components, may not be available to customers outside the United States.

This book is printed on acid-free paper.

1 2 3 4 5 6 7 8 9 0 DOC/DOC 0 9 8 7 6 5 4 3

ISBN 0-07-235389-9

Vice president and editor-in-chief: *Thalia Dorwick*
Publisher: *Jane E. Karpacz*
Executive editor: *Vicki Malinee*
Developmental editor: *Gary O'Brien*
Senior marketing manager: *Pamela S. Cooper*
Senior project manager: *Marilyn Rothenberger*
Production supervisor: *Enboge Chong*
Media technology producer: *Lance Gerhart*
Senior designer: *Violeta Diaz*
Cover designer: *Yvo Riezebos*
Cover image: © *PhotoDisc/Getty Images*
Art editor: *Jen DeVere*
Photo researcher: *Natalia Peschiera*
Senior supplement producer: *David A. Welsh*
Compositor: Carlisle Communications, Ltd.
Typeface: 10/12 New Baskerville
Printer: R.R. Donnelley/Crawfordsville, IN

Library of Congress Cataloging-in-Publication Data

Leisure programming: service-centered and benefits approach/ Christopher R. Edginton
... [et al.].— 4th ed.
    p. cm.
  Includes bibliographical references (p.) and index.
  ISBN 0-07-235389-9 (alk. paper)
   1. Recreation leadership. 2. Recreation—Management. 3. Leisure—Management. I.
Edginton, Christopher R.

GV181.43.L45 2004
796'.06'9—dc21

                                                    2003051410

www.mhhe.com

This book is dedicated in loving memory of
Gloria A. Hudson

Contents

PREFACE

The centrality of leisure programming to the mission of any leisure service organization cannot be disputed. Creating opportunities for individuals to experience leisure is the major focus of our profession. Knowledge of the elements involved in leisure programming is pivotal to our professional endeavors. The ability to plan, organize, implement, and evaluate leisure programs and services is key to the success of any leisure professional. In a sense, the creation of the opportunity to experience leisure is our reason for being and the major focal point of our profession.

Leisure Programming, fourth edition, provides a comprehensive overview of the elements found in the planning, organization, implementation, and evaluation of leisure programs and services. Effectively integrating theory with numerous examples and illustrations of best professional practice, this text is designed to assist both students and professionals in the process of leisure program development. The text is conveniently organized to guide individuals through the program planning process and is designed to provide a sequential exposure to various leisure program elements. Organized in fifteen chapters, the text provides a strong philosophical and theoretical foundation, yet at the same time effectively engages contemporary strategies used in the delivery of leisure services in public, private, and nonprofit organizations.

Promoting Quality and Excellence. As in previous editions, we have strongly emphasized the importance of creating quality services. We believe that our professional efforts must be tied to quality and excellence. Any leisure service organization or professional wedded to quality will outperform those focused elsewhere. In addition, we strongly believe that all leisure service organizations must focus their efforts on customers' needs, interests, wants, and desires. An organization with a strong focus on service committed to ensuring that the customers' needs have primacy—will be successful. We have emphasized the importance of such a focus, as well as the importance of establishing a benefits orientation to programming. Also, we believe that leisure programmers must manage to exceed expectations.

A Focus on Diversity and Inclusion. New to this fourth edition is a complementary focus on diversity and inclusion as essential features in the establishment of leisure programs. Not only are leisure service organizations mandated by law to ensure that participants have access to program and service offerings, but leisure service providers have a moral obligation to ensure that programs reach diverse individual interests and promote cultural, racial, and ethnic well-being. Leisure programming competencies that include diversity and cultural issues ensure that leisure programmers can meet the needs of people in a pluralistic society.

In this Edition. The fourth edition of *Leisure Programming* provides a thorough and complete perspective and review of theoretical concepts and elements of professional practice employed in the delivery of leisure services. The text includes many new features, including updated information regarding contemporary program practices and offerings throughout North America. As mentioned, a special emphasis has been placed on incorporating significant information regarding diversity and inclusion throughout the text. We have provided numerous examples in support of both the new and old information presented. In addition, chapters relating to leisure in contemporary society and leisure wellness and education have been substantially rewritten and updated with new references, citations, and examples. Further, the chapter on future trends and professional issues presents new directions influencing professional practice and directions.

Highlights of newly incorporated concepts, trends, and professional practices for each chapter are as follows:

CHAPTER ONE

- Comprehensive discussion related to how leisure experiences provide numerous benefits to individuals, groups, communities, and cultures
- Numerous examples of the how different leisure experiences provide multiple benefits
- Incorporation of Driver and Burns's (1999) conceptualization of the endless benefits of leisure
- Discussion of the negative consequences of leisure (opposed to the benefits) if such opportunities are designed poorly or if leisure programmers lack professional competencies
- Expanded discussion of how the tenets of building a philosophy of programming are related to providing leisure experiences or opportunities for people with disabilities and people from diverse cultures
- Example of how the Western DuPage Special Recreation Association, a cooperative extension of nine recreation and park districts in the western suburbs of Chicago, provides leisure programming for people with disabilities
- Twenty-four new references, twenty of which were written within the last five years

CHAPTER TWO

- Comprehensive discussion on building collaborative, cooperative partnerships with reference to twenty-first-century community learning center programs
- Reference to best professional practices in building quality programs utilizing the concept of QUEST from the City of Virginia Beach (Virginia) Parks and Recreation Commission
- Numerous examples and illustrations of contemporary programs and services from community park and recreation departments, nonprofit youth service organizations, and therapeutic recreation settings
- Distillation of program theories into a condensed, readable format; the new table condenses eight pages of discussion into two usable pages of information

CHAPTER THREE

- Comprehensive historical review of leadership theories from the 1930s to the present with emphasis on new collaborative models for the twenty-first century

- Extensive revision of information concerning leadership studies and models
- Up-to-date information about ethical practices for the leisure professional

CHAPTER FOUR

- Updated information concerning demographic characteristics of consumers
- Expansion of diversity categories
- New illustrations to reflect changing leisure behavior patterns

CHAPTER FIVE

- More effective integration of text materials with examples from professional practice
- Expansion of sources that can be tapped to indicate community needs
- Presentation of practical methods to garner community consensus on controversial decision-making issues

CHAPTER SIX

- Revision of values and mission section to reflect all sectors of the leisure service delivery system
- Inclusion of benefits-based programming process to illustrate the flow of goals and objectives to outcomes
- Discussion of the advantages and challenges of implementing benefits-based programming

CHAPTER SEVEN

- Thorough discussion on providing *customized, individualized* leisure services
- Inclusion of information on changes in how society's institutions impact on time factors associated with leisure programs
- Discussion of an integrated service strategy for delivering services by the city of Edmonton (Alberta, Canada)
- Discussion of the importance of programming to exceed expectations; the discussion is tied to the work of the University of Northern Iowa's *Camp Adventure*™ *Youth Services* program
- Inclusion of a program planning worksheet/checklist; such documents are useful in helping to ensure that steps in program planning are addressed in a systematic fashion

CHAPTER EIGHT

- New information and statistics concerning Americans' involvement in the arts
- Discussion of youth art programming provided by the Austin (Texas) Parks and Recreation Department
- Discussion of the Cincinnati (Ohio) Recreation Commission's unique youth literary program, "Mind Matters"
- Example of an innovative approach to offering aquatic services known as the "FISH" philosophy, which focuses on promoting customer service
- Expanded discussion supporting the establishment of wellness programs with information from the U.S. Surgeon General

- Updated list of the myriad of services offered under the umbrella of wellness
- New information from the literature concerning the extensive benefits of volunteering
- Discussion of the emerging area of youth programming, including a suggested program framework
- Discussion of the growth area of family programming, including a suggested program framework
- Many new examples and illustrations from professional practice, including examples from commercial leisure service organizations, national associations, park and recreation departments, and nonprofit organizations

CHAPTER NINE

- Examples of fee-based services and rental of equipment, areas, and facilities supporting the Commission for Accreditation of Park and Recreation Agency's standards
- Discussion of extreme sports
- Expanded definition of special events

CHAPTER TEN

- Expanded discussion of personal selling with a focus on the importance of friendship building; including additional information regarding personal selling and the pursuit of multiple objectives such as quantitative aspects of personal selling
- Discussion of the possibilities of rapid transmission of images through electronic means in support of program promotion, training, and implementation
- Discussion of desktop publishing with a focus on the importance of customizing promotional activities
- New information regarding computer-generated presentations
- Inclusion of a host of new examples and illustrations from commercial leisure service organizations, park and recreation departments, and nonprofit organizations

CHAPTER ELEVEN

- Up-to-date examples of putting budgeting theories into practice
- Comprehensive and contemporary citations concerning pricing categories used in leisure services
- Practical examples of budget worksheets used in leisure services
- New illustrations and examples to explain the budgeting process

CHAPTER TWELVE

- Discussion of service quality management and the link between service quality and the customer/leader interface
- Integration of an organizational empowerment model that can be implemented in leisure service delivery systems
- Overview of different communication styles among people from diverse ethnic cultures
- Revised and updated discussion of flow theory and management of the autotelic experience
- Detailed accounting of needed information on registration forms
- Many updated examples of leisure service delivery procedures and elements
- Twenty-six new references—seventeen of which were written within the last five years

CHAPTER THIRTEEN

- Discussion of the differences between quantitative and qualitative methods of collecting evaluative data
- Updated discussion of quality assurance and the link between quality assurance and evaluation
- Updated examples of evaluation techniques, such as qualitative evaluation forms, use of experts in consultative evaluation, and case studies
- New section that provides an overview of data collection methods for evaluation

CHAPTER FOURTEEN

- Discussion and case study of how leisure education is a function of leisure programming
- Articulation between leisure barriers and leisure constraints
- Extensive revision of contemporary leisure education models
- Discussion of two cross-cultural leisure education models
- Discussion of how leisure interpretive services can be a form of informal leisure education
- Over fifty new references—thirty-three of which were written within the last five years

CHAPTER FIFTEEN

- Synthesis of future trends from numerous leisure educators and program entities
- Case study of futuristic leisure programming from the city of Edmonton (Alberta)
- Discussion of how the terrorist attacks in the United States on September 11, 2001 will continue to influence leisure programming
- Expanded discussion of practical examples of future leisure programming

ACKNOWLEDGEMENTS

As is the case with any writing endeavor grounded in professional practice, writing this text required the assistance of individuals currently engaged in the practice of the profession to ensure that the materials are relevant, up-to-date, and reflect contemporary applications. Numerous individuals contributed to this endeavor and we would like to extend our appreciation and recognize them for their contributions. In particular, we would like to thank Dr. Ng Kinsun, Executive Secretary, Recreation & Sports and Camp Services, Chinese YMCA of Hong Kong; Rand Hubbell, Marketing Coordinator, Parks and Recreation Department, Maricopa County, Arizona; Nancy Woods, Parks and Recreation Department, Santa Barbara, California; Matthew R. Corso, Manager of Programs, Northern Suburban Special Recreation Association, Northbrook, Illinois; Genie Zakrzewski, Director of Parks and Recreation, St. Louis County Parks, Missouri; Stephanni J. Cohen, Creative Director & Marketing Coordinator, Cincinnati Recreation Commission, Ohio; Sara Hensley, Director, Department of Parks and Recreation, Virginia Beach, Virginia; Charles F. Connington, Superintendent of Recreation and Parks, Parks Board and Recreation Commission, Town of Clarkstown, New York; Nanci Williams, ORLOFF/Williams & Company, San Jose, California; Metha D. Sizemore, Outreach

Coordinator, Parks, Recreation and Neighborhood Services, City of San Jose, California; Kathleen Merner, Executive Director, Macon County Conservation District, Decatur, Illinois; Rebecca McAsey, Communications Department, Joliet Park District, Illinois; Joseph Wynns, Director, Indy Parks and Recreation, Indianapolis, Indiana; Andrew S. Kimmel, Director of Environmental Education & Public Affairs, Lake County Forest Preserves, Libertyville, Illinois; Peg Wilson, Superintendent of Recreation, Western DuPage Special Recreation Association, Illinois; Charles A. Malta, Parks and Recreation Manager, Parks and Recreation Department, City of Wooster, Ohio; Tina Burton, Community Information Specialist, Department of Parks, Recreation and Marines, City of Long Beach California; Jody L. Stowers, Director, Department of Parks and Recreation, City of Westerville, Ohio; Vicky Galea, Administrative Assistant, Department of Parks and Recreation, City of San Carlos, California; Michelle Howell, Project Coordinator, Forest to Ocean: A Voyage of Discovery, Halifax, Nova Scotia, Canada; Noreen Gupill; Project Coordinator, Forest to Ocean: A Voyage of Discovery, Halifax, Nova Scotia, Canada; Jill Brewer, Director, Department of Recreation, City of St. John's, Newfoundland, Canada; Nancy P. Pavona, Resource Development Supervisor, Department of Parks and Recreation. City of Virginia Beach, Virginia Beach, Virginia; Winnie Li, Manager, Promotion and Communications, Economic Development, Culture and Tourism, Toronto Ontario, Canada; Claire Tucker-Reid, General Manager, Parks and Recreation, Toronto, Ontario, Canada; Jill Brewer, Director of the Department of Recreation, City of St. John's, Newfoundland, Canada; Rhonda Booth & the Queen Elizabeth II Health Science Center Recreation Therapy Staff, Halifax, Nova Scotia, Canada; and Mike Blanchard, Proprietor, The Core, Cedar Falls, Iowa.

A number of leisure service organizations also provided us with materials. We would like to thank them for their contributions to this effort. Many of their promotional materials are included in the textbook, including examples of brochures, fliers, posters, and other promotional items. Some of the organizations that we would like to recognize include:

Chinese YMCA of Hong Kong
Parks and Recreation Department, Maricopa County, Arizona
Parks and Recreation Department, Santa Barbara, California
Northern Suburban Special Recreation Association, Northbrook, Illinois
Parks and Recreation, St. Louis County Parks, Missouri
Cincinnati Recreation Commission, Ohio
Parks and Recreation Department, City of Virginia Beach, Virginia;
Parks Board and Recreation Commission, Town of Clarkstown, New York
Macon County Conservation District, Decatur, Illinois
Joliet Park District, Illinois;
Indy Parks and Recreation, Indianapolis, Indiana
Lake County Forest Preserves, Libertyville, Illinois
Western DuPage Special Recreation Association, Illinois
YMCA of the USA, Chicago, Illinois
Parks and Recreation Department, Columbus, Ohio
Health Canada, Ottawa, Ontario, Canada
Parks and Community Services Department, Ft. Worth, Texas

Community Services, Edmonton Alberta, Canada

Recreation and Parks Department, Largo, Florida

Edmonton Arts Council, Edmonton Alberta, Canada

Tourism and Visitors Bureau, Cedar Falls, Iowa

Wellness and Recreation Services, University of Northern Iowa, Cedar Falls, Iowa

Iowa Northland Regional Council of Governments, Iowa

Community Recreation, Sport and Culture Needs Study, Prince George, British Columbia, Canada

Department of Parks and Recreation, Virginia Beach, Virginia

Department of Parks and Recreation, Wichita, Kansas

Park and Recreation Department, Dallas, Texas

Parks and Recreation Department, Waverly, Iowa

National Intramural-Recreational Sports Association

Department of Conventions, Art and Entertainment, City of San Jose, California

YMCA, Edmonton Alberta, Canada

Parks and Recreation Department, Norwalk, Iowa

Camp Adventure™ *Youth Services,* University of Northern Iowa, Cedar Falls, Iowa

'CHIPS' Black Hawk Gymnastics, Waterloo, Iowa

Hardin Area Chamber of Commerce & Agriculture, Hardin, Montana

North American Museum of Ancient Life, Lehi, Utah

National Park Service, US Department of the Interior, Washington, D.C.

The Church of Jesus Christ of Latter Day Saints, Salt Lake City, Utah

Parks and Recreation Department, City of Wooster, Ohio

The Department of Parks and Recreation, Calgary, Alberta, Canada

Parks, Recreation and Library Department, City of Phoenix, Arizona

Travel Montana, Helena, Montana

Convention and Visitors Bureau, Waterloo, Iowa

Leisure Services Commission, Iowa

Black Hawk County Conservation, Iowa

Lehi Swimming Pool

Girl Scouts of the U.S.A.–Mile Hi Council, Denver, Colorado

Disney Sports Attractions, Lake Buena Vista, Florida

Custard Battlefield Museum, Garryowen, Montana

Cultural and Racial Diversity Task Force, City of Calgary, Alberta, Canada

SIK-OOH-KOTOKI Friendship Society, Lethbridge, Alberta, Canada

Leisure Services, The City of Lethbridge, Alberta, Canada

Therapeutic Recreation Services, Trinity Regional Hospital, Ft. Dodge, Iowa

Helen Schuler Coulee Centre, Lethbridge, Alberta, Canada

Lethbridge Public Library, Lethbridge, Alberta, Canada

YMCA of Lethbridge, Alberta, Canada

Museum of the Plains Indian, Browning, Montana

The Glacier Institute, Glacier National Park, Montana

Glacier National Park, West Glacier, Montana

Canadian Red Cross Society, Ottawa, Ontario, Canada

Boy Scouts of America, Irving, Texas

Department of Recreation, Lehi, Utah

Parks, Recreation and Neighborhood Services, City of San Jose, California

Missouri Department of Natural Resources

Department of Natural Resources, State of Iowa

Mormon Frontier Foundation, Independence, Missouri

City of Independence, Missouri
Northfield Rotary Club, Northfield, Minnesota
Tourism and Visitors Bureau, Cedar Falls, Iowa
Historical Society, Cedar Falls, Iowa
Truman Presidential Museum & Library, Independence, Missouri
The Access Fund, Boulder, Colorado
Worlds of Fun, Kansas City, Missouri
Parks & Recreation, City of Westerville, Ohio
Department of Recreation, City of St. John's, Newfoundland, Canada
Parks & Recreation Department, City of San Carlos, California
HRM Parks & Recreation Services, Halifax, Canada
Rockingstone Heights School, Halifax, Nova Scotia, Canada
Dalhousie University, Halifax, Nova Scotia, Canada
The Nova Scotia Sea School, Halifax, Nova Scotia, Canada
Sports and Recreation Commission, Halifax, Nova Scotia, Canada
Portland Parks and Recreation
Department of Parks & Recreation, Des Moines, Iowa
Department of Parks, Recreation and Marine, City of Long Beach, California
Edmonton Federation Community Leagues, Edmonton, Alberta, Canada
YWCA Black Hawk County, Waterloo, Iowa
Carnaval de Québec, Quebec City, Quebec, Canada
Indian Nature Center, Department of Parks, Cedar Rapids, Iowa
YMCA, Ankeny, Iowa
Wilderness Inquiry, Minneapolis, Minnesota
Club Car Incorporated, Augusta, Georgia
Santa Clara County Parks, California
Economic Development, Culture and Tourism, Toronto, Ontario, Canada
National Recreation and Parks Association, Arlington, Virginia
National Program for Playground Safety, University of Northern Iowa, Cedar Falls, Iowa
American Association Retired Persons, Washington, D.C.
National Sporting Goods Association, Mt. Prospect, Illinois
The City of Edmonton Community Services, Edmonton, Alberta, Canada
Morale Welfare Recreation Department, U.S. Marine Corps, Okinawa, Japan
Madison School District, Madison, Wisconsin
Champaign Park District, Champaign, Illinois
Parks and Recreation, City of Dallas, Texas
BCI Burke, Fond du Lac, Wisconsin

At the University of Northern Iowa, Lynda Moore assisted with the production aspects of this book, including providing clerical assistance, organization, and grammatical clarity. Lynda operates with quiet patience, yet great enthusiasm for this and many similar projects. Without her assistance, this book would not have been possible. At McGraw-Hill, we appreciate the efforts of our Freelance Developmental Editor, Gary J. O'Brien. Gary assisted us by providing relevant information and establishing deadlines. We would also like to express our appreciation to Vicki Malinee, Executive Editor; Pamela S. Cooper, Senior Marketing Manager; and Marilyn Rothenberger, Senior Project Manager, all of the McGraw-Hill Higher Education group.

The authors would also like to thank several of our colleagues who provided a review and critique of the previous edition of the book. Their comments proved to be insightful, enabling the authors to improve, enhance, and upgrade information presented in a meaningful fashion. We would like to thank the following individuals for their time and effort: Clinton D. Longacre, Emporia State University; Daniel C. Gibble, University of Illinois; Tonia Van Staveren, Eastern Connecticut State University; Fred Green, Newberry College.

Family members and others are always instrumental in providing support for endeavors such as this writing project. For their support and encouragement, we would like to express our appreciation to Susan Edginton, Carole and Tom Flack, David and Jennifer Edginton, as well as our grandchildren Hanna Michelle Flack and Jacob (Jake) Jerod Edginton. The Edginton clan have been great contributors to many writing efforts over the years. Susan, Carole, and David now provide their professional expertise and knowledge to these projects, as well as their encouragement. Hanna and Jake provide inspiration and hope for the future. In addition, we would like to thank Dr. Donna Thompson and Dr. Sarah Rich for their friendship and continued interest in our professional activities. We would like to thank the Dieser family—in particular, Ricki, Chayce, Jonas, and Zachary for their time, support and encouragement in this project. In addition, we would like to thank the faculty and students of the Division of Leisure, Youth and Human Services, School of Health, Physical Education and Leisure Services at the University of Northern Iowa. Our colleagues and students have provided a rich environment that encourages intellectual curiosity, while at the same time, provides us with space to pursue our scholarly activities. Dr. Sam Lankford, Dr. Joe Wilson, Dr. Allison Stringer, Dr. Kathy Scholl, Dr. Betty van der Smissen, Dr. Doug Magnuson, Gordon Mack, and Christopher Kowalski—all have provided support to our endeavors and have helped us create a rich academic environment. In addition, we appreciate the support provided by the staff of the National Program for Playground Safety and *Camp Adventure™ Youth Services*.

This book is dedicated in loving memory of Gloria A. Hudson. Gloria Hudson, caring mother of Dr. Susan Hudson, had an unmatched zest for life. Her influence was widely felt. She was a dynamic, cheerful, enthusiastic cheerleader in our work environment. At Dr. Hudson's side, Gloria made her presence by her participation in our activities as a participant, observer, and sometimes, even organizer of our efforts a joy. She was the "queen of leisure programming." The events she organized and implemented reflected the best that we could ask for from any professional leisure programmer. Although she was only 5 feet tall, her influence was bigger than life. The fact that she was a family member and mother figure to all of us made her involvement even more special. We will all miss Gloria Hudson—she was a special person!

Leisure in Contemporary Society

LEARNING OBJECTIVES

1. To help the reader develop an understanding and awareness of the *role of leisure in contemporary society.*
2. To help the reader understand the basic *concepts associated with leisure, recreation, and play.*
3. To provide information useful in developing a *philosophy of leisure programming.*
4. To help the reader understand the *relationship between leisure services and the benefits sought by customers.*
5. To help develop an *awareness of the leisure experience as a service.*

INTRODUCTION

Leisure is a powerful force influencing life in contemporary society. Woven into the fabric of our culture, leisure concerns are reflected in our personal lives and in the political, social, commercial, and religious institutions that shape our lives. We seek leisure as a way of enriching, enhancing, and nourishing our lives. Leisure provides opportunities for relaxation, reflection, renewal, release, and restoration, and it serves to promote the growth, development, and general well-being of individuals. As Edginton et al. have written (1995: xi):

> Leisure is one of life's greatest gifts—an important dimension influencing the quality of an individual's life. Finding satisfaction within one's leisure experiences promotes a greater sense of well-being and increases one's sense of self-worth. . . . For society as a whole, leisure provides an ideal medium for the transmission of historical, social, and cultural values that promote desired norms, social orientations, and customs.

Leisure is a powerful force because of the multiple benefits it provides for individuals, groups, communities, and cultures. To illustrate, consider a quick case study of the Carnaval de Québec held in Québec City. Since 1955, the Québec Winter Carnival has been the world's largest winter celebration and the third-largest carnival festival after those in Rio and New Orleans (the carnival's main site welcomes close to 1 million participants each year). From a historical and cultural perspective, the first benefit of this leisure festival is that participants learn about historical and traditional life of Old Québec by participating in activities of the first winter carnival of 1894. Figure 1.1 presents a contemporary snow sculpture that simulates snow sculpture activities of the late 1890s. A second benefit from the Carnaval de Québec (2001–2002) is its economic impact: (1) $36 million in direct economic spin-offs; (2) $42.5 million in spending by visitors; and (3) the creation of 1,250 jobs per year. Beyond these cultural and economic benefits, the Québec winter carnival provides additional personal and social benefits, such as personal achievement, education, freedom, and community bonding.

Another example of the influential benefits of recreation and leisure is that of the Active Living Program that the Department of Recreation in the City of St. John's, Newfoundland (Canada) has developed. Although the Active Living Program has many dimensions (after-school programs, community development, fitness programs, special events), one program area focuses specifically on developing active and healthy children. The program challenges families to be active by participating in Active Living's leisure education program (Chapter 14 discusses leisure education programming). In particular, the leisure education program highlights how often children watch T.V. (26 hours per week) and provides basic guidelines on how an inactive family can become an active family involved in recreational activities (e.g., pick a time of day to fit in active living and stick to it). In essence, this leisure education program can provide three paramount benefits: healthy children, healthy parents, and healthy families. Figure 1.2, which is from the *Your Guide to Active Living* booklet (2002) (City of St. John's, Department of Recreation) provides a broad overview of this program.

Although research and scholarship have articulated the beneficial outcomes of recreation and leisure experiences (see Table 1.3), such benefits are readily apparent in everyday living. For example, the newspaper article shown in Figure 1.3 further augments the significant benefits of recreation and leisure services in contemporary life. This article (Fuson, 2002) highlights how a group of volunteers in Varina, Iowa developed the Freedom Quilt project after the World Trade Center buildings were attacked in New York City on September 11, 2001. On the first-year anniversary of the terrorist attacks, the Freedom Quilt project had given away 2,800 quilts to families who lost loved ones on that dreadful day. This leisure group is still planning on making 4,000 to 5,000 more quilts to donate

Figure 1.1   A Snow Sculpture from the Carnaval de Quebec, Québec City, Québec.

to families of the September 11th attack. The Freedom Quilt project has helped individuals deal with the terrorist attacks and has contributed to community unity.

Professionals involved in the creation and distribution of leisure programs have as their focus the planning, organization, and delivery of leisure experiences. *Leisure service programming* is the creation of opportunities for leisure experiences with consequent benefits. The programming of leisure opportunities provides a means

for individuals to seek novelty, variety, pleasure, challenge, renewal, and growth in their lives through participation in leisure experiences. The work of the leisure programmer is one of understanding individual needs, wants, and desires in order to create opportunities for individuals to take part in meaningful, creative, and ethically sound leisure experiences.

The cultural diversity, gender and ethnic differences, generational value orientations, varying family structures, income stratification,

CHILDREN & PHYSICAL ACTIVITY

Even though children are naturally inclined to move and play, many things in today's world stop them from being physically active. Television, video games, computers, cars, safety concerns and busy schedules have all contributed to the decline in physical activity among our children.

A recent study in the Canadian Medical Association Journal showed that from 1981 to 1996 the prevalence of overweight children increased by 92% in boys and by 57% in girls. Children are moving less and less and this is bad for their health.

- As many as 65% of all Newfoundlanders are insufficiently active for optimal health benefits.
- Children spend too much time being inactive. They watch television on average of 26 hours per week and spend approximately 30 hours per week sitting in school.
- Youth who are not physically active are more likely to smoke, drink, have poor eating habits and low self-esteem.
- Inactive children often become inactive adults and are more likely to develop heart and bone disease, diabetes and some forms of cancer.

BE AN ACTIVE LIVING FAMILY!

Children need opportunities to be active both inside and outdoors. As adults, we need to encourage our kids to be active. Listed below are some suggestions for becoming an Active Living Family.

Plan Ahead
Being inactive is a bad habit that requires a bit of planning to break! Pick a time of day or week to fit some active living in and stick to it! For example pack a brown bag supper once a week and walk to a park or a family member or a friend's house for supper!

Experiment and find a comfortable routine.
Don't have time — think again! The average high school graduate will spend 15,000 to 18,000 hours watching TV! Watch less, move more!
Take it slow at first.
Remember changes in lifestyle take time and a shift in attitude. Plan to do one short activity per week. Concentrate on participating regularly and enjoying yourself. Don't rush or force things. For example, if you are out for a family walk and your kids want to spend more time collecting rocks than walking-don't worry. You are making lifestyle changes and the more you and your kids enjoy Active Living the more likely you are to stick with it!

Monitor your progress & focus on your successes
It is natural to miss sessions from time to time. Work or other family responsibilities may get in the way and if you are really tired it is sometimes better to take a day off. Don't focus on your missed sessions but rather plan for your next success.
Keeping track of your successes can be as simple as making a note on your family calendar. Take a camera along and snap a photo every time your family does something active together. Once the photos are developed you can have a great time putting together an Active Living Family Scrap Book!

A family that plays together stays together!

LEISURE OPPORTUNITIES AND THE QUALITY OF THE ENVIRONMENT BUILD COMMUNITY PRIDE

Figure 1.2   Active Living Program, Department of Recreation, City of St. John's, Newfoundland.

Quilter *should* stop but doesn't

"Happiness is a journey, not a destination. Work like you don't need money. Love like you're never been hurt and dance like no one's watching"

For a family: Nielsen works on a quilt to give to the family of firefighter Gregory Saucedo. "I believe they are feeling our love when they wrap themselves around it," Nielsen says. "That's the biggest reward I get."

GREGORY THOMAS SAUCEDO
DOB 12-16-89
LADDER CO 5

Of course she should stop.

How much more can Betty Nielsen do?

She already has given away 2,800 quilts to family members who lost loved ones in the Sept. 11 terrorist attack. An additional 500 remain stored or stacked on chairs in the living room of her farm in rural Pocahontas County, awaiting distribution.

A year ago, Nielsen had made exactly two quilts herself; now she and her friends have made 351. A year ago, she had never been to New York City; now she has been there twice, both times to deliver quilts to family members. A year ago, the prospect of public speaking terrified her; now she regularly tells groups about her work.

Nielsen, 49, has driven herself to the point of exhaustion. She has lost 20 pounds. She no longer takes shopping trips to the mall.

"There's more to life than material things," she says. "Life is short."

Every day, you see, somebody else learns about the Freedom Quilt project, and how Nielsen and a group of volunteers gathered in a church basement in tiny Varina, Ia., population 90, and stitched quilts together because they thought they might comfort grieving relatives.

Those relatives send Nielsen their requests via e-mail, telephone calls and letters. The stories are heartbreaking. A new one arrives every day:

I lost my son and only child . . .

I'm still waiting for God to show me the way through the pain . . .

I told my Mom there was a possibility she could get a quilt, and she cried and said she would sleep with it in her arms . . .

So Betty Nielsen keeps at it. She asks for more donations. She believes she will need 4,700 more quilts to give one to every relative who wants one.

The mail brings other letters, too.

"How can I begin to thank you?" writes a Rhode Island mother whose daughter was killed. "You have no idea what this means to us."

Of course Nielsen should stop.

"But God always comes back and tells me to continue," she says.

—*Ken Fuson*

"How can I begin to thank you? You have no idea what this means to us."

— a Rhode Island mother whose daughter was killed

■ More submissions from Register readers can be found at: **DesMoinesRegister.com**

Figure 1.3 Newspaper Article (*Des Moines Register,* September 11, 2002) Regarding the Freedom Quilt Project in Varina, Iowa.

and technological advances that exist in North American society all provide dynamic and diverse challenges to leisure programmers. The task of leisure programmers is to meet the challenge of providing high-quality, high-impact services that are responsive to the needs of individuals. People today want and demand quality and value in service delivery. The leisure service programmer must be responsive in providing leisure experiences that are relevant, meaningful, ethical, and that maintain a high degree of excellence.

CONCEPTS OF LEISURE, RECREATION, AND PLAY

The definitions, interpretations, and "common-sense language" associated with leisure, recreation, and play are as value-laden and personal as emotional commitments, moral behavior, and

**EXHIBIT 1.1
THE HEALING INFLUENCE OF RECREATION:
Elizabeth Smart and the Smart family**

In the early morning hours of June 5, 2002 Elizabeth Smart was abducted from her bedroom in Salt Lake City. Nine months later, Elizabeth Smart was miraculously found in Sandy, Utah. Soon after her return, recreation and leisure activity was used to (1) help Elizabeth Smart and the Smart family heal and transition back to their everyday life, and (2) facilitate a community celebration. The use of recreation as a healing process is captured well in the following quotation from the Salt Lake Tribune newspaper (March 14, 2003): "After spending nine months in the mountains and the desert, on the streets of Salt Lake City, San Diego and who knows where else, Elizabeth Smart eased into her first 24 hours back home doing the things she always has. She fooled around on her harp, missing a few notes along the way. She watched her favorite movie. She tussled with her brothers and sisters. And she slept in her own bed." Elizabeth Smart also commented that she wanted to go horseback riding. A few days after Elizabeth Smart returned, a massive community celebration welcoming Elizabeth Smart home and thanking the vigilant community members was held in Liberty Park with numerous recreational activities, such as live bands, food, and fireworks.

spiritual beliefs. Often the terms *leisure, recreation,* and *play* are used interchangeably, but in fact are not synonymous. A number of sources provide definitions of these terms. A basic understanding of these concepts can be useful in developing a personal and professional philosophy for programming.

What Is Leisure?

Leisure is a difficult term to precisely define. It means different things to different people. However, central to most definitions of leisure is the notion of *freedom.* Leisure suggests freedom to pursue individual interests. Leisure is derived from the Latin *licere,* which means "to be free." From this word came the French word *loisir,* which means "free time." The Greeks used the word *scole* or *skole* to define "leisure." This word led to the Latin word *scola* and the English word *school.* Thus, it could be implied that for the Greeks, a close relationship existed between leisure and intellectual, physical, and spiritual development.

Today, we usually define leisure from seven primary orientations—as *free time;* as an *activity;* as a *state of mind;* as a *symbol of social class;* as *action;* as an *end in itself* (antiutilitarian); and *holistically.*

1. *Free Time*—Time can be divided into existence, subsistence, and discretionary time. Leisure can be viewed as an unobligated block of time—discretionary or free time—when we are free to do what we choose.
2. *Activity*—Leisure can be defined as the activities in which one participates during free time; for example, running, reading, volunteering, or swimming.
3. *State of Mind*—Leisure is a style of behavior or an attitude that can occur in any activity. The emphasis is focused on one's psychological mind-set or condition.
4. *Symbol of Social Class*—Leisure is defined by the desire to demonstrate one's ability to be at leisure as opposed to labor and to consume leisure goods and products.
5. *Leisure as Action*—Kelly (1996) suggests that leisure can be viewed as action that includes elements of time, activity, attitude, or state of mind. As he notes, leisure involves some implied action with direction. It also includes some element of self-determination.
6. *Antiutilitarian*—Leisure has also been defined as an end in itself, serving no instrumental value. Kelly (1996), building on the work of Murphy (1975), suggests that leisure is "an end in itself, not secondary to work, as self-expression and as fulfilling satisfaction."
7. *Holistic*—Leisure is a combination of some of the previously mentioned definitions of leisure, with particular emphasis on the individual's perceived freedom in relation to the activity and the role of leisure in helping the individual achieve self-actualization. In this model, everything has potential for leisure.

Brightbill (1960), Kaplan (1975), Dumazedier (1974), Nash (1960), Murphy (1974), Grey (1972), Butler (1976), Edginton et al. (1995), Kelly (1996), and Russell (1996) all provide insights on how leisure can be viewed. In defining leisure, Brightbill has examined leisure in relation to time, work, play, and recreation. He contends that leisure, in its relation to time, "is a block of unoccupied time, spare time, or free time when we are free to rest or do what we choose." Russell also suggests that leisure may be viewed as free time. She writes that leisure is "considered leftover time apart from that time a person is obligated to work" (p. 34).

Time can be divided into three segments: existence—the things we must do biologically to stay alive; subsistence—the things we must do to make a living (through work) or to prepare to make a living (through school); and discretionary time—the time that can be used according to one's own judgment. Though these types of time are used in very different ways, they are interrelated. Each segment of time is highly flexible, and each can be increased or decreased depending on individual circumstances. Included in the definition of leisure as time are the concepts of *true leisure* and *enforced leisure*. True leisure is internally chosen whereas enforced leisure is externally imposed on the individual.

Defining leisure in relation to the concept of work may appear to dichotomize work time and leisure time. This is not necessarily the case. Work can be a time for personal involvement, creativity, purposefulness, and usefulness. The use of time for amusement, entertainment, participation, and creativity is often called "recreation." Traditionally, society has suggested that recreation takes place during what we call "leisure time," and therefore it is closely associated with the concept of leisure.

Kelly (1996: 19), discussing leisure as an activity, suggests that it includes "games, sports, culture, social interaction, and some activity that looks like work but is not." According to Kelly, herein lies the paradox of defining leisure as an activity. Some activities look like work, some activities look like leisure. Obviously it depends on the context. The participant's perception and motivation must be considered. Interestingly, most leisure program classifications are built on the view of leisure as an activity. In this context, the work of the leisure programmer is one of organizing activities, events, and other services that provide opportunities for leisure experiences.

Kaplan has described several traditional concepts of leisure that he says are basic to an understanding of the subject (1975). The concept that Kaplan calls the "humanistic" model describes leisure as an end in itself, a state of being, or a positive condition of human beings. The "therapeutic" model, he suggests, shows leisure as a means, an instrument, or a control. In this way, leisure can be instrumental as a therapy, as a social control, and perhaps as a status symbol. The "quantitative" model describes leisure as being the time left over when the work that is necessary for maintaining life is finished. This concept appears to be the most widely referenced and utilized. The "institutional" concept distinguishes leisure from other social values and behavior patterns such as religious, educational, or political involvement and commitment. The "epistomologic" concept relates activities of leisure to aesthetic and analytic expressions of understanding of the world in which we live. The "sociologic" concept has as elements of the definition of leisure the view that leisure is an antithesis to work and a voluntary activity—including a range of possibilities from highly creative tasks to total withdrawal from involvement. From the sociologic view, "nothing is definable as leisure per se and almost anything is definable as leisure, given a synthesis of elements" (Kaplan 1975: 19).

Another often-cited leisure theorist is Joffre Dumazedier, who has suggested four broad definitions of leisure based on contemporary sociology. His first definition proposes that leisure is a style of behavior. As a behavior, leisure can occur in any activity—work, study, play—and any activity can become leisure. This concept has a psychological basis and refers to the attitude of some individuals rather than to the common behavior of all people. Leisure in this context does not define a specific sphere of activities and does not denote a measure of time. Dumazedier's second definition views leisure specifically in relation to work, suggesting that leisure should be equated with non-work. This view ignores other kinds of commitments and obligations that take place within a structure of time, such as family responsibilities. Dumazedier offers yet another definition of leisure that covers the sociospiritual and sociopsychological obligations that influence the individual. This concept would seem to embrace heterogeneous realities—those of individual rights and institutional duties. Control by religious institutions over free time has been diminished—perhaps freeing time for individually chosen activities for pleasure, possibly hedonism (Dumazedier, 1974: 37). Sociopolitical activities may provide the individual satisfaction through participation, but they are the "democratic duty" of the individual. Dumazedier's preferred definition is that leisure is a concept of time that is oriented toward a person's "self-fulfillment as an ultimate end." This concept of time evolution is not determined by the individual but is a product of economic and social evolution, with the individual retaining the right to dispose of it as he or she chooses.

Murphy has discussed leisure in relation to the two concepts of work and time (1974: 6). He suggests that leisure can be seen within the constructs of discretionary time, as a social instrument, in the classical tradition, as antiutilitarian (an antithesis to work), and as a holistic approach. These conceptual descriptions are not drastically different from those suggested by Kaplan.

Nash (1960: 89) viewed the use of leisure within specific activities on four levels: passive, emotional, active, and creative involvement. He attaches values to the kind of involvement and use of leisure time as the levels move from the bottom to the top of his pyramid configuration. Those involvements referred to at the base of his pyramid of leisure use are essentially negative in value and deemed undesirable.

Edginton et al. (1995: 7) offer a comprehensive view of leisure, suggesting that it is a "multidimensional construct in which one is relatively free from constraints, has a feeling of positive affect, is motivated by internal forces, and has a sense of perceived freedom." These authors tie leisure to the concept of life satisfaction and suggest that leisure may promote a sense of well-being, happiness, or quality of life.

The Conditions of the Leisure Experience

To understand leisure, it is important to try to define and measure conditions of the leisure experience. Some of the critical questions to be asked are: How do we measure leisure? Can it be measured? How can we determine if one is at leisure?

Social psychologists who study the interactions of the individual have indicated that several criteria can be used to define and measure the leisure experience. Four basic criteria are central to the leisure experience: *perceived freedom, intrinsic motivation, perceived competence,* and *positive affect.*

1. *Perceived Freedom*—Perceived freedom occurs when a person does not feel forced or constrained to participate in an experience and does not feel inhibited or limited by the environment. Perceived freedom is measured by the concept of locus of control. The greater the internal locus of control, the greater the perception that the individual has influence or is responsible for personal actions or behavior.

2. *Intrinsic Motivation*—Involvement in leisure pursuits that are initiated by the individual for personal feelings of satisfaction, enjoyment, and gratification are said to be intrinsically motivated. Extrinsically initiated participation reduces perceived freedom.

3. *Perceived Competence*—A person must perceive him- or herself to possess a skill or a degree of competence to engage in a leisure activity. Whether this perception exists in reality or not is irrelevant. It is the person's perception of his or her competence that is critical.

4. *Positive Affect*—Another criterion related to leisure is that of positive affect. Rossman (1988: 5) and Edgington et al. (1995: 4) refer to positive affect as the need for or extent to which individuals have the ability to exert influence within the context of the leisure experience. Rossman suggests that leisure programs unfold, and as they unfold, individuals need to have the ability to influence the animation of the experience.

In a sense, the work of the leisure programmer should be focused on creating the conditions that enable individuals to successfully experience leisure. It is interesting to note that most leisure experiences occur in "casual" settings. Samdahl (1992) has conducted research that indicates that for most of us, leisure "just occurs" and is not often characterized by special activities or events. We give great attention to planning, organizing, and implementing leisure activities but, as Samdahl suggests, these might be "relatively rare and exotic leisure occasions." Perhaps the challenge in programming is to focus not only on the creation of the rare and exotic, but also facilitating and influencing the casual and "just occurring" life events that have potential for leisure. This can be done by recognizing that the conditions of a leisure experience—perceived freedom, intrinsic motivation, perceived competence, and positive affect—can be facilitated by programmers in a variety of life spaces.

Elements in Creating the Leisure Experience

Creating a leisure experience essentially involves arranging or assisting the placement of an individual in a *social, physical,* or *natural environment.* This might involve the functions of planning and organizing, assembling of materials and supplies, arranging for the use of facilities, providing for leadership, and other actions that lead to the creation of opportunities for leisure.

1. *Social Environment*—The creation of the social environment might involve the planning and implementation of such activities as special events, festivals, and so on, that result in benefits such as aesthetic awareness, fantasy, fun, enjoyment, excitement, and social contact.
2. *Physical Environment*—Constructed facilities might include golf courses, swimming pools, fitness centers, tennis courts, parks, and other areas. Participation in these types of facilities offers the individual a sense of status and opportunities for physical conditioning and skill acquisition.
3. *Natural Environment*—There are many natural areas suited to outdoor recreation—ocean beaches, mountains, rivers, and so on. Participants can experience feelings of awe, beauty, spiritual awareness, challenge, and solitude in the natural environment.

Figure 1.4 illustrates the relationship among various environments that can be created by the leisure programmer and some of the potential outcomes or benefits from each type of environment. The topic of benefits will be discussed in depth in the What Do People Seek from Leisure? section later in this chapter. Although Figure 1.4 is a simplistic portrayal of the environments in which the programmer creates and distributes services, it does reflect the concept that programming involves the organization and manipulation (to be viewed in a positive sense) of different elements to produce leisure experiences of value and benefit to participants.

What Is Recreation?

Traditionally, the term *recreation* has been thought of as a process that "restores or recreates" the individual. It stems from the Latin word *recreatio,* which means "to refresh." Thus, the historic approach in defining recreation has been to consider it as an activity that renews the individual for work. This approach to defining recreation has several limitations, one of which is the fact that many individuals do not view recreation as an element related to work or used to enhance an individual's job performance.

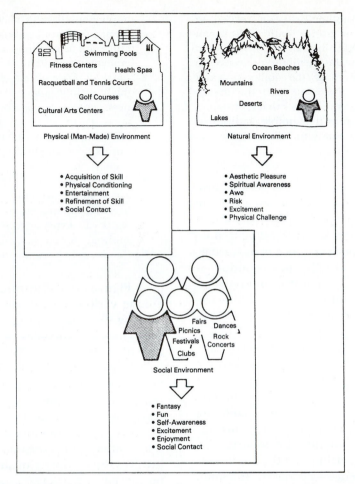

Figure 1.4 Leisure Environments. (From Bullaro, J. J., and C. R. Edginton. 1986. *Commercial Leisure Services.* New York: Macmillan.)

Most definitions of recreation focus on it as a form of activity. Neumeyer (1958: 261) suggest that recreation involves:

Any activity pursued during leisure, either individual or collective, that is free and pleasureful, having its own immediate appeal, not impelled by a delayed reward beyond itself or by any immediate necessity.

Hutchinson (1949: 2), while corroborating the activity approach, introduces an additional element of social acceptance:

Recreation is a worthwhile, socially accepted leisure experience that provides immediate and inherent satisfaction to the individual who voluntarily participates in an activity.

Kraus (1971: 261) presents several other definitions promulgated over the past years, including the following:

1. Recreation is widely regarded as activity (including physical, mental, social, or emotional involvement), in contrast to sheer idleness or complete rest.

2. Recreation can include an extremely wide range of activities such as sports, games, crafts, performing arts, arts, music, dramatics, travel, hobbies, and social activities. These activities can be engaged in briefly or in a sustained way, for single episodes or throughout one's lifetime.
3. The choice of activity or involvement is completely voluntary and not due to outside pressures.
4. Recreation is prompted by internal motivation and the desire for achieving personal satisfaction, rather than by "ulterior purpose" or other extrinsic goals or rewards.
5. Recreation is heavily dependent on a state of mind or attitude; it is not so much the activity one pursues as it is the reason for doing it and the way the individual feels about it, that makes an activity recreational.
6. Recreation has potential desirable outcomes; though the primary motivation for participation might be personal enjoyment, it can result in intellectual, physical, and social growth. This is not to say that recreation is automatically desirable; it might consist of activities that are dangerous, undesirable, or degenerative to the personality. However, when engaged in as part of a program of community recreation services, it is assumed that recreation is designed to provide constructive activity.

Thus, as one can see, recreation tends to be defined as purposeful, wholesome activity. Recreation, from a contemporary standpoint, is viewed as assisting individuals to have positive leisure experiences that help renew their spirit, restore their energy, and rejuvenate them as individuals. Recreation also is often linked with specific types of activities, such as games, arts, crafts, outdoor recreation, and others. It is assumed that people participating in such activities are "recreating."

What Is Play?

Play is viewed, generally speaking, as a positive form of human behavior. Many definitions of play have been offered during the last 100 years. There are no definitive concepts that are univer-

sally accepted. Kraus (1971), writing in *Recreation and Leisure in Modern Society,* has suggested the following definitions for play:

1. Play is a form of behavior that is generally regarded as not being instrumental in purpose.
2. Play is often carried out in the spirit of pleasure and creative expression.
3. Play can be aimless, disorganized, and casual, or highly structured or complex.
4. Play is commonly thought of as activity engaged in by children, but adults also play.
5. Play stems from an instinctive drive, although much play behavior is culturally learned.
6. Play is regarded as voluntary, pleasurable, and nonserious, although it can involve risk and intense commitment.
7. Play appears to be found in all cultures.
8. Play is linked to important social functions such as law, religion, warfare, art, and commerce.

DEVELOPING A PHILOSOPHY OF PROGRAMMING

Understanding various definitions of leisure, recreation, and play can provide a basis for a philosophy of leisure programming. A philosophy asks us what we value and what we believe in. We can develop a philosophy of leisure programming with the following questions in mind: What promise does leisure hold for people? Is it a gift to be enjoyed, resulting in happiness? Should leisure programs be accessible to all? Should the leisure experience result in specific ends or should it be unrestrained? These are questions to ponder in developing a philosophy of leisure programming.

Edginton et al. (1995: 100) note that the foundation of any organization is its philosophy. A philosophy of programming is useful from a number of perspectives; it helps leisure programmers find meaning as well as focus in their efforts. For a leisure service organization, a philosophy is useful in establishing direction as well as determining the methods and procedures to be employed in planning, organizing, and implementing leisure programs and services. A philosophy helps an organization define its relationship with its stakeholders, that is, customers, employees, the community, and other individuals, institutions, and agencies.

On what is a philosophy of programming built? It starts with the acknowledgment of a basic set of beliefs and values. These beliefs are shaped into tenets, which guide the development of a philosophy. In turn, the adoption of a set of tenets will influence the operational methods selected by the professional to create and distribute services. Table 1.1 lists a set of tenets that guide the professional in the formulation of a philosophical basis for programming. These principles highlight that leisure programmers must include leisure experiences for all people, including people with disabilities. In addition, leisure programmers should have a firm understanding of the Americans with Disabilities Act (ADA). Table 1.2 highlights key aspects of the ADA.

In regard to the first programming tenet (every customer has a right to pursue recreation and leisure in a manner that relates to individuals), many recreation and leisure organizations are providing inclusive programs to help people with disabilities experience leisure. For example, the Western DuPage Special Recreation Association (WDSRA), a cooperative extension of nine park districts in the western suburbs of Chicago, provides recreational opportunities for individuals with special needs via the following seven steps:

1. The person with special needs registers for a park district program of his or her choice.
2. On the registration form, the person with disabilities explains his or her special needs and suggests accommodations.
3. The participant then contacts the Manager of Inclusion at WDSRA.
4. The Manager of Inclusion, in cooperation with family members (if appropriate), discusses the type of inclusion support needed and makes necessary accommodations.
5. The participant starts the inclusive program with the necessary accommodations in place.

TABLE 1.1   Tenets for Building a Philosophy of Programming

1. Every customer has the right to pursue recreation and leisure in a manner that relates to individual needs.
2. The programmer should have an understanding of the wants, needs, desires, and expectations that the individual has in relation to the recreation and leisure experience and organization.
3. The programmer should provide programs that appeal to a full spectrum of potential customer groups.
4. Leisure is freedom—freedom from the bondage of time and physical toil and freedom to explore and express oneself.
5. Every individual must be viewed as having an equal opportunity to pursue and fulfill a leisure lifestyle.
6. Inherent in the leisure experience is the "pursuit of happiness"—the seeking of a sense of joy, wonder, accomplishment, and creativity.
7. The program should afford every customer a quality leisure environment that is safe, accessible, affordable, and pleasing.
8. Customers in recreation and leisure must be viewed in a holistic sense—not as a commodity to be quantified.
9. Every customer has the right to be treated in a dignified manner, with full respect for his or her heritage, age, sex, religion, condition of life, and ability.

TABLE 1.2   Key Information Regarding the Americans with Disabilities Act (ADA)

1. Passed as law on July 26, 1990 (Public Law 101-336).
2. Provides civil rights for people with disabilities.
3. Recognizes the rights of people with disabilities to equal access to all public services and accommodations, including recreation and leisure facilities (e.g., community pools, commercial resorts, parks).
4. Public organizations must provide reasonable accommodations (e.g., modifications, adjustments) that will enable a person with a disability to participate in a function or activity.
5. Most complaints about ADA violations are filed with the U.S. Department of Justice Civil Rights Division.

From: U.S. Department of Justice (2002). *Enforcing the ADA: A status report from the Department of Justice.* Washington, D.C.: Author.

6. An inclusion staff member periodically observes the program to provide support to the recreation participant.
7. Communication continues between the Manager of Inclusion, the Park District staff, and the person with special needs (and family, if appropriate) through a cooperative process.

The Department of Parks and Recreation in Virginia Beach, Virginia also provides inclusive programs so that people with disabilities can experience the benefits of leisure. Figure 1.5 provides an outline of this program.

These tenets for building a philosophy of programming underscore that leisure professionals must embrace diversity and have a relevant understanding of cross-cultural issues (e.g., every customer has the right to be treated in a dignified manner, with full respect for his or her heritage, age, sex, religion, condition of life, and ability). According to Allison (2000), *diversity* refers to variety and differences and consists of core and secondary dimensions. Core dimensions are powerful reflections of identity that are impossible or difficult to change. Examples of core dimensions are gender, race/ethnicity, and mental/physical abilities. Secondary dimensions interact with one's core dimensions, but are more mutable and variable over the life span. Examples of secondary dimensions include religion, education level, and geographic location. Understanding diversity, an important aspect of leisure programming, is exemplified in the following quotation by DeGraaf, Jordan, and DeGraaf (1999):

> . . .Recreation programmers must search to find ways to accommodate participants of a variety of abilities and varied backgrounds and beliefs. This includes such actions as hiring a diverse staff that represents people of various ethnic backgrounds in marketing materials; confronting participants and coworkers when they tell an ethnic joke; scheduling programs at times and locations that are accessible to a variety of constituents; and other such actions which protect the rights of all participants for equal access and participation in leisure programs (p. 70).

To this end, leisure programmers need to understand how people from diverse cultures (e.g., American Indians, Asian Americans) experience leisure so they can design culturally appropriate strategies for leisure experiences.

WHAT DO PEOPLE SEEK FROM LEISURE?

What do people seek from their leisure? What do they value and seek as benefits from the leisure experience? According to Driver and Peterson (1986), it is important to clarify succinctly what is meant by "values and benefits." These authors note that values and benefits refer to preferred conditions. They state that "by benefit is meant an improved condition or desired change of state" (p. 1). A value, on the other hand, is much more difficult to define. Values can be thought of as preferences or ideals that people have toward a particular idea, custom, object, or thing. In other words, values are ideals that people hold as being desirable.

Do people value leisure in North American society? Do they seek leisure? A long-standing goal of humankind has been the pursuit of happiness, freedom, and enjoyment of life. Early philosophers such as Aristotle, Cicero, and Seneca all espoused the importance of the pursuit of happiness. Aristotle, in particular, wrote that happiness was the most desirable state of life. Discussing Aristotle, Simpson (1989: 4) writes that the ultimate goal in life "for which all other ends were means . . . was happiness." Simpson goes on to note that, in defining leisure, Aristotle maintained that "the freedom from having to be occupied, was the necessary condition or activity for happiness" (p. 5).

Sylvester (1987: 184) has written that "included among the great ideas affecting the fabric of human existence are such notions as love, beauty, justice, goodness, freedom, and leisure." Thus, one can see that leisure, in the broadest possible context, is sought as vigorously as the other great ideals or values of humankind. Sylvester notes that "leisure is a creation of the human intellect, an idea that gives meaning to

Is an inclusive recreation environment the right choice for me?

Observe the program first-hand and ask yourself the following questions:

Am I interested in the program?

Am I comfortable and able to function appropriately (with or without assistance) in an inclusive environment?

Do I meet the minimum program requirements?

Does my current day (class or work) prepare me for an inclusive recreation environment?

What are minimum requirements for successful inclusion?

The same minimum requirements that apply to a person without a disability also apply to a person with a disability. These include:

- *Meeting age and registration requirements of the program*
- *Following the rules of conduct (with or without reasonable accommodation)*
- *Voluntary participation: recreation programs are voluntary in nature; participation will be encouraged and aided, but not forced*
- *Level of participation: with or without reasonable accommodations, participating in scheduled activities for at least 75% of the time*
- *Ability to use a consistent form of communication to indicate basic needs and follow simple directions (communication board, sign language, interpreter, writing, verbal, gestures, computer system, etc.)*
- *Ability to tolerate and function, with assistance, as a member of a larger*

social group (10 or more people) depending on the program

What is the inclusion process?

If an accommodation is necessary, you are asked to fill out the *Inclusion, Accommodation & Special Needs* form that is in the back of the Guide or on the website. This will be sent to one of the Department's Inclusion Specialists.

The Inclusion Specialist will design an accommodation plan that will aid you in successfully participating in the program.

What are examples of reasonable accommodations available to promote successful participation in a program?

- Adaptive equipment
- Interpreters
- Program adaptations
- Partial participation
- Inclusion Support Staff
- Ongoing in-service training for all staff
- Assistance with health services that do not require medical training
- Accessible transportation (when transportation is provided as part of the activity or program)

What is not part of Inclusion Support Services?

Inclusion does not provide the following:

- *A separate area or alternate activities for a significant portion (more than 25%) of the scheduled program*
- *Exemption from the rules and regulations that have been established for the safety of all program participants and staff (with or without reasonable accommodations)*
- *Guaranteed assignment, hiring or selection of a specific staff member*

- *Individualized therapy within a program*
- *Personal custom devices*

What are the other choices available for individuals with disabilities or life-altering challenges?

The Virginia Beach Department of Parks and Recreation offers recreation programs and services that cater to specific needs of an individual.

Therapeutic Recreation offers programs that promote and provide access to opportunities that offer therapy, skill development, and leisure education as well as facilitate participation in recreational activities.

PLAY Team offers prevention and intervention programs that support and encourage positive youth development for youth and their families.

For more information, call Therapeutic Recreation Programs or PLAY Team programs at 471-5884 (voice) or 471-5839 (TTY).

Figure 1.5 Inclusive Programming. Department of Parks and Recreation, Virginia Beach, Virginia.

experience." What we as human beings perceive to be of value and benefit shapes, guides, and molds our existence. Leisure is an ideal that is valued in contemporary North American society. We seek the benefits that can be derived from participation in leisure events, activities, programs, and services.

Benefits Sought from the Leisure Experience

Numerous benefits are derived from leisure. North American society places great emphasis on individual choice and preference. This factor influences what people value in their leisure and what benefits they seek from leisure experiences. Individual preferences are measured not only in the types of experiences individuals seek in leisure, but also in the intensity with which individuals pursue a given leisure experience. Even though one can identify broad societal leisure benefits and values, it is important to keep in mind that every individual expresses his or her values in different ways and with different degrees of intensity. As a society, we may seek

Inclusion Support Services

The Virginia Beach Department of Parks and Recreation believes its residents have a right to participate in community recreation. We are committed to creating equal access for anyone who may have a challenge or barrier. Parks and Recreation believes that inclusion is an ongoing process of creating a welcoming and safe environment for all of its diverse citizens. Reasonable accommodations are provided to enable an individual's successful participation in a program. Some minimum eligibility requirements must be met in order to participate.

Inclusion Support Services

Department of Parks and Recreation
Community Recreation Services
2289 Lynnhaven Parkway
Virginia Beach, VA 23456

Phone: (757)471-5884
TDD: (757) 471-5839
Fax: (757) 471-2330

Inclusion Support Services

Inclusion is an ongoing process of creating a welcoming and safe environment for all citizens. The Virginia Beach Department of Parks and Recreation is committed to creating equal access for anyone who may have a challenge or barrier.

When is inclusion the right choice?

Answers to commonly asked questions

Experience the Fun!
Virginia Beach Parks and Recreation

Figure 1.5 *Continued.*

"happiness" through leisure; however, the pathways to achieving this end may vary from individual to individual, community to community, and region to region.

There has been a considerable attempt to identify the benefits sought from leisure experiences. Driver and Bruns (1999) suggested that there are three types of leisure benefits: First, a leisure benefit provides an improved condition for an individual, a group of individuals (e.g., family, community), or another entity such as the physical environment. Examples of improved conditions from recreation and leisure include mental health among adolescents (Dieser and Ruddell, 2002), family functioning and togetherness (Shaw and Dawson, 2001), economic development in communities (Crompton, 1999), and improvement in the livability standards of communities (Edginton, 2000). Second, a leisure benefit prevents a worse condition through maintenance of a desired condition. For example, Witt (2001) summarized how recreational,

Lake County Forest Preserve Benefits

Natural areas, parks and recreation and cultural services provide many important direct and indirect benefits to the residents of Lake County. The preservation and conservation of natural resources provides a means of enhancing the quality of life for the public.

Forest preserves contribute to Lake County's positive image in many ways:

> Land purchased along streams and rivers provides:
> - wildlife habitat
> - recreation opportunities, and
> - flood relief.

Large open areas in preserves allow rainwater to recharge underground water supplies.

Trees and shrubs act as air conditioners, cooling and purifying the air.

Noise pollution is reduced in areas immediately adjacent to preserves.

Streams are cleansed of pollutants as they flow through natural areas of vegetation.

Forest preserves provide a natural buffer between villages, lessening the adverse impacts of urban growth.

Forest preserves give residents a feeling of civic pride and a spirit of belonging among the generations.

Home values, especially near preserves, appreciate more rapidly.

Tax dollars spent acquiring, developing and managing the preserves return to area businesses, creating direct and indirect job opportunities and economic vitality.

Preserve visitors support local merchants through purchases of sporting goods, picnic supplies and other items.

-over-

Lake County Forest Preserves
2000 N. Milwaukee Avenue
Libertyville, Illinois 60048
367-6640

LAKE COUNTY FOREST PRESERVES
Preservation, Restoration, Education and Recreation

Figure 1.6   Benefits of Forest Preservation. Lake County Forest Preserves, Libertyville, Illinois.

Natural habitats and open spaces are provided for plants and wildlife.

Preserves fulfill basic human needs to play and to recreate and offer a relatively inexpensive opportunity to relax with family and friends.

Research has demonstrated that businesses find it's easier to attract and keep highly-trained employees in areas with a strong commitment to quality of life and community values.

Some day soon, the only open spaces left in Lake County will be those preserved as parks and forest preserves.

Although experts don't agree on whether or not development pays for itself, they do agree on the need for balance between development and preservation. Too much, too fast, of either one is costly to the community.

Enjoy your Lake County Forest Preserves.
Dedicated to preserving the past and protecting the future.

Figure 1.6 *Continued.*

after-school programs can prevent youth from participating in negative events, such as illegal drug use or vandalism. Third, a leisure benefit is the realization of a specific, satisfying psychological outcome. For example, Mandin and Fox (2000) demonstrated how jazz musicians gain self-expression and self-actualization during serious leisure experiences. Figure 1.6 illustrates how the Lake Country Forest Preserve program of Libertyville, Illinois provides benefits in the three areas of an improved condition (e.g., large, open areas in preserves allow rainwater to recharge underground water supplies); prevention of worse conditions (e.g., preserve wildlife habitat); and positive psychological outcomes for people (e.g., preserves fulfill basic human needs to play and recreate and offer a relatively inexpensive opportunity to relax with family and friends). To this end, Table 1.3, adapted from the academic work of Driver and Bruns (1999),

TABLE 1.3   Benefits of Recreation and Leisure Experiences

I. Personal Benefits
  1. Psychological
    a. Better mental health and health maintenance
      i. Wellness
      ii. Stress management
      iii. Catharsis
      iv. Prevention of or reduced depression, anxiety, and anger
      v. Positive change in moods and emotions
    b. Personal development and growth
      i. Self-confidence
      ii. Improved cognitive and academic performance
      iii. Sense of control
      iv. Autonomy and independence
      v. Leadership
    c. Personal appreciation and satisfaction
      i. Sense of freedom
      ii. Self-actualization
      iii. Creative expression
      iv. Spirituality
      v. Appreciation of nature
  2. Psychophysiological
    a. Cardiovascular benefits
    b. Reduce or prevent hypertension
    c. Decrease body fat and obesity
    d. Increase muscular strength
    e. Reduced consumption of alcohol and tobacco
    f. Reduced serum cholesterol and triglycerides
    g. Improved bone mass

    h. Improved functioning of immune system
    i. Respiratory benefits
    j. Increase life expectancy
II. Social and Cultural Benefits
  1. Community satisfaction
  2. Cultural and historical awareness
  3. Ethnic identity
  4. Family bonding
  5. Understanding and tolerance for others
  6. Reduced social alienation
  7. Pride in the community and nation
  8. Social support
  9. Enhanced worldview
  10. Prevention of social problems by youth at risk
III. Economic Benefits
  1. Reduced health care costs
  2. Increased productivity at work
  3. Decreased job turnover
  4. Local and regional economic growth
  5. Contribution to national economic development
IV. Environmental Benefits
  1. Maintenance of physical facilities
  2. Husbandry and improved relationships with natural world
  3. Understanding human dependency on the natural world
  4. Development of an environmental ethic
  5. Environmental protection of biodiversity and ecosystems

Adapted from: Driver, B. L., & Bruns, D. H. (1999). Concepts and uses of the benefits approach to leisure. In E. L. Jackson & T. L. Burton (Eds.), *Leisure studies: Prospects for the twenty-first century* (pp. 349–369). State College, PA: Venture.

summarizes the multiple benefits of recreation and leisure experiences (to understand the benefits of leisure with greater depth and breadth, readers are encouraged to read the actual article by Driver and Bruns). Some of the potential personal benefits of leisure experiences follow:

1. *Personal Development*—This type of benefit refers to changes in attitudes, values, and skills. There are many possible benefits from participation in leisure experiences that can be obtained; some of these are improved self-concept, greater confidence, spiritual growth, creativity, learning, self-reliance, and self-actualization.

2. *Social Bonding*—Leisure experiences provide opportunities for individuals to interact with one another socially. Leisure activities and events often provide opportunities to meet new people, establish new friendships, support family unity, engage in group cooperation, and develop stronger bonds with friends and other associates.

3. *Physical Development*—Certainly many leisure activities can contribute significantly to physical fitness and physical well-being. Enhanced physical fitness, in turn, can result in better health, greater energy level and strength, improved coordination and balance, and increased stamina, as well as an improved sense of self-worth and well-being. Leisure activities that are fitness-oriented can

help individuals improve their self-image and dramatically influence their self-concept.

4. *Stimulation*—Leisure experiences provide individuals with opportunities for increased stimulation. In addition, they provide opportunities for individuals to use their curiosity and to expand their life horizons. Leisure experiences often provide individuals with new and novel situations that break the routine of their lives.

5. *Fantasy and Escape*—North Americans seem determined to engage in activities that offer opportunities for escape and fantasy. Leisure experiences help individuals escape the daily routine of life. Often individuals will use their leisure to escape into their own personal space. For many, the quickened pace of life produces the desire for tranquillity or escape from the roles that they occupy in their professional work lives.

6. *Nostalgia and Reflection*—Leisure provides individuals with an opportunity to reflect on and appreciate previous life experiences. Reflection on past life events is often reinforced through participation in leisure experiences such as family reunions. Much of the pleasure that we experience in life comes from recalling and reliving experiences that provided joy, satisfaction, and pleasure.

7. *Independence and Freedom*—Leisure activities promote the individual's sense of perceived freedom and independence. A measure of perceived freedom provides individuals with an opportunity to express themselves away from the constraints of daily living. This sense of freedom can serve to energize an individual, promote creativity, and provide an outlet for the use of one's untapped potential.

8. *Reduction of Sensory Overload*—Leisure experiences may provide an individual with an opportunity to buffer the sensory overload that comes from one's work, family life, and personal relationships. In this sense, the benefit of leisure would be to provide an individual with an opportunity to reduce tension, noise, confusion, and complexity.

9. *Risk Opportunities*—Leisure experiences may provide an opportunity for individuals to engage in risk-taking behavior. Many recreation activities require that individuals extend themselves to their fullest capabilities. Further, many leisure activities provide challenges that are adventurous, producing an element of risk. Exposing oneself to risk appears to be a way of expanding one's capabilities, coping with boredom, and increasing the exhilaration of life.

10. *Sense of Achievement*—One of the major benefits of the leisure experience is that it provides people with an opportunity to feel that they have achieved something. Leisure activities can be organized in a competitive way or to promote the personal best of each individual, or both. By learning a new skill, climbing a mountain, painting a portrait, running a race, making a new friend, or participating in an exercise program, one develops a sense of achievement. This often fosters pride and in turn builds self-confidence and self-esteem.

11. *Exploration*—Another potential benefit of leisure experiences is that of exploration. Many leisure experiences enable individuals to learn about new concepts and ideas. The leisure experience is an ideal way to examine and discover. Exploration can also refer to the idea of traveling to different locations for the purpose of discovery during one's leisure. Think of the child who attends summer resident camp and has an opportunity to learn facts about nature and the environment as well as to work with other people.

12. *Values Clarification/Problem Solving*—Leisure provides an opportunity for individuals to examine and clarify their perspectives, beliefs, or values. Often, the leisure setting offers an opportunity to examine concepts and ideas from a different perspective. This perspective may enable individuals to see new patterns of thinking, new ways of approaching problems, and new ways of interacting with others. Further, leisure environments also present individuals with opportunities to use their problem-solving abilities to successfully negotiate challenges. Participation in games is often a means for individuals to clarify values related to winning and losing, teamwork, cooperation, sensitivity toward others, and so on.

13. *Spiritual*—Some important benefits that can be sought from leisure experiences are spiritual ones. Many leisure activities provide opportunities for contemplation, reflection, devotion, and spiritual renewal. For example, being outdoors and experiencing the grandeur of nature can

present a person with feelings of awe, beauty, and humility. In fact, the natural environment has been described by Rolston (1986: 103) "as a cathedral." He further says that "an encounter with nature is the cradle of spirituality."

14. *Mental Health*—Because many leisure experiences are chosen freely and often result in positive outcomes and associations, they can contribute to an individual's well-being, including mental health. This is particularly the case when using leisure to relax, associate with other individuals, or engage in new and creative activities. It is often said that people should seek balance in their lives in order to promote good mental health. In fact, leisure programs and services are often used as therapeutic or healing strategies to help individuals improve mental health.

15. *Aesthetic Appreciation*—Closely associated with spirituality is the idea that leisure experiences promote aesthetic appreciation. Aesthetics focuses on beauty in art, nature, and other aspects of human existence. Leisure experiences provide opportunities for individuals to create or focus on activities that are pleasing to them from an aesthetic standpoint.

Although many benefits can be gained from participation in leisure programs and services, numerous leisure professionals and educators (e.g., Dieser, 2002; Dustin, McAvoy, and Goodale, 1999; Moore, 2002; Wearing, 1998) wisely posited that leisure services also provide negative experiences if they lack proper or competent programming. For example, a poorly designed outdoor recreation trip (e.g., lack of a risk management plan) can cause physical harm to participants. In additional, a playground that is not accessible to children who use wheelchairs can cause these children psychological harm, such as feelings of exclusion and isolation. A sampling of environmental impacts due to poor outdoor recreation programming and natural resource management includes the following:

- Increase of human and ecological disease due to dog litter in park and environmental settings (Barry, 2002)

- Physical and psychological harm (e.g., death, stress) to dolphins due to mass tourism (Orams, 1997)
- Loss of plant species in a conservation areas due to recreational activities such as hiking (Drayton and Primack, 1996)
- Black bear den abandonment during hibernation (which can result in bear starvation) due to winter recreation activities (Goodrich and Berger, 1994)

If leisure professionals are to design leisure experiences that increase positive benefits and decrease negative benefits, it is imperative that they gain a solid understanding of professional practice (e.g., evaluation, leadership) and a thorough understanding of the body of knowledge (e.g., leisure theory, programming strategies) in recreation and leisure services.

Leisure Programming and Benefits

Leisure programs can be thought of as the vehicles that professionals use to deliver benefits to customers. We might think that a facility, an activity, or an event is "leisure." However, none of these contain the elements that are central to experiencing leisure. It is by focusing on benefits and arranging physical, social, and natural environments in such a way as to facilitate leisure that we, as professionals, produce leisure opportunities. The first step in the process of facilitating leisure experiences for our customers is to understand the importance of benefits.

Customers do not buy facilities, activities, or services. They buy benefits or expectations of benefits. Benefits sought by individuals in today's society are varied and ever changing. Leisure is not a static state; it is dynamic in nature, providing challenges to programmers. The leisure service programmer is in the business of identifying and creating benefit packages that can lead the customer to a satisfying leisure experience.

Also, it is important to remember that the customer's expectations for a leisure activity can have a great deal of influence on the success or failure of the program. If the leisure service programmer claims that the benefits of a program will include fun, joyous, exciting, and pleasurable activities, but the program design does not produce these outcomes, then the individual participating will be disappointed and disinclined toward future participation. The expectation of benefits draws people to programs and services.

Leisure service organizations that view themselves in a broad context are far more flexible and have the ability to maneuver their resources to meet the needs of individuals. For example, if the Union Pacific Railroad in the mid-1800s had seen itself as being in the transportation business rather than the freight business, it might have put the first man on the moon. Charles Revlon of Revlon Cosmetics once noted that "in the factory we make cosmetics, in the store we sell hope." The AT&T Corporation changed the focus of its benefits to customers worldwide. It notes that it is in the "communications business, rather than in the business of making telephones." These organizations have focused their efforts to provide benefits in a broad context.

A good example of a leisure service organization that has attempted to define its benefits structure is the *Camp Adventure*™ *Youth Services* program. This organization provides contracted recreation programs to dependents of government personnel residing primarily overseas. The motto of the program captures the essence of the benefits structure promoted by *Camp Adventure*™. It reads, "*Camp Adventure*™ will be an environment of magic and delight, joy and laughter, wonder and discovery, fellowship and friendship, learning and sharing, and pride and achievement." This benefits structure shapes the development and implementation of the program design and also influences the promotional activities of the service. From a more intuitive standpoint, it also shapes the expectations that are established in building transactional and transformational relationships between children and youth served by the program and the camp directors, camp counselors, aquatics instructors, and other leaders. Exempli-

fying the importance of identifying the benefits of leisure services, the Sunnyvale (California) Parks and Recreation Department emphasizes benefits in its promotional flier, encouraging its customers "to try something new . . . this is the place to do it . . . for great trips, to be entertained, to be creative, to be adventurous, to be active."

THE LEISURE EXPERIENCE AS A SERVICE

Most people think of the delivery of opportunities for leisure experiences as a service; that is, most organizations and businesses providing leisure services fall within the service sector of society. Service industries, including leisure services, have grown dramatically during the past several decades. In fact, today the service/information sector of our society constitutes nearly 75 percent of all jobs in North America. Surprisingly, manufacturing accounts for only 13 percent of the workforce and jobs related to agriculture, only 3 to 4 percent.

What are the major characteristics of the service industry? How can service industry functions be separated from those of the manufacturing, agriculture, and information industries? First, let us consider the other components that make up the workforce in North America today. The manufacturing industry transforms raw materials or refined resources into finished goods for resale. Many businesses in this sector are involved in the creation of leisure goods, such as bicycles, bats, balls, skis, boats, exercise equipment, and leisure apparel. The agriculture industry produces food commodities. The information industry focuses primarily on the exchange of knowledge and facts between parties. On the other hand, service industries focus on transactions *between people*. In other words, service-related activities involve exchanges that often require dialogue, empathy, creation of a mood, motivation, and personal interaction.

What are the characteristics of a leisure service? There are numerous definitions as to what makes an enterprise a "service." Some of the more common characteristics of a leisure service follow:

1. *Transaction Between People*—A leisure service involves a transaction between individuals. It often involves a leader working directly with a customer by providing instruction, interpretation, direction, coaching, or some other form of exchange.
2. *Services Are Not Tangible*—A leisure service is not a tangible item; you can't touch it. It is an experience that is created by both the leisure service programmer and the individual experiencing leisure.
3. *The Customer Must Be Present*—Because the leisure experience is a personal one, the customer must be present in order to partake in the service. Leisure experiences, unlike leisure goods, cannot be stockpiled or warehoused.
4. *The Service Cannot Be Created in Advance*—The leisure service cannot be created in advance because it occurs at the moment of delivery. It is dependent on the direct involvement of the customer. Because it is delivered instantaneously, it cannot be experienced in advance of the event or be recalled. As a result, quality assurance must occur *before* the service is rendered.
5. *Leisure Services Are Labor Intensive*—Because leisure service requires interaction between individuals, it is very labor intensive. This means that the success of such services depends, almost exclusively, on having an adequate number of well-trained, highly qualified, "people-oriented" individuals to plan and implement the service.

Many leisure service organizations view themselves in the context of being service-oriented. In this sense, they perceive themselves as being focused on people. They are cognizant of the need to manage the transactions that take place between the providers of services and the customers they serve. The management of such transactions may very well spell the success or failure of an organization.

A good example of a focused service orientation is that of the Eighth U.S. Army Morale, Welfare, and Recreation program. This organization provides morale, welfare, and recreation services to military personnel and their families

assigned to army installations in the South Korea. Its motto is "People are our business." This organization sees its role as one of serving people. It has clarified its service orientation from the customer's viewpoint. Although this is an abstract concept, it helps focus the organization on benefits that are valuable to the customer.

Another example of a leisure service organization that has developed a service orientation is that of the YMCA of Columbia-Willamette located in Vancouver, Washington. This voluntary agency focuses its services on people by building its image around the motto "We build strong kids, strong families, strong communities." The concept of being focused on building "stronger" kids, families, and communities is reflected in this organization's stationery, brochures, fliers, and other promotional materials (see Figure 1.7).

The Sunnyvale (California) Parks and Recreation Department (1994: 3) also has at its core the ideal of customer service. Its philosophy of customer service is as follows:

> We believe in meaningful service. Each of our jobs centers around meeting human needs. So we believe that service excellence is both an attribute and an attitude. Simply put, we work at offering the competent and cheerful assistance which people who depend on us deserve—the same consideration and efficiency which we, as citizens and neighbors, expect from each other.

YMCA
We build strong kids,
strong families, strong communities.

Figure 1.7 Logo Promoting the Value Structure of the YMCA of Columbia-Willamette, Vancouver, Washington.

This is translated in the policy documents governing the operation of the organization. In discussing the parks and recreation department's commitment to the individual customer, the organization notes a need to demonstrate a "commitment to the individual customer, with an appreciation of the individual's rights, responsibilities, beliefs, sensitivities, needs and an acknowledgment that we need to listen and be responsive to each and every individual customer and a commitment to providing opportunities to the customer to provide input." Table 1.4 provides an outline of this strategy.

Another example of a service strategy is from the Morale, Welfare, and Recreation Department, U.S. Marine Corps, Okinawa, Japan. Its focus is "uplifting the spirits of their customers." The organization's motto, "Put your time in our hands!" (see Figure 1.8), suggests an open, welcoming relationship. To accomplish this end, it has developed a marketing strategic plan that links its communication services and customer research activities into a unified effort. Figure 1.9 depicts one of twelve monthly plans designed for MWR staff to guide their efforts. It includes the monthly objective as well as suggestions for special events, print and broadcast strategy, market research, sponsorship, and other actions.

The Anaheim (California) Parks, Recreation, and Community Services Department also has articulated clearly its mission and goals related to customer service. As indicated in Figure 1.10, every person is "considered a valued

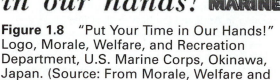

Figure 1.8 "Put Your Time in Our Hands!" Logo, Morale, Welfare, and Recreation Department, U.S. Marine Corps, Okinawa, Japan. (Source: From Morale, Welfare and Recreation Department, U.S. Marine Corps, Okinawa, Japan.)

TABLE 1.4 WHAT IS SUPERIOR CUSTOMER SERVICE?

"Customer service" is a way of approaching our work which places the highest value and strongest focus on meeting the needs of the people being served. A customer service orientation asks all employees, regardless of the specific tasks they perform, to consider people first, and to act with attitudes of respect, concern and responsiveness. Customers should also be expected to treat employees with respect, and providing good customer service to disgruntled customers may well involve referring them to a supervisor or providing complaint forms.

The actions required to deliver superior customer service will vary as widely as job descriptions. However, all actions will reflect our standards.

Customer Service Standards

- Consistently meet the customer's needs and go beyond what is required.
- Follow through on promises and commitments.
- Be visible, identifiable, and present to the public a clean, well-groomed image.
- Take the time to interact with the public and staff in a courteous, understanding, and caring manner.
- Be knowledgeable of the Department operations to which assigned, possess a basic understanding of City of Sunnyvale organization, mission and history, and be supportive of Department programs and policies.
- Be available to assist customers in completing their business or participation in Department services.
- Be sensitive to the cultural, ethnic, and ability differences of customers.
- Consider quality, customer convenience, and the perceived value and benefit in pricing and delivery of programs and services.
- Stand behind our work by continuing and considering expansion of the "Satisfaction Guaranteed" program.
- Design programs and facilities which take into account customers' accessibility, safety, convenience and customer needs and preferences.
- Present facilities to staff and the public in an attractive, clean manner.
- Inform the public of operational considerations that can affect their visit to Sunnyvale parks or participation in activities.
- Enforce rules and procedures to provide for the safe, peaceful, and enjoyable public use of areas and facilities while protecting property, facilities, and natural resources of the City, and notify the public of potential hazards.

From Sunnyvale Parks and Recreation Department, Sunnyvale, CA. Reprinted by permission.

April

Month of the Military Child

Objective
To increase awareness of and participation in Marine Youth Activities Programs.

Special Events
Family Fun Day - April 15; Islandwide Easter Egg Hunts - April 8

Holidays
April Fool's Day - Apr 1; Easter - April 16; Secretaries Day - April 26; Month of the Military Child

Print Strategy
- Use of posters, "Guidon", and "For Immediate Release" to promote Marine Youth Activities offerings including Center Membership, sports programs, customer rentals, miniature golf, birthday bashes, Camp Adventure, youth karate, dance & gymnastics classes.
- Use of outside pubs to promote Easter Egg Hunts,
- Signage, posters, booklet for Family Fun Day
- Usage of outside pubs for Family Fun Day, Easter Egg Hunts, Youth Centers & Camp Adventure
- Reprint MYA brochure & folder
- Update/Reprint of Camp Adventure brochure and poster

Broadcast Strategy
- Radio/Television spot for Centers - Costume rentals, birthday bashes
- Radio/Television spot for Family Fun Day & Easter Egg Hunts
- Radio/Television spot for Camp Adventure
- Radio/Television spot for Miniature Golf
- Radio/Television spot for Teen offerings

Sponsorship
- Carry out sponsorship for Family Fun Day
- Finalize sponsorship plans for Oura Wan Beach Bash
- Solicit sponsorship for Camp Hansen Hoedown
Plan sponsorship package for Camp Kinser Springfest and Super Sunday at Kin Blue

Coupon/ Promotions
- Discounts on golf, free meal for children w/parents' meals, one month free membership w/ yearly sign-up.
- Coupons for, and Mr. Gecko at, Family Fun Day

Market Research
- MILITARY CHILD(REN) - Focus Group to determine the specific needs of children of the military family.
- Survey on MYA membership, programs and effectiveness and ideas- Focus Group to determine what children want to do during Camp Adventure.
- Extensive research on how to involve teen-agers in Marine MWR activities, focus groups, surveys

Other MWR & Offbase Happenings
- Kadena Grand Opening of Boating
- Kadena Family Talent Contest
- Kadena Spring Arts Fair
- Kadena Easter Egg Hunt
- AAFES Easter Egg Hunt

Publicity Support Requests
are due to Marketing by March 1st for all events happening in April and the first week of May.

Figure 1.9 Monthly Marketing Objectives, Morale, Welfare, and Recreation Department, U.S. Marine Corps, Okinawa, Japan. (Source: From Morale, Welfare and Recreation Department, U.S. Marine Corps, Okinawa, Japan.)

**ANAHEIM PARKS, RECREATION AND COMMUNITY SERVICES
CUSTOMER SERVICE**

MISSION

Everyone who receives services from the Anaheim Parks, Recreation and Community Services Department is considered a valued customer. Each deserves to be treated with respect, honesty and expediency. Our employees are courteous, receptive, knowledgeable, and diligently strive to provide the best service possible with positive, proactive attitudes.

GOALS

Develop and maintain a customer service emphasis that addresses the needs of department external and internal customers and is adaptable to their changing needs.

Regularly evaluate services and programs utilizing customer feedback.

Discover and employ methods that give employees maximum flexibility in solving customer requests.

Contribute to the Department's overall positive image by building customer satisfaction and loyalty.

Develop and maintain an on-going training effort that will keep all employees current with the customer service values.

Establish commitment to the value of customer service at all levels of the organization.

Provide motivation and recognition within the department to maintain and enhance customer service as an ongoing value.

Figure 1.10 Customer Service Mission Statement, Anaheim (California) Parks, Recreation, and Community Services Department.

customer . . . each deserves to be treated with respect, honesty and expediency."

Effective leisure service organizations can be differentiated from those that are ineffective by the extent to which they have developed a service orientation. An important component of any leisure service organization is the *image* that it projects—not only to the customers it serves, but also to the broader community within which it operates. There is an old adage, "You are only as good as your name." When people hear the word *image* as it relates to leisure service organizations, several things come to mind—goodwill, excellence, people orientation, credibility, honesty, ethics, consistency, quality, value, and integrity. All these factors can impact on the

image of a leisure service organization. From a service perspective, the term *image* can be thought of as the managed perception of the way that the leisure service organization does business. Those organizations that *manage their image* are more successful than those organizations that do not.

Another key factor in building a successful service orientation is the development of a *customer-friendly* system. Customer-friendly means that the programs and activities, and systems used to deliver these services, are organized for the convenience of the customer, not for the organization and its members. To be customer-friendly means that the organization keeps the needs of the customer at the forefront of the work of the organization at all times. This approach involves developing specific processes that can be managed or scripted for delivering a service and then ensuring that these procedures are carried out in a convenient, consistent, and courteous manner.

Often it is the little things that make a difference in service delivery. Every aspect of an organization's services should be addressed, from the primary services to those services that support, complement, or add value to the work of the organization. Successful leisure service organizations are ones that develop strategies for the following: (1) program and activity interactions, (2) telephone interactions, (3) information exchange, (4) registration interactions, (5) office interactions, and (6) casual conversations. These strategies are more fully described in Chapter 12. All of these interactions can be scripted out to produce the desired benefit. Scripts (written information) that describe forms of interaction between the organization's staff and the customer help cue individuals to different elements in the environment and contribute to the creation of successful leisure experiences. Individuals can be cued by positive acknowledgments and by friendly, courteous, and informed interactions.

All of the procedures mentioned here can and should be addressed in written form. That is, they should be scripted out in writing in a detailed fashion. For example, at Disneyland and Walt Disney World, interactions between customers and the "cast" are written out in minute detail. The Jungle Cruise illustrates this point. Guides are meticulously trained in the narrative to be used in each of the journeys taken by guests participating in this attraction. Even acceptable deviations from the script are written out and must be strictly adhered to. The point is, nothing is left to chance in terms of creating positive relationships between the customer and those providing services.

The last major component in building a strong service orientation is ensuring that the organization has customer-oriented, frontline people. Without question, it is people that make the difference in an organization. Frontline people must be customer-oriented people. The critical interface that takes place between the customer and the leisure service leader, host, guide, interpreter, coach, or instructor is fundamental to ensuring a successful leisure experience. Every transaction that takes place between the customer and the leader may result in the creation of a positive leisure experience. There are many moments of "truth," and these moments can and must be anticipated and managed effectively.

Frontline people need to know that each individual must be treated as if he or she is a unique person. Each individual must be dealt with in a courteous manner and with a great deal of care and support. People are often displeased if they are made to feel that their needs are being handled in a routine fashion. Individuals requesting information, registering for a program, or participating in an activity need to feel as though they are the most important person being served by the leisure service organization.

Critical frontline positions in leisure service organizations are sometimes viewed as the least important within the agency. Part-time and seasonal employees often make up the bulk of individuals actually delivering services. Individuals occupying such positions usually receive minimum wages. Further, the resources invested in their training and development are low. With such a low investment, it is no wonder that organizations see a great turnover in individuals occupying these positions. Better strategies for promoting the value and worth of frontline staff must be developed if leisure service organizations are to effectively respond to the needs of customers.

A key element in improving the performance of frontline staff is building an awareness of the need to serve the customer in an attentive, courteous, and supportive fashion. This can be done by focusing the attention of frontline staff on the need for positive customer relationships. Positive relationships are built on the desire to serve people by being helpful, sincere, genuine, supportive, courteous, and competent. For example, one way of being helpful to customers is to be sure they are provided with accurate, up-to-date, and factual information in a timely way. For this to occur, frontline staff members must be provided with accurate information on a daily basis. They must also be trained to seek and verify the information they need from appropriate sources. Frontline people should be encouraged to solve problems, react with spontaneity and flexibility, and be able to recover from adverse situations with poise. Positive customer relationships are generated when frontline people are encouraged to show care and express concern for the welfare of others.

Customer-Driven Programs Promote Quality

Leisure service programmers need to be customer driven. Osborne and Gaebler (1992: 169) suggest that public organizations become "as customer-driven as businesses." These authors suggest that governments in particular build customer-driven systems. As they indicate "most customers know what is important to them" (p. 180). Osborne and Gaebler suggest the following:

- Customer-driven systems force service providers to be accountable to their customers.
- Customer-driven systems depoliticize the choice-of-provider decision.
- Customer-driven systems stimulate more innovation.
- Customer-driven systems give people choices between different kinds of services.

- Customer-driven systems waste less because they match supply to demand.
- Customer-driven systems empower customers to make choices and empowered customers are more committed customers.
- Customer-driven systems create opportunities for equity.

Quality is also an important variable to be sought in the provision of leisure services. Quality is a perception of excellence. The concept of quality will be discussed in more depth in Chapter 13. However, McCarville (1993) has identified a number of keys to quality programming that have emerged from the service literature. He has suggested seven interdependent steps that promote quality. They are:

1. Establish programming priorities.
2. Discover client needs.
3. Develop product accordingly.
4. Identify key program providers.
5. Identify key encounters with clients.
6. Train for flexibility, but when in doubt set standards.
7. Ask for help.

These steps indicate that being close to the customer is an important element that can impact the quality of the services of a leisure service agency.

Summary

Leisure is an important indicator of quality of life for North Americans. Individuals occupying professional positions as leisure programmers influence the leisure behavior and values of others. Leisure programmers are challenged to provide services that are linked to customer needs and that result in desirable benefits for those toward whom services are directed.

A key factor in succeeding as a leisure programmer is an understanding of the basic concepts of leisure, recreation, and play. Knowledge of these concepts is a fundamental building block in developing a philosophy of leisure programming. Leisure has been defined from many orientations. It has been defined as (1) an unobligated block of time, (2) an activity, (3) a state of mind, (4) a symbol of social class, (5) an action, (6) an end in itself, and (7) a holistic concept that suggests everything has potential for leisure. Recreation is usually thought of as a wholesome activity pursued during one's leisure. Play is thought of as a positive form of human behavior that does not necessarily serve instrumental purposes. It is pleasurable, and can be aimless or disorganized on one hand or structured or complex on the other.

The benefits that people seek from a leisure experience must guide the work of the programmer. There are numerous possible benefits—both economic and noneconomic. Economic benefits are concerned with the worth of services both from the standpoint of dollars generated and from questions of equity. Noneconomic benefits focus on the behaviors demonstrated or sought by individuals. Some noneconomic benefits of the leisure experience include personal development, social bonding, physical development, stimulation, fantasy and escape, nostalgia and reflection, independence and freedom, reduction of sensory overload, risk, achievement, exploration, values clarification, spiritual enhancement, enhancement of mental health, and aesthetic appreciation.

The delivery of leisure experiences is usually referred to as a "service." The creation of a leisure service often requires the development of a mood or an atmosphere and is usually dependent on some personal interaction between a leisure programmer and a customer. Leisure services are not tangible but are personal in nature. For a leisure service organization to be effective, it must be service-oriented. It must be customer-friendly and encourage positive, responsive frontline staff behaviors. An important part of developing a service-oriented strategy is managing the image of the leisure service organization so that it represents values related to effective delivery of leisure experiences.

Discussion Questions and Exercises

1. What roles do leisure programmers play in contemporary society?

2. What tenets would you use to build your leisure programming philosophy? How are these tenets linked to your own personal values and beliefs concerning leisure?

3. How are the tenets of building a philosophy of programming related to people with disabilities? Further, how does the Americans with Disabilities Act (ADA) affect leisure programming?

4. What are leisure benefits? Drawing upon the academic work of Driver and Bruns (1999), explain three types of leisure benefits.

5. Outline the multiple benefits that can occur from the Québec Winter Carnival.

6. Identify fifteen benefits sought by customers who participate in leisure experiences. Cite specific examples of how leisure service organizations can create these benefits.

7. Explain how outdoor leisure experiences can cause negative consequences when they lack proper or competent leisure programming.

8. What is a leisure service?

9. What are the characteristics of a leisure service? How can they be differentiated from leisure products?

10. What elements are necessary in building a service-oriented strategy in a leisure service delivery system?

References

Allison, M. T. 2000. Diversity in organizational perspective. In *Diversity and the recreation profession: Organizational perspectives,* edited by M. T. Allison and J. E. Schneider (pp. 3–18). State College, PA: Venture.

Barry, R. E. 2002, October. *The relationship between environmental cues at trailheads and intention to litter.* Paper presented at the National Recreation and Park Association Leisure Research Symposium, Tampa Bay, FL.

Brightbill, C. K. 1960. *Challenge of leisure.* Englewood Cliffs, NJ: Prentice Hall.

Bullaro, J. J., and C. R. Edginton. 1986. *Commercial leisure services.* New York: Macmillan.

Butler, G. D. 1976. *Introduction to community recreation.* 5th ed. New York: McGraw-Hill.

Carnaval de Québec. 2001–2002. *Annual report.* Québec City, Québec: Author.

City of St. John's Department of Recreation. 2002. *Your guide to active living.* St. John's, NF: Author.

Crompton, J. L. 1999. *Financing and acquiring park and recreation resources.* Champaign, IL: Human Kinetics.

DeGraaf, D. G., D. J. Jordan, and K. H. DeGraaf. 1999. *Programming for parks, recreation, and leisure services: A servant leadership approach.* State College, PA: Venture.

Dieser, R. B. 2002. A personal narrative of a cross-cultural experience in therapeutic recreation: Unmasking the masked. *Therapeutic Recreation Journal* 36(1): 84–96.

Dieser, R. B., and E. Ruddell. 2002. Effects of attributional retraining during therapeutic recreation on attributes and explanatory styles of adolescents with depression. *Therapeutic Recreation Journal* 36(1): 35–47.

Drayton, B., and R. B. Primack. 1996. Plant species lost in an isolated conservation area in metropolitan Boston from 1894–1993. *Conservation Biology* 10(1): 30–39.

Driver, B. L., and D. H. Bruns. 1999. Concepts and uses of the benefits approach to leisure. In *Leisure studies: Prospects for the twenty-first century,* edited by E. L. Jackson and T. L. Burton (pp. 349–369). State College, PA: Venture.

Driver, B. L., and G. L. Peterson. 1986. Benefits of outdoor recreation: An integrating overview. In *A literature review: The president's commission on Americans outdoors.* Washington, DC: Superintendent of Documents.

Dumazedier, J. 1974. *Sociology of leisure.* New York: Elsevier.

Dustin, D. L., L. H. McAvoy, and T. L. Goodale. 1999. The benefits equation. *Parks and Recreation* 34(1): 32–37.

Edginton, C. R. 2000. *Enhancing the livability of Iowa communities: The role of recreation, natural resource development and tourism.* Cedar Falls, IA: University of Northern Iowa Press.

Edginton, C. R., D. J. Jordan, D. G. DeGraaf, and S. R. Edginton. 1995. *Leisure and life satisfaction.* Dubuque, IA: Brown & Benchmark.

Fuson, K. 2002. Quilter should stop but doesn't. *Des Moines Register,* 11 September, p. 13.

Goodrich, J., and J. Berger. 1994. Winter recreation and hibernating black bears *Ursus americanus. Biological Conservation* 67: 105–110.

Grey, D. E. 1972. Exploring inner space. *Parks and Recreation* 7(12): 18–19, 46.

Hutchinson, J. 1949. *Principles of recreation.* New York: A. S. Barnes.

Kaplan, M. 1975. *Leisure theory and policy.* New York: John Wiley.

Kelly, J. R. 1996. *Leisure.* Boston: Allyn & Bacon.

Kraus, R. 1971. *Recreation and leisure in modern society.* New York: Appleton-Century-Crofts.

Mandin, T. G., and K. Fox, 2000 October. *Including play in serious leisure: Jazz.* Paper presented at the National Recreation and Park Association Leisure Research Symposium, Phoenix, AZ.

McCarville, R. E. 1993. Keys to quality leisure programming. *Journal of Physical Education, Recreation, and Dance* 64(8): 34–36, 46.

Moore, T. A. 2002. The parks and being loved to death and other frauds and deceits in recreation management. *Journal of Leisure Research* 34(1): 52–78.

Murphy, J. F. 1974. *Concepts of leisure: Philosophical implications.* Englewood Cliffs, NJ: Prentice Hall.

Murphy, J. F. 1975. *Recreation and leisure service.* Dubuque, IA: Wm. C. Brown.

Nash, J. B. 1960. *Philosophy of recreation and leisure.* Dubuque, IA: Wm. C. Brown.

Neumeyer, M. H. 1958. *Leisure and recreation: A study of leisure and recreation in their sociological aspects.* New York: Ronald Press.

Orams, M. B. (1997). Historical accounts of human-dolphin interaction and recent developments in wild dolphin based tourism in Australia. *Tourism Management* 18(5): 317–26.

Osborne, D., and T. Gaebler. 1992. *Reinventing government.* New York: Addison Wesley.

Rolston, H. 1986. Beyond recreation value: The greater outdoors preservation-related and environmental benefits. In *A literature review: The president's commission on Americans outdoors.* Washington, DC: Superintendent of Documents.

Rossman, J. R. 1988. Development of a leisure program theory. *Journal of Park and Recreation Administration* 6(4).

Russell, R. 1996. *Leisure pastimes.* Dubuque, IA: Brown & Benchmark.

Samdahl, D. 1992. Leisure in our lives: Enhancing the common leisure occasion. *Journal of Leisure Research* 24(1): 19–32.

Shaw, S. M., and D. Dawson. 2001. Purposive leisure: Examining parental discourse on family activities. *Leisure Science* 23(4): 217–32.

Simpson, S. 1989. Aristotle. In *Pioneers in leisure and recreation,* by H. Ibrahim. Reston, VA: American Alliance for Health, Physical Education, Recreation, and Dance.

Sunnyvale Parks and Recreation Department. 1994. *Our customer service strategy.* Sunnyvale, CA: Sunnyvale Parks and Recreation Department.

Sylvester, C. 1987. The ethics of play, leisure, and recreation in the twentieth century, 1900–1983. *Leisure Science* 9(3): 184.

U.S. Department of Justice. 2002. *Enforcing the ADA: A status report from the Department of Justice.* Washington, DC: Author.

Wearing, B. 1998. *Leisure and feminist theory.* Thousand Oaks, CA: Sage.

Witt, P. A. 2001. Insuring after-school programs meet their intended goals. *Parks and Recreation* 36(9): 32–52.

Programming Concepts

LEARNING OBJECTIVES

1. To help the reader define *programming* and programming concepts.
2. To help the reader gain a *perspective of the historical development* of leisure programming.
3. To assist the reader in gaining a knowledge and understanding of the *strategies used in the organization of leisure services*—governmental/political, voluntary, and market systems.
4. To help the reader identify and define *steps in the social-planning process*.
5. To help the reader gain knowledge of the *process of community development*.
6. To provide the reader with an understanding of *social marketing*.
7. To help the reader identify and define the *process of social action*.
8. To provide the reader with information concerning *theories of programming* as identified in the literature of our field.

INTRODUCTION

The major function of the leisure services profession is to provide leisure services (Rossman, 1995: x). It is the responsibility of the leisure services professional to not only understand, but to anticipate, the leisure needs of the customers by the organization it serves. Providing leisure experiences is the focus of the organization. In this sense, leisure programs should be thought of as the tools of the leisure services professional—the vehicle for service delivery. It is through the provision of programs that the leisure benefits sought by individual customers are achieved. Programs provide opportunities for customers to develop skills, form values, learn processes, and express themselves creatively, intellectually, socially, and physically.

What constitutes a program? The recreation and leisure program concept may have different meanings for different people. Is it a park? An aerobics class? A child care center? A craft show? An outreach program? An in-line skate park? A zoo (see Figure 2.1)? Or is it all these things? Does a program have to have the appearance of activity, or can it occur simply through the exchange of information between people? Is it possible for the participant to be passive? Broadly, a program can take almost any form within the framework of one's definition as to what constitutes a leisure experience.

Rossman (1995: 3) writes that "a program is a designed opportunity for a leisure experience to occur." Paraphrasing Rossman, we can think of programming as designing leisure opportunities by intervening in such a way as to create environments that maximize the probability that those who enter them will have leisure. Supporting this notion, Farrell and Lundegren (1993: 26) have written that leisure "programming is a process." Thus, we can think of programming as a process that enables individuals to experience leisure. Leisure programs often structure social opportunities between individuals, create physical environments that facilitate leisure, and provide individuals opportunities to enjoy the natural environment.

Figure 2.1 Zoo Brochure, Pueblo (Colorado) Zoo.

Leisure programs can be vibrant, dynamic, uplifting, or they can be passive, relaxing, quiet. As indicated, leisure programs take many forms and shapes, all directed toward helping customers achieve quality leisure experiences. As Russell (1982) writes, "programs are those magic moments of joyous participation that occur when the available and necessary resources have been stirred together just right by programming." As Farrell and Lundegren (1993) emphasize, "good programming does not happen; it is made to happen." Consistent with this idea is the notion forwarded by Bullaro and Edginton (1986). They note that provision of leisure services is a process that helps individuals attain leisure experiences that they perceive to be beneficial. According to these authors, "Creating the leisure experience involves arranging for or assisting people to be placed in a social, physical (man-made), or natural environment. This may involve planning and organizing, assembling materials and supplies, arranging the use of facilities, providing leadership, or other actions that lead to the creation of opportunities for leisure" (12).

LEISURE PROGRAMMING: A HISTORICAL PERSPECTIVE

Leisure, viewed in the context of the history of humankind, is pervasive. However, the delivery of leisure programs by professionals is relatively new, as is the systematizing of a body of professional knowledge or the standardization of a set of principles of professional practice. Some evidence exists that communities during the Middle Ages appointed individuals to organize events (Edginton et al., 1995: 62). Known as the "Lords of Misrule," such individuals organized festivals, religious events, harvest celebrations, and other activities. From a historical standpoint, leisure programming can be divided into three periods of time: the classical, the neoclassical, and the modern.

The Classical Era (1880–1939)

Europeans expended great energy to understand the implications of children's play in the mid-

1800s. Especially important was the work of German educator Friedrich Froebel, who directed his work toward systematizing play to make it more effective. He "knew that spontaneity must not be sacrificed to the system, as the great value of play intellectually and morally depends on the freedom of the individual in expressing its own purposes and carrying out its own decisions." Froebel's task involved the "systematizing of play under the leadership of adults, without robbing play of its perfect spontaneity and independence of action" (Hughes, 1897: 124). Thus, Froebel and, subsequently, others established a philosophical basis for the work of leisure programmers; that is, creating opportunities for spontaneity of action, self-direction, and freedom through play and leisure.

The leisure service profession in North America traces its historical roots to the late 1800s and early 1900s. The social conditions of the 1890s were so harsh that they set the tone for reform in the early twentieth century (James, 1993: 177). Jacob Riis (1890) wrote in his book *How the Other Half Lives* about the dismal social conditions in New York City. In a later book, he noted that "there was, in the whole of Manhattan, but a single outdoor playground attached to a public school and that was an old burial ground in the First Street that had been wrestled from the dead with immense toil" (Riis, 1902). A great concern for the welfare of children during this period of time resulted in the creation of a host of leisure programs. G. Stanley Hall (1904–1905) published a two-volume work entitled *Adolescence* that was a landmark document related to youth and youth programs. Emphasis was placed on "child-saving" activities. This era was characterized by provision of services directed toward immigrant, disadvantaged, poor, and other populations in need of philanthropic or government support. Most programs were found on playgrounds, in schoolyards, or in settlement houses.

In 1915, stressing the importance of programming, Henry Curtis wrote that "the playground that has no program achieves little."

Boden and Mitchell (1923) suggested that "programs are necessary to make playgrounds more interesting and efficient." During this era, leisure programming was predominantly focused on children. Most programs were seasonal. As indicated in the *Normal Course in Play* (Lee, 1925), "leisure time programs should continue throughout the entire twelve months of the year." The importance and value of programming was recognized, although the orientation was to the content of programs rather than the process. There was no integrated theory of programming; however, there was acknowledgment of the fact that activities should be classified by age. As Nash wrote in 1927, "the program of activities should be arranged to meet the various demands of groups of different ages . . . activities . . . [should] . . . be selected in light of age, needs, modified by conditions of time, space, climate, and leadership."

The period of time in the 1930s that was marked by the Great Depression in the United States also saw an attempt to respond to social conditions by creating leisure programs and services. National service and relief programs such as the Civilian Conservation Corps, the Works Progress Administration, and the National Youth Administration resulted in the creation of leisure programs, areas, and facilities. According to Lutzin (1973), the period of time of the Great Depression in the United States also saw the laying of a foundation for responsiveness to social problems and issues. He writes:

> It might be said that the era of the 1930s in many ways was a Golden Age for human services. This was the period when new and innovative programs were initiated to deal with social problems which had always been with us, but whose increased intensity and widespread population involvement made possible the development of public and legislative support for appropriate action (3).

The classical era of leisure programming spanned a period from the late 1800s until after World War II.

The Neoclassical Era (1940–1959)

During the neoclassical era of leisure programming following World War II, America experienced an unparalleled period of growth and prosperity. Gains in discretionary income and time resulted in a greater focus on quality of life issues, including the provision of leisure programs and amenities. The neoclassical era of leisure programming was characterized by the growth of programs and an acceptance of the importance of the provision of leisure services by the government. Programs became more diverse, targeting all populations from young to older persons. The focus of programming changed to providing "the greatest good for the greatest number" or attempting to serve all segments of society. The largest growth occurred in leisure programs in suburban middle class communities. As Wolfenstein (1955) notes, a "fun morality" in programming emerged, wherein play was to be viewed as free, voluntary, spontaneous, and egalitarian.

The importance of programming in organizational work also was emphasized. Meyer and Brightbill (1948) suggest that "the program of an agency is its most vital asset." During this era, an analysis of the procedures used in program planning emerged, as well as an emphasis in the professional literature about the importance of program development. Hjelte (1940) writes that "a program is only a plan. Program making involves charting activities in detail." In support of this position, Hutchinson (1949) indicates that "successful programming depends on sound principles of planning and a wide selection of activities." The neoclassical era also promoted the idea of a linkage between program benefits and activities. In 1940, Butler noted that "activities are the medium through which individuals satisfy their recreation desires and interests." Danford (1953) supported this viewpoint, suggesting that "activities, sports, dance, drama, and crafts are not ends; they are means . . . [the program] . . . is the sum of all organized experiences which aim to make a contribution to the enrichment of the human personality."

Clearly, a greater emphasis was placed on the development of programming principles during the neoclassical era. The level of sophistication of the work of leisure services professionals in providing programs had increased dramatically, as had the level of funding available for the provision of such services. There was greater variety in programming, more options, and an attempt to serve more diverse populations. As Danford (1953) noted, "the development of a program for the Boston Parmenter Street Chapel playground was a simple matter—all activities centered around the sandpile."

The Modern Era (1960–Present)

The modern era of leisure programming is host to a number of innovations and developments. One of the most significant developments in the evolution of leisure programming was the establishment of the second national workshop on recreation at Michigan State University in 1953. This workshop produced an important book— *The Recreation Program* (1954). A collaborative effort of several educators and practitioners established, for the first time under one title, a comprehensive resource focused on leisure programming. Emphasizing the importance of programming, contributors to this important document have suggested that "the heart of the recreation effort is program opportunity and enrichment."

The modern era has seen the emergence of a systematic body of professional knowledge and practice that has become identifiable and widely accepted and employed in the delivery of leisure services. In other words, the essential elements in the program planning process have been generally accepted and agreed upon by authors such as Farrell and Lundegren (1993), Edginton, Hanson, and Edginton (1992), Russell (1982), Carpenter and Howe (1985), and Rossman (1995). This expanded body of knowledge has provided theoretical models for leisure programming and also scientific inquiry regarding program formats and benefits. As Edginton, Compton, and Hanson wrote in 1989, "we must

build our professional body of knowledge by combining empirically verified information with practical knowledge and professional values to create a comprehensive, theoretical, and practical approach to the process of programming."

A key factor influencing professional practice in the modern era has been the application of principles of marketing to leisure programming. The 1970s and 1980s saw movement— championed by such authors as Edginton and Williams (1978) and Howard and Crompton (1980)—away from a social welfare orientation of service with a broad service strategy attempting to serve multiple segments of the population toward an emphasis on identifying discrete target markets. Greater importance was placed on privatization of services, contracting of services, and the provision of cost recovery activities. Program activities flourished in the areas of wellness and fitness, services for older adults, risk recreation, outdoor pursuits, tourism, and cultural arts. By the late 1980s and early 1990s, concern was also expressed for youth development. A return to a reemphasis on "child-saving" activities was in evidence.

Twenty-first century literature suggests a new, stronger emphasis on inclusion and diversity and a continued focus on youth programming. In addition, greater emphasis is placed on childcare and before- and after-school programs. The latter have been enhanced by funding through the 21st Century Community Learning Centers program. There are about 6,800 rural and inner-city public schools in 1,420 communities participating in this program, which is often operated in collaboration with other public and nonprofit agencies, organizations, local businesses, post-secondary institutions, scientific/cultural, and other community entities. Collaboration, cooperation, networking, and partnerships between and among public, private, and nonprofit organizations continue to be emphasized in the creation and delivery of leisure programs. Further, as the baby boomers mature and move into their fifties, their leisure interests and tastes continue to be

TABLE 2.1   Leisure Service Delivery: Governmental/Political System (Public)

Local	State	Federal
• Municipal (City) Parks & Recreation	• Parks	• National Park Service
• Township	• Forests	• U.S. Forest Service
• County	• Waysides	• Bureau of Land Management
• Conservation Districts	• Game & Fish	• U.S. Corps of Engineers
• Special Recreation Districts	• Conservation	• Dept. of Defense
	• Tourism	• Tennessee Valley Authority
	• Hospitals	• U.S. Fish & Wildlife
	• Prisons	• Bureau of Reclamation
	• Universities; Colleges	• Bureau of Indian Affairs
		• Soil Conservation
		• Veterans Administration
		• National Endowment for the Arts
		• National Endowment for the Humanities

dominant factors influencing leisure preferences. In particular, this generation continues its quest to be physically and spiritually well and to emphasize fitness, nutrition, and building meaningful relationships with others as well as an understanding of one's self.

Strategies Used in the Organization of Leisure Services

The way in which a leisure service organization chooses to allocate resources or make decisions depends on what it values. From a very simplistic standpoint, what we value will influence the types of strategies we use in organizing and delivering services. In general, there are three approaches to providing service: the *political/governmental system,* the *voluntary system,* and the *market system.* Following is a description of these approaches.

Political/Governmental System (Public)

The political decision-making process is a collective one in a democratic society. It often subordinates individual choice to the collective desires of the whole. In meeting leisure needs, *governments or political bodies draw resources from society and attempt to meet its needs.* Sometimes governments use a rational, logical, and systematic approach to making decisions. Other times governments are influenced greatly by special interest groups, pressure groups, or influential individuals. In some societies all the resources of the culture are concentrated in government. In other societies this is not the case. In the United States, vast amounts of resources are concentrated in government at the local, state, and federal levels. The United States spends more than $6 billion annually for park, recreation, cultural, and environmental services (see Table 2.1).

Voluntary System (Private Nonprofit)

North Americans have been and are still strongly committed to *the notion of giving time and talent on a voluntary basis to better community life.* Over the years, the result of this value system has been the emergence of literally hundreds of thousands of organizations, agencies, and institutions that provide leisure programs and services as a way of enhancing the community's well-being. These organizations are funded primarily by contributions, gifts, memberships, and most importantly, by the contribution of the time and talent of community members. Some voluntary organizations target their services to the community as a whole. Other organizations focus on specific target groupings, segmented by age, gender, or other variables. Many voluntary agencies promote specific values that are linked to religious, social, environmental, or other concerns.

TABLE 2.2   Leisure Service Delivery: Voluntary (Nonprofit)

National Collaboration for Youth	Disaster Organizations	National Health Council
• YMCA • YWCA • Camp Fire • Girl Scouts of the USA • Boy Scouts of America • Boys/Girls Clubs of America • Big Brother/Big Sister • 4-H • Junior Achievement • Boys & Girls Clubs of Canada	• American Red Cross • Volunteers of America • Salvation Army	• Volunteer hospitals • Health education training

Philanthropic Intermediaries	National Nonprofit Professional Associations
• United Way • Black United Givers • Hispanic Voluntary Contributors	• National Recreation & Park Association • Association for Volunteer Administration • American Camping Association • American Alliance for Health, Physical Education, Recreation, and Dance

Expenditures by the voluntary system in the United States are estimated to exceed $16 billion (see Table 2.2).

Market System (Commercial for Profit)

The market, or free enterprise, system is built on the assumption that the basis of decision making is the individual. In the case of leisure, the customer uses his or her discretionary funds to purchase goods and services that meet his or her needs. *The individual rather than the collective whole determines what to produce, how much to produce, and what the cost will be.* In addition, the individual customer decides what to consume, how much to consume, and what he or she is willing to pay. The market system in the 1900s, as conceived by Adam Smith (1910/1950) in the classic book *The Wealth of Nations,* is one in which an invisible hand guides supply and demand. The market system in America today is responsible for producing more than $450 billion in leisure goods and products (see Table 2.3).

Political/governmental systems, voluntary systems, and marketing-oriented systems use different strategies for creating and distributing leisure programs and services. Leisure service organizations have employed four major strategies over the past several decades in varying degrees to provide programs and services. They are *social planning, community development, social marketing,* and *social action.* Political/governmental organizations also employ all four strategies. *Social planning* is a task-oriented strategy that is directed toward solving problems. *Community development* is a process-oriented strategy directed toward helping individuals identify their own problems and assisting them with resources necessary to solve them. *Social marketing* is a strategy directed toward meeting anticipated consumer needs by directing services to them while at the same time meeting organizational goals. *Social action* is directed toward changing the basic distribution of resources by forcing the existing power structure to change its priorities and policies.

A leisure service organization may employ more than one of these strategies at one time. An organization must consider carefully the conditions that it is confronted with and wisely choose the strategy or strategies that best fit the particular community needs. For example, the rights of persons with disabilities are often best championed by assuming a strong advocacy posture. The social action strategy might be the best approach to ensure the organization and delivery of leisure services to these individuals within

TABLE 2.3   Leisure Service Delivery: Market (Commercial)

Participatory Facilities	Entertainment Services	Outdoor Facilities	Hospitality Facilities
• Tennis or racquet clubs • Ice rinks • Health spas or clubs • Fitness centers • Dance studios • Ballrooms • Bowling alleys • Movie theaters • Roller skating rinks • Miniature golf; driving ranges	• Racetracks; raceways • Sports arenas; stadiums • Rodeos • Circuses • Nightclubs • Movie theaters • Theme & amusement parks	• Ski resorts • Marinas; beaches • Campgrounds • Camping resorts • Resident camps • Ranches • Sports resorts	• Convention centers • Self-contained resorts • Hotels; motels • Guest houses • Bed & breakfast inns

Retail/Shopping	Food Services
Places: • Shopping malls • Conventional stores • Specialty shops Products: • Recreation vehicles • Sports equipment • Clothing • Toys & games • Home entertainment • Hobby supplies • Boats, canoes	• Restaurants • Cafes and coffeehouses • Food and beverage shops • Fast food establishments • Concession stands; refreshment services • Catering

a community. These strategies are presented here and their application in the provision of leisure services is highlighted.

Social Planning

Social planning, as previously indicated, is a task-oriented process directed toward rationally and logically distributing leisure services. It is a process of using the knowledge and expertise of professionals to plan, organize, and deliver services. The process of social planning is often referred to as *direct service delivery*. Basically, it involves the collection of pertinent information and data by physical and social planners. The analysis of this data provides information to planners in decision-making roles. To succeed as a social planner, one must often have the ability to work within large, bureaucratic structures.

What is the role of the professional using the social planning strategy with the individual or individuals receiving the service? Social planners look upon individuals within a community as the customers of their services. Their job is to understand and know the customer well enough to provide meaningful services. Conversely, customers also view their role as one of consumer. They are the recipients of the process of social planning. They may or may not be interested in becoming involved in the planning, organization, and promotion of services (see Table 2.4). According to Howard (1985), the major factor influencing customers is convenience of the service.

Leisure service professionals as social planners are involved in a number of tasks—technical, political, and social. Although there is no general consensus as to the specific tasks in which social planners should be involved, Lauffer (1974: 353) has identified eight approaches to the social-planning process. He suggests that the work of the planner can be viewed as the following:

TABLE 2.4 Social Planning as a Strategy for Delivering Leisure Services

Social planning is a task-oriented strategy directed toward rationally and logically distributing community resources. It is a process of using the knowledge and expertise of professionals to plan, organize, and deliver services (direct service delivery).

Goals	Problem-solving orientation to community needs, service
Basic strategy	Fact gathering followed by rational decision making regarding the distribution of resources
Professional roles	Program planner, fact gatherer, analyst, program implementer
Sector	Public, quasi-public, or private
Conception of population served	Consumers (we are the experts; people consume what we diagnose is good for them)

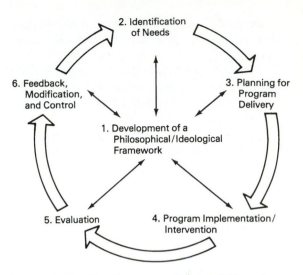

Figure 2.2 The Process of Social Planning

1. A way of connecting community influence toward achievement of a common goal.
2. A rational method of problem solving.
3. A process in which policy determined by a separate political process is translated into a set of operational orders for the execution of that policy.
4. A systematic ordering of the near future; a designing of the future.
5. Rational, goal-directed behavior seeking the optimum adaptation of means and ends as guided by a limiting set of social values.
6. A process whereby the planner feeds more information into the decision-making system.
7. Program development based on a process of goal selection and the progressive overcoming of resistances of goal attainment.
8. A means of directing social change through some form of coordinated program in order to further social well-being by attacking social and community problems. (Reproduced by permission of the publisher, F. E. Peacock Publishers Inc., Itasca, Illinois. From Fred M. Cox, et al., *Strategies of Community Organization,* 1974 copyright, p. 353.)

Social planning is a multistep process (see Figure 2.2). The initial step is the development of a philosophical/ideological framework. This often refers to the vision or mission of the organization—its value orientation. This is followed by the identification and assessment of customer needs; this is a fact-gathering and analysis process. The next step is planning for program delivery. This involves acquiring and transforming the resources necessary to produce services. Following this is the actual program implementation. We usually think of our services as falling into one of three categories: activities, places, or information. The next step is the evaluation of the program. There are two different approaches to this: formative and summative. The former is ongoing evaluation; the latter is evaluation conducted at the end of the program. Last, there is a need for some tie or feedback, modification, and control. This is a logical, rational, systematic approach to delivering leisure services.

One final note concerning social planning: No matter how logical and rational the process is intended to be, it is important to recognize that the resources of an organization are finite. That is, they have definable limits. Even though the process of planning may be well organized and carefully thought out, it is impossible to meet all the needs of all the people all the time. Our organization leaders as well as our leisure professionals must make difficult decisions regarding the distribution of scarce resources.

The city of Virginia Beach (Virginia) Parks and Recreation Commission (Virginia's First Commission for Accreditation of Park and Recreation Agency accredited program) has as its basic intention a vision of quality programs through the provision of park, land, facilities, and programs. The organization pursues its *QUEST* by emphasizing the following:

- Quality—Commitment to excellence
- United Vision—Clear sense of direction
- Effective Leadership—That guides a creative and competent workforce
- Response to customer needs through trust and communication
- Teamwork—Conviction that "it takes everyone's contribution"

This organization, with its voluntary advisory group serving as a sounding board, exercises influence throughout the community to improve and expand recreation opportunities. It offers a myriad of direct services, programs, and activities that are planned, organized, and delivered in accessible formats conveniently packaged for customers. The scope and range of programs organized by the agency are staggering—camps, outdoor education, cheerleading, basketball, services for the disabled, outreach programs, middle-school programs, before- and after-school programs, tennis, golf, ballet, tap, flamingo, Irish tap, salsa, jitterbug, swing, country line, ballroom, special events, fitness, football, soccer, art, adventure, softball, volleyball, walking programs, fitness assessment, crafts, racquetball, aquatics, pottery, ceramics, drawing (watercolors), computer use, drama, photography, dog obedience, guitar, massage therapy, cooking, gymnastics, karate, roller skating, tai chi, yoga, hockey, and many others.

Community Development

Community development is a process of enabling, or *indirect service delivery*. The strategy rests on the basic assumption that individual customers can be partners in the process of determining their own leisure destiny. In fact, community development suggests that individuals can learn the processes necessary to plan, organize, and implement their own leisure services based on their perception of their own needs. Basically, community development is focused on helping people help themselves.

Community development is not new to the leisure field. In the late 1800s and early 1900s, recreation and leisure services functioned as social service agencies and resulted primarily as a by-product of community concern for the welfare of the poor. Leisure services initiated through the developmental efforts of settlement houses represented one of the earliest attempts to improve the general welfare of the community and, as such, was one of the earliest forms of community development. Furthermore, early leaders of the play and recreation movement were not trained in play or recreation leadership but viewed themselves as social activists engaged in the process of community development. Contemporary recreation and leisure theorists have rekindled interest in the process of community development. They argue that the task-oriented approach to the organization of recreation and leisure services is less effective in the face of rapid and constant change and the emergence of humanism. Discussing the development of the recreation movement, Murphy (1975: 51–52) has written:

> The recreation movement has passed through several stages of professional development, including a phase dominated by the concern of park professionals for pleasant, passive surroundings in which people could enjoy leisure at their own pace; a period of time which included the propagation of an egalitarian "recreation for all" principle, which stimulated an almost compulsive concern for programs and activities, and the legitimizing of local government responsibility for recreation and leisure service; a tumultuous period of social upheaval and social unrest

which brought the movement back to issues of social concern and commitment to the provision of recreation designed to meet important social needs; and most recently a human developmental phase, which focuses on the individual and the need to build and nurture human services responsive to his needs. An ecologically based perspective, this evolving stage of the Recreation Movement is concerned primarily with the interrelationships among people in their physical and social environment and the way these relationships contribute to or hinder their ability to realize their human potential. The Recreation Movement, then, grew out of humanitarian concerns, and it appears that it has now come full circle, to an era which again is focusing on the individual. Recreation opportunities are increasingly being fostered with the intent to build and nurture arousing situations which are responsive to human needs. They are not seen as trivial, but as fundamental to the developing individual.

Thus, we see the resumption of the community development role as a strategy to be used in the organization of recreation and leisure services. At the heart of this shift in strategy is the recognition of the need to support alternative values in our society. The formulation and acceptance of alternative lifestyles are factors influencing the development of new forms of service delivery. There has also been an increased concern for the involvement of individuals in those decisions affecting their lives.

The role of the leisure professional involved in the community development process can be described in many ways. The professional can be viewed as a resource to individuals and community groups, providing valued information and insights. The professional can also be viewed as a teacher or coach, helping people clarify their values and instructing individuals in the skills necessary to work in groups. The community developer can be a coordinator linking various resources together within a community to assist individuals or groups in attaining their goals and objectives. A community developer can also be a friend or encourager to individuals and groups, serving as a source of inspiration.

The community development process should be viewed as a collaborative process. The community developer works directly with individuals on a face-to-face basis, encouraging them to identify and solve their own problems. The relationship between the community developer and the participating individuals requires mutual confidence, trust, and respect. The community developer does not try to "diagnose" the clients but helps them develop their own diagnostic skills and abilities. In this sense, the community developer can be thought of as a sharer and an activator in the process of an individual's or group's development.

It is important to draw a distinction between the work of a community developer and the work of a social planner. Perhaps the most important difference concerns the view that each has of the customer. The social planner views the customer as a consumer of his or her services. The role is to isolate individuals with needs and then intervene directly with services. The community developer, on the other hand, views participants as customers with whom he or she engages in an interactive process of problem solving. The social planner is primarily involved in fact gathering in an effort to determine the needs of the individuals being served. Once the appropriate information has been gathered, it is used in the decision-making process to develop a rational plan for the distribution of available or acquired resources. The community developer, however, maintains a basic strategy of change in which his or her role is to help through collaborative efforts. The community developer works with individuals and small groups, whereas the work of the social planner is primarily carried out in large, bureaucratic organizations. The skills needed by the social planner are primarily those of management and administration; the community developer's skills should be particularly strong in the areas of communications and small group behavior.

Specifically, community developers carry out four functions:

1. Community developers work toward stimulating individuals to think about and participate in not only their own personal development but also the development of the community in which they live.
2. Community developers work to develop the leadership capabilities of those with whom they work.
3. Community developers assist individuals by supplying information about the methods and procedures that an individual or group can use to bring about change within a community.
4. Community developers assist individuals in the formulation of values and the appropriate mechanisms with which to evaluate their progress toward the attainment of these values.

A good example of the community development process in action occurs when a leisure service agency works with a special interest club. In this situation, the agency attempts to organize information rather than activities and acts as a resource to the club, helping it evaluate its progress. Numerous programs can be shifted from a pattern of direct service delivery to an indirect program. In these days of financial constraints, this might be a useful pattern to explore. For example, why should a public service organization operate an adult softball league when the adults themselves have the ability to plan, organize, and implement the program? The staff resources saved in this area could be used in other program areas. How many leisure service organizations are prepared to let go of services in order to expand their community offerings (see Table 2.5)?

Communications and Community Development
The ability to communicate is a prerequisite to effectiveness as a community developer. Communication is essentially an exchange process that exists between people; it takes place only when the meaning of the message transmitted is clearly and accurately received by the recipient.

TABLE 2.5   Community Development as a Strategy for Delivering Leisure Services

Community development rests on the basic assumption that individuals can be partners in the process of determining their leisure destiny. It suggests that individuals can learn the processes necessary to plan, organize, and implement their own services based on their perception of their own needs. Community development focuses on helping people help themselves.

Goals	Self-help, teaching process skills, promotion of democratic values, service
Basic strategy	Assisting individuals to determine and solve their own problems
Professional roles	Enabler, catalyst, coordinator, teacher, value clarifier
Sector	Public, quasi-public
Conception of population served	Partners

Often people believe that communication has occurred because they feel that they have articulated their views clearly; however, it is important to remember that there is not only a sender in the communication process but also a receiver. If the receiver fails to grasp the meaning of the intended message or misinterprets it, then the communication process breaks down.

Because the community development process is a sharing process, the community developer not only must be an articulate sender but also must be able and willing to receive and understand the message transmitted by those with whom he or she works. The effective community developer double-checks the messages received to ensure that they have been received correctly; conversely, he or she checks to make sure that the messages communicated have been received as intended. The community developer doesn't build facilities or create activities but provides information and counseling in the broadest sense to individuals and groups. His or her raison d'être, as an expert in the communications area, is to ensure that the process of individual and collective development is achieved without communicative hindrance.

Assisting individuals in identifying and locating recreation and leisure opportunities can be seen as a process of helping to facilitate one's leisure. Therapeutic Recreation Services Department of Trinity Regional Hospital in Ft. Dodge (Iowa) has created a leisure resource directory that includes information regarding arts and crafts, bingo, bowling, club and member organizations, culture and the arts, dance, fitness, golf, parks, senior citizen activities, roller skating, softball/baseball, swimming, tennis, theatres, transportation, travel agencies and bureaus, county natural areas, and others.

Partners

The community developer must also have an understanding of group dynamics, especially small-group behavior. Since much of the community developer's work takes place in small groups, it is advantageous for him or her to be aware of the type and quality of interactions that are possible in such settings. This requires an awareness of the subtleties of individual behavior that may take place in group situations. The community developer might engage in positive manipulations of the individuals within a group to help them identify and solve their particular problems. This can be accomplished by tactfully addressing the dysfunction created when anti-group roles emerge and by encouraging those roles that are supportive of the group and are task oriented. The community developer needs to make the group experience a positive one. If a group is experiencing difficulties, the community developer should be able to use his or her skills to manipulate group behavior in such a way as to propel the group into a more positive direction.

Operational Assumptions of the Community Developer

The community development process is not a value-free process. A number of ideas or values may affect the interactions of people and, as such, may affect the role relationship that occurs between the community developer and the participant. Perhaps the most articulate statement of assumptions concerning the role of the participant and the community developer in the community development process is the following, developed by Biddle and Biddle (1965: 60–62):

1. Each person is valuable, unique, and capable of growth toward greater social sensitivity and responsibility.
    a. Each person has underdeveloped abilities in initiative, originality, and leadership. These qualities can be cultivated and strengthened.
    b. These abilities tend to emerge and grow stronger when people work together in small groups that serve the common (community) good.
    c. There will always be conflicts between persons and factions. Properly handled, the conflicts can be used creatively.
    d. Agreement can be reached on specific steps of improvement without destroying philosophical or religious differences.
    e. Although the people may express their differences freely, when they become responsible they often choose to refrain in order to further the interest of the whole group and of their idea of the community.
    f. People will respond to an appeal to altruism as well as to an appeal to selfishness.
    g. These generous motivations may be used to form groups that serve the welfare of all people in the community.
    h. Groups are capable of growth toward self direction when the members assume responsibility for group growth and for an inclusive local welfare.
2. Human beings and groups have both good and bad impulses.
    a. Under wise encouragement they can strengthen the better in themselves and help others to do likewise.
    b. When people are free of coercive pressures, and can then examine a wide range of alternatives, they tend to choose the ethically better and the intelligently wiser course of action.

c. There is satisfaction in serving the common welfare, even as in serving self-interest.

d. A concept of the common good can grow out of group experience that serves the welfare of all in some local area. This sense of responsibility and belonging can be strengthened even for those to whom community is least meaningful.

3. Satisfaction and self-confidence gained from small accomplishments can lead to the contending with more and more difficult problems, in a process of continuing growth.

4. Within the broad role of community developer, there are several sub-roles to be chosen, depending upon the developer's judgment of the people's needs:

a. Encourager, friend, source of inspiration, and believer in the good in people.

b. Objective observer, analyst, truth seeker, and kindly commentator.

c. Participant in discussion to clarify alternatives and the values these serve.

d. Participant in some actions—not all.

e. Process expert, advisor, conciliator, expeditor of on-going development.

f. The prominence of the community developer is likely to be greater in the early stages, then taper off toward a termination date, but it may increase temporarily at any time.

Finally, in summary:

5. When community developers work on a friendly basis with people, in activities that serve the common good;

When they persist patiently in this;

When their actions affirm a belief in the good in people;

When the process continues, even in the face of discouragement;

Then people tend to develop themselves to become more ethically competent persons;

Then they may become involved in a process of self-guided growth that continues indefinitely. (Excerpt from *The Community Development Process: The Rediscovery of Local Initiatives* by William W. Biddle and Loureide J. Biddle, copyright © 1965 by Holt, Rinehart and Winston, Inc. and renewed 1993 by Bruce J. Biddle, Loureide J. Biddle, and Katherine B. Austin, reprinted by permission of the publisher.)

Knowledge of these operational assumptions can be useful to the community developer in guiding individuals and groups, since they serve to illustrate a potential philosophical framework and role definition from which the community development process can take place. The assumptions made by Biddle and Biddle are not unlike the philosophical values that we hold in the recreation and leisure field. We, too, are concerned about creating opportunities for self-improvement, self-expression, and self-initiative.

Social Marketing

Over the past several decades, marketing has become a very popular topic in the leisure arena. We like the term *social marketing*. We choose this term for two reasons. The first is that *social marketing connotes an emphasis on the delivery of experiences rather than tangible products*. Most leisure experiences fall within the context of "social services." The second reason is that the primary thrusts of the leisure service movement—wise use of leisure, promotion of an environmental ethic, and enhancement of human dignity—take precedence over efficiency, profit, or other goals. However, this does not mean that leisure service providers ignore other desired ends, but rather have developed a priority structure that finds leisure professionals operating with a "social conscience." For example, profit is a goal sought in commercial outdoor recreation businesses. The social context that an outdoor vendor may operate in suggests a strong value orientation directed toward preservation and conservation of the environment. Marketing is built on the basic assumption that an organization should have as its basic strategic objective meeting customer needs. It is a way of aligning resources with needs, supply with demand. *Marketing is a philosophy that focuses the work of the entire organization on satisfying the customer* (see Table 2.6).

According to Kotler (1982: 64), "the true meaning of marketing is not hucksterism, making it possible to sell persons on buying things, propositions, or causes they either do not want or which are bad for them. The real meaning is

TABLE 2.6   Social Marketing as a Strategy for Delivering Leisure Services

Marketing is built on the assumption that an organization should have as its basic strategic objective meeting customer needs. It is a way of aligning resources with need, supply with demand. Marketing is a philosophy that focuses the work of the entire organization on satisfying the customer.

Goals	Satisfying customer needs, profit
Basic strategy	An analysis of needs, integration and initiation of marketing mix to meet these needs
Professional roles	Analyst, planner, implementor, promoter
Sector	Discrete target markets
Conception of population served	Customers, consumers, guests

the concept of sensitively serving and satisfying human needs. Perhaps the short-run problem of business firms is to sell people on buying the existing products, but the long-run problem is clearly to create the products that people need. By this recognition that effective marketing requires a consumer orientation instead of a production orientation, marketing has taken a new lease on life and tied its economic activity to a higher social purpose."

According to Rubright and MacDonald (1981), marketing involves a number of characteristics. These characteristics seem to apply in all sectors—marketing, voluntary, governmental/political—where leisure services are created and dispersed. The characteristics that appear to apply to all areas in which leisure services are delivered include the following:

Aggressiveness—An organization must have the capacity to seek new business instead of merely reacting to competition and then taking necessary action. An aggressive organization keeps up with new developments in its industry and takes risks if it can comprehend the ultimate benefits that may accrue for itself and its constituents.

A Continually Positive Attitude—If the overall agency attitude is characterized as negative, cyn-

ical, or sour, it is almost impossible to achieve a positive climate for marketing.

Contrariness to Tradition—Marketing makes things change because its presence means doing things differently, taking chances, discarding old habits, making or seeking new friends.

Initiative—An organization inclined to market cannot wait for clients to come to it; it can't assume that, just because it exists, it has no obligation to plan and develop its future.

Responsiveness—A marketing-oriented organization succeeds if it correctly perceives its targets; if it meets the needs of referrers, users, and staff members; if it knows its constituents' psychosocial underpinnings. The organization's response to impacting forces must not be reactive or arbitrary, but deliberate and calculated.

Planning—The organization must make this a major characteristic of its operation. Marketing is the study of the future, some say, and any bright future involves the ability to do sound planning (Rubright and MacDonald, 1981: 11–12).

There are essential differences in the marketing of services as compared to the manufacturing and the delivery of products; whereas products are tangible items, services are intangible, usually involving contact between one human being and another. Products can be seen, held, studied, tried on, tasted, or felt before using; in other words, the customer can sample the product before purchasing. Services, on the other hand, are more difficult to experience before actual consumption. In fact, to effectively meet the needs of individuals, a customer must anticipate the potential benefit to be gained from the service. Thus, services require interaction with the leisure professional, who presents the value of the leisure experience to the customer.

Some of the unique characteristics of service transactions are as follows:

1. Consumption or use is not possible without the participation of the seller.

2. Services are sold, then produced and consumed simultaneously.
3. The capacity to produce a service must exist before any transaction can occur. Services can't be stockpiled.
4. Universal performance standards are difficult to attain. "Not only do performance standards vary from one service seller to another, but the quality of a single-service seller may vary from buyer to buyer."
5. Since most services are paid for after they are performed and cannot be repossessed, service providers are very dependent on the good faith of the buyer (Rathmell, 1974: 6–8).

As previously mentioned, one misconception about marketing is that it involves selling. Marketing is more than just selling or promoting. Kotler (1982) has suggested that selling finds an organization focusing inwardly on its programs and services. Its primary goal is to achieve large numbers in terms of participation. The marketing orientation, on the other hand, is focused on consumer needs, wants, and desires. The work of the organization using a social marketing orientation is directed toward producing customer satisfaction. In contrast to

TABLE 2.7   The Marketing Mix

1. *Product.* The product refers to the type of service that is produced by the leisure service organization. There are five types of products—areas and facilities, activities, information, leadership, and equipment and supplies.
2. *Price.* The value of a service is often related to its price. There are multiple approaches to pricing.
3. *Place.* The time and location of a service is a critical factor in the marketing mix. Convenience is extremely important.
4. *Promotion.* Promotion is a process of communication between the organization and the customer. Promotional efforts let people know what is available and its cost, location, time, and benefits.
5. *Package.* Different programs and services can be packaged in different ways. This is referred to as the program format. The form can vary, yet the content remains the same.

the hard-sell approach, the marketing orientation is a process that involves integrating five components—the product (service/program), the place, the price, the way the product is promoted, and how the product is packaged—to produce customer satisfaction (see Table 2.7 and Figure 2.3).

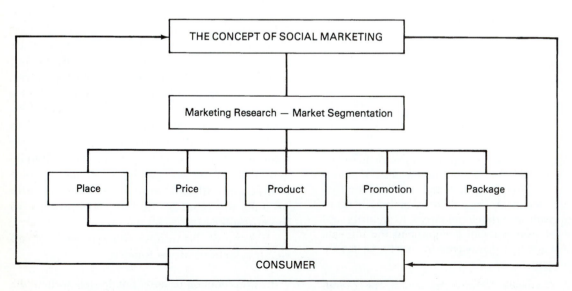

Figure 2.3   Social Marketing Mix.

Central to the idea of marketing is the identification of target markets. These are also referred to as "market niches." One of the central features of marketing is that an organization, to be successful, cannot be all things to all people. It must carefully determine what business it is in and what population it can best serve. To identify a target market, an organization will usually undertake the process of segmenting markets to understand specific customer needs to which it can effectively relate. Market segmentation usually is done by demographic and psychosocial variables. Demographic variables such as age, gender, and income are useful and psychosocial or lifestyle variables such as propensity or desire for risk, need for status, and others can be used to segment markets.

One of the interesting concepts to emerge in the marketing literature is that of the "product life cycle." This concept suggests that leisure programs have a definable life span (Figure 2.4). This life span can be viewed as having successive stages. When a service is first introduced, its acceptance by the marketplace is usually low. Over a period of time, if the service is successful, acceptance grows and reaches a point of maturity or saturation. At some point, adjustments need to be made in the way the service is packaged, promoted, or priced in order to accommodate changing environmental conditions. This must be done to ensure that the service remains viable over an extended period of time.

Leisure activities tend to have short life cycles. One could speculate that the novelty aspect of a new leisure program is an integral part of its attractiveness. Ellis (1973) suggests in his book *Why People Play* that novel, complex, and dissonant events elevate an individual's arousal and move an individual to an optimum level that is accompanied by pleasure. This pleasure is sustained for a relatively short period of time. Csikszentmihalyi (1975) suggests that individuals must be constantly challenged; otherwise they will become bored. Therefore, it would appear that new leisure programs challenge individuals

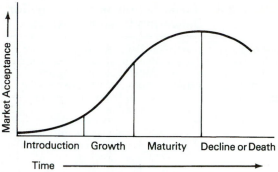

Figure 2.4   Product Life Cycle.

for a short period of time; eventually, people master the skills necessary to participate and move on to other, more challenging activities.

A final note on marketing—As previously indicated, marketing is concerned with consumer satisfaction. Thus, the focus of marketing activities is to determine which benefits individual customers perceive to be desirable. This is a dramatic shift from a focus on activities or facilities. Using this orientation, one could broadly suggest that we are in the "life satisfaction" business, not just in the business of providing facilities and distributing leisure programs.

Social Action

Social action is a strategy not widely considered to be among the repertoire of skills of most leisure professionals. *It presumes that there is a disadvantaged population, great social injustice, and a need to force the system, institutions, organizations, and agencies to change the ways they are distributing resources; hence, services.* The individual using the social action strategy operates outside the system. To be a part of the system would be inconsistent with the concept. However, we all see injustice in the way in which resources are distributed and, therefore, we are not able to distance ourselves from either the need to be involved or the effects of social action (see Table 2.8).

The social action strategy has been used successfully in advocating for the rights of persons with disabilities, for promoting the environ-

TABLE 2.8   Social Action as a Strategy for Delivering Leisure Services

Social action is a strategy that presumes that there is a disadvantaged population, great social injustice, and a need to force the system, institutions, and organizations to change the ways they are distributing resources, hence services. To be a part of the system is inconsistent with the concept.

Goals	Shift of power and resources
Basic strategy	Confrontation, crystallization of issues, identification of enemy targets
Professional roles	Advocate, broker, agitator, negotiator, organizer
Sector	All sectors of society
Conception of population served	Disadvantaged, victims

mental movement in North America, and for pursuing civil and human rights. In the latter cases, the right to leisure opportunities is seen as an important human right as recognized by the Universal Declaration of Human Rights.

The roles of the leisure professional when using a social action strategy are numerous and varied. Perhaps the most common role is that of the advocate. The advocate is a person who serves to champion or promote the rights of others. Often the person in this role helps identify the issues and organize people and resources to impact on the concern. Other roles that often are found are those of activist or agitator. Further, it is not unusual for the social action strategy to find an individual operating in the role of a negotiator or broker. These roles are not what we traditionally define as leisure professional roles. However, they certainly have the capacity to impact tremendously on the delivery of leisure services.

The social planning strategy and the marketing strategy view customers as consumers. Community development views the customer as a collaborator in the process. Social action views customers as individuals who are victims of society. A victimized population that is engaged in social action attempts to redress the power structure. Social action is often done through conflict or confrontation. It often requires direct action in the form of public protest and other expressions of concern to get the attention of decision makers.

How should a professional respond when confronted by individuals using the social action strategy? These groups and individuals can provide additional information and insight into problems with which they are concerned. On the other hand, certain individuals and groups act as pressure groups promoting ends that may not be in the interest of the entire community. The professional must assess needs and apply resources within economic and political realities accordingly.

Advocacy

Advocacy can be thought of as *a process that is directed toward the support of an individual or group viewpoint, program, or ideological position.* The purpose of the advocacy posture is to ensure that the individuals in decision-making positions are aware of and understand the program or service being proposed by the professional leisure planner. Discussing the relationship of advocacy to recreation, Nesbitt and Edginton (1973) offer the following information:

> Advocacy is a process directed toward improving the quality of goods and services rendered to consumers and an advocate [is] the person who generates and sustains the advocacy process. Functions include analysis, critique, planning, organizing, informing.

Thus, according to Nesbitt and Edginton, the advocacy mechanism is used not only as an informational tool but also as a means of improving the quality of services available to participants. In other words, the advocacy process is value-laden. It is directed toward substantially improving, via direct intervention, the welfare of individuals and groups addressed by the social activist.

The YWCA of Black Hawk (Iowa) County has embedded in its mission statement not only a call for direct service provision, but also for advocacy in education. Its mission includes promoting racial justice, dignity, freedom, and equity for all. Its local mission is consistent with the mission of the YWCA of the U.S.A., which advocates diversity and the creation of opportunities for women's growth, leadership, and power in order to obtain a common vision of peace, justice, freedom, and dignity for all people. The YWCA uses its collective power to eliminate racism wherever it exists, by any means necessary. The YWCA of Black Hawk County's efforts involve reaching out to the community through various advocacy efforts to assist individuals in making meaningful changes in their lives.

Corey (1971) has identified *five basic types of advocacy:* (1) *inside-nondirected advocacy,* (2) *outside-directed advocacy,* (3) *educational advocacy,* (4) *ideological advocacy,* and (5) *indigenous-liberation advocacy.* In inside-nondirected advocacy, the individual carrying out the advocacy process works within the bureaucratic organization that is providing services. The advocate's role is to represent not only his or her own viewpoint but also that of the customers represented. In other words, the professional in this case is advocating "for" people. In outside-directed advocacy, the professional plans "with," rather than "for," the customers he or she serves. The professional actively aligns his or her viewpoints with those of individuals (or a group) processing similar viewpoints. Educational advocacy involves the teaching of advocacy mechanisms so that others might carry out the process on their own. The fourth type of advocacy, ideological, finds the advocate focusing on ideals rather than on the actual felt or expressed needs of the customers. Many ideological advocates perform advocacy work that bears little or no relationship to the real or felt needs of those being advocated for. Nonetheless, the ideological advocate serves to facilitate initial exploration of alternative approaches for solving problems. The last type of advocacy, indigenous-liberation advocacy, involves the performance of the advocacy function by an independent group outside the realm of the social planning agency.

Edginton and Compton (1975) identify and define several roles that are carried out by people involved in the advocacy process. In the context of advocacy and special populations, the roles they identify are (1) *initiator, planner, strategist, or organizer;* (2) *investigator or ombudsman;* (3) *mediator, arbitrator, or negotiator;* (4) *lobbyist;* (5) *counselor;* (6) *technical or resource assistant;* (7) *educator;* and (8) *critic, analyst, or evaluator.* They define functions of each of these roles as follows:

> The *initiator, planner, strategist, or organizer* might come from within the special populations group or may be an outsider who specializes in such advocacy activity. This is a critical phase in the advocacy process, as the initial planning and strategies are usually the cornerstone of any movement. Sound planning and strategies usually yield success if followed by those carrying out the advocacy process.
>
> The *investigator or ombudsman* role is one in which individuals engage in fact finding, data gathering, and legal clarification in support of the rights of the members of our special populations. The role also includes identifying the current state of the art with respect to recreation, leisure, and cultural activities for special populations. In addition, it may involve preparing material for class action suits.
>
> The role of *mediator, arbitrator, or negotiator* is often placed in legal or governmental hands, but may also be handled by persons outside the two negotiating factions. This role is one which comes to the forefront when issues have been identified, requests for action have been clarified, and no subsequent response has come forth from the recreation, leisure, or cultural activity delivery system.
>
> The role of *lobbyist* is one that can be assumed by appointed and paid individuals, organizations, or other collective bodies. A lobbyist's function is to inform, gain attention, and persuade those making decisions about goods and services for a particular constituency. Particular attention must be paid to local ordinances, charters, state and federal laws, and regulations that directly affect the special populations consumer.

The *counselor* role is one which may be undertaken by an individual, either a consumer or an advocate. Counseling and guidance with respect to the quality and quantity of recreation, leisure, and cultural services is generic to efficient consumerism and advocacy. The counselor may work with one individual or a group. The counselor's job is to simply match resources with the individual or group needs.

The role of *technical or resource assistant* is involved with various functions such as financing, logistics, data gathering and compilation, identification, interpretation, and administration. This role may shift daily as the advocacy process emerges.

The *educator* role implies that there is an educational component to the advocacy process. Education, as an advocacy, focuses on the creation of societal awareness for the needs of the clientele represented. Working towards social reform, the object of this particular approach is to work within the existing political structure to represent the needs of special populations. The role of the advocate is to sell and/or educate each member of the society to be receptive and responsive to the pressing needs of those he or she represents. This approach has proved to be an effective and efficient method of bringing about change within our society. However, this method has also been viewed skeptically, as the interests of all the members of society are not inherently met.

Finally, the role of *critic, analyst, or evaluator* is one which is critical to any advocacy process. In order for the individual or organization to realize whether or not it has attained its objectives, the process of analysis or evaluation must take place. This process might be undertaken by a formal group which monitors progress toward stated objectives or may be an ongoing process which aids in identifying the quality and quantity of goods and services (Edginton and Compton, 1975: 27–29).

PROGRAM THEORIES

In the leisure literature, authors have detailed a number of theories concerning the way in which program services are developed. Knowledge of these program theories can be useful to both the student and the professional. Theories may help the student gain an understanding of the processes and procedures that professionals use in the development of activities, facilities, and other services. An understanding of these theories can be useful to leisure service professionals by enabling them to appraise their own methods of developing and selecting services. Ultimately, the professional might also be able to relate these theories to the type of organizational strategy selected for use within his or her agency.

Table 2.9, a summary of the work of Edginton, Hudson, and Ford (1999), describes various program theories. Over the past several decades, there have been nearly thirty-five program theories offered by various authors. These program theories are aimed at describing various approaches to providing leisure programs and services. As such, these theories provide a conceptual framework from which the leisure professional can guide his or her effort at creating leisure experiences. There is no one, preferred programming theory—several approaches can be combined within any given leisure service organization depending on its vision and mission. Some agencies will focus more on direct service delivery; others will find themselves serving as facilitators or advocates. A leisure service organization's focus will, in fact, have great bearing on the program theories it uses to guide and formulate how it plans, organizes, and delivers services.

MIXING ORGANIZATIONAL STRATEGIES AND PROGRAM THEORIES

Is one organizational strategy more appropriate than another? Is there one "best" program theory that the professional should use in his or her development of organizational services? The use of organizational strategies and program theories should be situationally or culturally specific. In other words, leisure service organizations must select strategies or program theories appropriate for their organization's particular needs and goals. The pragmatic professional should use any options available that will help

Table 2.9 Leisure Programming Theories

Program Theory	Author(s)	Description
Traditional approach	(Danford and Shirley, 1964)	Provides services that have been offered in the past, relying on former successes
Current practice approach	(Danford and Shirley, 1964)	Uses current trends to understand program needs
Expressed desires approach	(Danford and Shirley, 1964)	Uses participant information for program development
Authoritarian approach	(Danford and Shirley, 1964)	Professional executives make decisions regarding program design
Reaction plan	(Tillman, 1974)	Professionals wait and respond to demands generated by participants
Investigation plan	(Tillman, 1974)	Uses fact-finding methods to determine needs
Creative plan	(Tillman, 1974)	Promotes an interactive relationship between the participant and the professional for joint problem solving/sharing
Cafeteria approach	(Murphy, 1975)	Creates a menu of services and many program opportunities
Prescriptive approach	(Murphy, 1975)	Professionals diagnose the needs of participants, improving their leisure functioning
Trickle-down theory	(Edginton and Hanson, 1976)	Bureaucratic activities result in services trickled down through the organization
Educated guess theory	(Edginton and Hanson, 1976)	Professional hunches are used to plan programs
Community leadership input theory	(Edginton and Hanson, 1976)	Advisory and policy-making boards assist in program planning
Identification of need theory	(Edginton and Hanson, 1976)	Involves analyzing demographic information to determine need
Offer what people want theory	(Edginton and Hanson, 1976)	Involves reflecting "what participants want"; promotes communication and interaction between professionals and participants
Indigenous development theory	(Edginton and Hanson, 1976)	Promotes grassroots program development that uses community resources
Interactive discovery	(Edginton and Hanson, 1976)	Encourages joint problem solving; no subordinate/superior relationship; rather, a process of assisting others without imposing a value system
Sociopolitical approach	(Kraus, 1985)	Recognizes the influence of social and political pressures on the program planning process
Synergistic approach	(Carpenter and Howe, 1985)	Several organizations and agencies working together can offer better leisure experiences to a community or group that can any one organization or agency working alone

Continued.

Table 2.9   Leisure Programming Theories—*Continued.*

Program Theory	Author(s)	Description
Facilitative approach	(Carpenter and Howe, 1985)	Views participants as increasingly self-directed in their desires to increase and review their leisure functioning and pursuits
Consultative/contractual approach	(Carpenter and Howe, 1985)	Promotes the hiring of independent contractors and consultants who provide recreation opportunity
Quality of life or amenity approach	(Kraus, 1990)	Promotes leisure programs as a way of improving community life
Marketing approach	(Kraus, 1990)	Views programming in an economic context; a commodity to be aggressively promoted
Human services approach	(Kraus, 1990)	Promotes a social ethic and views programs as purposeful; links together community, health-related programs
Prescriptive approach	(Kraus, 1990)	Sees programming as an instrumental activity; a form of therapy
Environmental/aesthetic/preservationist approach	(Kraus, 1990)	Views programming as a mechanism to preserve the natural environment and protect historical heritage
Hedonistic/individualistic approach	(Kraus, 1990)	Stresses the pursuit of excitement and pleasure as focus of leisure programs; promotes creative expression
Programming by objectives	(Farrell and Lundegren, 1993)	Establishes the use of performance or behavioral objectives to guide program development
Programming by desires of participants	(Farrell and Lundegren, 1993)	Built on the assumption that participant needs can be identified and linked to program development
Programming by perceived needs of participants	(Farrell and Lundegren, 1993)	Promotes anticipatory planning and understanding the interest of individuals
Programming by cafeteria style	(Farrell and Lundegren, 1993)	Similar to Murphy (1975); encourages a smorgasbord of activities
Programming by external requirements	(Farrell and Lundegren, 1993)	Promotes utilization of normative standards or external criteria (e.g., CAPRA standards)
Symbolic interaction theory	(Rossman, 1995)	Focuses on programming the leisure experience and the queuing of objects in social settings
Benefits-driven approach	(Kraus, 1997)	Focuses on sharply defining the benefits and positive outcomes of leisure service

Source: Edginton, C. R., S. D. Hudson, P. M. Ford, 1999. *Leadership for recreation and leisure programs and settings.* Champaign, IL: Sagamore Publishing. p. 16–17.

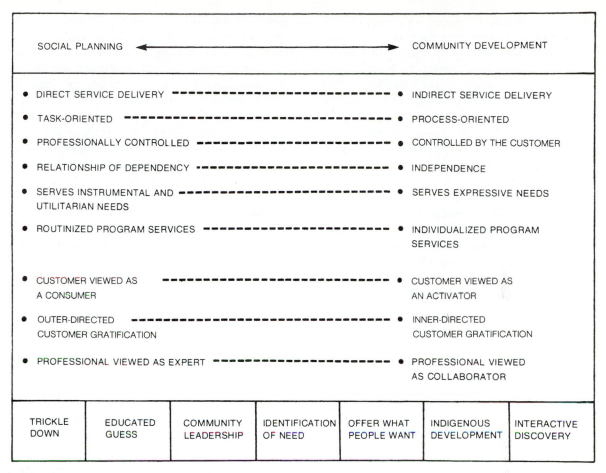

Figure 2.5 The Program Continuum.

him or her effectively and efficiently fulfill organizational responsibilities.

Figure 2.5, the program continuum, illustrates the relationship between the organizational strategies of social planning and community development and the Edginton/Hanson operational program theory paradigm. This figure suggests that organizational strategies and program theories can be viewed as existing on a continuum. At one end of the continuum is the social planning strategy of organizing recreation and leisure services. Related to this end of the continuum are the educated guess, trickledown, community leadership, and identification

of needs theories of program development. Generally speaking, professionals operating at this extreme of the continuum use primarily their own expertise in the development of services. They may or may not consult the customer. Their role is to organize direct services (that is, activities or facilities) and in some cases, to provide information. The social planning strategy of organizing recreation and leisure services, resulting in direct service delivery, is task oriented and professionally controlled. The professional is viewed as an expert; the customer is viewed as a consumer of services. The professional attempts to use his or her knowledge and perceptions of consumer needs to intervene with services. Services created via this approach tend to meet instrumental and utilitarian needs, comparable to Maslow's lower order needs. Such services do not promote satisfaction by fulfilling higher order needs related to growth, belonging, self-esteem and self-actualization.

Satisfaction from this type of recreation and leisure experience is dependent to a large degree on the actions of others; it is "other directed." The professional determines the course of events—the behavioral outcomes expected, the norms of gratification, and so forth. As a result, there is a tendency for the customer to become dependent on the professional for leisure gratification rather than to be self-reliant.

The community development strategy of organizing leisure services is found at the other extreme of the continuum. This strategy can be aligned with the indigenous development, offer what people want, and interactive discovery program theories of the Edginton/Hanson paradigm. Professionals using a community development strategy encourage the independent functioning of the customer. They are viewed as collaborators with the customer and as such, are involved in indirect service delivery. Professional community developers share their knowledge with the customer and help the customer define and attain leisure needs through his or her own efforts. The community development process serves to individualize program offerings, whereas the social planning approach concentrates and focuses on mass recreation and leisure experiences. Services tend to become routinized when the social planning model is employed.

At the community development end of the continuum, opportunities exist to meet humankind's expressive needs. Services that encourage shared decision making and the involvement of customers promote positive effect and build ownership. Such services can contribute to greater psychological growth and thus are related to higher-order levels on Maslow's hierarchy of needs. These services promote self-actualizing, growth-motivated needs. Strategies that involve people in decisions impacting on their lives may be more powerful than ones that leave the customer out of the decision-making loop. After all, as Samdahl (1988) has discovered, most leisure takes place in casual social occasions rather than in highly organized, exotic forms of recreation. It is obvious that individuals have more ownership in spontaneous social occasions within which they exert influence and control.

Although in our discussion we have dichotomized the relationship between the two organizational strategies (community development and social planning), in reality, this is not the case. Many organizations mix these strategies and theories to accommodate the specific and varying needs of their customers. For example, an organization might initiate interaction between customers with the professional in a dominant role, and gradually develop the relationship into one that facilitates the independent functioning of customers. It is also possible for individuals or groups operating within the framework of the community development strategy to influence an organization involved in direct delivery of services. A neighborhood association, for example, might organize itself around a given concern (i.e., the desire for a community center or for skills-oriented programs) and join with the local parks and recreation department in its development. In other words, the community development and social planning strategies may, in certain circumstances, complement one another; the most effective approach may involve the use of both strategies in varying proportions.

SERVICE ROLES

Murphy and Dahl (1991) suggest that a new cultural pluralism is emerging in the United States that will require a change in philosophical thinking in terms of the delivery of leisure services. According to these authors, the traditional model of direct service delivery will need to be

SERVICE ROLES	DIRECT SERVICE	INFORMATION REFERRAL	ENABLING FACILITATION	ADVOCACY
EXISTING SERVICE ROLES	• Conduct of fee classes for ethnic/ cultural groups • Provision for facility rental by ethnic/ cultural groups • Provision of ethnic/ cultural older adult social service programs	• Contracting private vendors • Contracting/hiring staff from ethnic/ cultural groups • Cooperative/ consultive interagency arrangements		
EMERGING SERVICE ROLES		• Appointing ethnic/ cultural persons to boards/commissions • Providing communitywide "Leisure Resource" information at every operation site	• Conduct of ethnic/ cultural awareness programs on regular basis for "whole" community • Conduct community leisure resource/ opportunity awareness programs for immigrant groups • Encourage self-help programs by neighborhood/ community ethnic/ cultural groups • Ensure leisure participation as option for everyone by meeting with indigenous community ethnic/cultural groups to learn about needs/ wants on provider bases	• Ensure participation by all ethnic/cultural groups by involving members in agency decision making • Ensure accessibility for ethnic/cultural groups by intervening in housing, transportation, and recreation concerns through proactive participation at City Hall, housing/ transportation authorities, etc. • Publication of brochures, catalogs, newsletters, flyers, etc. in multiple languages which reflect constituency

Client/Participant Dependence on Leisure Service Agency for Leisure Expression/Participation ⟵——————————————⟶ Client Independence from Leisure Service Agency for Leisure Expression/ Participation

Figure 2.6   The Service Continuum Model. (Source: From J. F. Murphy and R. F. Dahl, 1991. The Right to Leisure Expression, *Parks and Recreation* September, pp. 106–107.)

replaced by a more holistic approach. They suggest that the new leisure service delivery continuum includes four roles: direct service, information referral, enabling facilitation, and advocacy. Traditional direct service and information referral roles are being augmented by roles that assist individuals in making "self-directed choices and gradually transfer[ing] where possible, full responsibility for leisure planning and programming from the professional to the participant." This enables a process, according to these authors, that "fosters greater personal freedom and locus of control, two ingredients for leisure involvement" (see Figure 2.6).

Summary

From a historical perspective, leisure programming can be divided into three periods—the classical, the neoclassical, and the modern. The classical era was characterized by a great focus on play and on child-saving activities. There was great development in expanding services to include all age ranges, and the depression enabled a growth in facilities and services. The neoclassical era reflected gains in discretionary time and income and a great focus on quality of life issues. The modern era is best characterized as a period of time when marketing principles were applied to programming. Program gains were made in wellness and fitness, services for older adults, risk recreation, outdoor pursuits, tourism, cultural arts, and programs focusing on youth development.

The four basic strategies used in the organization and delivery of leisure services are social planning, community development, social marketing, and social action. The strategy or strategy blend used by the professional will have an effect on the planning process and on the program experience of the customer.

The professional who employs the social planning strategy uses his or her professional expertise and knowledge to identify customer needs and to plan programs accordingly. Thus, the locus of control in the process of program development remains essentially with the professional. Social planning is task oriented. The community development strategy demands grassroots participation and development. It is a process-oriented program strategy. The work of the professional who uses a community development

strategy is aimed at enabling the customer to assume the initiative for his or her own self-development. Consequently, the locus of control is not found within the organization but rather is located with the customer. Whereas the social planning method often results in a customer-dependent relationship, the community development strategy fosters customer independence.

Social marketing is a philosophical strategy directed toward meeting customer needs. This strategy involves integrating five components—the product, the place, the price, the promotion, and the packaging—to produce customer satisfaction. The social marketing effort implements the leisure experience while producing a strong degree of satisfaction. The social action strategy presumes a disadvantaged population. The leisure professional works as an advocate on behalf of disadvantaged groups, encouraging the redistribution of resources. Social action is often found in disabled, disadvantaged, or deprived population groupings. These four strategies can be blended in various ways to suit the needs of particular situations.

The leisure literature offers numerous theories in the area of program development. This chapter has described some of the more relevant theories and has incorporated them into a model delineating the results that are likely to occur with use of either the social planning or community development approaches to program planning and aligns relevant program theories along the continuum presented. The model points out that there are many ways to organize leisure services within these two basic strategies.

Discussion Questions and Exercises

1. What constitutes a leisure program? Trace the history of leisure programming.

2. Identify and discuss the differences among the political/governmental, voluntary, and market systems of leisure service delivery.

3. Select an agency from one of the categories listed in Table 2.1, Table 2.2, and Table 2.3. Schedule an interview with a professional engaged in the delivery of programs in each of these agencies and determine the following:
   a. The scope and types of program services offered
   b. The type of professional leadership utilized
   c. Methods of promotion
   d. Strategies used to deliver services
   e. Methods of program evaluation

4. Define *social planning*. Identify the steps in the social planning process.

5. Define *community development*. How does community development differ from social planning?

6. Define *social marketing*. What does the term "social" marketing mean in the context of the development of leisure services?

7. Contrast selling with marketing. What are the characteristics of marketing?

8. Define *social action*. What does the concept of advocacy imply?

9. Identify and discuss at least ten leisure program theories found in the literature.

10. Discuss how a leisure service organization can use social planning and community development simultaneously.

References

Biddle, W. W., and L. J. Biddle. 1965. *The community development process: The rediscovery of local initiative.* New York: Holt, Rinehart and Winston.

Boden, W. P., and E. D. Mitchell. 1923. *The theory of organized play.* New York: Barnes.

Bullaro, J. J., and C. R. Edginton. 1986. *Commercial leisure services: Managing for profit, service, and personal satisfaction.* New York: Macmillan.

Bulter, G. D. 1940. *Introduction to community recreation.* New York: McGraw-Hill.

Carpenter, G., and C. Z. Howe. 1985. *Programming leisure experiences.* Englewood Cliffs, NJ: Prentice Hall.

Corey, K. E. 1971. *A framework for advocacy planning.* Paper presented at Annual Conference of the American Institute of Planners, 25 October, at San Francisco.

Cox, et al., (1974). *Strategies of Community Organization.* Itasca, IL: F. E. Peacock Publishers, Inc.

Csikszentmihalyi, M. 1975. *Beyond boredom and anxiety.* San Francisco: Jossey-Bass.

Curtis, H. S. 1915. *The practical conduct of play.* New York: Macmillan.

Danford, H., and M. Shirley. 1964. *Creative leadership in recreation.* Boston: Allyn and Bacon.

Danford, H. G. 1953. *Recreation in the American community.* New York: Harper.

Edginton, C. R., and D. M. Compton. 1975. Consumerism and advocacy: A conceptual framework for the therapeutic recreator. *Therapeutic Recreation Journal* 9(1): 27–29.

Edginton, C. R., D. M. Compton, and C. J. Hanson. 1989. *Recreation and leisure programming: A guide for the professional.* Dubuque, IA: Wm. C. Brown.

Edginton, C. R., and C. J. Hanson. 1976. Appraising leisure service delivery. *Parks and Recreation* 11(3): 27, 44–45.

Edginton, C. R., C. J. Hanson, and S. R. Edginton. 1992. *Leisure programming: Concepts, trends, and professional practice.* 2d ed. Dubuque, IA: Brown & Benchmark.

Edginton, C. R., S. D., Hudson, and P. M. Ford, 1999. *Leadership for recreation and leisure programs and settings.* Champaign, IL: Sagamore Publishing.

Edginton, C. R., D. J. Jordan, D. G. DeGraaf, and S. R. Edginton. 1995. *Leisure and life satisfaction.* Dubuque, IA: Brown & Benchmark.

Edginton, C. R., and J. G. Williams. 1978. *Productive management of leisure service organizations.* New York: John Wiley.

Ellis, M. 1973. *Why people play.* Englewood Cliffs, NJ: Prentice Hall.

Farrell, P., and H. M. Lundegren. 1993. *The process of recreation programming.* State College, PA: Venture.

Hall, G. S. 1904–05. *Adolescence.* Vols. 1 and 2. New York: Appleton.

Hjelte, G. 1940. *The administration of public recreation.* New York: Macmillan.

Howard, D. R. 1985. An analysis of the market potential for public leisure services. *Journal of Park and Recreation Administration* 3(1).

Howard, D. R., and J. L. Crompton. 1980. *Financing, managing, and marketing recreation and park resources.* Dubuque, IA: Wm. C. Brown.

Hughes, J. L. 1897. *Froebel's educational laws for all teachers.* New York: Appleton.

Hutchinson, J. L. 1949. *Principles of recreation.* New York: A. S. Barnes.

James, T. 1993. The winnowing of organizations. In *Identity and inner-city youth,* by S. B. Heath and M. W. McLaughlin. New York: Teacher's College Press.

Kotler, P. 1982. *Marketing for nonprofit organizations.* 2d ed. Englewood Cliffs, NJ: Prentice Hall.

Kraus, R. G. (1997). *Recreation Programming: A Benefits—Driven Approach.* Boston: Allyn and Bacon.

Kraus, R., and J. Curtis. 1990. *Creative management.* 5th ed. St. Louis, MO: Mosby.

Kraus, R. G. 1985. *Recreation program planning today.* Glenview, IL: Scott, Foresman.

Lauffer, A. 1974. *Social planning in the United States.* In *Strategies of community organization: A book of readings,* edited by F. M. Cox, J. L. Erlich, J. Rothman, and J. E. Tropman. Itasca, IL: F. E. Peacock.

Lee, J. 1925. *The normal course in play.* New York: A. S. Barnes.

Lutzin, S. 1973. The evolution of the outreach program—How it all began. In *Outreach: Extending community service in urban areas,* by J. Bannon. Springfield, IL: Charles C. Thomas.

Meyer, H. D., and C. K. Brightbill. 1948. *Community recreation: A guide to its organization and administration.* Boston: D. C. Heath.

Murphy, J. F. 1975. *Recreation and leisure service: A humanistic perspective.* Dubuque, IA: Wm. C. Brown.

Murphy, J. F., and R. F. Dahl. 1991. The right to leisure expression. *Parks and Recreation,* September, 106–107.

Nash, J. B. 1927. *The organization and administration of playgrounds and recreation.* New York: Barnes.

Nesbitt, J. A., and C. R. Edginton. 1973. A conceptual framework for consumerism and advocacy in parks, recreation, leisure, and cultural services. Unpublished paper presented 11 January at Montclair State College, Upper Montclair, NJ.

Rathmell, J. M. 1974. *Marketing in the service sector.* Cambridge, MA: Winthrop Publications.

The Recreation Program. 1954. Chicago: The Athletic Institute.

Riis, J. 1890. *How the other half lives.* New York: Macmillan.

Riis, J. 1902. *The making of an American.* New York: Macmillan.

Rossman, J. R. 1995. *Recreation programming: Designing leisure experiences.* 2d ed. Champaign, IL: Sagamore.

Rubright, R., and D. MacDonald. 1981. *Marketing health and human services.* Rockville, MD: Aspen Systems.

Russell, R. V. 1982. *Planning programs in recreation.* St. Louis, MO: Mosby.

Samdahl, D. M. 1988. Leisure in our lives: Enhancing the common leisure occasion. *Journal of Leisure Research* 24(1): 19–32.

Smith, A. 1910/1950. *The wealth of nations.* New York: Dutton.

Tillman, A. 1974. *The program book for recreation professionals.* Palo Alto, CA: National Press Books.

Wolfenstein, M. 1955. Some variance in the moral training of children. In *Childhood in contemporary cultures,* edited by M. Mead and M. Wolfenstein. Chicago: University of Chicago Press.

The Leisure Service Programmer

LEARNING OBJECTIVES

1. To provide the reader with knowledge of the *criteria used in defining professional work.*
2. To identify and define *responsibilities of professional practice* for the reader.
3. To provide the reader with an understanding of the *concept of leadership.*
4. To enable the reader to gain insight into and appreciation for various *theories and empirical studies concerning leadership styles.*
5. To discuss the *relationship between professional values and leadership.*
6. To explore the various *roles of the leisure service programmer.*

INTRODUCTION

Individuals occupying professional positions in leisure service organizations play a key role in the successful planning, organizing, and implementing of activities and events. Such individuals are often referred to, in a generic sense, as leisure service programmers. The range and variety of activities that leisure service programmers engage in throughout the entire profession are broad. The work of a leisure service programmer may vary from supervising a specific program area to managing a facility. Leisure service programmers may engage in direct frontline face-to-face service delivery or they may find themselves serving as supervisors in an administrative capacity. The point is, the work of leisure service programmers is varied and situation specific, but always concerned with the development of leisure opportunities.

Leisure service programmers are responsible for organizing, promoting, implementing, or facilitating in some way the leisure experience for customers. The work of the leisure service programmer may involve actually leading the program or organizing some or all aspects of a service. Further, the leisure service programmer may serve as a facilitator, counselor, information provider, or developer of ideas. Leisure service programmers are pivotal to an organization's success. Their creativity, enthusiasm, competence, drive, and vision provide, in large part, the thrust that allows a leisure service organization to effectively meet and exceed its customers' anticipated needs.

This chapter examines the professionalism of the leisure service programmer, including the leadership styles that he or she might use and the roles that he or she might assume. Specifically, the terms *professional* and *leadership* are defined. In addition, the responsibilities of the professional and the importance of leadership to the leisure service field are discussed. Included are a number of significant research studies and models that deal with the subject of leadership.

THE PROGRAMMER AS A PROFESSIONAL

Professionals play a key role in North American society, and professional status is widely sought by a large number of occupations. Leisure services, as an occupation, strives toward professionalism; therefore, it is important to understand what constitutes a profession and why professional status is desirable. In this section, we explore and explain the necessary components of a profession, relating this information to the leisure service field. Furthermore, we determine to what extent the leisure service occupation meets the criteria of a profession as established by a number of noted authorities.

Primarily, the efforts of a professional are directed toward service rather than simply financial remuneration. In other words, the professional works to enhance the well-being of given individuals, motivated by altruistic values. The professional works with people because he or she is concerned with their development and growth rather than with their potential as a commodity to be manipulated or coerced.

Occupations can be viewed as existing on a continuum between the two extremes of professional and nonprofessional. Certain factors influence an occupation's status on the continuum. For example, the more recognition and status that an occupation is accorded by the public, the closer it will be to the professional end of the continuum. Edginton et al. (1999) described some of the other factors that affect the status of an occupation:

> *Discretionary Risk.* The status and recognition accorded an occupation is usually related to the amount of risk assumed by an individual practitioner in the process of intervention on the consumer's behalf. It may be suggested that the high status accorded to the medical profession is a direct result of the risk involved in protecting human life.
>
> *Consumer Knowledge.* The prestige of an occupation usually corresponds to the amount of knowledge that the public has of that given area of expertise. Simply stated, people are more in

awe of that which they know little about. The prestige and authority of professional practice in those occupations in which little consumer knowledge exists is evident.

Customer Values. Customers are more willing to accord professional status to those occupations which it values highly. If people value their leisure time more highly, greater status will be accorded the movement. If not, the prestige of the occupation will remain relatively stable. As the value of leisure time experiences increases, the status of the profession will increase (Edginton et al., 1999: 58–59).

Common Elements of Professions

Common elements are found in all professions. Four common elements that all professions possess are: (1) *an organized body of knowledge;* (2) *organizations and institutions that exist to transmit professional knowledge;* (3) *creation of professional authority as a result of public sanction;* and (4) *a code of ethics and standards to guide professional practice.* These four elements represent areas in which the leisure service occupation can improve to enhance its status and recognition as a profession. A discussion of each of these areas and the degree to which they have been achieved in the leisure service field follows.

An Organized Body of Knowledge

One of the primary prerequisites of a profession is that it serve society in a unique way. To perform a unique function, a profession must have a distinct set, or body of knowledge. We refer to the body of knowledge in the leisure service field as *professional knowledge.* Our professional knowledge is composed of three areas. The first area includes *information drawn from the scientific disciplines* such as sociology, psychology, anthropology, biology, and botany. This information provides us with our basic theoretical notion of humans, their environment, and the ways in which they interact. The next component of professional knowledge is drawn from the *values we profess and to which we subscribe.* In the leisure service field, for example, such values might include the right of all individuals to have access to leisure experiences, the

wise use of leisure time, promotion and protection of human dignity, and conservation and preservation of the environment. Professional values sometimes act as a filter, coloring any knowledge that is presented and influencing the extent to which we accept or reject even empirically verifiable scientific knowledge. The third area within our body of professional knowledge concerns *applied or engineered skills.* These are skills that the professional must have to perform his or her job. In the leisure service field, engineered and applied professional knowledge would include such skills as leading an activity, understanding the mechanics of the budget process, and knowing how to use public media to promote leisure programs.

The uniqueness of the body of knowledge of the leisure service field results from the blending of the resource areas around the phenomenon of leisure. The relationship between general scientific knowledge and professional practice is a linear one. As new bodies of knowledge are produced, the applicable or useful knowledge is incorporated into a professional framework (sometimes with modifications because of professional values). This process results in the development of quasi-theories of professional knowledge.

Professional knowledge is largely found in books, magazines, journals, manuals, technical and research reports, and statements by professional associations, agencies, and individuals. But, is this knowledge systematically organized? As the acquisition of knowledge accelerates (some say that it now doubles every five years), the existing organizational framework that traditionally centered around municipal park and recreation services has been expanded into several subareas such as program management, therapeutic recreation, outdoor recreation, sports management, tourism, youth development, and the social psychology of leisure. One constant should remain, however, and that is at the core of the expanded knowledge base in all of these areas is the understanding of the leisure phenomenon in individual's lives.

*Organizations and Institutions That Exist
to Transmit Professional Knowledge*

The next criterion to leisure services as a profession is that of existing organizations and institutions for the creation, exchange, and transmission of professional knowledge. Institutions and organizations provide the means by which knowledge can be verified, recorded, and passed "officially" between individuals and organizations in a systematic manner. Furthermore, once an area of study has gone through this process (become "institutionalized"), it is generally accepted as a routine service that is integral to the public welfare. Institutions and organizations allow us to formalize our commitment to a given concern—in this case, the provision of leisure services.

At the present time, numerous colleges and universities in the United States and Canada have programs in parks, recreation, leisure, tourism, sports management, and natural resource management. Development of formalized curricula in parks and recreation began at the college and university level in the late 1930s. Preceding the development of such programs were numerous career institutes and classes designed to train play leaders, including those organized and offered by Harvard University and the Playground and Recreation Association of America. The phenomenal increase of the number of curricula offered resulted in both a dramatic growth in the number of trained practitioners and increasing acceptance of the occupation as a profession (Stein, 1975).

In the United States, the American Institute of Park Executives (founded in 1904), the Playground Association of America (founded in 1906), and the American Recreation Society (founded in 1938) were some of the forerunners of the National Recreation and Park Association. The National Recreation and Park Association (in the United States) and the Canadian Park/Recreation Association serve as major professional organizations for the gathering and transmission of professional knowledge. All of these organizations, in their respective countries, draft and advocate positions or policies relating to leisure service. In addition, these organizations encourage the exchange of professional knowledge through the organization of conferences, institutes, and workshops, and through the publication of magazines, journals, and technical reports. Other organizations involved in the transmission of professional knowledge include the American Alliance of Health, Physical Education, Recreation, and Dance; the Resort and Commercial Recreation Association; the World Leisure and Recreation Association; the National Association for the Education of Young Children; the National School-Age Care Alliance; and the National Employee Services and Recreation Association. The publication of magazines, journals, and books by organizations transmits information regarding the leisure service profession. Some of the most visible periodicals in the leisure service field include: *Journal of Leisure Research, Leisure Sciences, Leisure Today, Employee Services Management, Leisure Studies, Therapeutic Recreation Journal, World Leisure & Recreation, Tourism Management, Annals of Tourism Research, Journal of Travel Research, Journal of Park and Recreation Administration, Parks & Recreation, Recreation Canada, Management Strategy,* and *Journal of Applied Recreation Research.* Access to many of these journals and magazines has been made easier through the technological advances of on-line subscriptions. Thus, professionals can have instant access to the latest scientific writings in professional journals such as the *Journal of Park and Recreation Administration.*

*Creation of Professional Authority
as a Result of Public Sanction*

The notion of professional authority can be viewed from two perspectives. First, the public at large can grant an occupation professional authority to intervene on behalf of, or in concert with, the customer without assuming full responsibility for its actions. If this is the case, the occupation is said to have the sanction of society. The occupation is given full authority to carry out its activities with limited interference. This is primarily because (1) society assumes that the professional has had extensive and thorough training; and (2) the customer has only limited knowledge of the occupation and the way in which it functions. Second, as an occupation achieves full professional status, it monopolizes services. Thus, the profession gains considerable authority because it is the only occupational group with acknowledged ability in a given area of demand. To recapitulate briefly, professional authority is created and exists when an occupation is sanctioned publicly.

Licensure, certification, or registration serve to document the fact that society accepts the authority of a profession (i.e., that the profession has the sanction of society). A license, certification, or registration program requires individuals to pass a professional knowledge examination, sets forth the rights and privileges of the professional, and establishes the boundaries and limitations of authority. For example, a license will grant an individual privilege to practice a profession but also will stipulate certain boundaries that, if disregarded, constitute malpractice or breach of confidence. In many states where leisure service agencies have started child-care and after-school-care programs, leisure professionals must conform to licensing requirements of the Department of Human Services in order to operate programs. However, in the majority of most program delivery areas in Canada and the United States, licensing has not occurred to any great extent. In contrast, there is an increasing number of well-developed professional certification programs at the state, provincial, and national levels. The National Certification Board of the National Recreation and Park Association (NRPA) offers a nationwide professional certification program requiring a written examination. Further, there is a well-developed professional certification program requiring testing for therapeutic recreation professionals operated by the National Council for Therapeutic Recreation Certification (NCTRC). To maintain professional certification from these organizations, individuals must pursue continuing educa-

tion activities as specified by the organization. In addition, depending on their area of specialization, leisure services professionals can be certified as certified recreational sports specialists (CRSSs) and certified commercial recreation professionals (CCRPs).

In the United States, the leisure service profession has attempted to sanction itself internally through university and agency accreditation processes. Whereas certification is the sanction of the individual, accreditation relates to the recognition of an organization or agency. The accreditation of college/university curricula began in the 1980s. Over 100 colleges and universities throughout the United States have met the voluntary standards set by the joint American Association of Leisure and Recreation/National Recreation and Parks Accreditation Board. In the mid-1990s, an accreditation process was begun for local public departments by the California Parks and Recreation Association (CAPRA). Since that time, there has been a slow but steady increase of agencies that have chosen to enhance their professional stature through this voluntary process.

While not all practitioners and educators have fully embraced the ideas of certification and accreditation, the profession as a whole has made steady progress to be recognized and sanctioned in the public arena.

Code of Ethics and Standards to Guide Professional Practice

Professional organizations establish a set of ethics or standards to govern the relationship that exists between the professional and those he or she serves, between the professional and the governing authority of employment, and between the profession and those in the profession. There is a need to establish norms of behavior by which the professional can exercise self-discipline because of the monopolistic nature and autonomy of professional practice. The leisure service field has been lethargic in the enforcement of behavioral standards. It was not until 1960 that the American Recreation Society (a forerunner of NRPA) established a code of ethics. Few professionals were aware of the content of this document and even fewer use the code as a mechanism for self-control. For these reasons, NRPA revisited this issue in the early 1980s and prepared an undated code of ethics, which included:

> General principles that applied to state recreation and park societies and affiliated professional organizations, and a set of special principles that related to such NRPA branches as the Society of Park and Recreation Educators and the American Park and Recreation Society. The general principles presented in this document were broad, including such statements as the need for the professional to be "of high moral character in fulfilling obligations to and protective of the public's trust" (Kraus, 1985: 333).

However, Shapiro's study (1986), found that fewer than eighteen state park and recreation societies had a written code of ethics, and almost none reported having a state code of ethics committee.

The National Recreation and Park Association continues to address the ethics issues with limited success. Better success in this area can be found at the local level, where a large number of public park and recreation departments have adopted policies and procedures that serve to guide the behavior of employees (see Figure 3.1).

The area of ethics and standards in the leisure services field needs further development. This is especially true in light of the field's evolution to a more humanistic-oriented philosophy, as evidenced in the contemporary leisure service literature and as demonstrated by the current practice of the profession. It is not enough simply to have a written code of ethics; there also must be commitment to the ideals presented in the NRPA document. Leisure service professionals would do well to promote the existing code of ethics and to be more fully aware of the ideals expressed therein.

An occupation may have satisfied all the criteria discussed here, but it still may not have achieved the level of status or recognition that some feel is appropriate. Even though the field of recreation parks and leisure services might have extensive professional preparation programs, a large body of knowledge, and a well-written code of ethics, certain other factors involving recognition may not apply to the leisure service field (such as risk, perhaps), thereby affecting the level of professional status attainable.

The Responsibilities of Professional Practice

As professionals, leisure service people must meet a number of responsibilities in order to operate in a professional manner. The guidelines presented here delineate responsibilities that, if fulfilled, can contribute to the development of individual and collective professional posture. These items by no means represent the only factors of which the professional must be cognizant, but should be viewed as elements on which the professional can build. The ten points presented are based on our practical experience and our direct application of these precepts in leadership, supervisory, and administrative positions in the leisure service field.

Placing the Needs of the Customer First

The most important responsibility of the professional is serving the needs and interests of the customer. This responsibility must carry over into all aspects of the professional's practice—planning, budgeting, and personal interaction. It needs to be an attitude that the professional not only practices but also conveys to subordinates so that the entire organization is directed toward meeting this goal.

Commitment to the Ideals of the Leisure Service Movement

The actions of the professional (resulting in program services) must be consistent with the philosophical aims of the leisure movement. The professional has the responsibility to promote the highest ideals of leisure as well as the productive use of leisure time. No single factor con-

---

NRPA Professional Code of Ethics

The National Recreation and Park Association has provided leadership to the nation in fostering the expansion of recreation and parks. NRPA has stressed the value of recreation, both active and passive, for individual growth and development. Its members are dedicated to the common cause of assuring that people of all ages and abilities have the opportunity to find the most satisfying use of their leisure time and enjoy an improved quality of life.

The Association has consistently affirmed the importance of well-informed and professionally trained personnel to continually improve the administration of recreation and park programs. Members of NRPA are encouraged to support the efforts of the Association and profession by supporting state affiliate and national activities and by participating in continuing education opportunities, certification, and accreditation.

Membership in NRPA carries with it special responsibilities to the public at large, and to the specific communities and agencies in which recreation and park services are offered. As a member of the National Recreation and Park Association, I accept and agree to abide by the Code of Ethics and pledge myself to:

1. Adhere to the highest standards of integrity and honesty in all public and personal activities to inspire public confidence and trust.

2. Strive for personal and professional excellence and encourage the professional development of associates.

3. Strive for the highest standards of professional competence, fairness, impartiality, efficiency, effectiveness, and fiscal responsibility.

4. Avoid any interest or activity that is in conflict with the performance of job responsibilities.

5. Promote the public interest and avoid personal gain or profit from the performance of job duties and responsibilities.

6. Support equal employment opportunities.

Figure 3.1 Professional Code of Ethics. From National Recreation and Park Association, Reston (Virginia).

---

tributes to the regression of the movement more than the gap that exists between professional philosophy or ideals and the actions of unprofessional practitioners.

Protection of the Customers' Rights

The relationship that exists between a professional and those he or she serves needs to be one of trust, mutual respect, and confidence. The professional protects the rights of the customer regarding privileged information or communication. Furthermore, the customer has access to any information that affects his or her well-being.

Acquisition of Adequate and Appropriate Knowledge Prior to Engaging in Professional Activities

The professional must have sufficient education and work experience to enable him or her to carry out the responsibilities of the job effectively. In addition, the professional must thoroughly research endeavors that he or she intends to pursue. Nothing is more frustrating to customers and other professionals than the individual who is ill-prepared and who has not adequately investigated the program area in which he or she is involved.

*Practice of the Highest Standards
of Professional Service*

The professional must endeavor to provide each customer or group with the highest possible quality of professional service. He or she should attempt to maintain consistent quality. This consistency of service will enable the professional to enjoy a reputation for dependability in terms of the quality of services provided.

*Continuous Upgrading of Professional
Knowledge, Skill, and Ability*

To maintain high standards of professional service, professionals must continuously seek out and acquire contemporary knowledge. Individuals must keep abreast of current trends, issues, and concerns. Frankly speaking, professionals who do not aggressively pursue new knowledge fail to serve their customers in the most effective and efficient manner possible.

Operating Ethically and Equitably

Leisure service professionals have the responsibility to be honest, forthright, and direct in their dealings with the public. Service providers should not attempt to mislead individuals through false publicity and information; nor should they discriminate between users or show favoritism to any individual or group. Professionals must not allow themselves to be coerced, bribed, or compromised.

*Maintaining a Collaborative Relationship
with the Customer*

Once an occupation has achieved full professional status, it is said to have monopolized services. When this occurs, the amount of control that the customer is able to exert over the profession is dramatically reduced. In fact, the customer's desires and concerns are often minimized, and the relationship that develops between the professional and the customer finds the latter in a subordinate role. Obviously, this is unacceptable in the leisure service field. Leisure service professionals must strive for a collaborative relationship. Collaborative interaction involves

dialogue—a *two-way* exchange of information. This approach is necessary to effectively translate the customer's interests and needs into tangible services or to assist the customer in the organization of programs.

Self-Regulation

It is the responsibility of the profession as a whole to establish standards for professional performance and to monitor its members in regard to these expectations. It is the responsibility of the individual to use these established professional standards as guidelines and to control and regulate his or her behavior accordingly.

*Contributing to the Development of
the Profession and Other Professionals*

The professional has a responsibility to share any special knowledge, skills, and abilities with others and to contribute his or her talents to the development of the profession as a whole. This can be accomplished through involvement in local, state, provincial, and national organizations, through the professional media, or through personal encounters. Established professionals should promote and encourage the development of younger, inexperienced professionals. The hallmark of a mature professional is the desire to share knowledge and experience enthusiastically with others. Such professional involvement contributes to the continuity and development of the leisure service movement.

CHARACTERISTICS OF SUPERIOR LEADERS

What are some of the characteristics of superior or excellent leisure service programmers? Seemingly, this is a difficult question to answer. Kouzes and Posner (1987: 16) have studied the characteristics that followers most admire in leaders. They have looked at more than 225 different values, traits, and characteristics. Table 3.1 presents a ranked list of the characteristics of superior leaders as noted by more than 2,600 individuals in industry. This table shows that the four highest-ranked characteristics are, in order,

TABLE 3.1   Characteristics of Superior Leaders

Characteristics	U.S. Managers ($N = 2,615$) =	
	Ranking	Percentage of Managers Selecting
Honest	1	83
Competent	2	67
Forward-looking	3	62
Inspiring	4	58
Intelligent	5	43
Fair-minded	6	40
Broad-minded	7	37
Straightforward	8	34
Imaginative	9	34
Dependable	10	33
Supportive	11	32
Courageous	12	27
Caring	13	26
Cooperative	14	25
Mature	15	23
Ambitious	16	21
Determined	17	20
Self-controlled	18	13
Loyal	19	11
Independent	20	10

From J. M. Kouzes and B. Z. Posner, *The Leadership Challenge: How to Get Extraordinary Things Done in Organizations.* Copyright © 1987 Jossey-Bass Inc., Publishers, San Francisco, CA. Reprinted by permission.

honest, competent, forward-looking, and *inspiring.* These findings were corroborated by other studies conducted in the public sector. These four characteristics can provide a basis for the work of leisure service programmers. Following is a discussion of each of these variables.

Honest. Operating with honesty or integrity is absolutely critical to establishing credibility as a leisure service programmer. A person's credibility is established in moment-to-moment, day-to-day interaction with others. We earn the trust and respect of others by operating in a way that is truthful, ethical, and principled (Kouzes and Posner, 1987: 18). Customers and other colleagues will follow an individual who they feel operates with integrity. We appreciate people whom we trust and in whom we can have confidence.

Competent. Competence refers to the leisure service programmer's ability to perform the role that he or she has been assigned. Competence can refer to a person's technical, conceptual, or human relations skills. These skills focus on the ability of an individual to get things done within a leisure service organization. An individual's technical skills provide him or her with the specific knowledge or details of a program area or format. Conceptual skills refer to an individual's ability to grasp and organize larger, broader issues associated with programming. Finally, human relations skills refer to a person's ability to interact successfully with others in a manner that moves the organization forward. As Kouzes and Posner note, "the abilities to challenge, inspire, enable, model and encourage . . . must be demonstrated if leaders are to be seen as capable" (1987: 19).

Forward-Looking. Forward-looking refers to the leisure service programmer's visionary or future perspective. Again, as Kouzes and Posner have written, "we expect our leaders to have a sense of direction and a concern for the future of an organization . . . Whether we call it a dream, vision, calling, goal or personal agenda, the message is clear: admired leaders must know where they are going" (1987: 20). Forward-looking, visionary leaders are able to translate their ideas, concepts, and dreams for tomorrow into a reality that is understandable, acceptable, and achievable.

Inspiring. To be inspiring is to be enthusiastic, energetic, and encouraging of the best efforts of others. Superior leisure service programmers are those who can inspire the best efforts of others. These programmers are individuals who can transform average talent and skill into outstanding performance. Enthusiastically sharing the potential impact of the leisure experience with others is often a key factor in the success of the programmer. The programmer's behavior has to convey to others the desired level of excitement, energy, and dynamism of the experience. We have all been associated with individuals who, because of their inspiring efforts, draw others to them and compel individuals to work or play with a greater degree of intensity, energy, and enthusiasm.

WHAT IS LEADERSHIP?

Leadership is a difficult and complex term to define; the word has many meanings and in fact has come to mean all things to all people (Rost, 1993). Further, leadership is often confused with management. Bennis and Nanus (1985), in their acclaimed book *Leaders: The Strategies for Taking Charge,* noted that "Managers do things right, leaders do the right thing." In discussing the distinctions between managers and leaders, Bennis and Townsend (1995: 6, 7) suggest the following:

- The manager administers; the leader innovates.
- The manager is a copy; the leader is an original.
- The manager maintains; the leader develops.
- The manager focuses on systems and structure; the leader focuses on people.
- The manager relies on control; the leader inspires trust.
- The manager has a short-term view; the leader has a long-term view.
- The manager asks who and how; the leader asks what and why.
- The manager has an eye on the bottom line; the leader has an eye on the horizon.

A definition of leadership can be viewed from a number of different perspectives. Some of the more contemporary leadership definitions found in the leisure services literature as follows:

> Leadership is the interpersonal influence exercised by a person or persons, through the process of communication, toward the attainment of an organization's goals (Russell, 2001).

> A dynamic process of interactions between two or more members of a group, which involves recognition, and acceptance of leader-follower rules by group members in certain situations (Jordan, 2002).

> Leadership involves influence, persuasion and moving people by their consent without authority (Bannon, 1999).

> Leadership is the process employed by the leader to assist individuals and groups in identifying and achieving their goals. Leadership may involve listening, persuading, suggesting, doing, and otherwise exerting influence on others (Edginton, Hudson, and Ford, 1999).

In all of these definitions of leadership, the emphasis is on establishing a vision and influencing the behavior of others. Leadership is a process in which customers and other professional staff members are moved toward a set of individual or organizational goals. Leadership is often viewed as an exercise of authority, a process of decision making and dynamic interaction. Leadership involves nourishing and enhancing others as well as persuading and influencing their behavior. It is a collaborative process that involves interaction between the leader and followers in a group setting. It often involves and results in cooperation and achievement among group members themselves.

Cordes and Ibrahim (1996:245) state that although each of the specialized occupations in recreation and leisure service requires particular characteristics and skills, all professionals need certain essential leadership characteristics, including:

- Ability to work effectively with others
- Insight into leisure trends
- Ability to develop interest and appreciation in others
- Sincere interest in public service
- Cooperative attitude and strong sense of dedication
- Common sense
- Ability to enjoy life
- Administrative skills
- Creativity
- Personable manner
- Trustworthy and respectful style
- Strong sense of values

Kraus (1985: 77–79) has written that leadership, as it relates to leisure service programming, involves four important elements. These elements are as follows:

> *Program Planning and Implementation.* This type of leadership involves the planning, organizing, implementing, and evaluating of leisure activities

and events. In other words, the leisure service programmer exercises leadership by managing all phases of the program planning process.

Direct Activity Leadership. This type of leadership involves the actual conducting of program activities, including providing activity leadership, group leadership, and counseling or enabling activities.

Provision of Related Program Services. This type of leadership involves working with other organizations to provide leisure services or related activities. These types of cooperative leadership experiences find leisure service programmers working to coordinate the resources of various organizations to meet the needs of individuals in a more holistic fashion.

Supervision of Special Facilities. Many leisure service programmers serve as leaders, supervising, managing, or actually leading programs and services at various types of leisure areas and facilities. Most notable is the work of individuals at outdoor recreation sites or special activity facility sites. Leadership in this type of setting may involve coordinating registrations, overseeing admissions, and providing general supervision.

LEADERSHIP STUDIES AND MODELS

Since the 1930s, researchers have undertaken studies that attempt to identify leadership patterns. These studies have emerged primarily from the areas of social psychology and business, although, more recently, some have emerged in leisure services. These studies and theories have provided an insight into the components of leadership style and situational variables that can impact the process of leadership. This section provides a historical summary of models and theories that have impacted the leisure services field (see Table 3.2).

The Benchmark Study: Lewin, Lippitt, and White

Lewin, Lippitt, and White reported what was perhaps the benchmark study on leadership in the *Journal of Social Psychology* in 1939. This classic study identified three key leadership styles—democratic leadership, autocratic leadership, and laissez-faire leadership (see Table 3.3). Interestingly, this study was conducted in the context of a leisure setting with a group of boys involved in model building projects. The researchers found that most of the boys reported liking the democratic and laissez-faire leaders more than the autocratic leaders.

Although this study was limited to a very narrow segment of the population—ten-year-old boys involved in voluntary club activities—the results of this research have been far-reaching in the leisure service profession. Many texts on leisure service leadership include a discussion of these leadership styles. The findings of this study's very limited sample suggest that a democratic leadership style is most desirable and effective in all situations. However, the ideal leadership style will vary according to the needs of a given situation, as will become evident with the review of other investigations into leadership styles and resulting group behavior.

The 1940s, 1950s, and 1960s: Defining Leadership Styles

In the 1940s, 1950s, and 1960s, several leadership models were proposed. Perhaps the most interesting concept emerging from these models was the idea that two types of leadership elements may constitute one style. These are referred to as either *task orientation* (also known as concern for production or initiating structure) and *people orientation* (also known as relationship orientation or consideration). Various authors have suggested that these styles can be mixed to provide accommodations of styles or that one's leadership style is on a continuum, with concern for task completion at one end of the continuum and concern for people at the other. A review of three studies/models that occurred during these decades will illustrate these concepts.

The Ohio State Studies

In an attempt to identify various dimensions of leadership behavior, the Bureau of Business Research at Ohio State University established a

TABLE 3.2   Leadership Studies and Models

Study/Model	Period	Major Contributors	Key Elements	Major Contributions	Other Remarks
Lewin, Lippitt, and White Studies	1930s	Kurt Lewin Ronald Lippitt Ralph White	Democratic leadership style; authoritarian leadership style; and laissez-faire leadership style.	Description of leadership styles	Beginning of the study in social psychology.
Ohio State Studies	1940s	Ralph Stogdill Alvin Coons	Initiating structure (task orientation); consideration (relationship orientation)	Discovery of integrating elements of leadership behavior—task (T) and human relations (HR)	Mixing of elements results in four styles: low HR, low T; high T, low HR; high HR, low T; high T, high HR
University of Michigan Studies	1940s	Daniel Katz Nathanial Naccoby Nancy Morris	Postulates that leadership is on a continuum	Continuum finds participant-centered leadership at one end and production-oriented at the other end	Participant-centered leadership promotes satisfaction
Contingency Model of Leadership Effectiveness	1960s	Fred Fiedler	Leadership style must be situationally determined	Style is determined by degree of favorableness to the leader by three factors: leader-member relations, task structure, and position-power	Provides empirical evidence that there is a need to match one's leadership style with situation elements
Path-Goal Theory of Leadership	1970s	Robert J. House Terence R. Mitchell	Directive leadership; supportive leadership; participative leadership; achievement-oriented leadership	Role of the leader is to "clear the path" to help achieve goals	Promotes the idea that there is no one best style of leadership
Tannebaum and Schmidt's Leadership Continuum	1970s	Robert Tannebaum Warren Schmidt	Leadership is on a continuum	Authoritarian, task-oriented leadership involves the leader making most of the decisions at one end of the continuum; at the other, the democratic relationship leader provides great freedom.	Promotes the idea that there is no one best style of leadership
Tri-Dimensional Leaders Effectiveness Model	1970s	Paul Hersey Keith Blanchard	Four basic styles: telling, selling, participating, delegating	Mixes task-relevant maturity into leadership discussion	Combines human relations orientation and task orientation with effectiveness

TABLE 3.2   Leadership Studies and Models—Continued.

Study/Model	Period	Major Contributors	Key Elements	Major Contributions	Other Remarks
Transactional and Transformational Leadership	1970s	James MacGregor Burns	Transactional leadership; transformational leadership.	Transactional leaders exchange one thing for another; transformational leaders lift people to focus on higher goal and needs.	Help individuals transcend self-interest.
Hitt's Dreamer and Doer Model	1980s	William Hitt	Four basic styles: victim, dreamer, doer, leader-manager.	An effective leader is both a dreamer and a doer, combining vision with implementation.	The essence of leadership is found in the ability to transform thoughts into action.
Leaders and the Learning Organization	1990s	P. M. Senge	Leaders are designers, stewards, and teachers.	Leaders are responsible for building organizations where people continually expand their capacities to understand complexity, clarify vision, and improve shared mental models.	Learning organizations are based on innovation, new ideas, creativity, networking, and shared decision making.
Collective/ Collaborative Leadership Model	1990s	C. Mabey	Leadership is not conducted in isolation; rather it is a shared, collaborative act, a partnership between individuals, groups, organizations, institutions, and communities.	Leadership is an influence relationship among leaders and collaborators who intend real changes that reflect their mutual purposes.	This type of leadership is more organic and fluid.
Leader Presence	1990s	Walter de Oliveira Christopher Edginton Susan Edginton	A leader may exert a positive presence and influence on others without directly pressuring them toward specific action.	The leisure service programmer builds a trust relationship and acts as a role model and a conveyor of values, goodness, and care.	This approach makes no attempt to pass judgment or talk individuals into a particular course of action.
Servant Leadership in Leisure Services	1990s	Don DeGraaf Deb Jordan Kathy DeGraaf	Applies Robert Greenleaf's characteristics of servant leadership to parks and recreation programming; major tenet is the idea that to lead is to first serve others.	Recognizes that leadership is an evolving characteristic within organizations where leaders become followers and participants become leaders.	Promotes teamwork, ethical caring behavior, and a sense of commitment.

TABLE 3.3   Characteristics of Different Approaches to Leadership

Authoritarian	Democratic	Laissez-Faire
1. All determinations of policy made by the leader.	1. All policies a matter of group discussion and decision, encouraged and assisted by the leader.	1. Complete freedom for group or individual decision without any leader participation.
2. Techniques and activity steps dictated by the authority, one at a time, so that future steps are always uncertain to a large degree.	2. Activity perspective gained during first discussion period. General steps to group goal were sketched; and where technical advice was needed, the leader suggested two or three alternative procedures from which to choose.	2. Various materials supplied by the leader, who made it clear that he would supply information when asked. He took no other part in work discussions.
3. The leader usually dictated the particular work task and work companions of each member.	3. The members were free to work with whomever they chose, and the division of tasks was left up to the group.	3. Complete nonparticipation by leader.
4. The dominator was "personal" in his praise and criticism of the work of each member but remained aloof from active group participation except when demonstrating. He was friendly or impersonal rather than openly hostile.	4. The leader was "objective" or "fact-minded" in his praise and criticism and tried to be a regular group member in spirit without doing too much of the work.	4. Very infrequent comments on member activities unless questioned, and no attempt to participate or interfere with the course of events.

From Kurt Lewin, et al., "Patterns of Aggressive Behavior in Experimentally Created Social Climates" in *Journal of Social Psychology,* S.P.S.S.I. Bulletin, Vol. 10, p. 271, 1939. Reprinted with permission of the Helen Dwight Reid Educational Foundation. Published by Heldref Publications, 1319 Eighteenth St., N.W., Washington, D.C. 20036-1802. Copyright © 1939.

series of leadership studies. Researchers developed an instrument called the *Leader Behavior Description Questionnaire* (LBDQ) to help them determine how leaders carried out their work. The LBDQ contained items that pertained to two dimensions of leader behavior: *consideration* and *initiating structure.* The consideration dimension was defined as involving actions indicative of friendship, mutual trust, respect, and warmth in the relationship between the leader and staff members (p. 21). In other words, it refers to the personal relationship that develops between the leader and the group. The second dimension, initiating structure, is defined as the leader's delineation of the role that each group member is expected to play, the establishment of well-defined patterns of organization and channels of communication, and the formation of methods for completion of tasks. In short, it refers to lead-

ership behavior that is directed toward the completion of a task.

Hersey and Blanchard (1977) have created a visual illustration showing the relationship of the consideration dimension to the initiating structure (Figure 3.2). The figure presents leadership as being bi-dimensional rather than uni-dimensional. The four quadrants of this model indicate that there are four different leadership styles involving initiation and consideration. A more complete explanation of this will be given later in the chapter.

Michigan Studies on Leadership Styles
In 1947, The University of Michigan Survey Research Center began a study to determine principles of leadership behavior that contribute to both the productivity of a group and the satisfaction that a group derives from participation. Generally speaking, this research group viewed leadership behavior as existing

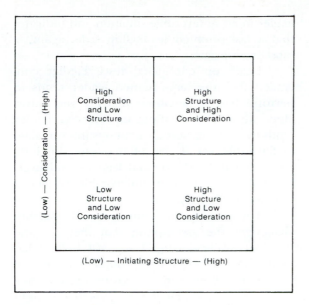

Figure 3.2 The Ohio State Leadership Quadrants. (From Hersey, Paul, and Blanchard, Kenneth H.: *Management of Organizational Behavior: Utilizing Human Resources.* 3rd ed. Englewood Cliffs, N.J., Prentice-Hall, Inc., 1977.)

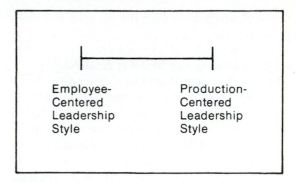

Figure 3.3 The Michigan Studies Leadership Style Continuum.

on a continuum (see Figure 3.3). At the one end of the continuum, the leader's behavior was employee-centered; at the other end, it was production-centered. Individuals who used an employee-centered leadership style were concerned with people and with establishing good human relations between themselves and their employees. With the production-oriented leadership style, individuals were concerned with the completion of a task. In leisure service activity, the production-oriented leader would be more concerned about the customer's accomplishments of a given skill, whereas the people-oriented leader would be more concerned about the sociopsychological growth and development of the customer. The objective of a leisure experience is often the acquisition of a given skill; however, the opportunity for social interaction is as important—or perhaps even more important—to the customer.

The leader's style will influence the outcome of participation.

Unlike the Ohio State studies, the Michigan continuum does not allow for the mixing of the two variables. It suggests that a leader who is more employee-centered will be less productivity-centered.

The Michigan Studies on Leadership Styles provided support for human relations-oriented leaders. The studies suggested that the more effective leadership style is one in which people are the major concern of the leader, subordinates are treated in a mature manner, are given responsibility and authority to conduct their tasks, and are not closely supervised (or, in a sense, coerced to complete their work activities). These studies also pointed out another important factor influencing leadership—that of the leader's superior. The leader behavior of the superior influenced the section leader's behavior toward his or her subordinates. Obviously, links among all levels of leadership in an organization ultimately affect the productivity of a group. One last point that emerged from the Michigan studies was that worker satisfaction was not found to be directly related to completion of tasks but to other factors. Perhaps the sociopsychological relationships that develop among individuals in a work group are of greater importance, in terms of satisfaction, than the material outcomes produced.

Fiedler's Contingency Model of Leadership

The Contingency Model of Leadership, developed by Fred Fiedler, relates an individual's leadership style to the performance of his or her group, hence, it indicates the leader's effectiveness. This model of leadership advocates a situational approach to the study of leadership behavior. The underlying premise of this approach suggests that different situations require different leadership capabilities and styles.

Fiedler's model suggests that the selection and utilization of an effective leadership style is dependent on the favorableness or unfavorableness of the situation. The favorableness (or unfavorableness) of a situation is determined, according to Fiedler, by three factors. The first factor is the *leadership relationship*. This variable is perhaps a leader's most important determinant of favorableness of a given situation. According to Fielder, "A leader who is liked, accepted, and trusted by his [her] members will find to make his [her] influence felt" (Fiedler, 1967: 150). Fiedler's second factor affecting the favorableness of a situation is the *degree of task structure* present. The task structure is the activities that are required of a group to fulfill its own goals or obligations as a subunit within a large organization. The last and least important of the variables affecting situational favorableness is the *power position* of the leader—his or her status within the organization.

Fiedler described three situations and determined which leadership style could be implemented most successfully in each. Figure 3.4 indicates the leadership styles appropriate for various group situations. The first situation finds the leader in a favorable leadership situation and suggests that a task-oriented leadership style will be most effective. The middle situation is one of intermediate favorableness for the leader and calls for a relationship-oriented leadership style. Fiedler's third situation finds the leader in an unfavorable situation and indicates that a task-oriented leadership style, again, is most appropriate.

Based on conducted tests, Fiedler concluded that the task-oriented leader tends to perform best in situations that are very favorable, while the relationship-oriented leader tends to perform best in situations intermediate in favorableness. Three of the tests also indicated that the task-oriented leader is relatively more effective in very unfavorable situations (Fiedler, 1967: 150).

The concept of contingency leadership challenges the assumption that there is one "best" style of leadership. It suggests, in fact, that there may be several appropriate leadership styles depending on the needs of a given situation. Furthermore, Fiedler suggests that it might be more effective to identify situations that fit the leader's style (and place him or her accordingly) than to invest large amounts of organizational resources on training or developing a leader to fit into a specific, existing situation.

Although Fiedler's model is useful in furthering our awareness of leadership styles and behavior, it can be criticized from several perspectives. First, his model views leadership styles as being either task-oriented or relationship-oriented and does not allow for a blend of the two (as does the Ohio State study). Second, his model is based on the supposition that people are rigid and fixed in their styles of leadership—that they cannot be flexible in their leadership styles and thus react appropriately in a variety of situations. This supposition denies the entire notion of human resource development in organizations.

The 1970s and 1980s: Effectiveness of Leadership Styles

In the 1970s and 1980s, leisure services researchers placed great emphasis on the effectiveness of leadership style. The idea of a leader's task-relevant maturity was introduced as a factor to be considered when adopting a particular style of leadership. The essential idea for-

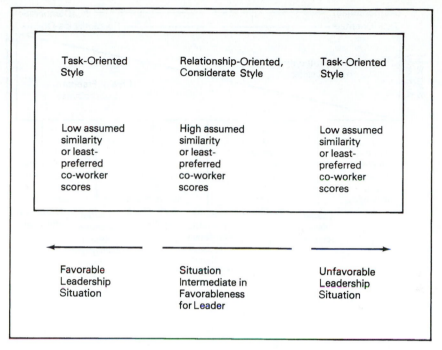

Figure 3.4   Fiedler's Contingency Model of Leadership. (From Fiedler, Fred E.: *A Theory of Leadership Effectiveness*. New York, McGraw-Hill, 1967, p. 14.)

warded is that no one, best leadership style exists. Four theories/studies that were proposed during this time will be examined.

Path-Goal Theory of Leadership

The Path-Goal Theory of Leadership is a recent approach to the study of leader behavior. Like the Contingency Model, this theory attempts to *identify the variables that influence the effectiveness of a given leadership style.* It offers four leadership approaches that can be used, in a situation-specific manner, to produce certain behaviors. According to House (1971), the theory involves the application of the following leadership styles:

1. *Directive Leadership*—This style is similar to the Lippitt and White authoritarian leader. Subordinates know exactly which is expected of them, and specific directions are given by the leader. There is no participation.

2. *Supportive Leadership*—The leader is friendly and approachable and shows a genuine human concern for subordinates.

3. *Participative Leadership*—The leader asks for and uses suggestions from subordinates but still makes decisions.

4. *Achievement-Oriented Leadership*—The leader sets challenging goals for subordinates and shows confidence in them to attain these goals and perform well (pp. 321–38).

In discussing the relationships between leadership styles and the tasks to be performed, House suggests that highly structured tasks require a different leadership style than relatively unstructured ones (Hersey and Blanchard, 1977: 103). He maintains that a high/low relationship leadership style is the most effective when tasks are relatively unstructured. However, when individuals are performing highly structured tasks, the most appropriate leadership

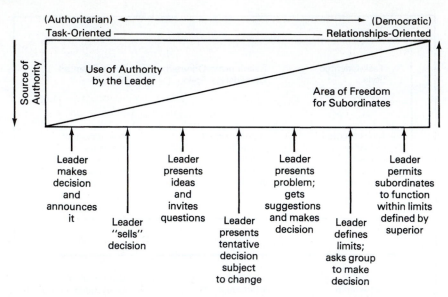

Figure 3.5 Tannenbaum and Schmidt Continuum of Leadership Behavior. (In Hersey, Paul, and Blanchard, Kenneth H.: *Management of Organizational Behavior: Utilizing Human Resources.* 3rd ed. Englewood Cliffs, N.J., Prentice-Hall, Inc., 1977, p. 92. Adapted from Robert Tannenbaum and Warren H. Schmidt, "How to Choose a Leadership Pattern," *Harvard Business Review* (March/April 1957), pp. 95–101.)

styles is one that is very supportive or relationship-oriented. When a task is highly organized and regimented, leaders find little need to reinforce task-oriented activities. Such tasks preclude the opportunity for individual creativity and flexibility; therefore, the worker must derive satisfaction from sources other than task performance. The major role of the leader, then, is to create a satisfying work environment in which workers can derive gratification from leader-member relationships (as opposed to gratification from task involvement and completion.)

Tannenbaum and Schmidt Continuum of Leadership Behavior

Robert Tannenbaum and Warren H. Schmidt have depicted leadership styles as existing on a continuum that ranges from an authoritarian, task-oriented leadership to a democratic, relationship-oriented leadership. Figure 3.5

illustrates this concept. As a leadership style along the continuum is applied by a given individual, the role of the leader—and the way in which this role is carried out—varies accordingly. An authoritarian leader is one who "makes decisions and announces them," as opposed to the democratic leader who presents problems, solicits suggestions, and then makes decisions, or who defines limits and asks the group to make decisions. Figure 3.5 shows that as the leadership style moves from authoritarian to democratic, the amount of subordinate freedom increases proportionately. Conversely, the leader's use of authority decreases as the style moves from authoritarian to democratic. As with other leadership models and theories, this continuum from Tannebaum and Schmidt recognizes the existence of two leadership components—one directed toward the completion of tasks and the other toward relationships between individuals. Frye and

Peters (1972) adapted this model to describe leadership behavior and client involvement in the area of therapeutic recreation.

Tri-Dimensional Leader Effectiveness Model

The Tri-Dimensional Leader Effectiveness Model is an extension and elaboration of the basic work carried out at Ohio State University in the 1940s. This model differs from that of Ohio State in that a third dimension—effectiveness—is added to the task and relationship behavior already described.

The third dimension, *effectiveness,* suggests the presence of certain situational demands that require a different style of leadership behavior. Some situations may call for an authoritarian style of leadership—a style with a high task orientation and a low relationship orientation—and other situations may need a more humanistic or democratic leadership style. The leisure service profession contains a variety of situations, each calling for the application of a particular style of leadership. Consider, for example, the leadership behavior required of an umpire or referee officiating at a sports program. The leadership required in this situation is highly task-oriented and authoritarian. The official cannot ask the teams to vote with him in making decisions regarding rule violations and completion of plays. On the other hand, the leadership behavior most appropriate in a senior citizen's center is quite different. In situations in which social interaction is desirable, the most effective leadership style would emphasize relationship behaviors and a democratic approach to leadership. Switching the application of either of these styles into the other situation would be inappropriate. As Hersey and Blanchard (1977) wrote:

> When the style of a leader is appropriate to a given situation, it is termed effective; when the style is inappropriate to a given situation, it is termed ineffective (105).

The Hersey and Blanchard Tri-Dimensional Leadership Effectiveness Model is presented in Figure 3.6. As shown in the model, the two dimensions—relationship behavior and task behavior—yield four, basic leadership styles: high task and high relationship, low relationship and low task, high relationship and low task, and high task and low relationship. When the effectiveness dimension is added, eight styles emerge—four in effective situations and four in ineffective situations (see Table 3.4). Thus, the role of leisure service programmer is to diagnose the situation and apply the appropriate leadership style. As Danford and Shirley state, "the difference between effective and ineffective styles is often not the actual behavior of the leader, but the appropriateness of the behavior to the environment in which it is used" (1964: 82).

Hersey and Blanchard's model takes into account the situational variables that are absent in other models, and as such, is a contingency model that emphasizes the use of a variety of leadership styles rather than the "one best" approach.

Burns's Transactional/Transformational Leadership Paradigm

A powerful way of thinking about leadership is to view the differences between *transactional* and *transformational* leadership (Burns, 1978). Transactional leadership is a more traditional approach to working with people. It has also been thought of as the *industrial* model of leadership. Transformational leadership, on the other hand, involves empowering people with a sense of mission that transcends narrowly focused personal interests.

Individuals engaging in *transactional leadership* are engaged in an exchange process. Leaders negotiate a relationship wherein an individual performs for a reward. Transactional leaders use a variety of rewards, including money and other reinforcements, to promote effort. The problem with this leadership style is that people are treated as a commodity or as pawns in an exchange process. They may or may not become truly vested in the vision or work of an organization. Such leadership usually produces an adequate level of effort, but does not necessarily produce

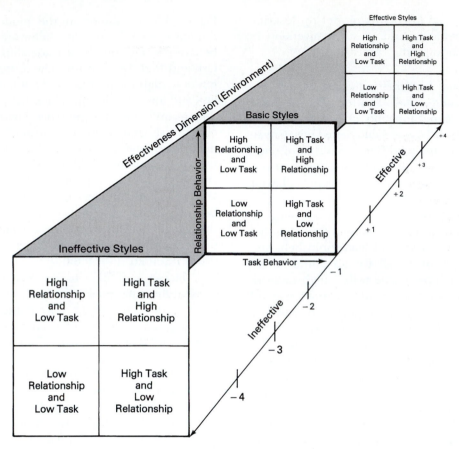

Figure 3.6 Tri-Dimensional Leader Effectiveness Model. (From Hersey, Paul, and Blanchard, Kenneth H.: *Management of Organizational Behavior: Utilizing Human Resources.* 3rd ed. Englewood Cliffs, N.J., Prentice-Hall, Inc., 1977, p. 106.)

an outstanding level of commitment, energy, effort, or performance.

Transformation leadership is built on a different set of assumptions. Transformational leaders work to empower other people by inspiring them to a higher sense of purpose or mission. Transformational leaders are concerned with individuals more than they are concerned with the exchange process of balancing work effort and rewards that can go on between individuals. The transformational leader works to raise the level of consciousness of individuals by helping them understand the broader implications of their efforts. For example, the work done by leisure service organi-

zations is central to producing a higher quality of life in North American communities. The transformational leader, by helping individuals to transcend their own self-interests, helps them reach higher levels of performance and, in turn, a greater sense of self-worth and self-esteem.

Hitt's Model of Effective Leadership

Building on the work of Bennis and Nanus, Hitt (1988) has developed a model of leadership that views the leader as a pragmatic idealist. The essence of leadership, according to Hitt, is to move an organization forward toward the right ends—to translate vision into action.

TABLE 3.4   How Others View the Effectiveness of the Basic Leader Behavior Styles

Basic Styles	Effective	Ineffective
High Task and Low Relationship	Seen as having well-defined methods for accomplishing goals that are helpful to the followers.	Seen as imposing methods on others; sometimes seen as unpleasant and interested only in short-run output.
High Task and High Relationship	Seen as satisfying the needs of the group for setting goals and organizing work, but also providing high levels of socioemotional support.	Seen as initiating more structure than is needed by the group and often appears not to be genuine in interpersonal relationships.
High Relationship and Low Task	Seen as having implicit trust in people and as being primarily concerned with facilitating their goal accomplishment.	Seen as primarily interested in harmony; sometimes seen as unwilling to accomplish a task if it risks disrupting a relationship or losing "good person" image.
Low Relationship and Low Task	Seen as appropriately delegating to subordinates decisions about how the work should be done and providing little socioemotional support where little is needed by the group.	Seen as providing little structure or socioemotional support when needed by members of the group.

From Paul Hersey and Kenneth H. Blanchard, *Management of Organizational Behavior,* 3rd edition, 1977. Reprinted with permission from the Center for Leadership Studies. Situational Leadership® is a registered trademark of the Center for Leadership Studies, Escondido, California. All rights reserved.

Hitt believes that leaders are individuals who have the ability to "transform vision into significant actions" (6). In this line of thinking, leadership is the driving force that provides the organization its vision and then helps move the organization to action to accomplish that vision. As Bennis and Nanus note, "leadership is what gives an organization its vision and its ability to translate the vision into reality." Thus, leadership has two elements: vision and action.

Figure 3.7 presents the two-dimensional elements of vision and implementation as adapted from the Hitt model, which proposes four types of leaders:

- Victim—Low on both vision and implementation; complains that the organization is unfair
- Dreamer—High on vision, but low on implementation
- Doer—High on implementation, low on vision
- Leader-Manager—High on both vision and implementation

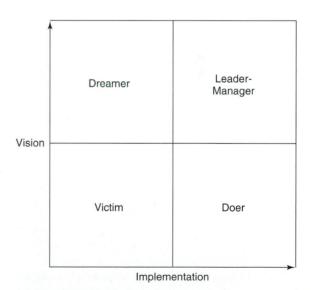

Figure 3.7   Hitt's Model of Leadership. (From Hitt, W. D.: *The Leader Manager: Guidelines for Action.* Columbus: Battelle Press. 1988.)

Visionary action is characteristic of the dreamer and implementation is characteristic of the doer. As Hitt notes, the leader is a dreamer and a doer, an individual who translates vision into reality.

The Contemporary Thought on Leadership in Leisure Services

Contemporary thought about leadership in leisure services is centered on collaborative models that emphasize the importance of relationships and partnerships. The models are based on the premise that leaders facilitate teamwork and group interaction in order to move the organization forward. In these models, the leader provides the presence or catalyst to get things done, but the actual action comes from individuals who are empowered to do the right things. The following models are examples of this new leadership paradigm.

Leaders and the Learning Organization

Segne's work, *The Fifth Discipline: The Art and Practice of the Learning Organization* (1990), provides key insight into the role of leadership in contemporary organizations. He suggests that to prosper, organizations must be "learning organizations." He describes learning organizations as including five learning disciplines—systems thinking, personal mastery, mental models, shared vision building, and team learning. He notes that the last two of these learning disciplines are engaged in by groups.

Learning organizations must be "organizations where people continually expand the results they truly desire, where new and expansive patterns of thinking are nurtured, where collective aspiration is set free and where people are continually learning how to learn together" (Senge, 1990). As Senge notes, people like to learn. The evolution from an industrial model to an information-based society creates opportunities for greater life satisfaction in all areas of life, as individuals are increasingly provided with opportunities for ongoing learning and growth.

Work, or perhaps what we might define as work/leisure, is increasingly viewed as having intrinsic value for individuals, and not just as an instrumental end.

Learning organizations will require a new perspective of leadership. Such organizations will be made up of individuals with a great sense of commitment. They will be populated with individuals of energy and enthusiasm who have a sense of shared responsibility for the effort of the whole. Learning organizations will be open organizations—open to change, to new ideas, to new ways of doing things. Organizations will have a vitality to them that encourages innovation, new ideas, creativity, personal commitment, networking, shared decision making, synergy, and group interaction that may transcend the work place and work hours.

Senge (1990) suggests that, traditionally, our leaders are viewed as "special people who set the direction, make the key decisions and energize the troops . . . leaders are heroes—great men . . . (and . . . women) . . . who 'rise to the fore' in times of crisis." His new view of leadership in learning organizations suggests that leaders are designers, stewards, and teachers (p. 340). Senge writes, "they are responsible for building organizations where people continually expand their capacities to understand complexity, clarify vision, and improve shared mental models—that is, they are responsible for learning."

Collective/Collaborative Leadership Model

Mabey (1994) offers a compelling, new view of the work of leaders in community settings that is defined as the *collective/collaborative* model of leadership. She suggests that the industrial model of leadership has three basic components: "it is an *individual* influencing a *group* toward a particular *goal.*" This model, according to Mabey, is too limiting in that leadership is not conducted in isolation. In most or all situations, leadership is a shared, collaborative act, a partnership, between individuals, groups, organizations, institutions, communities. As Mabey writes:

> the breakdown of the industrial model of leadership has been our need to extend our belief that one person can solve problems, that one institution can solve problems . . . When you say the word leadership, what you notice is people who do not talk about the relationship of leadership, they focus on the leader. The mode, however, is that leadership equals the leader . . . The United States is very individualistic; the way in which we view how rules are made, how law is made, how we function, is based on individualism not on collectivism (12, 15).

The collective/collaborative model of leadership is "an influence relationship among leaders and collaborators who intend real changes that reflect their mutual purposes" (Mabey, 1994). In this model of leadership, power is fluid, moving from one individual to another, depending on the situation. The challenge of leadership, according to Mabey, is one of converting "power to the followers" (p. 16). Collective/collaborative leadership transforms and empowers individuals. This form of leadership helps to "identify the resources and potential that exists and how you step in and help in a respectful way. . . . This type of leadership is more organic and fluid. It involves 'being connected, bringing people together' " (p. 16). It builds empowerment within groups, facilitating self-efficacy and control, and leaving people with the sense that they have significant influence.

According to Mabey (1994), there are several types of leadership because leadership must be connected to context—the context of self, team, organization, citizenship, or community (p. 20). The following discusses briefly the focus of each of these types of leadership and its outcome for the leader according to Mabey's collaborative/collective leadership model.

1. Personal Leadership—This type of leadership is focused on self-management and personal aspirations of the leader. It includes such skills as goal setting, decision making, time management, reflection, budgeting, life goals, and career planning. The leader builds self-worth, self-esteem, and individual competence. Outcomes related to self-efficacy of the leader include a feeling of importance, mastery, and achievement.

2. Team Leadership—The focus of team leadership is teamwork and collective action. Skills and competencies of the leader include team building, team development, recruitment of the team, group dynamics, interpersonal communications, delegating, accountability, and shared goal setting. Outcomes related to team leadership include understanding how to work together and building a spirit of cooperation.

3. Organizational Leadership—This type of leadership involves the role of the leader within the institutional setting. Skills and competencies of the leader related to this aspect of leadership include project management, organizational behavior, strategic planning/action planning, allocating resources, networking, conducting committee meetings, public speaking, staff selection/development, systemic change/organizational culture, managing information, and marketing/press relations. Outcomes related to effective organizational leadership include the ability of the leader to work with others and allocating resources to get something done.

4. Citizen Leadership—The leader engaging in effective citizen leadership actively participates in public life. Skills and competencies of the leader operating within this area include verbal persuasiveness, power mapping, issue competency, cultural competency, managing information, writing, advocacy skills/caucusing, networking/relationship building, asking questions, media relations, and social change strategies. Outcomes related to effective citizen leadership include political efficacy as evidenced by the ability of the leader to command the attention and action of persons in power.

5. Community Leadership—Community leadership focuses on identifying needs and resources and on facilitating the leadership of others to commit to action. Skills and competencies related to community leadership include

interpersonal communication, networking, community organization, community mapping, cultural competency, leader/group development, planning for transitions/successions, conflict resolution, public speaking, and grant writing.

Leading the Journey Leadership System
Another collaborative leadership model is the Leading the Journey (LTJ) leadership system. Belasco and Stayer developed this collaborative leadership paradigm and presented it in their book *Flight of the Buffalo* (1993). According to these authors, "all leaders face a challenge of leadership. The old models and paradigms no longer work" (16). The old paradigm of leadership, according to Belasco and Stayer, functions like a herd of buffalo. They note:

> Buffalo are absolutely loyal followers to one leader. They do whatever the leader wants them to do, go wherever the leader wants them to go . . . [the leader is] the center of power . . . because buffalo are loyal to one another; they stand around and wait for the leader to show them what to do. When the leader is not around, they wait for him to show up (16, 17).

The new leadership paradigm offered by Belasco and Stayer is compared to a flock of geese. This model promotes the importance of collaboration. Discussing team collaboration, Kayser (1994) found that the V formation used by flying geese enhances their range significantly. For example, when one goose falls out of the V formation, the drag is felt by the others immediately. Further, Kayser found that geese within the formation encourage the leader by honking and that geese rotate to the lead position. As Belasco and Stayer (1993) note:

> I could see the geese flying in their 'V' formation, the leadership changing frequently, with different geese taking the lead. I saw every goose being responsible for getting itself wherever the gaggle was going, changing roles whenever necessary, alternating as a leader, a

follower or a scout . . . when the task changed, the geese would be responsible for changing the structure of the group to accommodate . . . I could see each goose being a leader (18).

According to Belasco and Stayer, the new leadership paradigm is built around the following principles:

- Leaders transfer ownership for work to those who execute the work.
- Leaders create the environment for ownership where each person wants to be responsible.
- Leaders coach the development of personal capabilities.
- Leaders learn fast themselves and encourage others also to learn quickly.

Through collaborative leadership, rotating tasks, and supporting up/supporting down, the effectiveness of the entire group is enhanced.

The LTJ model of leadership is built on four basic activities. The first is to establish focus and direction—in other words, to develop a vision. The second objective is to remove obstacles and barriers that may impede performance. It has often been said that the role of the leader is to assist people in achieving their ends by removing the barriers or obstacles that prevent them from accomplishing effective performance. The third objective of the system is developing ownership—that is, encouraging a sense of responsibility throughout the organization. The fourth objective is to stimulate self-directed action—to encourage others to be leaders. This is accomplished by empowering people. Pantera (1995) has suggested that this leadership model can be applied to the park and recreation field, especially in working with youth.

Leader Presence
de Oliveira, Edginton, and Edginton (1996) have written that "intangible qualities of leadership are associated with terms such as visionary, passionate, caring, charismatic, warm, sensitive, and friendly." The conjunction of these characteristics forms what these authors refer to as

"leader presence." Drawing from the concept of presence found in Christian theology, these authors suggest that leaders can use their presence to influence others. This leadership concept has been successfully applied with hard-to-reach youth who do not attend planned or structured programs (de Oliveira, 1994).

What does the term *leader presence* mean? It is possible to sense or feel someone's presence, and in doing so, be touched by a positive or negative feeling. A leader may exert a positive presence and influence on others without *directly* pressuring them toward specific action.

For example, a leisure service programmer engaged in outreach might use the service delivery mode of leader presence and "hang out" with youth in areas that they frequent. The leisure service programmer models positive behavior and character, converses and clarifies, exerts his or her presence, and gets to know youth. Leaders in other settings might also exert a positive or negative influence on youth through presence—that is, through personal commitment, character, and values that are seen and felt by other people. Following is a description of the method of leader presence as practiced by youth leaders in Brazil with disenfranchised, disengaged youth.

> And [our work] will depend on this way of being, of being with, without bringing anything, only presence, but a constant and active presence . . . by active presence, we mean our presence of love, friendship and protection. A . . . presence which creates space for a dialogue, for the discussion of life problems (UNICEF/MPAS, 1983: 6).

This approach makes no attempt to pass judgment or to talk individuals into a particular course of action. Rather, the leisure service programmer builds a trust relationship and acts as a *role model*, a conveyor of values, goodness, and care. In this indirect manner, others (by observing and interacting with an exemplary individual with genuine care for them)

are encouraged to consider and clarify their values and consider the life example of the leisure service programmer.

Servant Leadership Approach

DeGraaf, Jordan, and DeGraaf (1999) have postulated that a new model of leadership is needed, one that puts serving others—including customers, employees, and the community—as the number one priority. They call this model the *servant leadership approach* and advocate that it should be the basis for programming and leadership in all types of recreation and leisure organizations—commercial, private, nonprofit, and public organizations.

The term *servant leadership* was first coined in 1970 by Robert Greenleaf. Spears (1995) identified servant leadership as an approach that "attempts to simultaneously enhance the personal growth of workers and improve the quality and caring of our many institutions through a combination of teamwork and community, personal involvement in decision making and ethical and caring behavior" (4). According to DeGraaf et al. (1999), "A servant leadership approach to delivering services encourages partnerships between constituents and professionals" (14).

The ten characteristics of a servant leader as defined by Spears (1995) include:

1. *Listening.* Servant leaders must make a deep commitment to listening intently to others. Listening, coupled with regular periods of reflections, is essential to the growth of the servant leader.
2. *Empathy.* Servant leaders strive to understand and empathize with others. People need to be accepted and recognized for their special and unique spirits. The most successful servant leaders are those who have become skilled empathetic listeners.
3. *Healing.* Learning to heal is a powerful force for transformation and integration. Many people have broken spirits and suffer from a variety of emotional hurts. Although this is a part of being human, servant leaders recognize that they have an opportunity to help make whole those with whom they come in contact.

4. *Awareness.* General awareness, and especially self-awareness, strengthens the servant leader. Awareness also aids in understanding issues involving ethics and values. It enables one to view most situations from a more integrated position.

5. *Persuasion.* Servant leaders rely on persuasion, rather than positional authority, in making decisions. Servant leaders seek to convince others rather than coerce compliance. The servant leader is effective at building consensus within groups.

6. *Conceptualization.* Servant leaders seek to nurture their abilities to dream great dreams. Servant leaders must seek a delicate balance between conceptualization and day-to-day focus.

7. *Foresight.* Foresight is a characteristic that enables servant leaders to understand lessons from the past, the realities of the present, and the likely consequence of a decision for the future.

8. *Stewardship.* Stewardship is defined as holding something in trust for another. Servant leadership, like stewardship, assumes first and foremost a commitment to serving the needs of others. It also emphasizes the use of openness and persuasion rather than control.

9. *Commitment to the Growth of People.* Servant leaders believe that people have an intrinsic value and must be included in decisions affecting their lives.

10. *Building Community.* Servant leaders are aware of the need to build community and actively seek to involve people in the process.

In the words of DeGraaf and others (1999), "leisure professionals must learn to be good leaders by learning to be good followers, by listening to participants and by helping them lead so we as leisure professionals can follow" (15).

THEORIES OF LEADERSHIP

The most important leadership models and research investigations into leadership have been fully described. However, several other general theories and approaches to the study of leadership are worthy of mention. One of the earliest theories of leadership is known as the *trait or great man theory.* Another theory widely used in the study of leadership behavior contends that leadership behavior is a *function of the group.* A third theory is known as the *situational theory of leadership.* We will discuss each of these general theories briefly and describe their relationship and applicability to the empirical investigations already cited.

Trait or Great Man Theory

This theory sets forth two conditions on which leadership can be based. First, individuals born to a high station in life are destined to become leaders, and second, some individuals are born possessing specific characteristics or traits that automatically enable them to emerge as leaders from any given situation. Most of the scientific investigations in this vein focused on identifying leader personality traits. After years of investigation, no conclusive results emerged. Therefore, research turned from study of the leader to study of those being led.

Leadership as a Function of the Group

This theory maintains that the function of the leader is to facilitate or encourage the work of the group. Group goals are achieved through positive interaction between the group and leader. As stated by Danford and Shirley (1964), the role of the leader within this context involves

> the performance of such acts as helping the group to establish goals, assisting it to achieve the goals, creating a friendly climate within which the interactions among members will be improved, providing the group with the facilities, equipment and supplies necessary for the attainment of its goals, and building a feeling of group unity and solidarity (p. 84).

This theoretical approach was emphasized in the Ohio State and Michigan studies, which focused on group perceptions of leadership behavior.

Leadership as a Function of the Situation

The situational approach grew out of the inadequacy of the trait and group theories. The basic premise of the situational theory is that several variables influence both the leader and the group in terms of performance, motivation, and satisfaction. Fiedler's Contingency Model of Leadership Effectiveness represents an effort to scientifically investigate this theory, and the Tri-Dimensional Leader Effectiveness Model is a situational model (emphasizing the need to respond to the environment when selecting a leadership style).

Discussing the application of the situational theory to leisure, Kraus and Bates (1975) have written:

> Since the competencies required in a leader are determined in large degree by the demands of the situation in which he is expected to function as a leader, the recreation administrator should study the situation carefully before assigning a leader to a specific task. He should ask himself this question: "Do the qualifications of this leader prepare him to meet the demands of this particular situation better than any other leader in our department?" At least an equal emphasis should be placed upon appraisal of the situation as upon appraisal of the leader. An individual might prove to be an excellent leader of a teenage club and a total failure of a club for the aged (p. 178).

A Word About Professional Values and Leadership

As previously indicated, one component of the professional knowledge of an occupation is its values and ideals. These values influence the provision of services. This is especially true in the leisure service field. An example of how professional values can influence provision of service is found in the playground manual of a Western municipal recreation department. In spite of the information gained from empirically based scientific investigations, this organization has chosen to emphasize subjective professional values above all. Table 3.5 sets forth a list of leadership qualifications desirable to this particular agency. These guidelines were presented to the entire staff as the basis for their actions. Some

guidelines are appropriate; others may be questionable. The manual excerpt illustrates how sociopsychological theories can be modified or bypassed because of adherence to subjective professional ideals. Particularly noteworthy is the statement "Is democratic" (relative to a quality necessary to being a good leader).

Leadership Ethics

Ethics and leadership go hand in hand (Hitt, 1990: 1). Many actions of leisure service programmers involve ethical decision making. Ethics can be thought of as standards of right or wrong. Another definition suggests that ethics are a set of moral principles or values. Ethical conduct and behavior are usually established by professional associations or societies that create codes of ethics. Such formal standards help guide the work of professionals and provide a benchmark against which they can evaluate decisions. Leisure service programmers will frequently make decisions that influence others; therefore, they must give careful consideration to the impact and consequences of their decisions.

The very nature of the leisure experience, emphasizing freedom and positive affect or the ability of individuals to influence their experience, requires decision making related to values and ethics. As Fain (1995) has written:

> The act of leisure begins with the question, "What ought I do?" Deciding what to do with this freedom of leisure is moral even when the decision ends in an amoral or immoral action. The fact that we make judgments about what is the right and the wrong use of leisure affirms this understanding and is why a leader will reason that one program is better than another (pp. 148–49).

Ethics and values are tied closely to one another. Values are principles or guidelines that individuals believe to be important in life (Edginton and Edginton, 1994). Thus, we can think of values as beliefs that are long lasting or enduring. Individuals have values, and organizations

TABLE 3.5 Professional Values' Influence Upon Leadership Behavior of the Recreation Leader

It may be true that to many Recreation Leaders, the art of leadership has come "naturally"; however, the majority of them, by far, are made—not "born." In other words, to be a good Recreation Leader takes not only a strong yen to be one and a keen love of good fun but also conscious, plugging effort and some self-examination.

Ask yourself which of the following qualifications, which are needed for a good leader, you can claim or can develop:

LOVES FUN and radiates the spirit of fun to the group.

LIKES PEOPLE and deals with them kindly and considerately.

IS DEMOCRATIC and gives the group a chance to share in making decisions.

IS GROUP-MINDED. Feels that individuals are important, but getting them to participate happily in the group is the job of a Recreation Leader.

IS PREPARED. Checks over information, tries out ideas, and rounds up more than enough material.

IS CREATIVE. Works under all kinds of conditions; can improvise and encourage others to do so.

IS HUMBLE, though confident. If not so confident, can be apprehensive or "just plain scared."

HAS FAITH in mankind. The best leader, whatever the goals, is attempting to bring more abundant life to those with whom he or she works.

Every leader finds that in attaining his or her goal, there are certain devices or techniques that bring better results than others. The "how-to-do's" are the skills and tools of the Recreation Leader's trade!

and institutions often promote a system of values. In the leisure field, the wise use of leisure as well as the conservation and preservation of the environment is valued, as is the promotion and protection of human dignity.

Some areas related to ethics and values that leisure service programmers must consider include the following:

The Ethic of Care. The primary focus of the leisure service programmer must be care of and concern for customers. In certain circumstances, care and concern for the customer may take precedence over rules, policies, and procedures.

Making Ethical Decisions. Leisure service programmers make decisions that impact others on an ongoing basis. There may be ethical dilemmas that the leisure service programmer must resolve when value structures collide. Decision-making processes are used by the leisure service programmer to increase the likelihood that sound, ethical decisions will be made.

Programming Ethics. Many ethical questions may emerge in regard to the establishment of programs and services. Issues of equity related to gender, socioeconomic status, ability, and other sensitive areas may require the leisure service programmer to evaluate the ethical foundation of programming efforts. Programming ethics may also involve issues related to quality and value.

Ethics and the Leader. Leaders have power and such power can be used unethically, as in the instrumental use of other people. On the other hand, power can be used wisely and well.

Ethics and the Customer. Relationships with customers must be conducted in an appropriate manner. Encouraging integrity, honesty, and respect of others in all interactions is paramount. Ensuring that the exchange that takes place between the leisure service programmer and the customer is handled in an ethical way is also important.

Ethics and the Environment. Leisure programmers value the environment. From an ethical perspective, it is an important responsibility to conserve and protect the environment and to use resources conscientiously.

ROLES OF THE PROGRAMMER

What does the leisure service programmer do? This question can be answered on both conceptual and operational levels. Conceptually, the programmer is involved in two basic types of service: *direct* and *indirect*. To implement direct program services, the programmer uses the social planning model of community organization. This approach (discussed in Chapter 2) suggests that the role of the programmer is to use his or her professional training and knowledge to diagnose the needs of the situation and to intervene in order to provide services. The second type of service, indirect, is based on the application of the locality development model of community organization. The role of the programmer in this strategy is to enable or encourage customers to assert their own skills in the initiation of programs and services that they feel will meet their needs. The purpose of this approach is to encourage self-help through collaboration between the professional and the customer. The customer has the ability to guide his or her own leisure destiny without the intervention of social welfare agencies.

Operationally, three professional roles result from our conceptual paradigm—the *activity leader,* the *program coordinator,* and the *community developer.* Because the strategy employed by activity leaders and program coordinators usually emphasizes their professional expertise, they are essentially involved in a direct service role. Community developers fall into the indirect service category because of their strategy of community organization and because they do not directly provide structured activities or facilities. In the remainder of this chapter, these three operational roles are discussed in depth.

Activity Leader

The face-to-face activity leader is one of the professional roles found within leisure service organizations. The number of full-time, face-to-face positions has declined over the years, and most of these positions today are part-time or seasonal. Therefore, the organization must focus on the function and importance of the role that the face-to-face leader plays in facilitating leisure programs and services.

What factors are involved in effective face-to-face leadership? This is a very difficult question to answer. The face-to-face leader may be involved in several different situations calling for a large variety of skills to fulfill his or her professional responsibilities. Because the leader works directly with customers, the factors that influence the patterns of interaction among individuals within groups are extremely important. The behavior among individuals in the group context is called "group dynamics."

Group dynamics can be described as the character and quality of interaction that takes place among individuals within a group and between individuals and other groups. How can the leader promote effective group dynamics? First, he or she can contribute to the effective functioning of the group by creating, promoting, and maintaining a positive group atmosphere. He or she can positively influence group atmosphere by being supportive of the group membership and by arranging the physical environment in such a way that individuals will feel secure. In addition, he or she can establish acceptable levels of behavior for the group and employ methods that secure and maintain that behavior. The leader should ensure that effective communication patterns exist within the group and should work toward establishing a feeling of esprit de corps within the group.

Although different situations require different leadership styles, the innate personality or behavior of the leader is an important factor in the development of his or her leadership style. Kraus and Bates (1975) have written that the leisure service leader's personality has great bearing on his or her ultimate success:

> He [or she] should be enthusiastic and lively in his [or her] presentation, so that his [or her] warm interest in the activity is communicated to group members. He [or she] should be well organized, and be able to help them enter into participation with a minimum of delay or confusion. He [or she] should be able to present the activity with the utmost clarity and efficiency. He [or she] should know it thoroughly, and have all the materials and equipment needed for participation ready. He [or she] should have control over the group, in the sense that its members look to him [or her] for help and direction (p. 178).

Numerous situations and settings require the application of general, face-to-face leadership skills. Playgrounds, recreation centers, camps, youth centers, senior citizens centers and programs, parks, nature centers, and athletic

TABLE 3.6   Organizing and Teaching Games—An Example of Engineered or Applied Skills

1. Get attention of everyone.
2. Use a warm-up before starting explanation procedures.
3. Give directions of game first, then announce the *NAME.*
4. Give *DEMONSTRATION* rather than *EXPLANATION.*
5. Get group into formation before giving demonstration and explanation.
6. If the rules are complex, first have a trial demonstration and then ask for questions.
7. Avoid repetition in your explanation.
8. *Do not* give explanations while in center of circle—too difficult for everyone to hear.
9. Coach while refereeing—try not to stop game.
10. Announce scores—it stimulates interest.
11. Use relays to teach skills.
12. Ensure success in games by having teacher be "IT" first.
13. Arrange competing teams equally in terms of skill and strength.
14. Avoid eliminating children from game when tagged; instead, give opposing team a point and allow those tagged to continue play.
15. Avoid monopolizing the game by re-tagging one another.
16. If child delays game by not attempting to reach base, have the group count slowly to five; if child is not on base at the count of five, he or she is considered out.
17. Avoid frequent changing of formations.
18. Avoid large groups; divide them into smaller groups to give children an opportunity to participate.
19. Gain attention by calling names or numbers.
20. Avoid situations where children are asked to *choose* partners.

IMPORTANT STEPS TO REMEMBER WHEN PRESENTING A NEW GAME ARE

1. Explain the game.
2. Demonstrate the game.
3. Ask for questions.
4. Do the game.
5. Evaluate the game.
6. Be enthusiastic.

fields are a few of the facilities, areas, and settings in which this type of leadership is presented. As a face-to-face leader, the leisure service professional comes into direct contact with the customers receiving the service. It is through the process of exchange between the leader and the customer that many leisure services are delivered.

Broadly speaking, leaders who perform the general, face-to-face activity leadership function are called *leisure service leaders.* Leisure service leaders are responsible for the organization and direction of activities and for the general supervision of facilities. Table 3.6 and Figure 3.8 represent two of the applied or engineered techniques used by the leisure service leader to lead activities. Table 3.6 focuses on the process of leading an activity; Figure 3.8 demonstrates the proper position of the leader relative to working with different group formations and activities. The general leisure service leader is expected to possess a broad knowledge of leadership skills and techniques (as opposed to a narrowly defined area of expertise). He or she must be able to direct games, lead contests, teach various skills, and supervise other activities.

The *leisure service specialist* is another kind of face-to-face activity leader. A person in this role functions within a very precise area of expertise and usually possesses substantial knowledge or training about a particular program area, population, or age group. When his or her expertise involves a specific program area, the leisure service specialist is probably teaching. An individual hired by a leisure service organization to teach tennis, for example, would most likely be a leisure service specialist. Such a person should have detailed knowledge of the rules, history,

These diagrams show the proper position of a leader when conducting activities in the following formations or conditions.

X—Represents the leader

Single-line formation

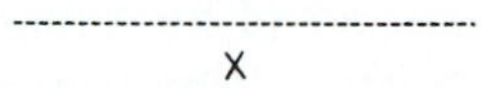

```
------------------------------------
              X
```

Double-line formation

```
              ------------------------------------
         X    ------------------------------------
```

Relay formation

```
         X    ------------------------------------
              ------------------------------------
              ------------------------------------
              ------------------------------------
```

Single circle   X ◯

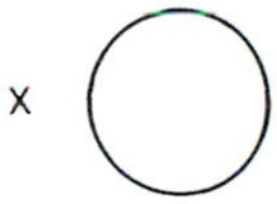

Two separate circle formations   ◯   X   ◯

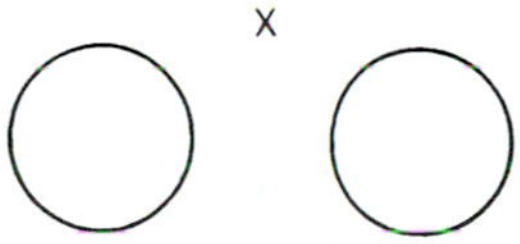

Double-circle (inside) formations

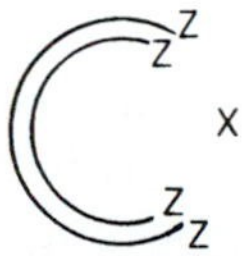

NOTE: During the explanation, the two circles break with Junior Leaders (represented by Z). This gives all participants a view of the leader. Join hands, re-form circle to start game.

Square or rectangle areas   X   ⊞

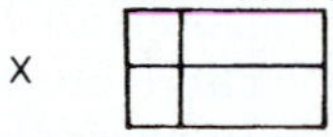

Stay in front of the group; never place yourself in middle of group. Always have group in front of you; do not allow participants to be behind you during explanation.

Figure 3.8   Proper Positions in Conducting Activities—an Example of Engineered or Applied Skills.

and procedures of the game. Often, he or she will have mastered the game itself. But most importantly, the individual must have the ability to transmit or teach the given skills or knowledge to customers. Another example of a leisure service specialist is the manager of an aquatic facility. An individual engaged in this type of work often not only possesses technical knowledge (for example, familiarity with the pool filtration system) but also is certified as a lifeguard and swimming instructor. This person interacts with individuals on a face-to-face basis, ensuring that they have an enjoyable, safe, and productive leisure service experience. A leisure service specialist also may have expertise in working with specific population groups—for example, a therapeutic recreation specialist. The therapeutic recreation specialist uses specialized knowledge of the etiology of disabilities as well as various procedures and techniques to provide programs and services for individuals with disabilities.

The face-to-face activity leader (whether possessing general leisure service leadership skills or more specialized recreation activity skills) is the main conduit through which the organization comes in direct contact with those who are consuming its services. Therefore, it is important to have activity leaders who are well qualified to handle the assignments they are given and who are well informed in the policies, practices, and procedures of the organization. Face-to-face activity leaders are hired because of their specific technical skill and ability and are not expected to have comprehensive, conceptual knowledge. To ensure a smoothly operating organization, the face-to-face activity leader should be made aware of his or her role in the organization and in relation to organizational goals. As stated by Graves (1977), "Beyond this, he [or she] should be able to view the activity, not just as a single event or experience taking place at a given time, but as a part of a continuing series of exposures and involvement in leisure pursuits for customers."

Neipoth (1983) has identified a number of roles that activity leaders might fill. These roles are diverse and can be situation specific. Some of the roles include serving as a *leader, teacher, group facilitator, advocate,* or *referral worker.* To this list, we also add serving as a *counselor, outreach worker, host/guide,* or *coach.* Following is a discussion of these roles.

Leader

As mentioned earlier, we often find leisure service activity leaders involved in general leadership roles. Leaders in this sense are individuals who provide direction, influence, and structure in a leisure service setting, often within a discrete program area, program format, or facility. Leisure service activity leaders are involved in leading and directing activities in such areas as arts and crafts, drama, sports, and so on. Leaders are often involved in working directly with target groups such as children on playgrounds or older adults.

Teacher

Leisure service activity leaders often provide instructional services. Teaching leisure skills to individuals involves identifying competencies, creating a comfortable learning environment, and encouraging others. The teacher also must want to select an appropriate method to convey information to individuals. The instructional format can be either formal or informal. Formal instructional environments in leisure service settings often involve the teaching of specific skills, knowledge, or values. The leader as an instructor uses various methods to communicate and develop the desired skills, knowledge, or values to the customer.

Group Facilitator

Leisure service activity leaders often work with groups to facilitate positive group interactions. There are numerous associations, clubs, special interest groups, and other types of groupings with whom leisure service activity leaders interact. Activity leaders in this situation help groups define goals, process information, develop identities, and establish and maintain procedures and methods for interaction.

Advocate

The leisure service activity leader as an advocate works to promote the interests of those individuals or groups that he or she represents. The advocacy function can involve representing others within an organization or providing information to individuals so that they may advocate on their own behalf or both. As Neipoth (1983) notes, "advocacy is the effort of a staff member to get changes made that will benefit others. . . . The staff member attempts to cause other people to make changes . . . that will benefit the people for whom the staff member is concerned" (p. 233).

Referral Worker

As a referral worker, a leisure service activity leader is involved in helping individuals get to or receive services that are needed but are outside the scope of the direct services provided by the leisure service organization. A leader must be perceptive enough to identify a person in need and then be able to effectively identify those services that might meet that need. Leaders in this sense must be sensitive to individuals and must also be resourceful in helping them identify and make contact with appropriate organizations.

Counselor

Often, leisure service activity leaders, especially those working in therapeutic recreation settings, engage in counseling. Counseling is generally directed toward helping individuals modify selected behaviors. Counselors often work to help individuals clarify values and develop problem-solving and conflict-resolution skills. Leisure counseling (leisure education) often involves helping individuals identify resources, develop skills, modify or enhance leisure lifestyle perspectives, and solve leisure-related concerns.

Outreach Worker

Outreach workers, according to, Edginton, Hudson & Ford (1999), are also known as roving leaders, youth counselors, street club workers, and street gang leaders. The outreach worker provides assistance in programs to individuals and groups in their own locale. In other words, he or she takes an activity service out of the facility and brings it directly to the customer, on his or her own turf and on the customer's own terms. The outreach worker attempts to provide services to individuals as an extension of the work of an organization. A good example of an outreach function is the "Meals on Wheels" program for the elderly.

Host/Guide

The host/guide carries out several responsibilities. Serving in this capacity, the leader may be charged with making customers feel comfortable, providing information, leading tours, and, in general, helping to make the leisure experience pleasant and satisfying for customers. The host/guide must have knowledge of an organization's functions, the ability to meet and communicate with customers in an effective and articulate manner, and the ability to anticipate and meet the needs of customers.

Coach

Coaching as a form of leisure service activity leadership involves a variety of different functions. Coaching entails not only enthusiastically encouraging and inspiring others, but also teaching and framing strategies for different game situations. Coaches promote and encourage values such as fair play and teamwork.

Program Coordinator

The role of the *program coordinator* or the *leisure service supervisor* is essentially one of middle management. In many organizations, it involves the actual creation and distribution of program services. We may find the program coordinator involved in planning, organizing, promoting, supervising, and evaluating programs. The process followed by the program coordinator in his or her work is depicted in the program planning model presented in Chapter 2. The work of the program coordinator is diverse, challenging, and exciting. On any given day, a program coordinator can engage in a variety of work activities—

appearing on a local television show to promote organizational activities, purchasing supplies and equipment necessary for the summer playground program, supervising activity leaders at several sites. The program coordinator serves many functions in the office, community, and numerous special locations. This position is frequently the major full-time, entry-level position available to individuals graduating from colleges and universities with a degree in leisure studies.

The responsibilities of the program coordinator within the leisure service organization can be administratively grouped together as follows: (1) *program area,* (2) *facility,* (3) *population group,* (4) *geographical area,* and (5) *a combination* of one or more of these.

Program Area

In many leisure service organizations, the program coordinator is given the responsibility for developing and implementing all services within a given leisure program area. In a municipal parks and recreation department, the program coordinator may be a sports supervisor who is responsible for organizing all sports activities for youth and adults. This could include competitive activities, such as leagues, tournaments, and play days; instructional programs, such as skill classes, clinics, and demonstrations; and organization and club activities, such as a swim-for-fitness club, a jogging club, or a soccer club.

Facility

A program coordinator may be given the responsibility for managing one type of facility, or a variety of facilities. For example, the program coordinator might be involved in the operation of a sports complex, a theater, a museum, a recreation center, an aquatic facility, an ice rink, or a park. Usually a person who manages a given facility is charged with the coordination of physical maintenance, program development, and general supervision (including control of drop-in use). The coordinator of a multiservice senior citizen facility, for example, might be responsible for structured programs, drop-in activities, medical and social services, transportation, meal programs, fund-raising, concessions, and maintenance. Leisure service organizations often have invested large sums of money in the development of physical resources. It is therefore vital that program coordinators have expertise in facility management.

Population Groups

The work functions of a program coordinator also can be organized according to population groups. This finds the programmer responsible for providing a complete and well-rounded offering of program services to a given population group (as defined by age, gender, or some other special characteristics). For example, a program coordinator working with population groups of different ages would develop such activities as preschool programs, children's programs, youth activities, and adult services. A program coordinator may also be assigned the responsibility of developing services for men or women, coordinating coeducational activities, or organizing program services for special groups such as persons with physical or mental disabilities.

Geographic Areas

Especially in larger communities, responsibilities for program coordination might be distributed geographically. This is usually done in an effort to maintain neighborhood cohesiveness and promote grassroots development. In addition, there is a movement toward decentralization of services in order to bring persons with decision-making powers closer to the recipients of services in a given geographic area. The decentralization of program services promotes accessibility of services and allows for the individualization of program offerings. The program coordinator operating within the decentralized model assumes many of the responsibilities just described (i.e., those associated with facilities, supervision, age group programming, and so forth).

Combination of Work Functions

As previously indicated, work functions within an organization are grouped together for administrative decision-making purposes. The structure of an organization—hence, its work assignments—is a reflection of its purpose and goals and the resources it has available to achieve these goals. Ideally, the work activities of a leisure service organization would be classified according to one of the four areas previously mentioned. However, in reality, an organization blends together its resources in the most efficient manner possible to achieve its goals. Therefore, we often find the work of a program coordinator organized around a combination of the previously described functions. For example, a recreation supervisor in a municipal park and recreation department of a middle-sized community might be responsible for the management of five community centers, summer playground programs, youth sports leagues, teen programming, and communitywide special events.

Although work functions can be classified in different ways, the actual tasks that are carried out by program coordinators are similar. Program coordinators must plan and organize the services for which they are responsible. This may involve determining customer needs, establishing objectives, hiring staff, and locating appropriate facilities and equipment. Once the services have been organized, program coordinators must promote the programs through use of the media and public relations resources. When the programs become operational, coordinators supervise the individuals they have hired to implement the service—providing both human and material support, encouragement, and assistance. Finally, program coordinators must audit and evaluate not only the efforts and work of their subordinates, but also their own efforts.

Obviously there is a certain amount of excitement in organizing and implementing a successful program. Program coordinators can be very gratified to see the results of their efforts being well received. However, it takes commitment and dedication to be successful. It may happen that program coordinators will carry boxes, make coffee, move furniture, sweep water off ball diamonds, and do other assorted tasks that are commonly absent from job descriptions in addition to managing human, fiscal, and physical resources in order to ensure the success of their programs.

Community Developer

The role of the leisure service professional as a community developer is not a new one. At the turn of the century, leisure service programs were promoted primarily by social agencies. Many leisure services resulted from early attempts to improve the "general welfare" of the community, especially for the poor. As such, the efforts of social workers in this area represented one of the earliest forms of community development. The massive, formalized growth of governmental intervention did not occur until the 1930s. Early leaders in the leisure service movement were not trained as play leaders; they were social activists, social organizers, or community developers. A movement is afoot within the leisure service field to again pursue the role of community developer and encourage people to take the responsibility and initiative for their own leisure concerns.

The adjectives used to describe a community developer are numerous. He or she has been called an enabler, a catalyst, a facilitator, a teacher, a change agent, a consultant, a stimulator, and a helper. In this context, we prefer the word *encourager* as the clearest description of the role of the leisure service professional operating as a community developer.

The leisure service professional as a community developer works primarily with community groups or associations that have been formed in response to an immediate concern or issue, such as the need for a swimming pool and community center or the rehabilitation of deteriorated park areas. These groups tend to be short-term, organized to solve specific problems. When a relationship between a community group and the developer has matured, the community

TABLE 3.7   Basic Functions of Community Workers

Advocacy—Community workers work with or on behalf of individuals and community groups to promote greater awareness of issues and concerns.
Analysis of Individual and Community Needs—Community workers use social indicators, surveys, demographic information, and other resources to analyze and interpret individual and community needs.
Conflict Resolution and Problem Solving—Community workers teach and work with individuals or community groups to identify and solve community problems as well as to determine ways to resolve conflict. This may involve mediation between parties.
Building Collaborative Relationships—Community workers attempt to build networks and effective alliances with individuals and community groups.
Training and Development—Community workers are involved in teaching and helping individuals and community groups develop skills to effect changes in their lives. The topics and subjects taught can be far ranging.
Counseling/Personal Support—Community workers may provide a wide array of counseling services and/or more informal personal support, including information, referral, advice, befriending, and enabling.
Promotion and Public Relations—Community workers are often called on to promote and bring attention to individual and community concerns. This may involve media work, public speaking, and other forms of communication.
Fund Development—Community workers often work with groups to help them identify sources of funding, develop proposals, and evaluate their efforts. Fund development may involve working with foundations, government agencies, or other donors.
Administrative Support—Community workers often provide support to individuals and community groups by engaging in record keeping, meeting facilitation, and other administrative/clerical activities. This may also include periodic reports to institutions, government bodies, and policy makers as required.
Outreach—Community workers usually extend themselves through some form of outreach. Their services may be provided in the neighborhoods, community facilities, homes, workplaces, and leisure settings where individuals are found.
Systems Access—Community workers act as the liaison between people who are disenfranchised or unable to effectively access institutions, agencies, or the political decision-making process.
Group Management—Community workers have a basic understanding of the principles and practices of group work, facilitation, community work, and community education. They are able to initiate and sustain group interactions and relationships and to enable community groups to assess and identify needs and determine a corresponding action plan.

developer should avoid co-opting the primary purposes of the organization. The relationship should be one of cooperation—a relationship in which the two bodies work together constructively, complementing each other's aims. Neighborhood and community associations may be involved in the management of services as well as in the execution of advocacy functions.

The encouragement of self-help and local initiative through the community development process is useful from several standpoints. First, it encourages citizen participation and, as such, makes governmental bodies and voluntary organizations more responsive to the needs of people. Second, the cost of providing services, especially innovative and creative new services, is becoming prohibitive, and the community development process increases available

resources to the organization. At the same time, it attempts to share the responsibility of the development of services with the customers.

The reviving of the community developer role in leisure service organizations requires the acquisition of a new and different set of knowledge and skills. A shift in the nature of services from a structure in which the professional serves as a direct provider to one in which he or she plays an indirect role as an encourager, changes the basic technology that is used in the leisure service profession. The role of the programmer, rather than emphasizing diagnostic skills and the methods and procedures used to provide services, becomes one requiring social skills in order to serve as a resource for individuals and groups. In other words, the community developer's work is not focused on the technical aspects of creating and distributing services but on the process of helping people to help them-selves. Table 3.7 lists the various functions of a community worker (developer).

Summary

In this chapter, we have examined the role of the leisure service programmer. The programmer is viewed as a professional. As such, he or she is involved in service. The professional performs his or her work in such a way that the needs of the customer are placed first. The relationship between the programmer and the customer is a collaborative one in which the programmer draws basic work gratification from the satisfying leisure experiences of the customer. The profes-sional programmer has usually attained a unique set of skills and knowledge through extensive college or university training. This unique infor-mation prompts society to recognize his or her authority and expertise in the area. As a profes-sional, the programmer has certain obligations, responsibilities, and duties. These are found in the profession's code of ethics or standards in the professional literature.

All programmers function as leaders. Knowledge of leadership techniques, skills, and theories is essential to the programmer. Leader-ship can be thought of as a process of influence that, when properly directed, helps a group or organization achieve its goals. The leadership style of the programmer is a key element influ-encing his or her success. Several leadership the-ories exist (e.g., trait, group, and situational). Contemporary scientific investigation has deter-mined that a contingency approach to leader-ship is the most effective. In other words,

leadership styles should be situation specific. There is no "best" leadership style; the most appropriate style will vary with the situation involved.

Finally, in this chapter, we have discussed, conceptually and operationally, the roles of the programmer. Two conceptual roles have been identified—the direct service role and the indi-rect service role. The direct service role implies structure and the use of professional knowledge in meeting people's needs. The indirect approach to services involves providing assis-tance to the customer and encouraging commu-nity initiative and indigenous leadership. Three operational roles that can be assumed by the programmer are also identified. Those individu-als employed on a full- or part-time basis to per-form the face-to-face leadership are called activity leaders. They are the prime conduit through which an organization interacts with its customers. Program coordinators are those indi-viduals who serve as middle managers in leisure service organizations. They are responsible for planning, organizing, and implementing services (e.g., employment of staff, promotion of activi-ties via mass communication) and acquisition of facilities and equipment. Community developers represent another operational role. The com-munity developer can be thought of as an encourager—an individual who works with peo-ple at the grassroots level.

Discussion Questions and Exercises
---

1. What are the four common elements that all professions possess?

2. Discuss the professional status of leisure occupations.

3. What is professional knowledge? Cite examples of the types of knowledge that are involved in its development.

4. What is leadership? What are the levels at which leadership occurs within a leisure service organization?

5. Identify and discuss four different characteristics of superior leisure service leaders.

6. What is the difference between direct and indirect services?

7. Identify and define four operational roles performed by leisure service professionals.

8. Identify and discuss how the responsibilities of a program coordinator can be grouped administratively within leisure service organizations. Locate an organizational chart for a public leisure service organization and analyze it in light of these administrative groupings.

9. What are some of the specific roles that leisure service activity leaders play? Provide an example of each of these roles in an actual leisure service organization.

10. Discuss the work of the leisure service programmer as a community developer.

References

Bannon, J. 1999. *911 management: A comprehensive guide for leisure service management.* Champaign, IL: Sagamore.

Belasco, J. A., and R. C. Stayer. 1993. *Flight of the buffalo.* New York: Warner.

Bennis, W., and B. Nanus. 1985. *Leaders.* New York: Harper and Row.

Bennis, W., and R. Townsend. 1995. *Reinventing leadership.* New York: Morrow.

Burns, J. M. 1978. *Leadership.* New York: Harper and Row.

Cordes, K., and H. Ibrahim. 1996. *Applications in recreation & leisure for today and the future.* St. Louis: Mosby.

Danford, H. G., and M. Shirley. 1964. *Creative leadership in recreation.* Boston: Allyn and Bacon.

DeGraaf, D. G., D. Jordan, and K. H. DeGraaf. (1999). *Programming for parks, recreation, and leisure services: A servant leadership approach.* State College, PA: Venture.

de Oliveira, W. 1994. We are in the streets because they are in the streets: The emergence and praxis of street social education in San Paulo, Brazil. Ph.D. diss., University of Minnesota.

de Oliveira, W., S. R. Edginton, and C. R. Edginton. 1996. Leader presence. *Journal of Physical Education, Recreation, and Dance* 67(1): 38–39.

Edginton, C. R., S. D. Hudson, and P. F. Ford. 1999. *Leadership in recreation and leisure services organizations.* 2nd ed. Champaign, IL: Sagamore.

Edginton, S. R., and C. R. Edginton. 1994. *Youth programs: Promoting quality services.* Champaign, IL: Sagamore Publishing.

Fain, G. S. 1995. Ethics, values and moral decision making in youth programs. In *Selected papers of the Academy for Youth Leaders,* edited by S. R. Edginton, C. R. Edginton, and W. L. Walser. Cedar Falls: Institute for Youth Leaders, University of Northern Iowa.

Fiedler, F. E. 1967. *A theory of leadership effectiveness.* New York: McGraw-Hill.

Frye, V., and M. Peters. 1972. *Therapeutic recreation: Its theory, philosophy, and practice.* Harrisburg, PA: Stackpole Books.

Graves, S. 1977. *The community development process.* Waterloo, Ontario, Canada: University of Waterloo.

Greenleaf, R. 1977. *Servant leadership: A journey into the nature of legitimate power and greatness.* New York: Paulist Press.

Halpin, A. W. 1959. *The leadership behavior of school superintendents.* Chicago: Midwest Administration Center, University of Chicago.

Hersey, P., and K. H. Blanchard. 1977. *Management of organizational behavior.* 3d ed. Englewood Cliffs, NJ: Prentice Hall.

Hitt, W. D. 1988. *The leader-manager: Guidelines for action.* Columbus: Battelle Press.

Hitt, W. D. 1990. *Ethics and leadership.* Columbus: Battelle Press.

House, R. J. 1971. A path-goal theory of leadership effectiveness. *Administrative Science Quarterly* 16.

Jordan, D. J. 2002. *Leadership in leisure services.* 3rd ed. State College, PA: Venture.

Kayser, T. A. 1994. *Team power: How to unleash the collaborative genius of work teams.* New York: Irwin.

Kouzes, J., and B. Posner. 1987. *The leadership challenge.* San Francisco: Jossey-Bass.

Kraus, R. G. 1985. *Recreation leadership today.* Glenview, IL: Scott, Foresman.

Kraus, R. G., and B. Bates. 1975. *Recreation leadership and supervision.* Philadelphia: W. B. Saunders.

Lewin, K., R. Lippitt, and R. K. White. 1939. Patterns of aggressive behavior in experimentally created 'social climates.' *Journal of Social Psychology* 10.

Mabey, C. 1994. Youth leadership: Commitment for what? In *Bold ideas: Creative approaches to the challenge of youth programming,* by S. L. York and D. J. Jordan. Institute for Youth Leaders, University of Northern Iowa.

Neipoth, E. W. 1983. *Leisure leadership.* Englewood Cliffs, NJ: Prentice Hall.

Pantera, M. 1995. The collaborative spirit can transform parks and recreation world-wide. *PERS Review 1*(2): 3–8.

Rost, J. C. 1993. *Leadership for the 21st century.* Westport: Praeger.

Russell, R. 2001. *Leadership in recreation.* 2nd ed. Boston: McGraw-Hill.

Senge, P. M. 1990. *The Fifth discipline: The art and practice of the learning organization.* New York: Doubleday.

Spears, L. 1995. Servant leadership and the Greenleaf legacy. In *Reflections on leadership: How Robert K. Greenleaf's theory of servant leadership influenced today's top management thinkers,* edited by L. Spear (pp. 1–16). New York: John Wiley & Sons.

Stein, T. A. 1975. *Report on the state of recreation and park education in Canada and the United States.* Arlington, VA: Society of Park and Recreation Educators.

UNICEF/MPAS. 1983. *Educador Social de Rua. Primeiro relato da experiência da Pastoral do Menor da Arquidiocese de São Paulo* (Street social educator: First report of the experience of *Pastoral do Menor* of the Archdiocese of São Paulo). São Paulo: UNICEF/MPAS.

Understanding Customer Behavior

LEARNING OBJECTIVES

1. To help the reader better understand *customer leisure behavior*.
2. To help the reader clarify how the relationship that develops between the individuals served and the professional is affected by *how participants are labeled*.

3. To identify *factors that influence customer decision making related to leisure*.
4. To gain knowledge of *lifestyle variables and their impact on leisure*.

INTRODUCTION

Understanding the customer is central to creating successful leisure programs. Knowledge of customer behavior can assist the leisure programmer in successfully meeting needs. Perhaps first and most important is the need for the organization to position itself toward service with a foundation of the knowledge of customer behavior. Numerous factors influence those served by a leisure service organization. Values, motives, lifestyle, and personality are all individual characteristics that can influence the decision to pursue one leisure experience versus another. Further, social influences, such as family, reference group, and the community can also have a dramatic impact on the decision-making behavior of an individual.

Knowledge of customer behavior is drawn from many different disciplines: psychology, sociology, and anthropology, as well as areas of study such as marketing. All of these areas provide a backdrop for organizing information concerning customer behavior. In the broadest possible context, the study of human behavior provides insight into those factors that motivate individuals and influence their decisions to participate in various leisure activities and events.

The task of analyzing human behavior and its relationship to leisure is a complex and imposing one. The study of human behavior is not as concrete as other areas of study, such as the physical sciences. For example, human subjects cannot be manipulated and controlled in an investigative effort the way that experiments are controlled in chemistry. However, the leisure service programmer must have some knowledge of how people pursue leisure through the lifespan and of other factors that may influence their decision-making behavior.

In this chapter, we investigate some of the factors that influence customer behavior as it relates to leisure. We first focus on the labels that professionals attach to individuals participating in leisure experiences. The purpose of this discussion is to help clarify how the relationship that the professional establishes with the customer is dependent on perceptions and assumptions about the nature of the interaction. Next, we provide a discussion of the factors influencing decision making regarding leisure activities and events. In addition, the chapter includes discussions about the implications of demographic information and life cycle variables as they influence leisure choices.

WHAT'S IN A LABEL?

The relationship that is established between a professional and the individuals that he or she serves is often reflected in the label that is attached to the person receiving the services. There are many common labels attached to an individual or group in the leisure service field. Some of the more common ones are *participant, patron, customer, client, member, user, visitor, guest,* and *consumer.* The use of one particular label versus another will have a direct bearing and impact on the association that is established. In fact, it may imply extent of freedom, dependence and independence, responsibility, patterns of communication, privilege, or acknowledgment of expertise or value assigned to either the leisure service professional or the person served by the organization.

The use and acceptance of terms describing the relationship between the professional and the person served by the organization should not be taken lightly. Why is this the case? The work of professionals can be greatly affected by how we view others and by our assumptions and expectations. Do we direct people or do we enable others? Are those we serve passive recipients or helpless individuals who require our expertise, skills, and methods of intervention to improve their lives? Or are they capable of exercising discretion and independent judgment and of making choices in meeting their own leisure needs? These are indeed difficult questions that have far-reaching implications for the nature of our work and its relationship to people.

An exploration of labels assigned to individuals served by leisure service organizations can be useful. Two graduate students at the University of Oregon, Stoll and Wheeler (1989), explore this concept in a paper entitled "Leisure Service Program Development." They write:

> As service providers we must be aware of categorizing people and its effect on services rendered. We are both enabled and limited by the words we use. Our service posture is related to our expectations of behavior, our communication patterns, and presumptions about the needs of those served. The labels we assign to people many times define the opportunities for service delivery and the way in which services are provided.

Following is a discussion of some of the common labels associated with the people being served by the leisure service field.

Client

A client is *an individual who passively receives recommendations of the programmer.* The client/programmer relationship is one in which individuals subordinate their own personal choices and defer to the expertise of the programmer. A client/professional relationship is one that implies a relationship of dependency; that is, individuals receiving the services are dependent on the application of the knowledge, skills, and values by the programmer to meet their leisure needs. The methods of treatment, the types of services, and the strategies used to deliver services are tightly controlled by the programmer.

The role of the programmer in this type of relationship is to diagnose the needs of the individual and then intervene with those services he or she feels are appropriate based on the use of professional expertise and judgment. In a client/professional relationship, the professional exercises a great deal of discretion in making decisions about what services would be useful or valuable to the individual. Thus, it may be inferred that the professional in this relationship exercises a discretionary risk. Decisions about which programs, strategies, or services are

to be offered are seldom shared between the client and the professional. Communication is one-way. The use of the word *client* is more often used in medical settings that are prescriptive in nature. Thus, one could find the concept of client in clinical, therapeutic settings.

Consumer

A consumer is *an individual who uses services.* In economic terms, a consumer is thought to be someone who uses goods or services in order to meet his or her needs. Consumers, by definition, engage in a process of exchange. They exchange something of value (e.g., time, money) to receive a service. The role of the programmer in this process is straightforward. The programmer creates and disperses a service, and the consumer absorbs the experience. Consumers do not have to subordinate their interests to the professional if they choose not to. Consumers are free to choose, to decide what services best meet their needs and whether they are willing to pay the cost of such services. In this relationship the consumer retains control over the decision to participate.

Within this context, a movement has emerged to protect the consumer from unsafe, unhealthy, and poorly organized services. This movement, known as *consumerism,* is directed toward having consumers influence the quality and value of services provided. Consumer activities in this arena often result in the establishment of regulations that protect their interests. A consumer/provider relationship can be a two-way relationship. With this relationship, the provider of services, in an attempt to more effectively meet the needs of the consumer, can discover ways of more effectively organizing services. The concept of consumer is used in most commercial recreation settings.

Customer

We think of a customer as *an individual who participates in a service on a regular basis.* Customers often develop relationships with providers that are mutually beneficial. The assumption is that if an individual is returning on a regular basis to a leisure service organization, his or her needs are being met. Stoll and Wheeler (1989) have written:

> The term customer implies a relationship based on needs satisfaction and loyalty in which benefit accrues to both the provider and the customer. Communication is assumed to be interactive in the sense of evolving some form of needs assessment (either formal or informal) and some form of evaluative feedback (as in "The customer is always right"). Expectations are that the customer will seek the provider's service for the satisfaction of a perceived need. The success of that transaction will be dependent upon such factors as the perceived quality and value of the experience, its timeliness, and price.

Customer/programmer relationships are built on developing satisfaction, trust, and loyalty. Because of the interactive nature of these types of relationships, the communication process is two-way. The provider of services must be willing to respond to felt and expressed needs of individuals. To be customer oriented means that the leisure service programmer develops a mutually beneficial relationship that considers the needs of the customer a central theme in the development of services.

In this book we have chosen to use the label *customer* because of its focus on needs satisfaction and the establishment of interactive relationships with individuals. Further, customer relationships require attention to quality, value, and convenience. Leisure service programs built around these themes are often successful. In a sense, using the term *customer* connects the leisure service programmer to the needs of the individual. A needs-focused leisure service organization will consistently outperform one that is other-focused.

Guest

A guest can be thought of as a party that is valued. Guests are often viewed in terms of behaviors that we as programmers exhibit when they come into our environments. A guest is *an individual who is treated courteously and respectfully, is given special care and attention, and is made to feel welcome in an environment.* Because we often associate the term *guest* with inviting individuals into our homes, we are assuming that such individuals are treasured, valued, and important to us. When an individual is considered a guest, the assumption is that the person will be treated with great dignity and that every attempt will be made to satisfy his or her needs. Thus, the professional takes a proactive stand in attempting to meet the needs of the guest. This association requires two-way communication and a desire to fulfill the needs of others.

The best illustration of this concept in the leisure service field is found in the relationship that is established between guest and service provider at Walt Disney World and Disneyland. At Disneyland, individuals are treated as guests, but the word *guest* is spelled with a capital *G*. The reputation for positive relationships that exists between the staff (actually called the *cast*) and individuals attending either of these two theme parks is legendary. Much of the success of Disneyland and Walt Disney World can be attributed to the establishment and maintenance of positive guest relations.

Member

Membership in an organization implies a sense of exclusivity. Thus, a person who is a member of an organization like the YMCA or YWCA is *an individual who has been given special privileges because the person has paid dues and/or been inducted in some fashion into a group or organization.* What kinds of unique privileges are accorded to an individual who has membership in an organization? In the context of leisure services, privileges take several different forms. First, being a member of an organization might provide a person access to facilities and services that are unavailable to other people. Membership may also enable an individual to associate with a prescribed group of people. Further, membership in an organization may result in greater individual attention, care, and service. The relationships that evolve between members and professional staff may be more personalized, focused, and directly related to the unique needs of the individual.

By becoming a member of an organization, an individual often embraces the philosophy, values, and goals of that agency. Membership in an organization generally requires active as opposed to passive interaction. Thus, the relationship that emerges between members and providers of services is two way, requiring active involvement. This sort of interaction may result in the member influencing and perhaps controlling the types, levels, or costs of services provided. The point is that individuals who hold membership in leisure service organizations can exercise control over their leisure experiences.

Participant

The label of *participant* has been used over the years as a generic term to denote individuals served by leisure service organizations. However, to participate means to share or take part in an activity or service. Thus, a participant is *an individual who is actively engaging in the process.* An individual may share in the successful implementation of a leisure activity by cooperating, providing social and emotional support to others, demonstrating teamwork, contributing ideas, solving problems, and engaging in other behaviors that contribute to the successful implementation of a leisure activity. The participant is a collaborator with the leisure service programmer. This collaborative relationship must be built on the basis of trust, two-way interaction, and respect.

From the perspective of the leisure service programmer, viewing an individual as a participant means that the professional must be willing to encourage sharing, open the process of decision making, and establish meaningful ways of involvement. This suggests the building of ownership or a sense of responsibility and desire for a positive outcome. Participation implies shared control.

Patron

The term *patron* has recently been applied to the area of leisure programming by Rossman (2002). A patron can be thought of as *an individual who buys services on a consistent or regular basis from a leisure service organization.* In other words, to be a patron suggests a certain amount of loyalty between the person receiving the service and the organization. In a sense, a patron is much like a customer. A relationship of satisfaction has been developed between the provider of the service and the patron that results in a continuing interaction.

Obviously, in viewing individuals as patrons, the leisure service programmer is seeking regular, continuous involvement. To encourage such involvement, the programmer must provide high-quality services that consistently meet the needs of the individual. Meeting the needs of the individual on a continuous basis is the foundation for building loyalty. When individuals patronize a particular leisure service organization, a relationship of mutual respect often develops. In fact, the word *patron* comes from the Latin *patronus,* which means "a person to be respected." There is another way of distinguishing a patron in relationship to a leisure service organization. A patron may be a person who voluntarily supports an organization with both time and money. The patron may not be directly involved as a recipient of programs and services. Instead, this person may contribute or secure resources to support opportunities for others, involve himself or herself in decision-making groups such as boards and committees, or represent the organization in the community at large as a proponent of the organization's purpose. The relationship of a patron with an organization is often long and enduring.

User

The term *user* is often applied to individuals who consume leisure services. To use something means to avail oneself of a service. Users are *individuals who involve themselves actively in a program or service on a regular basis.* In other words, the concept of the term *user* suggests a consistent pattern of involvement in leisure services rather than irregular use.

What is the relationship that emerges between the individual user and the leisure service professional? A user/professional relationship is one of need, dependency, and dependability. The leisure professional works to provide the service continuously in such a manner that the individual's needs for achievement, risk, and spontaneity are met. To be a user does not necessarily suggest a relationship of two-way interaction with the professional. Nor does it necessarily suggest a relationship of cooperation, trust, and mutual respect, but rather one that is built on the self-interests of the individual. In other words, the person "uses" a leisure product or service for his or her own ends.

Visitor

A visitor is *an individual who visits an area or facility or participates in a program.* Generally speaking, a visitor is thought to be an individual who comes to an organization's service, facility, or site. Such visitors may be invited, or their visits may occur more informally or spontaneously. Further, such participation may be either regular or infrequent. The interest on the part of the leisure service organization is that visitors become regular customers.

The status accorded to visitors is similar to that accorded guests. The expectation is that the visitor will be valued, treated courteously, and perhaps entertained, educated, or enhanced in some manner. The relationship that often develops between a leisure service programmer and a visitor is one of mutual respect, positive interaction, and support. The visitor often comes to see or participate in a unique geographic, cultural, or historical activity or site. Visitors often must be provided with support services and must be made to feel as if their participation is valued.

CUSTOMER DECISION MAKING

How do customers make decisions concerning leisure? What are the factors that influence their leisure preferences? These are, indeed, complex and difficult questions to answer. Only within the past several decades have researchers studying decision making in the field of marketing begun to develop a body of knowledge concerning this topic. Even less research has been devoted to the study of how people make decisions about leisure. The application of decision-making theory to leisure has only emerged within the last few years.

Purchasing Patterns of Customers

Decision making concerning leisure activities and preferences will vary in terms of intensity and motivation. Some decisions are made in a routine fashion, whereas others require extensive problem solving and investigation. Consider, for example, the following three scenarios. Each requires a different level of decision making on the part of the customer because of the potential effects resulting from the decision.

1. Dennis and Lyn are considering the purchase of a $75,000 recreation vehicle to be used during weekend and summer vacation months for excursions to the Lake of the Ozarks and Lake Superior.
2. Raul and Rosa are considering vacationing at a new coastal location this summer. For the past ten years they have vacationed at Salishan Lodge, but now are considering moving their vacation site to Driftwood Shores.
3. Bob and Sally must replenish their supply of golf balls. They have purchased *Titleist* brand golf balls for the past seven years and intend to purchase the same brand when they go to their local athletic supply store.

These three situations point out the difference in complexity of decision making related to leisure. The first decision involves a major purchase. It requires in-depth investigation. The couple will probably compare several products to determine their comparable quality and value. This approach to decision making can be thought of as *extended/information search.* Because the purchase is a major one, the couple is required to weigh the benefits of comparable products and engage in extended problem solving. Such a purchase is usually made only once or twice in a lifetime and not in a routine fashion.

The second situation illustrates another level of decision making. In this case, the couple is switching between comparable vacation sites. Perhaps they are seeking novelty in their vacation experience and have decided to try another resort. Just as easily as they have sought the new location for their vacation, they could switch back to their former site. We call this approach to decision making *product, service, or brand switching*. It involves limited problem solving. The decision making is less complex than in the first situation, but nonetheless requires some search and problem solving.

In the last example, the couple's purchase of golf balls represents a minimal investment of time and effort in the decision-making process. They are simply buying a product that they have previously purchased and with which they have been satisfied. This process of decision making is labeled *routine/repeat decision making*, or routine problem solving. They know that they like the product and that it will meet their needs. It is a simple decision to make and often occurs out of habit. The couple does not have to engage in conscious decision making. In fact, they are very loyal to the *Titleist* brand because it has met their needs in the past. Further, the actual cost of golf balls is low and, as such, represents a small investment.

These concepts are illustrated in Figure 4.1. This model presents two continuums—one related to decision-making complexity and the other related to the financial risk of the leisure purchase. The horizontal continuum for decision-making complexity places routine decision making at one end and extended decision making at the other end. The vertical continuum places low financial risk at one end and high financial risk at the other. Four sections are created from the intersection of the two continuums. The four sections are *routine/low risk, extended search/low risk, routine/high risk,* and *high risk/extended search*.

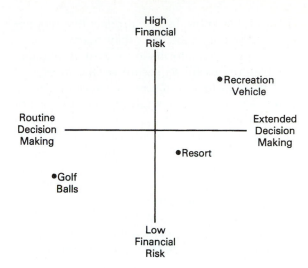

Figure 4.1 Decision-Making Complexity as Related to Cost of Leisure Products and Services.

The decisions discussed in the three scenarios can be placed in one of the four sections of the model. For example, in Dennis and Lyn's decision about a recreation vehicle, there is a large financial commitment to be made. Therefore, this decision would fall into the high risk/extended search category. In making this decision, they will shop carefully and spend considerable time and effort comparing the benefits of various vehicles.

In the second example, making a decision to switch to another resort, Raul and Rosa have less of a financial stake, but will engage in some comparison and decision making. Thus, their decision would fall into the extended search/low risk category. There is not as much financial risk in their decision making and the investigation into their purchase will not be as thorough as that of Dennis and Lyn.

The last example, involving the purchase of golf balls, falls into the routine/low risk category. In this instance, Bob and Sally will not spend time researching the product they are about to purchase; it is a routine decision based on past satisfaction with the product. It involves little financial risk and they know that the product that they are about to purchase will meet their needs.

Why is this information regarding purchasing patterns useful to leisure service providers? The point is that customers use information to make decisions. The complexity and intensity of decision making may vary from one situation to another, but nonetheless individuals process information and use it to choose between one service and another. The needs and lifestyles of individuals will greatly influence the information that they seek. Knowledge of such decision making patterns is extremely useful to leisure service organizations that are attempting to communicate the benefits of their services effectively to their customers.

Variables That Impact Customer Decision Making

Three important variables have an impact on customer decision making. These are known in the marketing literature as *involvement, differentiation,* and *time pressure.* Involvement refers to the extent to which a service or product reflects pertinence and relevance to the individual. In other words, involvement, as reflected by a particular service, tells us whether it reflects an individual's self-image, attitude, or selected set of behaviors. Such reflections on the part of an individual can influence decision making. For example, if customers perceive that a particular leisure product or service reflects or exemplifies their lifestyle, they may be moved to purchase it.

Differentiation deals with the availability of leisure products and services. Many similar leisure services and products are available in the marketplace. However, each of these services and products can be differentiated from the others in some way. Customers often look for subtle, unique features that distinguish one leisure service or product from another. They will make decisions based on those differences.

The last variable that affects decision making is time pressure. In certain situations, we are under constraints when making decisions concerning leisure products and services. Time pressures influence decision making in such a way

that convenience and location may become major determinants influencing the selection of a service. For example, a customer may find it easier to travel to a fitness club that is closer to home than to go to one across town that is more fully equipped and less expensive. Because of time constraints, customers often choose convenience.

All of these variables interact with each other. For example, convenience may, in fact, be a subtle way of differentiating one service from another. Such factors motivate and shape the decisions that people make regarding purchase of leisure products and services. Attention must be given to the potential impact of each of these variables in designing leisure activities and events and in communicating their potential benefits to individuals.

LIFE SPAN VARIABLES

Leisure service customers include individuals across the life span—from infancy to old age. The knowledge and understanding that the leisure service provider has about various age groups and cohorts in our society is crucial to the provision of programs and activities to meet the leisure needs and interests of our society. Behavioral scientists for generations have studied the human being to determine how individuals develop and function as they do. Because people in the field of leisure services must know as much as possible about individuals and groups of individuals, it is necessary to focus on the whole life span of human beings.

The subdiscipline of developmental psychology, which focuses on life span development, examines and investigates a broad range of factors that influence the development of human beings. Included as areas of study are physiology, genetic inheritance, psychosocial history, education, religion, family, home, community, socio-economic status, and culture. Figure 4.2 is an illustration of the determinants that influence human growth and development. The three "conventional" areas of investigation—physiological, psychological, and environmental—are described, but the area of metaphysical study is also included. The philo-

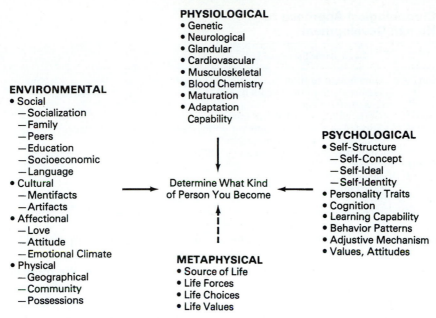

Figure 4.2 Determinants of Human Growth and Development. (*Human Development: The Span of Life,* 3rd edition by Kaluger/Kaluger, © 1984. Reprinted by permission of Prentice-Hall, Inc., Upper Saddle River, NJ.)

sophical area of metaphysics is generally more speculative in scientific research than the other areas of focus. It is included in this figure to acknowledge "the possibility of the existence of principles that underlie the study of the nature of humankind and its place in the universal scheme of things" (Kaluger and Kaluger, 1984: 70).

Developmental psychologists suggest that neither people nor their behavior remains constant. Throughout the life span, individuals change from year to year, from month to month, and even from day to day. The developmental scientist attempts to explore lifelong changes. Unlike child or adolescent development and adult psychology, developmental psychology examines the entire life cycle. Kaluger and Kaluger (1984: 2) indicate that "as life advances and experiences increase, both internal and external phases of behavior and growth change constantly." Traditionally, attention has been strongly focused on the growth and development of the young (children and youth). However, only "one-fourth of an

individual's life is spent growing up. Three-fourths of a person's life is spent in adulthood, growing older" (p. 473). The importance of focusing on the human life span is evident.

Human development is a multifaceted experience. It is the integration of age-graded, internal biological (physiological) and psychological processes, with external social (environmental) influences that occur for cohorts (generational groups). Knowledge and understanding about both internal development and maturation and external experiential differences are important to the leisure service professional for needs identification and assessment, program development, and the delivery of leisure activities and services to the leisure customer.

Age-Related Phases

Table 4.1 illustrates a chronological approach to human development. Although this approach is useful in categorization, it should be noted that each individual is unique in the process of devel-

**TABLE 4.1   Chronological Approach to
Human Development**

Life Stage	Approximate Time Period
1. Prenatal period	Conception to birth
2. Infancy	Generally the first 2 years of life
3. Toddlerhood	2–3 years of age
4. Early childhood	Generally 3 or 4 to about age 5
5. Middle childhood	Either 6–9 or 6–12, depending on the usage of the terms "late childhood" or "preadolescence"
6. Adolescence	Generally the teenage years (13–19)
7. Young adulthood	19–30
8. Middle adulthood	30–50 or 60
9. Later adulthood	50 or 60–75
10. Old age	75+

opment. Age categories simply allow the programmer to segment certain groups of people into units that may be more alike than dissimilar—for example, some toddlers mature faster than others but, in general, all toddlers exhibit similar physical, intellectual, emotional, and social (PIES) characteristics. Chronological age is only one measure of maturation. Turner and Helms (1979) have noted that as chronological age increases, age becomes a poorer criterion to use for comparative development. (see Exhibit 4.1)

Aging (the passage of years through all of life) involves developmental changes in definitive areas of life. Table 4.2 summarizes a multifaceted approach to human development. Physical development, mental development, and personality and social development by the individual integrate varied stages of growth and development. Developmental traits provide a basis for leisure program planners in designing leisure experiences. Program planning can be enhanced when the leisure service professional understands age-group characteristics in relation to human behavior (see Table 4.3).

The most critical age factor in the United States today is that older people are living longer than they ever have before. In 1900, the average life expectancy for an individual was 47.3 years. Now it is seventy-eight years for women and seventy-five years for men. In addition, individuals living beyond the age of sixty-five are expected to live an average of an additional 15.5 years. It is projected that in the year 2028, more than one-fourth of the American population will be over the age of sixty-five (Edginton, Hudson and Ford: 46).

EXHIBIT 4.1   Example of Children's Program

WATER WIZARD'S DAY CAMP

Hidden in the heart of San Jose is an experience for children that combines local history and the environment in an awesome outdoor adventure presented by experienced teachers. Explore the Guadalupe River habitat and wildlife, dive into water conservation, discover a bin of recycling worms, and uncover the past in our Historic Orchard and archeological dig.

The Friends of Guadalupe River Park & Gardens are once again presenting a series of Water Wizard day camps this summer for children ages 7–10. Each session of the camp consists of two days of activities in a fun and educational setting in Guadalupe Gardens. Art projects, games, and snacks all contribute to an enjoyable summer learning experience.

The cost of each camp session is $60 per child, the ratio of children to teachers is 10–1, and the maximum number of children per camp session is 30. The camps are held on Tuesdays & Thursdays, from 8:30am–12:30 pm, at the Garden Center in Guadalupe Gardens, 715 Spring Street, near the corner of Spring and Taylor. Five camp sessions are available between the beginning of July and the first week of August.

For more information, call the Education Coordinator for the Friends of Guadalupe River Park & Gardens, at 408–298–7657, or visit *www.grpg.org.*

TABLE 4.2   Multifaceted Human Development

	Physical Development	Mental Development	Personality and Social Development
Infancy & toddlerhood	Rate of physical growth is most rapid during first three years of life. Physiological maturation, which allows performance of tasks (i.e., locomotion, grasping, coordinated hand-eye movement and dominant handedness).	Cognitive abilities begin to be developed—thinking, perceiving and understanding. Beginning of sensorimotor skills—reaction, mental images, objects. Developmental patterns of speech and language.	Emotions emerging—fear, anxiety, and later anger and frustration. Prefer solitary activity (play) begin to investigate environment.
Early childhood	By fifth year, birth length is doubled and birth weight has increased by five times. Muscular growth and development result in coordination abilities and gains in small- and large-motor skill activities.	Thought is characterized by ego-centrism/self-centeredness. Cognitive abilities develop in relation to people, objects, events. Language acquisition enables multiword sentences and construction of ideas.	Self-concepts develop through interaction with family and peer groups. Expression of emotions verbally—resentment, anger; displays of jealousy, sometimes sibling rivalry. Activity becomes more socially oriented; active play, imitation, imaginary companions.
Middle childhood	Advancement in motor-skill abilities—large-muscle movement and refined coordination. Sense of physical self and awareness of bodily changes in efficiency of varied motor skills.	Emerging intuitive thought and comprehension; organization of information and problem solving. Advancement in language skills; developing ability to understand and adapt to environment.	Interaction with peers influences socialization. Emerging self-image, self-esteem, sex-role identification. Emotional maturity evolving, influenced by the individual's personality.
Adolescence	Pronounced growth spurt is experienced as children enter puberty. Maturation of primary sex characteristics. Continuing development of motor skill and coordination.	Intellectual growth; past learning experiences contribute to higher-level thought processes. Cognitive advancement includes the ability to apply reasoning and exercise insight.	Struggle to attain satisfying sense of identity. Factors influencing self-concept include value system, standards of conduct and sexual identity. Desire for individuality and independence. Peer group becomes important agent of socialization.
Young adulthood	Physical growth and development virtually completed. With maturation, gradual declines begin to occur—height, fatty tissue, sense of hearing, sense of sight.	Intellectual maturity reaches a high level of function, both quantitative and qualitative. Mental ability is maintained throughout life, but is influenced by intellectual function and individual idiosyncrasies.	Emotional security, extension of self, relating warmly to others, realistic perceptions and establishing a philosophy of life. Adults learn to overcome irrational childhood notions and parental dependencies.

Continued.

TABLE 4.2 Multifaceted Human Development—*Continued*.

	Physical Development	Mental Development	Personality and Social Development
Middle adulthood	Modest decline of physical abilities and noticeable bodily changes. Changes in sensory capacities. Some behavioral changes in both men and women.	Continued use and stimulation of intellect maintains adequate function. Ability to draw on previous experience demonstrates wisdom.	Stability of adult characteristics. Acceptance of self and others. Interest in striving for self-actualization. (In all areas, physical, mental and social development, is the influence of the midlife crisis.)
Later adulthood	Metabolic changes and slowdown in physiological processes. Older adults have the same diseases as younger age groups, but recovery may be slower or may not occur. Decrease in efficiency of sensory function in hearing and vision.	General knowledge and vocabulary tend to remain constant. Long-term memory remains constant with some change in short-term memory. (Individual variations in memory exist throughout the life cycle.)	Successful aging appears to be satisfactory psychological (inner) and socially oriented (outer) adjustment. Variety in personality type influences adjustment to old age.
Old age	Life's final developmental change—facing death. Death can and does occur at any age, but elderly people are more aware of its imminence.	Fear of the unknown. Sorrow from losses.	Loneliness. Sometimes loss of identity.

Adapted from Turner and Helms (1983).

Many leisure service organizations have responded to these changing demographics within the population. For example, the city of Long Beach, California Parks and Recreation Department provides an integrated array of services for senior citizens, including advocacy, health and nutrition, recreation, and social services (see Figure 4.3). Programs include activities (arts to weaving), blood pressure screening, camping clubs, coffee shop, counseling, consumer information, emergency food and housing, dial-a-ride, employment, elder abuse, dental care, house-sharing, homemakers, legal services, personal care, smoke detection, telephone reassurance, trips, visitation reassurance, volunteer opportunities, and weatherization information.

Traditionally, the leisure service field placed much emphasis on the planning and provision of services for children and youth. In addition to continuing to serve the young age groups in the population, leisure service organizations must enlarge their focus to better meet the needs of adult population groups. The leisure service provider must have comprehensive knowledge about demographic factors (described later in the Demographics section of this chapter) to be familiar with the interests, levels of health, financial abilities, family structures, cultural diversity, personality differences, and gender expectations of leisure customers to understand their leisure behavior and meet their needs.

Cohorts

A cohort is a group of individuals who were born in the same time interval (a range of five, seven, or ten years) and therefore share the same

TABLE 4.3   Age-Related Human Behavior

Group	Age	Characteristic
Preschool	Under 4	Dependent on others, short attention span, self-centered, major motor development, and desire for immediate reward.
Primary	5–7	Developing social relations and additional motor skills, imagination and exuberance, develops self-control, and becomes industrious.
Intermediate	8–12	Perseverance, diligence, and competency develop; play is serious business.
Early adolescence	13–15	Rapid physical growth, onset of puberty, sometimes awkward and self-conscious.
Youth	16–19	Develops individual identity, discovers talents. Strong likes and dislikes, group memberships, sets goals, and strives for independence.
Young adult	20–29	Seeks meaningful relationships, makes commitments, career choices, and uses a variety of recreation activities in the courtship ritual; may pursue outdoor and risk activities to test competency.
Adult years	30–49	Major productive years, child-rearing responsibilities and other social obligations. Looks to recreation for activity, diversion, status, and autonomy.
Pre-retirement adult	50–64	Reduction of intensity of some needs, generally secure, enjoys social outings, provides leadership in social-spiritual-civic and volunteer organizations.
Early retirement	65–79	Recreation often replaces work as reason for being. Can be active or passive, depending on health. General physical decline and more difficult to stimulate.
Later maturity	Over 80	Contingent upon health, can be a rewarding but semipassive way of life. Research has revealed that those who prepare for retirement and later maturity can prevent the despair associated with the loss of independence, isolation, and a lonely wait for death.

From F. C. Patterson, *A Systems Approach to Recreation Programming,* 1987, Waveland Press, Inc., Prospect Heights, IL. Reprinted by permission of Frederick Patterson.

Figure 4.3   Senior Programs and Services, City of Long Beach, California.

major experiences throughout their lives. Cohorts are faced with specific sets of life conditions during important and impressionable periods in their lives. In other words, cohorts (generational groups) have lived during the same time period and have experienced the same historical, social, economic, and political conditions during their life span.

Basic value creation is influenced and formed in early life. Primary influences on value development can include family, friends, school, religion, and geographic place of residence. An individual's basic personality is developed by the age of four. Up to the age of seven is the time of imprinting. The human influences and the life events that have occurred have imprinted on and are a permanent part of that individual. Early formation of values and modeling or exhibiting behaviors occurs during the ages of eight to thirteen. The values that were earlier imprinted may at this point be evident in the person's behavior and lifestyle. Socialization—that is, being with others and seeking the approval of others for individual behavior—occurs during the teen years, ages fourteen to twenty. By the time an individual reaches twenty years of age, his or her value system is strongly in place.

Cohort groups also experience personal life events—starting school, graduating from high school or college, finding a job and beginning a career, getting married, raising a family, reaching retirement—at about the same time. A focus on a cohort group infers that major specific societal, cultural, and personal experiences have affected and influenced the lives and development of the individuals in the group in ways unique from other cohort groups (Table 4.4).

Adult cohort values often are reflected in orientation to social structure, perception of political process, attitude toward the workplace, preference of lifestyle, and leisure needs and choices of leisure activities. What is "good," "right," or "normal" is different for different cohorts. Interests in specific areas of leisure programming or choices of particular activity formats are related to cohort values. Although a cohort seems to express common interests, which is important to the leisure professional, leisure service providers must remember that groups are made up of individuals, and individuals may differ in personal interests and leisure preferences.

Differences among individuals within a cohort result from individual experiences. Major events that occur in a person's life, called life change units (LCUs), may occur with greater frequency for some individuals than for others (Table 4.5). When these events do occur for individuals, it makes them different from others in their cohort. Experiential differences, individual intelligence, temperament and personality, social class, cultural influence, level of education, job and income, and racial and ethnic differences all contribute to forming the individuals who are our leisure service customers.

Demographics

The leisure phenomenon is extremely complex. Murphy et al. (1973: 85) observed that "the reasons for different individual expressions of (leisure) behavior are interrelated and exceedingly complex." The leisure service provider needs to examine individual behavior in relation to a variety of factors. Differences such as age, gender, personality, education, occupation, income, race and national identity, health, and marital status and family all have an impact on an individual's lifestyle and leisure behavior.

Age

As has been described previously in this chapter, primary influences related to age are physiological and psychological as well as social. Physiological characteristics include fine and gross motor skills, coordination, endurance, and level of acquired skill. These factors influence participation for individuals of all ages. Physical skills develop at varying rates across the life span and begin to decline as the person grows older. In addition, psychological development is related to age. The desire to function alone in activities as young children changes to the ability to be involved in cooperative activities and competition. Choice of leisure activity based on age is also influenced by the cohort that the individual is a part of and by the social and cultural expectations that exist.

Gender

Individuals become "socialized" by the society in which they live. In other words, certain expectations of leisure activity choices and behaviors are anticipated based on gender. However, in recent years, the differences have decreased and the involvement in similar leisure activities by both males and females (at all ages) is expected and accepted. For example, sport competition (individual, dual, and team) is available for both sexes, co-ed leisure activities are accessible; and creative arts and high-risk activities are pursued by both sexes.

Table 4.4 Cohorts and Generational Events[1]

Decades of Cohorts	Historical Events	Business and Technology	Social and Media Events	Music and Dancing	Famous People
Old age 1900–1909	Turn of century; Spanish-American War; McKinley assassinated	Severe unemployment; trolley cars; Model T Ford; electric light bulb	First airplane flight; first radio message; first World Series; yellow fever epidemic	Let Me Call You Sweetheart; Home on the Range; Sweet Adeline; the turkey trot	William McKinley, Teddy Roosevelt, W. H. Taft, Henry Ford, Orville and Wilbur Wright, Charlie Chaplin, Carrie Nation
1910–1919	First woman in Congress; World War I; communism started	Federal income tax; telephone invented; vitamins discovered; use of electricity	Panama Canal opens; Halley's comet; *Titanic* sinks	"Alexander's Ragtime Band"; "When Irish Eyes Are Smiling"; "Over There"; the fox-trot	Susan B. Anthony, W. H. Taft, Woodrow Wilson, Thomas Edison, Buffalo Bill Cody, Jack Dempsey, Jane Addams, Emma Goldman
1920–1929	Prohibition Act; Harding's Teapot Dome Scandal; League of Nations	Child labor laws; oil replacing coal; mechanical cotton picker; Wall Street collapse	Bootlegging; Lindbergh's Atlantic flight; Empire State Building	Vaudeville; "Yes, We Have No Bananas"; "Old Man River"; the Charleston	Woodrow Wilson, Warren Harding, Calvin Coolidge, Herbert Hoover, Babe Ruth, Andrew Carnegie, Margaret Sanger
Later adulthood 1930–1939	Great Depression; New Deal; Social Security Act	Bank panic; WPA— public works; color movies	Amelia Earhart solo across the Atlantic; John Dillinger; public enemy no. 1; Hindenburg explosion	WPA orchestras; "Brother, Can You Spare a Dime?"; "I've Got You Under My Skin"; the big apple	New York Yankees, Bing Crosby, Mickey Mouse, Babe Didrikson, Greta Garbo, Amelia Earhart
1940–1949	World War II; United Nations; GI Bill of Rights	Taft-Hartley Act; 40-hour week; first electric locomotive; first atomic bomb	Pearl Harbor attack; first black major league baseball player—Jackie Robinson; country of Israel	Big band sounds; "In the Mood"; "White Christmas"; "When You Wish Upon a Star"; jitterbug	Franklin D. Roosevelt, Harry Truman, Winston Churchill, Joseph Stalin, Bob Hope, Frank Sinatra, Eleanor Roosevelt, Katharine Hepburn, Clare Booth Luce
Middle adulthood 1950–1959	Korean War; Cold war; Truman fires MacArthur	Minimum wage 75¢ per hour; AFL-CIO merger; first earth-circling satellite; Salk antipolio vaccine	Racial segregation banned; school desegregation; development of television; two monkeys in space	Hit parade: "Rock Around the Clock"; "My Fair Lady"; Twist; rock and roll; Elvis Presley	Harry Truman, Dwight Eisenhower, George Meany, Grace Kelly, Perry Como, Rosa Parks, Julius and Ethel Rosenberg, Marilyn Monroe

Continued.

TABLE 4.4 Cohorts and Generational Events—*Continued*.

Decades of Cohorts	Historical Events	Business and Technology	Social and Media Events	Music and Dancing	Famous People
1960–1969	Civil Rights Act; assassinations of J. F. Kennedy, Robert Kennedy, Martin Luther King, Jr.; Vietnam War	Minimum wage $1.25 per hour; affluent economy; men on the moon; birth-control pill	Fifty-star flag; beatniks, hippies; Woodstock; student demonstrations; drug culture	Beatles; "Hello, Dolly"; "Moon River"; rock	J. F. Kennedy, Lyndon Johnson, Richard Nixon, Warren Burger, Martin Luther King, Jr., Neil Armstrong, Golda Meir, Jackie Kennedy, Martha Graham, Rachel Carson, Diane Arbus
Young adulthood 1970–1979	End of Vietnam War; Watergate scandal; 19-year-olds vote; Israel-Egypt accord	Minimum wage $2.65 per hour; oil embargo; inflation increases; test-tube baby	Nixon resigns; women's liberation; two popes die within 40 days	Rolling Stones; Country-western; Punk rock; disco dancing; "You Light Up My Life"	Richard Nixon, Gerald Ford, Jimmy Carter, Muhammad Ali; Hank Aaron, Pittsburgh Steelers, Gloria Steinem, Billie Jean King, Barbara Walters, Patty Hurst
Adolescence 1980–1989	Hostage crisis in Iran; President Reagan shot; Israel-PLO war in Lebanon; San Francisco earthquake; *Challenger* disaster; U.S. military action in Panama; fall of Berlin wall	Major recession; energy crunch subsides; inflation slows down; industry and business in transition; artificial heart; acid rain	Prince Charles marries; Princess Grace dies; home computers are big items; E.T.: The Extra-Terrestrial; Star Wars series; "Batman"; "Teenage Mutant Ninja Turtles;" children in daycare outside of the home	Rock subsiding; country rock; Barry Manilow; Dolly Parton; Flashdance; "Gloria"; Michael Jackson; rap music; "Dirty Dancing"; MTV	Ronald Reagan, Pope John Paul, Sally Field, Jesse Jackson, John McEnroe, Jane Pauley, Geraldine Ferraro, Christa McAuliffe, George Bush, Mikhail Gorbachev, San Francisco 49ers
1990s	Operation Desert Storm; midwest flooding; Oklahoma City bombing; war in Bosnia; Million Man March; U.S. government shutdowns; Atlanta Olympics; Republicans take control of U.S. Senate and House of Representatives; U.S. mili-	Minimum wage $4.25 per hour; VCRs; professional baseball salaries; Nintendo; World Wide Web; Internet; virtual reality; inline skates; murders in the workplace; American female astronaut	Major league hockey strike; O. J. Simpson trial; Major League Baseball strike; Forrest Gump; Lion King; "Bay Watch"; "Friends"; Menendez brothers trial; Prince Charles and Princess Diana divorce; AIDS/HIV; body piercing and tatooing;	Garth Brooks; line dancing; Branson, MO; macarena	Norman Schwarzkopf, Madonna, Boris Yeltsin, Michael Jordan, Bill Clinton, Tom Hanks, Bob Dole, Chicago Bulls, Colin Powell, Cal Ripken, Jr., Hillary Rodham Clinton, Mother Teresa, Newt Gin-

	tary in Somalia and Haiti; Los Angeles (Northridge) earthquake		baby boomers turn 50 years old; John F. Kennedy, Jr. marries; George Burns dies; drive-by shootings; coffee bars; blue M & Ms; women at the Citadel; "trash" talk shows; liposuction; cosmetic surgery			grich, Christopher Reeves, Bill Gates, Itzak Rabin, Howard Stern, Rush Limbaugh, Dr. Jack Kevorkian
2000	9/11 Twin Towers; 2000 election; terrorism; sniper attacks; anthrax scare; wild fires; child kidnappings; pipe bomber; First blind man ascends Mt. Everest; Erik W; cloning; North/South Korean exchanges; war with Iraq	Enron scandal; DVDs; .com; instant messages; digital photos; caller I.D.; stock market plunge; electronic marketing and banking; baby boomers retiring; GPS in cars; self-scanning groceries	August Cortrov; Harry Potter; Lord of Rings; Play Station/ Sega Scooters; Reality TV; 2000 Summer Olympics; Battle Bots; Jimmy Carter Peace Prize; Osbornes; Ice Skating Scandal	American Idol; Eminem; boy bands; Britney Spears; Dixie Chicks; Faith Hill; Kid Rock		Kurt Warner, George W. Bush, Barry Bonds, Lance Armstrong, Elizabeth Dole, Venus and Serena Williams, Steve Forbes, Osama bin Laden, Rudy Guiliani, Sammy Sosa

Adapted from *Human Development: The Span of Life*, 3rd edition by Kaluger/Kaluger, © 1984. Reprinted by permission of Prentice-Hall, Inc., Upper Saddle River, NJ.

Cohort differences are influenced by the major events that occurred during significant periods in a person's life.

TABLE 4.5 Life Change Units (LCUs)

Events	Scale of Impact (LCU)	Events	Scale of Impact (LCU)
Death of spouse	100	Son or daughter leaving home	29
Divorce	73	Trouble with in-laws	29
Marital separation	65	Outstanding personal achievement	28
Jail term	63	Spouse begins or stops work	26
Death of close family member	63	Begin or end school	26
Personal injury or illness	53	Change in living conditions	25
Marriage	50	Revision of personal habits	24
Fired from work	47	Trouble with boss	23
Marital reconciliation	45	Change in work hours or conditions	20
Retirement	45	Change in residence	20
Change in health of family member	44	Change in schools	20
Pregnancy	40	Change in recreation	19
Sex difficulties	39	Change in church activities	19
Gain in new family member	39	Change in social activities	18
Business readjustment	39	Mortgage or loan less than $10,000	17
Change in financial state	38	Change in sleeping habits	16
Death of close friend	37	Change in number of family	
Change to different line of work	36	get-togethers	15
Change in number of arguments		Change in eating habits	15
with spouse	35	Vacation	13
Mortgage over $10,000	31	Christmas	12
Foreclosure of mortgage or loan	30	Minor violations of the law	11
Change in responsibilities at work	29		

Reprinted by permission of the publisher from "The Social Readjustment Rating Scale" by T. H. Holmes and R. H. Rahe in *Journal of Psychosomatic Research,* II, 1967 by Elsevier Science Inc.

Personality

Who we are influences what we do. Personality is an expression of interests, values, and capabilities. Personality is affected by personal variables such as age, gender, and education. Within an individual's personality are the components that indicate preference for structure or spontaneity in life activities, for active or passive behavior, for aggressiveness and interest in competition or vicarious involvement, for familiar activities or high-risk challenges.

Education, Occupation, Income

Generally accepted is the suggestion that the higher the level of education an individual has, the broader the base of leisure knowledge, skills, and experiences he or she has. As level of education increases, the opportunity for exposure to a broader range of opportunities and activities exists. Educational level is closely related to occupation and income. The kind of occupation and, thus, the potential for income are generally influenced by the educational experiences of an individual. Further, cultural expectations exist in relation to some occupations. Specific leisure activity choices may be anticipated or expected of individuals in particular occupational groups. Another variable is the time factor that persons in different occupational groups must deal with. Self-employed and professional workers may have long working hours while individuals who work specifically structured hours may have more discretionary time. Available personal income may either limit or allow leisure activity choices. Spending for leisure may require a significant amount of money to initiate an activity or it may be spread over a long period of time. Choices of expenditures for leisure may be influenced strongly by the individual's personal survival needs.

Race and National Identity

Preservation of cultural heritage can be a strong influence on leisure choices made by individuals. Cultural attitudes in relation to social behaviors, competition, performing arts, and ethnic practices may pervade the involvement by minority groups in the general leisure activities of the community. Previous opportunities and experiences by groups of people in the general society will affect the leisure attitudes and behaviors demonstrated by those individuals.

Health

The overall health condition of individuals at any age will limit or allow leisure activity involvement. Pursuit of leisure activities may also contribute to the continuing good health of the leisure customer. Therapeutic involvement in leisure activities can be an avenue to improving health conditions. On the other hand, onset of health problems may contribute to the necessity for individuals to change their leisure behaviors and lifestyle. The increase in obesity, especially in children, is of great concern to the health of the country. Provision of active recreation program offerings is one of the most important ways to alleviate problems such as escalating adult and childhood obesity, the increased prevalence of "lifestyle-related" diseases like coronary heart disease, problems with high rates of anxiety and depression among teens, and maintenance of independent functioning in older adults.

Marital Status and Family

The home and family are the earliest influences on an individual's leisure choices and behavior. The structure of the family determines the opportunities for leisure involvement for both children and adults in the family unit. In society today, acknowledgment must be made of couples, couples with children, single individuals, single parents with children, blended families, extended families, and other living arrangements and family structures. It is significant within the context of family today that greater numbers of children, youth, and older adults are

with caregivers outside the home for greater periods of time than they are within the family unit. Family unit activities, as well as independent activities for individual family members, impact the leisure service delivery system in the community.

Place of Residence and Mobility

Single-family dwellings, high-rise apartment buildings, condominiums, and other kinds of residential living influence the accessibility to leisure programs and facilities for leisure customers. Distance, traffic arteries, and availability and modes of transportation have a definite impact on the ability of customers to use leisure services. The primary means of transportation in our society for many urban and rural residents alike is the private car. Some groups of leisure customers are more affected by place of residence and mobility than others. These groups include children, young teens, individuals with special needs and disabilities, and older adults who have never driven a car or who are no longer driving.

Examples of Trend Analysis

Consider the following statistics as related to demographic characteristics influencing leisure in the United States:

> *Diversity on the increase.* The U.S. population increased by 9.8 percent between 1980 and 1990, but proportions of various groups shifted significantly. For example, the white population increased by 6.0 percent, Hispanics by 53.0 percent, African Americans by 13.2 percent, Native Americans by 37.9 percent, and Asian/Pacific Islanders by 107.8 percent. It has been projected that early in the twenty-first century, virtually one-third of the U.S. population will be people of color; already nonwhites make up the majority of the population in all major cities (Cordes and Ibrahim, 1996: 166).

> *Immigrant population growing.* In 1990, 8 percent of the U.S. population (or 20 million people) was individuals who were not born in the United States, as opposed to 5 percent in 1970. Fourteen

percent of the population speaks a language other than English at home, as opposed to 11 percent a decade ago (Richie, 1996: 382).

Religion/Faith. Religion and faith exert a powerful influence over human behavior, including leisure activities (Cordes and Ibrahim, 1996: 123). Today, many religious institutions continue to promote and sponsor leisure activities to provide wholesome opportunities for their congregations. In some communities, church activities are the major source of recreation opportunities for people of all ages. Recreations programmers must be cognizant of the role that religious institutions play in their communities and seek to supplement, not supplant, these programs.

Aging of the population. The Bureau of the Census estimates that the number of Americans age sixty-five and over will increase from 34 million in the year 2000 to 70 million in 2030. The age group with the greatest rate of increase is the "old old"—those over age seventy-five (Kelly and Warnick, 1999: 11).

Family structure. The family structure is changing. Married couples have declined to 78 percent of families from 87 percent in 1970. Families maintained by a single parent (women) rose from 11 percent in 1970 to 18 percent in 1994 (Richie, 1996: 382).

Women and the labor force. Female employment increased from 15 percent for those aged twenty-five to forty-four in 1980 to 60 percent in 1990. The 60 percent proportion included married women with preschool children; the statistic rose to 75 percent for women with school-age children (Kelly and Warnick, 1999: 15). This has increased substantially the need for child care.

Population distribution. More individuals are living in metropolitan areas, although metropolitan areas are becoming more suburban. Eighty percent of all Americans live in metropolitan areas, with 61 percent of these individuals living in suburban environments. The populations of the south and the west increased above the U.S. average (Richie, 1996: 382).

Increases in education. Americans are more educated, with one in five individuals holding a bachelor's degree or higher. In 1970, only one in ten individuals was a college graduate. Education generally parallels earnings: The more education people have, the higher their wages (Richie, 1996: 382).

LEISURE BEHAVIOR

As this chapter has discussed, life span leisure behavior is affected by numerous social and cultural forces, social agents (other people), and individual experiences. Iso-Ahola (1980) conceptualized the development of leisure behavior as shown in Figure 4.4, which he labels the "process of leisure socialization." The figure illustrates the interaction of components that contribute to overall leisure behavior.

The leisure activity skills needed by the leisure customer across the life span have been articulated in the "leisure skill assessment" offered by Navar (1980). By designing programs that contribute to developing the following competencies, the leisure service provider can contribute to the physical, mental, and social well-being of the leisure customers being served (From N. Navar, "A Rationale for Leisure Skill Assessment with Handicapped Adults" in *Therapeutic Recreation Journal,* 14(4):21–28. National Therapeutic Recreation Society, Arlington, VA.).

1. Physical skill that can be done alone.
2. Physical skill that can be done with others regardless of skill level.
3. Physical skill that requires the participation of one or more others.
4. Activity dependent on some aspect of the outdoor environment.
5. Physical skill not considered seasonal.
6. Physical skill with carryover value for later years.
7. Physical skill with carryover opportunity that is vigorous enough for cardiovascular fitness.
8. Mental skill participated in alone.
9. Mental skill requiring one or more others.
10. Appreciation skill or interest area that allows for emotional or mental stimulation through observation or passive response.
11. Skill that enables creative construction or self-expression through sound or visual media.

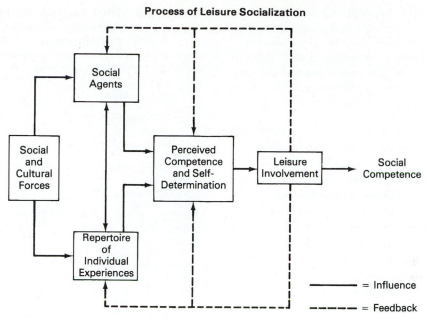

Process of Leisure Socialization

Figure 4.4   Development of Leisure Behavior. (Iso-Ahola 1980: 132.)

12. Skill that enables the enjoyment or improvement of the home environment.
13. Physical or mental skill that enables participation in a predominantly social situation.
14. Development of leadership or interpersonal skill that enables community service.

The source of leisure behavior is both intrinsic and extrinsic. Leisure behavior is influenced by the leisure competencies that an individual possesses and is encouraged by the availability of leisure activities and facilities. The variety of specific behaviors that leisure customers exhibit has been described by Murphy et al. (1973). The following is a synopsis of a broad range of these behaviors.

1. *Socializing Behavior*—Relating to others in a social experience in a social environment.
2. *Associative Behavior*—Gathering people around a common interest, sometimes in a formal structure like a club group.
3. *Acquisitive Behavior*—Interest and participation in acquiring or collecting things, such as a hobby.

4. *Competitive Behavior*—Within a structured set of rules and cooperative team work; interest in continuing to improve level of personal skill.
5. *Testing Behavior*—Competition against the natural environment; mental activities of problem solving.
6. *Risk-Taking Behavior*—Individual measures the risk and assumes reasonable chance of success and/or safety.
7. *Explorative Behavior*—Discovering new environments or rediscovering past adventure; involvement may be highly active or intensely passive.
8. *Vicarious Behavior*—Involvement via viewing the participation, performances, or works of others.
9. *Sensory Stimulation*—Experiences of intense sensory stimulation or manipulation of feeling, hearing, vision, or physical or emotional reaction.
10. *Physical Expression*—Physical activities that emphasize personal expression without emphasis on competition.
11. *Creative Behavior*—Creative expression through the arts and literature.
12. *Appreciative Behavior*—Responding to the outcomes of creative behavior—your own or someone else's; response to the natural environment; aesthetics.
13. *Variety-Seeking Behavior*—Diversion; a change from the normal routine, responsibility, and involvement.

14. *Anticipatory and Recollective Behaviors*—Participation includes planning and recalling in addition to actual involvement in an experience.
15. *Altruistic Behavior*—Demonstration of concern for others resulting in satisfaction and pleasure.
16. *Spiritual Expression*—Communion with others; expression of personal faith.

The information presented in Table 4.6 shows participation in selected sport activities.

Exercise walking remains a popular activity, followed by swimming. Many of the activities are focused on personal fitness and well-being, such as aerobic exercising, bicycling, calisthenics, exercise walking, exercising with equipment, racquetball, running/jogging, and swimming. In addition, a number of activities can be defined as individual, dual sports and/or outdoor activities, such as backpacking, bowling, fishing, golf, hiking, hunting, skiing, target shooting, and tennis. These categories speak to the nature of most activities that adults participate in, which are individually focused or carried out in pairs or small groups.

Another indication of the participation of adults in various art activities is found in Table 4.7. Visiting a historic park, an art museum, or a musical play are among the most popular activities. Table 4.8 & 4.9 presents information regarding actual participation in various arts activities. Most popular activities include needlework, buying artwork, photography, and painting.

Involvement in physical recreation and exercise activities can be related to physical expression, variety-seeking behavior, risk-taking behavior, testing behavior, or explorative behavior. On the other hand, a leisure customer's choice of arts performances and leisure activities may be related to socializing behavior, vicarious behavior, variety-seeking behavior, or appreciative behavior. Several kinds of leisure behavior may be intrinsic in each leisure activity a customer chooses. Although an individual may often select participation for one reason (i.e., competition, creative expression, or sensory stimulation), other behaviors are inherent in the activity.

TABLE 4.6 2001 Participation in Sport Activities—Ranked by Total Participation

Participated more than once (in millions)
Seven (7) years of age and older

Sport	Total
Exercise walking	71.2
Swimming	54.8
Camping vacation (overnite)	45.5
Fishing	44.5
Exercising with equipment	43.0
Bowling	40.3
Bicycle riding	39.0
Billiards/pool	32.7
Basketball	28.1
Golf	26.6
Hiking	26.1
Running/jogging	24.5
Aerobic exercising	24.3
Boating, motor/power	22.6
Weight lifting	21.2
Roller skating (In-Line)	19.2
Hunting with firearms	19.2
Dart throwing	16.9
Target shooting	15.9
Baseball	14.9
Backpack/wilderness camping	14.5
Mountain biking (on road)	14.0
Soccer	13.9
Softball	13.2
Scooter riding	12.7
Volleyball	12.0
Calisthenics	10.9
Tennis	10.9
Skateboarding	9.6
Horseshoe pitching	9.1
Football (touch)	8.9
Football (tackle)	8.6
Table tennis	8.4
Skiing (alpine)	7.7
Roller skating (2 × 2)	7.7
Canoeing	6.8
Mountain biking (off road)	6.3
Snorkeling	6.0
Step aerobics	5.7
Paintball games	5.6
Water skiing	5.5

Percent change is from 2000, na = Not surveyed in 2000
Note: 36.5 million people indicated they "worked out at club" in 2001, a 9.9% increase in 2000.

Source: National Sporting Goods Association, Mt. Prospect Il 60056 847.296 N 847.391.9827

TABLE 4.7   Attendance Rates for Various Arts Activities: 1992 [In percent. For persons 18 years old and over. Excludes elementary and high school performances. Based on 1992 household survey Public Participation in the Arts conducted January through December 1992. Data are subject to sampling error: see source.]

Item	Attendance at Least Once in the Prior 12 Months At—								Reading Literature[1]
	Jazz Perfor-mance	Cassical Music Perfor-mance	Opera	Musical Play	Non-Musical Play	Ballet	Art Museum	Historic Park	
Total	11	13	3	17	14	5	27	35	54
Sex: Male	12	12	3	15	12	4	27	35	47
Female	9	13	4	20	15	6	27	34	60
Race: White	10	13	3	18	14	5	28	37	56
Black	16	7	2	14	12	3	19	18	45
Other	6	12	5	11	10	6	29	23	42
Age: 18 to 24 years old	11	10	3	16	13	5	29	33	53
25 to 34 years old	14	10	3	16	12	5	29	36	54
35 to 44 years old	13	12	3	19	14	5	30	40	59
45 to 54 years old	11	17	4	22	17	5	29	41	57
55 to 64 years old	8	15	4	19	15	5	25	33	53
65 to 74 years old	7	14	4	17	13	4	20	29	50
75 to 96 years old	2	8	2	9	7	2	10	12	40
Education: Grade school	1	2	1	3	2	1	4	8	17
Some high school	2	3	1	5	4	1	7	15	32
High school graduate	6	7	1	12	8	2	16	26	49
Some college	14	14	3	21	16	6	35	43	65
College graduate	20	23	6	30	23	9	46	52	71
Graduate school	25	36	12	37	35	12	59	64	79
Income: Under $5,000	6	5	2	8	8	2	12	17	37
$5,000 to $9,999	5	6	1	7	6	3	14	16	40
$10,000 to $14,999	5	6	2	8	7	2	13	20	43
$15,000 to $24,999	9	11	2	14	11	3	23	31	50
$25,000 to $49,999	11	13	3	18	14	5	29	40	58
$50,000 and over	18	23	8	33	24	10	44	51	71
Not reported	11	13	4	18	15	5	28	33	50

[1]Includes novels, short stories, poetry, or plays.

Source: Data from *Arts Participation in America: 1982–1992*, U.S. National Endowment for the Arts.

Summary

The relationship that is established between the leisure service provider and the person receiving the services is often reflected in the label that is attached to the individuals being served. Some of the more common labels used in the leisure service field include participant, patron, customer, client, member, user, visitor, guest, and consumer. The label that is used may imply the level of dependence or independence, the expected patterns of communication, or the acknowledgment of expertise of both the leisure service provider and the person being served. The use of labels should not be taken lightly because it has a significant

TABLE 4.8   Participation in Various Arts Activities: 1992 [In percent, except as indicated. Covers activities engaged in at least once in the prior 12 months.]

Item	Adult Population (mil.)	In the Past 12 Months Percent Engaged at Least Once In—							
		Playing Classical Music	Modern Dancing[1]	Pottery Work[2]	Needlework[3]	Photography[4]	Painting[5]	Creative Writing	Buying Art Work
Total	185.8	4	8	8	25	12	10	7	22
Sex: Male	89.0	3	8	8	5	13	9	7	22
Female	96.8	5	8	9	43	10	10	8	22
Race: White	158.8	4	8	9	26	12	10	7	24
Black	21.1	3	8	8	15	11	5	6	12
Other	5.9	5	9	5	24	9	10	11	8
Age: 18 to 24 years old	24.1	6	11	9	18	11	19	14	13
25 to 34 years old	42.4	3	10	10	24	15	10	7	19
35 to 44 years old	39.8	4	7	10	25	13	10	8	27
45 to 54 years old	27.7	5	6	9	26	13	8	7	29
55 to 64 years old	21.2	5	6	6	27	10	6	5	26
65 to 74 years old	18.3	4	9	6	29	7	6	5	20
75 to 96 years old	12.3	3	5	3	26	2	4	2	17
Education: Grade school	14.3	1	4	2	22	3	1	(Z)	4
Some high school	18.6	1	4	7	25	5	5	3	11
High school graduate	69.4	2	8	8	25	9	9	4	15
Some college	39.2	6	10	12	26	15	13	11	27
College graduate	26.2	8	8	9	26	16	12	12	32
Graduate school	18.1	9	10	8	21	22	13	16	49
Income: Under $5,000	8.6	2	7	7	22	6	8	7	10
$5,000 to $9,999	15.2	2	7	4	27	7	8	7	10
$10,000 to $14,999	19.2	3	7	8	26	8	8	6	14
$15,000 to $24,999	32.9	4	9	8	26	9	10	7	17
$25,000 to $49,999	62.2	5	8	10	25	13	10	7	22
$50,000 and over	32.1	6	8	8	23	17	11	9	40
Not reported	15.6	4	8	8	24	12	11	9	24

Z Less than .05 percent. [1]Dancing other than ballet (e.g., folk and tap). [2]Includes ceramics, jewelry, leatherwork, and metalwork. [3]Includes weaving, crocheting, quilting, and sewing. [4]Includes making movies or video as an artistic activity. [5]Includes drawing, sculpture, and printmaking.

Source: Data from *Arts Participation in America: 1982–1992,* U.S. National Endowment for the Arts.

impact on how we view ourselves and others and on the assumptions and expectations made of each other.

Leisure customer decision making is influenced by three variables, described in marketing literature as involvement, differentiation, and time pressure. Involvement describes the extent to which an individual finds rele-

vance and interest in a particular leisure activity or leisure service. Differentiation relates to the multiple leisure opportunities that may be available from which the individual must choose. The third variable, time pressure, influences leisure choices based on both location and convenience of activities or services. Understanding leisure customer behavior

TABLE 4.9   2001 Youth Participation in Selected Sports with Comparison (4–10 year)
Participated more than once (in thousands)

	Year	Total	Change vs. 1991	Total age 7–11	Change vs. 1991	Total age 12–17
Total U.S.	1991	228,756		28,529		20,817
Total U.S.	2001	251,239	9.8%	20,350	9.8%	23,868
SPORT						
Baseball	1991	15,548		5,213		4,832
Baseball	2001	14,868	−10.2%	4,654	−10.7%	4,089
Basketball	1991	26,150		4,969		8,002
Basketball	2001	28,104	7.5%	6,352	27.8%	7,813
Bicycle Riding	1991	53,972		11,064		9,337
Bicycle Riding	2001	39,004	−27.7%	9,751	−11.9%	7,255
Fishing—fresh water	1991	41,778		4,345		4.052
Fishing—fresh water	2001	39,077	−6.5%	5,119	17.8%	4,494
Golf	1991	24,728		767		1,706
Golf	2001	26,637	7.7%	1,012	32.0%	2.264
Ice/figure skating	1991	7,921		2,036		1,861
Ice/figure skating	2001	5,344	−32.5%	1,528	−24.9%	1,320
Ice hockey	1991	1,809		209		517
Ice hockey	2001	2,193	21.2%	384	84.5%	441
Roller hockey	1993	1,471		413		577
Roller hockey	2001	2,235	51.9%	831	101.1%	688
Martial Arts	1991	3,231		889		485
Martial Arts	2001	5,132	58.8%	1,560	75.6%	975
In-Line Skating	1991	7,307		2,799		2,119
In-Line Skating	2001	19,225	163.1%	7,113	154.2%	5,056
Skateboarding	1991	8,011		3,589		3,012
Skateboarding	2001	9.623	20.1%	4,513	25.8%	3,965
Skiing (alpine)	1991	10,427		688		1,616
Skiing (alpine)	2001	7,660	−26.5%	613	−11.0%	1,455
Snowboarding	1991	1,577		265		572
Snowboarding	2001	5,343	238.8%	962	263.0%	1,640
Soccer	1991	9,992		3,737		3,577
Soccer	2001	13,886	39.0%	5,860	56.8%	3,833
Softball	1991	19,646		2,358		4,283
Softball	2001	13,213	−32.7%	2.484	5.4%	2,286
Tennis	1991	16,702		1,052		2,990
Tennis	2001	10,911	−34.7%	731	−30.5%	1,964
Volleyball	1991	22,586		1,784		5,082
Volleyball	2001	12,027	−46.8%	1,311	−26.5%	3,319

across the life span is basic to successful leisure programming.

Individual differences based on life span variables—which include age, gender, cohort, leisure skills, and leisure behaviors—are the factors that the leisure service professional must consider when developing leisure programs and services.

Leisure service customers include individuals across the life span, and their leisure behavior has been influenced by individual experiences and social and cultural forces. The personal leisure interests, personal leisure skills, and personal leisure preferences of individual leisure customers determine the leisure behaviors that they exhibit.

TABLE 4.10   10-Year History of Selected Sports Participation
Participated more than once (in millions)
Seven (7) years of age and older

SPORT	2001	1999	1997	1995	1993
Swimming	54.8	57.9	59.5	61.5	61.4
Camping	45.5	50.1	46.6	42.8	42.7
Exercising with Equisetum	43.0	45.2	47.9	44.3	34.9
Fishing	44.4	46.7	44.7	44.2	51.2
Bicycle riding	39.0	42.4	45.1	56.3	47.9
Bowling	40.3	41.6	44.8	41.9	41.3
Billiard (pool)	32.7	32.1	36.0	31.1	29.4
Basketball	28.1	29.6	30.7	30.1	29.6
Golf	26.6	27.0	26.2	24.0	22.6
Hiking	26.1	28.1	28.4	25.0	19.5
Roller skating (in-line)	19.2	24.1	26.6	23.9	12.4
Aerobic exercising	24.3	26.2	26.3	23.1	24.9
Boating motor/power	22.6	24.4	27.2	26.8	20.7
Running/jogging	24.5	22.4	21.7	20.6	20.3
Dart throwing	16.9	20.2	21.4	19.8	19.2
Hunting with firearms	19.2	17.1	17.0	17.4	18.5
Baseball	14.9	16.3	14.1	15.7	16.7
Softball	13.2	14.7	16.3	17.6	17.9
Mountain bike (on road)	14.0	15.1	16.0	10.5	10.5
Volleyball	12.0	11.7	17.8	18.0	20.5
Backpack/wilderness camp	14.5	15.3	12.0	10.2	9.2
Soccer	13.9	13.2	13.7	12.0	10.3
Target shooting	15.9	17.7	18.5	19.4	na
Calisthenics	10.9	12.6	11.10	9.3	10.8
Tennis	10.9	10.9	11.1	12.6	14.2
Roller skating (2 × 2)	7.7	8.2	10.9	14.4	15.3
Football (touch)	8.9	11.1	11.9	12.1	na
Shuffleboard	2.3	na	2.4	na	2.4
Mountain biking (off road)	6.3	6.8	8.1	6.7	4.6
Step aerobics	5.7	8.2	9.6	11.4	10.6
Table tennis	8.4	8.2	8.8	9.3	na
Ice/figure skating	5.3	7.7	7.9	7.7	6.9
Skiing (alpine)	7.7	7.4	8.9	9.3	10.5
Football (tackle)	8.6	8.4	8.2	8.3	na
Water skiing	6.0	6.3	6.3	6.5	4.9
Canoeing	5.5	6.6	6.5	6.9	8.1
Skateboarding	6.8	7.3	7.1	8.7	6.5
Hunting w/bow & arrow	4.7	5.8	5.3	5.3	na
Badminton	5.2	4.9	5.6	5.8	na
Archery (target)	4.7	4.9	4.8	4.9	na
Martial arts	5.1	5.1	4.9	4.5	3.6
Racquetball	3.4	3.2	4.5	5.0	5.4
Wrestling	3.5	3.8	2.2	na	na
Snowboarding	5.3	3.3	2.8	2.8	1.8
Sailing	2.7	2.8	3.4	3.9	3.8
Kayaking/rafting	3.5	3.0	2.9	3.5	2.1
Hockey (roller)	2.2	2.5	3.0	3.1	1.5
Muzzleloading	3.0	3.3	2.9	na	na
Cheerleading	3.7	na	na	2.9	na
Skiing (cross-country)	2.3	2.2	2.5	3.4	3.7
Scuba diving (open water)	2.1	2.3	2.3	2.4	2.4
Kick boxing	3.7	3.8	na	na	na
Boxing	1.7	1.3	0.8	1.4	0.7
Hockey (ice)	2.2	1.9	1.9	2.2	1.7
Shuffleboard	2.3	na	2.4	Na	2.4
Wind surfing	0.4	0.5	0.3	0.7	0.6

Source: National Sporting Goods Association, Mt. Prospect IL 60056 847.296 N 847.391.9827

─────────────── *Discussion Questions and Exercises* ───────────────

1. Discuss the physiological, psychological, and environmental determinants of human growth and development.

2. Examine the labels given to the persons for whom leisure services are designed. Describe the relationship between the leisure service professional and the person receiving the leisure service that each label implies: client, customer, guest, member, participant, patron, user, and visitor.

3. Leisure customer decision making can be influenced by three variables—involvement, differentiation, and time pressure. Describe how each of these may have an impact on leisure activity choices.

4. What is meant by a person being part of a cohort? Discuss the factors that influence generational differences among groups of people.

5. Demographics is a method of studying social factors that can be categorized. Discuss the way in which each of the following factors may have an impact on individual or group leisure behavior: age; gender; personality; education, occupation, and income; race and national identity; health; marital status and family; and place of residence and mobility.

6. Describe the leisure activity skills needed by an individual that will contribute to the physical, mental, and social well-being of that individual.

7. Murphy et al. (1973) described several leisure behaviors that leisure customers might exhibit through involvement in leisure activities. Discuss these behaviors and relate the behaviors to specific activities.

8. Discuss how changes throughout the life span have an impact on leisure behavior.

9. Interview at least two individuals in at least two different age cohort groups to determine how they approach their leisure.

10. Discuss the process of leisure socialization. What are some of the factors that might influence the way a person is socialized in his or her leisure?

─────────────── **References** ───────────────

Cordes, K., and H. Ibrahim. 1996. *Applications in recreation & leisure for today and the future*. St. Louis: Mosby.

Edginton, E., Hudson, S. and Ford, P. (1999). Leadership in Recreation and Leisure Service Organizations. Champaign, IL.: Sagamore.

Iso-Ahola, S. E. 1980. *The social psychology of leisure and recreation*. Dubuque, IA: Wm. C. Brown.

Kaluger, G., and M. F. Kaluger. 1984. *Human development: The span of life*. 3d ed. St. Louis: Times Mirror/Mosby College Publishing.

Kelly, J., and R. Warnick. 1999. *Recreation trends and markets: The 21st century*. Champaign, IL: Sagamore.

Murphy, J. F., J. G. Williams, E. W. Niepoth, and P. O. Brown. 1973. *Leisure service delivery system: A modern perspective*. Philadelphia: Lea and Febiger.

Navar, N. 1980. A rationale for leisure skill assessment with handicapped adults. *Therapeutic Recreation Journal* 14(4): 21–28.

Patterson, F. C. 1987. *A systems approach to recreation programming*. Prospect Heights, IL: Waveland Press.

Riche, M. F. 1996. How America is changing—The view from the Census Bureau, 1995. *The World Almanac*. Mahwah, NJ: Funk and Wagnalls.

Rossman, J. R. 2002. *Recreation programming: Designing leisure experiences*. Champaign, IL: Sagamore Publishing.

Stoll, M., and D. Wheeler. 1989. Leisure service program development. Term paper, University of Oregon.

Turner, J. S., and D. B. Helms. 1979. *Lifespan development*. Philadelphia: W. B. Saunders.

Turner, J. S., and D. B. Helms. 1983. *Lifespan developments*. 2d ed. New York: Holt, Rinehart and Winston.

Needs Identification and Assessment

LEARNING OBJECTIVES

1. To help the reader understand the *process of needs identification.*
2. To help the reader gain knowledge of the *processes involved in needs assessment.*
3. To help the reader gain an awareness of the *differences among needs, wants, values, and attitudes.*
4. To provide the reader with specific information about *tools and techniques for needs assessment* that are available to the leisure service professional.
5. To help the reader gain an understanding of *need typologies.*
6. To provide *specific examples of needs identification and needs assessment tools.*

INTRODUCTION

Needs identification and assessment focuses on understanding the individual and collective behavior of the customers whom the leisure service professional serves. Through needs identification and assessment, the leisure service professional can become aware of people's interests, opinions, attitudes, habits, desires, and knowledge regarding recreation and leisure.

Needs identification involves the determination of habit patterns, especially those concerned with individual leisure lifestyle. In other words, what does a person do during his or her leisure time? What recreation facilities do individuals use? When and how often do they use them? What facilities are *not* being used and why? In what organizations does a person have a membership? When does the person take a vacation?

Needs identification can be used to evaluate other factors relative to the delivery of leisure services and to determine the answers to such questions as: What is the quality of leadership that exists? What facilities are available and what is the quality of maintenance and development of these facilities? Identification and assessment of needs can reveal factors relating to both the customer (assessee) and the leisure service provider (assessor). When identifying needs, the leisure service provider must also be cognizant of existing leisure opportunities and services available to the individual and to society in general in any given community.

Figure 5.1 proposes categories of evaluative questions that can be used in the needs identification and needs assessment process. These are proactive questions; that is, they are questions and considerations that must be reviewed prior to program design and implementation. In general, these questions ask: Who is to be served? What strategies should be used to serve them? How are programs and services to be organized and implemented? and, What results are to be achieved? The corollary to this approach of identification and assessment of needs is found in Chapter 13.

BASIC CONCEPTS

It is important to distinguish the differences in meaning among such terms as *leisure needs, wants,* and *desires.* In this chapter, we focus on the concepts of needs identification and needs assessment. These two terms, while similar, also have different meanings and carry different implications in terms of leisure service program planning and development. Six basic concepts, or terms, can be useful in developing strategies to plan programs more effectively, under the generic heading of "needs." These are: (1) needs, (2) wants, (3) values, (4) attitudes, (5) needs identification, and (6) needs assessment. Brief definitions of each of these concepts follow.

Needs

A need can be thought of as an individual *physical, psychological, or social imbalance.* As Edginton, Hudson, and Ford (1999) have noted,

> When an individual has an imbalance—physically, psychologically, or socially—he or she has a need. Physiological needs are those deficiencies associated with biological drives, such as the need for food, water, sex, and sleep. Physiological needs reflect the desire of individuals to maintain an internal equilibrium. Psychological and social needs are more difficult to assess, but equally important. The need for companionship, social interaction, safety, love, self-esteem, self-worth, self-actualization, recognition, power, and achievement are all examples of psychological and social needs (p. 75).

In other words, needs reflect the discrepancy between the "ideal" state—physically, psychologically, and socially—and the current condition of the individual in the environment within which he or she is functioning. We all have needs; we all act on these needs; and movement toward alleviating these deficiencies propels human behavior. Just as an individual has a "need state," so do communities, regions, nations, and whole societies.

Purpose	Categories of Needs Identification and Assessment Questions			
	Goals	**Strategies**	**Program Elements**	**Results**
To Aid Decision Making	Who is to be served? What are their <u>needs</u>? What <u>problems</u> have to be <u>solved</u> if the needs are to be met? What <u>funds</u> are available for work in this area? What <u>research findings</u> have a bearing on problem solving in this area? What relevant <u>technology</u> is available? What <u>alternative goals</u> might be chosen?	Are the given <u>objectives</u> stated operationally? Is their accomplishment <u>feasible</u>? What relevant <u>strategies</u> exist? What <u>alternative strategies</u> can be developed? What are the potential <u>costs and benefits</u> of the competing strategies? What are the <u>operating characteristics</u> of the competing strategies? How <u>compatible</u> are the competing strategies with the system? How <u>feasible</u> are the competing strategies?	What is the <u>schedule</u> of activities? What are the <u>personnel</u> assignments? What's the program <u>budget</u>? What potential <u>problems</u> attend the design? What are the <u>discrepancies</u> between the design and the operations? What <u>design changes</u> are needed? What <u>changes in implementation</u> are needed?	What <u>results</u> will be achieved? Will they be <u>congruent</u> with the objectives? Will there be any <u>negative side effects</u>? Will there be any <u>positive side effects</u>? Do the results suggest that the goals, designs, or process should be <u>modified</u>? Do the results suggest that the project will be a success?

Figure 5.1   A Matrix for Identifying and Analyzing Evaluation Questions.
(Source: Stufflebeam, D. L., 1974. *Meta-Evaluation,* Kalamazoo, MI: The Evaluation Center: Western Michigan University, 18.)

It has been stated that play is a universal need. People have the need to play regardless of their social status, age, or psychological or physiological state. As George Bernard Shaw has written regarding play and age, "Man does not cease to play because he grows old—he grows old because he ceases to play." Another way of looking at need is that it is a state that is desired or necessary. A need occurs when something is lacking in a person's life. Leisure needs occur when people lack the opportunity for play, access to leisure spaces, opportunities for meaningful social interaction, freedom, and the opportunity to choose; hence, to experience, leisure.

Wants

To want something is to desire it or to wish for it. Thus, we can think of a want as *something that is per-*

ceived as being needed. Wants can be differentiated from needs in that they are desired by the individual, but are not necessary to sustain life or well-being. Wants are often based on an individual's previous experience and knowledge, whereas a need may be influenced more by an individual's physical, psychological, or other similar demands. When a person expresses a "want" to participate in a particular leisure activity, he or she is expressing a preference or desire for engagement that he or she perceives will be beneficial. However, wanting to participate in an activity and actually having that experience meet a need are two different conditions that may or may not be linked.

Values

A value can be thought of as *a principle, guideline, or standard of quality that an individual, community, or society considers to be worthwhile.* We all make value judgments about our leisure preferences and experiences. These value judgments help us discern the relative worth of a leisure experience. Values can be thought of as assumptions that we make about what is or what ought to be. Often, values determine the way in which individuals will direct their energy and resources.

People place strong values on their leisure pursuits. Values related to leisure may be tied to status that is placed on a leisure experience. In addition, the value that a person places on a leisure experience often triggers an emotional response concerning its relative worth. Examples of ways in which people attach value to a leisure experience might include the degree to which they are committed to pursuing the activity; for example, how much they are willing to pay in relationship to the service they receive and the location of the experience that they choose (skiing in Aspen, surfing in Hawaii, or vacationing at Club Med in Mexico).

Values are difficult to measure. An individual can be asked what he or she values, but it is often easier to draw conclusions from the way people act. Leisure values are an important factor to measure and study in the needs identification and assessment process.

Attitude

An attitude is *a feeling or state of mind.* Leisure is often defined as a condition or state of mind. By understanding how people feel about their leisure, we can better understand what they would like to do during their leisure.

Leisure attitudes are often likened to opinion and can be thought of as a disposition to respond in a certain way. For example, individuals may hold the attitude that any form of participation in a leisure activity should be tolerated because it is an expression of freedom. To such individuals, freedom and individual license to engage in whatever behavior they see fit is synonymous with leisure. Contrary to this may be a prevailing societal value that certain restraints must be exercised in pursuit of

leisure (e.g., off-road vehicles should not have free access to all environments, but rather should be restricted to designated areas). Attitudes, like values, are emotionally charged, complex, and may or may not be linked to actual behavior or actions.

Needs Identification

Needs identification describes the leisure service requirements that may exist in a given social or geographical area (Siegel et al., 1987: 71). Needs identification strategies are designed to provide data that will enable program planners to determine the extent and kinds of needs in a specifically defined area. This process can be thought of as *a means of taking inventory of leisure wants, needs, behaviors, values, attitudes, and resources.* We discuss various ways to identify needs later in the next section, Needs Assessment.

The importance of the needs identification process is that it provides a basis for actual needs assessment. Before judgments can be made as to which needs and values should be addressed, or what leisure resources must be improved or created, programming professionals must know the status or state of these variables. The value of information collected in the needs identification process depends on its authenticity and reliability. The information must be as accurate and consistent as possible. In other words, every effort must be made to make sure that the information collected accurately reflects the state of people's thinking and the status of resources that currently exist.

Needs Assessment

Needs assessment is the application of judgment to assess the significance of the information gathered in order to determine priorities for program planning and service development. In other words, once all the relevant information has been collected, programming professionals make some *judgment as to the target groups to be addressed and the resources to be secured and delivered.* In addition, the assessment process can be useful in making judgments on the continuance, the termination, or the development of programs and related resources.

What are some of the factors that can influence the assessment process? First, and perhaps most important, is the vision or mission of the organization itself. Although the needs identification process may uncover different needs, values, and attitudes, an organization may choose to address only those that are consistent with its mission. For example, a social welfare organization may differentiate its services and target more of its resources toward disadvantaged groups. A second factor is the availability of resources. It is important to realize that any leisure service organization must live within certain parameters or constraints related to resources. Still another factor that may influence needs assessment is the broader community attitudes that may exist regarding the solving of community problems. Even if a need exists and it appears to be a strong priority, prevailing social, political, or economic variables may make it inappropriate to create a viable program to meet the need. For example, think of the popularity of swimming in communities across North America. Because of this popularity, it is difficult to imagine that there are communities that do not have accessible swimming programs and facilities. Yet, it may not always be feasible, based on the economic environment of a community, to provide needed swimming activities.

Although the needs identification process requires knowledge of a number of sophisticated strategies to collect information, the assessment area is where professional expertise and judgment of a set of individuals comes into full play. It is one thing to have information available as a leisure program planner; however, it is another thing to know how to evaluate such information. An even more complex task is to organize information and subsequent judgments into an understandable and coherent plan that can be supported by the customers served by a leisure service organization. Judgments regarding the distribution of resources, directed at meeting needs, requires wisdom,

experience, creativity, and vision. Further, once a course of action has been identified, it often takes perseverance, determination, and drive to see that the program succeeds.

MAKING ASSESSMENTS

What kinds of tools and techniques are available to the leisure service profession to engage in the needs assessment process? Most leisure service organizations use a combination of instruments to determine needs so as to produce different perspectives on needs. One instrument may be very useful at measuring individual leisure needs, while another may provide a broader perspective of community needs.

Careful consideration should be given to the selection and development of the instruments used. If the instruments do not give an accurate measure (called *validity*) of the leisure deficiency being studied, or if the instruments fail to give a consistent measure (called *reliability*) of the same phenomenon, valuable organizational resources can be wasted. Often the selection of inappropriate instrumentation results in the lack of correlation between the customer's needs and the services that the organization delivers to its customers. This problem can be a difficult one to remedy, not only because of the problem in selecting valid and reliable instrumentation, but also because of other variables. For example, a customer's understanding and willingness to participate in the needs assessment process can be a powerful factor in its success.

Most needs assessment processes use a variety of approaches. Some of the common needs assessment procedures that can be employed in the leisure service field are *social indicators, social surveys,* and *community group approaches.* The following section, social indicators, describes these categories.

Social Indicators
Social indicators are quantitative measures that establish the need for a service. In other words,

TABLE 5.1   Types and Sources of Social Indicators

Types	Sources
1. Standards	1. National organizations
2. Demographic information	2. State and provincial organizations
3. Socioeconomic variables	3. State, provincial, and federal government
4. Health statistics	4. Census reports
5. Education trends	5. Government publications
6. Population density	6. Trade associations
7. Family characteristics	7. Political interest groups
8. Marriage patterns	8. Special interest groups
9. Housing characteristics	9. Religious organizations
10. Community participation	10. Futurist organizations and businesses
11. Delinquency rates	11. Others
12. Suicide rates	
13. Drug and alcohol use	
14. School dropout rates	
15. Others	

these types of measures involve *the development of standards and the correlation of the needs of a consumer group with these standards.* Standards have been established especially for determining needs in providing leisure facilities. For example, the National Recreation and Park Association (NRPA) and the federal government in the United States have developed documents that can be useful in helping communities determine facility availability and accessibility. Another approach is the comparative approach. Information collected from other leisure agencies or businesses can be analyzed to determine need.

Table 5.1 defines types and sources of social indicators that can have an impact on the delivery of leisure programs and services. A number of different types of information can be collected in the needs assessment process. Normally the information used is secondary data—in other words, data that has been gathered beforehand and not specifically for the expressed purposes of the current analysis.

Information can be gathered from a variety of sources to shed light on a particular problem. For example, information can be gathered locally and then combined with other sets of data that have been obtained from national sources. The combination of these two approaches can be useful in assessing need. Many different types of information can be collected. For example, knowledge of the amount of individual or family discretionary funds available may impact the types of leisure activities that can be purchased by customers or that might require a subsidy to ensure access for customers. Some of the types of information that are often available include standards, demographic information, socioeconomic variables, and others.

Much of this information is available from convenient and accessible sources. For example, census data can be found at most public libraries or on-line at www.census.gov. The U.S. government designates selected libraries throughout the United States that serve as repositories for government publications and documents. These are usually located in conjunction with major state colleges and universities. National organizations such as the National Recreation and Park Association (NRPA), the American Association for Leisure and Recreation (AALR), and the Canadian Parks/Recreation Association (CP/RA) all produce written documents that can be useful in the needs assessment process. (website, for these organizations can be accessed at www.nrpa.org, www.perd.org/aalR, and www.cpra.org.)

In recent years, futurist associations have provided composite information regarding social indicators in the leisure field. Such publications as *Leisure Watch* and *Leisure Industry Digest* provide summaries of leisure trends and expenditures in the leisure market. Trade journals such as *Athletic Business* and *Recreation, Sports and Leisure* often provide invaluable statistics concerning expenditures, trends, and new developments in the leisure market. Other organizations such as political interest groups, special interest

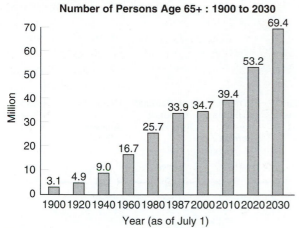

Number of Persons Age 65+ : 1900 to 2030

Figure 5.2 Number of Persons Age 65 and Older.
(Source: Data from the U.S. Bureau of Census, 1997.)

groups, and religious organizations compile facts and figures in support of various issues and concerns they value. These types of organizations can be tapped. For example, the American Association of Retired Persons (AARP; 1988) annually produces a pamphlet entitled *A Profile of Older Americans*. This document contains a wealth of information that has been researched and compiled by this organization and serves to illustrate the type of information available from special interest groups (the AARP web site is www.aarp.org). A sample of this type of information is found in Figure 5.2, which shows U.S. Bureau of the Census data.

Social Surveys

Social surveys are often used by leisure service organizations to assess need. Leisure service organizations use this strategy to gather information about individual and collective leisure preferences, opinions, and attitudes. Surveys provide *a method of collecting demographic information and the opportunity for correlation of such information with leisure preferences.*

Information concerning expressed and felt desires can be translated into an analysis of a

demand for leisure programs, services, and facilities. When we ask individuals to tell us what activities and facilities they currently participate in, and in which ones they would like to participate in the future, we are able to compare expression with the existing resources and forecast potential demand. Surveys can also be useful in providing the leisure service organization with information concerning the level and extent of services that a customer group might support. For example, with questionnaires, we can determine whether taxpayers would be willing to support a referendum for facility development or land acquisition. Another example might be a youth-serving agency asking its members if they would support a membership fee increase. A leisure service business might want to survey its constituents to determine a need for expanded services.

Figure 5.3 outlines an eleven-step process used by the Bend (Oregon) Metro Park and Recreation District to conduct a needs assessment. The survey provided an opportunity for community involvement in the planning and decision-making processes of the district. The study also provided the Bend Metro Park and Recreation District board of directors and professional staff with empirically based information to assist in decision-making processes. Specifically, the survey involved the following goals.

1. Identification of the scope and depth of opportunities available for use for leisure in the public domain.
2. Identification of the activities in which individuals say they participate.
3. Identification of the activities individuals say that they currently do not participate in but would like to at some future date.
4. Identification of what additional leisure facilities and recreation and leisure programs should be developed by the Bend Metro Park and Recreation District.
5. Determination of what individuals believe is the present effectiveness and efficiency of the Bend Metro Park and Recreation District in providing services.

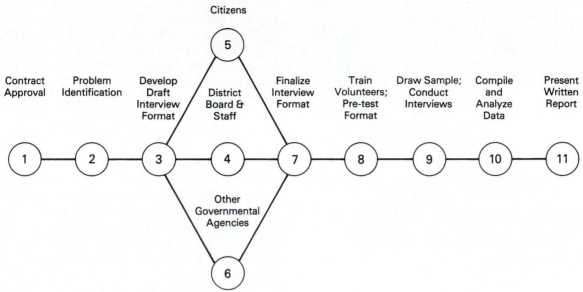

Figure 5.3   Format for Market Research, Bend (Oregon) Metro Park and Recreation District.

6. Determination of what factors influence initial and repeat participation in the services and facilities offered by the Bend Metro Park and Recreation District.
7. Identification and definition of barriers that prevent participation in services and facilities operated by the Bend Metro Park and Recreation District.
8. Identification of public opinions concerning future fiscal support for various programs and services of the Bend Metro Park and Recreation District.
9. Identification of demographic information useful in predicting leisure behavior of district residents.
10. Identification of psychographic (lifestyle) variables useful in predicting leisure behavior of district residents.
11. Identification of the current time use of the residents of the Bend Metro Park and Recreation District with an eye toward understanding patterns of leisure time use.

The procedures employed in conducting this survey in Bend involved use of the personal interview format, conducted by telephone. A representative sample of the residents of the Bend Metro Park and Recreation District was drawn from the latest set of telephone directories, representing the telephone exchanges within the district. The number of telephone listings drawn from the entire population was done in a systematic fashion beginning at a random starting point. This was followed by the selection of every nth residential number listed. The total number of households selected was representative of the entire district population.

The interview format was developed by initially interviewing the professional staff, followed by discussions with:

1. The Bend Metro Park and Recreation District Board of Directors
2. Community groups and individuals
3. Other public agencies (governmental)
4. Other interested parties

The final format was approved by the Bend Metro Park and Recreation District Board of

Directors as recommended by the professional staff and the consultants. Individuals conducting the telephone interviews were trained in appropriate telephone interview techniques. The survey and telephone interview techniques were pretested to ensure reliability and validity. The interview process took place during the span of two days. Callbacks were used to make contact or to complete an interview when necessary.

The final report that was presented included:

1. A summary statement of findings
2. Discussion of the purposes and objectives of the study
3. Discussion of the methodology employed, with attention to the representativeness of the sample
4. Discussion of survey findings with summary tables, reporting statistical information such as frequency distributions, percentages, mean scores, and median scores
5. Recommendations for review by the Bend Metro Park and Recreation Board of Directors and professional staff

The telephone survey that was used included a number of questions dealing with activity participation, barriers to activity and facility use, and questions concerning opinions about future developments. (See a sample of another telephone survey in the appendix of this text.)

There are some drawbacks to using surveys. Individuals often do not respond as they really think and feel. Also, surveys measure the attitudes, interests, and opinions of people at a particular moment or period of time. Changes may become apparent after programs and services are actually implemented. Another drawback is that much of the information collected using a survey yields quantitative information. However, leisure is a qualitative experience and the commitment that people make to a particular leisure event varies in intensity. This in turn influences their commitment. Nonetheless, surveys are a very valuable method used in the needs assessment process. Virtually every leisure organization uses this procedure.

A more recent use of the survey format in leisure service organizations is to measure customer satisfaction. The Willamalane Park and Recreation District (Springfield, Oregon) conducts telephone surveys on a quarterly basis to assess, among other things, levels of customer satisfaction. The programming staff views the gathering of this information as fundamental to its work in understanding customer needs. According to one staff member, "One of the important elements in the process of marketing is determining the extent to which we actually satisfy the needs of those that we serve. This is an important yardstick we use in measuring our success."

A convenience survey used by the U.S. Marine Corps Morale, Welfare, and Recreation Department that is directed toward identifying individuals' areas of interest as well as their name, address, and other vital information is found in Figure 5.4. This survey asks individuals to provide information in order to be included on the MWR Department's mailing list. Individuals filling out the form receive a free gift, choosing from such options as bowling passes, a bucket of balls at a driving range, or $5 off a dinner activity at one of its clubs.

Community Group Approaches

North Americans have a strong tradition of being involved in decisions that influence their lives. From a historical perspective, town hall meetings were one of the earliest forms of participatory democracy. These public forums were built on the assumption that all members of the community should have an active voice and opportunity to influence community affairs. This tradition continues today in some communities, especially in the northeastern portion of the United States where major community decisions are still made at town hall meetings.

In more recent years, the strategies and techniques employed in soliciting community input have become less informal, more sophisticated, and more fully developed, planned, and

Get on Marine MWR's
Mailing List

and receive a FREE GIFT!

Please fill this out

Sponsors Name: _____ Birth Month _____

Spouse: _____ Birth Month _____

Mailing Address: _____

_____

Duty Station: _____ Rotation Date: _____

Duty Phone: _____ Home Phone: _____

Are you? active duty ❑ civilian ❑ accompanied ❑ unaccompanied ❑

Rank: (or civilian equivalent)

E1-3 ❑ E4-5 ❑ E6-9 ❑ CWO ❑ O1-03 ❑ O4-06 ❑ 07-010 ❑

Names, Age(s) and Birth Month of Children: _____

_____

_____

_____

Please check your areas of interest:

❑ aerobics	❑ aquatics	❑ arts & crafts	❑ athletics/fitness
❑ auto hobby	❑ basketball	❑ bingo	❑ boating
❑ bowling	❑ bus service	❑ car insurance	❑ delivery service
❑ dining out	❑ education	❑ golf	❑ karate
❑ libraries	❑ nightlife	❑ races	❑ racquetball
❑ recycling	❑ scuba	❑ softball	❑ travel service
❑ volleyball	❑ weightlifting	❑ youth activities	❑ other

Bring home a box-full of news and info about the latest MWR happenings!

Marine MWR wants to make your tour on Okinawa FUN! So, effective in March, we're bringing "FUN" home to you like never before.

When you get on our mailing list, we'll send you information on all the activities and events you're interested in. And that's not all, we'll also send you our monthly magazine, For Immediate Release.

Simply fill out this card; fold and staple or tape it (make sure Marine MWR address is on the outside); then drop it in the mail today! **You'll want to hurry—the deadline is February 8, 1995.**

Fill us in and receive your choice of the following *(please check one)*

_____ Two FREE Bowling Passes

_____ $5 OFF Dinner Coupon

_____ FREE Bucket of Balls at
Kishaba Driving Range

Where do you get most of your recreational information! (check all that apply)

❑ Banners

❑ For Immediate Release

❑ Okinawa Marine/Guidon

❑ FEN Radio

❑ Posters

❑ Shogun

❑ Stars and Stripes

❑ FEN TV

❑ This Week on Okinawa

❑ Other

Figure 5.4 Interest Survey, Morale, Welfare, and Recreation Department, U.S. Marine Corps, Okinawa, Japan.
(Source: From Morale, Welfare and Recreation Department, U.S. Marine Corps, Okinawa, Japan.)

organized. In fact, in North America today, leisure service professionals use a myriad of approaches or strategies to solicit and identify the ideas, opinions, and values of a community. The great value of these strategies is that they provide *an active opportunity for community members or customer groupings to express their opinions, to make their needs known, and to be involved in decision-making and planning processes.*

Generally speaking, five community group approaches have been identified in the literature. These are: *community forums, focus groups, nominal group technique, Delphi technique,* and *community impressions approach.* The following is a discussion of each of these strategies and their application in leisure service organizations.

It has been suggested that the community group approach is less expensive than other approaches to assessing community needs. However, this approach often involves the use of highly trained facilitators and is not necessarily efficient from a time perspective. Soliciting meaningful input from customer groups within a prescribed time limit is often difficult. When limits are established, it often prevents a thorough discussion of ideas, concepts, opinions, or needs. Other problems associated with the community group process can occur when groups are over- or underrepresented. For example, a domineering group of individuals can force its perspective on others, even the majority, if it is not properly handled within the context of the group process chosen. Despite some of these limitations, the community group process is found throughout North America today.

Community Forums

A community forum can be thought of as an open meeting. Although community forums can be called for discussion on a wide variety of topics or subjects, they also can be called to discuss specific projects, services, or problems that may warrant attention. In general, community forums allow for the expression of opinions by community members, customer groups, or groups with special concerns. In fact, community forums provide opportunities for unattached or unaffiliated citizens to express their viewpoints.

A community forum is usually called by the leisure service organization requiring input from customers. The role of the leisure service professional is to listen while at the same time communicating necessary information concerning proposed or existing projects, services, and programs. Most community forums involve a lively exchange with a free-flowing expression of opinions and ideas. Community forums that are misused often result in individuals feeling that they have been manipulated or used as pawns in order to induce customer acceptance of the work of professionals or politicians. On the other hand, community forums can provide an opportunity for coalition building and the development of a greater awareness of the projects, programs, and services of an organization. A good example of the community forum process took place in Denton, Texas where the Parks and Recreation Department staff was attempting to get community input on a five-year master plan for facilities development. The department first did a random phone survey to prioritize facility needs identified by the staff and get citizen input on any additional facilities that the public felt were needed. It then held four public forums in various parts of the city to validate the findings of the survey and to help create the final comprehensive list of facilities for the master plan. The use of public forums in this manner helped to generate support for the bond initiative that was needed to fund the facilities. The process also ensured that the facilities were a priority in the public's view as well as that of the staff.

Focus Groups

Customer focus groups are another way of soliciting input concerning needs and wants. Such groups are established to provide a method of gauging customer reaction to a wide variety of concerns. Not only do focus groups have the ability to provide information concerning the types of services that may be desired, but they also can be valuable in assisting the leisure services professional in finding ways to promote activities, determine the prices, and assist in other areas related to program design and implementation. In addition, customer focus groups can be a source of information about competitive services. Customer focus groups can alert the professional to changes that may be occurring in the marketplace and thus enable a leisure service organization to continue to maintain its competitive or cooperative activities.

One of the advantages of focus groups, as opposed to other ways of collecting information about customers, is that they can be set up to operate on a continuous basis. Further, customer groups can be established to focus on specific programs or facilities that a leisure service organization might operate. Several groups may function simultaneously. For example, a voluntary leisure service organization may have focus groups that deal with such diverse program areas and management concerns as youth activities, health promotion programs, resident camps, product sales, and facility use.

There are a number of challenges in forming focus groups and in holding them together. First is the danger of bias creeping into the recommendations made by groups because they are not representative of the customers served. Another difficulty is maintaining continuous interest in the work of the group. Of course, this can be alleviated to a certain extent by making sure that the recommendations of the focus group are listened to and implemented; their input must have impact. Focus groups can also be costly to establish and maintain. It often takes time to gain the trust of individuals in order to ensure that the concerns of the customer are of primary importance. This requires time, energy, and human resources; in effect, there is a real cost to an organization.

Howard (1989: 18) noted that the use of focus groups was especially valuable in the management of fitness and health centers. According to Howard, "focus groups can be incredibly insightful in showing how members are experiencing a fitness center. Focus groups typically consist of six to nine people and a moderator who asks questions and records answers . . . focus group members are less inhibited about speaking their minds if their group meets at some place other than the fitness center and the moderator is a neutral third party." Focus groups are a way of developing feedback from customers to monitor the work of a leisure service organization or a specific leisure program or service.

Nominal Group Technique

The nominal group technique procedure is a model approach to program planning and program development. Basically, the nominal group technique is a noninteractive workshop that is designed to maximize creativity and productivity and to minimize the argumentative style of problem solving and competitive discussion (Siegel et al., 1987: 90). This technique involves a systematic process for defining problems, identifying barriers, and determining solutions. The nominal group technique contains the following steps:

1. *Problem Identification*—The first step in the process is to determine the problem or problems to be resolved.
2. *Ranking*—The next step is to rank the problems. This enables discussion of a wide variety of issues.
3. *Response of Critical Reference Groups*—Critical reference groups in this final step include customers, experts, and organization professionals.

Nominal groups consisting of eight to ten individuals are posed questions and asked to respond with ideas. These ideas are recorded and displayed for review by the entire group. Usually this is done in a round-robin fashion with each member of the group having the opportunity to offer one idea until all ideas have been recorded. No comments are made during this period; the purpose is to encourage idea generation. Following this procedure, idea clarification is pursued during a discussion period. Then each member of the group is asked to identify and rank the five most important ideas. This allows for the prioritization of concerns without a competitive modality. As Siegel et al. (1987: 90) note, "It allows each member time for reflection and thought. It encourages the generation of minority ideas; it avoids hidden agendas; it imposes a burden on all present to work and contribute and to have a sense of responsibility for the group; it facilitates creativity; it allows for the airing of personal concerns; and . . . it does not allow any one person or point of view to dominate."

The National Program for Playground Safety teaches a variation of this process as a method to help community groups come to consensus about what items to include on a playground (see Exhibit 5.1). All members of the group are encouraged to generate ideas. Through a ranking procedure, members categorize these items as first, second, third, and fourth in importance. This system has worked well with numerous groups—everyone comes to the table with his or her own wants and needs and the result is a consensus without conflict.

EXHIBIT 5.1 GETTING THE ROCKS

This is a consensus-building process used to determine the elements most important to the group. Although the National Program for Playground Safety uses this process to determine design elements for playgrounds, the authors have used it in various other situations such as development of mission statements and action plans where group consensus was important. A more complete description of this process can be found in the *SAFE Playground Handbook* available through the National Program for Playground Safety (www.Playgroundsafety.org).

THE PROCESS

Step 1: Generating Ideas

1. Have each member of the group make an individual list of all elements of play that he or she feels are important. Allow about five minutes for this process.
2. Have each member of the group give one thing from his or her list to add to the group master list. Do not encourage discussion of items at this time, merely list items on paper.
3. Continue with each member making additions to the list until everyone has depleted his or her individual list. Keep the group on task. The elements are not listed in order of importance but do need to be numbered starting with number 1. Try to end with an even number.
4. Try diligently to get all group members to add elements of play to the master list. It is important to get the entire group engaged and talking early on in this process in order to ensure overall satisfaction with the finished results. Once the list is completed, the next step is to vote.

Step 2: Voting

1. All members of the group will participate in the voting process. If there is an even number of people in the group, have the group decide how a tie is broken—have them tell you.

2. It is important at this stage to allow any conversation to carry on as long as it takes to allow the group to come to a majority level of consensus. As the facilitator, you will simply ask which of the two elements being considered is the most important and then record the vote.
3. This process requires three rounds of voting. For round one, divide the list in half. Compare the first item on the list (#1) with the first item on the second half. For example, if the initial list had 20 items, the first half of the list would contain items 1–10; the second half of list would contain items 11–20. You would compare 1–11; 2–12; 3–13; and so on. Put an X next to the item that you consider to be the most important and an 0 next to the other.
   a. Round two uses the same process but compares the first and second items, then the third and fourth, fifth and sixth, seventh and eighth, and so on.
   b. Round three continues the process but this time compares the first item with the last item. Thus, in our example, #1 is compared with #20, #2 is compared with #19, #3 is compared with #18, and so on.

Step 3: The Final Tally

1. When you are finished with step 2, each item on the list should have three marks beside it. The possible combinations are: XXX or XXO or XOO or OOO.
2. The items with three "X"s are the most important elements of play for this group. These play elements are significant in that they constitute the core of this group's priority values. These elements should be the first included in the design. The two "X"s, one "X"s and three "O's" are all important but their ranking indicates in what order they should be included in the design. Thus, if the playground is developed in phases the three "O"s would go in the last phase.

Delphi Technique

The Delphi technique is another strategy that can be used by leisure service professionals to gather information about needs. This procedure allows for systematic input of information on specific areas of focus. The Delphi technique procedure is usually used in areas having an impact on broad policy formulation. It helps in the process of making value judgments wherein decisions require broader, more expansive thinking. Basically, the Delphi process provides a format for exploring questions and opinions and then summarizing information.

Siegel et al. (1987: 90) have written that the Delphi technique involves five steps. These steps are as follows:

1. *Identification of Key Issues*—The first step in the Delphi procedure is to develop a questionnaire that identifies the key issues.
2. *Panel Experts*—The next step in the process involves giving the questionnaire to key individuals to complete and return to the initiators of the process.
3. *Tally Results*—Results of the returned questionnaires are tallied to summarize areas of agreement and disagreement.
4. *Items of Disagreement*—The panel of experts receives a second questionnaire containing items of disagreement and the reasons for the initial judgments that were made.
5. *Repeat of Process*—The first four steps are repeated until an agreement can be reached.

A major advantage of using the Delphi technique is that it provides a systematic way of allowing input by individuals on specific issues. In addition, the Delphi process is useful because it is methodical in nature. In other words, it is a way of ordering the process by which information is gathered within an organization. It provides focus on a set of specific issues or concerns and enables an organization to derive responses or opinions to issues that have been identified. Another major reason that the Delphi technique is useful is that respondents can maintain their anonymity. In other words, the identification of

a particular customer can be held in confidence. The value here is that individuals are presumed to respond more freely and openly when their identity is not known. Thus, the Delphi technique is a controlled way of garnering feedback on issues related to need.

There are some drawbacks in using the Delphi technique. The major drawback seems to be a lack of specific guidelines in the use of the strategy. For example, how many times must questions be returned to respondents in order to develop the final focus? Another problem lies in maintaining the anonymity of the participants. Obviously, the individuals responding to the questionnaire will be known to some parties. In fact, the question could be asked, should the respondents be anonymous? Often, people working in tandem or groups operate creatively, producing synergistic solutions to problems and issues.

A prime example of the application of the Delphi technique in the leisure service field was a survey of customer opinion of the "operation, needs, and future directions of the Parks and Recreation of the City of Lake Oswego, Oregon." The study was aimed at forecasting future plans and developments as well as ascertaining attitudes regarding current operations. The Delphi technique was used as a method for arriving at consensus and determining priorities directly related to the future direction of the organization.

The method used in this procedure by the city of Lake Oswego involved several steps. Initially, a questionnaire was mailed to a group of respondents who remained anonymous to each other. These participants gave short opinion statements that were synthesized into a second questionnaire. The second questionnaire was sent to the respondents who then ranked all the concerns, their own as well as the others, and this data was compiled to make a third questionnaire. The third questionnaire had the rankings from the previous survey and allowed the respondents a chance to amend their prior rankings. From this process emerged a consensus of the entire group surveyed. Before explaining to the participants the procedures that would be undertaken, the city justified the procedures. The reasons for specific procedures relating to the overall technique were then more evident.

The Delphi technique has, in the past, been used most frequently in situations which professional groups or narrowly defined populations were asked to give advice hinging on their professional expertise. The researchers' efforts were an attempt to serve the same purpose in the city of Lake Oswego. These individual respondents had ideas that were especially important in establishing future plans.

One of the main features of the Delphi is its "democratic" quality. Without having to bring people together, the Delphi brings opinion together in the same way that New England town meetings did. It also creates an equality of individual opinion, allowing each respondent to have equal say. The method acts as a communication medium as well as a fact-gathering instrument. Each participant has the opportunity to review the generalized opinions of others, becoming better informed and at the same time seeing his or her own separate ideas within the context of the larger group. The Delphi also has a practical value. The results gained constitute a very usable reflection of opinion, from which substantive conclusions may be drawn and suggestions can be made. To better understand the process of the Delphi technique, following an outline of the specific procedures of the study in the city of Lake Oswego.

Date(s)	Action
October 9	Initial study team visited the community. Coordinated study plan with city manager and staff. Agreement signed.
October 18	Letter sent to twenty individuals whose names were provided by the city. Each person was invited to participate and provide ten names of knowledgeable and concerned citizens who might enjoy participating.
October 23–29	Follow-up phone calls to those among the twenty who had not responded. Research and preparation of FIRST Delphi questionnaire.
October 30	FIRST questionnaire sent to 119 citizens—list provided by city and the "Snowball Sample." The FIRST questionnaire was deliberately open-ended, seeking (1) areas of satisfaction and/or dissatisfaction, and (2) suggestions for changes, additions, and/or improvements for the Parks and Recreation Department. The FIRST survey was designed to provide an information base for the development of the SECOND questionnaire.
November 10–20	Continuous follow-up phone calls.
November 20–24	Fifty-seven FIRST questionnaires returned. Each specific response cataloged in card file that became the reservoir of opinion from which the SECOND questionnaire was constructed. Opinion correlated into subject topics and specific concerns that formed the outline of the SECOND questionnaire.
November 26	The SECOND questionnaire sent to fifty-seven respondents who agreed to participate. Respondents asked to rank both topics and more specific concerns within the three broad categories of administration, areas and facilities, and programs. A ranking did not necessarily imply endorsement but simply an order of priority. The SECOND questionnaire was as precise as possible, without sacrificing any of the concerns raised in responses gathered in the FIRST questionnaire.
December 5–10	Follow-up phone calls to those who had not returned the SECOND questionnaire.
December 13–16	Forty-eight SECOND questionnaires returned, of which forty-three were usable. Tabulation of data, establishing both average and rank-ordered priorities. From these rankings the THIRD questionnaire was developed.

December 17	THIRD questionnaire sent to same fifty-seven respondents as the SECOND questionnaire. The THIRD questionnaire gave the rankings of the SECOND and asked respondents to reevaluate their earlier opinions and rank them again.
December 30–31	Follow-up phone calls to those who had not returned the THIRD questionnaire.
January 7–10	THIRD questionnaire tabulated. Organization of data collected.
January 10–13	Report writing.
January 16	Review final draft with city representatives.
January 20	Presentation of final report to city.

Community Impressions Approach

The community impressions approach to identification and assessment of needs finds the leisure service professional working with specific groups that have been identified as having the greatest level of needs. It is a strategy that is committed to involving a group in the process to help reduce its own need. The community impression approach often involves key members in the community who can speak on behalf of or represent effectively the group in need. Leisure service professionals using this approach find themselves in a proactive role, reaching out to customer groups to help them solve their problems.

Community impression groups are often organized as special interest groups. For example, a neighborhood association may already exist that can provide information on needs in a given geographic location. A sporting group, like a softball association, may provide a nucleus of a group that could provide input into decisions concerning facility development or utilization. Special interest groups often are very vocal in advocating that their needs be met. They can be well organized, politically sensitive, and astute in promoting their own self-interest. On the other hand, these types of groups may lack political sophistication, financial resources, and organizational know-how. In other words, within a community, these special interest groups run the gamut in terms of their levels of complexity and effectiveness.

These methods do not stand in isolation of one another. Rather, a combination of methods and strategies can provide an integrated profile of community needs. Exhibit 5.2 is an example of an integrated approach used in Edmonton, Alberta.

Other Strategies

Bullaro and Edginton (1986: 215–17), discussing commercial leisure services, have suggested a number of methodologies that can be employed by commercial leisure service organizations in identifying and assessing leisure needs. The authors offer several simple, inexpensive, and effective strategies to collecting market-oriented information related to needs. The strategies they suggest are as follows:

1. *One-on-One, Face-to-Face Interviews*—Basically, this approach involves talking to people one-on-one and listening to what they have to say. Bullaro and Edginton note that leisure service professionals can contact potential subscribers to or buyers of their services in order to ask questions and engage in brainstorming.
2. *Telephone Interviews*—Another procedure for collecting information is to sample potential customers using a telephone interview format.
3. *Direct-Mail Questionnaires*—Direct-mail questionnaires that do not take more than five minutes to complete are an effective way of gathering marketing information concerning needs.
4. *Combination Mail/Telephone Surveys*—This approach to gathering information consists of sending the customer a questionnaire in

EXHIBIT 5.2   INTEGRATED NEEDS ASSESSMENT, CITY OF EDMONTON, ALBERTA.

How We Developed the Integrated Service Strategy

Research and Analysis: Our research included surveys and questionnaires on service needs, core values research and expert opinion papers. We also looked at reviews of costs and benefits, business forecasts, best practices, neighbourhood data and relevant literature.

Talking with Edmontonians: We held community service area meetings, focus groups sessions, one-on-one interviews, household surveys and questionnaires, key content interviews and discussion forums.

Full Consultation: A complete draft of the strategy was shared with an extensive list of individuals and groups in January 2000. We asked for public input through questionnaires, open houses, public information booths, focus groups, print, television and electronic media.

The community provided information and ideas for revisions to the strategy. Public review allowed us to validate and revise the strategy content based on comments from diverse community perspectives. These findings then enabled improvements of our efforts.

INPUT AND CONSULTATION HIGHLIGHTS

Staff, Public and Stakeholder Input Phase November 1998 – August 1999	Preview Phase September 1999 – December 1999	Draft Strategy Review Phase January 2000 – February 2000
• Random Household surveys • Public Questionnaire • Staff/Public Workshops • Focus Groups • Consultation with Special Interest Groups • Interviews: business, community, government & academic leaders • Core Values Survey • Extensive Research and Report Development	• Staff Focus Groups • Community Services Advisory Board Preview Session • Department and Corporate Preview Sessions • Department Staff Information Sessions	• Public Response Survey Distribution • Open Houses • Stakeholder Roundtables • Public Focus Groups • Public Information Displays • Special Meetings and Presentations • Public Notices and Media Releases • Web Site Information and Survey Response Tool

advance and then following it up with a phone call. The result is that the customer is able to become familiar with the questions being asked and therefore is less suspicious of the motive or intentions of the needs assessment effort.

5. *Primary or Secondary Data Sources*—Another way of gathering information on needs is to use primary or secondary data sources. Public libraries, government agencies, businesses, and trade associations are all useful sources, as we mentioned earlier in this chapter.

6. *Trade Shows*—Trade shows are a valuable way of testing the market. Trade shows attract people interested in particular kinds of products to meet their customers' needs. The potential of a given product or service can be gauged to some extent on the reaction of individuals attending the trade show.

NEED TYPOLOGIES

Perhaps the most cited theoretical construct pertaining to human needs is that of Abraham Maslow. Maslow (1943) has suggested that needs are hierarchically ordered. At the base of the hierarchy are the primary physiological needs of the human being (e.g., food, sex, shelter), and

Figure 5.5 Maslow's Hierarchy of Needs.

at the apex of the hierarchy are those needs that are related to the psychological factor of self-actualization (sense of pride, sense of achievement, and so on). Maslow's hierarchy of needs is diagrammed in Figure 5.5.

In terms of the conceptualization of leisure needs, a number of problems exist in the application of Maslow's hierarchy. The first of these problems has to do with the hierarchical ordering of needs. Such life factors as food, shelter, sex, recognition, and creativity are not, in reality, divided into sectors but are often overlapping and occur simultaneously, although proportionately; there will be differences between them. For example, a person may have to reach a certain level of existence to be generally "self-actualized." A second problem in using the hierarchy is related to its application

to leisure services. Maslow's identification of needs does not give any indication of the way in which these needs are expressed. It is somewhat difficult to operationally define how needs come into existence. Are they expressed by the participant, or have they come into existence as a result of the professional's diagnosis of the deficiencies of the participant? Traditionally, the problem has not been in recognizing the type of needs that Maslow has identified but in applying the model in an operational sense. Notwithstanding these concerns, the hierarchy is obviously a useful way of identifying and categorizing the different types of needs that individuals have.

Another conceptual framework within which needs are identified is based on a holistic perspective. Figure 5.6 illustrates fundamental

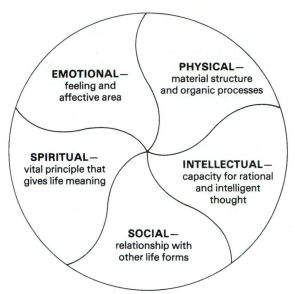

Figure 5.6 Total Person—the Continuous, Dynamic Interaction of Five Vital Areas.

human needs as viewed in their integrated relationship to each other, in the five basic aspects of living: physical, emotional, social, intellectual, and spiritual (Brill, 1973). Holistically, life is a dynamic process and therefore the needs and fulfillment of needs in each of these dimensions continually changes for every individual person.

Identification of need using either of these concepts as it relates to leisure is difficult for both the individual leisure service customer and the leisure service provider. The leisure service provider must be aware of the total individual and attempt to facilitate opportunities for satisfaction at varying levels of need. It is also necessary for the leisure service provider to recognize and be sensitive to a large number of variables that have direct impact on individual needs. These variables include interests and abilities; wants, values, and attitudes; and gender, age, cultural background, and other factors.

A taxonomy of potential individual leisure expressions in these five aspects of living is given by Murphy and Howard (1977) in Table 5.2. This suggestion of perceived needs provides a base for creating leisure service environments that facilitate opportunities for fulfillment in all aspects of individual needs.

TABLE 5.2   POTENTIAL RECREATION OUTCOMES

Physical	Psychological-Emotional	Social	Intellectual Educational	Spiritual
relief of tension	anticipation	interpersonal relationships	mastery	ecstasy
relaxation	reflection	friendships	discovery	mind expansion
exercise	challenge	trust	learning	transcendence revelation
motor skill development	accomplishment	companionship	insight	release
rehabilitation	excitement	involvement	intensified skills	contemplation
fitness	achievement	fellowship	new experience	meditation
coordination	aesthetic appreciation	communication	developing avocations	wonderment
physical growth	self-image	group and family unity	cultural awareness	
muscle tone	introspection	develop sense of community	learning about one's self-evaluation	
rejuvenation	security	compatibility	synthesis	
testing of body capabilities	pleasure	appreciation	problem solving	
	self-confidence	cultural sharing		
	self-actualization	concern for others		
	enjoyment	belonging		
	exhilaration	interaction		
	self-expression			

From J. F. Murphy and D. R. Howard, *Delivery of Community Leisure Services.* Copyright © 1977 Lea & Febiger, Philadelphia, PA. Reprinted by permission.

Other Sources that Can Indicate Community Needs

In addition to the five traditional community approaches that have been discussed, there are a few other ways to discern public needs and wants. While atypical, programmers should not ignore these sources. They include:

- *Task Forces*—Many times, a particular need or problem may arise that warrants a specific response. As a result, an agency or governmental entity will appoint a selected group of citizens to work specifically on the situation. The result might be a recommendation for a new service, program, or facility. An example of this is a youth task force appointed by the city to deal with problems associated with an abundance of latchkey children in the community.
- *Hearings*—Unlike public forums, hearings tend to be reactive, not proactive, in nature. They usually occur when some community-wide issue has become controversial enough that government officials feel it is important to get community input prior to making a decision. Examples include the extension of a controversial program sponsored by the parks and recreation department (i.e., midnight basketball leagues), the inclusion of services that go against public sentiment (i.e., video games in community recreation centers), and placement of facilities (i.e., a softball complex in an aging neighborhood).
- *Litigation*—Although we tend to be a litigious society, lawsuits can indicate that an agency was negligent in fulfilling an important need in the community. For instance, if a public agency is cited as violating the Americans With Disabilities Act (ADA), it is an indication that it has not made its facilities accessible to all members of the community.
- *Legislation*—Sometimes the need of the community is strong enough that it is written into law. For instance, the need for providing children with safe playgrounds was strong enough in California that the state adopted the U.S. Consumer Product Safety Guidelines into its state codes.

It is important for the programmer to stay informed about these additional sources of community input as they can serve as an important catalyst to provide needed activities and services.

The leisure services literature (DeGraaf, Jordan, and DeGraaf, 1999; Edginton, Hanson, Hudson, and Edginton, 1998; Rossman and Schlatter, 2002) has incorporated work by Bradshaw (1972) and Godbey (1976) to develop five categories of social needs: *normative, felt, expressed, comparative,* and *created.* These needs are discussed in the following sections.

Normative Needs

Normative recreation needs can be defined as more or less *precise and objective standards that are set up by experts* in various fields associated with recreation and leisure. In other words, normative needs represent value judgments that are made by professionals in the leisure service field (such as criteria for open space standards). A number of standards are used in the determination of normative needs, including the "desirable relationships between areas, population, user groups, time, distance, staff, sites, and so forth." These normative needs, stated as standards, are usually expressed in quantitative terms—for example, normative needs for park acreage in a community are usually expressed in terms of the amount of park acreage desirable per 1,000 population, such as, a community of 100,000 should have 1,000 acres of parkland.

The use of normative needs as a *single* determinant of need can be criticized on a number of points. First, the development of standards is usually based on individual (or small group) value orientations. That is, the individuals involved in the determination of standards are influenced by such factors as their own socioeconomic status, cultural heritage, and so forth. As a result, these standards could not be applied, with any degree of validity, to the population as a whole. The next problem arises from the notion that services ought to be distributed equally throughout every community and neighborhood within each community. Different communities and neighborhoods may require different quantities and qualities of recreation and leisure services. All people do not have the same needs, desires, and interests; thus, the application of a universal set of standards can create problems.

In connection with the concern just discussed is the assumption that we can also define *normatively* those services that ought to be provided. Standards usually include the kinds of facilities that a public leisure service organization ought to provide (such as parks and playgrounds). Overattention to these types of suggestions might preclude the possibility of meeting other needs that are not mentioned on the "normative" list.

Normative, by definition, refers to the standards that reflect the needs of the majority of the population. However, such a perspective may not reflect or cater to the needs of certain minority populations, such as the physically challenged. The Americans With Disabilities Act of 1990 is having a far-reaching impact on all human and leisure services, and facility and program accessibility. Until recently, government buildings (including many park and recreation facilities) did not allow for accessibility of the facility to the disabled.

Felt Needs

Felt needs can be defined as *the desires that an individual has but has not yet expressed actively*. In other words, felt needs are based on what people *think* they want to do, rather than what they are actually doing or have done in the past. Felt needs are often a reflection of the normative needs that have been defined by social agencies (e.g., governmental, leisure service organizations). In many cases, felt needs are limited by the individual's knowledge and perception of available leisure service opportunities. However, mass communication has expanded the individual's potential for knowledge, perceptions, and experiences ordinarily outside his or her realm of existence. As a result, felt needs, on one hand, are limited by an individual's perception of opportunities but, on the other hand, can be based on fantasy.

The concept of felt needs can be used by leisure service organizations in a number of ways. First, it enables consumers to express their desire for those activities, programs, and services in which they would like to participate at some future time. This provides the leisure service organization with an indication of what the consumer would like to do, or plans to do, in the future. Such information can be useful in the planning, development, and distribution of resources within the decision-making framework of the leisure service organization.

Second, the use of the felt needs concept reduces the amount of dissonance that the participant experiences relative to his or her participation in organizational services. If an individual has a desire to play tennis and instead is offered only other programs, he or she experiences dissonance. According to Godbey (1976), "Individuals will be happier participating in what they perceive they want to do during their leisure than they will if their leisure options are dictated to them by the professional" (p. 10).

The major limitation of using felt needs in a pure sense as the sole determinant of program services is that they are limited to the perceptions and knowledge of the individual participant or participants. Another limitation of the utilization of felt needs as a guide to the distribution of resources is the fact that, from an idealistic standpoint, leisure service organizations would like to please everyone; however, from an organizational standpoint, the availability of resources limits the fulfillment of this idea.

Expressed Needs

Those *activities in which individuals actually participate* are known as expressed needs. An individual playing, knitting, or swimming is engaged in the fulfillment of his or her needs. By actually participating in an activity, an individual provides the leisure service manager with knowledge as to his or her current leisure preferences, tastes, and interests. Expressed needs are felt needs "put into action." However, in order for individuals to express their needs, they must first be able to conceptualize what their needs are, and then visualize how these needs might be fulfilled. For example, an older adult who is lonely and desires companionship may translate this feeling (felt need) into action (expressed need) by going to the senior center in his or her community.

If expressed needs are used as the sole determinant of an organization's planning process—hence, its distribution of resources—a number of problems might occur. First, if programs and services are based on expressed needs (what people are doing), practitioners preclude the initiation of new services and programs within their organization. An unstated, faulty assumption exists on their part that the services presently available are meeting all the needs of their consumers. However, since participants' behavior is limited by the specific programs that are available, it must *necessarily* conform to the services that are offered. This presents a circular dilemma—the participants attend the services available, and the practitioners limit their services to the consumers' behavior; thus, consumers continue to have their behavior defined and molded by the current service offerings of the leisure service organization.

On the other hand, if an organization only provides activities that participants have previously attended, it will be certain of the reception that the offered programs and services will receive. Consequently, there will be little waste of resources or effectiveness. Efficiency—in regard to the *specific* programs attempted—will be maximized.

Comparative Needs

The comparative need approach to needs assessment in program development can be defined as a method whereby an organization compares the services it offers to a given population and the behavioral outcomes of these programs with similar populations and their services. In this way, an organization may be able to identify those areas in which it is deficient and can improve services to lessen such deficiencies. For example, a leisure service organization may want to improve services in order to overcome social or environmental dysfunctions in the community it serves. By comparing its own program offerings with those of a community that is effectively offsetting social problems, the leisure service organization may be able to identify services that could alleviate existing dysfunctions. Of course, the assumption here is that only communities with similar population characteristics will be compared. The comparative need process not only can be used to overcome dysfunctions, but it also can be viewed in a positive sense—enabling an organization to expose its population to beneficial experiences.

Another way to apply the comparative need approach is to identify the differences in leisure experiences among groups in a community or neighborhood. For example, differences may exist between the services provided for special groups and those provided for the rest of the population. Assuming that people who fall within the categories known as "special groups" have the same rights to leisure services as others, an organization using the comparative need approach would be able to see the differences that occur in terms of services—and the results of those differences. The organization could then provide appropriate services to the individuals affected or could make special efforts to integrate them into existing programs so that they could fulfill their leisure interests.

Care must be practiced when utilizing the comparative need method in needs assessment and program planning. It is faulty reasoning to assume that what works well in one situation will automatically be effective in another. Furthermore, the intensity of the service needed may vary a great deal among populations or groups within communities. Another problem to consider is the reality that each community may not have the necessary resources to pursue the fulfillment of equal services. As a result, sometimes comparative needs assessment may serve as an ideal that communities may strive for rather than as an effective way of immediately dealing with dissimilarities that exist among population groups in communities.

Created Needs

Leisure service agencies and organizations exist to plan and offer programs to individuals in the community. These programs and services, as has been indicated throughout this section of the book, are based on several approaches to the identification of needs. Godbey (1976) suggests that the professional engaged in the program planning process must also consider the created need. His concept of created need implies the following:

> Agencies can create leisure interests and values independent of what people do, [what] they want to do, or have supplied to them during their leisure. Created need refers to those recreation activities which [agencies and organizations have] . . . introduced to individuals in which they will subsequently participate at the expense of some activity in which they previously participated (p. 13).

In other words, created need refers to *those programs, services, and activities solely determined by the organization and accepted by the participant without question, desire, or prior knowledge.* For example, a municipal park and recreation agency might initiate a day-care center for senior citizens (who live at home with their relatives), thereby creating a need in the community for such a service. Once the leisure service agency starts programs such as this, the community is awakened to a need heretofore unrealized; the community then will depend on the continuance of such programs.

The created needs approach to need assessment can be useful to the participant as well as to the organization as a method of defining needs. Many individuals are grateful to organizations for helping them identify an area of interest or need that they had not previously considered. In a sense, the approach is a form of leisure education that is an important component of many recreation and leisure service organizations. The organization also benefits by serving as an agency that creates opportunities for stimulation and enrichment. As a result, individuals may look to the organization as a vehicle for providing innovative experiences.

Summary

This chapter has focused on the concepts of needs identification and needs assessment. Understanding people's needs, wants, interests, values, and attitudes can have a positive impact on the effectiveness of leisure programs and services. Needs *identification* describes the processes that leisure program planners use to determine the extent and kinds of consumer needs that are within a specifically defined social or geographical area. Needs *assessment* is the process of judging which consumer needs will be addressed in a priority scheme within an organization. In other words, needs identification helps leisure service professionals understand what concerns must be addressed and needs assessment helps professionals prioritize their efforts.

A variety of different strategies can be employed to make assessments. Some of the approaches that can be taken include identifying social indicators, using social surveys, and employment of several community group approaches including use of community forums, focus groups, the nominal group technique, the Delphi technique, and community impressions approach. Task forces, hearings; and legislation, are other approaches to community needs assessment. Still other methodologies that can be applied are one-to-one interviews, telephone interviews, and direct-mail questionnaires.

Various typologies have been developed to help understand needs. Perhaps the most consistently applied needs typology is Maslow's hierarchy, which arranges needs from the most basic physiological needs to those factors dealing with the psychological needs of self-actualization. In the leisure service field, different frameworks or typologies have been developed to explain needs. Some of the categories include normative needs, felt needs, expressed needs, comparative needs, and created needs. Understanding these needs typologies can be useful in helping identify consumer needs and responding with appropriate leisure services.

Discussion Questions and Exercises

1. Define *needs identification*.

2. Define *needs assessment*. How can you differentiate needs assessment from needs identification?

3. Define *needs, wants, values,* and *attitudes*.

4. How can social indicators be used in establishing the need for a service?

5. Organize a survey of a specific social grouping to determine its leisure needs. Develop a questionnaire similar to the one found in the appendix.

6. What is a customer focus group? Identify how customer focus groups can be applied to the delivery of leisure services. Locate a focus group used in a leisure service organization and describe its structure and operating procedures.

7. Compare and contrast the nominal group technique with the Delphi technique for assessing needs. Describe the conditions that would be favorable to the use of each of these strategies.

8. Discuss how Maslow's hierarchy of needs can be applied to understanding leisure behavior.

References

American Association of Retired Persons. 1988. *A profile of older Americans*. Washington, DC: American Association of Retired Persons.

Bradshaw, J. 1972. The concept of social need. *New Society* 19 (496):640–43.

Brill, A. 1973. *Working with people: The helping process*. Philadelphia: J. B. Lippincott.

Bullaro, J. J., and C. R. Edginton. 1986. *Commercial leisure service: Managing for profit, services, and personal satisfaction*. New York: Macmillan.

DeGraaf, D., D. Jordan, and K. DeGraaf. 1999. *Programming for parks, recreation and leisure services: A servant leadership approach*. State College, PA: Venture.

Edginton, C. R., A. Hudson, and D. M. Ford. 1999. *Leadership in recreation and leisure service organizations*. New York: Wiley.

Edginton, C. R., C. Hanson, S. Hudson, and S. Edginton 1998. *Leisure programming*. 3rd ed. Boston: WCB McGraw-Hill.

Godbey, G. 1976. Recreation and park planning: The exercise in values. Paper presented, January, at University of Waterloo, Waterloo, Ontario.

Howard, D. R. 1989. Turning a member's bad experience into a good one. *Athletic Business* 13(13).

Maslow A. H. 1943. A theory of human motivation. *Psychological Review,* July, 370–96.

Murphy, J. F., and D. R. Howard. 1977. *Delivery of community leisure services: A holistic approach.* Philadelphia: Lea and Febiger.

Rossman, J., and B. Schlatter. 2002. *Recreation programming: Designing leisure experiences.* 4th ed. Champaign, II: Sagamore.

Siegel, L. N., C. C. Attkisson, and L. G. Carson. 1987. Need identification and program planning in the community context. In *Strategies of community development.* 4th ed. Edited by F. M. Cox, J. L. Erlich, J. Rothman, and J. E. Tropman, 71–97. Itasca, IL: F. E. Peacock.

Stufflebeam, D. L. 1974. *Meta-evaluation.* Kalamazoo, MI: Evaluation Center, Western Michigan University.

Establishing Direction:
Developing Goals and Objectives

LEARNING OBJECTIVES

1. To provide the reader with information useful in *establishing direction within an organization.*

2. To help the reader gain *appreciation of the role that an organization's culture plays in the provision of leisure services.*

3. To help the reader understand the processes in *establishing vision and mission statements.*

4. To help the reader gain insight into the process of *establishing program goals and objec-* *tives,* including those related to program development, promotion and sales strategies, and financial strategies.

5. To provide the reader with information and strategies for *developing performance objectives* emphasizing desirable behaviors and levels of achievement.

153

INTRODUCTION

An important part of leisure programming involves the establishment of direction for the work of professionals. In a broad context, we can look at this on two levels. The first level is the direction that the organization establishes for itself overall. This broader philosophical direction will influence the types of programs and services an organization delivers, the target groups it serves, the benefits it promotes, and the values it encourages. The second level is the direction that is established for each individual program or service offered by the agency. We often refer to these types of direction statements as goals and objectives.

Why is it important for the leisure service programmer to have a grasp of the concepts related to the creation and maintenance of an organization's culture? As an employee within the organization, the programmer must ensure that his or her goals and objectives are congruent or in line with those of the organization. Programs and services developed within an organization must reflect the broader intentions of the leisure service organization. Specific program goals and objectives must be related to and reflect the broader values of the organization.

Why is establishing direction for the work of a leisure service organization important? From an overall organizational perspective, the direction that an organization establishes helps define how its resources will be used. Also, the overall philosophical direction of the organization establishes the "culture" that exists within it. As Edginton (1987: 6) has noted, "the culture of a leisure service organization may be the most powerful factor influencing its success or failure." An organization's culture can influence the work of employees, the quality of services, the transactions that take place with customers, and the image that it establishes with its public.

The culture of an organization may occur by happenstance or it may be planned and cultivated. Careful planning can produce desired organizational behaviors that result in superior levels of service, innovation, productivity, and positive public image. These are all hallmarks of successful organizations; organizations that are perceived as contributing in positive ways to society by providing valued goods and services. Leisure service organizations that reflect on their culture are able to be progressive and aggressive in adapting to change and building strong and lasting relationships with their customers.

When setting direction for programs or services, establishing program goals and objectives helps link the benefits to be produced with the procedures to be employed to accomplish them. Program goals and objectives allow us to define exactly what services we are going to create, how we will create these services, when we are going to produce them, and how we will measure whether we have produced them as intended. Program goals and objectives move the work of the leisure service organization from complex, broad, general, global patterns to more discrete, measurable, specific, and concrete actions.

There are a number of specific reasons why leisure service organizations must establish program goals and objectives. First, program goals and objectives link customer needs with organizational services. Second, they provide a mechanism for linking means and ends—means being procedures and ends being outputs. Third, program goals and objectives provide a basis for measurement and evaluation. Finally, they offer a way to focus resources so that priorities can be established and decisions made about concerns such as program equity, value, and quality.

This chapter discusses the establishment of the overall direction of a leisure service organization and presents specific information on the establishment of program goals and objectives. The success of a leisure service organization and its subsequent program efforts may very well depend on clear articulation of the intentions of leisure programs and services. The work of an organization can be enhanced dramatically with common agreement as to the direction that the enterprise should take. With these two concerns in mind, the material in this chapter offers both theoretical and practical information that can be applied in various leisure service settings.

ESTABLISHING AN ORGANIZATION'S CULTURE

The *culture* of a leisure service organization refers to the prevailing norms, customs, values, and behaviors that are exhibited by its members. This culture can have a great deal of impact on the work of an organization. For example, some organizations are guided by a strong service ethic while others are not. Some organizations are profit-oriented while others are nonprofit. Certain leisure service organizations direct their energies and efforts toward building the character of youth; some organizations emphasize leisure as a therapy treatment.

Visionary Organizational Cultures

Collins and Porras (1994), writing in their book *Built to Last: Successful Habits of Visionary Companies*, suggest that successful organizations—ones that could be defined as visionary companies—develop a strong ideology, sense of community, sense of passion, commitment and devotion to the ideals of the organization, shared values, and other similar factors.

Organizations like Walt Disney, Nordstrom's, American Express, Hewlett-Packard, Mariott, Sony, and IBM have developed such cultures. Collins and Porras (1994) suggest that there are some timeless, fundamental principles that distinguish these organizations from comparable organizations. According to these authors (p. 122), the characteristics of such organizations include the following:

- Fervently held ideology
- Indoctrination
- Tightness of fit
- Elitism

Such organizations are also characterized by a great deal of "experimentation, trial and error . . . [and] . . . optimism" (p. 8).

One of the critical factors in building a successful culture within an organization is a strong commitment to an ideology. At Hewlett-Packard, they call it the "HP Way." At Nordstrom's they call this ideology "The Nordstrom's Way." Within the University of Northern Iowa's *Camp Adventure*™ Youth Services program, it is called "The *Camp Adventure*™ Way." In each of these organizations, the basis of the establishment of the organizational culture was not the creation of products or services, but the creation of an ideology or philosophy that guided the work of the organization. "Bill Hewlett and Dave Packard's ultimate creation wasn't the audio oscilloscope or the pocket calculator. It was the Hewlett-Packard Company and the HP Way" (Collins and Porras, 1994: 30).

The *Camp Adventure*™ Way is a formula developed by the organization to guide the work of individuals participating in its effort (see Figure 6.1). As indicated in the introductory statement of the document, the *Camp Adventure*™ Way is referred to as "a formula for success." It is a way of emphasizing "the little things that make a difference." To promote its ideology, the *Camp Adventure*™ Youth Services program also has developed another set of principles, known as the "Panther Way" (the panther is the mascot of the University of Northern Iowa). These two statements as well as other documents help shape the culture and ideology of the organization. In a sense, this organization does not see itself as just providing youth programs, but sees itself as transforming the lives of youth and making a lasting, positive impact on their development.

Following the establishment of an organization's guiding principles that help define its culture, the organization must put these principles into action. To be successful, the organization must translate the ideology into action. As Hitt (1988: 6) says, "successful managers transform vision into significant actions."

Culture Statements

The following statements have been derived from several different types of leisure service organizations, representing the different systems provid-

Camp Adventure™ College
Development Program

THE *CAMP ADVENTURE*™ WAY

We have a formula for success. We call it The *"Camp Adventure*™ Way." We have been successful because we have found a way to emphasize the little things that make a difference. The *"Camp Adventure*™ Way" can best be described in the following statements.

- **Quality and Excellence.** Quality and excellence are achieved when the services we offer are the best that can be provided. There is no substitute for competence.

- **Attention to Detail.** It is the little things that make a difference between superior organizations and mediocre performance.

- **Support and Protect the Family.** Trust and support of one another is a key to success. Concentrate on what's important–the children we serve and each other.

- **Child/Leader Interaction.** There is no greater area of importance than providing quality interaction with our participants. Be sincere, generous, caring and helpful.

- **Anticipate Needs.** Don't merely respond to participants needs. Learn to anticipate them in advance and meet them <u>before</u> they make a request.

- **Resourcefulness.** Learn to be adaptable, and creative in responding to the various conditions and environments in which you are placed.

- **Cooperation.** Cooperate and do not put up barriers with your co-workers, superiors or our contract partners.

- **Planned, Well-Organized Activities.** The key to *Camp Adventure*™ is planning and organizing. Prepare for success and you will succeed.

- **Attitude, Attitude.** Positive attitudes are important. Be enthusiastic, energetic and zestful. Remember, if you enjoy what you are doing, that quality will rub off on others.

- **Pride.** Belief in what you are doing is contagious. Pride is having a high opinion of *Camp Adventure's*™ worth and your efforts.

Camp Adventure™ attempts to create a caring and sharing environment which provides for the personal growth of both campers and staff. *Camp Adventure*™ is your opportunity to make a difference and *"Catch the Magic!"*

Figure 6.1 *The Camp Adventure™ Way, Camp Adventure™ Youth Services,* University of Northern Iowa.

ing leisure programs and services—the political/governmental sector, the market sector, and the voluntary sector. In each of these statements, the values being imparted establish the tone for the work of professionals within the organization. They represent attempts to establish the organizational culture—the norms, customs, values, and behaviors—of individuals within the organization.

The first statement is from the city of Long Beach (California) and describes "what we believe." In other words, they have outlined the values that influence the work of their organization. Figure 6.2 outlines their belief system. As noted in this document, they believe that their "business is service." The document further imparts the importance of commitment to values such as participation, communication, integrity, loyalty, innovation, responsibilty, and pride.

Figure 6.3 is a statement taken from the commercial sector and delineates the corporate

The City of Long Beach
WHAT WE BELIEVE

The City's Business is Service
We are committed to providing service to our diverse
community in ways that are helpful,
caring, and responsive.

Working Together to Serve
We believe that the success of our organization depends
on teamwork, mutual trust, and honesty achieved
through commitment to the following values.

Participation
by
citizens and City team members in setting and attaining the
City's goals.

Communication
with
one another and with citizens.

Courtesy
in
all personal relations.

Integrity
in
everything we do.

Loyalty
to
our community, to this organization, and to each
team member.

Innovation
in
meeting the present and future needs of the City.

Responsibility
as
a team for efficient and effective delivery of services.

Pride
in
our work, in our dedication to public service,
and in being the best we can be.

Figure 6.2 What We Believe, The City of
Long Beach, California.

vision for BCI Burke, a playground manufacturing company. After being a family-owned business for eighty years, the company was sold and the new owners attempted to bring "new-economy" ideas to a decidedly "old-economy" company culture (Berg, 2002). According to the new company president, Tim Ahern, "The company has a great tradition and a great core of people, and we were counting on that to build on. But there was a huge cultural difference between what we came in with and what people were accustomed to" (Berg, 2002: 4). After a rocky start, the company has moved forward to increasing its market share every year since 2001. Many credit the turnaround to the instilling of core values (figure 6.3) that defined what kind of company BCI Burke was going to be. As Ahern states:

> It was a way of deciding where we're going and how we're going to get there. It says, This is what we stand for. An it all really boils down to four things: You treat people with dignity and respect, you do the right thing, you hold yourself accountable, you perform. If you do all those things, you'll be fine. If you don't do those things, you're going to have problems (p. 4).

The last statement is from *Camp Adventure*™ *Youth Services. Camp Adventure*™ is a successful model for providing contracted leisure services for children, youth, and teens. The "Values and Traditions" statement found in Figure 6.4 outlines the organizational expectations for leaders, specialists, directors, and supervisors. These values and traditions are integral to the success of the program and every attempt is made to ensure that individuals not only understand, but also embrace, these precepts. The *Camp Adventure*™ management team is entrusted with the responsibility of maintaining the values and traditions of the organization as a way of ensuring the continued development of a high-quality, high-impact series of contracted leisure services for children, youth, and teens.

Not only is an agency's organizational culture related to the formal organization with corresponding rules and guidelines, but there is also an informal organizational culture that may influence the behavior of employees. In other

BCI Burke's Core Values

Integrity—We demand of ourselves and others the highest ethical standards, and our products and processes will be of the highest quality. Our conduct as a company and as individuals within it will always reflect that highest standards of integrity. We will demonstrate open, honest and ethical behavior in dealing with customers, clients, colleagues, suppliers and the public. The Burke name is a source of pride to us, and should inspire trust install with whom we come in contact.

Respect For People—We recognize that people are the cornerstone of Burke's success. We will treat our employees, sales representatives and customers with respect and dignity. We will treat listen to the ideas of our colleagues and respond appropriately. We seek a business that fosters personal and professional growth and achievement. We recognize that communication must be frequent and candid, and that we must support other with the tools, training and authority that they need to succeed in achieving their responsibilities, goals, and objectives.

Teamwork—We know that be a successful company, we must work together. We want all of our colleagues to contribute to the best of their abilities, individually and in teams. Teamwork improves the quality of decisions and increases the likelihood that good decisions will be acted upon. Teamwork sustains a spirit of excitement, fulfillment, pride and passion for our business, enabling us to succeed in all our endeavors, and continually learn as individuals and as a corporation.

Leadership—Leaders advance teamwork by importing clarity of purpose, a shared sense of goals, and a joint commitment to excellence. Leaders empower those around them by sharing knowledge and authority, and by recognizing and rewarding outstanding individual effort. Leaders are those who step forward to achieve difficult goals, envisioning what needs to happen and motivating others. They utilize the particular talents of every individual and resolve conflict by help others to focus on common goals. Leaders build relationships with others throughout the company to share ideas, provide support and help to ensure that the best practices prevail throughout Burke.

Innovation—In our drive to innovate, we support well-conceived risk-taking and understand that it will not always lead to success. We embrace creativity and constantly pursue new opportunities. We look for ways to make our products and services more useful to our customers, and our business practices, processes and systems more efficient and effective.

Performance—We strive for continuous improvement in our performance. When we commit to doing something, we will do it in the best, most complete, most efficient and most timely way possible. Then we will try to think of ways to do it better next time. We will measure our performance carefully, ensuring that integrity and respect for people are never compromised. We will compete aggressively, establishing challenging but achievable targets, and rewarding performance against those targets. We wish to attract the highest-caliber employees and sales representatives, providing them with opportunities to develop their full potential and share in the success that comes from winning in the marketplace.

Figure 6.3   BCI Burke Core Values.

words, the norms, customs, and values of an organization are not necessarily found only on a piece of paper; they are also found in the actions of leaders and others within the organization. At times, discrepancies may occur between what is stated in writing and what is actually practiced. However, the closer the informal culture is to the formal organizational culture, the greater the possibility that the organization will move forward in a positive and productive fashion.

CAMP ADVENTURE™

"Values and Traditions"

"We Value Excellence"
- We strive to produce the impossible; our staff has few preconceived notions. If they believe it can be done, it happens.
- We value an individual's commitment, motivation and dedication.
- Excellence is an attitude that results in superior performance.

"We Care About Kids"
- Our bottom line is our front line leaders.
- We promote positive, caring child leader interactions.
- Sincerity, genuineness and caring are our hallmarks.

"We Are All Part of the *Camp Adventure*™ Family"
- Teamwork, as reflected by caring, sharing, and helping one another is a hallmark of the program.
- Any group of people that work together as a team are far more successful than people operating individually.
- We protect one another by looking out after each person's interests, needs and respecting their personal concerns.

"Well-Planned Means Well Executed"
- We believe in complete and thorough planning as a prelude to program implementation.
- Our attention to detail reflects our commitment through planning.
- There is no substitute for planning; it is the keystone to success.

"We Create Magic Moments"
- Our goal is to create magic moments for children that last a lifetime.
- We strive to produce fun, joyful, exhilarating and treasured experiences.

"Today's Children Are Tomorrow's Leaders"
- Our staff members serve as positive role models for children.
- Positive, purposeful, play activities that develop leadership skills are our focus.

"Our Contractors Are Our Partners"
- We strive to produce mutually beneficial services.
- We value those we work with and seek their professional expertise and knowledge to enhance services.
- We strive to create a win/win situation with our partners.

"The *Camp Adventure*™ Name Means Quality"
- Our name is a guarantee of quality services.
- Extensive planning and staff development produce quality experiences for our partners.
- We produce high quality, high impact services that make a difference in children's lives.

"Enthusiastic and Energetic Leadership"
- Our staff is dynamic, moving, energetic and committed.
- *Camp Adventure*™ staff are high on life, high on kids.

"*Camp Adventure*™ is Innovative and Creative"
- We believe our success stems from commitment to innovation.
- Creativity is encouraged in all of our spontaneous and planned programs.
- *Camp Adventure*™ is never the same from one year to the next; it is constantly evolving to meet the needs of kids today, as well as the needs of our partners.

"We Believe in the Power of Play"
- Play is enriching, it helps enhance and sustain life.
- Our social play environments emphasize fun and laughter, joy and delight, adventure and discovery.
- Play is a shared experience between children and leaders.

"You Have to Earn It to Wear It"
- Our staff earns the right to wear their *Camp Adventure*™ uniforms by affirming our values.
- They train diligently and must demonstrate a high level of competence.
- They must demonstrate their commitment to the ideals of the program.

Figure 6.4 Values and Traditions, *Camp Adventure™ Youth Services,* University of Northern Iowa.

Vision and Mission Statements

The broad, overarching goals of an organization are usually reflected in vision and mission statements. The purpose of such statements is to reflect the value system of the organization. These statements provide philosophical direction to a leisure service organization. They can emerge from the cognitive as well as the spiritual or intuitive domain. They are usually written to be bold, broad, and inspiring, giving direction to the efforts of individuals at all levels within the organization. They also serve as a way of communicating to customers the intentions of a leisure service organization.

Such statements are useful from a number of perspectives. First, they provide common direction for individuals within an organization. They are thus useful in guiding the daily behavior of employees. This is especially important in setting standards for the way employees will interact with customers. Second, these statements are often motivational and inspirational in nature. They inspire employees to achieve higher levels of performance because the employees become dedicated to an ideal and are able to channel energies in prescribed directions. Such statements enable employees to develop a sense of purpose and value for work efforts.

In addition, these statements are very useful in decision making. They enable an organization to understand its parameters, focal points, target population, and scope of service delivery. Such statements are also valuable in that they empower employee behavior. If the values of an employee are consistent with the values of an organization, the employee is capable of independent action. Finally, such statements provide for continuity of purpose over the years. This can be especially useful in retaining the focus of an organization during times of rapid change. The Girl Scouts of the U.S.A. may, for example, change their activities, reward structure, or leadership methods, but they never lose the focus of their broader, more global intentions, such as character development of youth.

Vision Statements

Vision can be thought of as the power of forward thinking. *Vision statements attempt to create a mental image of the future desired state of the organization.* Vision statements often are written in such a way that they focus on potential benefits to be gained by association with a particular leisure service organization. Vision statements should draw individuals to the organization and its services and should inspire, motivate, excite, and stimulate them. Vision statements should project an image of the organization's worth to individuals, the community, and the region that the organization serves.

Peters (1987) writes of several steps that should be employed in developing vision statements. These steps serve as a guideline for individuals and organizations wishing to develop such statements:

1. Effective visions are inspiring.
2. Effective visions are clear and challenging—and about excellence.
3. Effective visions make sense in the marketplace and by stressing flexibility and execution stand the test of time in a turbulent world.
4. Effective visions must be stable but constantly challenged—and changed at the margin.
5. Effective visions are beacons and controls when all else is up for grabs.
6. Effective visions are aimed at empowering our own people first, customers second.
7. Effective visions prepare for the future, but honor the past.
8. Effective visions are lived in detail, not broad strokes (pp. 401–4).

Developing a vision for an organization or refining an existing one provides the leisure service programmer with a unique opportunity to shape the destiny or future of an agency. By relating program and service efforts to an organization's vision, individuals are linked to a far more compelling, challenging, and exciting effort. When operating as a part of the whole, consistent with the vision of an organization, the leisure service programmer is positioned to draw on the resources and energy of the entire operation. Programming efforts become more satisfying, meaningful, and valuable when tied to a broader, stronger concept. (Figure 6.5). shows the vision statement for the Cincinnati (Ohio) Recreation Commission.

Mission Statements

Mission statements are often thought of as synonymous with vision statements. Like vision statements, they provide overall direction to an organization's effort. They usually spell out the

Vision

The Cincinnati Recreation Commission will excel in the delivery of recreational services to the people of Cincinnati.

Figure 6.5 Vision Statement, Cincinnati Recreation Commission.

Mission

The Cincinnati Recreation Commission is dedicated to providing recreational and cultural activities for all people in our neighborhoods and the whole community. We believe that by enhancing people's personal health and wellness, we strengthen and enrich the lives of our citizens and build a spirit of community in our City.

Figure 6.6 Mission Statement Cincinnati Recreation Commission.

broad ends or aims that the organization attempts to achieve.

There are some differences between vision and mission statements as they have been developed and applied within leisure service organizations. The most apparent difference between vision statements and mission statements in the leisure service field is in the motivational aspect or tone of the statement. Mission statements tend to be direct, pragmatic, and focused in terms of the types of services to be provided or broad features related to potential benefits. Mission statements also tend to be much shorter and more direct than vision statements. Vision statements, as mentioned, attempt to be more motivational in nature, employing emotional terms and phrases to project the direction of the organization. Even though the differences between these two types of statements are subtle, they have a great deal of impact on the development and evolution of a leisure service organization. Figure 6.6 shows the mission statement for the Cincinnati Recreation Commission. Compare this with Figure 6.5 to see the differences between the Commission's vision statement and its mission statement.

Mission statements define the primary work of a leisure service organization. They help an organization define its scope and function in terms of services to be provided and benefits to be achieved. Mission statements may also focus on target groups or populations. Like vision statements, they are useful documents in not only shaping the work of an organization, but also communicating the organization's intentions internally and externally.

What are the characteristics of mission statements? A number of important elements are found in most mission statements:

1. Mission statements are short and direct statements that are focused in terms of the work of an organization and its aspirations.
2. Mission statements often focus on specific types of services, markets, and benefits to be produced by the leisure service organization.
3. Mission statements may reflect a focus on quality and excellence or other variables that influence the way in which services are delivered.
4. Mission statements often reflect organizational values that provide direction to the overall work of the organization.
5. Mission statements are often difficult to measure and quantify because they are written in broad, global terms.

Mission statements serve as a basis for professional practice. Ultimately, the goals and objectives of a leisure service organization are linked to its mission statement. Thus, mission statements provide a beginning basis for determining the direction of an organization and its areas of focus. In the delivery of local governmental park and recreation services, organizations often focus on the provision of "parks, leisure, and cultural services as a way of improving the quality of life" of those served. In a youth-serving organization like the YMCA, the focus of the mission statement might be to "improve and positively influence conditions that affect the quality of life for the people we touch." In a leisure service business organization, the mission statement might read, "to provide high quality services while at the same time earning a profit in order to return value to our customers."

Mission statements will vary greatly depending on the type of organization and its general purpose. We have listed here mission statements from various leisure settings. The examples presented represent several different types of leisure service organizations.

Eugene YMCA (Eugene, Oregon): The Eugene Family YMCA is an association of individuals from this community and around the world—youth and adults of all ages, ethnic backgrounds, and faiths, united in a common effort to put Christian principles into practice, where the spirit of love for all people is shown through thought and deed.

City of Aurora, Recreation Division (Aurora, Colorado): To provide recreation activities and cultural, human, and special services that: Contribute to the physical, mental, and social development of our citizens; meet the needs and interests of our citizens with quality service at a reasonable price; complement services and programs of other public/private agencies; contribute to the quality of life in our community; effectively utilize available resources; provide a challenging and rewarding environment for employees; maintain a level of earnings to support our growth; and sustain the confidence of those we serve.

Indianapolis Parks and Recreation Department (Indianapolis, Indiana): The Indianapolis Department of Parks and Recreation will improve the quality of life of citizens and their neighbors by preserving land, facilities, the environment, and our natural heritage and by creating significant opportunities for recreation, conservation, education, and relaxation for now and future generations.

Courage Center (Golden Valley, Minnesota): The mission of Courage Center is to promote the maximum independence, personal responsibility, self-esteem, and dignity of people who have a physical or sensory disability, with primary emphasis on individuals with severe or multiple disabilities. Courage Center provides pioneers and promotes vital and caring programs in rehabilitation, independent living, and recreation at the appropriate regional, national, or international level.

Anaheim Parks, Recreation, and Community Services Department (Anaheim, California): The mission of the Anaheim Parks, Recreation, and Community Services Department is to provide a comprehensive system of parks, open space, recreation, and human services programs designed to enhance the quality of life for residents of Anaheim.

Davenport Park and Recreation Department (Davenport, Iowa): The City of Davenport Park and Recreation Department is committed to enhancing the quality of life through responsible stewardship of resources and the provision of leisure opportunities to the community.

Hartman Reserve Nature Center (Cedar Falls, Iowa): The Hartman Reserve Nature Center is dedicated to the preservation and protection of this unique, natural area and to the promotion of a better understanding of our environment.

City of Kettering Parks, Recreation, and Cultural Arts Department (Kettering, Ohio): The mission of the Parks, Recreation, and Cultural Arts Department is to improve the quality of life for all residents of Kettering by providing a wide range of leisure and cultural activities, special events, facilities, and services that encourage health, fitness, relaxation, enjoyment, cultural enrichment, and learning as well as providing opportunities for community involvement. It is also the purpose of the department to improve the quality of the City's urban setting by enhancing the appreciation and care of the national environment through maintenance and development of open space, parks, roadside areas, government grounds, and medians.

Joliet Park District (Joliet, Illinois): The Joliet Park District's mission is to enhance the quality and availability of leisure opportunities to meet the diverse needs of the community through the efficient and economic provision of recreation programs, facilities, and park areas for the benefit of future and current generations.

These nine mission statements reflect many of the common characteristics noted earlier. They are short and to the point. They serve to focus the work of each of these organizations or programs. They identify the benefits to be pursued as a result of development of programs and services. Such mission statements are extremely important in the development of programs and services. They provide the philosophical underpinnings for the work of leisure service programmers. They are the basis on which programs and services are created and distributed. They serve as broad guidelines that are useful in developing more specific goals and objectives.

PROGRAM GOALS AND OBJECTIVES

Most leisure service programmers are required to establish goals and objectives to be used as part of the planning process in the development of programs and services. Establishing goals and objectives links the day-to-day work of the programmer with the broader philosophical direction of the leisure service organization for whom he or she works. This linkage legitimizes the work of the programmer. By linking program goals and objectives to the broader philosophical directions of an organization, the programmer is empowered to access the resources of the agency. The programmer can bring to bear the influence and resources of the organization to develop and implement leisure program offerings.

Establishing goals and objectives allows the leisure service programmer to determine what results are desirable. Goals and objectives that are established in general terms are difficult to measure and to implement. Therefore, the more specific that goals and objectives become, the greater the probability that they can, in fact, be measured. One of the first things that leisure service programmers must remember when establishing goals and objectives is that they must be specific and focused.

One of the steps that follows the establishment of goals and objectives is to communicate them to various individuals. By communicating goals and objectives, leisure service programmers can often build consensus for their efforts within an organization and to the target populations served by the agency. Effectively communicated goals and objectives help build a common framework for action.

Setting Goals and Objectives: Areas for Consideration

Leisure service programmers can focus their goal setting in several broad areas. It is important to recognize that there are many component parts to developing a program. The activity must be selected, the format developed, and the evaluation techniques chosen. In addition, strategies for promoting the program must be developed, and careful consideration must be given to the way in which the program is financially managed. In general, there are three broad areas that the leisure service programmer will want to consider when developing goals and objectives for a given program or service: *program development, promotion and sales strategies,* and *financial strategies.*

Program Development

At the heart of the goal-setting process is the establishment of goals and objectives for the program or service to be created and delivered. Goal and objective statements related to program development would focus on such questions as: Who are the recipients of services?

TABLE 6.1   Recreation Program Principles, Champaign (Illinois) Park District.

1. Provide program opportunities for all ages, sexes, and interests.
2. Provide for varying levels of skill and ability, basic skills emphasized. Work with all participants and not the skilled few.
3. Empasize programs with a carryover value, activities that the participant can continue on his or her own, such as lifetime sports, creative arts, etc.
4. Provide programs that challenge the participant.
5. Provide opportunities for noncompetitive as well as competitive, for passive as well as active programs.
6. Balance program offerings on an annual basis and between indoor and outdoor activities.
7. Provide communitywide events as well as activities conducted at neighborhood locations.
8. Offer individual opportunities as well as mass activities.
9. Encourage community participation in program planning and develop and utilize volunteer leaders.
10. Encourage community awareness of program offerings.
11. Develop an awareness of all recreation opportunities within the community in order to complement rather than duplicate programs of other agencies.

From Champaign Park District, Champaign, IL. Reprinted by permission.

What are the services? What leadership resources are required to execute the program? What will the program consist of? Where will the program be located? What will be the length and duration of the program? These and other questions form the basis for the establishment of goals and objectives in this area. The Champaign (Illinois) Park District has developed a set of recreation program principles that provide general direction to the work of the organization. These principles can be thought of as "program development goals." Table 6.1 presents these recreation program planning principles, which were drawn from their planning for parks and recreation documents. For example, one of their goals states that there is a need to provide a balance of activities relating to a variety of skill levels. Another goal suggests the importance of emphasizing programs with a carryover value.

Another example of a set of recreation program principles with a different orientation is provided by the Madison (Wisconsin) School-Community Recreation Department. This program philosophy statement ties leisure activities to the school system. As such, programs and services have a strong educational component (see Table 6.2).

Promotion and Sales Strategies

Another important area in which goals and objectives are established is that of promotion. In establishing goals and objectives in this area, efforts should be undertaken to identify ways of communicating with target markets. Goals and objectives statements in this area would focus on such questions as: What channels of promotion should be used in communicating with customers? What specific tools or methods of promotion (e.g., fliers, brochures) will be used? At what time(s) should the information be disseminated or released? Goals and objectives related to promotion may detail not only promotional actions, but how these actions relate to revenues desired.

Financial Strategies

Every leisure service program has a break-even point. The development of goals and objectives related to expected revenues and expenditures is extremely important. Basic questions here might include the following: Should a profit be earned? Should the program be subsidized by the agency? What equity factors must be considered when developing fees and charges for programs? How are funds to be received and dispersed? In public agencies, tax dollars have

TABLE 6.2 Recreation Program Principles, Madison (Wisconsin) School-Community Recreation Department.

Recreation in the Schools

The state of Wisconsin, through forward looking legislation passed in the early part of the 20th century, is the national leader in provision of community recreation services through local school districts. Madison's decision to provide these services as a function of public education, made in 1926 and strongly supported ever since, implies some additional directions and obligations for community recreation:

• Recreation programs should directly reach children in the schools.
• Recreation programs should take full advantage of school resources: people, facilities, and funds for initiating, implementing, and evaluating services.
• Recreation programs should help all community people, especially those not directly reached by daytime school offerings, receive a direct return on their investment in the school system by providing opportunities responsive to their interests.
• Recreation programs should exemplify educational ideals: high quality teaching, prefaced by careful preparation and based on sound learning principles; provision of physical, social, and psychological environments conducive to desired outcomes; and sound administrative and policy making practices which ensure continuing support for services vital to full human development.

Department Purposes

With these understandings as a base, the staff of the Madison School-Community Recreation Department summarizes the department's purposes as follows:

• To provide year-around recreation opportunities which are accessible to all residents of the Madison Metropolitan School District, responding to expressed interests and making maximum use of all available resources in the School District.
• To educate community citizens, with emphasis on children and youth of school age, on the value of learning and practicing lifetime leisure skills and appreciations.
• To serve as a community resource and catalyst for recreation services: providing referral information, organizational expertise, and planning with other agencies, organizations, and citizen groups in order to more fully meet the recreational needs of all community residents.

Source: Madison School District, Madison, Wisconsin.

become scarce, and in the marketplace, customer discretionary dollars have become scarce. Contributed dollars to voluntary organizations become more and more difficult to obtain. The establishment of goals and objectives that relate to careful financial planning has become increasingly important within leisure service organizations. A good example of an organization linking its mission statement, goals, and objectives into one integrated unit is found in the Morale, Welfare, and Recreation Marketing Department, U.S. Marine Corps, Okinawa, Japan. This effort is directed at enhancing "promotional and sales strategies" and deals with communications, research, and, in general, their linkage to the group's customers. Its marketing strategic plan, briefly introduced in Chapter 1, presents a coordinated effort aimed at linking the mission of the marketing department with its goals and objectives. These statements are found in Table 6.3.

Goals and objectives are not established in a vacuum. Ideally, the leisure service programmer will work with various individuals when developing goals and objectives. They should reflect the opinions and needs of both individuals within the organization and those external to the organization, since program goals and objectives are a way of linking customer needs to the work of the organization.

TABLE 6.3   Marketing Goals and Objectives, Morale, Welfare, and Recreation Department, U.S. Marine Corps, Okinawa, Japan.

Mission:

To uplift the spirits of our customers by providing world class communication, products, and customer research in a timely manner and in a format that identifies with our target audience.

Goal:

Increase the overall usage of and participation in Marine MWR facilities, programs, and special events.

Objectives:

- To unite Marine MWR Marketing efforts by concentrating our promotion, publicity sponsorship, and research efforts on one focus each month.
- To exploit all possible avenues for communicating with our customers and tracking the effectiveness of any vehicles used.
- To enhance the visual perceptions of Marine MWR with the staffing and equipping of a visual merchandiser.
- To identify and track our customer's perceptions and satisfaction levels and consistently work to improve our image by providing timely resolutions to customer complaints, communicating our commitment to our customers, their return on investment, and their importance in everything we do.
- To continuously research our customers and document their needs, wants, and desires and communicate those needs to the management staff of Marine MWR. Use all methods available including advisory councils, surveys, focus groups, telephone, personal interviews, and other options that become available.
- To improve the communication between the marketing staff and the managers of Marine MWR, so as to better provide the products and services needed to support their marketing needs.
- To provide customer service training to all Marine MWR employees on uplifting the spirits of our customers by going beyond their expectations, and taking steps to avoid/handle unsatisfied or irate customers.

Source: Morale, Welfare and Recreation Department, U.S. Marine Corps, Okinawa, Japan.

A key feature of program goals and objectives is the idea that they enable the programmer to *focus* his or her activities. Focusing on program goals and objectives creates a mechanism to guide the work of the professional. Rather than wallowing in uncertainty, leisure service programmers are able to clearly understand what they are trying to accomplish, how they are trying to accomplish it, and how their work will be measured. Likewise, this focus enables the customer to understand what services are to be produced, what benefits will be available, and what resources are to be employed. Thus, goals and objectives increase accountability for the programmer and help customers assess the extent to which their needs are being addressed.

Common Characteristics of Program Goals and Objectives

The terms *goals* and *objectives* are often thought to be synonymous. However, most definitions of goals suggest that they are broad statements, whereas objectives are more specific and measurable. When referring to program goals and objectives, we differentiate between these terms. *Program goals are broad statements that define the leisure services to be produced.* They are the aims or ends toward which the leisure service professional directs his or her activities. *Program objectives are specific statements that are measurable and have some dimension of time.* In developing program objectives, the leisure service programmer will usually consider what is to be done, how it is going to be done, when it is going to be done, and how it will be measured. A program objective describes the way in which the accomplishment of a goal can be carried out and measured—just as program goals are linked to the mission of the leisure service organization.

Some of the common characteristics of both program goals and objectives are as follows:

1. *Specific*—Program goals and objectives are specific, clear, and concrete. They help put the vision or mission of a leisure service organization in operation.
2. *Measurable*—Program goals and objectives must be measurable. There must be some way to determine whether the desired results have been achieved.
3. *Pragmatic*—Program goals and objectives also must be pragmatic; that is, they must be attainable and reality based.
4. *Useful*—Program goals and objectives must have worth; that is, they must be worth the effort needed to accomplish the end. They must be of value to the customers being served, to the leisure service programmer, and to the organization as a whole.
5. *Linked to Needs*—Program goals and objectives must be linked to the needs of customers and the organization's vision or mission.

Well-defined and articulated program goals and objectives make things happen within organizations. They not only provide direction for events and activities that the leisure service programmer may wish to have occur, but their establishment often actually produces the momentum necessary to move the organization in a specific direction. As indicated, program goals and objectives help identify programs to be developed, ways of promoting activities and events, and financial strategies to be employed.

Most program goals and objectives are written in terms of benefits or outcomes to be realized by the customer; as a result, they are written as performance objectives. A performance objective has the same qualities and attributes as a program objective. However, in addition to the factors just described, *performance objectives are written in terms of the behavior that is to be demonstrated by the customer* as a result of his or her involvement in a program or service.

Because performance objectives refer to the actual behavior to be demonstrated by the customer, they must be stated in terms of what the consumer is to know and what he or she is to demonstrate. Essentially, the programmer attempts to change or maintain certain types of defined customer behaviors by directly intervening with a program or service or by providing assistance as an enabler to help the customer in his or her leisure pursuits. Performance objectives focus on the behavior of the customer rather than on the actions of the programmer. In other words, performance objectives are not written to include the programmer's actions (such as intervening, enabling, and the like). They are written only to identify and measure the behavioral changes displayed by the customer.

Another key characteristic of performance objectives is that the behavior learned by the customer must be observable in order to be measured. One cannot measure that which is not seen. An example of a psychomotor skill that could be demonstrated (by the customer), observed, and measured is a free throw in basketball. A customer in leisure program activities, in order to fulfill a performance objective related to a physical skill, would be expected to demonstrate a described level of proficiency. Using the example of free throws, the customer might achieve a level of proficiency with the successful completion of eight out of ten free throws. A leisure program customer might display a cognitive skill through the application of knowledge. For example, the knowledge that sports officials have gained or possess can be evaluated in terms of their performance on a written test regarding the rules and regulations of the sport they officiate.

In another performance objective, the customer may be expected to demonstrate behavior in the affective domain (e.g., displaying an intangible such as enjoyment). What is enjoyment, and how can such an intangible element be measured?

It is possible for programmers to set standards and definitions for enjoyment that are based on their own specific interpretations and perceptions, and then measure enjoyment in this way. For example, the programmer might define enjoyment at a youth drop-in center as the number of smiling and laughing individuals, the length of time that the customers stay at the drop-in center, and the frequency with which they attend the center. In this way the programmer can, at least theoretically, attempt to measure enjoyment. This, in turn, may help in the evaluation of activities for these types of programs because the programmer has operationally defined intangible behavior in a tangible, measurable form.

Obviously, it is easier for the leisure professional and the customer to conceptualize the use of performance objectives in relation to tangible behaviors, such as the demonstration of a physical skill or the display of acquired knowledge. It is much more difficult to evaluate—hence, measure—feelings, values, and emotions. The difficulty in measuring intangible behavior and the comparative simplicity in measuring tangible behavior may account for the major emphasis on efficiency-oriented evaluative techniques (such as counting the number of customers) and for the dominance of programs that lend themselves to measurement by these types of performance objectives. In order to measure the essence of the leisure experience, increased emphasis should be placed on the quantification of intangibles such as enjoyment, social interaction, and excitement.

According to Edginton and Hayes (1976: 21), four factors are involved in writing performance objectives:

1. What must be known or done by the customer?
2. How is the customer to demonstrate a specific behavior?
3. What are the factors or conditions that might affect the customer's acquisition and demonstration of a specific behavior?
4. What is the minimum level of acceptable achievement for the customer's performance of a given behavior?

In writing performance objectives, the leisure programmer must first state exactly what is expected of the customer. These expectations or behavioral outcomes can be referred to as *terminal behaviors*. Terminal behaviors are the ends, events, or actions that the customer will eventually demonstrate. The professional must state the terminal expectations using an action verb. For example, "To hit the ball" is an example of a desired terminal behavior, and the action verb describing that behavior is the word "hit." This is not an easy task. When writing objectives, it is easier to focus on the actions of the programmer or on the process rather than on what the customer is expected to know or do. Edginton and Hayes (1976: 21) have indicated that "there is a tendency to focus on leisure activity as an end in itself rather than as a means to an end." It is important to remember that the customer must be aware of exactly what he or she is to know or do in terms of facts, ideas, physical movement, problems to be solved, and other factors that can be identified.

Another step in the process of writing performance objectives is to specify conditions or circumstances that may affect the acquisition of knowledge or demonstration of a skill. The objective should specify the form that the activity must take or the nature of the instruction that will be applied. In developing performance objectives, one is dealing with individuals or groups. Because individuals and groups vary in terms of values, interests, desires, needs, skills, and knowledge, each performance objective must account for these differences. Examples of adaptations and modifications that are based on individual and group differences include leadership styles, activity progression, game and contest rules, and the social and physical setting in which the activity takes place. Spelling out the special conditions or circumstances under which an action is to take place is especially important in dealing with special populations. For example, disabled individuals in wheelchairs play basketball using modified game rules.

The final step in writing performance objectives is consideration of the level of achievement required by the participant. For example, it is not sufficient to describe only what the participant is to do or know (such as "hitting the ball"); the programmer must also specify the level of proficiency to be achieved in hitting. This can mean the distance the ball must be hit, the accuracy of the hitter, or the number of hits per attempts. By specifying the achievement level required of the participant, the programmer can more specifically define the type of behavior expected. Likewise, we are quantifying the outcome in more precisely measurable terms. An example of the process is found in Table 6.4.

Identification of these four components serves both the customers and the organization. Customers benefit because they are able to visualize what it is they are trying to achieve through involvement in a recreation or leisure activity. The organization can benefit from the use of performance objectives in terms of its accountability. In other words, the organization is forced to define exactly what it is trying to do in terms of behavioral changes in people. When questioned as to the purpose of their organization, many leisure service agencies respond, "We exist to provide recreation and leisure activities to all members of the community." By using performance objectives, an organization can go a step further and define not only in general terms the activities it offers, but also in more specific terms the behavioral outcomes that can be anticipated for the individuals that participate in these activities.

At this point, we should also introduce some of the problems associated with performance objectives. First, they are extremely time consuming to formulate. In addition, they require an organization to deal with people on an individual rather than a mass basis. Given the present structuring and financing of public recreation services, this may be difficult and considered inefficient. Performance objectives also require a precise degree of structure in their formulation and implementation. According to some individuals, this robs potential from

TABLE 6.4 Writing Performance Objectives

Step 1—State the performance objective with a *verb* that defines the accepted behavior: "The customer *will demonstrate* proficiency in skiing . . ."

Step 2—State the *method* of performance by which the participant can demonstrate: *by traversing* a giant slalom course . . ."

Step 3—State those *factors or conditions* that may affect the attainment or achievement of the objective: "of 4,000 feet in *length,* with a *vertical drop* of 1,200 feet . . ."

Step 4—Indicate in each *performance* objective how it is to be *measured:* "covering the course in under five *minutes.*"

"The customer will demonstrate proficiency in skiing by traversing a giant slalom course of 4,000 feet in length, with a vertical drop of 1,200 feet, covering the course in under five minutes."

From *Taxonomy of Educational Objectives: Handbook I: Cognitive Domain,* Benjamin Bloom, et al. Copyright © 1956, renewed 1984 by Longman Publishers. Reprinted by permission.

a recreation and leisure experience. For example, spontaneity and freedom of interaction are two highly valued attributes of the leisure experience. By overstructuring, we may reduce the possibility that experiences featuring these attributes will be available. The problem is not one of overstructuring but of operationally defining terms such as *spontaneity.* We strongly recommend that organizations and individual leaders employ the concept of performance objectives, even if in a modified form.

Benefits-Based Programming Goals

One way to see the interplay among goals, performance objectives, outcomes, and awareness is to revisit the Benefits-Based Programming (BBP) model introduced in Chapter 1. Figure 6.7 provides an overview of the BBP model as modified by Rossman and Schlatter (2002).

Development of Target Goals

The first phase of the BBP model is to develop issue and target goals. These goals are those that

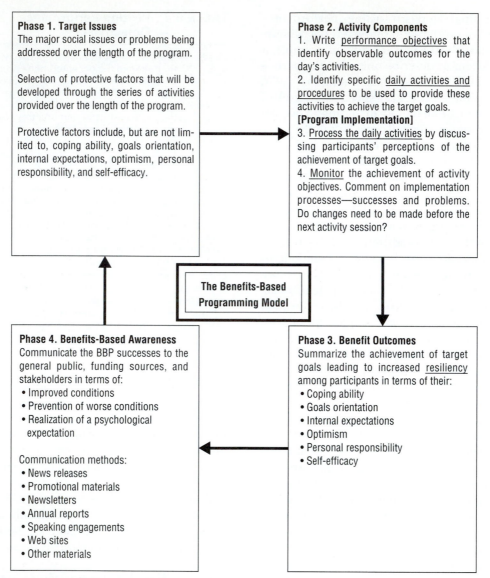

Figure 6.7 Benefits-Based Programming Model.
Adapted from Benefits-Based Programming Model (Allen and McGovern, 1997) by Rossman and Schlatter, 2002.

have been identified by the agency's stakeholders and will become the focus for program development. Examples of social issues might be the high incidence of latchkey children in a neighborhood, the prevalence of gang-related activity in a specific section of town, or the absence of healthy exercise opportunities for independent seniors. As Rossman and Schlatter (2002) state, "A key point to remember is that benefits-based recreation programs alone will not always address the issue entirely. Widespread community involvement is required to adequately confront all facets of a social issue" (p. 57). However, the advent of BBP gives leisure service programmers a tool to help them become integrated into the social fabric of the community and become part of the community's problem-solving processes. Once programmers identify the issue, their next step is to develop target goals. These goals must contain two features: First, they must be logically connected to the social issue. For instance, if the issue is one of safety of latchkey children, the goal should not be to make sure that all latchkey children are fed an afternoon snack. In this instance, there is no logical, easily identifiable link between the issue and the goal. Second, the goal statements must be written to facilitate the development of protective factors—those factors that protect the individual from harm. Thus, the target goals written for a program concerning latchkey children need to be clear on how children who participate in a proposed program will develop resiliency skills, attitudes, behaviors, or coping mechanisms (McMillan and Reed, 1994). Allen and McGovern (1996) have developed a BBP planning sheet to assist programmers in formulating target goals (see Figure 6.8). Once the programmer has written the target goals, he or she proceeds to the second element of the BBP model: the activity component.

The Activity Component

The activity component is comprised of four subcategories: (1) performance objectives, (2) daily activities and procedures, (3) processing of activities, and (4) monitoring. A brief summary of these four categories follows:

1. *Performance Objectives*—As mentioned earlier in this chapter, performance objectives provide the who, what, where, and hows that are expected. Because BBP is an outcome-based design, it is essential to have well-written performance objectives that provide a measurement for the success or failure of the program.
2. *Daily Activities and Procedures*—This is a written plan that provides the operational details of what

BBP Planning Sheet

Program:
Target Issue:
Time:
Program Synopsis:
Facility Needs:
Supplies:
Target Goals (Protective Factors to be Addressed;
* = Primary, + = Secondary)

_____ Self-efficacy
_____ Goal orientation
_____ Personal resposibility
_____ Optimism
_____ Internal expectations
_____ Coping ability
_____ Other

Partnering Agencies (Contact Person)

_____ School	_____ Social services
_____ Law enforcement	_____ Other
_____ Church	

Figure 6.8 BBP Planning Sheet. (From Allen, L., & McGovern, T. (1996, October). *Implementing a benefits based recreation program.* Paper presented at the NRPA Congress for Recreation and Parks, Kansas City, MO.).

must occur so that customers can achieve the benefits of the program. It also provides documentation should the program need to be duplicated. This helps to present a systematic series of activities that maximize customer benefit.

3. *Processing*—This subcategory is carried out by program staff to help participants link their feelings and experiences with the target goals. Time is set aside for discussion at the end of each activity session. Figure 6.9 shows an example of processing questions that Allen and McGovern (1996) developed for a youth-at-risk program.
4. *Monitoring*—This is a daily activity that is the responsibility of the leisure service staff in charge of the program. Staff need to constantly monitor the link between the objectives and the target goals to ensure that program intervention and modification are not needed.

The Benefit Outcome Component

In this component, programmers evaluate the overall outcomes as they relate to the target goals. To implement this component, they must develop a comprehensive evaluation plan. Chapter 13 will cover the evaluation methods appropriate for this component. If the outcomes have a direct link to the target goals, then the purpose of instituting the BBP model has been met.

Benefit-Based Awareness

According to Forest (1999), a fourth component—awareness—should be added to the BBP model. This component involves "the establishment of a comprehensive marketing effort that effectively communicates the significance of the programs and services offered by the recreation service providers" (p. 42). By providing information to the public about how parks and recreation services benefit the community, the department becomes integrated into the civic fabric. By this means, services and programs become viewed as a necessity, not a frill. Promotion techniques will be covered in Chapter 10.

To BBP or Not to BBP?

This short presentation on the Benefits-Based Programming model illustrates the linkages between goals and objectives. The BBP model is initiated by developing target goals and is predicated on having measurable performance objectives. As such, it is a clear example of the necessity of both goals and objectives in developing programs.

Implementing the BBP model can be time-consuming. It requires a large amount of documentation—record keeping, reports, and

Asking the right questions is often the key to good processing. Listed below are questions that may help you in becoming more comfortable with processing.

1. How did you feel when you had to trust someone else to keep you safe?
2. How did you decide whom you would trust?
3. What did it feel like to cooperate with other members of your group?
4. How did you (your group) make decisions?
5. How well did you do?
6. What did you say to yourself?
7. In what ways did you criticize or support yourself?
8. What type of feedback did you receive or give to others?
9. In what ways do you differ from other group members?
10. What was your greatest success today?
11. How can you use something you learned today in other situations?
12. What did you learn about yourself during this activity that you want to work on in the future?

Figure 6.9 Processing Questions. (From Allen, L., & McGovern, T. (1996, October). *Implementing a benefits based recreation program.* Paper presented at the NRPA Congress for Recreation and Parks, Kansas City, MO.).

monitoring—in order for the program to adequately show the benefit outcomes. In addition, it is fairly prescriptive in nature, which may act against the idea of creativity and spontaneity in the leisure experience. The point is that not every program offered by an organization needs to utilize the BBP model. But for those programs directly tied to social issues in the community, it has been proven to an effective means of benefiting both customers and the identity of park and recreation departments in communities.

Summary

In this chapter, we have discussed the importance of establishing direction for the work of the leisure service organization and that of the leisure service programmer. In a formal sense, the direction that an organization establishes is reflected in its vision statement, mission state-

ment, program goals, program objectives, and performance objectives. Organizational goals are essential for (1) establishing the final end toward which the organization and the programmer direct their resources; (2) providing an indication of how the intended result or end will be achieved; and (3) serving as a control indicating whether the desired ends have been achieved.

The culture of a leisure service organization is usually established by developing a vision statement. Vision statements are bold, motivating statements that reflect the values of an organization. A vision statement is useful in establishing the ideals that an organization wishes to pursue. It becomes an important mechanism to communicate the intent of the organization to its own employees internally as well as to those groups it serves externally. Closely related to vision statements are mission statements. Mission statements in the leisure service field tend to be written in a shorter, more pragmatic, more direct, and more focused fashion than vision statements.

Program goals, program objectives, and performance objectives are methods for linking the work of the leisure service organization to its broader vision. They are much more specific than either mission or vision statements and they can be operationalized. Program goals can be thought of as broad statements that direct the work of the programmer. Program objectives are more specific, concrete statements that can be measured. Performance objectives have the same properties as program objectives, except that they are stated in terms of the desired behaviors to be demonstrated by the customer.

The NRPA Benefit-Based Program model is an example of how the linkage between goals and objectives can help to reposition agency programming within a community. While the BBP model can help an agency deal with social issues, the prescriptive nature of the process may not be suitable for all of an agency's programs. However, it can provide a framework and serve as an example to tie goals and objectives together in a meaningful way.

Providing direction to an organization is an important step in leisure service programming. Organizational resources are used more efficiently when planning professionals have a clear understanding of what they are trying to create, what behaviors they are trying to produce, or what outcomes they desire. Further, the needs of the customer are more clearly linked to the work of the organization.

Discussion Questions and Exercises

1. Why is establishing direction important for the work of a leisure service organization?

2. What is meant by the *culture* of a leisure service organization? How does the culture of the leisure service organization have an impact on its programs and services?

3. What is the difference between a vision and a mission statement?

4. Write a vision statement for a leisure service organization or program area of your choice.

5. Explain the difference between goals and objectives.

6. How might goals and objectives vary when developing them for: (1) programs; (2) promotion and sales strategies; and (3) financial management? Develop a set of goals and objectives for each one of these areas for a given leisure service activity.

7. What are some of the common characteristics of goals and objectives?

8. What are performance objectives?

9. What four factors are involved in writing performance objectives?

10. Develop a taxonomy of behavioral outcomes that can be used in writing performance objectives.

References

Allen, L. R., and T. D. McGovern. 1996, October. *Implementing a benefit-based recreation program.* Paper presented at the NRPA Congress for Recreation and Parks, Kansas City, MO.

Allen, L. R., and T. D. McGovern. 1997. BBM: It's working. *Parks and Recreation* 32(8), 48–55.

Berg, R. 2002, September 10. Playmakers. *Marketplace Magazine* 13(14): 1–4.

Bloom, B. S. 1956. *Taxonomy of educational objectives: Cognitive domain.* New York: McKay.

Collins, J. C., and Porras, J. I. 1994. *Built to last: Successful habits of visionary companies.* New York: HarperBusiness.

Edginton, C. 1987. Creating an organizational culture. *Management Strategy* 11(1): 6.

Edginton, C. R., and G. A. Hayes. 1976. Objectives in the delivery of recreation services. *Journal of Leisurability* 3(4): 21.

Forest, K. K. 1999. Benefits-based Programming. *Illinois Parks and Recreation* 30(5): 41–42.

Hitt, W. D. 1988. *The leader-manager: Guidelines for action.* Columbus: Batelle Press.

Peters, T. 1987. *Thriving on chaos.* New York: Alfred Knopf.

Rossman, J., and B. Schlatter. 2002. *Recreation Programming: Designing Leisure Experiences.* 4th ed. Champaign, IL: Sagamore.

Program Development

LEARNING OBJECTIVES

1. To provide the reader with an understanding of the factors involved in the *total program planning process.*

2. To help the reader gain an understanding of *program areas.*

3. To help the reader gain an understanding of *program formats.*

4. To help the reader understand how *the specific content of a program contributes to the development process.*

5. To provide information concerning factors related to the *timing, facility needs, supply and equipment needs, and cost of a leisure program.*

6. To provide the reader with information concerning the concept of *activity analysis* and its relationship to leisure programming.

7. To recognize the place of *risk management* in all program planning activities.

INTRODUCTION

The program development step in the total program planning process integrates the customer needs that have been identified with the goals and objectives that have been determined. It then focuses on the factors that are crucial in constructing both individual programs and the total scope of programs and services made available by the leisure service organization. The same elements in the development procedure can be applied in all situations where program construction takes place. In other words, whether the leisure service professional is organizing a swimming class, a softball tournament, a travelogue series, a ballet performance, or a communitywide weekend arts festival, the same methodology can be applied to the development of the activity. Whether the program being developed is for a small number of individuals, for several groups of people, or for a large number of leisure customers, common elements in the development process are applicable to all situations.

Rossman (1994) has developed a program design model with three basic steps (see Figure 7.1). The first step involves establishing design goals and understanding the leisure experience. In this initial step, the leisure service programmer focuses on the expected leisure outcomes to be produced. The next step deals with the design aspects of the program. The focus is on the elements that influence the character of a program, including: the patrons (customers); the place of the program; objects found in the setting; rules, rituals, customs, and norms that impact on the interaction; relationships that bind consumers together; and the animation of the event. This step focuses on the means of program design. The last part of the process is the actual plan or process, which Rossman refers to as "design tactics." In this process, the programmer develops plans and alternative scenarios that can occur during the program process.

PROGRAM DESIGN ELEMENTS

Similar sets of program design elements are found in the organization of most leisure experiences. Though not listed in any order, the following factors are common to all program design efforts. With the specific customer group(s) in mind, the leisure service professional will focus on: program area, program format, program content, time factors, facilities, setting, equipment and supplies, staffing, cost, promotion, activity analysis, risk management, and special

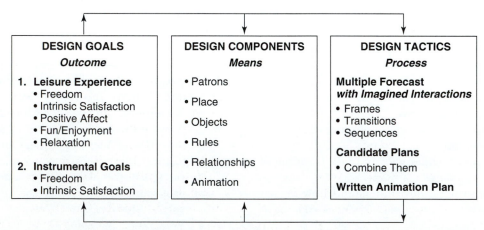

Figure 7.1   Program Design Model—Sequential Order of Design Process.
(From J. R. Rossman, 1994, *Recreation Programming,* 2nd ed. Champaign, IL: Sagamore.)

considerations (for example, responding to individuals with disabilities in compliance with the Americans With Disabilities Act).

Each factor's prominence and degree of influence in the development of a specific program will vary with the situation. For one leisure organization, for example, the cost of staffing and the resulting cost to the customer may be of primary importance. In another situation, securing the facilities and creating the setting may be most crucial to the development step, or developing and facilitating a program promotion plan may be of greatest importance to constructing a particular program or event. Whatever the situation is and whatever the specific program is, all the factors listed here are important to the program development step. Two of these factors are considered in greater detail later in the book: program areas are discussed in Chapter 8 and program formats in Chapter 9. They are introduced here as a part of the program development step in the program planning process.

Program Areas

The term *program areas* refers to how leisure program activities are categorized or classified in the context of this book. Chapter 8 provides a detailed discussion of the way in which leisure activities can be identified. The areas of programming included in this book are: the arts, incorporating visual arts (including crafts), performing arts, and new arts; literary activities; aquatics; sports, games, and athletics; outdoor recreation; social recreation; self-improvement/education activities; wellness activities; hobbies; travel and tourism; and volunteer services (see Figure 7.2). Through needs identification and assessment and through determination of goals and objectives, the leisure service programmer selects the area(s) of programming that will be the focus for development.

Program planners in leisure service organizations attempt to provide a broad spectrum of programming in a variety of program areas. Consideration must be given to the several customer

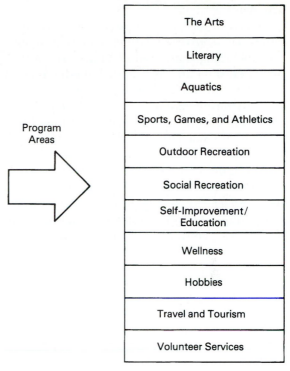

Program Areas →

- The Arts
- Literary
- Aquatics
- Sports, Games, and Athletics
- Outdoor Recreation
- Social Recreation
- Self-Improvement/Education
- Wellness
- Hobbies
- Travel and Tourism
- Volunteer Services

Figure 7.2   Areas of Programming.

groups for whom an agency plans. In addition, leisure service program planners attempt to develop and maintain a balance of programming in order to meet the greatest number of customer needs and interests. In other words, activities in several areas of programming can be developed by the leisure service organization. For example, sports, wellness activities, aquatics, arts and crafts, volunteer activities, travel and tourism, and hobby groups can all be included in the programming offered by a specific organization. At the same time, activities at several skill levels can be provided for customers. An example of this is in aquatic programming, where specific opportunities are often offered for beginning swimming, intermediate swimming, advanced swimming, diving instruction, synchronized swimming, and lifesaving courses. This variety of activities for different skill levels can be applicable in all programming areas.

The Arts

Programs in the arts embrace all creative disciplines. *Visual arts* can be thought of as decorative arts, including both graphic and plastic forms. Activities could incorporate such mediums as oil painting; pen and ink drawing; stone, metal, and clay structuring; tapestry making; block printing; and wood carving. A *craft* may be distinguished from other visual arts in that it results in a product that serves a utilitarian purpose. Some examples might include leather craft, sewing, embroidery, tie-dyeing, candle making, pottery, snow and ice sculpturing, fly tying, and furniture refinishing. The *new arts* involve creative use of twenty-first century technology. They may include computer art, photography, and music synthesizers. The *performing arts* involve artistic expression in which the individual is the mode of expression. Performing arts include such activities as acting, singing, and dancing. The participant must be involved in the activity, although it is of no consequence whether an audience is present. Modern dance, pantomime, puppetry, opera, barbershop quartets, symphony orchestras, and dramatizations are all examples of performing arts.

Literary Activities

Literary activities are leisure opportunities that emphasize literary, mental, and linguistic activities. Literary activities facilitate communication through writing and speaking, and may include the study of English and foreign languages; creative writing and composition; oral reading of poetry, short stories, or plays; book reviews and discussion; and study of literature. In addition, this area of programming may encompass development of oral histories, storytelling, and study of family genealogies.

Aquatics

Although aquatics may fit well into the category of sports, games, and athletics, it is such a large area of programming for many leisure service organizations that we have listed it here as a separate category. This area of programming encompasses swimming, diving, water aerobic activities, water games, lifesaving instructions and practices, and aquatic instructions. It also includes other water-related activities such as canoeing and boating and the safety practices related to these activities.

Sports, Games, and Athletics

Any physiological activity that requires gross and fine motor muscle control may be categorized within this cluster. Track and field, rifle shooting, archery, golf, weight lifting, handball, badminton, volleyball, softball, and water polo are all examples of this classification.

Outdoor Recreation

Outdoor recreation and leisure activities are natural, resource-oriented activities. Some that strongly depend on the use of natural resources are sailing, fishing, camping, hiking, climbing, and hunting.

Social Recreation

Social recreation involves activities that are created in order to bring about interaction between individuals. Social recreation programs may involve the use of other areas (such as those already mentioned) to contribute to its objective. Generally speaking, the setting is most important in social recreation programming.

Self-Improvement/Educational Activities

Activities in this programming area can be broad in scope and interest. Discussion groups of all kinds may be included: current events, politics, financial planning, and home improvements, to name a few. Specific instructional opportunities included in this category may focus on family life, child rearing, presenting a new self-image, interviewing skills, and interpersonal communication.

Wellness Activities

Wellness activities in leisure programming include physical fitness activities as well as changes in health behaviors such as weight reduction, cessation of smoking and chemical intake, and dietary concerns and adaptations. Wellness also includes social and emotional good health and lifetime practices and activities that contribute to a positive lifestyle and living environment.

Hobbies

A hobby is a leisure activity that is pursued with interest over an extended period of time. Two classifications of hobbies are collecting and creative. Common items accumulated for a collecting hobby are stamps, coins, guns, books, antiques, nature objects, dolls, and models. Creative hobbies include writing, composing, cooking, and gardening.

Travel and Tourism

As a program area, travel and tourism encompasses the movement of persons from their immediate surroundings and places of residence to other locations for the purpose of interacting with the physical and social environment. This may include viewing and interacting with natural physical features, manufactured structures, and the human culture of the area.

Volunteer Services

Volunteer programs involve utilizing skills and abilities during leisure time for the purpose of giving to others. Whereas other individuals may receive satisfaction from directly participating in an activity, volunteers receive their satisfaction from service rendered to others.

Program Formats

The program format is the way in which an activity is organized and structured for delivery to the customer. Obviously, the format used to organize an activity will have a great deal of influence on its appeal to the customer. To make an overall program attractive and desirable, activities within the program areas must be organized using creative and appropriate program formats.

Individual programs within the several program areas should be formatted to cater to broad sections of the population in order to meet the needs and interests of a variety of groups of people. Leisure programming formats include: *competitive, drop-in, class, club, special event, workshop, interest group,* and *outreach* (see Figure 7.3).

A feature that makes leisure programming dynamic is that activities in many of the programming areas can be offered in a variety of formats. At the same time, formats can be mixed to add interest to activities that are provided. The program area of sports can be used to illustrate the application of formats to program activities. Basketball, volleyball, softball, or other sports activities can be offered competitively through leagues and tournaments. Skill development in these activities may be facilitated through structured instruction in a class format. Open facilities with nonscheduled activities offer opportunities for drop-in participation, while workshops and seminars present opportunities for sports coaches and officials to be trained to lead the sports activities. Sometimes there is a fine line between formats used for a particular activity. For example, a sports tournament could be both a special event and a competitive event or just one of the two. A matrix that shows the application of formats to program areas is included in Chapter 9.

Competitive

Many leisure activities, especially sports, games, and athletics, can be competitive in nature. Competition can stimulate interest and provide motivation among participants. This is not only true for sports but also applies to other program areas. Program planners, when scheduling leisure activities that focus on competition, should take into consideration the relative skills and abilities of the participants involved and correspondingly adapt the level or intensity of competition. Common methods used to organize program areas into competition include leagues, tournaments, and contests.

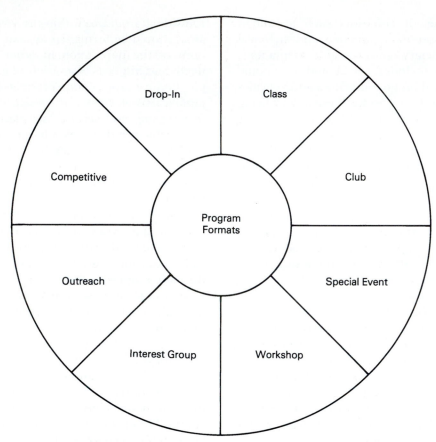

Figure 7.3 Leisure Programming Formats.

Drop-In/Open

Drop-in/open formatted activities provide the participant with an element of freedom in contrast with activities that operate on rigidly fixed time schedules. Generally speaking, activities are arranged in a manner that allows them to be either ongoing or spontaneous. Utilization of a gymnasium track for jogging and use of a library for reading are examples of drop-in programming.

Class

Another method of organizing leisure activities is through instructional classes. Classes are more formal than the drop-in approach. They usually involve hiring an instructor who teaches within a given subject area. Although the class setting may be formal in comparison with other program forms, the emphasis is one of individual concern and attention.

Club

A club consists of a group of people who are associated for a common purpose. The club membership usually provides its own leadership, organization, and perhaps finances. A club is customarily a self-contained unit unless facilities are needed to operate. Leisure service organizations often provide facilities to meet the interests of individuals within clubs. Furthermore, they can provide initial stimulation for the formulation of a club around a specific area of interest (e.g., organizing an introductory meeting or providing in-kind services, such as storage space or clerical help).

Special Events

A special event is a method of organizing an activity in a unique manner. Ranging from simply executed activities to elaborate and lengthy productions, the special event is a method of stimulating interest. Special events include exhibits, parades, festivals, demonstrations, and carnivals.

Workshops/Conferences

The workshop/conference is a method of organizing activities and people into a format that allows intense participation within a short period of time. The duration of a given workshop/conference is usually determined by the amount of material to be covered. They usually last a maximum of two weeks and, in many situations, are organized for much shorter periods of time. A conference is a meeting at which individuals with common interests gather to discuss issues, to disseminate information, and to make decisions.

Interest Group

An interest group may have some of the characteristics of a club; however, interest groups are usually a collection of individuals that is formed around an activity issue or a program area. Special interest groups usually have their own leadership. The lifespan of an interest group may vary from meeting together one or two times to a more ongoing existence. Several individuals may serve as resource people for the group according to the interest for which the group was formed. Groups may form in relation to social needs, social issues, community projects, leisure interests, and so on.

Outreach

Many programs and services are organized around the utilization of facilities rather than around people and their needs. Outreach programs meet people in their own locale. Emphasis is placed on taking the activity to the participant rather than on having the participant come to the activity.

Program Content

Once the leisure programmer has identified the program area in which a service will be offered, determined the specific activity to be presented, and selected the format that will be used to implement the program, he or she needs to develop the specific content that the program will have. To have continuity in planning programs, a leisure service organization may wish to have a common format for program descriptions so that similar information will be included in all activity planning. With a format to follow, the planner can be more certain of including necessary and appropriate information for each activity that is developed.

Both long-range planning and short-range planning are necessary to bring a program to implementation. The long-range planning may include general information about the program goals and objectives, the customers for whom the program is being planned, the time for the program to be offered, and the general content for the sessions that make up the program. Figure 7.4 is an example of a long-range program plan that includes a plan for offering the program over a two-year time period. A short-range plan, on the other hand, focuses on the individual sessions that will take place during the program. Figure 7.5 shows the plan that is applicable to each session. In other situations, a short-range plan may offer even greater detail than the example. In an instructional (class) program, the short-range plan would describe in detail exactly the content that would be covered each class session, the materials necessary to carry out the session, and the anticipated outcomes from the session. Chapter 9 contains an example of a detailed short-range plan in the description of the class format.

When writing long-range plans and short-range plans, the leisure programmer and the

Program Area:	Travel and Tourism
Program Form:	Drop-In
Name of Program:	Travel Adventures
Customers:	All Members of the Community
Program Goal:	To provide a variety of travel experiences through film, videos, slides, and speakers.
Program Objectives:	To enable individuals to "travel" the United States and the world.
	To bring the culture of distant places to the local community.
	To stimulate discussion and exchange of travel experiences among those in attendance.
Time:	Second Wednesday each month, September through June Two sessions each month; 1:30 P.M. and 7:00 P.M.

First Year:
"Around the World"

Sept. — North to Canada
Oct. — Mysteries of the Orient
Nov. — Exploring Spain and Portugal
Dec. — Christmas in Scandinavia
Jan. — Enchanting Egypt
Feb. — Secrets of the Soviet Union
Mar. — The South Seas: Tahiti and Samoa
Apr. — Intrigue of India
May — Winter in Australia
June — Ethnic Fest

Second Year:
"Exploring the USA"

Sept. — The Meandering Mississippi
Oct. — Cactus and Other Desert Flowers
Nov. — New England Winter
Dec. — Snow-Capped Mountains of the USA
Jan. — Romantic Cities: New Orleans
San Antonio
San Francisco
Minneapolis
Feb. — Southwest USA
Mar. — Lakes of the USA: Superior, Meade, Champlain, Crater
Apr. — Summer in Alaska
May — Festivals and Fun: Eugene (OR) Bach Festival; St. Paul (MN) Winter Carnival; Traverse City (MI) Cherry Blossom Festival
June — Heritage Days

Figure 7.4 Long-Range Program Plan: Travel Adventures.

activity leader must always keep in mind the specific customers for whom the activity plan is being developed. Knowledge and common sense must be exercised in all situations so that the goals and objectives are realistic, the contents are intrinsic to the program, and the planned activities are age appropriate and group appropriate. For example, a leisure service organization might offer a beginning swimming class for young children and another one for adults.

Although the desired outcomes of comfort in the water and beginning swimming skills are the same for both groups, the approach to accomplishing those outcomes would be different in working with the two diverse age groups.

Generally speaking, individuals involved in the planning and supervision of leisure programming are not expected to teach or lead, or be involved in the face-to-face delivery of program activities. Their primary task and responsi-

---

Objectives for each session:
To provide an atmosphere of comfort.
To facilitate interaction between customers and speaker.
To encourage interaction among customers.

Equipment and supplies:
Chairs, coffee pot (and necessary supplies), refreshments, A/V equipment — projector, screen, VCR, and TV.

Outcomes:
A positive social environment.
Customers interested in attending "Travel Adventures" another time.

Figure 7.5 Short-Range Program Plan: Travel Adventures.

bility is to help identify the need for the activity and to pull together the resources (human, material, and monetary) that are necessary to implement the program. The leisure programmer secures (hires) qualified staff (full-time or part-time) in order to plan specific program content and carry it out. In addition, the leisure programmer has the responsibility to reserve the facility and to coordinate the availability of the equipment and supplies that are necessary to implement and carry out the planned program. He or she also has the responsibility to make decisions about the budget for the specific program, both the potential disbursements for staff and materials and the potential of revenue from the customer and other sources.

It is important to remember that the customer can make valuable suggestions regarding the content of the program. Individuals who are involved in the formulation of the learning experience will be more interested in the activity and more highly motivated; hence, more effective learning will take place. This practice can be applied in the leisure programming context. The leisure programmer and the activity leader should interact with potential customers or the individuals in specific programs to gain an understanding of their needs and attitudes. The customer, through dialogue with the program leader, can gain a better understanding of the goals and the methods employed in implement-

ing the leisure experience. In certain situations, customers may want to design their own program content; in other situations, they may wish to interact with the leader to develop the experience. In the former case, a drop-in format may be most appropriate; in the latter instance, a structured format may be more effective.

Customized, Individualized Services
Increasingly, we live in a society in which customers expect programs and services to be customized to their individual needs and preferences. There was a time when leisure services were massed produced—one program model was assumed to fit the needs of many, if not all. However, we now live in a very diverse society. Strategies in leading programs must reflect the fact that individuals respond differently to different methods of instruction and leadership. Individuals often require services to be provided at times and locations that are convenient to their schedules. Further, the way in which the program is actually implemented may vary from individual to individual.

Leisure service organizations are seeing greater demand for services that are geared to the individual. This includes individual assessments, private lessons in all program areas, and the provision of areas, facilities, and equipment in which individuals can be active on their own. For example, in organizing a fitness class, one might assume that the content and pace, as well as presentations of materials, could follow one standard format. Many fitness programs start with the assumption that customers must be assessed or tested individually. Following analysis, a customized, individualized program is established. A variety of fitness equipment and routines can be varied to meet the conditioning needs of an individual.

In addition to customizing services, other support activities are often bundled together to reflect the need for additional individualization. Again, using the fitness example, an individual might require support in the form of child care, transportation, food services, and provision of clean apparel to participate in the program. Such support services are often selected on the basis of need and individual interest. One individual might require child care, whereas another may not.

Time Factors

Time is an overriding factor in the program development process. The time factor both influences and is influenced by the other elements of program planning. For instance, determining the time to start planning, deciding the time the program will begin, and scheduling the time (day and time of day) that the activity will take place are all extremely important. Because of the importance of time in leisure program planning, it is necessary to examine several components of the time factor.

A timeline for planning will serve as a guide for the leisure programmer. The timeline may be as long or as short as the planner decides to make it. It may be as detailed or as brief as the leisure programmer desires. For example, a timeline for program planning may begin with the needs identification and assessment phase, move to the task of developing goals and objectives, then include the program development process and the program implementation stage, and conclude with program evaluation. On the other hand, a timeline may be created only to guide the leisure programmer through the phase of program development; or a timeline for the "life of the program" (implementation) may be written. A timeline is an outline or list of tasks to be carried out, including people to contact, facilities to reserve, materials to secure, and promotion to be distributed; all of which will be designated with a specific time as to when the task should be completed. Figure 7.6 gives an example of how a timeline can be prepared.

Other time factors that are a part of planning are time of day, time of week, week and month of year, and length or duration of each activity session or the whole program. These time decisions cannot be made in isolation from other factors; they are influenced by the program area and specific activity being planned. The format that will be used to implement the activity influences time decisions. The customers for whom the activity is being planned and the facility in which the program will take place also influence how the time factors are established. There is an interrelatedness of many elements in time planning.

Changes in how society's institutions are organized can have a dramatic impact on the time factors associated with leisure programs. Two examples support this idea. The first is the way the work is organized. Increasingly, we find individuals working in varying schedules. The traditional 8-to-5 workday is evolving as a result of flextime—compressed work hours and other strategies aimed at supporting employees' need for more options in the workday. These strategies provide the opportunity for alternative scenarios for offering leisure programs and services. The second institutional change is the implication of year-round school schedules on the more traditional seasonal format that many leisure service organizations have used over the years. For example, there has been a greater emphasis on establishing programs operating during the school year that provide extended child care during an "off semester," which may now occur during the fall or spring.

Consider one program—swimming lessons for children—to illustrate the decisions that

Event: Community Concert

I. 12-16 weeks prior to event
   A. Reserve facility
   B. Sign contract with performer
   C. Determine budget

II. 9-11 weeks prior to event
   A. Order printing of tickets
   B. Order advertising
   C. Reserve necessary A/V equipment
   D. Contact radio and TV stations

III. 6-8 weeks prior to event
   A. Discuss all performance needs with facility management
   B. Know regulations at facility—security, fire, crowd management, etc.
   C. Release initial advertising and publicity

IV. 4-7 weeks prior to event
   A. Distribute additional advertising and publicity
   B. Monitor ticket sales—fill mail orders
   C. Continue in contact with facility management and follow up
      on equipment reservations

V. 1-3 weeks prior to event
   A. Continue to monitor ticket sales—hold mail orders for pickup
   B. Set up interviews with performer by local media
   C. Monitor all last-minute details

VI. Day of event
   A. Check with facility to know that all seating, concessions, equip-
      ment, etc., are in place
   B. Provide for the performer's convenience—motel, dressing room,
      food, etc.
   C. Monitor all necessary details
   D. Attend concert

VII. Immediately following event
   A. Pay all bills
   B. Return all borrowed equipment
   C. Write and send thank-you letters
   D. Write critique of strong and weak points of planning and
      implementation
   E. Close financial record and prepare report

Figure 7.6   Program Development Timeline.

TABLE 7.1   Varied Time Structuring for Ten-Session Programs

Time Structure	Program Idea
Once a week for ten weeks	Creative Dramatics for Children
Twice a week for five weeks	Adult Aerobics
Five times a week for two weeks	Summer Swimming Class
Twice a day for five days	Cheerleading Camps
Two days, five hours each	CPR Training
One day for ten hours	Sports Official Recertification Workshop
Twice a month for five months	Square Dance Club
Once a month for ten months	Travelogue Series

must be made in relation to time. Several questions must be asked and answered. What time of year is the program to be offered? If it is offered both during the school year and during the summertime, how will this change the time planning? How many sessions will be offered? How long will each session be? What time of day will the program be offered? How many times a week will the program meet? In order to answer these questions, the planner must keep in mind when the customers (children) are available. The planner must also know when parents or other significant adults are available to get the children to the program. During the school year, the times that children are likely to be available for participation are on weekdays after school into early evening and on weekends. During the summer, children would probably have greater flexibility of time and be available for longer periods of time. How frequently should the swimming sessions be offered? Once a week for ten weeks, twice a week for five weeks, five times a week for two weeks? Table 7.1 suggests various ways in which ten activity sessions could be structured.

Farrell and Lundegren (1983) have suggested that scheduling can be thought of in specific patterns. The first pattern involves the seasons of the year or natural annual time blocks such as holidays. These blocks of time may also include traditional program planning, which falls into eight-to-ten-week time periods. This pattern of planning seems to accommodate the class format and structured competitive sports leagues, and facilitates a plan for periodic pro-

motional and program registration activities. A second scheduling pattern may have more of a monthly or weekly focus. Ongoing programs, such as club groups that meet on a regular basis, weekly programs, special events, and monthly themes fit into this pattern. This pattern of programming enables the leisure programmer to accommodate special interests and to emphasize particular kinds of programming in concentrated periods of time. Further, this programming pattern may appeal to the drop-in customer more than other programming options. The Beidleman Environmental Center operated by the city of Colorado Springs (Colorado) Parks and Recreation Department publishes a spring calendar listing programs available on a monthly basis. Figure 7.7 presents the schedule for the month of April. The Northbrook (Illinois) Park District publishes a monthly calendar of events. The third pattern for scheduling focuses on the lifestyle patterns of leisure customers. Days of the week are divided into time-use patterns.

Farrell and Lundegren have divided daily time-use patterns into five blocks of time (from P. Farrell and H. M. Lundegren, *The Process of Recreation Programming*, 2nd edition, 1983. Macmillan Publishing, New York, NY. Reprinted by permission of Leisure Studies, University Park, PA). These five time periods include:

1. *Morning Session*—This time slot is a possible activity period for senior adults, preschool children, swing-shift workers, housepersons, and

april

Saturday, April 1
GARDENING FOR COLORADO TRANSPLANTS
9-11:00 a.m.

Join the staff from Los Robles Garden Center for a hands-on gardening workshop. Learn what can be successfully grown in our semi-arid Pikes Peak region, then take a brief tour of nearby Los Robles. For interested gardeners of all ages, reservations required.

Saturday, April 8
WATER-A MOVING EXPERIENCE
10:00 a.m.-2:00 p.m.

Join us for our spring opening! Explore WATER- a moving experience! Bring your sack lunch. Experiment with bubbles; sing with the Colors of Life; listen to storyteller Judith Daley as she weaves water tales and explore Mesa Creek with Alex Vargo, Colorado College biologist (bring an extra pair of tennis shoes and rainwear); or hike the El Paso Canal with Curt Poulton. There will be hands-on activities for children and a book fair sponsored by Once Upon a Mind. For everyone, young and old, no reservations required.

The PIKES PEAK LIBRARY DISTRICT presents...
The Kennedy Center
IMAGINATION
CELEBRATION

Tuesdays, April 11,18 and 25
BASIC BIRDING BY EAR (3-part series)
7-9:00 p.m.

This three-session course will cover the two dozen birds that account for most of what we hear in our parks and back yards. In a relaxed atmosphere we will listen to examples of each bird while viewing slides. We will discuss useful cues and tricks of the trade and review and test ourselves with quizzes. Participants will be invited to join in field trips and point counts organized by the Nature Conservancy in their Aiken Canyon property. Your $15.00 donation to the Aiken Audubon Society, 740 W. Caramillo, 80907 will confirm your reservation and help pay for materials and refreshments. For adults, reservations required.

Tuesday, April 18
BASIC BIRDING BY EAR-part 2
7-9:00 p.m.

This is the second of the three-part series. You must be registered for the entire series to participate in this evening's workshop. Please see April 11 for details.

Call 578-7088 for program reservations-Fax 719-578-6717
3

Figure 7.7 Spring Calendar of Events, Beidleman Environmental Center, City of Colorado Springs (Colorado) Parks and Recreation Department.

others. The activity rarely begins before 9:00 A.M. and is usually completed before noon, although a meal may be a part of the program activity.

2. *Early Afternoon Session*—This time period may well attract the same clientele as those listed above. Some programs may incorporate a rest hour here, or the institution may choose this time period for special medication or treatments, such that immediately after the noon hour activity generally is at a lower level. After this normally slower period, it can be expected that activity periods will be popular.

3. *Late Afternoon Session*—This may be the busiest time during the school year in which children of school age will require programs and participate in recreational activities. During the summer months, however, this [may] not be a highly participatory time.

4. *Early Evening Session*—Aside from varying work shifts in the area, this remains a most popular time for recreational activity. There are many elements in a person's life that compete for this time of one's day. Television, part-time jobs, community service work, social clubs, family get-together time, school activities and studying, church work and fellowship groups, and socializing with peers; all tend to be competitors for activity during evening discretionary hours.

5. *Late Evening Session*—Depending on the bedtime habits or possible curfew regulations in the area, this time block could extend well into the early morning hours. Although this tends to be an adult time period, there are many areas of the country in which younger children are out until well past midnight.

To these five blocks of time we would add three more:

6. *Early Morning*—This is a time period popular with leisure customers who wish to "get into" their leisure activities before their workday or other daily activities begin. This time block, perhaps 5:00 A.M. to 8:00 A.M., is used by leisure customers at leisure facilities or in their own home.

7. *Noon Hour*—People who have busy schedules often choose this time to engage in leisure activities. Though it may not be a lengthy period of time, it is a busy time block at many different leisure facilities.

8. *Evening Dinner Hour*—This time period of leisure activity participation can be inserted between late afternoon and early evening. It encompasses the time between 5:00 P.M. and 7:00 P.M., and may be included in the customer's personal schedule between daytime and evening commitments and activities.

Societal changes continue to have an influence on the way in which leisure programs are scheduled and on the times that leisure facilities are available to customers. Some work schedules may require longer workdays, but fewer workdays per week. Further, some places of employment may have employee work schedules that differ from week to week. Other places of employment may shut down at the same time each year, and all employees are given the same vacation time period. With such flexibility in work schedules, leisure service organizations must build flexibility into program scheduling to serve leisure customers. Concentrating leisure activities into shorter periods of time (e.g., scheduling a workshop over a three-day weekend instead of on three consecutive Saturdays may be more attractive to the leisure customer).

The availability and usability of a specific facility also influences the scheduling of particular programs and services for leisure customers. Figure 7.9 is an example of the way in which the four primary physical activity areas in a YWCA are scheduled. Program planners may also wish to group activities so that customers can be involved in more than one program during the time they are at the facility. For example, by following the schedule in Figure 7.8, an individual could participate in four activities on Thursday morning. The customer could work out in the gym beginning at 7:30 A.M., use the body shop at 8:00 A.M., participate in lap swim at 8:45 A.M., and enjoy the whirlpool at 9:30 A.M. Figure 7.9 is a schedule for A Day in the Park sponsored by the Champaign (Illinois) Park District. In this pro-

BUILDING SCHEDULE
March 27 – June 4

WA = Water Aerobics
LS = Lap Swim
OP = Open Plunge
MAX = Modified Aquatic Exercise
AE = Arthritic Exercise

FP = Family Plunge
LS/OP = Lap Swim, Open Plunge
(Lap swimmers must yield to plunge participants)
S55 = Swimnastics 55

SS = Senior Swim
OG = Open Gym
BS = Body Sculpting
CWT = Circuit Weight Training
SWT = Senior Weight Training

	POOL	WHIRLPOOL	GYMNASIUM	BODY SHOP
MONDAY	6:30 a.m. – 8:00 a.m. LS 8:00 a.m. – 8:45 a.m. WA 8:45 a.m. – 9:30 a.m. LS 9:30 a.m. – 10:15 a.m. OP 10:15 a.m. – 11:00 a.m. MAX 11:00 a.m. – 11:45 a.m. WA 11:45 a.m. – 1:00 p.m. LS 2:00 p.m. – 2:45 p.m. AE 4:45 p.m. – 5:30 p.m. WA 6:15 p.m. – 7:00 p.m. WA	6:30 a.m. – 8:00 a.m. 8:45 a.m. – 10:15 a.m. 11:45 a.m. – 1:00 p.m. 5:30 p.m. – 6:15 p.m.	7:30 a.m. – 9:00 a.m. OG/Adult 11:30 a.m. – 1:30 p.m. OG/Adult members only 1:30 p.m. – 5:00 p.m. OG/Adult/Youth 6:30 p.m. – 8:30 p.m. TKD	6:30 a.m. – 10:00 a.m. Open 10:15 a.m. – 11:00 a.m. BS 10:45 a.m. – 4:45 p.m. Open 4:45 p.m. – 5:30 p.m. 5:45 p.m. – 6:30 p.m. CWT 6:30 p.m. – 8:45 p.m. Open
TUESDAY	6:30 a.m. – 7:15 a.m. WA 7:15 a.m. – 8:00 a.m. OP/LS 8:00 a.m. – 8:45 a.m. WA 8:45 a.m. – 9:30 a.m. LS 9:30 a.m. – 10:15 a.m. OP 11:00 a.m. – 11:45 a.m. WA 11:45 a.m. – 1:00 p.m. LS 1:00 p.m. – 1:45 p.m. SS 3:00 p.m. – 4:00 p.m. LS 4:45 p.m. – 5:30 p.m. WA 6:15 p.m. – 7:15 p.m. WA	7:15 a.m. – 8:00 a.m. 8:45 a.m. – 10:15 a.m. 11:45 a.m. – 1:00 p.m. 3:00 p.m. – 4:00 p.m. 7:00 p.m. – 8:45 p.m.	6:30 a.m. – 9:30 a.m. OG/Adult 11:30 a.m. – 1:00 p.m. OG/Adult members only 1:30 p.m. – 3:00 p.m. OG/Adult 3:00 p.m. – 4:30 p.m. OG/Youth 7:00 p.m. – 8:30 p.m. TKD	6:30 a.m. – 10:30 a.m. Open 10:30 a.m. – 11:15 a.m. SWT 11:15 a.m. – 5:30 p.m. Open 5:30 p.m. – 6:30 p.m. CWT 6:30 p.m. – 8:45 p.m. Open
WEDNESDAY	6:30 a.m. – 8:00 a.m. LS 8:00 a.m. – 8:45 a.m. WA 8:45 a.m. – 9:30 a.m. LS 9:30 a.m. – 10:15 a.m. OP 10:15 a.m. – 11:00 a.m. MAX 11:00 a.m. – 11:45 a.m. WA 11:45 a.m. – 1:00 p.m. LS 1:00 p.m. – 1:45 p.m. S55 2:00 p.m. – 2:45 p.m. AE 4:45 p.m. – 5:30 p.m. WA 5:30 p.m. – 6:15 p.m. OP 6:15 p.m. – 7:00 p.m. WA	6:30 a.m. – 8:00 a.m. 8:45 a.m. – 10:15 a.m. 11:45 a.m. – 1:00 p.m. 5:30 p.m. – 6:15 p.m.	7:30 a.m. – 9:00 a.m. OG/Adult 11:30 a.m. – 1:30 p.m. OG/Adult members only 1:30 p.m. – 3:00 p.m. OG/Adult 3:00 p.m. – 5:00 p.m. Adult Basketball 6:30 p.m. – 8:30 p.m. TKD	6:30 a.m. – 10:00 a.m. Open 10:15 a.m. – 11:00 a.m. BS 10:45 a.m. – 4:45 p.m. Open 4:45 p.m. – 5:30 p.m. CWT 6:30 p.m. – 8:45 p.m. Open
THURSDAY	6:30 a.m. – 7:15 a.m. WA 7:15 a.m. – 8:00 a.m. OP/LS 8:00 a.m. – 8:45 a.m. WA 8:45 a.m. – 9:30 a.m. LS 9:30 a.m. – 10:15 a.m. OP 11:00 a.m. – 11:45 a.m. WA 11:45 a.m. – 1:00 p.m. LS 1:00 p.m. – 1:45 p.m. S55 3:00 p.m. – 4:00 p.m. LS 4:45 p.m. – 5:30 p.m. WA 6:15 p.m. – 7:00 p.m. WA 7:00 p.m. – 8:45 p.m. OP	7:15 a.m. – 8:00 a.m. 8:45 a.m. – 10:15 a.m. 11:45 a.m. – 1:00 p.m. 3:00 p.m. – 4:00 p.m. 7:00 p.m. – 8:45 p.m.	6:30 a.m. – 9:30 a.m. OG/Adult 11:30 a.m. – 1:30 p.m. OG/Adult members only 1:30 p.m. – 3:00 p.m. OG/Adult 7:00 p.m. – 8:00 p.m. TKD	6:30 a.m. – 10:30 a.m. Open 10:30 a.m. – 11:15 a.m. SWT 11:15 a.m. – 5:30 p.m. Open 5:30 p.m. – 6:30 p.m. CWT 6:30 p.m. – 8:45 p.m. Open
		Special events sometimes cancel scheduled open gym and plunge times. Please watch the building for posted signs about schedule changes.		
FRIDAY	6:30 a.m. – 8:00 a.m. LS 8:00 a.m. – 8:45 a.m. WA 8:45 a.m. – 9:30 a.m. LS 9:30 a.m. – 10:15 a.m. OP 10:15 a.m. – 11:00 a.m. MAX 11:00 a.m. – 11:45 a.m. WA 11:45 a.m. – 1:00 p.m. LS 1:30 p.m. – 2:15 p.m. AE 4:45 p.m. – 5:30 p.m. WA 5:30 p.m. – 6:30 p.m. LS 6:30 p.m. – 8:45 p.m. FP	6:30 a.m. – 8:00 a.m. 8:45 a.m. – 10:15 a.m. 11:45 a.m. – 1:00 p.m. 5:30 p.m. – 8:45 p.m.	7:30 a.m. – 9:00 a.m. OG/Adult 11:30 a.m. – 1:30 p.m. OG/Adult members only 1:30 p.m. – 3:00 p.m. OG/Adult 3:00 p.m. – 5:00 p.m. OG/Youth 6:00 p.m. – 8:45 p.m. Volleyball	6:30 a.m. – 10:00 a.m. Open 10:15 a.m. – 11:00 a.m. BS 10:45 a.m. – 4:45 p.m. Open 4:45 p.m. – 5:30 p.m. 5:45 p.m. – 6:30 p.m. CWT 6:30 p.m. – 8:45 p.m. Open
SAT.	8:00 a.m. – 8:45 a.m. WA 12:30 p.m. – 1:30 p.m. LS 1:30 p.m. – 3:00 p.m. FP	12:30 p.m. – 3:00 p.m.	12:30 p.m. – 3:00 p.m.	8:00 a.m. – 3:00 p.m. Open
		Gym and pool rentals are available.		

Figure 7.8   Building Schedule, YWCA of Black Hawk County, Waterloo, Iowa.

BRING YOUR FAMILY AND JOIN THE FUN AT

A DAY IN THE PARK

Saturday, July 17
7:00 a.m. - 4:00 p.m.
Hessel Park, 500 W. Kirby Ave.

CHILDREN'S ACTIVITIES

Children's Activities:	10:00 - 4:00
Hayrack Rides	
Face Painting	
Olive Garden "Pasta Art"	
Games by Mothers Against Drunk Driving	
Ambucs Games	
PuttPutt Golf ®	
Petting Zoo	
Camel Rides ($2)	
Moon Bouncer ($1)	
Dunk Tank ($.50/3 balls)	
"Say It Big" Clown	12:00 - 2:30

ENTERTAINMENT

Flashback	11:00 - 12:00
Keith Page Magic Show	12:00 - 12:30
Gator Alley	12:30 - 1:30
Keith Harden (solo)	1:30 - 2:15
Red Letter Day	2:30 - 3:30
Boneyard Creek Cloggers	3:30 - 4:00

FOOD

Free Pepsi
Popcorn & Sno-Cones (C-U Special Recreation)
Ambucs Hamburgers, Brats, Ice Cream
Olive Garden
Bidwell's, Lemon Shake-ups, Tenderloins, Onion Rings
Carlos O'Kelly's

See reverse side for map.
For further information contact the
Champaign Park District at 398-2550.

OTHER EVENTS

WDWS Live Broadcast	All Day
Gigantic Flea Market & Crafts	7:00 - 4:00
Pancake Breakfast	7:00 - 10:00
Golf Clinic by Dave Huber, Pro	7:30
Hot Air Balloon	8:00 - 10:30
6-on-6 Co-rec Volleyball Tournament	9:00
3-on-3 Basketball Tournament	9:00
Catlin H. S. Pompettes Cake Walk	9:00
Tennis Clinic with Punam Paul, Pro	9:30, 11:00, 1:00
Radio Controlled Car Demo	10:00
Don Branson, Midget Car Racer	10:00 - 2:00
Dog Training Club of C-U Demo	10:00
Champaign Public Library Bookmobile	10:00
Fire Truck (possible spray)	10:00
D.A.R.E. Police Car	10:00
Hyong's Moo Do Academy	11:00 & 2:00
Tae Kwon Do Demonstration	
Central Illinois Aerospace Rocket Club	11:00
Chess Club Challenge	11:30
YMCA/Irish Gymnastics Demo	1:00
Pepsi Hot Shot Contest	1:30
Bubble Gum Blowing Contest	2:00
Water Balloon Toss	2:30
Tug Of War Competition	3:00
Hot Air Balloon Ride Giveaway	3:30
C-U Astronomical Society	
Prairie Paddlers	

Figure 7.9   A Day in the Park, Champaign (Illinois) Park District.

gram, the timing of each event is important, requiring great coordination. The diagram shows all the locations for each of the events, which also requires a high level of planning to ensure that the customers have access to each event within the area.

Another time factor that is a part of our society is the concept of "time deepening." Godbey (1985: 18) indicates that time deepening "has three related aspects: undertaking an activity more quickly, undertaking more than one activity simultaneously, and using time more precisely." An activity undertaken more quickly may be to play racquetball over the noon hour instead of playing in a volleyball league in the evening; watching television while eating or having a business conference on the golf course is involvement in more than one activity at a time; and calling before 8:00 A.M. to schedule the tennis court at 4:40 P.M. illustrates using time more precisely.

Leisure customers must be understood for who they are and for the time segments that are a part of their lifestyles. The common ways in which we group individuals—as older adults, employed people, home managers, college students, children, junior and senior high school students, singles, married couples, single parents, and families—influence how we schedule leisure opportunities for these groups. The leisure programmer must be sensitive not only to the activity interests and needs of these groups of customers but, perhaps more important, to the time availability and restrictions that leisure customer groups have. Figure 7.10 presents a schedule for a community center's swimming pool. Attention is given to meeting the varying needs as well as the varying interests of different age groups.

Facilities

Leisure service facilities, in this context, include both *buildings* and *land areas*. In other words, structures such as recreation centers and swimming pools and areas such as ballfields and golf courses are all included when referring to leisure service facilities. The location, the design, the availability, and the accessibility of any facility is what contributes to its usability for both structured and spontaneous participation in leisure activities. For example, the proximity of facilities to people who wish to use them, the hours of the day and days of the week that they are open, and the convenience of parking personal cars or using public transportation are all factors that make the use of leisure facilities possible for leisure customers. Transportation to leisure programs can be challenging for individuals and groups, especially to outlying areas and facilities. The East Bay Regional Park District in Oakland, California, operates a program known as the Parks Express (see Figure 7.11). This program provides low cost prescheduled transportation for nonprofit groups in conjunction with the local authority. In this way, fewer people are excluded from participating in activities.

Although many facilities in communities are designed and used for leisure services and programs, many other facilities also lend themselves to use for leisure activities. In many communities, school facilities have traditionally been primary leisure service areas. Schools have been built for educational purposes and therefore offer a wide variety of spaces for leisure use. Schools have gymnasiums, swimming pools, locker rooms, athletic areas, tennis courts, arenas, auditoriums, craft areas, meeting rooms, libraries, kitchens, dance studios, theaters, and parking lots, which make them desirable leisure service areas. Further, in many communities, public utility buildings, banks, churches, social and human service organizations, and shopping malls have meeting spaces, auditoriums, and in some cases, gymnasiums and playing courts, which are available to organizations and community groups to use for leisure programs and activities. Commercial recreation facilities in communities, which may include bowling alleys, fitness centers and spas, movie theaters, ballrooms, and restaurants are sometimes available for use by outside groups for leisure service programs.

Community Center Pool Fall Schedule   September 18 – February 4

Monday	Tuesday	Wednesday	Thursday	Friday	Saturday	Sunday
6-9 Lap Swim	Daily Lifeguard Break: 7:30 – 7:35 a.m.					
9:15 – 10:00 Parent-Tot Adult	9:00 – 9:45 Arth. Aquatics	9:15 – 10:00 Parent-Tot Adult	9:00 – 9:45 Arth. Aquatics	9-10 Open Swim	9-9:25 Parent-Tot 9:30-9:55 Pre Sch	
10-11:30 Senior Swim	9:50 – 10:35 Aquasize 10:45 – 11:30 Open Swim	10-11:30 Senior Swim	9:50 – 10:35 Aquasize 10:45 – 11:30 Open Swim	10-11:30 Senior Swim	10:00 – 10:40 Beginner 10:45 – 11:25 Adv. Beginner	
11:30 – 1:00 Lap Swim 11:30 – 1:00					11:30 – 1:30 Lap Swim	
1-2 Maintenance	1-2 Special Pops Open Swim	1-2 Maintenance	1-2 Special Pops Open Swim	1-2 Maintenance	1:30-6:30 Open Swim	
2-3 W.E.B.	2 – 2:30 Maint. 2:30-3 Pre Sch	2-3 W.E.B.	2 – 2:30 Maint. 2:30-3 Pre Sch	2-5 Open Swim		
3-5 Open Swim	3:05 – 3:50 Beg/Adv Beg 3:55-4:55 Int Swim BWS or EWS	3-5 Open Swim	3:05 – 3:50 Beg/Adv Beg 3:55-4:55 Int Swim BWS or EWS		4 - 8 Free Admission	
5-6:30 Lap Swim 5-6:30						
6:30 – 8 Swim Team	6:30 – 7:15 Beg/Adult/A.Beg. 7:15 – 8:00 W.Aerobics/Int	6:30 – 8 Kayak	6:30 – 7:15 Beg/Adult/A.Beg. 7:15 – 8:00 W.Aerobics/Int	6:30 – 8 Swim Team	6:30 – 8 Lap Swim	
8-9 Masters 9-10 Open Swim	8-10 Scuba or Water Safety	8-9 Masters 9-10 Open Swim	8-10 Scuba or Water Safety	8-9 Masters	**Look for revised Schedule During the Holidays (Fall Break, Thanksgiving, Christmas) **Pool Closes at 5:00 pm on Friday 9/22/89	

Figure 7.10 Community Center Pool Schedule.

The kinds of facilities and areas that a leisure service organization has available for use will obviously determine what kinds of programs and activities the organization can provide for its customers. For example, the list of areas and facilities in Figure 7.12 identifies the resources available to the customers served by the Chapel Hill (North Carolina) Parks and Recreation Commission. Obviously, to have aquatic activities in a community, some kind of aquatic facility needs to be available in proximity to the potential customers. This is an example of a specialized facility required for specific programming. On the other hand, many activities could take

place in a variety of spaces with some adaptability. The ideal place for tennis to be played is on a court designed for that purpose. However, tennis can be played on a grass surface, on hard surface areas such as a parking lot or a gymnasium floor, and when space is short, on the roof of a building that has been prepared for that purpose and that has a fence high enough to keep both the balls and the players on the roof.

The design and maintenance of any facility contribute greatly to the usability of that facility. Leisure service programmers may not have had the opportunity to be involved in the design of an existing facility. In other words, some leisure

PARKS EXPRESS

Sponsored by East Bay Regional Park District.

Figure 7.11 Parks Express, East Bay Regional Park District, Oakland, California.

service facilities may have originally been designed and built for a purpose other than their present use. Some school buildings are renovated to become recreation centers. Sometimes stores or other places of business have

been converted to senior citizen centers. Creative imagination and good judgment are attributes that a programmer must have to make maximum use of any facility that is available. Cleanliness, good lighting, comfortable temperatures, use of attractive colors on walls, ceilings, and window covers, appropriate floor surfaces, and monitoring and prevention of vandalism contribute to respect for property by the customers and the desire to use the facility.

The question may be asked, Is a leisure facility a leisure program? A facility is not a program per se, but all leisure activities must have some kind of facility. On the other hand, unless a leisure facility is put to its best and highest use with good programming, the facility is of little value. Therefore, the need for a facility in order to create a program and the need for a program in order to make use of a facility make these two factors crucial in program development and delivery.

Figure 7.13 presents a parks guide from the city of Olympia (Washington) Department of Parks, Recreation, and Cultural Services. This document lists various facilities available, including picnic spaces, picnic tables, nature trails, playgrounds, basketball courts, tennis courts, athletic fields, running tracks, public art areas, wading pools, rest rooms, and horseshoe pits.

Setting

Closely related to the factor of areas and facilities for leisure programming is the setting in which the activity will take place. Whereas areas and facilities may refer to the physical structure of buildings, sports fields, and parks, the setting encompasses the physical and social environment within these facilities. As was mentioned earlier, the design and maintenance of any facility contribute to its usability and the environment that it creates. Outdoor maintenance of a building is as important as the maintenance that is necessary to set aside a special area for that activity only. On the other hand, many kinds of physical activities can take place in a gym, high ceiling or not. Games and relays,

Town of Chapel Hill
Recreational Areas & Facilities

	Lighted Tennis Courts	Picnic Area	Athletic Fields	Basketball Goals	Play Equipment	Nature Trails	Fitness Trails	Recreation Center	Swimming Pool	Free Play Open Space	Volleyball Courts
1. Hargraves Park	3	•	•	•	•			•	•	•	P
2. Umstead Park	*1	•	•	•	•	•	•	•		•	•
3. Oakwood Park	1	•		P	•					•	
4. Cedar Falls Park	6	•	•	P	•	•	P	P	P	•	P
5. Ephesus Park	6	•	•	•	•	P	P			•	
6. Legion Field			•							•	
7. Phillips Park	4	P									
8. Jones Park		•			•	•					
9. Westwood Park					•						
10. Lincoln Center				•☆					•		
11. Gomains Play Area		•			•						
12. Burlington Play Area		•			•					•	
13. Community Center Park		•		•☆	P				•	•☆	•	•

14. Plant Road Administrative Offices
15. N.C. Botanical Garden
16. Chapel Hill High School
17. Seawell Elementary School
18. Phillips Junior High School
19. Estes Hills Elementary School

20. Ephesus Elementary School
21. Carrboro Elementary School
22. Glenwood Elementary School
23. Frank Porter Graham Elementary School
24. Culbreth Junior High School

P Proposed Facility
☆ Indoor Facility
• Existing Facility
* Not Lighted

200 Plant Road, Chapel Hill, N.C. 27514 • 968-2784

Figure 7.12 Areas and Facilities Guide, Chapel Hill (North Carolina) Parks and Recreation Commission.

exercise programs and running, badminton and tennis, and cheerleading and gymnastics all are "at home" in the gymnasium. Discussion groups, craft classes, lectures, and meetings could also take place in the gym if other spaces are not available, although customers would be better served if these activities were held in meeting rooms or classrooms within a facility. Instead of eliminating a particular leisure activity because the "ideal" space is not available, adapt the activity or adapt a space, or both, and create the most suitable setting in which the activity can take place.

Taking program activities out of traditional settings and carrying them out in new settings can add interest to programming. Moving a theatrical production off the elevated stage in an auditorium and offering it in a "theater-in-the-round" or "theater-in-the-park" setting may attract more and different customers to the program. Moving an after school program for children from an established leisure facility to an elementary school may make the program accessible for more customers because of the proximity of the activities to the children. Using the outdoors for outdoor activities instead of taking

PARKS GUIDE

City of Olympia Parks ●	Picnic	Picnic Tables	Nature Trails	Playgrounds	Basketball	Tennis Courts	Athletic Fields	Running Track	Public Art	Wading Pool	Restrooms	Horseshoe	Acres
1 10th & Decatur (undeveloped)		O		O	O						O		6.14
2 Bigelow	●	●		●	●				O		●		1.89
3 Capitol Lake		●		●	●						●		10
4 Garfield Nature Trail			●										5
5 Governor Stevens			●										6.2
6 Grass Lake (undeveloped)			O										163.5
7 Harry Fain's Legion	●	●		●									2.3
8 Japanese Garden									●				.45
9 L.B.A.	●	●		●	●	●	●	●	●		●		22.15
10 Lions	●	●		●		●		O			●		3.44
11 Madison Scenic													2.36
12 Old Washington (Oly. Schl. Dist)					●		●				●		1
13 Park of the Seven Oars									●				.27
14 Percival Landing		●							●		●		1.85
15 Priest Point	●	●	●	●	●					●	●		282
16 Stevens Field	●	●				●	●	●			●		5.5
17 Sunrise		●		●	O						O		6.5
18 Watershed			●										171
19 Woodruff		●			●	●					●		2.46
20 Yauger	●	●	●	●			●	●			●	●	40.5
21 East Bay (undeveloped)													1
State Park Land ▲													
1 Capitol Campus									▲				20
2 Interpretive Park			▲								▲		17
3 Marathon Park	▲	▲									▲		2.1
4 Sylvester									▲				1.5

O Planned/In Progress

Information subject to change without notice

Figure 7.13   Parks Guide, City of Olympia (Washington) Parks and Recreation Department.

them indoors, offering programs in locations closer to the customers, and adapting both the setting and the activity, as suggested in the previous paragraph, will enable the leisure service organization to demonstrate more flexibility and variety in programming.

Social environments are more important to leisure experiences than the physical settings in which they take place. Although the physical setting contributes significantly to the social environment, the human factor is the primary element in the leisure experience. The individual customer, the leisure service provider, the other individuals in the same leisure activity, and all other customers within the same facility have an influence on the outcome of the leisure experience. The leisure professional must consider many elements in the planning process.

Depending on the leisure activity being planned, the planner must decide who will be included in the program. If the program is for children, will it always be for both girls and boys, or is it appropriate to offer a program just for girls or just for boys? Another necessary consideration is to be aware of what groups of customers may be using a facility at the same time. When there is open swimming at a pool, should all age groups be in the water at the same time? Maybe all customers would be better served with designated times in the scheduling for young children only, families only, or teens and young adults only.

Individual customers have individual preferences about the social environments in which they choose to participate. How groups are structured, how many people are in the group, how much individual attention a customer may prefer or wish to avoid, and how many and what kind of customers may be at a facility at the same time are factors that influence the participation choices that people make. The leisure programmer must be conscious of the "mixture" of both program activities and kinds of customers that are in a facility at the same time. Although leisure activities are broad in scope and many facilities are designed for multiple use and leisure experiences, the settings in which leisure

programs take place must be selected with appropriate planning and good judgment.

The interaction between the leisure service providers and the customers in any setting is important to the social environment that is created. The leisure programmer, the activity leader, the custodian, the office manager, the locker room attendant, the organization executive director, and other organization staff all contribute to providing services to the customers. How each of these individuals interacts with (or ignores) the customer contributes to the quality of the leisure experience for that customer. Congeniality, concern, accessibility, providing service, and caring about individual customers establish the social environment in a leisure service organization.

Equipment and Supplies

In addition to facilities and settings, it is necessary to have equipment and supplies to implement leisure program activities. Equipment is generally thought of as those items that are permanent and reusable, while supplies are materials that are consumed during activities and cannot be reused. In other words, equipment can range from basketball backboards to tennis rackets, from scissors and easels to record players and VCRs, from coffee pots and clip boards to tables and chairs. Supplies are those items needed each time a particular activity is carried out, such as craft materials, chalk for athletic fields, chemicals for swimming pools, award ribbons and trophies, and all other materials that are depleted at the end of the activity.

Attainment of equipment and supplies by leisure service organizations is primarily accomplished in three ways: wholesale or retail purchase, having customers supply the materials for themselves, or scrounging to acquire items at little or no cost from a variety of sources. Some organizations may use only one of these methods while others may use all three. The cost of the necessary equipment and supplies, the availability of the materials, the ages of the customers involved, and the philosophy of the organization are all factors that determine the method(s) of acquisition that an organization uses.

Contributing to the availability of equipment for leisure programming is the practice of sharing equipment. This can be accomplished in several ways. In a leisure facility that has similar programming for a variety of groups, it is only practical to use the same equipment. In other words, if there is one volleyball league for men, one league for women, and a coed league, the use of the same nets and standards is logical. Use of the same volleyballs may also be possible, unless the level of competition by one group or the other dictates the use of a different quality ball. Another example of equipment sharing is a situation in which several units within an institution use audio/visual equipment periodically. Rather than supplying each unit with equipment that is seldom used, units could share the A/V equipment through a coordinated sign-out system. A third example of equipment sharing would be new softballs provided for adult softball leagues and then used for children's programming after they have been "broken in." Because most leisure service organizations must monitor expenditures and equipment inventory carefully, multiple use of equipment for several programs is necessary.

The equipment and supplies needed for a particular program activity will have an influence on the cost of offering the program. If the activity involves equipment that has been or can be used repeatedly, the cost involved may be less than if supplies must be acquired each time the program is offered. The leisure program planner and the activity leader should have a plan of regular and ongoing maintenance and repair of the program equipment. In addition, there should be a structured system to monitor the inventory of supplies that the leisure service organization has or will need to secure.

Staffing

Staffing is the process of securing the human resources for program delivery. Personnel and staffing decisions are an ongoing activity in all

Figure 7.14 The Three Levels of Leadership.

leisure service organizations. At the same time, staffing decisions must be made in relation to each program that is planned. Several considerations must be kept in mind as activity staffing decisions are resolved. The leisure program planner must determine the level of knowledge, skill, and ability needed by the activity leader and, in some cases, the age of the leader in relation to the customers with whom the leader is working. Although these factors will not be discussed in detail here, they are inherent in the process of selecting staff.

Traditionally, there are three levels of leadership in leisure service delivery (see Figure 7.14): the administrative level, the supervisory level, and the face-to-face level of leadership. The program-planning activities within a leisure service organization primarily involve the supervisory level (programmer) and the face-to-face level (direct activity leader.) On the other hand, the staffing of programs and services is a comprehensive activity within the organization. At whatever level and for whatever purpose staff is being secured, several procedures are involved.

Planning, recruiting, selecting, training, supervising, evaluating, and compensating are all necessary elements in the staffing process (see Figure 7.15). A brief description of these elements follows.

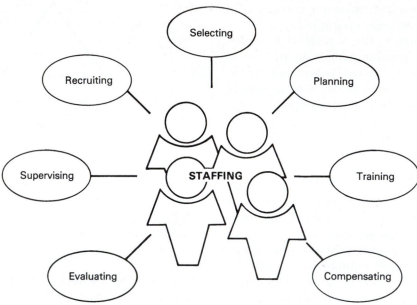

Figure 7.15 Elements of the Staffing Process.

Planning
This involves an analysis of the job, the determination of the tasks and responsibilities of the job, and the qualifications required of the person who fills the position. A job description should be developed that includes information about all of these factors.

Recruiting
Leisure organizations can use both internal and external strategies to find applicants for available positions. A leisure service organization might distribute information to current staff and customers, to community groups, to community organizations, to school and colleges, to job placement departments, and to employment agencies. Leisure service organizations often use local media, such as newspapers, to recruit staff.

Selection
The hiring of staff is generally accomplished through the application and interview process.

Training
Once individuals have been selected for program leadership, it is necessary to orient them to the organization and to train them for the position.

Supervision
Supervision of activity leaders is carried out by the program planner and takes place during the development and implementation phases of the programming.

Evaluation
In this ongoing process, there are two types of evaluation: formative and summative. Formative evaluations contribute to the growth and development of the individual staff person. Summative evaluations enable the person to know how well he or she has accomplished job expectations.

Compensation
Compensation for work comes in many forms, including monetary compensation, individual

acknowledgement, public recognition, or even internal satisfaction.

In many leisure service organizations, the program activity staff is composed of part-time and seasonal employees, both paid and voluntary. As indicated earlier in the content section, leisure service professionals in the supervisory/programmer role are often not the direct activity providers. However, we recognize that in many organizations the program planner also functions as the direct program provider. Also, it is necessary to recognize that some leisure service organizations pay all the personnel within the organization; other organizations have a combination of paid and voluntary personnel; in some, professional paid staff supervise volunteers or volunteer leadership supervises paid professional staff and activity providers.

Cost

Determination of the cost of leisure program activities is based on both the program's expenditures and its potential for income. Program expenditures include staff salaries and wages, equipment and supplies, facility or physical space maintenance, promotion, and all other overhead costs that must be accounted for such as postage, facility rent, and so on. On the other hand, program income may come from several sources. These include the organization's general budget, customer fees and charges, purchase of equipment and supplies from the organization by the customer, and special contributions from other sources.

Both the expenditures and income for leisure program activities are influenced by several factors. Area of programming, program format, setting, facility needed, equipment and supplies necessary, the level of specialization and expertise required of the activity leader, the age of the customer, and the customer's ability to pay all influence program cost. In addition, the philosophy and practice of the organization in relation to funding has an impact on program cost. The organization may have a "pay as you go" system, a membership fee with additional program fees, a membership or service fee that includes all program participation costs, or the outright purchase of programs and services by the customer; the extent to which program cost is affected will depend on which system is used.

Chapter 11 provides much greater detail about program cost and securing equipment and supplies, and provides a discussion about determination of wages and salaries for program staff.

Promotion

Promotion is the communication of the leisure service organization with the leisure customer. Communication involves a communicator (the leisure service organization), a message (information about programs and services), channels of distribution (advertising, publicity, personal selling, public relations, and sales promotion), and an audience (the target group) that the organization wants to receive the message. Chapter 10 discusses promotion in great depth, but promotion is included here as an important element in the program development process.

All elements of the program development phase are crucial to providing program activities. However, the most dynamic planning and innovative programming will go for naught without detailed planning and implementation of promotion. Although the development of promotion may be built into the program development timeline, it may also be necessary to develop a timeline for the program promotion element itself. To develop promotion, leisure programmers must avail themselves of expertise that may exist within the leisure service organization as a whole or within the institution of which leisure services may be a part. It is also necessary for leisure service programmers to become familiar with persons and resources in the general community that will facilitate the promotion process.

The program planner must become involved in determining for what audiences particular promotional materials need to be developed. Channels and tools to distribute the information must be selected. As stated earlier, a timeline for the promotion process should be set and adhered to. As in many of the phases of the program development process, several persons may be involved in the promotion process, and therefore, adequate time to complete tasks must be anticipated and designed into the planning.

Activity Analysis

Activity analysis is the procedure of breaking down and examining the inherent characteristics of an activity. This process provides the means by which the leisure programmer and the leisure customer can determine whether the customer is capable of meeting the requirements necessary to take part in the activity safely and effectively. In addition, activity analysis shows whether the activity contributes to meeting goals and objectives for the customer.

When an individual is involved in an activity, behavior occurs in three domains—psychomotor (physical/action), cognitive (intellectual/thinking), and affective (emotional/feeling). In other words, activities require the customer to use muscular or motor skills to perform an action or carry out a task; to demonstrate understanding, recall, and problem solving to accomplish an expectation; and to display feelings that reflect character.

The nature of each specific activity may emphasize one performance domain more than the other two. However, each domain of behavior is present to some degree in all activities. When a person is involved in swimming, the psychomotor domain is most obvious, but at the same time the individual must cognitively make appropriate judgments about safe behavior in the water and may affectively show satisfaction with improvement in a swimming skill. In another example, passive participation at a symphony emphasizes the affective domain of enjoyment, while some knowledge of the music or musical instruments contributes to the experience, and the physical action is getting to the concert.

Another area of behavior that is considered in activity analysis is the amount of social interaction or social skills needed to participate.

Avedon (1974) described social interaction patterns, including:

1. *Intraindividual*—Action taking place within the mind of a person, or action involving the mind and part of the body, but requiring no contact with another person or object. Examples of this social behavior might be daydreaming or twiddling one's thumbs.
2. *Extraindividual*—Action directed by the individual toward an object in the environment, and requiring no contact with another person. Walking, reading, or playing solitaire are examples of this action.
3. *Aggregate*—Action directed by the person toward an object in the environment while in the company of other persons, but no contact or interaction with the other persons is necessary. This behavior is exemplified by playing bingo, attending a movie, or painting a canvas.
4. *Interindividual*—Action of a competitive nature directed by two persons toward each other. This action includes playing badminton or board games.
5. *Unilateral*—Action of a competitive nature among three or more people, with one person being the antagonist or "it." A variety of games and activities with an "it" are examples of this social interaction.
6. *Multilateral*—Action of a competitive nature among a group of three or more persons, with no individual as the antagonist. This action includes card games or board games.
7. *Intragroup*—Action of a cooperative nature by two or more persons attempting to reach a mutual goal. Music groups and drama groups are examples of cooperative action.
8. *Intergroup*—Action of a competitive nature between two or more intragroups. Competitive team sports activities are intergroup actions. (Source: Data from E. M. Avedon, *Therapeutic Recreation Service: An Applied Behavioral Science Approach*, 1974, Allyn and Bacon, Inc., Needham Hts., MA.)

Farrell and Lundegren (1983: 72) note that in addition to the behavioral domains and patterns of social interaction, the comprehensive activity analysis model also examines the level of leadership necessary, the equipment that is required, the duration of time for the activity, the facilities needed, the number of participants involved, and the age of the participants. The function of activity analysis is to provide the information needed to match the needs of the individual with the types of activities that will contribute to the successful accomplishment of goals and objectives. In so doing, activity analysis provides an accountable manner in which to provide activities. It seems ridiculous, but too often activities are offered with no consideration of their consequences. Activity analysis is based on preplanning to ensure that appropriate activities are provided to the customers.

Risk Management

Risk management in program development is the anticipation of situations, not problems, and the exercise of reasonable care and judgment as a precaution to reduce or eliminate hazards and risks. Risk management is not limited to individual program planning within a leisure service organization; the management of risk is a comprehensive management tool in the total operation of the organization. It is applicable to total program development and individual program development at the same time.

Nilson and Edginton (1982: 35) have said, "The basic goal of a risk management program is to identify and evaluate risks with an eye toward reducing or eliminating the agency's financial loss." The sources of risk within a leisure service organization, according to Nilson and Edginton, include contracts, programs, facilities, participants, employees, and equipment. Though finances are not listed as a source of risk, losses in any of the areas listed ultimately lead to a financial loss of some (sometimes severe) magnitude. Financial loss will occur whenever there is deterioration or destruction (vandalism) of property and equipment; negligence or dishonesty by staff; injury or the loss of life to customers; and catastrophic events, such as natural disasters or accidental occurrences such as fires.

Risk management in program development is needed to protect the leisure service organization, the organization's staff, and the customers that are served by the organization. According to Kraus and Curtis (1990), to minimize the risk of lawsuits common in society today, a leisure service organization must have a well-organized plan for risk management and accident prevention. The organization must be responsible for adequately maintained facilities and equipment at all times. There must be a specific plan for the routine monitoring and maintenance of all physical facilities and areas and all equipment. Organization staff must provide appropriate accident prevention supervision for all services, programs, and activities. As a part of supervision practices, there must be a planned follow-up procedure when problems do arise. In addition, leisure customers need to be protected from their own ignorance in the use of leisure areas, facilities, and equipment. The leisure service organization must use more sophisticated approaches to educating the public in regard to environmental values and criminal acts.

Figure 7.16 illustrates the process of risk management. Kaiser (1986) has indicated that for risks to be managed, they must be identified, evaluated, and treated (selected), and a management plan must be developed. Nilson and Edginton (1982) include a fifth step in the risk management process: the ongoing review and evaluation of the whole process itself. Kaiser focuses on risk treatment, which he also refers to as risk selection. According to Kaiser, choosing the "method for risk treatment is based on the frequency of the occurrence and severity of loss" (p. 232).

Risk treatment methods are risk avoidance, risk reduction, risk retention, and risk transfer. *Risk avoidance* is the possible elimination or cancellation of a leisure program or activity, or the closure of a facility by the leisure service organization. Making the decision of risk avoidance weighs the advantages of the activity or facility against possible undesirable results. *Risk reduction*

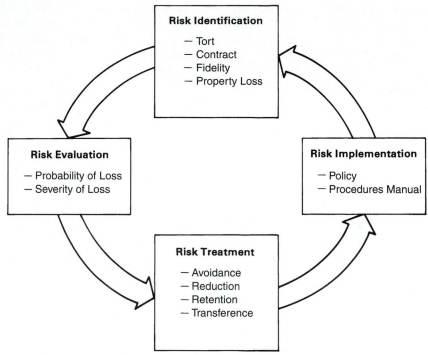

Figure 7.16 Risk Management Process. (Kaiser 1986: 229.)

attempts to lower the chance that a loss will occur and to reduce the severity if a loss does occur. It may be possible to reduce risk by developing safety rules for operation of facilities and equipment, conducting periodic safety inspections of facilities and equipment, aggressively using preventive maintenance, training staff in safety procedures, and developing emergency procedures (Kaiser, 1986). These items are discussed in greater detail later in this section.

Risk retention means that the leisure service organization assumes a level of loss. Risk retention can be either passive or active. Passive retention means that the organization is not aware of the risk and therefore does not attempt to manage it. Active risk management occurs after the risk has been identified and the leisure service organization has decided how to manage it. Kaiser (1986) indicates that risk retention, when coupled with loss prevention and an insurance program, has the greatest potential for the

leisure service organization. *Risk transfer* is shifting the risk to another party. This generally occurs when the risk may be of high frequency or carries the potential of high financial loss. Risk transfer may be instigated by shifting the facility or program to another source or by transferring the risk of loss to another party, as in the case of insurance coverage.

A systematic plan with control procedures is mandatory to carrying out risk management practices. Listed earlier were guidelines to reducing risk. Kraus and Curtis (1990) have considered these factors in some detail (From R. G. Kraus and J. E. Curtis, *Creative Management in Recreation, Parks and Leisure Services,* 4th edition. Copyright © 1990 Times Mirror/Mosby College Publishing. Reprinted by permission):

1. *Systematic Reporting and Record Keeping*—Reports and records are a means of monitoring trends and trouble spots within the leisure service

organization. Systematic record keeping may also give an indication of where improvements in problem situations are occurring. Although reporting and record keeping is an orderly processing of information, there still are the possibilities of the unusual and unanticipated incidents occurring.

2. *Facilities Inspection and Hazard Abatement*—Inspection and hazard abatement is peculiar to each situation and setting in which it should be carried out. For example, on the playgrounds, all equipment must be inspected to ascertain that it is in proper working order and that all parts of the equipment are maintained and replaced when necessary. In leisure facilities, on the other hand, walks, steps, floor surfaces, lighting, storage spaces, exits, and so on must all be inspected and managed to reduce hazards.

3. *Participant Safety Briefing and Preparation*—The leisure service organization must exercise the responsibility of informing customers and helping them understand the inherent risks involved in inappropriate behavior and incorrect use of leisure areas, facilities, and equipment.

4. *Staff Training and Goal Setting*—Risk management can be effective only when all staff members are aware of it and are committed to maintaining a safe environment and program. Staff orientation and training provide an introduction to risk management, but a focus on risk management must be continued at staff meetings, during personnel evaluation, and in other management procedures. Staff should be involved in setting risk management goals and objectives and in reporting and recording information to protect both the leisure customer and leisure service personnel. It should be noted that leisure service providers may be at higher risk for injury because they become involved in emergency and lifesaving situations and procedures.

5. *Emergency Procedures*—Specific procedures for first aid, accidents, and other emergencies should be precisely laid out for all staff in a leisure service organization. Because leisure service providers function in such a variety of places and situations—from mountainsides to swimming pools and sports arenas, from health care facilities to bowling alleys—procedures for action must be clearly defined and understood.

Emergency procedures should be regularly practiced at leisure areas and facilities; appropriate public relations procedures should be exercised in emergency situations; and necessary first-aid supplies and transportation arrangements should be available in all settings.

The reasonable approach in risk management suggests that leisure service providers should not dwell on all the negative possibilities that could happen, but should exercise appropriate planning for the probabilities that exist for hazards and problems. Kozlowski (1988: 58–59) advises that "the most important element under the reasonableness standard is the concept of foreseeability . . . address the foreseeable hazards, rather than worrying about every conceivable mishap." Alleviating the hazard is common sense. In order to create safe leisure environments, the Oak Lawn (Illinois) Park District, in cooperation with neighborhood park advisory committees and the Oak Lawn Police Department, has created a neighborhood park watch program known as Eagle Eye (see Figure 7.17). The program is directed toward ensuring that incidents of vandalism, unruliness, and other wrongful acts are reported. Eagle Eye watchers who report incidents remain anonymous. The program encourages individuals to participate in such a way as to have control of activities taking place in their own neighborhoods.

Special Considerations

We have identified diversity and inclusiveness as important strategies to be sought in the organization of leisure programs. As indicated in Chapter 1, the Americans With Disability Act (ADA) prohibits discrimination on the basis of disability and applies to the provision of leisure service. Public Law 336 of the 101st Congress, enacted July 26, 1990, prohibits discrimination and ensures equal opportunity for persons with disabilities in employment, state and local government services, public accommodations,

Figure 7.17 Eagle Eye Neighborhood Park Watch Program, Oak Lawn (Illinois) Park District.

commercial facilities, and transportation. Leisure programs cannot discriminate on the basis of disability. An excellent example of an organization dedicated to assisting individuals with disabilities to participate in leisure programs is that of the West DuPage (Illinois) Special Recreation Association. Exhibit 7.1 provides an overview of the work and philosophy of this organization. Its many and varied program offerings serve preschool children through senior adults.

BUILDING A FRAMEWORK FOR SERVICE DELIVERY

An important element in planning for the delivery of leisure programs is to establish a framework for service delivery. Highly successful leisure service organizations are those that have a strong vision that is clearly developed and understood by all stakeholders. Leisure organizations that keep a strong focus on service and quality will outperform those that are focused elsewhere. Quality services occur because the organization's framework includes a well-conceived strategy that focuses on the customer. Such a framework also demands that frontline staff is customer oriented and that the organization has a system in place that is designed for the convenience of the customer and not its employees.

Designing a framework for service delivery requires an understanding of environmental factors that influence an individual's leisure preferences and needs. This often involves a close monitoring of the social, economic, political, and cultural environment. It also requires a keen understanding of key community values and aspirations. Not only does a leisure service programmer need to understand what results are to be achieved but, more importantly, what expectations people hold for the quality, quantity, and value of services to be provided. It also often requires leisure programmers to think "out of the box." It may require future forecasting and the development of a strategy that enables resources to be deployed in collaborative ways.

EXHIBIT 7.1   Inclusive Programs Through WDSRA

Western DuPage Special Recreation Association (WDSRA) serves more than 6,000 people of all ages with and without disabilities in over 1,000 annual recreation programs, special events, and trips. The nationally acclaimed, not-for-profit organization is a cooperative extension of the Bloomingdale, Carol Stream, Glen Ellyn, Naperville, Roselle, Warrenville, West Chicago, Wheaton, and Winfield Park Districts.

WDSRA complies with the American With Disabilities Act (ADA), which prohibits discrimination on the basis of a disability. WDSRA will make reasonable accommodations in recreation programs to enable participation by an individual with a disability who meets essential eligibility requirements. The recreation programs offered by WDSRA will be available in the most integrated setting appropriate for each individual.

WDSRA and its member park districts believe that all individuals should be provided with leisure opportunities that allow for performance at their highest level of ability. We understand that not every person who has a special need desires WDSRA programming. In cooperation with our member districts, WDSRA staff will be happy to assist and advise any resident who is interested in participating in a local park district program.

WSDR will contact the appropriate park district staff and work with the instructor to assure the individual experiences a smooth transition in the inclusion process. All of these services are provided at no cost to the individual.

Source: Summer Programs 2002 (2002). Western DuPage Special Recreation Association. Carol Stream, IL. p. 9

The City of Edmonton (Alberta, Canada) has developed a integrated service strategy for delivering community services including park and recreation activities and programs (see Figure 7.18). The city's report, *Towards 2010—A New Perspective: An Integrated Service Strategy*, presents a service delivery framework. This framework identifies community values to be pursued as well as external and internal drivers of change. The service strategy in turn calls for an integrated organization built on roles that find individuals sharing knowledge, brokering services, sharing funding, coaching others, and acting as stewards. Service themes to be emphasized include placing citizens first, community building, focused efforts, urban wellness, promotion of ribbons of green and blue, and the creation of community places. Key result areas include: (1) community building; (2) citywide support; (3) housing; (4) strategic and business applications; (5) social, recreation, and cultural programs and (6) operation and maintenance of parks and open spaces; park development and preservation; enterprise facilities and community facilities.

Programming to Exceed Expectations

Our focus in this chapter has been to identify all of the various steps in the process of program development. Program development is not necessarily done in a linear fashion; that is, the leisure professional may work on several different tasks simultaneously in order to plan, organize, and implement a leisure program. There are times when the planning of a program unfolds in a linear fashion; or the program planner might be able to plan and organize program development in a step-by-step, sequential manner. However, leisure programmers are often required to engage in multiple tasks simultaneously—they are required to work on parts of the development of a program while keeping in mind the end results they desire.

When developing a program, we have advocated the importance of focusing on the achievement of benefits and the importance of building activities and services around a benefit structure. In doing so, the leisure professional is able to stay focused on the end results desired and, as such, manage toward these desired ends. It is important to note that one has to not only manage toward results-oriented benefits, but must also keep in mind the expectations that individuals have for a given leisure experience. In fact, it may be as important to manage toward expectations as toward results.

Service Delivery Framework

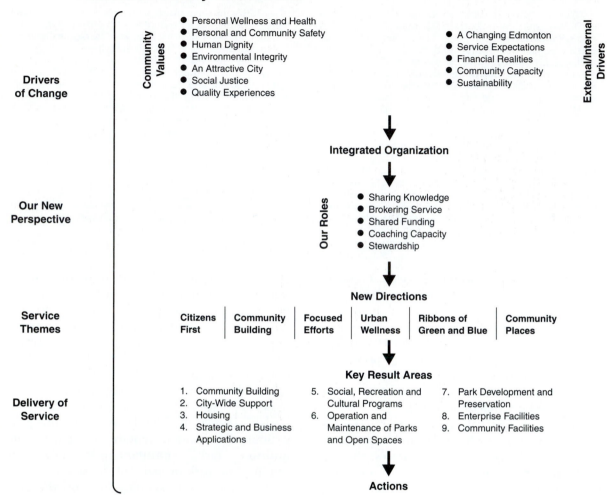

Figure 7.18 A Service Delivery Framework.
(From *Towards 2010—A New Perspective: An Integrated Service Strategy,* City of Edmonton, Alberta (Canada) Community Services, 2000. Reprinted by permission of the City of Edmonton, Alberta, Canada.)

Camp Adventure™ Youth Services, a service-learning program operated from its headquarters at the University of Northern Iowa, has adopted a program philosophy of exceeding expectations. Using a concept known as *Total Quality Program Planning* (see Chapter 12 for a complete description), this organization works to incrementally improve its delivery of services on a day-to-day basis, so as to not only meet, but exceed, customer expectations. Each frontline staff member is challenged to find a way to make the delivery of programs and services better today than it was yesterday. Leisure programmers need to be careful not to inflate expectations and then fail to deliver on their promises.

PROGRAM PLANNING WORKSHEET

This form is to be completed and submitted to your supervisor for each program being done. This is due no less than eight weeks prior to the planned event. You will be held accountable for all dates and responsibilities associated with your program.

Program Name: _____

Program Design

Circle One: Special Event   Trip   Daily Program   Tournament   Other

                      Youth   Adult   Senior

Day/Date of Event _____   Time of Event _____

Minimum # _____   Maximum # _____

Registration/Reservation Deadline _____   Cost _____

Program Description/Special Instructions
_____
_____
_____

Amount of Petty Cash or CAF Request _____

Equipment needed
_____
_____

Program Tasks
Target
Date

_____   ( )   Cost out program

_____   ( )   Phone calls for volunteers, donations and speakers.

_____   ( )   Confirmation letters for volunteers, donations and speakers. (1 month prior)

_____   ( )   CAF or petty cash request (1 month prior)

Figure 7.19   Program Planning Worksheet, Seatack Community Recreation Center, City of Virginia Beach (Virginia) Department of Parks and Recreation.

A number of leisure service organizations provide guidance in the form of checklists or program planning worksheets to assist individuals in the program development process. Figure 7.19 is a program planning worksheet used by the Seatack Community Recreation Center in Virginia Beach (Virginia). Such checklists are useful in providing guidance to ensure that each of the steps in the process of program development are addressed. They also provide a mechanism for supervisory guidance, coaching, and even control (see Exhibit 7.2).

EXHIBIT 7.2   Going the Extra Mile to Help Others

On a recent evening, my social group had rented a city picnic shelter in Ames. On arrival, the group tried to plug in coffeepots only to discover that the electricity was not working.

A call to the city parks office soon brought an employee named Scott. He determined the problem, but it wasn't something that could be fixed immediately.

Scott apologized and promised a refund of the shelter fee. He then left but returned 20 minutes later with coffee for everyone.

We felt that was above and beyond the call of duty.

Source: Keys, E. (2002, October 20). *How* Iowans Went the Extra Mile to Help Others. *Des Moines Register*, p. 1E

Summary

Program development is the integration of identified needs and the program goals and objectives that have been developed. Some specific factors are generic to all program development efforts and applicable to any situation. The program development factors that have been discussed in this chapter include: program area, program format, program content, time factors, facilities, setting, equipment and supplies, staffing, cost, promotion, activity analysis, risk management, and special considerations. The emphasis given to all or to each of these factors is relative to the specific planning situation.

Program areas are the way in which activities are categorized, while program formats are the way in which activities are structured for program delivery. Activities in all areas of programming may be formatted in a variety of ways to make programming more dynamic for the leisure customer. Program content includes goals and objectives and a description of activities that will take place during a specific program, whether it is a one-time event or takes place in several sessions. Time factors in program development are inherent in the whole process. Time-use patterns of leisure customers and availability of facilities and settings influence the outcome of the leisure experience.

The leisure service environment, which includes facilities, settings, equipment and supplies, and staffing, is crucial in program delivery. The availability and accessibility of facilities, the physical and social environment of the setting, and the acquisition of equipment and supplies all contribute to the quality of the program. Staffing is providing the human resources necessary to implement the program. Within the programming process, the leisure programmer will work with activity leaders in implementing many of the leisure program activities. Program costs include both income and disbursements and are influenced by other factors such as staff salaries and wages, supplies and equipment, and so on. Promotion of programs is the way by which the organization communicates with leisure customers. Promotion is the development of information that is delivered to an audience using varied means of distribution.

Risk management in leisure program development is the anticipation of situations and the exercise of reasonable care and judgment to reduce or eliminate risks. Managing risk is facilitated by the leisure service organization that develops a specific risk management plan as a tool of operation within the organization. When programmers organize leisure experiences, they should establish programs that support the special needs of individuals. Creation of barrier-free environments in support of the Americans With Disabilities Act is a preferred strategy.

─────────── *Discussion Questions and Exercises* ───────────

1. List the planning factors included in the development of leisure programs and activities.

2. Discuss the way in which emphasis on particular factors may vary in different programming situations.

3. Explain the domains of behavior and social interaction patterns in the activity analysis procedure. What is the value of activity analysis in program development?

4. What is risk management? How can the management of risk be implemented within the leisure service organization?

5. Discuss the differences between facilities and settings. Explain the relationship between them.

6. (a) Write a timeline for the development of a summer softball league, or (b) develop a timeline for planning a daylong bus trip for older adults.

7. Explain the difference between equipment and supplies in leisure programming. Give several specific examples of each.

8. Take one program activity from a specific program and suggest how it could be offered in four different program formats.

9. What is the difference between the long-term plan and the short-term plan when developing program content?

10. Explain the purpose of promotion. What factors are included in the process of communication?

─────────── *References* ───────────

Avedon, E. M. 1974. *Therapeutic recreation service: An applied behavioral science approach.* Englewood Cliffs, NJ: Prentice Hall.

Farrell, P., and H. M. Lundegren. 1983. *The process of recreation programming: Theory and technique.* 2d ed. New York: John Wiley.

Godbey, G. 1985. *Leisure in your life: An exploration.* 2d ed. State College, PA: Venture Publishing.

Kaiser, R. A. 1986. *Liability and law in recreation, parks, and sports.* Englewood Cliffs, NJ: Prentice Hall.

Kozlowski, J. C. 1988. A commonsense view of liability. *Parks and Recreation,* September, 56–59.

Kraus, R. G., and J. E. Curtis. 1990. *Creative management in recreation, parks, and leisure services.* 4th ed. St. Louis: Times Mirror/Mosby College Publishing.

Nilson, R. A., and C. R. Edginton. 1982. Risk management: A tool for park and recreation administrators. *Parks and Recreation,* August, 34–37.

Rossman, J. R. 1994. *Recreation programming.* 2d ed. Champaign, IL: Sagamore.

Program Areas

LEARNING OBJECTIVES

1. To acquaint the reader with information concerning *program areas, including categorization and classification systems.*
2. To impart to the reader knowledge of *the arts and literary activities* as program areas.
3. To provide the reader with information concerning *aquatics* as a program area.
4. To enable the reader to understand *sports, games, and athletics* as a program area.
5. To offer the reader information about the *outdoor recreation* program area.
6. To provide the reader with a greater awareness of *social recreation* as a program area.
7. To help the reader understand the program area of *self-improvement/education.*
8. To help the reader gain an understanding of *wellness* as a program area.
9. To provide the reader with information concerning *hobbies.*
10. To help the reader understand *travel and tourism* as a program area.
11. To provide information concerning *volunteer activities.*

INTRODUCTION

In this chapter, the categorization and classification of leisure service program activities is the focus of discussion. There are a variety of ways in which leisure service activities may be classified. Activities may be grouped according to the amount and kind of involvement by the customer (i.e., passive or active); within physical, mental, and social contexts (i.e., high risk or low risk, structured or unstructured, planned or self-directed, individual or group); on the basis of the general environment in which the activity takes place (i.e, indoor or outdoor, seasonal—summer, fall, winter, or spring); and on the basis of facility or setting (e.g., courts, courses, fields, recreation centers, studios, parks, camps). Leisure activities may also be classified on the basis of the customer's age, gender, or both.

Another of the methods of classifying activities is based on types of activities. A number of authors have identified activity areas. For example, Russell (1982) has identified activity areas as follows: sports and games, hobbies, music, outdoor recreation, mental and literary recreation, social recreation, arts and crafts, dance, and drama. Farrell and Lundegren (1983) offer the following categories: arts, crafts, dance, drama, environmental activities, music, sports and games, and social recreation. Sessoms (1984) classifies recreation activities as follows: music, dance, dramatics, literary activity, sports and games, nature and outings, social recreation, and arts and crafts. Rossman (1989) has suggested a classification system that includes sports, individual activities, fitness activities, hobbies, art, drama, music, and social recreation. Another classification system is offered by Farrell and Lundegren (1991: 172). They suggest that program areas include: arts, crafts, dance, drama, environmental activities, music, sports and games, social recreation, and volunteerism. More recently, Chase and Chase (1996: 123) have suggested eight program areas including: 1) adventure challenge; 2) community/social/environment; 3) crafts; 4) fitness/health/wellness; 5) hobbies; 6) lifelong learning (fine arts, reading, writing, etc.); 7) outdoor living/outdoor skills/camping; and 8) sports/games.

Another system by which activities can be categorized is based on goal structure. Depending on the goal structure of the individual involved, activities can be classified as competitive, individualistic, or cooperative. Sheffield (1984) has indicated that in the competitive structure, in order for one customer to accomplish his or her goal, other customers must be prevented from accomplishing theirs. In the individualistic goal structure, the customer's successful goal attainment is not related to any other customer's goal attainment—all may accomplish their goals, none may accomplish their goals, or some may accomplish their goals. Cooperative goal structure is a mutually inclusive goal and can be accomplished only when all customers involved accomplish their individual goals (see Table 8.1).

Categorizing activities by partitioning, using statistical procedures like factor analysis, multidimensional scaling, or some other statistical method, is another approach to classification. These typologies often focus on benefits or outcomes, or the reasons that people are motivated to participate in such activities. As MacKay and Crompton (1988) note, terms such as *relaxation, achievement, intimacy, power,* or *socialization* define clusters of activities.

MacKay and Crompton (1988) suggest six typologies to delineate leisure program activities based on *activity characteristics:*

1. *Nature of the Service Act*—examines whether the program is directed at people or things, and whether the act is tangible or intangible.
2. *Type of Program Relationship*—refers to formal relationship with customer, such as membership, and whether the service delivery is continuous or discrete.
3. *Potential for Customization*—illustrates the potential for tailoring programs to meet individual customer needs and whether there is high participant-provider contact or low participant-provider contact.

TABLE 8.1   Examples of Multiple-Option Programming

Activity	Competitive Goal Structure	Individualist Goal Structure	Cooperative Goal Structure
Swimming	Swim meet or water polo league	WSI/Lifesaving course or aquacise	Synchronized swim or water games, water ballet
Aerobics	Best original routine contest	Aerobic Fitness class	Cumulative job or partner aerobics
Cooking	Chili cook-off	Cookbook of "my best" recipes	Clambake or fish fry
Bird-watching	Christmas bird count	"Hunting with a camera" outing	Establishing a bird sanctuary
Needlecraft	Needlecraft show with prizes	Folk art technique class	Commemorative or "city" quilt
Tennis	Challenge ladder	Practice board for solo usage	Tennis marathon
Cycling	BMX racing	Bike care class	May Day bike ride
Orienteering	Orienteering meet	Wilderness survival skills clinic	Partner/team orienteering
Creative writing	Short story contest	Open workshop on creative writing	City history project
Flower arranging	African violet show	Plant care classes	Garden club
Woodworking	Pipe carving contest	Auction "find a treasure" trips	Carve a totem pole
Painting	Juried show	Face painting at art festival	Town hall mural
Social dance	Break dance contest	Aerobic fitness	World record/fund-raising dance-a-thon
Choral group	All-city chorus tryouts	Musicians' hotline program	Community sing-alongs
Basketball	HotShot tournament	Weekend coaching clinic	All touch/no scoring/no standing

From L. Sheffield, Are You Providing Multi-Option .? in *Parks and Recreation,* May 1984, pp. 56–57. National Recreation and Park Association, Arlington, VA.

4. *The Nature of Demand for a Program*—relates both to the supply or capacity to make a program available and the quality of the program that is offered.

5. *Attributes of the Program*—describes the relative importance of people (providers) and facilities to the customers' perceptions of programs.

6. *The Program Beneficiaries*—are often determined by the source of the programs and services—public or private—and by the level of use the customer may expect to receive at various facilities.

These classification systems are designed to facilitate generalizations about leisure activities and programs and to contribute to the development of theory in program development.

For the purposes of discussion in this chapter, the program areas are classified in the following way: the arts, including performing arts (music, dance, drama), visual arts (including crafts), and new arts; literary activities; self-improvement/education; sports, games, and athletics; aquatics; outdoor recreation; wellness activities; hobbies; social recreation; volunteer services; and travel and tourism. A brief description of each of these program areas is presented in Chapter 8. We recognize the interrelatedness of all program areas—for example, music and dance are as much a part of theatrical production as is the dramatic performance of the actor. Often no distinction is made between sports and outdoor recreation. The person who has trained to become skillful in mountain climbing cannot be categorized only within the realm of outdoor recreation activity and not categorized in sports as well.

Chapter 9 presents a discussion of what we call *format of programming*. A program format is the way in which an activity is organized for implementation. Formats of programs include class, competitive, club, drop-in, special event, outreach, interest group, and workshop/conference. Table 9.5 on pages 303–304 is a matrix illustrating the application of program formats to program areas to create program activities.

THE ARTS

Expression of natural culture is highly visible through the arts. Today, the arts are flourishing. In the early 1990s, Naisbett and Aburdene (1990:62) projected that ". . .the arts would replace sports as society's primary leisure activity." However, information from the *Statistical Abstracts of the United States* (2001) clearly shows that although there has been great growth in the arts, participation in selected sports activities far exceeds participation in the former. It is estimated that there were 240 million individuals participating in sport activities compared with 87.6 million individuals participating in art-related activities such as Broadway shows, non-profit theater performances, and opera and symphony orchestra concerts (U.S. Census Bureau, 2001). This does not include attendance at museums, historical sites, and similar institutions. However, growth in the arts is undeniable. Consider the following:

- The number of performing arts companies has steadily increased in the past decade (U.S. Census Bureau, 2001).
- There has been growth in the number of independent writers, artists, and performers (U.S. Census Bureau, 2001).
- Museums, historical sites, and similar institutions continue to grow in terms of the number of employees and estimated expenditures of dollars (U.S. Census Bureau, 2001).

- From the United States and Europe to the Pacific Rim, wherever the affluent information economy has spread, the need to reexamine the meaning of life through the arts has followed (Naisbett & Aburdene, 1990:62).
- More people as a percentage of the population are collecting art today than ever before, even during the Renaissance (Naisbett & Aburdene, 1990:68).
- As the arts become more important in society, individuals, corporations, cities, and towns will increasingly decide their fate under the influence of the images, personalities, and lifestyles of the arts (Naisbett & Aburdene, 1990:78).

It is apparent that the arts are likely to play an increasing role in the lives of North Americans and the work of leisure service professionals.

Art—a term that embraces all the creative disciplines—can be manifested in leisure service activities in a number of ways. Acknowledged divisions within the arts designate more clearly the uniqueness of this program area. Broadly, the performing arts (in which the participant is the mode of artistic expression) include music, dance, drama, literature, poetry, and writing. The visual arts (also called fine arts) include painting, sculpture, architecture, engraving, etching, woodcutting, lithography, printing, and crafts. In the visual arts, it is the product of the artistic expression that is important. The new arts—including photography, television, radio, films or cinema, and recordings—use a technological medium as the form of expression.

The Performing Arts

Music

Throughout history, music has been an integral part of human culture. Like all arts, music is a means of self-expression and communication. Music can be thought of as a form of human expression that involves the arrangement of sound in interesting, beautiful, moving, or pleasing patterns. Music can be produced by voice, by instruments, or by some combination of these.

According to Arnold (1976: 199), "In music the unskilled person can reach the heights of artistry in well-directed chorus singing first-rate music." Music provides the power of expression—the ability to express feelings such as joy, sorrow, and enthusiasm. Music enhances the feelings in experiences and associations familiar to us—such as holidays (Christmas, the Fourth of July) and athletic events. In describing the beauty of music as a value of music, we must recognize it for its own sake, without attaching a personal or social significance to what music is and what it can do.

Numerous other values of music are suggested by Danford and Shirley (1970: 237):

1. It is universally accepted as a highly desirable activity.
2. It can be enjoyed alone or in a group.
3. Music appeals to all ages.
4. Its cost ranges from nothing to whatever a person wishes to pay.
5. It helps to create friendships and a sense of unity.
6. It provides emotional release and relaxation.
7. Of all the arts of communication, music is one of the most expressive.
8. A wide range of skill from the neophyte to the master is possible with a high degree of enjoyment accruing at each level.
9. It brings into the lives of people an element of refreshing beauty.
10. Music contributes to a developing sense of personal adequacy by providing reassuring experiences of success.
11. Music contributes to a person's cultural development.
12. It contributes to the morale of both the individual and the group. (Source: Data from H. Danford and M. Shirley, *Creative Leadership in Recreation*, 2nd edition, 1970, Allyn & Bacon Inc., Needham Hts., MA.)

There are so many kinds of music within our culture that nearly everyone can relate to one form or another: classical, semiclassical, opera, popular, rock, soul, bluegrass, jazz, country, blues, and folk music. Literally thousands of organizations, groups, and individuals are involved in playing, singing, and producing music. The range of instruments and styles of singing are too numerous to be listed here. Instruments range from the homemade drum to the electronic synthesizer—and everything in between. Most instruments—strings, brass, woodwinds, percussion—not only can be used as they were designed, but also can be amplified or be electronic in design.

What about music as a leisure activity? Music has a very important place in all leisure service organization programs. How does music in recreation settings differ from music in other settings? If we choose to define a difference, perhaps music in the leisure setting is less formal. However, this does not preclude emphasis on skill development and the pleasing production of sound. In the leisure program area, "the overall aim is to show how much better and richer life can be through the influence of music rather than to produce polished musicians" (Danford and Shirley, 1970: 236). The better a person understands something, the more he or she will enjoy and appreciate it, and so it is with music. The opportunity to listen, play an instrument, sing, or otherwise have a musical experience will contribute to a person's familiarity with music and increase the level of his or her interest. For example, an individual may find it easy to become involved in an athletic event after having experienced the same physical activity at an earlier time. Similarly, a person who has had a previous musical experience is better able to relate to music.

A taste for music can be cultivated through a gradual experiential approach. Obviously, not all people will like all kinds of music, but a person can better choose what musical sounds are most pleasing to him or her after a broad exposure to various types of music.

Numerous music activities can be offered through leisure service programs. Farrell and Lundegren (1991: 201) suggest that music experiences can be classified in five ways. Table 8.2 presents the five types of music experiences—*appreciation, instrumental, mechanical, vocal,* and *concomitant activities*—and suggests some exam-

TABLE 8.2 Five Types of Music Experiences

Appreciation	Instrumental	Mechanical	Vocal	Concomitant Activities
Attending performances	Orchestra	Electronic synthesizer	Choir Chorus	Composing
Listening to reproductions	Band	Computer-generated music	Soprano	Conducting or directing
Studying music	Strings		Alto	Accompanying vocal areas
Acting as a patron or sponsor to activities	Brass Woodwinds		Tenor Bass	Acting as a librarian Acting as a business manager
	Percussion		Mixed voice ensembles	
	Mixed instrument ensembles			

Source: Adapted from Farrell, P. & Lundegren, H. M. (1991). *The Process of Recreation Programming*. State College: Venture. p. 202.

ples. Leisure experiences in music can be carried out individually or in groups. There can be opportunities for individual lessons as well as performances, in groups or solo.

Summer concerts are a popular leisure activity for many North Americans. The St. Louis (Missouri) County of Department of Parks and Recreation sponsors a full program of music concerts at park locations throughout the summer months (see Figure 8.1). This agency provides a full range of concerts including ones focused on the blues, country music, jazz, folk, swing, and Zydeco. For example, the "Blues on the Mississippi" concert series provides low-cost entertainment throughout the summer on both weekdays and weekends at Jefferson Barracks Park.

Dance

Dance can be thought of as a form of human expression through movement, usually in time with music. Dance is a manifestation of the human need to move. It usually involves movement in rhythm, often with special groups of steps. Dance is associated with the human experience, especially as a ritualistic activity that humans often carry out repeatedly with great feeling. As a ritualistic activity, dance is often associated with acts of celebration or ceremony.

There is often great joyful expression associated with dance. Further, dance provides a way to transmit culture from one generation to the next, as in the teaching of folk dances. It has been used to symbolize the activity of life by all peoples and cultures. Dance can be used to express joy, sorrow, love, war, reverence, and other emotions. Arnold (1976) distinguishes between movement and dance this way:

> Movement is a conscious or unconscious non-verbal communication that comes from the inner being in response to some intrinsic or extrinsic stimulus. Dance is a spontaneous or artistic (constructed) movement or series of movements that is an expressed reaction to an intrinsic or extrinsic stimulus.
>
> The fundamental movements common to man are also the movements that are present in dance. These are jumping, darting, expanding, contracting, turning, running and sliding (Arnold, 1976: 71).

Dance has developed in many ways, but examining dance as a folk expression and as a structured performing art can enable us to understand its evolution. Early dances depicted such happenings as the disappearance of the sun and the rising of the moon, hunt scenes, and

Figure 8.1 Summer Music in the Parks, St.Louis County (Missouri) Department of Parks and Recreation.

ceremonial events. In more recent history, American folk dance was fashioned around the culture of many nationalities and took place at social events such as barn raisings, harvest gatherings, celebrations of statehood, and many more (Arnold, 1976: 73). Folk dances that have been taken from the folk art and advanced to a higher degree of skill and performance have become "performing folk art"—ethnic dances. Participation in this activity took on a new form when scholars, dance masters, and musicians began to structure the performance and teaching of dance. As a result of this structuring, a very scientific study of dance and movement emerged, and dance began to develop as a structured performing art (p. 73).

Dance as a leisure activity has many values for the individual participant. Dance is a physical activity and is sufficiently active and vigorous to contribute to physical fitness. Involvement in dance activity can release tension, develop grace and control of the body, and may lead to body changes—toning and trimming. Dance also offers an opportunity for creativity. Many forms of dance lend themselves to self-expression and interpretation. Dance further offers an opportunity for social interaction. Tillman (1973: 168–69) lists other values of dance as a leisure program activity. He suggests that dance may enable the individual to develop an appreciation for beauty, recognize and understand culture, relax and escape, develop rhythm and coordination, and have an opportunity for a new experience. Table 8.3 lists many different types of dances that can be included in programming.

Drama
Drama reflects, interprets, and enriches life by enabling the individual to express his or her feelings and understanding of life. Drama is an imitation of life.

> Man has always been a storyteller. It is the most personal and direct way that he passes on his culture. More personal than the printed word, more direct than the symbolism of dance and

**TABLE 8.3   A List of Activities
in a Dance Program**

Aerobic dance	Folk dance
Ballet	Free rhythms
Ballroom dance	Identification rhythms
Chorus line dance	Jazz dance
Circle dance	Line dance
Clog dance	Longways dance
Country dance	Modern dance
Concert dance	Modern jazz
Contemporary/popular dance	Precision movement drills
Couple dance	Rap dance
Creative dance for children	Rock-and-roll dance
Creative fitness rhythms	Round dance
Creative rhythms	Show dance
Dance mixers	Social dance
Disco dance	Social or ballroom dance
Dramatic rhythms	Solo dance
Drill and dance routines	Square dance
Ethnic dance	Tap dance

music. He needs only his voice and body to create that pure self-expressive art called drama.

It is self-expressive creativity because it allows man to interpret his environment and feelings to others with techniques and styles that not only communicate but entertain. Unlike dance, music, or literature, it must have an audience to sustain meaningful participation. Man can retire to solitude and talk to himself with music, dance, and crafts, but drama demands others to witness it (Tillman, 1973: 281).

Dramatics as a performing art encompasses two broad areas—formal and informal. Tillman offers the following description of formal dramatics:

> Formal dramatics involves a written script, lines to be memorized, a director who interprets the play and directs action, emphasis on staging and costuming, and major consideration given to the entertainment of an audience and its reaction to a finished product (Tillman, 1973: 281).

Informal dramatics is a broad term that encompasses a wide variety of activities: imaginative play, make-believe, story dramatization, pantomime, impromptu work, extemporaneous pre-

sentations, shadow plays, puppetry. The emphasis in informal dramatics (also called *creative dramatics*) is on the person involved and not on the audience.

Values of participation and involvement in dramatics can be far-reaching and very personal. Participation in drama may extend the horizons of the participant by stimulating his or her imagination and by allowing an opportunity to momentarily be "someone else." Drama allows for interpersonal exchanges and group interaction as well as for personal expression. It is an important part of cultural life—a reflection of many lifestyles. Consequently, it enables persons to better understand their own lifestyle and to appreciate lifestyles different from their own. Because of the scope of drama, it can appeal to all age groups, both as direct participants and as spectators. See Table 8.4 for a list of drama activities that can be included in programming.

The integration of the arts is as important as the expression of each art individually. Examples of integration are highly evident throughout the arts. For example, production of drama might incorporate dance choreography, visual arts display (set construction), and decoration and costume design in addition to the performance of the actor. The performance of dance may inspire the artist to interpret the expression on canvas or in sculpture; the dancer interprets the music that may, in turn, be an interpretation of words, ideas, and feelings from literature and poetry. Relative to the various program areas of the arts, recreation and leisure service organizations should provide opportunities for the participant to develop an appreciation of the arts in the passive as well as the active sense. In an active sense, participants should be able to learn, develop, and apply skills within the arts.

The Visual Arts

When defining art within the context of the visual arts, we are speaking of the decorative arts—beautiful objects for their own sake—and crafts—beautiful objects for utilitarian use. *Crafts* can be viewed as the utilization of materi-

TABLE 8.4 A List of Activities in a Drama Program

Art/music festivals	Marionettes
Blackouts	Mime
Book reviews	Mobile theater
Ceremonials	Monodrama
Charades	Monologue
Children's theater	Musical comedy
Choral speaking	Musicals
Choral speech	Observances
Classic/great books programs	One-act plays
Clowning	Operetta
Comedy hour	Pageants
Community theater	Pantomime
Costume design	Peep box
Creative drama	Plays
Creative play	Poetry
Creative writing	Property management
Debate society	Puppet therapy
Demonstrations	Puppetry
Directing	Reading groups
Dramatic games	Readings
Dramatizations	Science fiction
Face painting	Scriptwriting
Festivals	Shadow plays
Fiction	Short stories
Film	Shows
Filmmaking	Skits
Finger plays	Stagecraft
Formal drama	Storytelling
Grand opera	Stunts
Imaginative play	Summer stock
Impersonations	Symphonic drama
Improvisation theater	Tableaux
Juggling	Theater
Light opera	Theater-in-the-round
Linguistic activities	Three-act plays
Magic tricks	Toastmasters
Makeup	Video making

als to produce items having a utilitarian value. *Art* can be defined as utilizing materials in a graphic or plastic demonstration of a symbol or concept. Simply stated, a craft can be handled and used, while art displays a perception. It is obvious that arts and crafts cannot be understood as precisely different areas of involvement. Separately or together, they are an outlet for human expression and provide a vehicle for the inherent desire of the individual to create.

Communication is one of the primary values of arts and crafts. Through the development of craft objects, a person can communicate with others and the environment and express his or her personality and the culture that has contributed to the development of that personality. Individuals involved in using materials to create art display varying levels of skill, technique, and interpretation. However, the specific piece or production that is the outcome of the art experience is not as important as the satisfaction that the individual achieves through the creating experience.

Communication through arts and crafts can take place through creativity, self-expression, or integration. Creativity involves the ability to change or modify existing components to produce a new or different end result. For example, an individual may see in a gnarled piece of walnut the possibility of a finished clock case; an individual may redesign a coat into a pair of slacks; a person may visualize pottery in a piece of clay, or see trees and a stream on a canvas. Self-expression can occur whenever the opportunity exists for the individual to demonstrate his or her feelings. In arts and crafts, this occurs when an individual shapes an object or creates a product that reflects his or her personality. The concept of self-expression is present in many areas of leisure service activity, but in arts and crafts, a visible object is produced as a result of a personal emotional expression.

Specific art and craft activities can range from items of simplicity to those of great complexity. Crafts can include crewel embroidery, leather tooling, knot tying, copper enameling, making bread dough items and burlap flowers, and so on. Art can include finger painting, drawing in charcoal, painting with acrylics, sculpting in clay and marble, etching on glass, or molding in silver or bronze. There are several categories within arts and crafts into which activities may be grouped. Shivers and Calder (1974: 7) suggest the following: the graphic and manipulative types of art (printmaking, papier-mâché, sculpting, casting, mosaics, and ceramics) and craft (leather crafts, woodcrafts, metal crafts, weaving, sewing, nature crafts, rug hooking, crafts from recycled materials, and theater crafts).

Arts and crafts have gained prominence and increased participation as a result of the "culture explosion" in our society. Another reason for the popularity of arts and crafts as a leisure service activity is the desire of many people to "get back to the basics." People choose to make craft items as utilitarian products—pottery, weaving, knitting, crocheting—rather than consume mass-produced items. Arts and crafts reflect the need to personalize one's lifestyle by creating and consuming objects that are unique. Leisure service organizations may be a vehicle for individuals to learn the skills of arts and crafts and to produce, demonstrate, display, and sell many of the items they create.

An example of an award-winning art experience is sponsored by the Austin (Texas) Parks and Recreation Department. Called Totally Cool, Totally Art (TCTA), the program provides visual arts classes to middle-school children up to sixteen years of age. The programs goals include: (1) providing safe places/sense of belonging; (2) providing opportunities for new experiences in order to increase participants' knowledge, skills, and possible interest in art as a career field; (3) increasing teens' trust and respect for other teens, adult mentors, artists, and other authority figures; (4) increasing teens' ability to work cooperatively with other teens and communicate effectively in a group; and (5) increasing teens' ability to make creative and positive choices through self-expression (Witt, 2000: 65–66).

The Britt David Cultural Arts Studio, operated by the Columbus (Georgia) Parks and Recreation Department, provides a full range of activities. Programs include pottery classes for children and teens, photography, puppet shows and workshops, stained glass classes, and weaving classes. The center also promotes demonstrations and shows for artists to exhibit their works. Young Rembrandts, a children's drawing program, provides opportunities for artistic expression. It also provides "added values . . . For example, preschoolers show increases in reading readiness and visual perception skills; older students and teens show vast improvement in concentration levels, problem-solving abilities, critical thinking skills; and adults report increased appreciation for the environment, stress reduction, and calming meditative-like experiences." The city of Kettering (Ohio) Parks, Recreation, and Cultural Arts Department holds an annual Holiday Arts and Crafts Show (see Figure 8.2). The San Antonio (Texas) Department of Parks and Recreation operates a Mural Program as a way of beautifying and showcasing the community. The program serves as a vehicle for participation of community youth in the actual painting of murals so that neighborhoods use their existing resources and talents in a positive way.

An example of a public art exhibit is provided by the city of Cedar Falls (Iowa) Tourism and Visitors Bureau. This organization has created an information piece that serves as a guide to public art in the community. Known as "Gardens to Main Street," the program is directed toward helping individuals to recognize the contribution of visual arts to the community. The program encourages an awareness and appreciation of regional artists and offers the public an opportunity to share in their vision. Cedar Falls, Iowa is considered to be one of America's best small art towns. Figure 8.3 presents a guide to the public art exhibit.

The New Arts

The new arts—in which an individual uses a technological apparatus of some kind to carry out an activity or produce an outcome—can include photography, computer programming, filmmaking, television production, and other media. The artist uses a DVD, MP3 camera, a computer terminal, a videocassette recorder, or some other technological device as a vehicle for artistic expression.

Photography—whether it results in photographs, slides, videotapes, or motion pictures—is an artistic means of self-expression. Through photography, an individual can reveal feelings, attitudes, and interests that are visible in the subjects chosen and in the ideas expressed.

Figure 8.2 Holiday Arts and Crafts Show, City of Kettering (Ohio) Parks, Recreation, and Cultural Arts Department.

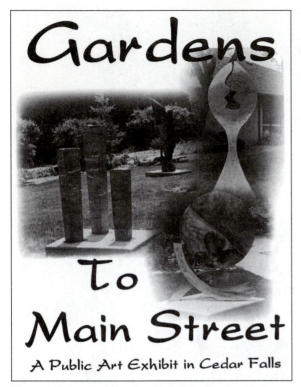

Figure 8.3 Public Art Exhibit, Cedar Falls (Iowa) Tourism and Visitors Bureau.

Informal photography can be a vehicle for capturing a mood, an emotion, a situation, an event, or an object. Photography also can be an expression of color, motion, distance, shapes, and texture. The resulting pictures may express joy, sorrow, fear, contentment, weariness, love, and many other emotions. The individual's knack for creating pictures can be displayed through techniques of slow-motion, animation, and stop-motion as well as through various kinds of photography, such as microphotography and telephotography. Furthermore, displaying the results of photography in panoramic views, close-ups, single or multiple screens, and dissolves can demonstrate the person's ability to communicate with photographic visuals.

Radio and television are vehicles for expression that utilize verbal and visual communication. An individual's inventiveness may lead to the pro-duction of materials such as scripts and videotapes that are original in concept and treatment. Simulated radio allows planning of dramatization, writing and reading, performing music, or producing sound. Videotape systems are a means of recording performance, producing animation, and capturing action and sound. With television production, the person or persons involved may have immediate feedback and observation of results.

With appropriate knowledge and skill, a person can design computer-generated animation through free-form sketching at a terminal, or images can be created through description in numerical or mathematical terms. Computer programs provide a means through which the user may engage in creative expression.

A person's leisure expression in the new arts, as in all the arts, can be as individual and creative as the person using the device allows it to be. As in all artistic expression, the limitations are controlled only by the individual's imagination.

The availability of the technology needed to produce new art has increased to make program planning and participant involvement more accessible. Some of the technological media (such as cameras) are readily available to individuals and organizations, while other devices (such as computers) may be available for use on a limited basis.

LITERARY ACTIVITIES

Numerous program offerings can be included within the area of literary activities. These activities are grouped into categories such as writing, communication, reading, foreign studies, and discussion groups. Writing activities include the original writing of plays, poetry, short stories, novels, and personal communications. Writing activities may lead to such experiences as sharing what has been written (e.g., through reading sessions) and performing the written material. Communication activities can take the form of public speaking, debate, broadcasting, group discussions, storytelling, recording tapes for the visually impaired, and other activities. Book clubs, great books seminars, and discussions of Shakespeare or American literature since 1900 are some of the reading activities that could be developed for recreation and leisure. Interpretive reading, book reviews, a magazine corner, and library visitations are other activities. Foreign studies might involve the study of language, culture, economics, and the social history of countries throughout the world; they might also encompass folklore, mythology, classics, and translations. Discussion groups within a recreation and leisure setting could cover any topic ranging from philosophy or Peruvian art to the Bible or English poets. The categories mentioned here in no way preclude the development of other activities. In all program areas, the potential activities are limited only by the planning capabilities of the recreation and leisure professional.

The Cincinnati (Ohio) Recreation Commission operates a unique program focused on literary arts. The basic philosophy of this program is that the "mind matters." The educational programs are geared to motivate, inspire, nurture, and develop individuals (MIND). The Commission's literary arts program emphasizes the spoken and written word. In programs geared for youth, classes, presentations, and workshops encourage individuals to express themselves to peers and adults. The program provides a broad range of literary arts activities that inspire children to appreciate prose and poetry of all genres, and motivates children to express themselves by developing speaking, writing, and storytelling skills (www.cincyrec.org) (see Figure 8.4).

SELF-IMPROVEMENT/EDUCATION ACTIVITIES

Of emerging importance in the leisure services field is a growing array of personal self-improvement activities and programs. Many of these literary, mental, and linguistic activities—which result in personal development and individual or group improvement—are generic to this category. Individuals engage in self-improvement activities for the primary purpose of developing either cognitive, communicative,

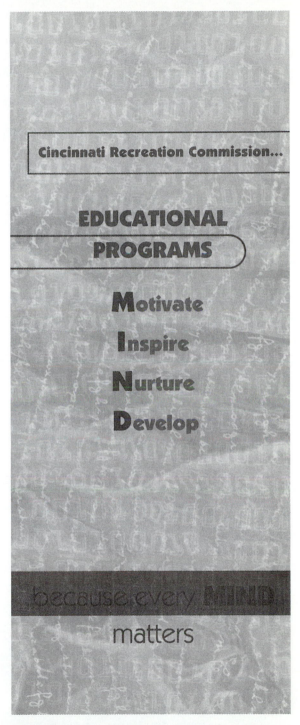

Figure 8.4 Literary Program—The Mind Matters, Cincinnati (Ohio) Recreation Commission.

or affective skills. For example, a self-development activity may lead to a change in behavior that might result in the improvement of the individual as shown in his or her work, home, or leisure environments and relationships.

The primary sponsors of self-development activities have been individual specialized businesses, corporate schools, community and technical colleges, the voluntary sector, and churches. Also, a number of book clubs provide specialty books and tapes featuring self-improvement. Religious organizations provide not only literature but also retreats and mass rallies to build spiritual values and positive lifestyles. For example, marriage and family encounters have become popular program responses to the rising divorce rates in North America. Another commercial venture in self-improvement is training programs organized by institutes and private enterprises.

The scope of programs in the self-improvement area is wide. It includes such diverse activities as continuing education, avocation sales promotions, marriage and family development, and intellectual development through games. Assertiveness training may enable an individual who has assumed a subservient role—whether in a work, family, or leisure setting—to gain a better sense of self-worth.

Women's needs, rights, and roles are other areas in which an array of programs and services has developed. In keeping with the rapidly changing roles for women, a number of books and training programs have emerged to encourage positive personal development. The topics are broad, including such areas as management challenges and techniques, sexual behavior, gender definition, and total lifestyle management.

Marriage and family retreats have become extremely popular. Participation in these programs has been encouraged by religious and other organizations as a means of promoting positive relations within the home. The setting is usually a camp or outdoor area—a contrast to the regular living environment. These daylong or weekend programs are a way of restoring and shaping positive individual feelings as well as family relations.

Intellectual development through games is widespread. *Outburst, Trivial Pursuit, Scrabble, Word Yahtzee, Monopoly,* and other table games may improve intellectual skills. In addition, computer technology has spawned such intellectual challenges as *Sim City* (a simulation of a growing community) and other software innovations. Local, state, regional, and national organizations actively promote these activities through newsletters, competitions, and demonstrations.

A new program of the Disney Corporation, the Disney Institute, is focused on providing learning activities for all ages. The Disney Institute is a "resort with a creatively charged atmosphere where you can engage your body, excite your mind and expand your horizons (Swartz, 1996: E9). This program features eighty different daily programs that focus on a variety of topics, including entertainment arts, performing arts, sports and fitness, culinary arts, environment, lifestyles, and story arts. This concept is built on the idea of the Chautauqua Institute, which features self-development classes and events.

Another activity that has become popular over the last several years is genealogy. This study of one's family history and lineage is a time-consuming activity. Individuals and groups spend hundreds of hours examining and clarifying their "roots" and their family trees. In North America, this activity has been supported by the public libraries, where census information and other appropriate records (e.g., birth, death, business) are usually made available.

SPORTS, GAMES, AND ATHLETICS

A sport is an activity that demands a combination of physical skill, endurance, alertness, purpose, and enthusiasm. Performance of a sport represents an accomplishment for which the body has been trained and for which the person must work to become skillful. In most sport activities, the person uses a specifically designed piece of equipment (such as a ball, a racquet, a bat, or a wicket) and carries out the activity on a field or area of a determined shape and dimen-

TABLE 8.5   List of Individual, Dual, and Team Sports

Individual Sports		Dual Sports	Team Sports
Archery	Weight lifting	Tennis	Hockey
Golf	Trap shooting	Boxing	Crew racing
Bowling	Riflery	Wrestling	Basketball
Swimming	Hunting	Badminton	Volleyball
Diving	Fishing	Handball	Baseball
Gymnastics	Sky diving	Racquetball	Softball
Skating	Hang gliding	Squash	Football
Skiing	Surfing		Soccer
Hiking			
Track and field			

sion, on which there may be permanent equipment. Sports activities may take many forms and are defined in several categories (see Table 8.5 and Exhibit 8.1).

An example of a website with information regarding sports, games, and athletics is PE Central (http://pe.central.vt.edu/). This website has a wealth of practical tips and suggestions on sport and physical activity.

A sport can be classified as an individual activity—that is, an activity that is carried out by an individual without a partner, team, or opponent (such as golf, archery, gymnastics, swimming, track and field, and so on). An example of a leisure service activity that incorporates several individual activities is the Peachtree City (Georgia) Youth Triathlon. This activity was conceived to promote fitness as a lifestyle for youth and serves youth ages seven to fifteen. Another example is the Elm Classic, a 5 K walk and 10 K run cosponsored by the Elmhurst Park District and the Elmhurst Family YMCA in Illinois. The

EXHIBIT 8.1   Soccer: "The Beautiful Game"

Around 6 A.M. Wednesday, I was ecstatic. The United States soccer team had just pulled off the world's biggest sports stage, the World Cup tournament, played this quadrennial in South Korea and Japan.

I giddily prepared for work and dressed in my USA team shirt, ready to share my excitement with my fellow Americans.

I realize this is not Argentina. We are not a soccer-crazed country. I knew better than to expect a scene like in Dakar, Senegal, after their national team defeated France, but I was hoping for something, anything. I went into Quik-Trip hoping to see at least one other fan and celebrate with them. Nothing. I went to work wishing that my weeklong boosterism would produce one person who cared. Nothing.

A few hours after the stunning result, the Associated Press ran a story on-line chronicling the apathy of Americans toward what many analysts were calling one of the biggest upsets ever in the world of soccer. We are preoccupied with the Stanley Cup, the NBA finals, terrorism and our mundane routines. Sports talk radio was filled with people who not only didn't care, but questioned the sanity of anyone who did.

It was disheartening. If this team can't get us excited about soccer, maybe nothing will.

One common knock on soccer is the lack of scoring. It is far more difficult to score in soccer than any other sport because an attacking team is usually outnumbered 2 to 1 at the offensive end. But even a low-scoring game features many scoring chances, outstanding defensive plays and spectacular saves by the goalie.

Give this game a chance, folks. Soccer players are the most physically fit athletes in the world, our national team is playing well at the World Cup level and this international game gives us a chance to learn about and appreciate other cultures. Kids today play soccer more than any other sport. Watching it with your kids will give them a greater appreciation for what has been called "the beautiful game."

United States soccer needs and deserves our support.

Brothers, M. S. (2002, June 16). Soccer: 'The Beautiful Game.' The Des Moines Register. p. 30P program also features a 1 K Kids' Run/Walk. The U.S. Marine Corps (Okinawa, Japan) Morale, Welfare, and Recreation Department sponsors an annual Olympics. Events include iron man (individual and team), *Rollerblade* dash, accuracy soccer kick, softball home run derby, *Frisbee* toss, aerobathon (individual and team), and three-point shootout. The program offers male and female divisions.

Dual sport activities are those that require at least two people to implement the activity. Such activities as wrestling, tennis, badminton, and fencing are dual sports. Team sports are those for which a group of people is needed to carry out the activity. Some team sports are soccer, basketball, football, baseball, volleyball, and hockey. An emerging team sport is roller hockey. The city of Long Beach (California) operates roller hockey programs at more than ten locations.

There are numerous other ways of identifying sports by category. For example, there are combative sports—boxing, wrestling, karate, and judo. There are vehicle sports—auto racing, motorcycling, and snowmobiling—and other kinds of locomotive sports—sailing, yachting, horseback riding and horse racing, hang gliding, parachuting, tobogganing, bicycle riding, and sky diving. Some sports rely on the environment as an impetus (such as mountain climbing and river rafting). Classification of sports can also be based on the kind of equipment used (such as ball games and net games) or the season (e.g., winter for skiing, sledding, and ice skating) or some other distinction (such as water sports— swimming, surfing, diving, water skiing, canoeing, and sailing). An example of a sports activity dependent on equipment is in-line skating. The Services Division at Hickam Air Force Base has organized an in-line skate party with instructors, music, and skate games. Many other sport activities, such as bowling, riflery, weight lifting, and fly casting, fit best into a miscellaneous category.

An interesting approach to providing sports programs is offered by the Clearwater (Florida) Fun and Fitness Academy. This commercial organization provides a wide range of sport and nutrition programs in a variety of formats, including clinics and camps. The organization's philosophy focuses on training "children to be physically fit and healthy while having fun!"

Games can have many different characteristics (see Table 8.6). They can be physical activities of low organization, often requiring only a low level of skill; usually these games have a few simple rules and are of short duration. Conversely, some games can be quite complex. Games can be carried out in an individual, dual, or team situation. They can be active, as in dodgeball and tag, or inactive, as in guessing and word games. There are numerous board games in which it is necessary to practice the decision-making process by solving complex problems. Three basic elements are usually present in game situations: luck (as in rolling the dice for a board game), physical endurance (as in running and playing tag), and skill (as in throwing darts or tossing rings).

> There is . . . [a] . . . difference between sports and games even more fundamental than the degree of organization. When children play games they quit when tired. The participant in a sport, provided he is truly an athlete, a competitor in the highest sense of the term, continues after he is tired, even to the point of complete exhaustion (Danford and Shirley, 1970: 188).

There is perhaps a fine line of distinction between sports and athletics.

> A sport may be either competitive or noncompetitive (swimming, for example); in the case of athletics, however, the definition is limited to the competitive aspect of sports. Whereas swimming may be engaged in as a sport for recreation, technically this sport becomes athletics when it is organized for purposes of competition (Donnelly et al., 1958: 3).

TABLE 8.6   Low-Organized Games, Table/Board Games, and Mental Games

Low-Organized Games	Table/Board Games	Mental Games/Puzzles
Dodgeball	Checkers	Guessing games
Tag	Chess	Construction puzzles
Two deep	Backgammon	Crosswords
Run-for-your-supper	Kalah	Word games
Newcomb	Chinese checkers	
Four square	Box hockey	
Deck tennis	Battleship	
Relays	Aggravation	
Goal games	Card games	
	Dominoes	

The Champaign (Illinois) Park District operates a myriad of competitive sport programs, including adult softball leagues (see Figure 8.5).

Walt Disney's Wide World of Sports Complex hosts ASA FastPitch Softball Tournaments (http://disneyworld.disney.go.com). The flyer shown in Figure 8.6 encourages public park and recreation department leaders to post the materials so that coaches and teams can participate in the event. This is an example of how a private leisure business works to promote its for-profit interests with public agencies.

> Sports or athletics may be defined in terms of the participant's motivation, or by the nature of the activity itself. Sport is a playful activity for some participants, while others place it in the context of work or an occupation. Moreover, the boundaries of sport as an activity blend into the more general sphere of recreation and leisure (Ball and Loy, 1975: 12).

Contributing to the organization of a sport for competition are factors such as duration of play, accumulation of points, achievement of a predetermined score, or completion of a specified course. In athletic competition, the primary object is to perform physically with strength, endurance, and agility, along with knowledge that gives one individual the advantage over his or her opponent. Table 8.7 delineates the characteristics of play, recreation, contests, games, sports, and athletics.

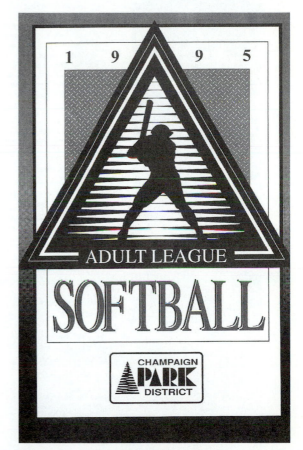

Figure 8.5   Adult League Softball, Champaign (Illinois) Park District.

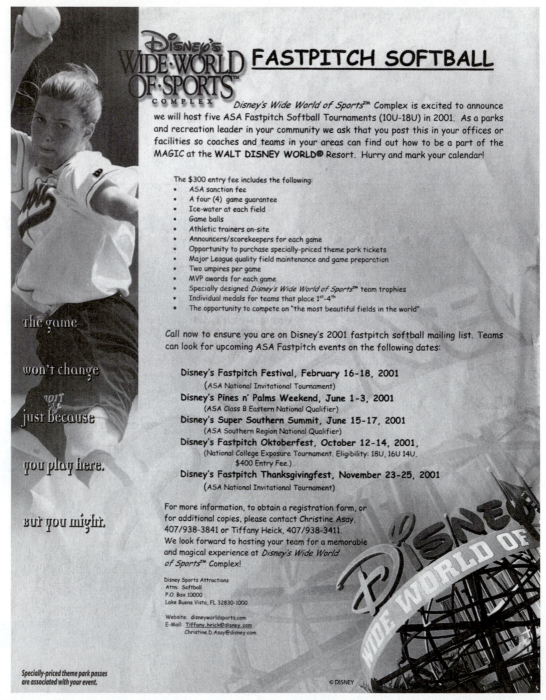

Figure 8.6 Fast Pitch Softball Tournament, *Disney's Wide World of Sports*™ Complex, Lake Buena Vista, Florida.

TABLE 8.7   Profiles of Activities Denoted by Central Concepts

Determining Attributes	Play	Recreation	Activities Denoted By: Contest or Match	Game	Sport or Athletics
1. Activity exclusive of concerns and influences emanating from outside of contest of activity	X				
2. Existence of fantasy or make-believe	X				
3. Actor or actors commence activity at will	X	X			
4. Actor or actors limit act in space and time	X	X			
5. Actor or actors terminate activity at will	X	X			
6. Activity not necessarily utilitarian in project (may be devoid of economic, material, prestige, power, or status-achievement goals)	X	X			
7. Competition not a necessary component	X	X			
8. Activity characterized by a necessary degree of spontaneity (not restricted by formal or informal rules of procedure)	X	X			
9. Relevance of role restricted to boundaries of activity	X	X	X		
10. Individualistically focused and oriented	X	X	X		
11. Actor or actors involvement in activity necessarily voluntary	X	X	X		
12. No imperative formal hierarchical arrangement of roles and positions	X	X	X	X	
13. Physical exertion not a necessary component	X	X	X	X	
14. Preparation for participation in activity not a necessary component	X	X	X	X	
15. No formal stabilized history or tradition necessary	X	X	X	X	
16. Activity inclusive of concerns and influences emanating of outside of context of activity		X	X	X	X
17. Nonexistence of fantasy or make-believe		X	X	X	X
18. Actor or actors may not commence activity at will		X	X	X	
19. Actor or actors may not terminate activity at will			X	X	X
20. Actor or actors do not have prerogative to limit activity in space and time			X	X	X
21. Activity utilitarian in product (emphasis on attaining economic goals, prestige, power status, self-esteem)			X	X	X
22. Competition necessary component			X	X	X
23. Activity necessarily characterized by formal or informal rules, regulations, restrictions, or limitations that must be followed			X	X	X
24. Activity not necessarily voluntary; may be forced			X	X	
25. Relevance of role not restricted to activity			X	X	
26. Activity necessarily collective in character			X	X	
27. Preparation for participation in activity necessary				X	
28. Formal history; recognized records and traditions				X	
29. Physical exertion a necessary component				X	
30. Imperative formal hierarchical roles and positions				X	

Edwards (1973: 59) suggests that as a person moves from play to sport, the following occurs:

1. Activity becomes less subject to individual prerogative, with spontaneity severely diminished.
2. Formal rules and structural role and position relationships and responsibilities within the activity assume predominance.
3. Separation from the rigors and pressures of daily life becomes less prevalent.
4. Individual liability and responsibility for the quality and character of behavior during the course of the activity is heightened.
5. The relevance of the outcome of the activity and the individual's role in it extends to groups and collectivities that do not participate directly in the act.
6. Goals become diverse, complex, and more related to values emanating from outside of the context of the activity.
7. The activity consumes a greater proportion of the individual's time and attention because of the need for preparation and the degree of seriousness involved in the act.
8. The emphasis on physical and mental extension beyond the limits of refreshment or interest in the act assumes increasing dominance. (From *Sociology of Sport* by Harry Edwards, © The Dorsey Press, 1973. Reprinted by permission of Wadsworth Publishing Co., Belmont, CA.)

There is a tremendous potential for positive physical, social, and psychological growth as a result of participation in games, sports, and athletics. Games—whether they involve children or adults—can initiate various kinds of behavior and outcomes. Involvement in a game situation may enable a person to learn to take turns, to accept and follow directions and rules, to experience both winning and losing, to learn new skills, to develop abilities for decision making, to practice fair play and consideration of others, and to feel the spirit of cooperation. The leader's role in the organization of games is to involve all participants as successfully as possible, to implement complementary group structures, and to encourage the participant to realize that

the process of playing the game is more important than winning or losing.

The values acquired through participation in sports are as broad and varied as the number of individuals involved. Because the primary concern of a leisure service organization should be with the individual, certain values should be emphasized in individual and group sports participation. Sports have great carryover value for a person throughout life. As with nearly all leisure activities, participation in sports need not be terminated at any time. Although it would seem that society has traditionally emphasized team sports, it is easier to continue involvement in individual and dual sports; this is because involvement can be continued on an individual basis or with one or two other people more easily than with one or more teams. Sports contribute to the individual's health and physical well-being and help develop feelings of self-confidence, self-esteem, happiness, and personal satisfaction. Participation in sports enables the individual to function as a member of a group or team—fostering feelings of acceptance, camaraderie, and cooperation. Participants in sports learn to follow rules and to accept authority and the decisions of others.

Many national and state professional societies and associations have in place a number of programs that leisure organization can utilize. For example, the National Association for Sport and Physical Education (NASPE), in collaboration with Sportime and Human Kinetics, has developed a program called *Sport for All*. This program provides children ages three to ten with age-appropriate, sports-related skills. Similarly, the National Recreation and Park Association (NRPA), in conjunction with Hershey, sponsors *Hershey's Youth, Track and Field Program* and an innovative youth sports camp program entitled *Let's Play Sports* that is operated collaboratively with *Sports Illustrated for Kids* magazine.

The National Alliance for Youth Sports has developed an extensive set of standards to assist in providing a positive sport experience for children and youth. The standards were developed as guidelines to assist individuals and organizations in providing a wholesome and safe youth sport environment. As indicated in the National Alliance for Youth Sports' booklet entitled *National Standards for Youth Sports: Modifying the Sports Environment for a Healthier Youth,*

> While sport for children is generally a positive experience, too often, history has shown that youth leagues have been created with an atmosphere of professionalism, e.g., the vicarious parent, the overzealous coach, leagues organized with championships as their main focus continue to exist. The National Standards for Youth Sports were developed to provide all youth groups with a focus on what is best for children in their growing, learning years (n.d., p. 2).

The National Alliance for Youth Sports has developed eleven standards to guide the management of sport youth groups. Each standard is supported by implementation strategies. The standards are as follows:

1. Parents must consider and carefully choose the proper environment for their child, including the appropriate age and development for participation, the type of sport, the rules in the sport, the age range of the participants, and the proper level of physical and emotional challenge.
2. Parents must select youth sports programs that are developmental and organized to enhance the emotional, physical, social, and educational well-being of their children.
3. Parents must encourage a drug-, tobacco-, and alcohol-free environment for their children.
4. Parents must recognize that youth sports are only a small part of a child's life.
5. Parents must insist that coaches be trained and certified.
6. Parents must make a serious effort to take an active role in the youth sports experience of their child, providing positive support as a spectator, coach, league administrator, and/or caring parent.
7. Parents must be positive role models, exhibiting sportsmanlike behavior at games, practices, and home while giving positive reinforcement to their child and support to their child's coaches.
8. Parents must demonstrate their commitment to their child's youth sports experience by annually signing a parental code of ethics.
9. Parents must insist on safe playing facilities, healthful playing situations, and proper first aid applications, should the need arise.
10. Parents, coaches, and league administrators must provide equal sports play opportunity for all youth regardless of race, creed, sex, economic status, or ability.
11. Parents as coaches, fans, and league administrators must be drug-, tobacco-, and alcohol-free at youth sports activities.

Sports in our society have become a social institution, a tradition, and a reflection of our cultural and ethnic heritage. Social scientists have defined and analyzed sport in conjunction with other social institutions (such as education, health, religion, politics, and economics). The professionalization and commercialization of competitive athletics and sports have permeated our culture and social structure. Whether one is a spectator or a participant, sports touch nearly everyone's life.

Sports, games, and athletics—as a part of organized leisure services—are reaching the greatest number and the widest variety of participants of any program area or activity. Opportunity for personal involvement can be made available through organized recreation and leisure services, whether the participant is young or old, male or female, able-bodied or differently abled, large or small. Examples of some very basic modifications of sport activities that exist in order to broaden the opportunity for participation are slow-pitch softball, slow-break basketball, T-ball, and lightweight football. Adaptations of this type are made in order to allow greater numbers of persons to participate.

AQUATICS

The program area of aquatics is an important dimension in the management of many leisure service organizations. Swimming is one of the most popular activities pursued by individuals in their leisure. Many leisure service organizations have built a large portion of their program effort around aquatics. For example, the Red Cross, the YMCA, and the National Safety Council, in conjunction with Ellis and Associates and the National Recreation and Park Association, have all developed instructional aquatic programs directed toward improving individual safety in and around the water. The program's objective is "to provide a positive, fun-filled opportunity to learn skills that will reduce the number of drownings and provide life-long aquatic enjoyment." It is not unusual for an organization that emphasizes aquatics to employ a number of full-time aquatic program specialists and many part-time and seasonal staff members.

Most aquatic programs are built around three goals. The first is to provide a safe aquatic experience, the second is to encourage individuals to have fun and enjoyment, and the third is skill development. Depending on the facilities available, some aquatic programs will emphasize fitness, competitive swimming, and other benefits. An excellent example of a well-rounded aquatic program is that operated by the Willamalane (Oregon) Park and Recreation District. This organization manages two swimming pool complexes. One of the complexes (a leisure pool) features a wave-generating pool, a lap pool, a kiddie pool, a slide, and a whirlpool that can accommodate up to fifty people. Their other pool, a more traditional operation with one water slide, features opportunities for competitive swim, lap swim, water aerobics, and swim lessons. Both swimming pool complexes are inviting and encourage participant involvement in a safe and enjoyable environment.

A broad range of aquatic services can be provided by a given leisure service organization. Most are dependent on having adequate pool facilities; however, many locations can provide safe adaptations that extend their services by encouraging the creativity of their aquatics staff. Programs often associated with aquatics are listed here.

Instructional Swim—Instructional swim lessons for all ages are a mainstay of many leisure service organizations. Both the American Red Cross and the YMCA have excellently structured, progressive programs in the learn-to-swim area. Most of these programs are focused on children, but adult swimming classes or even parent/infant classes are other possibilities.

Open Swim—The open swim format enables people to use the aquatic facility to swim or enjoy the aquatic environment. Drop-in swim programs often attract large numbers of individuals, requiring attention to appropriate safety procedures and methods.

Competitive Swim—Competitive swimming programs cater to individuals desiring a more intensive aquatic experience. Competition between teams promotes increased performance and can build esprit de corps among team members. Competitive swimming programs are also valuable in helping participants establish individual standards reflected in their desired levels of performance. Competitive swim programs are often thought to cater only to elite swimmers, but a good program will provide entry points for individuals of many skill levels.

Aquatic Exercise Programs—Fitness-oriented programs, including water aerobics, lap swimming, and others, have become very popular. Aquatic environments provide low-impact resistance to force and, therefore, as a medium of exercise can be pursued comfortably by individuals with varying levels of fitness.

Small Craft Instruction and Safety—Learning how to maneuver small crafts in and around aquatic environments safely is another activity managed by leisure service organizations. Lessons in kayaking, canoeing, windsurfing, sailing, and so forth are all potential instructional areas available to leisure service organizations.

Aquatic Games—Numerous games can be played in aquatic settings. These can range from relatively simple activities, such as low-organized games, to more complex athletic events like water polo. Aquatic games can bring increased interest to this program area and can stimulate fun, competition, and enjoyment. Aquatic games can also serve as a method of progressively teaching skills in a fun manner. They can also be used to promote fitness.

Social Activities In and Around the Water—Water is a magnet to many individuals. Combined with social recreation activities, it can provide a pleasant atmosphere for parties and other functions. Such programs should be organized to promote both safety and enjoyment. Many organizations will rent out their swimming pool complexes to groups for social functions. These rentals can be important sources of income for leisure service organizations.

This is by no means an all-inclusive list of aquatic activities. Aquatic programs operated by public leisure service organizations are used to generate enough revenues to pay for the operation of the aquatic programs and facilities. However, in recent years, there has been a general decline in the revenue position of aquatics programs. Perhaps this is not due to a decline in the interest of people in aquatics, but rather to a lack of dynamically designed facilities that are in step with contemporary needs. Today, an aquatic facility must be more than just a body of water; it must be creatively programmed to effectively draw individuals.

The Boulder (Colorado) Park and Recreation Department offers a number of swim programs, including lap swim, master swim, family swim, senior swim, and open swim. The city of Long Beach (California) Parks, Recreation, and Marine Department operates such programs as lap swim, adult recreation swim, all-age swim, water exercise, water aerobics, deep water exercises, scuba diving, beach swimming, diving, and swimming lessons. In addition, they provide lifeguard training and water safety instructor courses. The City of Kettering (Ohio) Parks, Recreation, and Cultural Arts Department organizes learn-to-swim programs, lifeguard training, water walking, water workouts, scuba diving, and drop-in swimming as part of its offerings (see Figure 8.7).

Figure 8.7   Aquatics Programs, City of Kettering (Ohio) Parks, Recreation, and Cultural Arts Department.

There has been tremendous growth in the popularity of water parks. Many are private leisure complexes. The Lost Island Water Park in Waterloo (Iowa) provides a full range of aquatic attractions. In addition, it includes a mini golf course and a go-cart track. Aquatic resources include the Polynesian Plunge, a 60-foot-tall water slide, the Samoan Splash—a 40-foot-tall water slide with a more circuitous route, Tsunami Bay water slide, the Lazy River—a water tube ride, Starfish Cove—a play area and activity pool, and the Tahitian Tree House—an outdoor climbing set with water (see Exhibit 8.2)

EXHIBIT 8.2

LOST ISLAND: A REAL "FIND"

The Lost Island water park could be a real "find" for the area's convention business, particularly for youth and adult athletic tournaments and events, according to Martha Place, Executive Director of the Waterloo Convention & Visitors Bureau.

Place couldn't quantify the park's projected economic impact yet. But she said the bureau's already been marketing the water park to land athletic tournaments, such as a youth baseball tournament coming to the city this summer.

When those tournaments come to town, "The young person is not spending their whole time at the soccer field or the tennis court," Place said. "We really have to expand our marketing efforts. We talk about the (Bluedorn Science) Imaginarium, we talk about the water park. That's just much extra that the kid and their families can do.

It becomes very important for us, really. The same could be said for the adult sports market, she said. When a man's age 35 and over softball tournament comes to town, "they bring their families and they're not at the ballpark all day. They're looking for other things to do." Attractions such as the water park "really help us sell this location," she said. "Those attractions really come in handy for us.

Kinney, P. (2001, May 9). Building on a Theme: Family Fun at the Lost Island Water Park Slated to Open May 26. The Waterloo-Cedar Falls Courier, p. 6.

The City of Roseville (California) Parks & Recreation Department utilizes an innovative approach in offering its aquatics program. Known as the FISH Philosophy, this approach was developed by the ChartHouse International Learning Cooperation. The program has four basic components:

1. *Play*—It's about having fun, enjoying yourself, being spontaneous and creative.
2. *Make Their Day*—It's about doing something special for your customers and co-workers. Make it a day to remember!
3. *Be There*—It's about being totally focused on the moment and on the person or task with which you are engaged. When we are fully present with our customers and with each other, we are listening deeply and important opportunities do not escape us.
4. *Choose Your Attitude*—It's about accepting full responsibility for all of our choices, even our attitude at work. A positive attitude is a decision we make moment to moment.

This program is aimed at improving customer satisfaction and operates in a fashion consistent with the major theme of this book, which focuses on providing quality services.

The William Lutsky YMCA of Edmonton, Alberta, Canada provides a full range of aquatic programs and services in its family community center. In particular, it offers a number of programs that focus on assisting individuals in developing greater fitness through aquatic services. Some of the aquatic programs provided include Aquafit, Deep Water, Gentle Aqua, and 50+ Aqua. Aquafit is a shallow-water cardio workout. The deep-water program is a high-energy workout at the deep end of the pool; participants use flotation belts. The Gentle Aqua program focuses on building muscle strength and promotes a full range of motion, using the water as natural resistance. The 50+ Aqua provides a shallow-water workout for this age group. In addition to these water-based fitness programs, this YMCA offers athletic conditioning, body strength, cardio interval, cycle/cyclefit/super cycle, dyna band, hip hop, on the ball, power walk/low impact, stability ball, step, strength circuit, stretch, tae boxing, tai chi, yoga, and 50+ land programs.

OUTDOOR RECREATION

The term *outdoor recreation* is usually associated with activities that take place in the out-of-doors. As Ibrahim and Cordes (1993: 4) suggest, outdoor recreation finds "interaction between the participant and an element of nature."

There are a number of ways to classify outdoor recreation pursuits. One classification divides activities into resource-oriented outdoor recreation pursuits and activity-oriented outdoor recreation pursuits. Still another way of viewing outdoor recreation activities is to classify them by the type of natural resource in which the activity takes place. Ibrahim and Cordes (p. 312) suggest that outdoor recreation activities take place in different environments or natural features, including land-, water-, and air-based activities.

The mere movement of activity-oriented programs to the outdoors does not make them outdoor recreation (resource-oriented). Many activities can certainly be enhanced by being carried out in the outdoor environment, but only activities that depend on the natural environment for their occurrence are truly outdoor recreation. A number of objectives should be considered in planning for outdoor recreation in our society. The majority of people in our urban society do not have much contact with the outdoors; therefore, they need opportunities to develop appreciation for nature in order to become aware of the importance of preservation practices and sound conservation. Participation in outdoor experiences should lead to individual satisfaction and enjoyment. Outdoor recreation experiences should also provide opportunity for diversion and relaxation. Developing physical fitness occurs in outdoor recreation through involvement in activities that are vigorous and taxing—moving participants beyond their usual levels of exertion. Our society has placed a great emphasis on physical fitness, and outdoor recreation allows many opportunities for fulfilling this need. "The fact that today's outdoor recreator must share his or her resources with many other people requires the development of desirable patterns of social outdoor conduct" (Jensen, 1977: 8). Development of desirable behavioral patterns for life in the "crowded" environment should encourage a comfortable sharing of natural recreation resources and preserving of resources in an ecological balance.

Other terms are often associated with the term *outdoor recreation activities*. Many of these terms overlap one another. They include:

Adventure Education. This type of education program focuses on outdoor activities that have some element of risk, such as whitewater rafting, ocean kayaking, sailboarding, and rappelling.

Adventure Tourism. This concept combines "fitness, environmentalism, multiculturalism, and travel" (Edginton et al., 1995: 123).

Conservation Education. This is education that focuses on assisting individuals to understand concepts related to wise use of natural resources.

Eco-Tourism. Eco-tourism, also known as eco-travel or eco-tours, involves the travel to unspoiled, remote, and pristine areas and enjoyment of such areas in a way that is environmentally sound and does not compromise the environment. Conservationists, governments, and individuals in the hospitality industry may cooperate toward this end.

Eco-Vacations. Eco-vacations involve the participation of individuals in vacations that involve volunteering "their labor to work in the out-of-doors (trail maintenance, research related to botany or animal life)" (Edginton et al., 1993: 410).

Ecology. Ecology involves understanding the relationship between living things, including human beings, and their environment.

Environmental Education. Environmental education is a broad concept that is directed toward teaching individuals about the environment in its broadest sense, including information regarding the interplay of humans, technology, and natural resources.

Environmental Interpretation. Environmental interpretation refers to the process of explaining aspects of the environment in their native habitats. An interpretive naturalist provides insight, education, or otherwise interprets plants, animals, minerals, and other living things in their native habitats.

Natural History. Natural history refers to the general study of animals, plants, and other things in nature.

Nature Education. Nature education focuses on learning related to natural resources. This is also sometimes referred to as nature recreation.

Nature Study. This form of education involves the study of specific animals, plants, and other things and events in nature.

Outdoor Education. Outdoor education implies commitment to the concept of providing educational experiences for individuals that help them build a land ethic as well as an awareness of our nature environment.

Outdoor Pursuits. This term refers to outdoor activities that are, generally speaking, non-mechanized.

Outdoor Schools. Outdoor schools provide a resident camp experience for individuals wherein they can learn, in an educationally focused program, about issues and factors related to the environment as well as to social living.

The scope of outdoor recreation activities and experiences is as large as the environment itself. Outdoor recreation experiences can encompass such activities as sailing a yacht, paddling a canoe, walking in the park, climbing a snow-capped mountain, visiting a rose garden, touring the Everglades, studying the geology on the banks of a small stream, seeing geological formations in the Grand Canyon, planting a garden, observing the wildlife, smelling the rain in the forest, and viewing the sunset across a plowed field. Recreation experiences in the outdoors may involve physical activity, intellectual discernment, and aesthetic appreciation (*Recreation program book,* 1963: 238). Horseback riding, skiing, hiking, climbing, hunting, fishing, swimming, diving, boating, building fires, and outdoor cooking all involve physical activity. Intellectual discernment is evident in outdoor recreation activities such as visiting interpretive centers; hearing naturalists describe areas of a park (or of a forest, desert, or body of water);

and studying and observing areas of natural, cultural, scientific, and historical significance. Aesthetic appreciation and awareness can be demonstrated through outdoor recreation activities such as painting, photography, writing, recording of sounds, landscaping, and creating natural craft items. It is important to note that "one cannot provide outdoor recreation. . . . It is possible to provide opportunities for, or resources and facilities for, but it is next to impossible to provide outdoor recreation as such all neatly packaged and predigested" (U.S. Department of Commerce, n.d.: 10). Table 8.8 presents a partial list of outdoor activities.

The Schaumburg (Illinois) Park District's Spring Valley Nature Sanctuary provides a full range of outdoor activities. Some of its programs are Kids Conservation Club, After-School Nature Series, Farm Life for Kids (activities include games and chores done by children in the 1880s), Nature Spots for Moms and Tots (craft projects, songs, finger games, all focused on nature activities), Owl Walks, Sundays at the Cabin (interpretation of a log cabin), A Traveling Quilt Exhibit, Nature Activities for Teachers and Scout Leaders, and Gardening, as well as a series of trips and tours. They also produce a newsletter called the *Natural Enquirer.* The Joliet (Illinois) Park District operates the Pilcher Park Nature Center. The nature center is a log cabin located in a secluded natural setting that provides opportunities for a variety of different programs and activities. Programs include syruping demonstrations, spring bird count, gardening, Earth Day celebration and park clean-up project, canoeing, and designing with nature. The center distributes a newsletter entitled *Raccoon Tales* (see Figure 8.8). The Boulder (Colorado) County Parks and Open Space Department operates an area known as Walden Ponds and Wildlife Habitat. This area provides opportunities for the public to view wildlife habitats as well as explore geologic formations.

Wilderness Inquiry (WI), a Minneapolis, Minnesota-based, nonprofit organization, provides a wide array of programs and services tied

TABLE 8.8 A Partial List of Outdoor Activities

Adventure education	Ice skating	Safety and survival courses
Air surfing	Interpretative activities	Sailing
Alpine skiing	Jet skiing	Sailboarding
Archery	Jogging	Sand sculpturing
Aquatic safety	Kayaking	Scuba diving
Backpacking	Kites	Sightseeing
Ballooning	Kite fighting	Skeet and trap shooting
Beach activities	Luge	Ski camping
Beach volleyball	Motor boating	Ski orienteering
Bicycling	Mountain biking	Ski touring
Bicycle touring	Mountain climbing	Skiing
Bird-watching	Mountaineering	Skin diving
Board sailing	Nature art	Skydiving
Boating	Nature education	Sledding
Bow hunting	Nature interpretation	Snorkeling
Bungee jumping	Nature photography	Snowboarding
Bushwhacking	Nature study	Snowmobiling
Camping	Navigation	Snow play
Canoeing	Nordic skiing	Snow sculpturing
Caving	Ocean kayaking	Snowshoeing
Climbing	Off-road motorcycles	Spearfishing
Collecting berries	Off-road vehicles	Speed skating
Collecting firewood	Organized camping	Spelunking
Cooperative tripping	Orienteering	Sunbathing
Conservation education	Ornithology	Surfing
Cross-country skiing	Outdoor pursuits	Survival skills
Curling	Outdoor survival skills	Target shooting
Cycling	Outdoor swimming	Tent camping
Day hiking	Paddling	Tobogganing
Diving	Parachuting	Touring
Downhill skiing	Parasailing	Trail hiking
Ecological activities	Photography	Tubing
Environmental education	Picnicking	Upskiing
Environmental interpretation	Pleasure boating	Visiting historic sites
Family gatherings	Pleasure driving	Visiting prehistoric sites
Fishing	Primitive camping	Visiting museums
Fitness walking	Rafting	Volksmarching
Flower gathering	Rapelling	Walking
Gardening	Recreational vehicles (RV) camping	Waterskiing
Glacier climbing	Resident outdoor school	White-water rafting
Golfing	Rifling	Wildlife observation
Hang gliding	River camping	Wildlife photography
Heli-skiing	River running	Wilderness trekking
High ropes adventure	River safety	Windsurfing
Hiking	Rock art hunting	Winter camping
Horseback riding	Rock climbing	Winter skiing
Hot air ballooning	Rockhounding	Wreck diving
Hunting	Ropes courses	Yachting
Ice boating	Rowing	
Ice fishing	Running	

to outdoor environments (www.wildernessin-quiry.org). Founded in 1978, the organization has served over 150,000 individuals including individuals with disabilities. The organization's focus involves ". . . providing opportunities to experience wilderness for everyone who wants to go." WI organizes a wide variety of programs dedicated to promoting the involvement of individuals in outdoor pursuits for people of all ages, backgrounds, and abilities. Programs include

Raccoon Tales

Issue I, 1995 — Official Newsletter of the Joliet Park District • Pilcher Park Nature Center

It's Maple Syrup Time

◆◆◆

Syruping Demonstrations March 18 & 19

◆◆◆

Scout Breakfast March 25

◆◆◆

Pancake Breakfast March 25 & 26

Expanded Hours!

Pilcher Park Nature Center Hours

The Joliet Park District is pleased to announce the Nature Center's expanded hours:

Monday 9am-4:30pm
Tuesday 9am-4:30pm
Wednesday 9am-4:30pm
Thursday 9am-8pm
Friday 9am-4:30pm
Saturday 10am-4pm
Sunday 10am-4pm

Technology Touches Maple Syruping
by Jerry Olson, Chief Naturalist

The Pilcher Park Nature Center has been making maple syrup at the park for 18 years. From the beginning, we have not tried to duplicate the pioneer methods of kettles over an open fire. Being able to get in out of the weather and actually make enough syrup for a breakfast made that method obsolete. Therefore, we purchased an evaporator. An evaporator is a sophisticated pan on a stove that utilizes gravity to move the liquid. Other changes in the maple syrup process have continued to occur. They are all geared towards making syrup of a higher quality and more cost effective. We would like to keep you, our followers, abreast of these techniques.

The first step in maple syrup production is the tapping of the trees. This requires drilling a 3 inch deep hole into the tree and then inserting a metal tube called a spile for directing the sap. Initially in maple syruping, the hand brace and bit were used but were quickly replaced by power drills as they came on the market. Large backpacks containing batteries were carried for the energy source to run the drill. The latest catalog from the maple syrup supplier has a light weight air cooled, two cycle engine to do the job.

A big step in cutting labor costs has occurred in the second stage of collection. Plastic tubing connecting the spile to the collection tank with a suction pump creates the force to bring the sap along the lines. This eliminated hours of collection.

Storage of the sap for a brief time period until it can be cooked has always been a problem. Bacteria finds sap an excellent medium to grow and multiply in. Science has found that ultra violet light is deadly to the bacteria so an inline treatment unit increases storage time and the quality of the syrup.

We have known for some time that we could increase our sugar content of the sap by discarding any ice found in the sap buckets. The ice is just water as the sugar molecule does not freeze but remains in liquid form. A 40 to 1 ratio is the norm in cooking maple syrup so any way we can decrease that is to our advantage.

Recent technology has developed a machine which completes a process called reverse osmosis. This process increases the sugar content significantly without cooking the sap, which cuts down on the time in the evaporator and saves on fuel.

The Nature Center has jumped into the 20th century of modern technology by plugging extension cords together and using our electric drill in the woods. The other updated technologies we haven't quite fit into our budget; specifically, $9,000.00 for the reverse osmosis machine. Hope to see you at the maple syrup pancake breakfast.

INSIDE

Figure 8.8 *Raccoon Tales* Newsletter, Joliet (Illinois) Park District.

outdoor skills workshops (canoeing, dog sledding, cross-country skiing), Mighty Mississippi Passport (designed to promote stewardship of the river, the passport includes over 100 events including canoeing, river boat ride, birding, hiking, and restoring native habitat), family programs, youth programs, Gateway to Adventure (opportunities for individuals with cognitive disabilities including training, outdoor skills workshop, extended outdoor adventures, and post program, networking, and support program and design training (education, training and consultation), facility and trail assessments, and information and research and presentations and exhibits (see Figure 8.9).

The Indian Creek Nature Center in Cedar Rapids (Iowa) is a private, nonprofit center that provides environmental education for people of all ages (www.indiancreeknaturecenter.org). The center promotes cooperation and collaboration with other organizations. This nature center includes 210 acres with four miles of trails in woodlands, prairies, wetlands, and forests. A remodeled 1932 dairy barn serves as an interpretive center and houses exhibits and an auditorium. The grounds also contain a butterfly habitat, sugar maple house, composting display, herbal gardens, frog pond, bee hives, bat houses, bluebird trail, sugarbush, and restored prairie. The Indian Creek Nature Center provides many workshops aimed at serving Cub Scout groups, such as workshops that focus on assisting Scouts earn various achievements and badges (see Figure 8.10).

The Pilcher Park Nature Center operated by the Joliet (Illinois) Park District is an example of a complex that provides a full range of services including hiking trails, the Nature Center, an artesian well, a greenhouse, and a horticultural center. The Bird Haven Greenhouse established in 1929 displays outdoor/indoor plants including an indoor tropical room and cactus house. The Andrew B. Barber and Clarence D. Oberwortmann Horticulture Center provides for a variety of exhibits as well as space for program learning opportunities. The Flowing Well

originated in 1927 and serves as a natural resource of cultural and historic value to the community (see Figure 8.11).

The Fort Worth (Texas) Botanic Garden is sponsored by the Parks and Community Services Department and serves as the oldest botanic garden in the state of Texas. It was conceived during the Depression as an outdoor library of plants and contains more than 2,500 native and exotic species of plants located on 108 acres. Self-directed leisure experiences are available at a very low cost, including tours of Rose Gardens of European designs, Fragrance Garden, Perennial Garden, Japanese Garden, and the Trail Garden. There are many pathways through the various gardens and displays. Facilities also include a conservatory, an exhibition greenhouse, a restaurant, and a gift shop (see Figure 8.12).

Camping opportunities are made available by the Santa Clara (California) County Parks and Recreation Department (www.parkhere.org) (see. Figure 8.13). This public park and recreation organization provides numerous natural areas with such leisure amenities as reservable campsites, restrooms, hot shower facilities, fresh tap water, fire pit barbeques, RV sites, picnic areas, and youth camping areas. Natural attractions provide opportunities for hikers, bikers, fishermen, and equestrians. There are many geographic and natural features of interests in the various park settings.

Several factors influence the significance of outdoor recreation in our society today. Population and urbanization, mobility, work and leisure, income, education, and technology are all elements that influence the direction and the existence of our rapidly changing society. The number of people living in a given area has a strong influence on patterns of utilization of natural resources. The growing urban areas, as well as the changing makeup of our society, concern not only sociologists and demographers but also those responsible for the development and delivery of outdoor recreation and leisure services. The demand for space (green areas), clean air, and water resources for out-

Figure 8.9 Nonprofit Organization Adventure Offerings, Wilderness Inquiry, Minneapolis, Minnesota.

CUB SCOUT WORKSHOPS
AT
INDIAN CREEK
NATURE CENTER

FALL & WINTER 2002-2003

6665 Otis Rd. SE
Cedar Rapids, IA 52403
PHONE: 319-362-0664
FAX: 319-362-2876
E-MAIL:NatureCenter@aol.com
www.indiancreeknaturecenter.org

A Special Place for Wildlife, Plants,
and People

Figure 8.10 Cub Scout Workshops, Indian Creek Nature Center, Cedar Rapids, Iowa.

Figure 8.11 Pilcher Park Nature Center, Joliet (Illinois) Park District.

Figure 8.12 Ft. Worth Botanical Garden Visitor's Map, Parks and Community Services Department, Ft. Worth, Texas.

Figure 8.13 Pocket Guide to Camping, Santa Clara County (California) Parks.

EXHIBIT 8.3   Outdoors Program for Girls Offered This Summer

If you are a girl and want to discover your strengths, join GUTS (Girls Understanding Their Strengths) this summer.

The outdoor leadership program for girls will sponsor two weeklong adventures to instill in them the skills they need to make a difference in the world. The program will use mentoring, workshops, and outdoor challenges to build the self-esteem, initiatives and strengths of young women.

The trips will be age-specific: one for junior high school girls, ages 11–13 and the other for high school girls, ages 14–17. Activities will include backpacking, canoeing, rafting, rock-climbing and orienteering. The trips will be based in the Jocko Valley, 40 miles northeast of Missoula and will be held July 16–21 and July 23–28. The fee is $200. Scholarships are available according to financial need. The deadline for enrollment has been extended to June 20.

For more information, call Women's Voices for the Earth at 543-3747 or stop by the office at 114 W. Pine Street.

Outdoors Program for Girls Offered This Summer (2002, June 13). *Missoulian.*

door recreation is extremely critical. The primary public transportation system, which is the use of personal automobiles, exerts massive pressure on outdoor recreation providers. Development of sophisticated roads and highways for access to specific areas and provision of extensive parking areas for cars and recreational vehicles, boat trailers, campers, and motor homes consume large areas of land space. The ability of people to travel long distances to use resource-oriented recreation areas is a by-product of society's mobility. The decline in the amount of work necessary to earn income for personal economic maintenance has increased the average individual's amount of discretionary time. The amount and kind of work that people do and the amount and length of leisure time they have available influence their leisure activity choices. These are important factors to be considered in planning for outdoor recreation.

Leisure service organizations both in the private sector and at all levels of government have an increasingly important role in the area of outdoor recreation programs and services. The management of people along with natural resources is a primary contemporary concern (Jensen, 1977: 45–46). Outdoor recreation areas should be identified and preserved for that purpose; the utilization of resources for recreation, conservation, and preservation should be a high priority. The leisure service movement must become more active in the area of ecology. We should assume strong positions in leadership and advocacy on behalf of and in cooperation with those individuals and groups concerned with ecological problems.

WELLNESS

Wellness is a program area that has emerged over the past several decades. Wellness programs operated by leisure service organizations have taken on increasing importance, paralleling the rising interest in health, fitness, and well-being. Not only is wellness an individual concern, but it is also a concern of organizations. Increasingly, the health of an organization's employees is recognized as having a bearing on its effectiveness and efficiency. Organizations are concerned with employees' absenteeism, morale, and job performances as well as with medical claims that are forcing increases in insurance rates. Today, many organizations are employing wellness specialists with the hope of reducing or minimizing these undesirable health-related factors.

Orsega-Smith, Payne, Katzenmeyer, and Godbey (2000:69) suggest that the following factors should be considered in promoting the need for healthy living; and hence, supporting the establishment of wellness programs:

- The United States now ranks thirty-seventh in the world in the overall quality of its health care.

- About 15 percent of all money spent in the United States is for "health" purposes and, in a rapidly aging population, the ratio of spending on older people is seven to 100 times as much as for younger people.
- Obesity is at an all-time high, as one out of every three Americans is overweight.
- Approximately one-third of all American adults reports having no leisure time physical activity.
- The leading causes of death are now mainly those over which individual behavior habits and attitudes exert some influence. While pneumonia, tuberculosis, and diarrhea or enteritis were the leading causes of death in 1900, a century later the leading causes are heart disease, cancer, and stroke. More than 80 percent of the factors that determine our state of health have to do with our environment, our relations with friends and enemies, the quality of our education, our status in the community, and how we think about ourselves.

In 1996, the U.S. Surgeon General highlighted the benefits of regular physical activity on the health and well-being of individuals. The report suggested that Americans should include thirty minutes or more of moderate to intense physical activity on all or most days of the week. Even though Americans recognize that physical activity is helpful, 60 percent of U.S. adults do not exercise regularly and 20 percent of the U.S. adult population is not active at all. The report also pointed out that nearly half of American youth ages twelve to twenty one are not vigorously active on a regular basis.

The report indicates that adolescents, young adults, adults, and older adults, both male and female, can benefit from moderate physical activity. Physical activity does need to be strenuous to be beneficial. The report pointed out that individuals can obtain significant health benefits with a moderate amount of physical activity that can prevent premature death, illness, and disability. Physical activity greatly reduces the risk for illness or death from the heart disease, diabetes, colon cancer, and high blood pressure. Further, regular physical activity can reduce

depression and anxiety and, in general, contribute to overall well-being.

Not only are wellness programs important in terms of the work environment, but they contribute to individuals throughout the life span. For example, wellness programs offered by leisure service organizations improve the physical health and intellectual performance of children. It is especially important because many children and adolescents are increasingly less likely to be involved in school physical education programs. Certainly, wellness programs enhance quality of life for adults and older citizens. Such programs prevent or delay the onset of certain chronic diseases, assist in the maintenance of one's functional autonomy, enhance cognitive functioning, and provide access to important networks.

The wellness program area is known by several terms. *Wellness* is an all-encompassing term that embraces many different kinds of activities. It is far broader than, for example, the term *physical fitness*. Another term that is often heard is *lifestyle management,* which is a broad term, like wellness, yet lacks focus. Also often used is the term *health promotion*. Health promotion focuses on the promotion of positive health behaviors. Health promotion activities include any combination of educational or other interventions that produce healthier individuals.

What is wellness? Wellness is difficult to define; it means different things to different individuals. From one person's perspective, wellness may be viewed as a process that helps individuals enjoy their lives more fully. Schlaadt (1983: 20) has written that wellness is a lifestyle dedicated to following desirable health practices and achieving optimal health. Another person may look upon wellness as a program of intervention focused on reducing the risks present in one's environment. Lawrence Green, former director of the Office of Health Information and Health Promotion, Department of Health and Human Services, has suggested that wellness is "any combination of health, education, and related organizational, economic, or political interventions designed to facilitate behavioral and environmental changes conducive to health" (Girdano, 1986: 5–6). Wellness can also be viewed more narrowly: It can be focused on a single dimension of a person's life, such as physical, emotional, or social well-being, or other kinds of well-being.

From our perspective, wellness is a broad concept that is tied to helping people formulate values and then act on them, through the provision of a variety of activities and services. As Behrens (1983: 1) has written, wellness "begins with people who are basically healthy and seeks the development of community and individual measures to help them develop lifestyles that can maintain and enhance their state of well-being." Wellness programs (such as nutrition, physical fitness, leisure education, and stress management) are different from health protection (occupational safety, toxic agent control, and accidental injury control) and preventive services (high blood pressure detection, immunization, and family planning). Participation in wellness programs is usually voluntary. Wellness programs "provide people with information, education, opportunities for behavioral change and/or incentives to help and encourage them to make the best possible choices about lifestyles they practice" (Behrens, 1983: 1). A wellness program that is organized by a leisure service organization should deal with three elements. These are as follows:

Information—Leisure service organizations can provide individuals with information related to their well-being. This information can concern the ill effects of a poorly managed lifestyle and can direct individuals to appropriate activities and services that can help them develop and maintain a greater sense of wellness and well-being.

Values Clarification—Another way that a leisure service organization can assist individuals is by helping them clarify their wellness-related values. To promote a permanent change in behavior, people must be motivated. Ideally,

individuals ought to be able to see the value of a healthy life, but often are unable to motivate themselves even in the face of overwhelming evidence that would suggest that their present behaviors are unhealthy. People are influenced by societal factors and habits that lead them to focus on short-term activities that provide immediate gratification rather than on longer-term goals related to wellness.

Activities, Programs, and Services—An important contribution that leisure service organizations make is in the structuring of opportunities for participation in wellness programs and activities. Not only can leisure service organizations directly create activities that they plan, organize, and implement, they can also work with a variety of different community agencies to cosponsor events. A leisure service organization can also serve as a clearinghouse, helping to identify and refer individuals to other programs, agencies, and resources.

These strategies suggest that leisure service organizations can engage in a wide variety of wellness-related services. The diversity of wellness activities provided by leisure service organizations may address a variety of different health, lifestyle, and well-being concerns. In one community, a leisure service organization might be narrowly focused on one type of activity or service, such as a fitness program. In another community, a leisure service organization might have a broader approach, providing a more comprehensive wellness program that includes hydrostatic weighing, cholesterol screening, nutrition classes, counseling, and various fitness activities.

What kinds of activities, programs, and services are normally associated with wellness programs? A myriad of services can be offered under the umbrella of wellness services. The following is a list of program areas adapted from Hoeger and Hoeger (2002: 6) that can be incorporated into a wellness program:

- Physical fitness
- Smoking cessation
- Sexuality
- Nutrition
- Spirituality
- Cancer prevention

- Safety
- Stress management
- Medical/physical exams
- Cardiovascular issues risk-reduction
- Health education

- Substance abuse control
- Leisure education
- Weight reduction
- Women's health
- Support groups

Another perspective on the types of activities, programs, and services associated with a wellness program is provided by the University of Northern Iowa's Wellness Promotion/Health Education Program (*Wellness/recreation center operating plan,* n.d.). The program serves students and employees of the university and is multidimensional in scope, organized to promote a thoughtful balance of mind, body, and spirit and to promote healthy behavior choices. Their services provide information, skill acquisition, and ongoing support for positive health behaviors. The program framework is as follows:

1. *Fitness and Nutrition Management*—Fitness and nutrition programs are designed to assist in the development of and provide ongoing support of regular, healthy eating and exercise habits.
2. *Medical Self-Care*—Medical self-care programs and services are designed to assist students and employees in their roles as primary caretakers of their health, addressing both preventive care and treatment processes.
3. *Relationship and Social Skill Building*—Relationship and social skill building programs are designed to help students and employees develop additional ways of becoming more effective teams.
4. *Mental and Spiritual Health Enhancement*—Mental health includes both emotional and intellectual health components with programs designed to encourage their full development. Intellectual activities are designed to stimulate thought processes in ways that may broaden and heighten understanding and vision.
5. *Substance Abuse Education and Prevention*—Substance abuse education and prevention programming is designed to create a new cultural norm for low-risk use of alcohol and other substances.

6. *Sexual and Reproductive Health Care*—Sexual and reproductive health care programs are designed to provide information that will assist students in making value-based decisions about their sexual health and behaviors.
7. *Safety and Emergency Response Training*—American Heart Association and Red Cross classes in CPR, first aid, lifeguard training, and blood-born pathogen training are available to all students and employees.
8. *Social/Leisure Activities*—Social/leisure activities are two-fold: 1) skill acquisition opportunities designed to promote an active lifestyle by assisting participants in acquiring sufficient skills for the enjoyment of recreational activities; and 2) events and programs designed to provide healthy and alcohol-free opportunities for fun.

Leisure service organizations often work in conjunction with other community agencies to provide services. It is not always possible for a leisure service organization to have all the resources necessary to structure a comprehensive wellness program. The strategy taken by the organization may be one of facilitating the work of divergent community groups to build a comprehensive community effort. Even if the leisure service organization is not the major motivating factor behind the provision of services, it will want to support the efforts of other organizations in building wellness programs. Many mutually beneficial relationships can be derived from working with the community resources that are in place. Some of these community groups include the following:

1. *Voluntary Agencies*—Local heart, cancer, lung, diabetes, and arthritis associations can provide material, staff time, space, and consultation.
2. *Special Interest Groups*—The American Red Cross and the YMCA/YWCA are placing a national focus on health promotion and may have material, courses, or teachers available. Alcoholics Anonymous and Al-Anon may offer assistance in handling crises. Groups such as the safety and dairy councils have many useful materials. The National Retired Teachers Association's

volunteers might provide "people power" for special activities or have individuals to teach courses.

3. *Hospitals*—A growing number of hospitals have lifestyle, occupational health, and employee assistance programs designed especially for implementation in local businesses and industries.

4. *Public Health Departments*—Many public health departments have health educators and some have developed special programs for worksites.

5. *Colleges and Universities*—Teachers and students may be able to offer assistance in planning and evaluation, determining training methodologies, and course content. Students may be able to develop and teach courses or research specific topics as part of their course work or to gain experience. Look especially for students in health education, public health, exercise physiology, or nutrition. Medical and nursing students also may be willing to help.

6. *Professional Organizations*—Local medical, dental, and hospital associations may have materials and may be able to direct individuals to people or groups that offer worksite programs or can offer consultation.

7. *Community Organizations*—Community organizations such as the United Way have been a valuable resource in the development of communitywide guides listing available health promotion programs. This kind of guide is useful to all local businesses and its development helps facilitate cooperation and information exchange among local businesses and program providers.

8. *Civic/Service Groups*—The Lions Clubs have a national program aimed at preventing blindness, and local groups may have a variety of resources to draw upon. Local Jaycees, Rotary Clubs, Kiwanis, and a wide range of other civic and service organizations may be valuable sources of volunteers, materials, and support.

9. *For-Profit Groups*—Groups such as Weight Watchers or Take Off Pounds Safely may schedule meetings at or near worksites. Other organizations are eager to supply material or speakers for use in employee health promotion programs. Many for-profit groups will provide a whole package of programs for your employees.

10. *Extension Services*—Most extension services have a nutritionist as well as a health subcommittee who could be helpful in developing in-house programs. Some also have services in other content areas. To find your local cooperative extension service office, look in the white pages of your phone book under county or city government.

Any or all of these types of organizations can provide invaluable information, assistance, and support for the development of a wellness program. Leisure service organizations should work actively to foster ties that are in the best interests of those whom they serve.

Wellness Programs—Agency Examples

Schaumburg (Illinois) Park District's Woodlake Fitness Club is an excellent example of a fitness center operated by a community organization. Amenities within this facility include exercise bikes, rowing machines, stair climbing machines, treadmills, aerobic studio, saunas, whirlpools, indoor lap pool, steam rooms, and tanning salon. Services include personal training, corporate seminars, individual fitness assessments, and nursery. The center's newsletter, entitled "corporate*rec*review," is targeted for the business community in the areas of employee fitness and recreation. Courts Plus, a center for health, sports and fitness operated by the Elmhurst (Illinois) Park District, offers a wide variety of programs, including tennis, racquetball, handball, wallyball, basketball, track, fitness, aerobics, aquatics, and water aerobics. A variety of programs are targeted for different ages and groupings of individuals, including women on weights, senior weight training, youth fitness, family fun aerobics, teen aerobics, and self-defense workshops.

A unique fitness program is the MSCR/Goodman-Rotary Senior Fitness Program, sponsored by the Madison (Wisconsin) School Community Recreation Department in cooperation with the Madison Downtown Rotary Club. This collaborative effort provides a wide variety of fitness activities for older persons, including exercise classes, walking club, tai chi classes, chairbound fitness classes, mall walking clinic, water exercise classes, health awareness

EXHIBIT 8.4   He's Fit for High Office

Like him or not, you've got to admire President Bush for his running ability.

Not just his running for office, his actual running. Most fitness runners of his age (56) couldn't keep up with him.

The president hadn't talked much about his running until granting an interview to *Runner's World* for the magazine's current issue. The interview reveals not a casual jogger but a serious runner who presses his limits. Bush told the magazine he runs five or six times a week and keeps a treadmill aboard Air Force One so he can work out on long flights. He told of forming a sort of club, complete with T-shirts for members of his entourage who were able to keep up with him on a three-mile run on his Texas ranch in 100-degree heat. He has the resting heart rate of an elite marathoner.

Bush discussed what every runner know—how the activity relieves stress and clears the mind. He indicated that it also helped him give up smoking and alcohol.

Bush said he granted the interview to encourage Americans to exercise more—a worthy cause, especially after the surgeon general identified obesity as a national epidemic.

The president does have one advantage over most people in maintaining an exercise regimen. He's got a job in which he's in charge of his own schedule. He can make it part of his day without having to punch a time clock or schedule around his boss' whims. And, attended to by the White House Staff, he is not burdened with the household chores that eat up the free time of most people. Still, Bush said almost anyone can find time to exercise if they really want to, and that's probably true. He suggested that corporations provide time for their employees to exercise, because a healthier work force is a more productive work force.

That may not be the kind of corporate reform people have in mind these days, but it might help some people follow the president's good example.

Et Cetra (2002, September 6). He's Fit for High Office. The Des Moines Register, p. 6A.

programs, golf programs, and exercise programs focused on individuals with arthritis. The city of Kettering (Ohio) Parks, Recreation, and Cultural Arts Department organizes a beginning resistance training program for women. The program is a personalized activity and is limited to three students per session (see Figure 8.14). The Colorado Springs (Colorado) Parks and Recreation Department operates a combined aquatic and fitness center. Programs include water rehabilitation, fitness training, water exercise, deep water aerobics, pre- and post-natal conditioning, senior fitness, water walking, jogging, conditioning, cardiovascular fitness, weight training, and fitness assessment.

Another example of a wellness program is the Health Fitness Program operated by the Willamalane Park and Recreation District in Springfield, Oregon. This comprehensive health fitness program is available to all members of the community and includes the provision of a well-equipped fitness center. The program enables individuals to participate in an individualized fitness program (IFP) in which the fitness staff design programs for customers to meet their fitness and lifestyle goals. Other programs include

calisthenics, Swedish massage, aerobic dance, aerobic fitness, water fitness, aerobic water and prenatal fitness, fluid movement (calisthenics in the water), and hydrostatic weighing (see Figure 8.15). Special events such as the Willamalane Turkey Stuffer are designed to engage customers in a holiday fitness run or walk.

The YMCA of Lethbridge (Alberta), Canada provides a full range of fitness classes for adults. Activities include power walking, stretching, aerobics, "kardio" kickboxing, body shaping, ski and sport conditioning, "waterfit," basketball, badminton, squash, fun runs, racquetball, golf, and tai-chi. In addition, the organization provides a number of adult fitness workshops. Individual fitness and nutrition consultations are available, as well as testing, fitness appraisals, massage therapy, and orientation to assist individuals in using cardio machines and weight rooms. Figure 8.16 provides an overview of the basic fitness services the organization offers.

The Cincinnati (Ohio) Recreation Commission, along with many other municipal park and recreation departments throughout the United States and Canada, provides fully developed fitness programs. Membership at the Fit-

Figure 8.14 Wellness Program for Women, City of Kettering (Ohio) Parks, Recreation, and Cultural Arts Department.

HYDROSTATIC WEIGHING

An accurate method of measuring your percentage of body fat.

Contact Health Fitness Instructors, Kerri Januik or Mark Dannis to schedule an appointment. Hours for testing are Saturdays from 9:00 a.m. to 1:00 p.m.

Phone 726-4368
for appointment or more information.

Prices:
Fitness Center Member............... $ 7.50

Nonmember
In-District.......................................$10.00
Out-of-District.............................$15.00

Figure 8.15 Hydrostatic Weighing, Willamalane Park and Recreation District, Springfield, Oregon.

Named the "best fitness center" by *Cincinnati Magazine,* membership includes access to weight machines, free weights, treadmills, elliptical cross-trainers, stationary bikes, Stairmasters, rowing ergometers, rowing tank, locker rooms, and showers. Other programs include personal training, health and fitness assessments, spinning classes (endurance program on stationary cycles), karate classes, and therapeutic massage.

Hobbies

A hobby is an activity that an individual pursues over a period of time with intense interest, primarily for the pleasure it brings. This would seem to define many leisure activities; however, the area of hobbies is a discrete program area in the way it develops and is pursued. Perhaps it is the quality of the individual's interest in the activity—its intensity and longevity—that is especially characteristic of the hobby concept. Hobbies are usually separate from an individual's professional pursuits, although not necessarily so.

Hobby activities can be broadly classified in several ways, so that the scope of activities can be better understood (see Table 8.9). Any given hobby may fall within more than one classification; or the same hobby might be classified a certain way for one person and a different way for another person. The hobby classifications included within this section are, by and large, all-inclusive. These classifications include collection hobbies, creative hobbies, educational hobbies, and performing hobbies (*Recreation program book,* 1963: 182–87). Other terms or categories might include construction hobbies, learning hobbies, demonstration hobbies, or hobbies for sale; however, the four classifications covered here (collection, creative, educational, and performing) encompass most hobbies.

Collection hobbies are probably derived from the natural human tendency to gather or accumulate things. People collect just about anything and everything found in the environment—from glass doorknobs to celebrity signatures. Collectors often classify themselves according to what they collect (e.g., antique collectors, stamp

ness & Rowing Center at Sawyer Point provides participants with a number of important values. There are no start-up fees, no long-term contract is required, and the facility is open conveniently before, during, and after business hours.

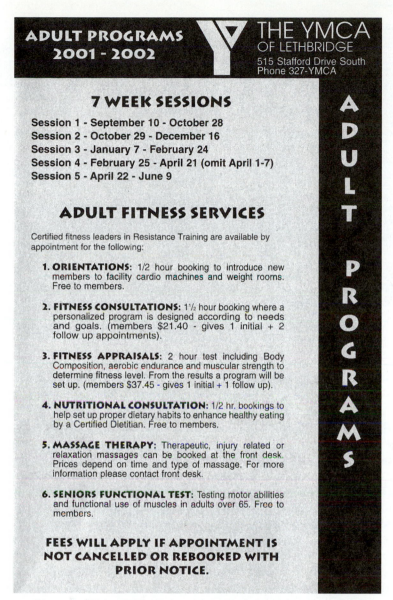

Figure 8.16   Fitness Classes, The YMCA of Lethbridge, Alberta, Canada.

collectors, art collectors, relic collectors, memorabilia collectors, firearms collectors, comic book collectors, quilt collectors).

Creative hobbies offer a different type of involvement than collection hobbies. People have a psychological drive to make, construct, and create. They find pleasure and satisfaction in the resulting object or product. The need to be creative often is fulfilled through vehicles such as painting, writing, using a computer, composing, inventing, making craft objects, cooking, sewing, or dancing. Hobbies that emphasize the learning of skills and acquisition of knowledge are called educational hobbies. Incidental and

TABLE 8.9   Classifications of Hobbies

Collection	Creative	Educational	Performing
Art	Carving/whittling	Archeology	Acting
Autographs	Ceramics	Art	Backgammon
Automobiles	Cooking	Astronomy	Checkers
Campaign buttons	Knitting	Beekeeping	Chess
Canes	Macramé	Crafts	Dancing
Church bulletins	Metal work	Drama	Fencing
Coins	Models	Meteorology	Golf
Christmas plates	Music	Mineralogy	Horseback riding
Dolls	Composing	Mountain climbing	Running
Flat irons	Playing	Music	Sailing
Glassware	Singing	Ornithology	Singing
Marbles	Painting	Reading	Skiing
Matchbooks	Photography	Skating	
Medals	Rug making	Tennis	
Music	Sculpture	Travel	
Phonograph records	Sewing		
Postcards	Short stories		
Recipes	Diary		
Rocks	Plays		
Scissors	Poems		
Sheet music	Woodworking		
Stamps	Writing		

experiential learning occurs in whatever we do—the experience of creating is educational; the practice of collecting can lead to many opportunities in which to learn more about the items collected.

Performing hobbies are based primarily on the use of physical skills in such activities as dance, sports, crafts, and musical performance. This kind of hobby involvement enables individuals to gain satisfaction from performing alone or with others.

As leisure service programs, hobbies have values that are different from those of other program areas. Few hobby activities require the acquisition of any specialized skills by the participant. Although some skills may be involved, these usually can be developed by the individual when needed in order to progress in the hobby. On the other hand, some educational and performing hobbies require highly developed levels of knowledge or skill or both. Hobbies may require very little outside stimulation or demand in order to create and sustain lasting interest and continued pleasure. Individual involvement

in hobby activities may also serve as a device for relaxation and reduction of boredom during limited leisure time, a means of compensation (by excelling in a hobby), a channel for development of interpersonal relationships and sociability (by meeting and being with other people involved in a hobby), an opportunity for youth to test interests for future career involvement, and a chance for adjustment by the older adult who has recently retired.

As we stated earlier, it is natural for a person to want to collect objects, to pursue various new learning experiences, and to seek opportunities for creative self-expression. Therefore, involvement in hobbies is very much a part of cultural tradition. However, there may be factors that affect, to some degree, the pursuit of hobbies. Both the social and physical environment may determine, in some situations, what kinds of hobby involvement will be appropriate. Religious beliefs, educational opportunities, and family values may be strong influences on the development of a hobby. The physical environment will affect the kinds of hobbies that people may be able to pursue in a given location: A large urban area is likely to offer better museum and library facilities to the person interested in studying European artists than is a small community that is some distance from the urban center; access to open fields, wooded areas, and country roads makes it easier for the person who is interested in hiking. The technological developments, level of affluence, and accessibility to resources will affect the knowledge and skills that people will contribute toward their involvement in hobbies. Leisure service organizations can provide opportunities for hobby development by making various program area activities available to participants for the development of skills and knowledge, and by making facilities available for such things as displays, demonstrations, sales, hobby shows, and exposure to different types of hobbies. A popular hobby among children and youth today is collecting trading cards—baseball, basketball, football, and others. Figure 8.17 shows a program offered by the Morale, Welfare, and Recreation Department of the U.S. Marine Corps in Okinawa, Japan. The program offers an opportunity for children to display and trade their cards.

SOCIAL RECREATION

In the social recreation program area of leisure activities, sociability is intended to occur as the primary function of the event and the setting. Social recreation uses all program areas to accomplish its objectives. It can include sports, games, drama, music, dance, arts, crafts, and outdoor recreation. The forms and kinds of activities may vary; however, the key factor is the reason for participation (social interaction) rather than the activity itself. Social recreation de-emphasizes competition. Many of the activities might be competitive in nature, but socializing is more important.

Settings for social recreation activities vary greatly. Socializing may be the primary emphasis at conferences, workshops, campfires, clubs, parties, picnics, family reunions, and banquets. Emphasizing sociability in a social recreation situation is a prime way to accommodate a wide variety of ages, interests, and abilities within a group. Ford (1970: 134) has indicated that we view a group in one of two ways: either as a horizontal group or as a vertical group. A horizontal group is composed of people with similarities in age, experience, skills, interests, or knowledge. Examples of horizontal groups would be Girl Scouts, sororities, certain clubs, or associations of related professionals. A vertical group is composed of people with varied ages, skills, and interests. Examples of this kind of group would be a family reunion, a father-daughter banquet crowd, or a playground party.

Individuals participating in social recreation activities do not need to possess specific knowledge or skills prior to involvement in the program. Most social recreation activities require only simple skills; they have few rules and can be used with various kinds of improvised equipment. Social recreation activities should include several general types of activities such as first-comers, ice-breakers, mixers, active games, and quiet activities. First-comer activities involve all customers as they arrive for the event so that they need not feel awkward or uncomfortable. A first-comer activity can be entered into at any time without having to wait for a specific time to begin. The activity may be done individually or in small groups, and it may be competitive or noncompetitive. Icebreakers serve to involve all participants; the intention is to enable the shy, inhibited person to feel more comfortable. Icebreaker activities usually occur with everyone doing something similar for the purpose of mutual fun and sociability. Mixer activities are designed to provide participants with an opportunity to socialize with one another for the purpose of direct communication and as a means of getting acquainted. Active games involve team play of a more active physical nature than most other social recreation activities. These games may involve running, tagging, dodging, or throwing. Inactive games usually are played while most customers are seated;

Figure 8.17 Trading Card Day, Morale, Welfare, and Recreation Department, U.S. Marine Corps, Okinawa, Japan. (Source: From Morale, Welfare and Recreation Department, U.S. Marine Corps, Okinawa, Japan.)

they may include dramatic games, creative actions, guessing games, and noisy games.

In planning social recreation events, certain factors should always be considered. Ford has suggested that a social recreation event should follow a "social action curve" (Ford, 1970: 134). There should be a low level of excitement as the customers arrive for a social recreation activity; the event should build to a higher level of excitement about midway through the event (based on the activities that take place). Toward the end of the event, the level of excitement should decline. The social action curve shows a definite beginning and end for a social recreation event. Another pattern that should emerge in planning social recreation events is the progression from pre-event planning to carrying out the event and finally to a post-event evaluation. In many situations, there are specific procedures for participant evaluation immediately after the event has taken place.

Many values inherent in social recreation events are different from other forms and areas of leisure service activities. Social recreation events can be implemented in conjunction with other program activities (such as planning a banquet to follow a sports tournament, planning a social event in coordination with a dance recital or an art exhibit, or initiating a campfire at the end of each week at camp). Social recreation events can be planned for staff—as first-aid and safety training workshops for playground staff, values clarification retreats for agency staff, and pre-camp orientation for camp staff. Social recreation events (like all recreation events) are for the benefit of the participant. The social recreation group process can foster the development of group solidarity and feelings of loyalty and belonging. Social recreation events can bring out special interests and latent talents of the participants. The Northbrook (Illinois) Park District provides a children's party service. The party packages include programs, equipment, refreshments, and leadership. Some of the parties offered by this park district include a play acting party, clay play party, dance party, sports

Figure 8.18 Children's Parties, Northbrook (Illinois) Park District.

party, music party, aerobics party, jewelry party, theater party, T-shirt painting party, ice skating party, makeup and dress-up party, cheerleading party, junior miss pageant party, and rock star talent show party (see Figure 8.18).

VOLUNTEER SERVICES

One of the highest forms of recreation is to use part of one's leisure to do something for someone else. This is facilitated by the volunteer program of the recreation agency . . . If the recreation agency does not have a program of volunteers it does not have a complete recreation program, for to many, volunteer service is a means of recreation (*Recreation program book*, 1963: 316).

A volunteer performs various services, accomplishes specific tasks, and carries out numerous responsibilities without remuneration. There is great variance in the number of volunteers, the use of volunteers, the necessity of volunteers, and the recognition of volunteers within leisure service organizations. However, volunteers function in three general areas: *administrative, program-related,* and *service-oriented.* A form of volunteerism that is increasingly offered within leisure services organizations is that of "service learning" for youth. Service learning offers youth opportunity to serve others and at the same time gain new skills and knowledge.

Volunteers involved in *administrative* responsibilities work very closely with the professional executive staff in determining policies, supporting program areas, raising funds, and supervising expenditures. Often persons functioning as volunteers at the administrative level have been appointed by elected officials or elected by members of the organization. These persons serve as board or committee members within the organizations. For example, an administrative volunteer might serve as a member of the board of directors of a voluntary youth organization (e.g., the YMCA) or as a member of the board (or of a commission) within a municipal leisure service department.

Program-related volunteers deal directly with program activities, often in a face-to-face leadership capacity. Volunteers working within the area of program activities may have specific responsibilities in planning and implementing programs in addition to directly carrying out planned program activities. The ways in which program volunteers can be involved in recreation and leisure service activities are literally endless. The primary determinant in the kinds of involvement possible for the volunteer is the type of leisure service organization with which

the volunteer is associated. Numerous youth organizations within our society were created and have been traditionally maintained by extremely strong, effective, voluntary leadership. These organizations include the YWCA, YMCA, Boy Scouts, Girl Scouts and Girl Guides, 4-H Club, and Camp Fire Boys and Girls. Most of the leadership within these organizations is voluntary—most visibly at the program level. Within public leisure service organizations (such as municipal agencies), volunteers at the program level can become involved as teachers, coaches, officials, program specialists, counselors, and leaders. Volunteers are sought to work in all program areas. Some volunteer involvement at the program level may be short-term (such as a week of counseling in a day camp) or long-term (such as teaching in the cultural arts program) or seasonal (such as coaching an athletic team).

Volunteers who function in a *service-oriented* capacity may have varied responsibilities, which can include typing, preparing large-scale mailings, making an inventory of equipment and supplies, repairing buildings, preparing campgrounds, and coordinating library and resource services. A service volunteer may also practice his or her professional skills to the benefit of the organization—for example, a doctor who gives assistance in a youth sports program physical examination clinic; an attorney who gives legal advice; an accountant who audits the books of an organization; a public relations worker who designs publicity materials; or a dietitian who consults on meal planning for congregate meals. All of these responsibilities and tasks require specialized skills and professional knowledge.

Volunteers are recruited primarily on the basis of their value to the organization; however, the organization must never lose sight of the value that such an opportunity will hold for the volunteer. The organization can seek out volunteers through several sources. Sources for recruitment include former members or program participants in the organization, community volunteer bureaus, educational or religious organizations, service organizations, civic groups, youth clubs and organizations, and retired persons.

Phoenix, Miller, and Schleien (2002:26, 28–29) have reviewed the literature and reported on the extensive benefits of volunteering. Consider the following:

- Approximately 56 percent of adults age eighteen or older volunteered for a total of 19.9 billion hours in 1998;
- It is estimated that 49 percent of students in grades 6–12 participated in volunteer services;
- In 1998, volunteers provided services equivalent to 9 million full-time employees at a value of $225 billion;
- Youth volunteerism helps build social connections with others—a perception that one can influence outcomes and moral political awareness;
- Volunteerism seems to increase social and personal responsibility among youth;
- Volunteerism is associated with a reduction in teen pregnancy and positive school-related outcomes;
- Volunteerism reduces alienation among youth and results in more positive attitudes toward adults, self-acceptance, moral development, and social and personal responsibility; and
- Volunteerism significantly increases intrinsic work values and increases perceived importance of community involvement among youth.

Although planning for volunteers and recruiting them are two crucial phases of volunteer program development, the selecting, orienting, training, and recognition of volunteers are also extremely vital. Volunteers should be selected in much the same way that staff persons are selected—on the basis of application, interview, and demonstration of skills and knowledge. It is important to know why the person has chosen to volunteer and if the volunteer is willing to accept supervision, direction, and guidance in carrying out responsibilities. Orienting the volunteer to organization philosophy, purpose, objectives, and policies should be followed with specific training as to the nature of the volunteer's tasks and how they are to be carried out.

The volunteer should have a written job description to reinforce his or her training. In addition to preparing the volunteer to function appropriately and effectively within the organization, the leisure service professional must be able to function effectively in a supervisory capacity to accept the volunteer as part of the organization and to provide appropriate reinforcement for services that are accomplished.

The City of Milpitas (California) Leisure Services Division operates a Milpitas Volunteer Partners (MVP) program (see Figure 8.19). This program provides opportunities for individuals to work with persons of all ages in activities ranging from theater performances to therapeutic recreation. The program includes volunteer opportunities in 500 activities. The city of Colorado Springs (Colorado) Parks and Recreation Department runs a Volunteers in Parks program. Figure 8.20 presents a brochure that emphasizes working as a volunteer coach. Figure 8.21 presents guidelines for the Teen Volunteers in Parks (VIP) program, which presents volunteer opportunities to teens in a positive way. Figure 8.22 is an example of the volunteer opportunities offered by the Hearst Center for the Arts, operated by the Department of Human and Leisure Services in Cedar Falls, Iowa. An application form for volunteers from the Foothills Park and Recreation District, Lakewood, Colorado, is found in Figure 8.23.

The Indy Parts and Recreation in Indianapolis (Indiana) sponsors a program aimed at drawing volunteers to assist in the maintenance of gardens in Holliday Park. This program provides an opportunity for individuals to volunteer their time to enhance various horticultural projects in the park. Individuals are provided with tools or can bring their own. They are encouraged to join others on Saturdays from 9 A.M. until noon for the volunteer project. Figure 8.24 provides a list of dates and projects for volunteers.

Voluntary service has value for the individual who volunteers and for the organization. Voluntary service enables some individuals to perform skills and demonstrate

Figure 8.19 Volunteer Partners, City of Milpitas (California) Leisure Services Division.

Figure 8.20 Volunteer Coaches, City of Colorado Springs (Colorado) Parks and Recreation Department.

knowledge with which they are familiar and confident. For others, volunteering may offer an opportunity to discover latent skills and talents. Volunteering may be especially rewarding for individuals who are no longer involved in paid, professional responsibilities (such as retired persons, homemakers and househusbands, or disabled persons), offering them an opportunity to extend their professional expertise. All volunteers are offered the enjoyment that comes from contributing. The value of volunteers to a leisure service organization is broad in scope. Through the involvement of volunteers, an organization strengthens its ties with the community that it serves. Volunteers

CITY OF COLORADO SPRINGS
PARKS & RECREATION DEPARTMENT

TEEN VOLUNTEERS IN PARKS (VIP) PROGRAM

"EVERYTHING YOU ALWAYS WANTED TO KNOW ABOUT WORKING WITH TEEN VOLUNTEERS BUT WERE AFRAID TO ASK ..."

OR

STRATEGIES FOR SUCCESS WITH TEEN VOLUNTEERS

Congratulations on your past successes in working with teen volunteers. In 1992, over 100 teens participated in Parks & Recreation Department summer programs, donating over 4,000 hours of valuable service to our department, and to our community. These figures reflect a growing nationwide trend toward teen volunteerism.

You, as a supervisor, can make the difference in a teenager's volunteer experience -- making that experience a great one for both of you, or a dismal time for all. No one volunteers to do a bad job. By following a few simple principles, the time together will be satisfying and worthwhile for staff and volunteer alike.

"What Teen Volunteers Need"

1. Teen volunteers need to be treated with respect. The goal is not to treat teen volunteers as "non-paid staff," but to treat staff as volunteers! Those teens who finally make it to your program have been carefully screened and interviewed. You have the "cream of the crop" working for you!

2. Teen volunteers need your patience, tolerance, and acceptance of those qualities that make each of them a unique individual.

3. Teen volunteers need to be known. Try to know the name of each teen volunteer and say "hello" when they arrive for work. It's hard to recognize a volunteer's efforts each day if you can't remember their name.

4. Teen volunteers need to be heard, listened to, and have their opinions valued by your attention.

5. Teen volunteers need your help in getting off to a good start by:

   • Introducing yourself and any other supervisor to whom they might report.
   • Touring the facility or workplace, explaining where to put personal belongings, where to sign in and out, where to find restrooms, and/or where to park.
   • Explaining the procedure for calling in sick; whom they should call, what phone number, best time to call, etc.
   • Knowing which supervisor can/will answer questions that arise on the job.
   • Being updated on changes or happenings at the site that may impact them.
   • Knowing what to do if tasks are completed early.

Figure 8.21 Teen Volunteers in Parks (VIP) Program, City of Colorado Springs (Colorado) Parks and Recreation Department.

6. Teen volunteers need your understanding that age is not a fair indicator of a person's level of ability or responsibility. Each teen volunteer will have a wide range of talents and experience. Some will need little direction, others will need more. Comparisons are both unfair and inappropriate.

7. Teen volunteers need work that fits their interests and offers opportunities for personal development and meaningful service.

8. Teen volunteers need well-defined roles and job descriptions; written and verbal. Be prepared to repeat instructions several times in the early days of your program. It may take teens a few days to feel comfortable enough with their surroundings that they can hear everything they are told.

9. Teen volunteers need to be involved in planning whenever possible.

10. Teen volunteers need to feel appreciated for their efforts; say "thank you" each day.

11. Teen volunteers need ongoing feedback on their performance and assessment of agreed-upon expectations. Try to motivate your teen volunteers with a positive working environment, and praise for a job well done.

12. Teen volunteers need good role models. If a volunteer's behavior seems inappropriate, make sure it is not YOUR actions that they are modeling.

13. Teen volunteers need to know that unsatisfactory job performance will result in disciplinary action.

14. Teen volunteers need privacy for correction or discipline. Correction and constructive criticism should be offered gently, honestly, and at the end of the workday when co-workers have left the site.

15. Teen volunteers need a protected work atmosphere. They are not expected to deal with media, unhappy parents, or emergency situations -- staff are paid to supervise these types of circumstances.

16. Teen volunteers need staff to display appropriate and professional behavior toward co-workers, by remembering these things:

   • Staff should be prompt, cooperative, helpful, honest, well-groomed and dressed appropriately for work. Staff should leave personal problems at home.
   • Staff should NOT criticize co-workers or supervisors, should not waste time, should not make personal phone calls, should not use unacceptable grammar, and should NEVER use profanity.
   • Department policy states that paid staff NEVER date teen volunteers for the duration of the summer program in which both persons are working.

Many of our paid staff (you) were once teen volunteers. Try to remember the uncertainty you felt and appreciate the challenges teen volunteers are facing.

Volunteers are a precious commodity. They give their very best when they get the very best from you!

Figure 8.21 *Continued.*

VOLUNTEER OPPORTUNITIES

The James & Meryl Hearst Center for the Arts offers exhibits, interesting programs and challenging classes for people in the community. Get involved with the volunteer program and Cedar Falls Arts Alive (membership support organization for the Hearst Center). Become acquainted with the benefits it offers you.

You are invited to explore new challenges and directions through volunteer opportunities offered at the Hearst Center:

★ As an <u>Office/Information Specialist</u>, you will meet visitors and assist with Office/Clerical work.

★ Assist an instructor and gain experience in the classroom as a <u>Classroom Associate</u>.

★ Learn more about Art! Help tour guides and teach studio activities by volunteering as a <u>Tour Associate</u>.

The volunteer program offers opportunities for *you to get involved.*
★ Call now for more information and stop in to see the Center.

James & Meryl
HEARST CENTER FOR THE ARTS
304 West Seerley Boulevard
Cedar Falls, IA 50613
319-273-8641

The James & Meryl Hearst Center for the Arts is a municipal arts center, a division of the Department of Human & Leisure Services, City of Cedar Falls.

Cedar Falls Arts Alive, Inc., membership support organization for the James & Meryl Hearst Center for the Arts, provides the center with operational and volunteer support.

Figure 8.22 Volunteer Opportunities, Hearst Center for the Arts, Department of Human and Leisure Services, Cedar Falls, Iowa.

Volunteer Application Form

Foothills

Appointment Applied For	Date of Application

How Did You Learn About Us?
- ❑ Advertisement
- ❑ Employment Agency
- ❑ Friend
- ❑ Relative
- ❑ Walk-In
- ❑ Other _____

Last Name	First Name	Middle Name
Address	*Number*	*Street*	*City*	*State*	*Zip Code*
Telephone Number(s)	*Home*	*Work*			

Education	Elementary School					High School				Undergraduate College/University				Graduate/ Professional			
Years Completed	4	5	6	7	8	9	10	11	12	1	2	3	4	1	2	3	4
Diploma/Degree																	

Are there any special skills and /or certifications which you possess that would benefit the District?
_____
_____
_____

Are you CPR certified? ❑ Yes ❑ No   First Aid certified? ❑ Yes ❑ No

Please list your hobbies, interests, etc.
_____
_____
_____

What community affiliations do you belong to? (churches, clubs, other organizations)
_____
_____

Previous volunteer experience (description of work and years employed)
_____
_____

Figure 8.23 Volunteer Application Form, Foothills Park and Recreation District, Lakewood, Colorado (continued on page 263).

What do you hope to gain through your volunteer experience? _____

_____

_____

Are you willing to give Foothills Park and Recreation District a time commitment of 6 months?
❏ Yes   ❏ No

Days and times available _____

_____

Do you foresee any conflict with your current occupation? _____

_____

Current occupation _____

Previous employment (Description of work and years employed; limit to last 10 years only)

_____

_____

_____

_____

_____

List two reference people whom we may contact:

_____

Name   Address   Phone

_____

Name   Address   Phone

List any other information that you feel is pertinent about yourself or your volunteer experience

_____

_____

_____
Applicant's Signature

┌───┐
│ *Please return to:*   │
│ Foothills Park and Recreation District   │
│ 2200 S. Old Kipling Street   │
│ Lakewood, CO 80227   │
│ 303-987-3602   │
└───┘

3/6/95 DT
Volunteer disk

Figure 8.23 *Continued.*

Figure 8.24 Volunteer Opportunity, Indy Parks and Recreation, Indianapolis, Indiana.

can add enthusiasm to organizational plans and programs, and can contribute specialized skills and knowledge to enhance existing activities. Volunteers also offer additional human resources to carry out existing programs or to enlarge and extend services.

TRAVEL AND TOURISM

Tourism is a growing program area for leisure service organizations. Edgell (1990) writes: "tourism in the 21st century will be a major vehicle for uplifting people's aspirations for a higher quality of life . . . tourism also has the potential to be one of the most important stimulants for global improvement in the social, cultural, economic, political, and ecological dimensions of future lifestyles." What exactly is tourism? What is travel? These two terms are often used interchangeably. *Travel* involves the movement of people from one location to another and *tourism* involves the provision of attractions and support services to assist individuals. The U.S. Department of Commerce (n.d.: 3, 7, 11), in the publication *Tourism and Recreation: A State-of-the-Art Study,* has suggested several definitions for the word *tourist,* such as the following:

> A tourist or pleasure traveler is defined to be anyone who has traveled away from home for pleasure purposes; . . . a person, not on business, who stays away from home overnight; [and a person who travels with] an element of recreation in mind.

The U.S. Department of Commerce's Travel and Tourism Administration (n.d.: 9) provides the following definitions for *visitors, tourists,* and *excursionists.* Adapted from this source, they are:

- *Visitor.* A visitor is a person visiting a location other than that which is their usual place of residence for any reason other than following an occupation remunerated from within the country visited. This definition covers two classes of visitors—tourist and excursionist;
- *Tourist.* A tourist is a temporary visitor staying at least twenty-four hours in the location visited and the purpose of whose journey can be classified under one of the following headings: 1) leisure, recreation, holiday, health, study, religion, and sport; 2) business, family, mission, meeting; and
- *Excursionist.* An excursionist is a temporary visitor staying less than twenty-four hours in the location visited (including travelers on cruises).

The individual's motivation for or purpose in taking the trip would be the most important factor characterizing the tourist. Other terms defined

EXHIBIT 8.5   Disney World Tops Family Destinations

According to *Family Fun* magazine, Walt Disney World in Orlando, Florida and Yosemite National Park in California are the top two destinations in the magazine's reader's poll.

This marks the second year in a row the Disney theme park topped the list. Its California cousin, Disneyland in Anaheim, placed fifth.

Outdoor adventures also are crowd-pleasers. In addition to Yosemite, Yellowstone National Park in Wyoming, Montana and Idaho; the Great Smoky Mountains National Park in Tennessee and North Carolina and Acadia National Park in Maine all ranked in the top 12.

Rounding out the list are Washington, D.C., the San Diego Zoo; Monterey Bay Aquarium in Monterey, California; SeaWorld Orlando in Orlando, Florida; the Statue of Liberty in New York City and New York's American Museum of National History.

Disney World Tops Family Destination (2002, March 19). *The Des Moines Register,* p. 6B.

by the Commerce Department study included: *outing*—"an occasion on which persons are away from home for the major part of the day"; *trip*—"an occasion on which persons are away from home at least overnight"; and *vacation*—"an occasion lasting four or more days" (p. 9).

Is there a definable difference between the tourist and the leisure activity customer? The degree of difference will depend largely on the characteristics of the individual tourist. Just as leisure customers are involved in activities within their immediate vicinity, most tourists are involved in a variety of activities in the course of their travels, and both are participating in these activities in their leisure time. Consequently, the difference between the tourist and the leisure customer is more a matter of locale than anything else. The Department of Commerce study suggests the following:

> Recreation is conceived of in the generic sense of the word, the 're-making' or 're-creating' of an individual through the use of leisure time in such a fashion as to restore or rebuild what has been depleted or exhausted in his makeup and to add to his knowledge and abilities with the purpose of a fuller, more satisfying life.
>
> Both the tourist and the recreationer add to their stock or knowledge and experience as a result of their activities. The recreationer . . . frequently needs to acquire new skills, or new abilities in order to engage in a particular form of recreation . . . Tourism consists primarily of travel for pleasure purposes, it does not normally involve a large measure of physical exertion, nor does it involve the acquisition of new skills (p. 10).

The Commerce Department study suggests, interestingly, that it is possible to be both a tourist and a service customer—a tourist, being a person who is traveling from place to place for pleasure, may be called a recreationer when he or she participates in any activities at those places where he or she may choose to stay. In our sedentary society are many who travel to find an activity that is physically challenging (e.g., skiing, surfing, scuba diving, and mountain climbing). "With equal zest, others travel to find the challenges to the mind that appear in contrasting one's own feelings and actions against those of people in other . . . [areas] or . . . countries" (Milne, 1976: 20).

The travel and tourism industry in the United States, Canada, and throughout the world has a major impact on the economy. Travel is one of the major industries of the United States, and in many countries of the world it is the major industry. In the coming decades, steadily increasing leisure time will make travel more important. The numerous kinds of services necessary to accommodate tourists (such as self-contained resorts, commercial lodging establishments, theme parks, eating places, auto service areas, and amusements) are supplied by private enterprise.

The program area of travel and tourism, under the auspices of the local community leisure service organization, can include both informative and participative activities. The organization could provide travel literature, travel films, "armchair" travel groups, and short or long-term travel opportunities, involving a few hours, a short trip of several days, or extended travel here or abroad. Leisure service organizations can serve an especially useful function by providing opportunities for those who cannot ordinarily travel on their own or who find it difficult to do. For example, the organization could initiate a ski trip for teens, a trip out of town to a major sports event for boys and girls, an excursion to a safari zoo for children, or a trip to Hawaii for a group of retired individuals.

California Cruisin' Yacht Charters, located at Cabrillo Isle Marina in San Diego (California), is an example of a for-profit leisure organization (www.californiacrusin.com). This leisure business provides several trips and tours and combines its services with the provision of boat and breakfast accommodations. Programs include harbor tours, custom charters, and sunset cruises (see Figure 8.25).

Blank (1989) has identified a number of examples of tourist attractions. He notes that the list is far from comprehensive but does define some of the elements that attract and hold tourists for a leisure experience. Among these are: (1) natural resources or a natural feature, (2) economic activity, (3) an ethnic/cultural makeup, (4) historic features, (5) climatic attractions, (6) religious attractions, (7) outdoor recreation, (8) specialty tourist attractions (e.g., stadiums, race tracks), and (9) events. Programmers can build on each of these attractions to create a comprehensive leisure experience. For example, historical features might include a religious attraction as well; a natural resources experience might also offer a climatic attraction.

EMERGING AREAS OF PROGRAM IMPORTANCE—YOUTH AND FAMILY PROGRAMMING

Two emerging areas of great importance to leisure service programs are youth program-

Figure 8.25 Tour Opportunities, California "CRUISIN" Yacht Charters, San Diego, California.

ming and family programming. There are many reasons why these two areas have become so important for leisure service organizations.

Social indicators suggest that youth have a great deal of time available outside of school and general life maintenance. In fact, youth have a great deal of discretionary time, much of which is spent without any adult supervision. Further, concerns regarding violence, crime, delinquency, sexual activity, and lower rates of achievement have made youth a focus. A prevailing philosophy through the twentieth century was that youth could be managed by providing them with fun, engaging activities. The "fun morality" has given way to a new ethic suggesting that youth should be embraced as important assets to any community and that we should work in a proactive way to assist them in their journey to adulthood.

Family dynamics have changed dramatically in the last several centuries. Consider the emergence of single-parent families, blended families, as well as the de-emphasis of living in extended family units. Divorce rates among, couples, marriage at a later date, the co-habitation of couples without being married, dual-income families with and without children, have all changed the nature of family life. Family life is in a state of flux, ever-changing with new dynamics emerging on a continuous basis. Families are often in transition, less stable; in a sense redefining what it means to be a family member. The redefinition of North American families has caused leisure services to rethink how it can meet the challenges of new and different types of family units, as well as strengthen traditional family values.

A Framework for Youth Programming

Edginton and de Oliveira (1999) have suggested a program framework for youth development. They suggest the following in organizing a comprehensive delivery of youth development services:

Academic Enrichment—Assist youth by proficiency improvement and/or by adding to enriching their knowledge base or skill.

Leisure Activities—Provide a full range of leisure activities in all program areas using all program formats is a purposeful way of promoting instru-

mental-, developmental-, or entertainment-focused services.

Leadership Development—Offer programs aimed at providing opportunities for youth that place them in leadership roles and assist them in identifying, discovering, and developing knowledge skills and competencies designed for leadership.

Service Learning—Provide a carefully monitored experience with intentional learning goals that include an opportunity for action and reflection (praxis).

Outreach Services—Direct programs at youth in their environments at times and places that are convenient.

Life Skill Building—Offer services that develop life skills to assist youth in their transition to adulthood; focus on human relations, finance, decision-making, developing resilience for threatening-life influences, etc.

Health Promotion—Focus on promoting healthier living including fitness, nutrition, sexuality, self-image, etc.

Peer Mentoring—Focus on youth leading youth.

Vocational/Career/Employment—Assist youth in finding their "calling" and assist individuals in establishing career goals or even employment.

Clubs/Special Interest Groups—Offer formal and informal clubs and special groups that provide youth with a sense of place, belonging, loyalty, etc. Peers and peer groups have a great influence on the formulation of youth identity.

A Framework for Family Programming

Promotion of quality time among family members is an important use of leisure. Great emphasis is placed on ensuring that parents play with their children in a meaningful way. Family recreation doesn't necessarily require great expenditure of funds, but rather ensures that family members spend quality time together. There is no universally acknowledged program framework for family recreation programming. Every life activity possesses opportunities for family members to be engaged in meaningful ways with one another. However, some general ideas for family recreation programming include the following:

Family Life Skills and Development—The development of life skills can help family members live, play, and work productively. Activities could include a focus on decision making, simple chores, problem solving, telephone etiquette, financial management, conflict resolution, assertiveness skills to avert peer pressure/abuse, and critical-thinking skills.

Family Hobbies—Hobbies are activities pursued with interest over an extended period of time. There are many hobby activities that the family share.

Family Collections—Collections are a form of a family hobby. Again, in any family unit, there may be many individual items that family members can collect or can share collectively.

Family Cultural Activities—Cultural activities are often uplifting, informative events that can be shared with family. Attending a concert or a play, visiting a museum, or attending ethnic/holiday/geographic/cultural/religious festivals or special events are good ways of building family cohesiveness.

Family Literary Activities—Literary activities can often serve as a focus for family activities. Journaling, reading a book together, going to the library, holding story time, as well as other creative activities can serve to encourage families to work together harmoniously.

Family Trips and Tours—Family vacations or holidays of any duration, even short trips together as a family unit, are valuable leisure experiences. Visiting museums, galleries, exhibits, natural wonders, fairs, farmers' markets, flea markets, festivals, parades, zoos, and even something as simple as a picnic and hike in the park bring families together.

Family Physical Activities—Families can participate in many physical activities and sports to enjoy with one another. Bowling, golf, bicycling, walking, croquette, kite flying, swimming, tennis—virtually any physical activity can be a shared family experience. Learned behavior among youth can be important beacons for future leisure behaviors.

Family Arts and Crafts—There are many different kinds of arts and crafts activities that can be shared among family members. Painting, drawing, sculpture, ceramics, photography, macrame, pumpkin carving, and holiday decorations are all examples of arts and crafts activities that can have a family focus.

Family Outdoor Activities—Activities that take place in the out-of-doors often build family cohesiveness, especially those that surround traditional parent/child or youth interaction, such as participating in youth service organizations. Planting a garden, developing outdoor skills, camping, fishing, swimming, horseback riding, snowboarding, cross-country skiing, and making snow angels are all examples of these types of activities.

Family Service Activities—There are many opportunities for families to volunteer in the service of others. Taking family time to give to others represents a powerful value that can serve to shape family life.

Family Time Capsules—Building a sense of one's family heritage and helping family members appreciate one another are essential component in building a strong family unit. Focusing on family heirlooms, jointly developing a family scrapbook, having family members develop a sense of appreciation for their family history, and promoting extended family relationships help build strong units.

Family Social Activities—Families are our primary social unit. Developing social activities within which family members can share time with one another in meaningful ways is essential. Participating in simple activities like board games, family puzzles, and family celebrations such as birthdays support the development of the family as a social unit.

Summary

This chapter has provided information regarding leisure program areas. Program areas refer to a way of categorizing and classifying activities. In this chapter, activities have been categorized in the following way: the arts, including performing arts (music, dance, drama), visual arts (including crafts), and new arts; literary activities; self-improvement/education; sports, games, and athletics; aquatics; outdoor recreation; wellness activities; hobbies; volunteer services; and travel and tourism.

The arts embraces various creative disciplines. The performing arts, for example, finds the participant to be the mode of artistic expression. The visual arts, also called fine arts, include activities such as painting and sculpture. The new arts involve use of and assistance from some form of technological medium. Music, dance, and drama are an important part of human history and have allowed individuals to express themselves and transmit culture. Crafts usually result in a useful product that is also decorative in nature.

Literary activities involve writing, communication, and reading. Self-improvement/educational programs include literary, mental, and linguistic activities directed toward individual or group improvement. Often such activities are focused on special interest areas such as women's rights, marriage and family retreats, and educational tourist-related programs.

In leisure service organizations, sports, games, and athletics are popular program services. Activities take many forms: People can engage in sport activities on an individual basis as well as in dual sports and team sports. Games can be differentiated from sports in the levels of organization and skill required; that is, games require lower organization and a lower skill level. Sports activities may be competitive or noncompetitive, although most sport activities are offered in some type of competitive format. Leisure service organizations are also involved in provision of aquatic programs and services. Swimming is a very popular activity, with leisure service organizations offering programs that encourage safety, fun, and skill development.

Outdoor recreation programs are those that take place in the out-of-doors. They involve some interaction between the participant and an element of nature. Programs are broken into two broad categories—activity oriented and resource oriented. A variety of terms can be applied in this area that influence program development, including adventure education, adventure tourism, conservation education, eco-tourism, eco-vacations, environmental education, nature education, outdoor education, and outdoor pursuits.

Wellness is a program area that has emerged in the past several decades, paralleling a rising interest in health, fitness, and well-being. Wellness programs are diverse and include such activities as physical fitness, nutrition, leisure education, weight reduction, smoking cessation, stress management, alcohol and drug awareness, health issues, and medical self-care.

Hobbies is a program area that finds individuals pursuing activities with intense interest. Hobbies can be broken into several classifications, including collection, creative, educational, and performing. Social recreation promotes social bonding with other individuals. Social recreation uses many other program area activities for the purpose of promoting sociability. Volunteer services are often a part of leisure service organizations. Volunteers serve in administrative, program-related, and service-oriented roles within organizations. Travel and tourism, as a program area, promotes opportunities for individuals to participate in a variety of activities that encourage movement to a destination attraction. Such attractions can promote natural resources, economic activity, cultural groupings, historical events, climatic attractions, religious interests, or events.

Discussion Questions and Exercises
---

1. What is a program area?

2. Identify at least three categorization/classification systems.

3. What is the difference between the performing arts and the visual arts? Provide specific examples.

4. What is a craft?

5. Distinguish literary activities from self-improvement/education activities.

6. What are the salient characteristics that distinguish games from sports and athletics?

7. Identify major aquatic services. What is meant by the statement, "The leisure service programmer must work creatively to program aquatic complexes in our contemporary environment"?

8. Identify four classifications of hobbies and provide examples of each.

9. What is social recreation?

10. What are the steps in organizing and implementing a volunteer service program? Why do you think volunteer services has been included as a program area?

References

Arnold, N. D. 1976. *The interrelated arts in leisure.* St. Louis: C. V. Mosby.

Ball, D. W., and J. W. Loy. 1975. *Sport and social order: Contributions to the sociology of sport.* Reading, MA: Addison-Wesley.

Behrens, R. 1983. *Worksite health promotion: Some questions and answers to help you get started.* Office of Disease Prevention and Health Promotion, Public Health Service, Department of Health and Human Services. August.

Blank, U. 1989. *The community tourism industry imperative.* State College, PA: Venture.

Chase, C. M., and J. E. Chase. 1996. *Recreation and leisure programming.* Dubuque, IA: Eddie Bowers Publishing.

Danford, H., and M. Shirley. 1970. *Creative leadership in recreation.* 2d ed. Boston: Allyn and Bacon.

de Oliveira, W. & Edginton. C. R. Youth and Human Services. In Harris, H. S. & Maloney, D. D. (1999).

Human Services: Contemporary Issues and Trends. Boston, MA: Allyn and Bacon. 255–268.

Donnelly, R. J., W. G. Helms, and E. D. Mitchell. 1958. *Active games and contests.* New York: Ronald Press.

Edgell, D. L. 1990. *International tourism policy.* New York: Van Nostrand.

Edginton, C. R., et al. 1995. *Leisure and life satisfaction: Foundational perspectives.* Madison, WI: Brown and Benchmark.

Edwards, H. 1973. *Sociology of sport.* Homewood, IL: Dorsey Press.

Farrell, P., and H. M. Lundegren. 1983. *The process of recreation programming: Theory and technique.* 2d ed. New York: John Wiley.

Farrell, P., and H. M. Lundegren. 1991. *The process of recreation programming: Theory and technique.* 3d ed. State College, PA: Venture.

Ford, P. 1970. *A guide for leaders of informal recreational activities.* Iowa City, IA: University of Iowa.

Girdano, D. A. 1985. *Occupational health promotion.* New York: Macmillan.

Hoeger, W. K., and S. A. Hoeger. 2002. *Principles and labs for fitness and wellness.* 6th ed. Belmont, CA & Wadsworth/Thompson Learning, p. 450.

Ibrahim, H., and K. A. Cordes. 1993. *Outdoor recreation.* Dubuque, IA: Brown & Benchmark.

Jensen, C. R. 1977. *Outdoor recreation in America.* 3d ed. Minneapolis, MN: Burgess Publishing.

MacKay, K. J., and J. L. Crompton. 1988. Alternative typologies for leisure programs. *Journal of Park and Recreation Administration* 6(4): 52–64.

Milne, R. S. 1976. *Opportunities in travel careers.* Louisville, KY: Vocational Guidance Manuals.

Naisbett, J., and P. Aburdene. 1990. *Megatrends 2000: The new directions for the 1990s.* New York: Morrow.

National Alliance for Youth Sports. n.d. *National standards for youth sports: Modifying the sports environment for a healthier youth.* West Palm Beach, FL: National Alliance for Youth Sports.

Orsega-Smith, B., L. Payne, C. Katzenmeyer, and G. Godbey, 2000. Community recreation and parks: The benefits of a healthy agenda. *Parks & Recreation* 35(10): 68–74.

Phoenix, T., K. Miller, and S. Schleien. 2002, October. Better to give than to receive. *Parks & Recreation:* 26–32.

Pritchard, A. 2000, February. Go fish. *Parks & Recreation* 35(2): 64–67.

Recreation program book. 1963. Chicago: The Athletic Institute.

Rossman, J. R. 1989. *Recreation programming: Designing leisure experiences.* Champaign, IL: Sagamore.

Russell, R. V. 1982. *Planning programs in recreation.* St. Louis, MO: Mosby.

Schlaadt, R. G. 1983. Wellness or lifestyle management. *The ACHPER National Journal,* (winter).

Sessoms, H. D. 1984. *Leisure services.* 6th ed. Englewood Cliffs, NJ: Prentice Hall.

Sheffield, L. 1984. Are you providing multiple-option programming? *Parks and Recreation,* May, 56–57.

Shivers, J. S., and C. R. Calder. 1974. *Recreational crafts: Programming and instructional techniques.* New York: McGraw-Hill.

Swartz, M. 1996. Different program: Disney Institute—a resort for active vacationers. *Waterloo–Cedar Falls Courier,* 25 February, 1996.

Tillman, A. 1973. *The program book for recreation professionals.* Palo Alto, CA: National Press Books.

U.S. Census Bureau. 2001. *Statistical Abstracts of the United States: 2001.* 121st ed. Washington, DC: U.S. Government Printing Office.

U.S. Department of Commerce. n.d. *Tourism and recreation: A state-of-the-art study.* Washington, DC: Government Printing Office.

U.S. Department of Health and Human Services. 1996. *Physical activity and health: A report of the Surgeon General.* Atlanta, GA: Centers for Disease Control and Prevention, National Center for Chronic Disease Prevention and Health Promotion.

Wellness/recreation center operating plan. n.d. Cedar Falls, IA: University of Northern Iowa School of Health, Physical Education, and Leisure Services, 19–21.

Witt, P. A. 2000, March. Its totally cool, totally art. *Parks & Recreation* 35(3): 64–75.

Program Formats

LEARNING OBJECTIVES

1. To help the reader define and understand the *program format concept.*
2. To demonstrate the relationship between *program formats and customer satisfaction.*
3. To help the reader gain an in-depth knowledge of *various types of program formats* including competitive, drop-in or open, class, club, special event, workshop/conference, interest group, and outreach formats.
4. To provide the reader with *specific examples of program formats.*

INTRODUCTION

A program format is another variable under the influence of the leisure service programmer. Selection of program format is important because different program structures produce different types of experiences for individuals. In order to effectively implement various activities, a leisure service organization should first make a concerted effort to review the wide variety of available program formats. Individual customers may prefer some program formats to others; certain formats may be more effective as a means of implementing the program.

Ideally, customers should be able to choose from a variety of formats to meet their leisure needs. For example, one customer may be more interested in swimming in a structured format such as a class, whereas another may prefer an open or drop-in format and a third customer may seek a competitive experience. The formatting or structuring of an experience can have a direct impact on the satisfaction of a customer. As a result, careful consideration must be given to the structuring of activities.

In this chapter, we discuss a number of factors related to the formatting of programs. First, we discuss how program formats are defined. Included are various definitions as presented by leading program theorists in the field. The relationship between program formats and customer satisfaction is explored. Finally, we offer examples of various program formats. Program formats to be discussed include competitive, drop-in or open, class, club, special event, workshop/conference, interest group, and outreach.

WHAT IS A PROGRAM FORMAT?

A program format is the way in which a leisure experience is organized. Think of a program format as its general structure. The program format is the configuration or way in which *experiences are sequenced and linked to one another to increase the likelihood that customers will achieve desired benefits.* In certain program formats, different outcomes are emphasized. For example, in one situation, the leisure service programmer may want to emphasize the skill acquisition components of an experience. In another situation, the programmer might want to emphasize the competitive aspects of an experience. Each of these examples would require the design of a different program format to achieve the desired outcome.

Program formats have been addressed in the literature that deals with leisure service programming. Farrell and Lundegren (1991: 101) suggests that the term *program format structure* refers to "what form the leisure experience takes." According to Farrell and Lundegren, the program format chosen will be directly related to the experience desired for the customer. They suggest five program formats: (1) self-improvement; (2) competition; (3) social; (4) participant spectator; and (5) self-directed.

A similar view is offered by Russell (1982). She says that a program format is the structure through which the activity is presented. Russell suggests still other ways of structuring programs. She writes that some of the more common program formats available to the leisure service programmer include: (1) clubs, (2) competition, (3) trips and outings, (4) special events, (5) classes, (6) open facility, (7) voluntary service, and (8) workshops, seminars, and conferences. Each of these program formats varies in terms of its purpose and general characteristics. Some allow for a continuous, uninterrupted leisure experience whereas others are short in duration, catering to lifestyles that require convenience (p. 212).

Still another approach to categorizing program formats has been offered by Kraus (1985: 186). He suggests that the program format is the form that an activity takes in the planning and scheduling process to meet a customer's needs. Kraus identifies eight potential program formats that can be employed by a leisure service organization: (1) instruction, (2) free play or unstructured participation, (3) organized competition, (4) performances, demonstrations, or exhibitions, (5) leadership training, (6) special interest groups, (7) other special events, and (8) trips and outings. He suggests that within a given recreation activity, a diverse number of program formats can be employed and that the format selected by a given leisure service organization may be directly related to its philosophical orientation. For example, Kraus notes that an "organization that bases its operation on the marketing orientation will concentrate on programs that yield revenue in one form or another" (p. 191). Kraus further notes that the selection of a program format should be completed through an intelligent process of planning and implementation (p. 191).

Rossman (1995: 53) suggests that program formats are linked with the type of roles that leisure service programmers play in the programming process. He identifies the following program formats: (1) self-directed noncompetitive; (2) clubs and groups; (3) open house drop-in; (4) competition leagues and tournaments; (5) special events; and (6) skill development. Programs that are self-directed versus those that require skill development demand different roles on the part of the leisure service programmer. Operating in the role of a *direct provider,* the leisure service programmer assumes "an increasing role in the development and operation of the program, while the individual [customer] assumes a lesser role" (p. 53). Conversely, the leisure service organization operating as a *facilitator* finds the individual customer assuming a greater role in the development and operation of the program.

These classification systems can be useful to the leisure service programmer in defining the ways in which a leisure experience can be structured and organized. The challenge to leisure service programmers is to link the most appropriate program format with the needs of the customer. Increasingly, efforts directed at segmenting needs in the marketplace have forced a more specific customization of experiences. Such a process of customization requires that the programmer be knowledgeable about the different structures that are available to deliver leisure experiences.

PROGRAM FORMAT AND CUSTOMER SATISFACTION

One of the most compelling reasons for careful selection of the leisure program format is that it may be directly related to the satisfaction that individuals derive from a leisure experience. In other words, a direct relationship may exist between the program format selected by a leisure services programmer and the satisfaction derived by the individuals participating in the experience. Do competitive programs deliver the desired outcomes sought by us and by those we serve? Do instructional programs provide individuals the expected levels of satisfaction in the leisure experience? Questions like these must be addressed by the leisure service programmer in the program planning process.

One of the key issues that we, as a profession, are concerned with is the satisfaction experienced by individuals participating in a leisure environment. We can define leisure satisfaction as the pleasure that one derives from participation in an organized leisure service program. As Beard and Ragheb have written, leisure satisfaction can be thought of as "the positive perceptions or feelings which an individual forms, elicits, or gains as a result of engaging in leisure activities and choices" (1980: 22). Rossman (1984) has suggested that program satisfaction can be discussed by identifying eight potential outcomes—achievement, physical fitness, social enjoyment, family escape, environment, economy, relaxation, and fun—and can be directly linked to leisure program formats.

Perhaps the most definitive study concerning the relationship between program format and customer satisfaction was conducted by Rossman (1984: 39–51). Rossman examined the typologies for classifying leisure program formats and their impact on customer-reported levels of satisfaction. Studying a range of customers from eleven to eighty-nine years of age (a mean age of 35.5), he found that customer satisfaction is greater when leisure programs are organized in formats that relate to certain benefits to be derived. For example, in studying the satisfactions derived from consumer involvement in programs that were environmentally oriented, Rossman discovered that satisfaction is increased in the open facility and special event program formats. Satisfaction with the benefit identified as social enjoyment is most likely achieved in the special event program format and is least likely achieved in instructional classes. Opportunities for family escape are most likely to be achieved in either directed programs or open facilities and least likely to be realized in leagues and tournaments.

As Rossman points out, the implications of this study for leisure service programmers is clear. He notes, "it seems clear that when the manager selects a program format for structuring a program, he or she is predetermining the probability that some satisfactions will be realized by the participant while limiting the probability that others will [occur]" (Rossman, 1984: 48). Obviously, the selection of a program format has a great deal of impact on the satisfaction derived from a leisure experience by a customer. Careful consideration must be given to linking the appropriate program format with the benefits to be achieved.

Another study focusing on the relationship of program format and participant satisfaction was conducted by Hupp (1985). Using the same model as Rossman, Hupp studied the impact of program format on the leisure satisfaction of a sample of women fifty-five years of age and older. She found that leader-directed programs produced the lowest level of satisfaction. On the other hand, programs that were organized in a drop-in format provided a higher level of satisfaction. In her study, customers indicated that achievement, relaxation, and environment contributed significantly to their levels of satisfaction with programs.

Again, this study confirms the importance of the selection of an appropriate program format to produce desired outcomes. As Hupp writes, "senior center directors and personnel involved with programming . . . could utilize these study findings in the planning and implementation of leisure programs" (Hupp, 1985: 93). Leisure programs for senior citizens should be formatted to produce the types of experiences and levels of satisfaction most desired by this population. Hupp's study points out the need to consider the programs and formats that will produce the most satisfaction for customers.

FORMATTING PROGRAMS

As indicated, leisure experiences can be formatted in a number of ways. Knowledge of program formats provides the leisure service programmer with information that can be useful in creating successful leisure experiences that meet the needs of customers. This portion of the chapter provides detailed information about eight different program formats: *competitive, drop-in or open, class, club, special event, workshop/conference, interest group,* and *outreach program formats.*

Competitive

In the competitive format of leisure activity, *a person's performance is judged in terms of established standards of performance or the performance of another person.* Competitive performance can be categorized in several ways. Individuals can compete against themselves to gauge their level of performance and work toward their own further development of skill and improvement in performance. An individual can compete against an opponent—either in parallel performance or direct face-to-face competition; this latter activity might be accomplished as an individual, in dual performance, or as a member of a team against another team. An individual can also compete against nature or the environment; this type of competition is carried out in such activities as hunting, fishing, mountain climbing, skiing, white-water canoeing, and hang gliding. Competition in some activities, such as skiing, can involve both human and environmental opponents.

There are two fundamental modes of competitive behavior. First, competition can take place in the form of a *contest*, which is a comparison of ability in parallel performance. By parallel performance, we mean that opponents do not interfere with the performance of each other. Some examples of contests are dance contests, spelling contests, bowling contests, and archery contests. The performance of one opponent does not affect the performance of the other opponent. A *game* is another form of competition—one that has direct, face-to-face opposition between competitors. The interference or strategy of one opponent or of a team directly affects the performance outcome of the other opponent(s). Obvious examples of game situations are tennis, softball, football, chess, and checkers.

> Contests differ from games in three significant ways. *First,* in a contest there is no interference with the contestant by his opponent(s), whereas in a game there is constant and deliberate interference with his [or her] plans and plays. *Second,* strategy and deception have no place in a contest, while games are full of unexpected situations, strategy, and deception—it is part of a game to outwit one's opponents and confuse them as to what one intends to do. *Third,* a contest presents few if any situations in which the player must exercise choice as to his or her moves, whereas games are filled with opportunities and emergencies calling for choice (Donnelly, Helms, and Mitchell, 1958:3).

Several plans can be used to organize games and contests for competition. One plan for competition can be a *meet*. In a meet situation, one's skills are matched against another's and individual scores are acknowledged; individual scores may also be combined for a total team score. Examples of this type of competition are a golf meet, swimming meet, or track meet. Another plan for competition is that of the organized *league*. In this plan of organization, all individuals or teams are scheduled to play an equal number of games against all other opponents in the league. A league is the plan of competition used for many team sports. Final standing is determined by the most number of wins or the

greatest number of points by an individual or a team. *Tournaments* are another plan of organization for competition. This kind of competition can take several forms to determine the final winner or winners. The elimination tournament is the most common kind of tournament. There is both a single elimination tournament and a double elimination tournament. Contestants are drawn by lot and matched by pairs on a draw sheet. In the single elimination tournament (see Figure 9.1), the individual or team is eliminated after losing only one game in the tournament. The contestant remaining undefeated is the winner. In the double elimination tournament (see Figure 9.2), initial pairings are determined in the same way as in the single elimination, but a contestant must lose twice before he or she is eliminated from competition. The consolation tournament (see Figure 9.3) is an elimination tournament made up of contestants who have been defeated in the first round of play. They may continue playing in a bracket from round one and a contestant must be defeated twice before being eliminated. Still another type of tournament used in competition is the ladder tournament (see Figure 9.4). This is a popular form of tournament for individual and dual activities. In the ladder tournament, contestants' names are posted in rank order, and contestants

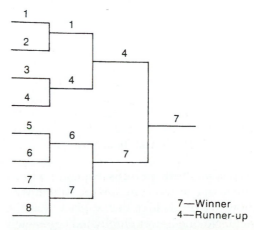

Figure 9.1 Single Elimination Tournament.

Winners' Bracket

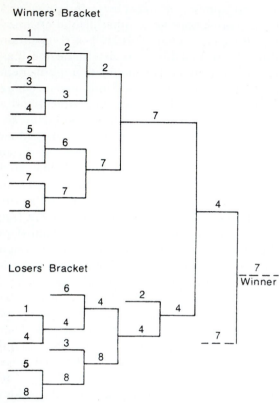

Losers' Bracket

Figure 9.2 Double Elimination Tournament.

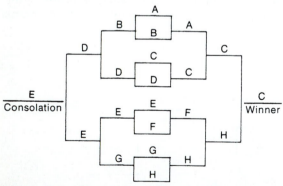

Figure 9.3 Consolation Tournament.

Figure 9.4 Ladder Tournament.

Patrick		Susan
James		Michael
Todd		Kyle
Sara		David
Molly		Joanna
Zeke		Jessica
Ann		Deb

Figure 9.5 Challenge Tournament.

can challenge those persons who are placed above them one or two rungs on the ladder. Winners move up the ladder to the place that the loser held. No one is ever eliminated completely from this type of tournament. Initial placing of

contestants on the ladder may be accomplished by having the contestants sign up for competition on a "first come, first listed" basis. Variations of the ladder (nonelimination) tournament may be used for activity competition (see Figures 9.5 and 9.6). A very popular kind of tournament frequently used in leisure activities is the round-robin tournament (see Figure 9.7), in which each contestant plays every other contestant successively. This is the kind of tournament often

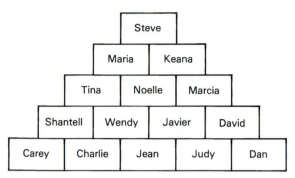

Figure 9.6   Pyramid Tournament.

Five Team Schedule

1–2	1–3	1–5	1–4	2–3
3–4	2–5	2–4	3–5	4–5
Bye 5	4	3	2	1

Six Team Schedule

1–2	1–4	1–6	1–5	1–3
3–4	2–6	4–5	6–3	5–2
5–6	3–5	2–3	4–2	6–4

Rotation System

	1	2	3	4	5	6
1	X					
2		X				
3			X			
4				X		
5					X	
6						X

Figure 9.7   Round-Robin Tournament.

used in league play. All contestants play the same number of games, and no contestant is eliminated from the tournament. This kind of tournament is difficult to manage if there are many contestants. The solution to handling large numbers is to organize more than one league.

The Joliet (Illinois) Park District sponsors an annual open tennis tournament. The program is organized as a round-robin tournament and follows U.S. Tennis Association rules. The event includes singles, doubles, and mixed doubles. There are divisions for boys age fourteen and under; junior men age eighteen and under; men—open and over age forty; girls age fourteen and over; junior women age eighteen and over; and women—open and over age forty (see Figure 9.8).

Several factors must be considered when employing competition in leisure service programs. Competition is perhaps one of the most commonly used as well as one of the most controversial forms of program activity. Although competition is an important part of leisure because of the values it has for both competitors and spectators and because of the place it has in our society, it is also very controversial because it has often been abused. Competition in leisure activities is a continuation of the competition met by most people in all life experiences, especially in education and work situations. Successful competition is thought to prove a person's worth. Competition has value in that it can be a motivator for continued performance and self-improvement on the part of the person involved. Competition also offers an opportunity for vicarious involvement on the part of spectators attending a competitive event. Competitors are often rewarded for their accomplishments; however, the importance of reward should not be emphasized.

The leisure service organization professional who plans competitive program activities must acknowledge all the levels of skill and interest that program participants might exhibit. Competitive activities must be organized in such a way as to accommodate all persons who wish to participate. There are many ways of "equalizing" competition among participants. Within tournament competition, players can be seeded—in this case, for the assumed advantage of the better player who has proved himself or herself in competition. In some sports (such as bowling

Figure 9.8   Open Tennis Tournament, Joliet (Illinois) Park District.

and golf), the score for the poorer player can be given a handicap, which means the poorer player's score has been made more equal to that of the better player. Some other sports activities, as mentioned earlier, have been adapted to offer more people opportunities for competition. These adaptations include slow-pitch softball, slow-break basketball, and teams organized according to the sizes of the players. Another equalizing factor that can be used is classification of teams according to the size of the city they come from or of the school they represent. The Joliet (Illinois) Park District provides a girls' basketball league for 6th, 7th, and 8th grades or girls twelve to fourteen years of age. The program operates during the summer months, with each team playing ten games. Figure 9.9 presents information about this program.

Drop-In Open, and Rental

Drop-in or open facility participation in leisure activities can take place at specific recreation facilities, such as community centers or tennis courts, or it might involve visits to libraries, museums, or botanical gardens. Because the nature of involvement in leisure is often spontaneous and not specifically planned, there must be opportunities and places for drop-in involvement. Drop-in participation may be stimulated by the desire to continue involvement in an activity after association with a class, team, or group is no longer possible or feasible. It might be engaged in by an individual who does not feel "ready" to associate with or make a commitment to a group for the purpose of regular involvement. *Drop-in activities do not have to follow a particular schedule and need very little supervision or leadership.* Equipment and materials may or may not be provided. This form of activity may be available in many areas of programming. Drop-in activity implies that there is a facility or area where the individual can participate. Drop-in opportunities may be available for all age groups, throughout the year—at times and places most accessible to the individual who will participate.

Within the community setting (such as a recreation center), gymnasium and game room facilities often are available on a drop-in basis. The swimming pool is frequently open for "splashes." Many kinds of craft room facilities (such as the ceramic potter's wheel, a drawing board, or an easel) can be available to the drop-in participant. Many times, facilities have supervisory personnel to maintain order and safety in the physical areas and craft areas and to provide information in response to questions concerning the activities and equipment. When people are using facilities during a drop-in time, they may be expected to supply their own equipment (for sports and games) or their own materials (for crafts). This makes it possible for the facility to be available at little or no cost to the customer. Golf driving ranges, tennis courts, outdoor sports courts, and playing fields are easily available for drop-in use when not scheduled for other events and activities. Much of the participation that occurs at mobile units and locations is on a drop-in basis.

Drop-in activities do not require any commitment on the part of the customers, often dismissing the need for registration and roll taking. Since leisure time availability varies for many individuals, drop-in activities are valuable because they can complement varying schedules. In time slots such as the early morning, lunch hour, mid-afternoon, and late evening, the majority of customers may not be available for scheduled program activities, but others might find these to be convenient times to engage in leisure activities on a drop-in basis. Opportunities for drop-in participation in recreation and leisure activities also enable many persons to move more easily into structured programs after becoming familiar with what is available.

The Commission for Accreditation of Park and Recreation Agencies (CAPRA) Standards in the Area of Program and Services Management (6.0) suggests that it is important to provide opportunities for individuals on a fee basis or free sign-up (Edginton and O'Neill, 1999: 183). The standards state that ". . . common examples of rental of equipment or a facility are picnic pavilions, ice skates, skis, boats, videos, outdoor gear, clown costumes and safety equipment" (183). The U.S. Air Force Services unit at Hickam AFB, Hawaii operates an equipment rental service available to those it serves. Rental items include party equipment, sports equipment, water sports equipment, camping equipment, and bikes. The Hickam AFB Recreation Equipment Issue Center also provides numerous

Figure 9.9   Example of a Competitive Program, Joliet (Illinois) Park District.

Figure 9.10 Hickam AFB Recreation and Equipment Issue Center, Hickam AFB, Honolulu, Hawaii.

Figure 9.11 Area and Facility Rental Opportunities, Long Beach (California) Parks, Recreation and Marine.

products that can be purchased including cameras, hats, coolers, towels, fanny packs, clothing, and other miscellaneous items (see Figure 9.10). The City of Long Beach (California) Parks, Recreation & Marine Department actively promotes the rental of its areas and facilities for such special occasions as wedding receptions, company picnics, birthday parties, Quniceñeras,

meetings, Bar Mitzvahs, class picnics, and family reunions (see Figure 9.11). The City of Fort Worth (Texas) Parks and Community Services Department reserves park sites for both public and private use. (www.forthworthgov.org/pacs/fvpacsd) (see Figure 9.12).

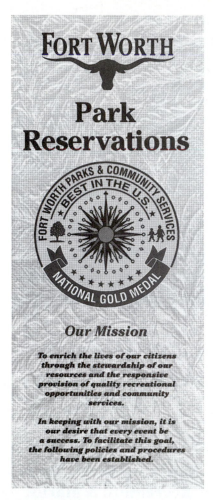

Figure 9.12 Park Reservations, Fort Worth (Texas) Parks & Community Services.

Class

The class program format used in leisure activities is a *highly structured teaching/learning situation.* A class can be defined as a group of persons meeting together to study the same topic over a specific period of time. Teaching and learning presumably occur through participation in all forms of activities; we call this *incidental learning.* However, in a class situation, opportunities for learning are directed through predetermined content development. As a result, designated outcomes of learning can be more easily mea-

sured. Although most program formats in leisure settings tend to be open and informal, class situations require certain elements of structure and organization. The class situation is a shared experience between the teacher (leader) and the learner (customer), but the teacher must assume specific responsibilities in developing the learning environment.

Included in the learning environment are such factors as the physical conditions and surroundings, the intellectual atmosphere, the emotional climate, and the social structure. The physical environment in a class situation includes location, size, and shape of the room; color and lighting; heating and ventilation; acoustics and furniture arrangement; and all equipment, supplies, and materials needed for the class. In order to comfortably accommodate class participants, the leader should take the characteristics of each given class into consideration. For example, a class for older adults should take place in an area or facility that offers easy access (preferably without steps), soft but adequate lighting, bright and pleasant colors, comfortable chairs and tables, easy access to restroom and telephone facilities, and audio/visual teaching aids that can be both easily heard and easily seen. When planning for children, the leader should realize that using appropriately designed and sized furniture will accommodate the children most comfortably.

The intellectual atmosphere of a class situation includes the teaching materials that are used and the individually directed learning experiences that are available. General organization of the learning experience fosters a more comfortable feeling for the class member. The emotional climate in a class involves the sensitivity of the teacher in meeting individual needs of the students for security, acceptance, and emotional involvement. A desirable emotional climate encourages person-to-person relationships among individual class members and between individuals and the teacher. Social structure in a class situation refers primarily to the method of leadership that prevails. Is the class carried out in a democratic manner with input from both teacher and learner? Is the class structured more loosely with little direction from the leader? Or is the class structured tightly with little input from the customer? Appropriate integration of the elements within the learning environment into the class form of activity enables both teacher and learner to share alike in a dynamic learning experience.

Several methods of presenting course content can be employed in the class situation. In deciding which methods to use, initial consideration must be given to the size of the class group, the nature of the material being presented in the course, and the situation in which it is being presented. Some of the ways in which teachers might present information include lecture, lecture with visual aids, use of videotapes and films, demonstration of projects and/or procedures, direct individual participation by the class members, and participation by class members in groups. All of these teaching methods can be employed within sessions.

It is the teacher's responsibility to practice good planning for his or her classes. Good planning takes into account the scope of the program activity to be covered, the goal that is to be reached, and the means of achieving that goal. A plan can be either a rigid design or a flexible arrangement, but the most effective planning seems to incorporate both specifics and alternatives. The effective teacher should understand why good planning is necessary. Both teacher and learner will reap the benefits of planning when a class (or session of classes) takes place.

It is necessary to develop both long-range and short-range planning. In leisure activities, class sessions often are planned to extend over a period of time. Classes might meet once a week for ten weeks or twelve weeks, or twice a week for four weeks or six weeks, and so on. Long-range planning, then, would cover the total number of weeks that the class will meet, and short-range planning, the content of each class period. In other words, the teacher should have a plan for the entire session as well as having daily plans.

Following is an example of a plan for a six-week session of a children's art class in painting.

Long-Range Planning

1. Name of class: Children's Art Class in Painting
2. Participants: Boys and girls, seven to ten years of age.
3. Length of time: Six weeks. The class will meet once a week for one hour.
4. Goal: To enable the child to become familiar with varied media and techniques related to painting.
5. Weekly sessions:
   a. Week 1—Finger Painting
   b. Week 2—Straw Painting
   c. Week 3—Squeeze Painting
   d. Week 4—Soapsuds Pictures
   e. Week 5—Sand Painting
   f. Week 6—Painting with Acrylics

Short-Range Planning

Week 1—Finger Painting
1. Objective: To allow the child to create a colorful painting without knowing how to paint.
2. Materials: shelf paper, scissors, spoon, sponge, finger paint.
3. Teaching procedure:
   a. Cover the entire working surface with newspaper.
   b. Cut the shelf paper to the desired size.
   c. Wet the paper with a sponge.
   d. Smooth the surface of the paper with your hand.
   e. With a spoon, drop some paint on the surface.
   f. With your hand, spread the paint over the surface.
   g. Using different parts of your hand, form a design (Shivers and Calder, 1974: 117).
4. Outcomes:
   a. A happy participant.
   b. A visible object, a painting.

Week 2—Straw Painting
1. Objective: To enable the child to produce a painting without using his or her hands.
2. Materials: drawing paper, straw, paintbrush, paints.
3. Teaching procedure:
   a. Cover the work area for protection of the surface.
   b. Place a drop of paint on the paper.

Learn the skill you need to

TEACH AEROBICS

FITNESS INSTRUCTOR CERTIFICATION PROGRAM

It's FREE!
**every Tuesday and Thursday
7-8 pm, Kinser Gym**

This 12-week class covers aerobic terminology, history,
anatomy, physiology, and common injuries.

EXPAND YOUR SKILL AND TEACH THE BEAT!

For more information call 637-1114 or make CONTACT at 645-2628.

Put your time in our hands!

Figure 9.13 Example of a Class, Morale, Welfare, and Recreation Department, U.S. Marine Corps, Okinawa, Japan. (Source: From Morale, Welfare and Recreation Department, U.S. Marine Corps, Okinawa, Japan.)

c. Hold the bottom of the straw 1/4 inch from the drop of paint and blow into the straw.
d. Place another drop of paint on the paper.
e. Blow the drop around the paper.
f. Finish the design (Shivers and Calder, 1974: 119).
4. Outcomes:
a. A fun and creative experience.
b. A painted design to take home.

In the planning process for class implementation, the teacher (leader) confers with the program supervisor, plans for the customers as well as with them, and reviews and evaluates the outcomes. For many customers, the class form of program activity represents their initial exposure to the activity. It may determine whether that person continues into other classes involving that same activity. Consequently, careful planning and implementation are extremely important. An example of a program organized in a class format is the Fitness Instructor Certification Program offered by the U.S. Marine Corps' Morale, Welfare, and Recreation Department in Okinawa, Japan. This program provides free instructions in aerobic terminology, history, anatomy, physiology, and common injuries (see Figure 9.13).

The City of Edmonton (Alberta, Canada) Community Services Program provides instructional classes designed to assist children in learning to play hockey. The program, for six- to eleven-year-olds, is designed as an alternative to organized and competitive hockey. An example of the flyer used to promote is shown in Figure 9.14.

Club

People are gregarious and, as a result, seek opportunities to be together in congenial social situations such as those found within the club program format. A club consists of *a group of persons organized for some particular purpose.* Clubs in leisure settings are most likely to be formed on the basis of age group or activity interest, or for the exchange of information and ideas. For example, age group clubs in leisure service organizations often exist for older adults or for children. Many clubs are

---

EDMONTON

Children's Learn to Play Hockey
Winter 2002

This program is designed for 6 – 11 year olds as an alternative to organized and competitive hockey. Drills will focus on stick handling, passing, receiving, shooting, strategy and defensive and offensive skills.

Location:	Tipton Arena
	10981 81 Avenue
Times:	Wednesdays
	3:45 – 4:45 pm
Dates:	January 9 to March 13
	(10 weeks)
Cost:	$40/child
Code:	43625

Call 496-2966 to register
Or drop in to 1st floor Circle Square
11808 St. Albert Trail
Monday-Friday, 8:30-4:30 p.m.

Edmonton THE CITY OF · COMMUNITY SERVICES

Figure 9.14 Children's Learn to Play Hockey, City of Edmonton, Alberta, Canada Community Services.

organized because of a special interest in an activity such as foreign cooking, rugby, bridge, jogging, or quilting. Clubs initiated for the exchange of information and ideas might be based on discussion of current events, evenings at the theater, or operation of ham radios. The purpose here is not to try and categorize each type of club group but to indicate the variety that is possible.

As a form of program activity, the club can have value for both participant and organization. A club experience can be a very educational one. Being with other people in a situation of this nature may enable the individual to broaden his or her ideas and interests and encourage individuals to learn from one another. Congeniality and cooperation do not require total agreement from all members at all times; people can learn from differences of opinion. Within a club, individuals have an opportunity to learn both leadership and "followership." People may learn to lead intelligently, and followers may be taught not to follow blindly. There are also opportunities for individual specialization—more so than in many other forms of activity.

Several principles of organization should be considered when developing a club. Within a club, customers function as a group and there is a long-term association of the group members. A group that is organized into a club should establish objectives and purpose for the organization. The club itself exists for the members and not for the leisure service organization professional. Clubs that are organized should be appropriate for the community in which they exist and membership in the club should not become cliquish and restrictive. This is especially true if the club functions within a public leisure service organization. Membership dues and financial commitments should not be excessive for the customers. The cost of belonging to a particular club will be greatly determined by the nature of the club and the interests and activities the customers pursue. A person who belongs to a group of Broadway theater-goers is going to spend more money than the person who is in a jogging group; supplies for a gourmet cooking club will probably cost more than those for the Saturday morning bird-watching club. Appropriate budget allowances on the part of the leisure service organization should be made for clubs, just as for other activi-

ties, so that the club members do not have to assume the entire cost of the club's existence.

Because clubs function in a different way than other forms of program activity, there must be internal organization among their members. Internal organization can be very formal or somewhat informal, but the pattern of organization should follow some order. The constitution and by laws of a club are the written orders of organization that clubs develop according to their intended purpose. "The Constitution lays down the fundamental principles on which the club is to operate. The By-Laws establish the rules of guidance by which it is to function. The By-Laws may be more easily amended and altered than the Constitution" (Milligan and Milligan, 1942: 27). A constitution and a set of bylaws are given here in very brief outline form. The club supervisor or leader may wish to expand on these items. The source used most frequently as a reference for parliamentary procedure is *Robert's Rules of Order.*

Outline for Constitution

Article I—Name

Article II—Purpose

Article III—Membership

Article IV—Officers

Article V—Executive Board

Article VI—Meetings

Article VII—Amendments

Outline for Bylaws

I—Membership

II—Dues

III—Duties of Officers

IV—Executive Board

V—Committees

VI—Quorum

VII—Order of Business

VIII—Parliamentary Authority

IX—Amendment

Figure 9.15 Example of a Club Format, Champaign (Illinois) Park District.

The club format of activity within a leisure program attempts to accommodate some of the varying interests of the program participants. Clubs can be limitless in the kinds of participants that they serve and in the kinds of activities and interests around which they may be formed. In the club format, more of the leadership and program planning may be assumed by the participants in conjunction with the leisure service professional than in other forms of program activity. The Champaign (Illinois) Park District offers a Saturday Theater Club. This program provides opportunities for individuals to engage in acting, storytelling, and theater games. Focused on children ages eight to twelve, the club is organized so that a small number of individuals (a maximum of ten) participate in the activity to ensure a positive interaction and high quality development (see Figure 9.15).

Special Event

Depending on the leisure service professional's interpretation of program areas and formats, the special event is sometimes considered a program area. We shall consider it as a program format—a way in which activities can be offered. A special event can be thought of as *an unusual or extraordinary activity or happening of some importance.* A special event deviates from the normal routine and often requires careful and extensive planning. Special events might have a special purpose tied to seasons, holidays, celebrations, or other community interests. Special events are a potent way of drawing attention to an activity. They often generate great interest, publicity, enthusiasm, and participation. Special events might cover activities that do not fall within the other forms of leisure programs already suggested.

Edginton and O'Neill (1999:219) have suggested that special events are ". . . occasions drawing individuals together to enjoy a recreation or education experience that is meaningful, significant and relevant to their well being." Discussing the characteristics of special events, they have written that special events are:

- A specifically planned and focused event;
- A singular occurrence, an unusual or extraordinary activity or happening of some importance; deviating from the routine or normal; a one-time or infrequently occurring event outside the normal program of activities of the sponsoring or organizing body; an opportunity for a recreation experience outside the normal range of choices or beyond everyday experience;
- A "crowd" participating, either by specific invitation or open invitation; or
- A publicized occurrence of finite length.

The special event needs to allow for the participation and involvement of all the individuals attending it. This factor should be considered in the planning of the special event. For example, if the special event is "Wild West Days" on the summer playground, there should be activities for boys and girls and for those age groups utilizing the playground. If the special event is a day of

"Pioneer Life on the Prairie" for an entire community, everyone in the community should have some activity in which they can be involved.

Special events can be planned and implemented by leisure service organizations as an introduction to program activities. For example, a special event such as a parade may open a week of competition for youth drum and bugle corps. Or a communitywide square dance may be the culminating activity for a weekend celebrating early American history with quilting, candle making, maple sugaring, and shoeing horses. Special events can be planned at any time during the program year to stimulate community interest or add interest to current programs. Events of this nature make a leisure service organization much more visible within the community; they also can service large numbers of community residents in a unique and attractive way.

In planning special events, the leisure service professional should capitalize on as many traditional bases as possible. For example, the seasons—winter fun, blossom time, lazy summer days, autumn leaves—are natural themes for special events. Traditional holidays and other days are standards for special event programming—for example, Fourth of July, Kwaanza, Cinco de Mayo, St. Patrick's Day, Memorial Day, and Martin Luther King's birthday. It seems easier—even for the seasoned leisure program planner—to list special events and let them describe themselves than to attempt to justify the importance and value of special events within any organization's program (see Table 9.1). Examples of special events are shown in Figures 9.16 and 9.17. The U.S. Marine Corps' Morale, Welfare, and Recreation Department in Okinawa, Japan, holds a pickle-eating contest for youth. The city of Kettering (Ohio) Parks, Recreation, and Cultural Arts Department sponsors a Benefit Celebrity Fashion Show with proceeds benefiting the United Cerebral Palsy organization.

The Santa Clara (California) County Parks and Recreation Department and the Silicon Valley Parks Foundation present the Fantasy of Lights special event. The program consists of thirty holiday lighting displays. This collaborative program features the work of a public park and recreation agency, a nonprofit voluntary organization, and a 501 (c) (3) public charitable corporation whose mission is to generate funds and support for the country parks and recreation department. This program provides opportunities for a variety of sponsors to align themselves with the work of these organizations (see Figure 9.18).

The Beach Bash Splash sponsored by the Virginia Beach (Virginia) Parks and Recreation Department is another example of a special event (http://ezreg/vbov.com). The program focuses on the beach scene and includes music, food, and activities. Figure 9.19 shows a flyer that advertises the activity. Another example of a special event is California Coastal Cleanup Day, which is sponsored by a variety of different organizations and businesses, including the City of San Jose, Santa Clara County Parks, Santa Clara Valley Water District, California Coastal Commission and Watershed Watch, Safeway Stores, Santa Clara Valley Urban Runoff Pollution Program, Actera, Prieta Resource Conservation District, West Valley Clean Water Program, Community Impact, Plata Arroyo Neighborhood Association, and the cities of Gilroy, Morgan Hill, Mountain View, and Saratoga.

The Tampa (Florida) Recreation Department advertises its special event activities on an annual basis. Some of its annual special events include an international festival, senior games, Halloween Fun Fest, Santa Fest and parade, Martin Luther King Family Festival, creative arts theater, 5 K and 15 K running events, children's parade, concert series, story telling festivals, 3-on-3 basketball tournament, and a program known as Bark in the Park (for people and their dogs).

Workshop/Conference

The workshop/conference is another program format utilized by leisure service organizations. Generally speaking, a workshop can be thought

TABLE 9.1 Examples of Special Events

Holidays and Special Days	The Arts	Ethnic and International	Animals
Christmas	Battle of the Bands	Spanish Night	Fishing Derby
Thanksgiving	Fiddlers' Contest	French Riviera	Dog Show
Easter	Barber Shop Singing	A Night in Venice	Cat Show
Valentine's Day	Art in the Park	Cinco de Mayo	Pet Show
St. Patrick's Day	Hobby Show	Scandinavian Vikings	Farm Animal Show
Fourth of July	Craft Auction	Scottish Kilts	Unusual Pet Show
Washington's Birthday	Film Festival	Irish Sweepstakes	
Lincoln's Birthday		British Jubilee	**Instructional**
Martin Luther King's	**Sports and Games**	Flight to Tokyo	Workshops
Birthday	Punt, Pass, and Kick	Midnight in Moscow	Clinics
Dominion Day	Hit, Throw, and Run	Canadian Sunset	Symposia
Queen Victoria Day	Junior Olympics	Greek Islands	Demonstrations
Halloween	Table Tennis Tournament	German Polka Day	Lectures
Ides of March	Gymnastics Clinic	African American Culture	Forums
April Fool's Day	Marble Madness	Day	Conventions
May Day		Jewish Festival	Conferences
Father's Day	**Special Days**		
Mother's Day	Hobo Day	**Locomotion**	**Promotionals**
Flag Day	Outerspace Day	Tractor Pull	Open House
Arbor Day	Wildwest Day	Soapbox Derby	Master Demonstration
	Backward Day	Sports Car Rally	Exhibition Games
Seasons	Gay Nineties	Bicycle Derby	Sports Skills Contests
Winter Carnival	Roaring Twenties	Steam Engine Days	Basketball Free Throws
Spring Fling	Fifties Day		Punt, Pass, and Kick
Summer Evening	Circus Day	**Specialties**	Football
Fall Frolic	Clown Parade	Freckle Contest	Catch, Throw, and Run
First Day of Spring		Bubble Gum Blowing Contest	Grand Openings
Midsummer's Night		Watermelon Seed Spitting Contest	Pep Rallies
		Pie-Eating Contest	
Extreme Sports		Egg Throwing	
Skateboarding		Treasure Hunt	
Wakeboarding		White Elephants	
BMX		Scavenger Hunt	
Freestyle Motorcross			
Surfing			
Snowboarding			
Speed Climbing			
Skiing			

of as *a program form with an intense content conducted over a relatively short period of time.* The workshop/conference can be used for instructional purposes or for problem solving. As an instructional vehicle, the workshop format allows individuals to focus on a number of specific topics that are of interest to the participants. As a means of organizing individuals or groups of people around a specific issue or concern, the workshop is an excellent way of arousing public interest and attracting publicity. Many different techniques for disseminating information can be used, ranging from the traditional lecture method to small group discussions. The planning methods used in organizing a workshop/conference, institute, seminar, clinic, or convention are similar.

What are the advantages in using the workshop/conference as a program form? First, it allows individuals to become intensely involved and to focus on specific topics, issues, or concerns in a short period of time. In this way an

Figure 9.16 Special Event—Pickle-Eating Contest, Morale, Welfare, and Recreation Department, U.S. Marine Corps, Okinawa, Japan. (Source: From Morale, Welfare and Recreation Department, U.S. Marine Corps, Okinawa, Japan.)

Figure 9.17 Special Event—Benefit Celebrity Fashion Show, City of Kettering (Ohio) Parks, Recreation, and Cultural Arts Department.

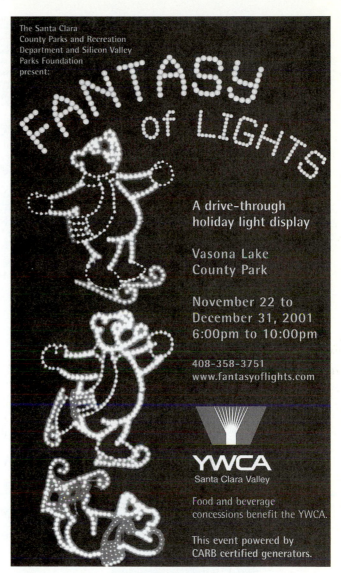

Figure 9.18 Fantasy of Lights, The Santa Clara County (California) Parks and Recreation Department and Silicon Valley Parks Foundation.

individual is able to concentrate his or her learning on a continuous, uninterrupted basis—an obvious advantage for the customer. In other forms used—especially in the class method—learning is spread over an extended period of time with sessions of short duration. The interruption that takes place between class sessions may detract from the learning experience. The second advantage is that workshops/ conferences usually focus on small-group interaction. As a result, individuals have the opportunity to express themselves and to work in accordance with their unique purposes.

We have suggested that the planning methods used in organizing workshops, conferences, institutes, seminars, clinics, and conventions are essentially the same. Yet, each type of meeting has a somewhat distinct set of char-

acteristics, and it is best to keep those characteristics in mind in order to plan effectively. Table 9.2 illustrates six types of meetings— their various functions and general characteristics. In addition to these general types of

Beach Bash Splash

Saturday, May 11, 2002

2:00—3:30 p.m.

Kempsville Recreation Center

800 Monmouth Lane
Virginia Beach, VA 2346
Phone: 474-8492
TTY: 471-5839
Email: pool@vbgov.com

All ages are invited to have a blast at our Beach Bash Splash! Our beach theme will include beach music, pizza, and fun for all! Those under 9 must be accompanied in the water by a responsible person age 15 or up.

$2 per person.

Class #33451

Make reservations at the front desk.

Or, if you know your client barcode (membership number) and family PIN, register with EZreg. Visit http://ezreg.vbgov.com or call 219-2FUN.

Experience the Fun!
Virginia Beach Parks and Recreation

Figure 9.19   Beach Bash Splash, Virginia Beach (Virginia) Parks and Recreation Department.

EXHIBIT 9.1   White Sox Plan Sleepover for 250

Comiskey Park's outfield grass will become a real Field of Dreams for 250 White Sox fans for games on June 8 and 9 against Montreal.

Sleepover Night costs $250 a person, entitling the ticket holder to lower-deck-reserved seats for the games on Saturday and Sunday, a fireworks display, a picnic, a silent auction of Sox memorabilia, a midnight snack, a baseball movie on the scoreboard, continental breakfast, and a workout in the field.

Guests must bring their own sleeping bags and pajamas, but an outdoor shower will be installed, said Rob Galls, White Sox marketing official.

In case of rain or cold, the sleeping area will be removed to a covered portion of the park.

"But I'm sure that most of the 250 who get in will be determined to stay put. It will have to be pretty cold for them to abdicate the outfield," Gallas said.

The idea originated with promotional guru Mike Veeck, who held his first baseball sleepover in 1997 at Fort Myers, Florida.

Veeck said the event allows the public to reclaim their stadiums.

BILLPEN (2002, May 28). White Sox Plan Sleepover for 250. *The Des Moines Register,* p. 2C.

TABLE 9.2   Types of Meetings

Type	Usually Used For	Characteristics
Convention	Annual meetings	All general sessions and committee meetings—mostly for giving information and voting on official business; may use subgroups within general session
Work conference	Planning, fact finding, or problem solving	General sessions and face-to-face groups; high participation
Institute	Training	General sessions, some face-to-face groups; staff provides most resources
Workshop	Training	General sessions and face-to-face groups; participants are resources
Seminar	Group of experienced people, or resources share experience	High participation, usually face-to-face group; leader is discussion leader, not just content expert
Clinic	Clinical exploration of some particular subject—participants usually in trainee role and clinic leaders in training role	Usually face-to-face, but may be general sessions and face-to-face

Bickhard, 1956: 29.

meetings, a number of different small-group meetings exist within the broader framework just presented (see Table 9.3). Each grouping can be seen as a mode of communication. Certain groupings facilitate one-way communication; others are useful in establishing a dialogue between individuals. The selection of a particular type of grouping will depend on the objective. For example, if a group is trying to resolve an issue or concern, it can be organized to encourage fact finding and problem solving through two-way communication. On the other hand, in a teaching-learning situation, each individual can function independently toward completion of a work project (reflecting one-way communication).

One illustration of the application of the workshop/conference in the delivery of leisure

TABLE 9.3   Small-Group Meeting Formats

Grouping	Kinds of Subject Matter	Group or Number of Participants
General sessions	Information giving Orientation Reporting to total group Voting Business meetings Demonstrations Speeches, lectures	Total conference group
Plenary sessions	General session with official action (business meeting, delegate assembly)	Total official group (voting members)
Work groups	Working with a problem or aspect of a problem to come up with action, recommendation, or finding; report usually expected; may meet once or several times	Usually not more than 20—to allow for maximum participation; group composed heterogeneously from conference groups
Special interest groups	Composed of people with common interests in a problem or with a common back-home job; exchange of opinions, experiences, ideas; usually no action required although finding may be produced	10 to 20 to allow for maximum participation
Occupation groups	Special interest groups built around back-home jobs of members	
Application groups	Designed to apply new learnings or information received to other situations of the members	7 to 15
Skills practice groups	Found in workshops and institutes; designed to give members practice opportunities in subject being studied (leadership training, conference leadership)	12 to 18
Training groups or process groups	Specialized form used in some human relations workshops, where subject is study of group process and behavior in groups	12 to 20
Off-the-record groups	Small groups designed to give participants opportunities to react to the conference; no reporting required, but may become informal channel to conference staff for gripes, suggestions; an official conference bull session	5 to 10
Orientation groups	Small groups that meet once at beginning of conference for introduction and orientation	5 to 10

Bickard, 1956: 29

service programs is the Community Conference on the Cultural Arts held in Fremont, California. This conference was established to serve as an inventory of leisure interests in the community, to inspire interest, and to give people an opportunity to meet and address experts and community officials concerning the area of cultural activities. It was an attempt to link social environmental planning with the community's physical planning. A number of nationally and internationally prominent leaders in the cultural arts field spoke at the general sessions of the conference. In addition, discussion groups were organized around ten cultural arts areas covered by the conference. This is an excellent example of how the conference method of organizing a program can be used in a recreation and leisure service organization.

Interest Groups

Interest groups are very similar to clubs in organization and structure. We can think of an interest group *as a collection of individuals that has formed around an activity, issue, or program area.* Usually interest groups generate their own leadership and may exist in a less structured way than a club format does, and the lifespan of an interest group may be shorter in duration than that of a club group. Kraus (1985: 188) suggests that leisure service organizations can be supportive of these types of groups by either sponsoring or encouraging their formation.

Over the past several decades, there has been a rise in the number of special interest groups that are organized around leisure concerns. Many of these are not only organized around specific leisure activities, but have been formulated to meet specific issues and concerns, such as the preservation and conservation of the environment. For example, the Indianapolis (Indiana) Parks and Recreation Department offers a program known as "Greenpieces"—Environmental Youth Group. This program is directed toward helping youth understand environmental issues and apply them in their own communities. Activities include structured classes, meetings, and service learning projects (see Figure 9.20). Often, special interest groups will form in a neighborhood and be focused on issues and concerns that have an impact on that geographic area's social and physical amenities.

Edginton and Ford (1985: 257–59) have suggested that different types of community groupings or special interest groups can be addressed by leisure service organizations. Some of these types of groups include: (1) neighborhood associations; (2) sports associations; (3) youth groups; (4) cultural associations; (5) activity or program advisory groups; (6) advocacy associations; and (7) service, civic, or fraternal organizations. They suggest that the work of the leisure service programmer is one of helping individuals develop their own abilities, skills, and knowledge. The process that they recommend is that of enabling. *Enabling* is focused on helping special interest groups learn the processes necessary for conducting their own affairs. The work of the leisure service programmer involves the provision of guidance, organization, access to resources, and encouragement. Following is a list of some of the roles that a leisure service programmer might play in working with special interest groups.

Networking Agent—In this role, the programmer links the special interest group with resources necessary to meet its needs. Such resources may include other people, funds, areas and facilities, information, supplies, and equipment.

Organizer—Helping special interest groups organize is a critical role for the leisure service professional. Organizing involves the selection of goals, objectives, and, in turn, the creation of a structure and roles for individual members of the group. Organizing may also involve helping a special interest group coalesce around specific concerns and issues.

Encourager/Coach—Working as an encourager or coach, the leisure service programmer provides motivation to group members as well as feedback to help the group attain its goals. Often the leisure service programmer will serve as a sounding board for a special interest group. The role of the programmer is to use his or her knowledge and values to guide the group toward appropriate ends.

Facilitator/Process Expert—Perhaps one of the most important roles that a leisure service programmer will play in working with special interest groups is that of helping the group learn process skills. How are meetings conducted? How does a group become officially sanctioned? What kinds of rules, procedures, or bylaws might be established to assist the group in governing itself? Facilitating involves working with groups to help them develop these skills so that they can operate independently in the future.

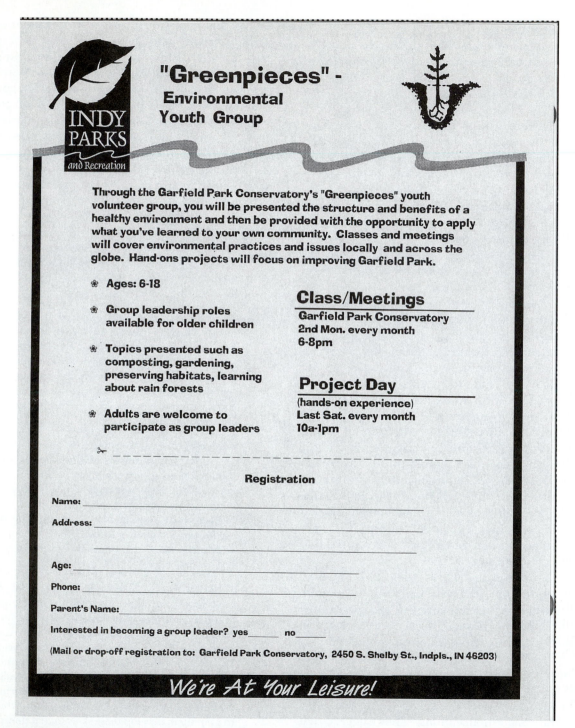

Figure 9.20 Special Interest Group, Indy (Indianapolis, Indiana) Parks and Recreation Department.

When working with special interest groups, the leisure service programmer usually interacts with six to ten individuals. Helping these individuals understand the processes that are involved in group operations becomes important. More than likely, participation in a special interest group has occurred on a voluntary basis. Keeping the special interest group together and operating in a smooth, responsive manner to individual group member needs can be a challenge. Often, special interest groups can become dominated by one or more individuals. Such cliques can affect group harmony and cohesion. The leisure service programmer can work with group members to help them learn more effective processes of decision making as well as ways to remain sensitive, responsive, and aware of the individual needs of others in the group. As Edginton and Ford (1985: 267) have noted, "two factors that often drive people from involvement in . . . [special interest] groups are the feelings of being under-involved or overwhelmed." Thus, the leisure service programmer can play a critical role in helping nurture group cohesion by making special interest group members aware of their impact on one another. This can be effected by the interpersonal skills that are developed within the group. Such group process skills as sharing information, providing feedback to others, and decision making can be influenced by the work of the leisure service programmer.

One of the process areas that can be especially critical in facilitating special interest groups is that of conflict resolution. Conflict is almost inevitable whenever two or more people interact. People often disagree with one another, not only regarding the general goals of a special interest group, but also on the processes used to achieve desired ends. The leisure service programmer can assist groups by helping them understand ways of resolving conflict in a positive fashion. Such activities find the programmer working to help individual group members compromise and collaborate in a positive fashion.

Outreach

In a society as mobile as ours, it is assumed that individuals can travel easily or move from one location to another to participate in leisure activities. Yet, there are large numbers of individuals who—for economic, social, physical, or psychological reasons—cannot travel to avail themselves of leisure services. A role within leisure service organizations and other social agencies is that of extending services to individuals outside traditional modes of delivery—a concept known as *outreach*.

In the leisure service field, many organizations limit their services to the facilities, areas, and structures developed for the purposes of delivering services. Traditionally we think of parks, playgrounds, recreation centers, swimming pools, and athletic fields as places in which services are provided to a community. To receive services or to participate in activities, the participant is required to travel to the given activity or service. Reliance on a facility-oriented approach for provision of services ignores the vast potential for leisure opportunities in the home, on the street, in churches, storefronts, and libraries, as well as in other areas more accessible to the customer. *The outreach concept enables an organization to expand and extend its services to broader segments of a population.* In this way, an organization is able to reach out—meeting people on their turf, within their culture, and according to their particular needs. Outreach efforts of leisure service organizations are often designed to reach out to individuals who are: (1) alienated from services; (2) currently excluded from services; and (3) not knowledgeable about services (Bannon, 1973). Outreach does not simply involve the provision of a set of activities. Rather, outreach "may involve a complex web of activities, programs, services, and personal interactions which respond to situation-specific, site-specific, and individual-specific needs" (Edginton and Edginton, 1996).

According to Edginton and Edginton (1996), outreach as related to youth can be viewed from several different general orientations, as follows:

- *Outreach as an Activity/Program*—Outreach can be viewed in terms of the programs and activities in which individuals, including youth, participate. Activities and programs that may be within the context of outreach include mobile programs, job skills training, parenting programs, resistance education, and other endeavors designed to "reach out" to youth with meaningful programs and services.
- *Outreach as Intervention*—Outreach can also be viewed as a form of intervention designed to effect social and personal outcomes. The outreach leader using this approach attempts to intervene with programs and services to meet social, physical, and other needs of individuals, including youth.
- *Outreach as a State of Mind/Attitude*—Outreach can be viewed as an attitude that influences the planning/program efforts of an organization and its leaders—an attitude of inclusion. It can involve the use of resources, processes, and structures to reach out to all individuals, not just those who already attend activities. For example, collaboration with other organizations on behalf of youth, referral, use of needs assessments, marketing, and other actions may be based on an attitude of inclusion. This view of outreach also might include advocating for youth and youth issues within the organization and the community.
- *Outreach as Presence*—This view of outreach focuses on the concept of presence—that is, the influence and impact of the positive presence of one individual on another. Unobligated interaction between a leader and young persons within which the youth are free to meet their needs primarily on their own terms (de Oliveira, Edginton, and Edginton, 1996) is an example of presence. The concept of leader presence involves free choice in terms of choosing or not choosing to acquire input, guidance, and engage in self-development. The concept of leader presence sees the leader modeling values and dialogue that encourage others to think about their own values, moral judgment, and life choices. The leader does not directly suggest options to youth, but rather serves as a personification of positive values.

- *Outreach as Defined by Time and/or Location*—Outreach has been described as activities, programs, and services offered outside the typical organization's boundaries of time and space. Mobile programs—directed mobility as well as detached services—are tied to this view of outreach. Detached services and directed mobility will be discussed later in this section. Also, this view ties outreach to program schedules that are not typical.
- *Outreach as a Holistic Approach*—This view of outreach maintains that many methods have potential to reach out in a manner that positively impacts individuals, particularly youth. It recognizes that the most effective outreach approach can vary with the situation or individuals participating. Programmers with a holistic view might attempt a variety of formats, activities, and approaches to draw youth into activities to serve their needs.

The outreach concept depends heavily on direct personal contact between the workers of an agency and the customers within the latter's environment; thus, leadership is an extremely important factor. Quite often, individuals employed as outreach workers come from the population group with whom they are working. This is especially true of the roving leader working with inner-city youth.

> Specialized training in recreation is not (necessarily) required, and in fact, the background and personal qualities of (outreach) workers are usually considered to be more important than formal credentials. Theoretical knowledge of group dynamics, . . . or social work is not as important as knowledge of the (social) milieu, personal experience, and character traits that are needed to work with (a given population) (Kraus and Bates, 1975: 266–67).

This is not to say that specialized training in recreation cannot be extremely useful in these types of settings, but that the qualities mentioned are the most important qualities in working with outreach groups.

There are a number of ways in which outreach programs can be employed. For example, the Meals on Wheels program, primarily serving the elderly within a community, reaches individuals in their own homes. Another service of a similar nature is the congregate meal program for the elderly, which makes meals available to groups of persons in close proximity to their homes. In both cases, contact with the outreach worker (or with peers, in the latter case) can be of equal or greater significance than the meals themselves, at least in a psychological sense. Health and medical services can be delivered to the community through such outreach programs as visiting nurse services and neighborhood clinics.

The outreach concept has been used extensively throughout North America by organizations that are a part of the voluntary sector. Many traditional youth agencies make their programs easily accessible to their customers in locations such as schools, churches, housing developments, and community meeting places. Girl Scout programs during the lunch hour in a school, a Boy Scout meeting in the evening at a church, a Boys-Girls Club basketball league at a housing complex, and a Big Brother/Big Sister program meeting at a community center are examples of the outreach delivery system concept.

Public leisure service organizations have implemented the outreach concept through the use of mobile recreation units. Outreach programming through the use of mobile recreation units has enabled many organizations to extend their services significantly. See Table 9.4 for a list of outreach and mobile leisure programs.

Edginton and Edginton (1996) have provided a list of ways in which leisure service organizations can reach out to youth. These include mobile services and detached leader services, parents as partners, home-based programs, contracted services, free-form programming, and school-based services. All of these approaches are based on a foundation of youth development; however, they each have a slightly different approach to accomplishing this goal.

Mobile Service Delivery—Mobile service delivery involves the transporting of programs, services, vehicles, equipment, and supplies to remote or

TABLE 9.4 A List of Outreach and Mobile Leisure Programs

Adventure challenge outreach	In-line skating round-up	Portable stages
Aerospacemobiles	Internet outreach	Puppet theaters
Artmobiles	Job team training	Puppets present
Bandwagons	Karaoke time	Rites of passage programs
Bookmobiles	Life skills for success workshops	School-to-work transition program
Circusmobiles	Life skills workshops	Science fun
Craftmobiles	Livingroom mobiles	Sciencemobiles
Design your own mobile program	Magic mania	Show time
Eco-Carnival	Mentoring for success	Showagons
Entertainment outreach	Mobile swimming pools	Sports spectacular
Espresso factory van	Mobile computer labs	Sportsmobiles
Filmobiles	Mobile ice skating rinks	Star search
Fitness/aerobic celebration	Mobile roller rinks	Starmobiles
Health and drug awareness	Mobile in-line skating parks	Starwagons
outreach	Movie-in-the-park	Teen street fairs
High tech/information	Nature creations	Vocational inside information
superhighway	Naturemobiles	Wide games
Hobby supershow	Outdoor schools	Youth special interest clubs
Hobbymobiles	Parents as partners	Youth wheels
Holiday festivals	Pets and pals	Youth work networks
Information and counseling	Playland	Zoomobiles
mobiles	Playmobiles	
Information shops	Portable shells	

outlying areas to serve youth. Mobile service delivery also includes "directed mobility," which brings in youth from outlying areas to a central location to participate in programs and services. Not only is it possible to take programs and activities to selected remote areas, but an organization can transport youth with similar interests to a single, central or common area to pursue activities and services. This is often done in the area of sports.

Detached Youth Work—The detached leader is an outreach worker who goes out and works with youth "on their turf." The detached leader seeks to involve disengaged youth in positive, constructive activities, to appropriately refer them to other agencies for support of specific needs, or both. Once involved, the detached leader attempts to lead youth into more traditional facility-based services and programs.

School-Based Youth Services Programs—It is important that the community takes an active approach in assisting children and teens after school, not only by providing activities that are fun and that promote social bonding and teamwork, but also to provide services that support them in many areas of their lives. School-based services offer a "one-stop-shopping" approach to services for teens and include such programs and services as counseling, social/recreation opportunities, health care, academic assistance, and employment counseling.

TABLE 9.5 Program Matrix

Program Areas	Class	Competitive	Club	Drop-In
Visual Arts	Drawing Class	Pottery Contest	Miniatures Whittling Club	Visit to Art Museum
New Arts	Photography Class	Film Festival	Radio Club	Photography Lab
Performing Arts (Dance)	Tap Dance Class	Dance Marathon for Charity	Square Dance Club	Boom-Box Music for Dancing
Performing Arts (Drama)	Puppet Class	Debate Contest	Dinner Theater Group—Once a Month	Costume Design Shop
Performing Arts (Music)	Guitar Lessons	Battle of the Bands	Older Adults Kazoo Band	Listening to Classical Music
Literary	Spanish Lessons	Topical Debate	Current Book Club	Library Reading Room
Sports, Games, and Athletics	Beginning Golf Class	Softball Tournament	Soccer Club	Tennis Courts
Outdoor Recreation	Orienteering Class	Cross Country Obstacle Ski Club	Sierra Club	Picnics
Hobbies	How to Get Started on a Hobby	Matchbook Collectors Contest	Electric Train Owners Club	Hobby Shop Slot Car Racing
Travel	Reading Topography Maps	Sports Car Rally	Antique Car Club	Sightseeing
Social Recreation	Quilting Tips for Beginners	Pie-Eating Contest	Saturday Group	Conversation
Voluntary Service	Orientation to Working with Children	Taking a sports Team to Play at Correctional Institution	Candy Stripers	Tutoring for Students
Wellness	Aerobics	Fun Run	Weight Loss	Open Gym
Aquatics	Water Aerobics	Swim Team	Masters Swim Club	Open Public Swim

Parents as Partners—According to the Nebraska Department of Education (1993), "Parents are the most influential people in children's lives." Children learn and grow in a variety of different settings—at school, in the community, on the playground, in youth centers and facilities, and *at home*. The reach of learning and development is broad; it is a process that does, and should, occur throughout the young person's day and throughout his or her life. Helping youth develop into confident, independent, and active individuals who grow and learn should be the goal of teachers, youth leaders, parents, and the community.

Home-Based Activities—One innovative approach to extending the reach of services involves designing materials that can be sent to children and youth in their homes. Outreach to individual homes can include a fun-o-gram, hobby-o-gram, craft-o-gram, or discovery-o-gram. Parents or caregivers can act as facilitators.

Free-Form Programs—The youth leader can be challenged to provide ongoing youth services to areas with no suitable facilities. What types of activities can be carried out in this setting? "Kids' Club" trips, which children plan and design themselves, can be organized with youth who reside in outlying or remote areas. Sports, games, and arts and crafts activities can be organized with materials stored at the homes of volunteer parents.

Intergenerational/Multigenerational Programs—Intergenerational programs are designed to bring

Special Event	Outreach	Workshop/Conference	Interest Group
Art in the Park	Craft Sale at Residence for Elderly	Conference for Teachers on Painting China	Arts Focus Group
Computer Art Display	Photography on Display in Mall	Conference on Television as Art Form	Photography Group
Black Dance Troupe Concert	Teen Dance at a Shopping Center Parking Lot	Workshop on Ethnic Dancing	Jazz Dance Group
Community Theater Production	Shakespeare in the Park	Creative Dramatics for Children	Mime Troupe
Barbershop Quartet Concert	Christmas Caroling	Master's Workshop	Choral Group
Rare Book Exhibit	Bookmobile	Workshop on the Works of Shakespeare	Library Advocates
5 K Run	Rollerskate Mobile	Workshop for Youth Sports Coaches	Sports Boosters
Winter Carnival	Day Camp	Family Conference on Boat Safety	Gardening Club
Hobbyists Trade Show and Sale	Mobile Display of Stamps and Coins	How to Know the Value of Books Workshop	Hobby Interest Group
Driving Along the Autumn Trail	Travelogs	How to See Europe by Train Workshop	Senior Travel Program
Progressive Dinner	Friendly Visitors	Bridge Club Workshop	Partners Program
Recognition Dinner for Volunteers	Reading to Visually Impaired in Their Homes	Role of Volunteers in the Community Conference	Volunteers in Action
Health Promotion Fair	Health Exams/Check-up	Conference on Smoking Cessation	Walking Group
Swim meet	Aquatics Mobile	Safety in Pool Clinic	Polar Bear Group

together young people and older individuals to promote the development of relationships and to facilitate the achievement of selected program goals. These types of programs offer mutual care and concern, added supervision, and benefits such as mentoring. Service learning programs can be used as a vehicle to bring together generations as well. Older persons can help reach out to youth and vice versa.

Mentoring Programs—Mentoring programs link youth with individuals in the community who can help them gain information and knowledge and provide them with personal support. It is often a one-on-one relationship that is both a friendship and a learning opportunity. Mentoring programs can be highly formalized and involve community businesses, or they can be more informal and geared toward personal support, rite of passage activities, and building life skills. For example, engineers at the local John Deere plant volunteer to mentor youth of color in the Waterloo, Iowa area. They have periodic meetings and learning opportunities for the participating youth. Dairy Queen links up adults and youth through its PALS program and thereby gives young people opportunities for adult support.

Internet Outreach—The growing popularity of the Internet offers new opportunities for outreach to youth. Organizations may be able to offer activities and information via the Internet, and youth can access such information as desired. Organizations may also be able to offer information to facilitate the use of the Internet by youth for pur-

poses of growth and development. For example, an organization's home page might have information that links youth to program information and topics of interest. A number of schools, including high schools, have computer labs with Internet capabilities that students can access, and an increasing number of homes have such capability.

Information Shops—Centrally located, drop-in centers that offer information on subjects of interest to teens can be an effective form of outreach. The National Youth Agency in the United Kingdom offers what it calls *The Information Shop* as a means of outreach to young people in fifteen locations. The Information Shop offers leaflets and other information sources for youth on such topics as education, employment, environment, family, health, housing, justice, money, and sport. In addition, counseling is available at The Information Shop and data are collected on the nature of counseling inquiries. The Information Shop method of outreach to youth can be an effective form of "one-stop-shopping" for information about issues of importance to youth.

An integration of program areas and program formats is presented in Table 9.5. This matrix demonstrates the application of the various program formats within the major program areas. It is a graphic illustration of the broad scope of program possibilities that can be implemented to suit the varying needs of customers.

--- *Summary* ---

This chapter has reviewed the topic of program formats. A program format can be thought of as the way in which an activity is structured or organized. The manipulation of program formats provides the leisure service program with another variable to control in the process of program planning and development. It is important to recognize that different program formats produce different benefits for individuals within a given leisure experience. The formats that a leisure service programmer chooses may have a

direct impact on the success or failure of the event. Therefore, close attention must be given to choosing the appropriate structure for an activity to ensure that customer satisfaction is achieved.

The idea of program formats has been identified and discussed in the recreation literature. Most authors support the view that a program format is the structure or form that the activity takes. The literature does not suggest consistency in identifying different types of program formats. However, many common structures used in organizing leisure services are identified by the authors surveyed. In this book, the program formats discussed have included competitive, drop-in or open, class, club, special event, workshop/conference, interest group, and outreach. The format that a program takes is directly related to customer satisfaction.

Knowledge of program formats is essential in the work of the leisure services programmer. One program format found in leisure service organizations is competition. The competitive program format finds individuals pitted against themselves or others in a situation in which performance is measured. The drop-in or open facility format is one in which little or no structure or face-to-face leadership is provided. When a program is organized to emphasize educational or instructional objectives, it is usually called a class. The club program format is one in which leadership comes from within a group focused around a particular program area. Special events are usually high-energy programs of a short-term duration. Workshops, conferences, and seminars provide an opportunity for an exchange of information in a short time and with intensity. Special interest groups are similar to clubs and yet are unique in that they focus on issues and concerns rather than on a program area like a hobby. Finally, the outreach program format is one in which the professional takes the services to the customers in their homes or neighborhoods.

Discussion Questions and Exercises

1. What is a program format? Why are program formats important to the leisure services programmer?

2. What is the relationship between customer satisfaction and the format chosen for a program?

3. Describe and present examples of the competitive program format.

4. What responsibilities does the leisure service programmer have in plan-ning and implementing an open facility or drop-in format? What concerns for customer safety need to be taken into consideration when using this format?

5. Using the lesson plans described in the chapter, develop both a short- and long-term outline for conducting an instructional class in two different program areas.

6. Locate and analyze the bylaws from a recreation club sponsored by a leisure service organization.

7. Describe the characteristics of the special event program format.

8. What is the difference between the workshop/conference format and the class format? Develop a working outline for a workshop or conference dealing with managing one's leisure lifestyle.

9. How can special interest groups be distinguished from clubs? What are the similarities and differences?

10. How might emerging technology have an impact on program formats? How can new technological developments put program formats into effect?

References

Bannon, J. J. 1973. *Outreach: Extending community services in urban areas.* Springfield, IL: Charles C. Thomas.

Beard, J. G., and M. G. Ragheb. 1980. Measuring leisure satisfaction. *Journal of Leisure Research* 12(4): 20–30.

Bickhard, R. 1956. *How to plan and conduct workshops and conferences.* New York: Association Press.

de Oliveira, W., S. R. Edginton, and C. R. Edginton. 1996. Leader Presence. *Journal of Physical Education, Recreation and Dance* 67(1): 38–39.

Donnelly, R. J., W. G. Helms, and E. D. Mitchell. 1958. *Active games and contests.* New York: Ronald Press.

Edginton, S. R., and C. R. Edginton. 1996. *Youth outreach and service excellence.* U.S. Army Child and Youth Services.

Edginton, C. R., and P. M. Ford. 1985. *Leadership in recreation and leisure service organizations.* New York: John Wiley.

Edginton, C. R., and J. P. O'Neill. 1999. Program, services, and event management. *Management of park and recreation agencies,* edited by van B. der Smissen, M. Moiseichik, V. J. Hartenburg, and L. F. Twardzil Ashburn, VA: National Recreation and Park Association.

Farrell, P., and H. M. Lundegren. 1991. *The process of recreation programming.* State College, PA: Venture.

Hupp, S. L. 1985. Satisfaction of older women in leisure programs: An investigation of contributing factors. Ph.D. diss., University of Oregon.

Kraus, R. G. 1985. *Recreation program planning today.* Glenview, IL: Scott, Foresman.

Kraus, R. G., and B. J. Bates. 1975. *Recreation leadership and supervision: Guidelines for professional development.* Philadelphia: W. B. Saunders.

Milligan, L. R., and H. V. Milligan. 1942. *The club member's handbook.* New York: New Home Library.

Nebraska Department of Education. 1993. *The primary program: An overview.* Lincoln, NE: Nebraska Department of Education.

Rossman, J. R. 1984. The influence of program format choice on participant satisfaction. *Journal of Park and Recreation Administration* 2(1): 39–51.

Rossman, J. R. 1995. *Recreation programming: Designing leisure experiences.* Champaign, IL: Sagamore.

Russell, R. V. 1982. *Planning programs in recreation.* St. Louis: Mosby.

Shivers, J. S., and C. R. Calder. 1974. *Recreational crafts: Programming and instructional techniques.* New York: McGraw-Hill Book Co.

Program Promotion

LEARNING OBJECTIVES

1. To make the reader aware of *the program promotion process* and its relationship to effective program planning.
2. To help the reader become aware of *the communication process and its relationship to program promotion.*
3. To provide the reader with knowledge of *five key channels for promoting programs and services.*
4. To provide the reader with an understanding of *the tools available for promoting programs and services.*
5. To provide *examples of program promotion tools* used by various leisure service organizations.

INTRODUCTION

Program promotion is a key element in effective program planning. Promotion can be thought of as communication. "The most essential purpose of this communication is to inform, to let people know what programs and services are being offered by a leisure service delivery system. A second function of promotion is to persuade" (O'Sullivan, 1991: 113). As Rossman (1995: 244) writes, a promotional program will fulfill one or more of the following functions: "to inform, to educate, to persuade, or remind." He suggests that the persuasion aspect of a promotional program is different from the other three forms in that persuasion attempts to bring about a change in behavior or attitude (p. 244). If the customer is not made aware of what the organization is offering and where and when it is being offered, there is very little chance that the program will succeed. Therefore, the effective employment of various promotional channels and tools is essential in order to support the efforts of the leisure service organization. Although program promotion involves a great deal of effort, it is also a very rewarding activity for the professional in that it involves creativity and resourcefulness and results in tangible evidence of success (e.g., media coverage). In this chapter, the importance of communication in the program promotion process is explored, and promotional channels and tools are identified and defined.

COMMUNICATION PROCESS

The successful promotion of a program hinges on the professional's ability to communicate effectively with people. *Communication is an exchange between two entities (such as two individuals or an individual and an organization) that carries meaning.* The exchange process is the vital link that enables an individual to express his or her needs to the organization and allows the organization to identify its program services. This communicative exchange can take place through verbal expression or visual stimuli. Communication can take place through the written word (brochures, news releases, annual reports, etc.), or can be nonwritten (slides, audiotapes, computer, internet, personal appearances, etc.).

The process of exchange that exists between the leisure service organization and the customer must be a two-way process. Effective communication means that the organization communicates *with* the prospective customer rather than *to* the prospective customer. That is to say, the communication process is not complete until the prospective customer acts on the message that he or she has received. The customer digests and evaluates the information being sent and either accepts or rejects it, based on his or her own values, norms, interests, and needs.

The processing of information for promotional purposes can be conceptualized by viewing the model presented in Figure 10.1. This process has four elements: the communicator, the message, the channel of information distribution, and the audience. The *communicator* is the leisure service organization—its professional staff and other associated members (such as persons in policy-making positions). In addition, program customers (current and prospective) can also serve as communicators. In general terms, the message communicated by a leisure service organization is one of improving quality of life through the wise use of leisure. Specifically, the *message* communicated will depend on the particular activity and the values to be derived from involvement. For example, the message used to promote a jogging class will center on physical fitness benefits, physical and mental challenges, relaxation, and so on. *Channels* used to distribute information include advertising, publicity, sales promotion, personal selling, and public relations. These topics will be defined shortly. Finally, this model suggests that the communicator direct his or her message through various channels to a selected *audience,* or target population. In other words, the communicator asks the question: Toward whom is the information being directed—an age group-

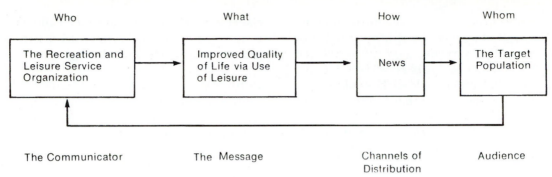

Figure 10.1   A Model for Processing Information.

ing, a geographic area, a lifestyle clustering or interest group, or males or females?

Through the communication process, information is targeted toward individuals in an attempt to stimulate involvement in a particular program service. As prospective customers become aware of the information communicated to them, they may relate to it in terms of their own needs and view it as a way of fulfilling those needs. The promotional process often not only informs individuals but also persuades them. Frequently, the persuasion aspect is viewed negatively, with the assumption that promotional efforts are only for the benefit of the provider of the service. In some instances—few, we hope—this may be the case. It is probably more apparent in the area of some commercial recreation enterprises, where profit may have a higher priority than the welfare of the customers. However, most leisure service organizations have a humanistic philosophy; as a result, they are interested primarily in the provision of services that are beneficial both to the customers and the organization. In this sense, the promotional effort is not directed toward the exploitation of individuals but toward the provision of services that are in the best interest of the consumer.

CHANNELS FOR PROMOTING PROGRAMS AND SERVICES

Five channels can be used in the promotion of programs and services: *advertising, publicity, sales* *promotion, personal selling,* and *public relations.* These channels have some common characteristics—especially in terms of the media employed—and should be utilized simultaneously; however, each serves distinctly different ends. To successfully promote a program, the professional should carefully design a strategy that incorporates each of these channels in an effective manner. Promotional efforts should be well planned; the productive professional should avoid an ad hoc approach.

Advertising

What are the distinctive factors that characterize advertising? Nylen (1975: 4) has suggested that most definitions include three basic factors. He writes:

1. Advertising is a paid message, as contrasted, for example, with publicity, which is not.
2. Advertising appears in the mass media. (Mass media or public advertising carriers such as television, magazines, and newspapers.) By contrast, selling by a salesman is a public message that does not appear in a public medium.
3. Advertising has as its purpose informing or persuading people about a particular product, service, belief, or action. For marketers, the dominant use of advertising is to sell products and services.

Based on these factors, it might be concluded that advertising is *a paid message, delivered via the mass media, and aimed at persuading and influencing individuals* to become involved in the consumption of a service or to adopt a belief or idea. Basically, advertising is accomplished through the use of newspapers, television, radio, magazines, and other tools such as billboards, placards on public transportation, grocery bags, and restaurant place mats.

O'Sullivan (1991: 123–24) suggests several factors for creating good advertising. She writes, "the message itself is a very important component of the advertisement." It should create attention and promote interest on the part of the customers targeted for a program. Further, the advertisement "should also foster a desire to take part in the program or service" (p. 124). Last, an advertisement should lead to action on the part of the customer. This is known as the AIDA approach—attention, interest, desire, and action.

Advertising is an important aspect of a leisure organization's promotional efforts in that it enables the organization to reach large numbers of people rapidly with its message. This channel of promotion has been used primarily by commercial enterprises as a mechanism to persuade individuals to join in various pursuits, and the principles and methods involved can be applied successfully to the public and nonprofit sectors. Advertising can be beneficial in a number of ways. It increases the customer's awareness of programs and services available. The customer also is able to make comparisons among the services offered based on quality, cost, and location.

There are basically two types of advertising—direct action and indirect action. *Direct action advertising encourages the individual to act immediately on the information presented.* For example, direct action advertising might inform the prospective customer of the need to sign up immediately for swimming lessons at the local pool or for day camp at the YWCA. *Indirect action advertising tries to create long-term interest in a service.* In other words, an indirect advertisement merely cites the availability of certain services or programs available from an organization. Spe-

cial advertising for Park and Recreation Month in July or Boy Scout Week in March are examples of indirect action advertising.

Publicity

"Publicity [may be] the most enduring promotional channel, the least expensive and perhaps easiest to use" (Rubright and MacDonald, 1981: 169). It consists of *media coverage of the events, activities, and services of a leisure service organization.* "Publicity embraces news releases and features, speakers' messages, and press conferences. Agencies find countless outlets for news releases in daily and weekly newspapers, in regional tabloids, in an ever-growing number of radio stations and in some television markets" (p. 169). The organization that uses publicity effectively conveys information to various media sources in such a way that the organization is presented in a favorable light to the public. Newspaper coverage of a public meeting in which policy issues are discussed, a feature story highlighting the efforts of an individual within the organization, a picture of the winning junior softball team—these are all examples of productive and positive publicity. On the other hand, an exposé on ineffective management practices or an editorial condemning an organization and its efforts could wound an organization severely.

How does one develop a favorable publicity posture? Many tools can be employed—news releases, photographs, press conferences—to provide the various media sources with positive information. Basically, the professional must sell the media on the newsworthiness of the various events and activities of his or her organization. To accomplish this, the professional should actively cultivate sources or contacts within the various media. Obviously publicity is not paid for, so the organization is placed in a competitive position for space in the newspaper and for radio time and TV time. An organization should compete by exemplifying excellence and by extending itself courteously to the media.

Does the organization or professional create news? The answer to this question is definitely yes. However, creating news does not imply the staging of news. News is created by providing programs, by informing the media of the programs, and by conveying to the media the human interest features of these programs.

Another kind of publicity generated by a leisure service organization is the brochures, fliers, reports, and newsletters that are distributed at various times and for various purposes to customers and potential program users. Although there is cost involved in producing these publicity items, it is generally less expensive than if the information were delivered through advertising.

Sales Promotion

At times, an organization will want to stimulate consumer interest in a service beyond advertising and publicity. To generate this kind of interest, organizations will often organize special promotional activities. These types of activities are referred to as sales promotions. *Items for sales promotions are designed to promote and persuade potential and existing customers rather than to merely educate them.* Most sales promotion pieces ask for an immediate or decisive response or action from the customer. Sales promotion items can include special mailings, attractive applications or survey forms, or special invitational materials that may be left in shopping malls, posted in public buildings, or distributed at churches, medical facilities, grocery stores, and other public places. The information distributed might invite immediate participation, allow opportunity to visit specific facilities, or describe how to take advantage of the organization's services. Other sales promotion items can include pencils, notepads, buttons, T-shirts, toys, caps, and similar articles that present frequent and attractive reminders about the organization.

Other important tools that can be employed in a sales promotion campaign include sampling, coupons, contests, and demonstrations. Edginton and Williams (1978:

272–73), in defining each of these concepts and discussing their application to recreation and leisure service organizations, have written:

> *Sampling* is an attempt to presell the consumer. For example, an organization attempting to promote arts and crafts lessons for children might want to allow the children to participate in one class free of charge. This provides the child with the opportunity to sample the experience, with the idea that he will be influenced to participate in an entire series of lessons.
>
> The *coupon* concept has been greatly utilized in the promotion of products, but has yet to reach its full impact in the area of social services. The one area in which coupons have been effectively used in the delivery of leisure services is senior citizen participation. Many organizations provide reduced rates for senior citizens (often during a given time of day or day of the week) providing they have a special card or coupon. This senior citizens example is actually profitable to the organization in two ways. Not only does the organization attract a group of consumers who are ordinarily unavailable to it, but it also enhances the public image.
>
> *Contests* have also been used to stimulate consumer interest in a service. Participation in a contest may result in cash prizes, food, and so on for the winner or winners. An example of the constructive use of a contest in the delivery of leisure services is the traditional Easter egg hunt (oftentimes augmented with special prizes for locating certain items). Sometimes a competitive program form is used in the provision of the service. A flower-arranging contest will motivate people to participate in the activity. Using the contest is also a promotional method directed toward creating enthusiasm and interest in the activity.
>
> *Demonstrating* a service to the target market is still another method used in sales promotion. To create interest for a class in judo instruction, a demonstration might be arranged to take place at an intermission during a sporting activity, at a shopping mall, or at a school assembly. Essentially, this method allows the consumer to see the skills, attitudes, and other benefits that can be derived from participation in the activity.

Sales promotion activities, if successfully arranged, enable an organization to generate a great deal of interest and enthusiasm for their service. These types of activities represent short-term promotional efforts and should be used sparingly rather than on a continuous basis, or they will lose their edge.

Personal Selling

One of the most effective channels of promoting programs is that of personal selling. Usually, personal selling involves *making direct, face-to-face contact with an individual or group*. One should not underestimate the potential of the direct personal contact. It is perhaps the most pervasive, effective form of promoting a program's service.

In leisure service organizations, personal selling is not directly identified as such. It most commonly occurs within the context of public speaking to various community groups. It also occurs when prospective customers make direct contact with organizational staff members for information or clarification. What makes a successful "salesperson" for the organization? Basically, an effective salesperson must be personable and be able to relate to people. He or she must be aware of customer needs and know how to communicate effectively the ways in which the services of the organization can meet those needs. This implies that a good salesperson understands not only people but also how the organization's service line can be employed to meet individual needs. The successful salesperson tailors his or her presentation to the audience, environment, and other relevant factors. "Personal selling is often one of the more pleasurable and self-rewarding channels of promotional communication. It permits organization personnel to experience the impact that the agency is making on its customers" (Rubright and MacDonald, 1981: 170).

Personal selling often involves building relationships with customers. We often refer to the importance of friendship building as well as fund development. Individuals engaged in personal selling are not only involved in persuading the customer to purchase a service or buy a membership, but are also involved in promoting program opportunities specifically and the work of the organization in the general sense. As a result the seller must determine the extent of his or her sales pitch to an individual. In some cases, the sale will be informational; in others, immediate, direct purchase will be encouraged. It is important to remember that those engaged in personal selling often pursue multiple objectives. In addition to the quantitative aspects of the organization's sales objectives, qualitative factors might also be considered such as providing a high level of customer care, presenting an image of professionalism, and maintaining a strong safety record.

Public Relations

Public relations should be viewed as an important organizational tool. Although in some circles public relations may not be considered as a channel of promotion, we include it here as a crucial aspect in the development of positive public attitudes toward the leisure service organization. Touching every part of an organization's operations, public relations deals with items such as the caliber of services, the manner in which the public is dealt with on the phone, the manner in which leaders interact with customers, and so on. Because public relations is involved in so many organizational areas, it should not be left to chance.

As a management process, *public relations efforts are directed toward engendering goodwill toward the organization and establishing an understanding of its operations*. Public relations efforts seek to develop a positive rapport with the public served by establishing management policies and practices conducive to the public interest and well-being. Such policies might deal, for example, with the following topics by specifically delineating guidelines for staff and employee behavior:

1. Interactions with the public;
2. Standards for dress and grooming;

3. Standards for building and grounds maintenance;
4. Rules regarding press release clearance; and
5. Clearance for special projects.

The good name of an organization is its greatest asset. An organization should try to cultivate good community relations in order to attract customers. A negative public image will, obviously, seriously affect the ability of an organization to serve a community effectively.

TOOLS FOR PROMOTING PROGRAMS AND SERVICES

The leisure service organization can utilize many tools to promote its programs and services. Throughout the rest of this chapter, a number of such tools are detailed—including use of newspapers, brochures, logos and emblems, awards and citations, annual reports, electronic information, information and press kits, exhibits, displays and demonstrations, novelty items, public speaking, fliers, newsletters, stationary advertising, radio and television, telephone, and videotape and slide presentations.

To be successful and productive, promotional tools should have several characteristics. Rubright and MacDonald (1981: 160–62) have listed the following: Tools are written or prepared for specific targets and communication channels; reflect or suggest program and service benefits; may indicate organizational missions and goals; have an acceptable tone, style, and character; are concisely written and edited; persuade or inform; elicit some action or participation by the customer; and have a distribution plan. "Tools must direct the customer from unawareness in order to convince an individual to try the service, repeat its use, and recommend it to others."

Further, in the development process for promotional tools, Rubright and MacDonald (1981: 162) list several factors that must be considered and decided on in order to determine the most appropriate tools for disseminating information. The process must include determi-

nation of the specific purpose of the tool, what promotional objectives are to be reflected by the tool, the target group to be reached by the tool, the methods of distribution, designation of the individual to prepare the tool, designation of how production will be accomplished, and decisions regarding how the tool will be evaluated.

Newspapers

One of the most important tools for the delivery of information is the newspaper. The majority of leisure service organizations are based at the local and neighborhood levels and, as such, they depend greatly on distribution of information via one or more newspapers. Basically, there are five classes of newspapers: national, daily, weekly, shopper's guides, and special audience newspapers. The local daily community newspaper is most frequently used by leisure service organizations in the promotion of its services.

1. *National Newspapers*—National newspapers such as *USA Today, Christian Science Monitor, The National Observer, The Wall Street Journal,* and *The Sporting News* are papers that are aimed at a broad cross section of individuals and do not focus on a particular geographic area. This type of newspaper can be used to draw national attention to an organization's unique programs and services. If the thrust of a leisure service organization is national in nature—such as the national offices of local youth agencies—use of this type of media presentation can be particularly effective.

2. *Daily Newspapers*—The daily newspaper usually originates in a specific locale; thus, its primary news thrust is on the locality or geographic area it serves. It is not unusual for a daily newspaper to assign one of its reporters to cover the activities of a local leisure service organization. The impact and potential of working with a local daily newspaper cannot be overstated.

3. *Weekly Newspapers*—The fastest growing type of newspaper is the weekly. Weekly newspapers are often found in suburban areas surrounding a large city. Sometimes the weekly newspaper is simply the Sunday edition of the major city newspaper or newspapers, subscribed to by

residents in a wide geographic area around the city. In working with a weekly newspaper, the professional must be much more careful and precise in his or her planning. Timing is very important for the appropriate release of information. This procedure is a bit tricky when a newspaper comes out just once a week; one does not want to release information too soon so that it loses its impact or too late so that individuals are prohibited from planning ahead to any degree.

4. *Shopper's Guides*—Shopper's guides are usually distributed on a weekly or monthly basis, with their main focus being sales of items and services. These papers usually contain little editorial or news commentary. The professional should, however, investigate the shopper's guides that are distributed in his or her area to determine their formats and whether they might be conducive to dissemination of information regarding recreation and leisure services. The City of Olympia (Washington) Parks, Recreation, and Cultural Services Department holds an "Ethnic Celebration," featuring live entertainment, food, informational displays, crafts, and demonstrations related to a number of different ethnic groups.

5. *Special Interest Newspapers*—Newspapers are not necessarily organized only on a geographic basis. Often, especially nationally, newspapers are specialized around a particular interest population. For example, if a leisure service organization was organizing a special event such as a coin or stamp hobby show, it could publicize the event in regional and national newspapers that cater to people with these interests. There are many publications for individuals interested in such activities as table tennis, swimming, or track and field.

It is important that the professional build a good working relationship with the newspapers. Whether seeking coverage of news-making items, seeking to disseminate public service information, or purchasing advertising, the professional must be aware of the methods and procedures that are necessary to facilitate the specific coverage desired. This involves knowing whom to contact and how to deliver information to the newspaper in the most appropriate manner. Newspaper personnel should be viewed as allies. If they perceive the professional to be an honest, efficient, and competent manager, they will in turn be likely to act in a similar manner. The professional should be cognizant of the newspaper's deadlines, limitations, and interests. One thing that irritates any newspaper is misinformation. The professional should double-check all information emanating from his or her department to ensure that it is accurate as well as concise, brief, and to the point.

Often, newspaper personnel are taken for granted and do not receive support, positive feedback, or other evidence of recognition for their efforts. The leisure service professional should be appreciative of the support he or she receives from newspaper reporters. Members of the press should always be viewed as invited guests. They should never be asked to purchase tickets or pay admission. Complimentary tickets to activities are a standard rule of thumb in dealing with the press. It is also beneficial to send a note from time to time, expressing your support and appreciation. The occasional thank-you note should be a part of organizational etiquette.

The News Release

Releasing information to the newspaper is often done via a formal news release. A newspaper does not have the resources to write all the organization's stories, and in some cases, it would not be to the organization's advantage. Thus, leisure service professionals must learn to prepare news releases. A news release can be thought of as the assembling of facts and information into a coherent written statement.

How do you write a news release? Very carefully! It must be written in a concise, factual, and direct manner. When preparing news release copy, one asks the questions, Who, What, When, Where, Why, and How? The standard for preparing a news release is to use the inverted pyramid format, as illustrated in Figure 10.2. The first

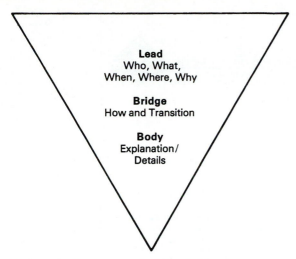

Figure 10.2 Inverted Pyramid for News Releases.(From: Ryan, Katrine Fitzgerald. [Summer 1988.] Getting the word out to the media through news releases and news advisories. *Voluntary Action Leadership.*)

paragraph is the lead paragraph and should answer the most important of the "*W*" questions. The lead paragraph is one sentence in length. The second paragraph can be called the bridge paragraph and is a transition to the detailed information in the news story. The next few short paragraphs should provide the reader with additional factual information, in descending order of importance. If it is necessary for the news release to be edited, the news professional usually edits from the bottom up; therefore, the order of information in the news items can be critical.

It is important to keep in mind some writing tips when preparing news releases. Ryan (1988) indicates that news releases should be written with short sentences, short paragraphs, and short words. Be very concise and factual when including times, places, phone numbers, people's names, and other program information. A news release should be written as an objective report and is not the place for subjective, descriptive adjectives such as "wonderful," "very good," or "enjoyable."

Whenever possible, one should create an official form on which the press release will be written. Why? Because newspapers receive literally hundreds of news items per day. When an agency's news is received at the newspaper's office, it should be distinctive, recognizable, and easily distinguished as a press release.

The news release should be typed on the agency news release form following these guidelines: leave a margin on all sides of the typed copy; type all releases double-spaced and on one side of the paper only; if a second page is needed, type the word "more" at the bottom of the first page; do not split a paragraph at the bottom of a page—end the page with the end of a paragraph and start the next page with a new paragraph; be sure that the organization's name is at the top of the page; at the end of the release, type "-30-" or "###"—these symbols mean "the end" to a news editor. A title on the news release will help the news editor quickly understand the subject matter of the release. Undue time should not be spent writing the title because the news editor will write a headline for the story according to space, type style, layout, and production. The news release form should include the name of the organization, a phone number, and the name of a contact person. Making it as easy as possible for the newspaper to contact the organization will contribute to ensuring that the news will be used and that it will be published accurately. Figure 10.3 shows an example of a press release from the City of Long Beach (California) Parks, Recreation & Marine. This press release provides information regarding the city's Juneteenth Jubilee 2002 Gospel Celebration. Figure 10.4 shows a press release from the Lake County (Illinois) Forest Preserve encouraging parents to enroll their children for summer camp. Figure 10.5 is a publicity support request form used to generate marketing information for the staff of the Morale, Welfare, and Recreation Department of the U.S. Marine Corps in Okinawa, Japan.

news　Parks, Recreation & Marine
2760 Studebaker Road, Long Beach, CA 90815-1697
562.570.3234 • fax 562.570.3189

Date: May 17, 2002
FOR IMMEDIATE RELEASE

"Creating Community Through People, Parks, Programs and Partnerships"™

JUNETEENTH JUBILEE 2002
set for Martin Luther King, Jr. Park in Long Beach

Non-stop entertainment and gospel music is planned for Long Beach Parks, Recreation and Marine's annual Juneteenth Jubilee celebration on Saturday, June 15, 10 a.m. to 4 p.m., at Martin Luther King, Jr. Park, 1950 Lemon St., Long Beach. Headliners for the event are gospel entertainers Donald Taylor and One Voice, the Family & Friends Gospel Ensemble, Praise - an a cappella Gospel Ensemble, Infusion - an a cappella Ministry of Song, along with other special guest performances and local churches.

Juneteenth Jubilee 2002 Gospel Celebration includes a family-style barbecue with traditional foods for sale. Kids can have fun jumping in the moon bounce and having their faces painted. Vendors will sell crafts and other items and city departments and local agencies will be on hand to provide information on community programs and services. There will also be a Carnival the whole family can enjoy from June 14 through June 16 as part of the Juneteenth Jubilee 2002 Celebration.

Juneteenth Jubilee 2002 is the Long Beach observance of the 136th anniversary of the signing of the Emancipation Proclamation. It was June 19, 1865, when word reached the people of Texas that President Lincoln had signed the proclamation freeing slaves two years earlier on January 1, 1863. Jubilation of the news turned into yearly celebrations and homecomings for those who had been separated from family and friends. The annual celebrations became known as Juneteenth.

Juneteenth Jubilee 2002 Gospel Celebration is presented by the Long Beach Parks, Recreation and Marine Department and cosponsored by the Long Beach Department of Health Services and Partners of Parks. For information on Juneteenth Jubilee 2002, call (562) 570-4405.

#

Note to Media:
This release is available in electronic format.
Please contact Tina Burton at chburto@ci.long-beach.ca.us
or call (562) 570-3234. This phone number is not for publication.

Figure 10.3　News Release, Long Beach (California) Parks, Recreation & Marine.

News Features

News features deal with information concerning a person, an activity, or an idea. News feature stories are not generally written and submitted by the leisure service organization itself, but because newspaper organizations are looking for human interest stories, the leisure service organization can suggest ideas for feature sto-

ries. It is not unusual for leisure service organizations to be involved in interesting and meritorious activities or events. Newspapers are also interested in issues and may want to run a feature on an issue that concerns the recreation and leisure service organization. Often a leisure service organization will have several special events during the year, and frequently one or

2000 North Milwaukee Avenue Libertyville, Illinois 60048-1199 Telephone 847-367-6640 Fax 847-367-6649

LAKE COUNTY FOREST PRESERVES

Preservation, Restoration, Education and Recreation

NEWS RELEASE

FOR IMMEDIATE USE

MAY 21, 2002

CONTACT:
Lynn Hepler, Manager
Outreach & Stewardship
847-968-3331

PARENTS SIGN UP NOW FOR SUMMER CAMPS
AT YOUR LAKE COUNTY FOREST PRESERVES

Summer is just around the corner and enrollment for summer camps and day programs at your

Lake County Forest Preserves is open and spots are still available!

Give your children a special chance to explore interests that aren't covered by regular classes or

standard day camps. Scoop a pond, check out life on a pioneer homestead, learn to fish, and more!

A variety of unique Forest Preserve day camp programs offer activities for children ages four to

14. All programs are led by professional Forest Preserve educators. Summer camps and day programs

are offered at six Forest Preserve locations throughout Lake County.

Beat the spring rush, sign up now to best ensure your spot. To receive your free brochure

detailing all program offerings or to register, call the Lake County Forest Preserves at (847) 968-3321.

#

U:\EnvEducation&PublicAffairs\MEDIA\Media02\News Releases\May\SummerCampSignup.doc

Figure 10.4   News Release, Lake Country (Illinois) Forest Preserves.

more of these events can serve as the subject for a feature story. A news feature article does not usually have to appear on a specific date; thus, it is more flexible and has fewer time constraints than the press release does.

How do special news features come to be written? A news story of interest or significance to the community will be picked up by one of the reporters on the staff of the local newspaper. Large leisure service organizations often employ individuals whose responsibilities include public relations. These individuals are involved in the organization of feature stories to be inserted in the newspapers. As indicated, it is not often that the public relations officer or leisure service professional will actually write a feature story; rather,

MWR PUBLICITY SUPPORT REQUEST

1.) Fill in all requested information. Please be neat, detailed and meet the following deadlines.
2.) Your PSR request must reach Marketing a minimum of 8 weeks prior to your event.
3.) PSR must be approved and signed by your General Manager.
4.) PLEASE CALL MARKETING IMMEDIATELY WITH ANY CHANGES AT 645-2068

PSR# _____

SUBMITTED BY: _____ PHONE: _____

CAMP: _____ FACILITY: _____

EVENT: _____ EVENT LOCATION: _____

DATE: _____ TO: _____ TIME: _____ TO _____ FEE: $ _____

SIGN UP FROM: _____ TO _____ AT _____

LATE REGISTRATION ON-SITE (Y/N) _____ TIME _____

TYPE OF AWARD (S) _____

T-SHIRT DESIGN NEEDED (Y/N)_____ TICKETS NEEDED? (Y/N) _____ QTY _____

OPEN TO: UNIT _____ CAMP _____ SOFA _____ ALL _____ CLUB MEMBERS _____

POC: _____ PHONE: _____ EXPECTED ATTENDANCE: _____

DETAILS: (What makes your event special? Please specify entertainment, type of food, etc. Use back if necessary.)

_____

_____

_____

General Manager's Signature: _____

Tentative Schedule to be filled out by Marketing and returned to you.

PRINT - Bretta Berger 645-3970/2764

Posters	_____	Sign	_____	Calendars	_____
Banners	_____	T-shirts	_____	Tickets	_____
Lamination	_____	Framed	_____	Program	_____
Brochure	_____	Ads	_____	Brief	_____
Press Release	_____	Other	_____	Other	_____

BROADCAST - Rick McGlothlin 645-3970/2068

TV Billboard	_____	Radio Reader	_____	Live Remote	_____
Television Spot	_____	Radio Spot	_____	TV News	_____
TV Interview	_____	Radio Interview	_____	Other	_____

NOTE: Most event information will be automatically released to "Japan Update", "This Week On Okinawa", "Shogun", "Okinawa Marine" and FEN.

Figure 10.5 Publicity Support Request Form, Morale, Welfare, and Recreation Department, U.S. Marine Corps, Okinawa, Japan. (Source: From Morale, Welfare and Recreation Department, U.S. Marine Corps, Okinawa, Japan.)

he or she is usually employed in facilitating its development—gathering facts, organizing facts, and choosing relevant photographs.

Editorials and Letters to the Editor

Editorials or letters to the editor often have no middle ground. Either the person writing the editorial or letter to the editor is very much in favor of or is very much opposed to certain aspects of the work of the leisure service organization. The primary source for letters to the editor is the community at large, whereas editorials are generated by the newspaper organization. Although it is not often practiced, a leisure service organization itself can initiate editorials or letters to the editor. Sometimes newspapers can be encouraged to support interesting activities or projects in the form of an editorial. The leisure service organization does not write its own editorial; rather, the local newspaper is encouraged to investigate a given subject. A leisure service organization may wish to have a local newspaper editorialize on the need for constructive playground environments. The leisure service organization can accomplish this by gathering statistics and other relevant information, plus examples of the value of well-organized and well-supervised play areas, and presenting them to the editor of the local paper. Of course, ultimately, the editor will decide whether the subject reflects his or her interests and those of the paper, and whether the subject is one that he or she wishes to elaborate on in an editorial.

Letters to the editor that concern the leisure service organization and that are written by other parties can be either positive or negative. How should the professional respond to a negative letter to the editor? Although the professional might like to rationalize that individuals who write letters to the editor are cranks who should be ignored, that is not a productive way to deal with such opinions. Every effort should be made to investigate the accusations, determine their cause, and make contact with the individual or party concerned, either personally or in writing. Every effort should be made to correct any error or to satisfy the displeased individual.

The letter-to-the-editor format can also be used by the leisure service professional to publicly thank individuals who have assisted his or her organization in terms of time or money. The work of leisure service organizations often goes unrecognized, and this is a relatively easy way to publicly express appreciation.

Sports and Athletic News Information

Information concerning sporting and athletic events is often handled in a slightly different manner than other news information. Sports editors frequently like to have a complete informational package concerning the organization's sporting event(s)—whether a league, meet, or contest—prior to the actual implementation of the activity. This often includes the presentation of complete team rosters or a list of contestants prior to competition. In addition, it is not unusual for a sports editor to request individual and team pictures prior to an activity. With this information in hand, the sports reporters can construct stories that are colorful, comprehensive, and accurate without actually being present at the event. Newspapers often have a special form to record box scores for sports events that the leisure service organization is required to use when reporting these activities. If a form is not required, sports results may (in certain newspapers) be called in via the telephone. Figures 10.6 and 10.7 are examples of sports information standings and scores as they might appear in a local newspaper. Figure 10.8 is an example of a coupon published in a newspaper asking for individuals to identify others for recognition in youth sport programs.

Photographs

The statement may be trite, but it is true—"A picture is worth a thousand words." A picture can communicate actions, feelings, and events better than any written description. Pictures taken at intervals during a given program can show its progress. Pictures attract attention whereas a caption may not. Although different types of pictures are discussed here, it is important to capture action whenever possible. Most newspapers today do not want formal photographs and prefer to have informal photos (e.g., a team in action rather than in a lineup).

Photographs of individuals within the leisure service organization are often used by newspapers. There are two types of photographs that the organization might want to keep on file—the formal staff photograph and the action photograph. The formal photograph is taken by a professional photographer and can be used to complement any article concerning that individual. The action photograph, of course, shows the individual "on the move" within an organizational activity, program, or event. The organization might want to keep several action

HOCKEY

Lane Amateur Hockey Association
At Lane County Ice

LEAGUE RESULTS — Team Athletics 3, Shooter's Pub 2. Good Times 4, Cascade Medical 1. Angus Inn 7, Guido's-U of O 4. Angus Inn 7, Shooter's Pub 2. Team Athletic 3, Cascade Medical 2. **LEAGUE STANDINGS** — Angus Inn 2-0-0: 4 pts. Good Times 2-0-0: 4 pts. Team Athletic 2-0-0: 4 pts. Cascade Medical 0-2-0: 0 pts. Guido's-U of O 0-2-0: 0 pts. Shooter's Pub 0-2-0: 0 pts.

Lane Amateur Broomball Association
At Lane County Ice

LEAGUE RESULTS — Team Genetics 3, Sacred Heart 1. Whittier Mutant Warriors 3, Whittier Ravens 1. Russ Fetrow Engineering, Inc. 4, Weyerhauser Paper 0. **LEAGUE STANDINGS** — Russ Fetrow Engineering 1-0, Whittier Mutant Warriors 1-0, Team Genetics 1-0, Sacred Heart 0-1, Whittier Ravens 0-1, Weyerhauser Paper 0-1.

BMX

Emerald Valley BMX
At Eugene
AGE-GROUP RESULTS
Oct. 18

7-EXPERT — 1, Sean Zorn. 2, Leon Medart. 3, Keith Bowers. **11-INTERMEDIATE** — 1, Katie Burke. 2, Jacob Pipkin. 3, Shanna Adams. **11-EXPERT** — 1, Kaleb Watson. 2, Brett McAllister. 3, Joe Parrott. **12-EXPERT** — 1, Jeremy Cutright. 2, Jon Barron. 3, Marc Reed. **15-INTERMEDIATE** — 1, J.J. Lemasters. 2, Davis Crump. 3, Brady Morris. **16-EXPERT** — 1, Cris Marsh. 2, Jason Tonner. 3, Kan Saner. 12 **AND UNDER-CRUISER** — 1, Cris Marsh. 2, Marc Reed. 3, Katie Burke.

Oct. 20

5 AND UNDER-NOVICE — 1, Tyler Lyons. 2, Jason Wood. 3, Mark Medart. **6-EXPERT** — 1, Vance Tarusan. 2, David Oakes. 3, Steven Faver. **7-EXPERT** — 1, Sean Zorn. 2, Leon Medart. 3, Brad Smith. **9-INTERMEDIATE** — 1, Jacob Pipkin. 2, Jeff Moorehead. 3, Cory Elgin. **11-EXPERT** — 1, Joe Parrott. 2, Kaleb Watson. 3, Steven McCullam. **13-NOVICE** — 1, Chip Wilbur. 2, Craig Brown. 3, Jeff Doyle. **13-EXPERT** — 1, Jeremy Cutright. 2, Devin Wolfe. 3, Jesse Howes. **15-NOVICE** — 1, W.C. Gomer. 2, David Crump. 3, Brady Morris. **16-EXPERT** — 1, Scott Naive. 2, Jim Guynes. 3, Chris Lute. **15-16 CRUISER** — 1, Scott Naive. 2, Chris Lute. 3, Cris Marsh. **7-8 GIRLS** — 1, Lisa Biggs. 2, Krystal Vickers. **9-10 GIRLS** — 1, Katie Burke. 2, Lisa Jackson.

SOCCER

Eugene Parks & Recreation
Fall Leagues
MEN

A RESULTS — Smith Family Bookstore 2, Wil. Val. Papa's Shooters 1. Eugene Stars 2, Bavarians 2. **A STANDINGS** — Bavarians 2-1-2, Wil. Val. Papa's Shooters 3-2, Smith Family Bookstore 3-2, Eugene United F.C. 2-2, Eugene Stars 0-3-2.

B RESULTS — Macaroni Ponies 2, Oh Cannibal Slab In Nacho 1. Outer Limb 0, Feets Plus 0. Don Juan Restaurants 3, Black & Blue 0. **B STANDINGS** — Don Juan Restaurants 3-3, Feets Plus 2-2-2, Black & Blue 3-3, Outer Limb 2-0-4, Oh Cannibal Slab In Nacho 2-3-1, Macaroni Ponies 1-4-1.

C RESULTS — SSC 4, Pleasant Hill's Angels 1. Wingnuts 5, Printer's Addition 0. McKenzie Study Center 4, Johnny Lasso 4. **C STANDINGS** — Pleasant Hill's Angels 4-1-1, Wingnuts 3-1-2, SSC 3-2-1, McKenzie Study Center 2-3-1, Printer's Addition 2-4, Johnny Lasso 1-4-1.

WOMEN

A RESULTS — Bavarians 5, Players A 0. Oasis Fine Foods 6, Springfield Soccer Club 1. **A STANDINGS** — Oasis Fine Foods 4-0-1, Bavarians 3-1-1, Springfield Soccer Club 1-4, Players A 1-4.

B RESULTS — Precision Graphics 8, Queens 2. Papa's Pizza 1, Players-Alpine Foods 0. Fircrest Flyers 13, Friendly's 0. **B STANDINGS** — Fircrest Players 5-1, Papa's Pizza 4-1, Players 3-2-1, Precision Graphics 3-2-1, Friendly's 1-5, Queens 0-5.

RUNNING

Road Run Calendar

SUNDAY, NOVEMBER 4 — Dream of Roses, all-women's 10k and 2-mile fun run-walk & race-walk beginning at 10 a.m. at Chemeketa Community College. The entry fee is $4 by Oct. 27, $8 after; add $7 for long-sleeve T-shirt, $10 for sweatshirt. For more information, call Phidippides Running Store in Salem at 399-7057.

THURSDAY, NOVEMBER 22 — Willamalane Turkey Stuffer, 5k beginning at 8:30 a.m. at the Lively Park Swim Center, 6100 Thurston Road, in Springfield. The entry fees including custom shirt, pancake breakfast, turkey raffle and wave pool swim are $12 by Nov. 17, $15 after; $5 and $8 without shirt. For more information, call 726-4368.

BASKETBALL

Eugene Parks & Recreation
Fall Leagues
3x3
MEN

A RESULTS — Community Markets d Pushing "30" 30-11, 31-15. Kappa Sig d Sultan's Of Swish 30-13, 30-20. **A STANDINGS** — Community Markets 4-0, Fishers Farmers Insurance 2-1, Kappa Sig 2-2, Pushing "30" 1-3, Sultan's Of Swish 0-3.

B RESULTS — Over The Hill Gang 30-23, 32-17. Brakers d Lead Feet, forfeit. Bill, Andy, Jim & Steff 30-27, 30-28. Jones & Roth d Hackers 31-28, 30-24. **B STANDINGS** — Jones & Roth 3-0, Hackers 2-1, Brakers 2-1, Over The Hill Gang 2-1, Bill, Andy, Jim & Steff 2-1, Lead Feet 1-2, Ideal Steelers 0-3, Second Wind 0-3.

SOFTBALL

Eugene Parks and Recreation
Fall Leagues
FINAL STANDINGS
COED

B STANDINGS — Vise Squad 5-0, Summertime Brews 3-2, Selectemp Sluggers 3-2, Pecadilloes 2-3, Foul Play 2-3, Mr. Morton 0-5.

C-1 STANDINGS — Late For Dinner 5-0, Mary Kay Cosmetics 4-1, Tino's 3-2, G.W. Finishing 2-3, Bellair 1-4, Play It Again Sports 0-5.

C-2 STANDINGS — Charlie's Raiders 5-0, Sharp Shooters 4-2, Centaurs 3-2, Central Lutheran Danelanders 2-3, Commercial Air 2-3, Northwest Spirit 0-5.

D STANDINGS — Tecdus 4-1, Aco Wood Works 4-1, Guys & Dolls 3-2, The Mutants 2-3, Pounders 2-3, Helium Heads 0-5.

E STANDINGS — Relief Pitcher-Brew Crew 5-0, Great Harvesters 3-2, Good News Bears 3-2, New Way Electric 3-2, Ad-Art Design 1-4, Women's Care Associates 0-5.

F STANDINGS — Altair Slammers 4-1, Bohemia Axe-Kickers 3-2, Parcs Fools 3-2, Terminators 2-3, Artisan Automotive 2-3, OSL Players 1-4.

G STANDINGS — Gardners' Quicksilver 5-0, Aliens 3-2, Kerry's Mitt Wits 3-2, Liberty Savings 2-3, Sluggers 1-4, Kneflights 1-4.

H STANDINGS — The Duck Heads 5-0, Beer Bellies 3-2, The Simpsons 2-2, Centennial Bank 2-2, Oregon Research Institute 1-4, Brites-Cascade Security 1-4.

VOLLEYBALL

Eugene Parks and Recreation
Fall Leagues
COED

A RESULTS — That Spankin' Team d Koch Chiropractic Center 16-14, 15-4, 12-4. T.C.I. Cablevision d Green Valley Guardians 7-15, 15-13, 7-5. Boy Dough & Flow Busters d Strange Crew 15-7, 7-15, 14-12. **A STANDINGS** — That Spankin' Team 3-0, Koch Chiropractic Center 2-1, Boy Dough & Flow Busters 2-1, Green Valley Guardians 1-2, T.C.I. Cablevision 1-2, Strange Crew 0-3.

B RESULTS — Kings Table d Spicey Spikers 15-5, 15-8, 15-9. UGO d Hands in Pocket 15-11, 15-9, 9-7. Smith Family Bookstore d Franks 15-9, 15-13, 14-12. **B STANDINGS** — UGO 4-0, Franks 2-2, Hands in Pocket 2-2, Smith Family Bookstore 2-2, Kings Table 2-2, Spicey Spikers 0-4.

C-1 RESULTS — Metal Clad Builders d Soft Dinks-Hard Bumps 15-12, 15-12, 10-12. Jacuzzi Bunch d Sunday Service 15-1, 15-6, 12-10. Patchwork d Absolutely Positively 6-145, 15-8, 15-4. **C-1 STANDINGS** — Soft Dinks-Hard Bumps 3-1, Metal Clad Builders 3-1, Jacuzzi Bunch 3-1, Sunday Service 2-2, Patchwork 1-3, Absolutely Positively 0-4.

C-2 RESULTS — The Dooley Bunch d Full Coverage 15-9, 12-15, 12-5. Net Monkeys d Chocolate Thunder 3-15, 15-11, 15-11. At Your Service d Eugene Debs 15-8, 15-9, 11-9. **C-2 STANDINGS** — The Dooley Bunch 4-0, Full Coverage 3-1, At Your Service 2-2, Chocolate Thunder 1-3, Eugene Debs 1-3, Net Monkeys 1-3.

C-3 RESULTS — Odd Ones Out d Twenty-Thirty Something 15-3, 15-13, 15-5. Good Timers d Giants 15-1, 6-15, 15-13. BC d Pepsi 15-3, 15-13, 15-3. **C-3 STANDINGS** — Pepsi 2-1, Good Timers 2-1, BC 2-1, Odd Ones Out 2-1, Giants 1-2, Twenty-Thirty Something 0-3.

C-4 RESULTS — SLIME d Net Gains 16-14, 15-2, 15-6. NaCl d Uncle Slam 15-4, 17-15, 11-13. Dig This d R-G News Busters 15-13, 15-11, 11-15. **C-4 STANDINGS** — NaCl 4-0, Dig This 3-1, R-G News Busters 2-2, Net Gains 1-3, Uncle Slam 1-3, SLIME 1-3.

C-D RESULTS — Gecko d Sand Box Bullies 15-2, 15-3, 15-3. Cap Outs d West Side 15-6, 15-3, 15-3. Richardson Sports d Bell Hardware 15-6, 3-15, 15-5. **C-D STANDINGS** — Gecko 4-0, Cap Outs 3-1, Sand Box Bullies 2-2, Richardson Sports 2-2, Bell Hardware 1-3, West Side 0-4.

Figure 10.6 Sample of Box Score Information, Eugene (Oregon) *Register Guard.*

photographs of its employees and update them to correspond with specific articles.

Group photographs or group action scenes are also often used by newspapers. Newspaper editors usually like horizontal photographs that result in a two-column illustration. These photographs should be submitted as 8-inch-by-10-inch glossies when possible, although newspapers with excellent photographic and editorial staffs can use 4-inch-by-5-inch photos without seriously affecting the clarity of the picture when it is reproduced in the newspaper. Generally speaking, it is best to use uncluttered backgrounds (unless a background is needed for perspective).

Photo captions should be included with each photograph submitted to a newspaper. One should not assume that newspaper editors will be able to identify individual photographs. A photo

NOTES/ANNOUNCEMENTS

WILLAMALANE BASKETBALL — The Willamalane Park & Recreation District will hold an organizational meeting at 7 p.m., Wednesday, Nov. 7, at the Memorial Building, 765 N. A St. in Springfield for all new teams planning to play in the winter basketball leagues. Team representatives should be present to discuss team fees, league format and registration procedures. For more information, call 746-1669.

KIDSPORTS VOLLEYBALL — Registration is available for the 1990 Kidsports volleyball program. Practice begins this week with the six-week season ending with a tournament on Dec. 7-9. The program is open to boys in grades 3-8, girls in District 4J grades 3-5 and girls in grades 3-8 in other school districts. The fee per player is $16. Registration forms are available at the Kidsports offices in Eugene (2190 Polk St.) and Springfield (1030 G St.). A late-night registration will be held from 5:30-7 p.m. Tuesday at Petersen Barn, North Eugene High School (Room 206), Sheldon High School and the Eugene-Springfield Kidsports offices. For more information, call 683-2373 (Eugene) or 746-0403 (Springfield).

KIDSPORTS FOOTBALL TOURNAMENT — The 1990 Swede Johnson Memorial Kids Bowl season-ending football tournament for tackle football will be held next Sunday. All games will be held at Autzen Stadium beginning at 1 p.m. Admisson is $2 for adults, $1 for seniors age 55 and older and free for youths 18 and younger. For more information, call 683-2373.

EUGENE PARKS AND RECREATION BASKETBALL — Registration for Eugene Parks and Recreation fall basketball leagues begins Tuesday, with league play beginning in December and continuing through the first week in March. For more information, call 687-5333.

STORM THE STAIRS BENEFIT — Recreation and Intramurals (RIM) at the University of Oregon and Sacred Heart Hospital's U-Can Center are sponsoring a "Storm the Stairs" event from 10:45 a.m.-1 p.m., on Sunday, Nov. 11, at Autzen Stadium. Part of the National Collegiate Drive to Cure Paralysis, proceeds from the pledge-oriented event will go towards purchasing rehabilitation equipment for the U-Can Center. The idea will be to collectively set a "world record" for vertical distance by climbing stairs at Autzen Stadium. In addition to stair climbing, there also will be demonstrations and recreational activities. For more information, call RIM at 346-4113.

WILLAMETTE VALLEY BABE RUTH — Willamette Valley Babe Ruth is accepting applications for coaching positions in the 9-12 Bambino, 13 Prep and 13-15 Babe Ruth leagues to be formed in the spring of 1991. Send applications to Roger Boothe at 3215 Meadow Lane, Eugene 97402. An organizational meeting is planned for 7 p.m., Wednesday, Nov. 7, at the Marist High School cafeteria. For more information, call Roger Boothe at 689-3443 and 484-7080, or Thomas Westfall at 686-9041 and 484-9509.

HUNTER EDUCATION — The River Road Park and Recreation District will hold a hunter safety course on Nov. 6, 7, 8 and 12-15 at the district facility at 1400 Lake Drive. The cost is $1 for district residents and $1.50 for all others. For more information, call Michael DeRobertis at 688-4052.

BOYS' POWER VOLLEYBALL — The Columbia Empire Volleyball Association, the local affiliate of the United States Volleyball Association, is looking to form a local team for its boys' power volleyball program. Anyone interested in organizing a team, playing or coaching, call Jerry King at 684-3108 or Reuben Chong at (206) 687-4845.

Figure 10.7 Sample of Sports Notes and Announcements, Eugene (Oregon) *Register Guard.*

Youth Sports recognition

If you're the coach or publicist for a youth sports program, fill out the form below or a reasonable facsimile.

Organization: _____

Coach or publicist _____

Your phone: _____

Name of meet and significance (local/area, state, regional or national):

_____

_____

The Courier will print the names of local and area youths among the top three finishers in a meet limited to local/area competition, the top 10 in a meet that is regional, state or national. Coaches may attach a 25-word comment and/or photo about winners of local events or the top three finishers in regional, state or national competition). **For team sports use the space below for pertinent information.**

Athlete's name	age	specific event	finish	time/score

Send to: **Youth Sports, Waterloo Courier, P.O. Box 540, Waterloo, IA 50704** (Use another sheet of paper for comments if necessary.)

Figure 10.8 Youth Sports Recognition Form, Waterloo (Iowa) *Courier.*

caption can be typed on a separate piece of paper and taped to the back of the photograph. The caption should not be written on the back of the photograph; this risks the transfer of felt-tip or ballpoint smudges to the front of the picture. Nor should a caption be taped to the front of the picture; this can cause damage to the image area of the photo. If the need arises to write something on the back of a photograph, a hard surface should be used to eliminate damaging impressions. When the photograph involved is an individual's picture, the caption need only name the individual and organization or position. If the photograph is of a group, all names as well as positions and the event and date of the event should be listed. Sometimes the photograph itself will tell the story; other times, the professional will have to be more elaborate in his or her interpretation of the photograph.

The advent of digital cameras and camcorders provides for the rapid transmission of images by e-mail or placement on a leisure services organizational website. *Camp Adventure*™ *Youth Services* often uses the digital camera to create images of staff development programs or special events such as its annual DessertFest program. Staffers immediately incorporate these images onto the website at the end of the evening. This provides for immediate feedback and reinforcement of the day's events. Participants often receive such images favorably as a way of immediately recapturing the excitement of the event.

Newspaper Advertising

As a vehicle for advertisements, the newspaper is important to profit-oriented as well as nonprofit leisure service organizations. Leisure services such as theaters, amusement parks, commercial bowling alleys, and other enterprises utilize newspapers extensively. Nonprofit organizations occasionally purchase paid advertisements or have benevolent or public-spirited businesses in the community sponsor such advertising space in a newspaper.

Newspapers have several ways of calculating advertisement costs. Some newspapers, for example, have a flat rate—that is to say, the newspaper charges the same rate per area unit for advertising regardless of volume or size of the advertisement or the frequency of the advertisement. More often, a newspaper will charge a lower rate per unit for larger advertisements or advertisements that appear a certain number of times. The basic rate for advertisements is determined by measuring the proposed advertisement in terms of column inches or agate lines. (There are fourteen agate lines to the column

inch.) Once the newspaper has determined this basic measurement, it will charge for space according to its own rates.

The process of creating an advertisement should be done in conjunction with the newspaper advertising staff. The leisure service professional needs to provide the advertising specialist with as much information as possible about the service and the market toward which it is directed. Rather than simply listing the activities of a leisure service organization, an advertisement should build around a central idea or theme. The central idea concept can be thought of as the verbal or visual device around which the advertisement is written. A theme often helps capture the attention of the newspaper audience that the professional is hoping to attract. Figure 10.9 is an example of a newspaper display ad from the City of Long Beach (California) Parks, Recreation & Marine.

Brochures

One of the most widely used and effective tools for disseminating information is the brochure. A brochure is a printed work bound together in such a way that it highlights programs, areas, facilities, and activities or presents information that enables people to find desired leisure experiences. Brochures come in all sizes, colors, shapes, and designs. In many respects, they have become a mainstay in the promotion of many leisure service programs.

In creating a brochure, the professional recreation and leisure service staff member or members must deal with a number of basic questions including:

1. *Brochure Content*—The leisure service programmer must ask himself or herself, What is the purpose of the brochure? Are we promoting an activity, a set of activities, or a facility, or are we disseminating information concerning other leisure opportunities? The professional must be acutely aware of precisely what he or she wants to convey in order to decide what a given brochure should contain.

Publication: **Beachcomber**
Run Date: **Friday, May 17, 2002**
Size: 3 col. x 8" (24 col. in.)
Advertiser: Long Beach Parks Recreation & Marine
Contact: Tina Burton 562.570.3234

Figure 10.9   Display Advertising, Long Beach (California) Parks, Recreation & Marine.

2. *Timing*—Timing deals with the question, What is the most appropriate time to produce the brochure to ensure timely distribution and maximum visibility and impact? It may be best to produce a brochure on a seasonal basis when promoting the schedule of activities of a municipal park and recreation department; conversely, it may be more effective to have a brochure available on a continual daily basis when promoting the use of a given facility (e.g., a swimming pool, an ice rink, or a drop-in center). No universally accepted set of rules exists for the proper timing of brochures. Obviously the timing of a brochure for a specific event is crucial, but timing is highly situational and must be managed by the leisure service professional.

3. *Format and Design*—The manner in which information will be arranged and presented in a brochure is of great importance. Will the brochure contain pictures or graphic designs? What colors will be employed—will it be multi-colored or limited to one color? Is the intent of the brochure to be striking and bold in appearance or more subtly persuasive? The type of design chosen will reflect on the material presented. For example, a bold design may indicate that the programs detailed will be bold in nature, whereas a soft approach may indicate to the public that the program involved is "relaxing," "classy," or "intellectual." What size will the brochure be? Will it be magazine size? A small booklet form? Folded in three panels?

4. *Distribution*—How does the leisure service professional intend to reach his or her target public? How will the public gain access to the information provided by the professional? Will the brochure be mailed? If so, to whom? If the brochure is to be made available to individuals visiting a facility, where should these brochures be located within the facility? Should the brochure be made available to service clubs, community organizations, the Chamber of Commerce, and groups within the community such as the Welcome Wagon? Should the brochure be distributed through the school system? These types of questions must be asked each time a brochure is disseminated.

5. *Cost*—Obviously the amount of money available to an organization for the production of brochures will affect the quantity and quality of its brochures. It is interesting to note that profit-oriented organizations spend a great deal of their budget for advertising and publicity whereas nonprofit and governmental organizations do not. However, these organizations are starting to sell advertising space in brochures to finance production.

The following discussion contains helpful suggestions for putting together brochures. It is important to remember that the professional is attempting primarily to inform his or her target public. As such, the brochure should be instructive, informative, and eye-catching. Information written for a brochure should be concise and to the point. The information should be accurate—including all necessary names, locations, and phone numbers. Nothing is more embarrassing to the professional than a brochure that contains an erroneous phone number or other misinformation.

The contents and format of a brochure will vary. For example, a brochure promoting an activity will often include a description of the activity, its cost, the time of the activity, its location, and perhaps its instructor. This type of brochure may also contain application or registration forms and information, depending on the circumstances. Brochures describing facilities might include a description as well as a diagram of the facility. Pictures and designs are often used to make a brochure distinctive or to emphasize the attractiveness of the facility or activity. For example, a picture of children playing in a swimming complex may communicate far more effectively than a written message would. Clip art is frequently used and can highlight information and add attractiveness to brochures.

The selection of a printer or design firm is important not only from the standpoint of cost but also in terms of production. Printing firms can often be very helpful to the professional in the selection of type—its size and most appropriate style. When laying out the brochure, it is important not to waste space or overcrowd the material. The printer can help the professional organize his or her material in an orderly fashion that will be clear to the individual reading the brochure. Once the decision has been made as to the content, the type of paper, the size of type, the number of pictures, and other designs to be used, the layout of the brochure can proceed.

In working with artists, typesetters, and printers, the professional will be asked to provide the following information:

1. *Artist*—Most artists base their fees on the amount of time involved in designing the publication and the amount of preparation

required for the final camera-ready art. A graphic artist may or may not be an illustrator as well. The artist will want to know:

   a. Type of design work required: basic conceptual design; layout; paste-up of a dummy; preparation of camera-ready art; illustrations; hand lettering.

   b. Number of pages of final product.

   c. Time: how soon the work will be needed.

2. *Typesetter*—Typesetters usually base their fees on the system of typesetting they use, the time it takes to set the material, and the number of manuscript pages. The typesetter will want to know:

   a. Number of manuscript pages.

   b. Typeface: for body copy; for headlines.

   c. Specifications: size of all type; leading (spacing) between lines; column widths.

   d. Anticipated number of author's alterations, if any.

   e. Time: how soon the work will be needed.

   f. Paste-up: will the computer graphics specialist do the paste-up.

3. *Printer*—Printers need to know paper stock specifications as soon as possible so that they can order the paper early enough to meet time constraints. To avoid delays, it is best to select a paper that is easy to obtain. The printer will want to know:

   a. Size of publication (e.g., 8 1/2 by 11 inches; 5 by 8 inches).

   b. Number of copies.

   c. Number of colors of paper or ink.

   d. Type of paper for both cover and text.

   e. Type of binding.

   f. Number of photographs.

   g. Any difficult registration jobs (a fine line running next to a color border, for example).

   h. If a proof is needed.

   i. Time: how soon the work will be needed.

The advent of desktop publishing provides a great deal of flexibility for leisure service organizations today. Through the use of various graphics packages such as Photoshop, Freehand, and Quark Express, it is possible for an organization to create its own brochures. In this way, an organization can customize its brochures and other materials and direct them toward specific audiences. In addition, the speed in which the organization can produce materials can be enhanced depending on its capabilities. Further, when coupled with websites, the brochure can be produced in electronic format. The electronic generation of brochures allows for the use of various special effects such as Quick Time videos and voice transmissions.

Leisure service organizations generally use four types of brochures. Brochures are used to identify and define activities, to provide information concerning the design and layout of areas and facilities, and to promote other recreation and leisure resources. The fourth type of brochure is created by combining two or more of the first three types of brochures together. For example, seasonal brochures not only define activities of the leisure service organization, but also identify and provide information concerning its facilities. Furthermore, the dependent relationship of many activities to a specific type of facility often requires these two types of information to be joined in a single brochure.

A number of brochures are used to promote leisure services. One common brochure is the comprehensive, seasonal program brochure. These brochures are built around the seasons of the year and mailed to individuals or households on a quarterly basis. Brochures come in many sizes and shapes.

In any community throughout North America there are a wide range of activities and events. Services are offered through public agencies, nonprofit organizations, businesses, or a combination of community organizations and interest groups. Often the promotion of a community's events is handled through its tourism and visitors bureau and/or its Chamber of Commerce. The Dubuque (Iowa) area Chamber of Commerce Convention and Visitors Bureau publicizes a wide range of leisure activities and events in its annual spring and summer brochure. The brochure identifies the varied and many festivals and events that occur during this time period. The brochure describes nearly 120 festivals and events and provides contact information (*www.TravelDubuque.com*).

Figure 10.10 Brochure, Santa Cruz (California) Beach Boardwalk.

The Santa Cruz (California) Beach Boardwalk is a popular commercial leisure service attraction and destination. Figure 10.10 shows a brochure that emphasizes its major roller coaster attraction (www.beachboardwalk.com).

Figure 10.11 shows a cover of a brochure featuring the unique Hickory Hills Park, which is operated by the Black Hawk (Iowa) County Conservation Board (*www.co.black-hawk.ia.us/dept/conservation*). This brochure contains a map, a description of the park and its location, as well as a presentation of the various leisure and recreation opportunities available including camping, picnicking, boating, sand volleyball, fishing, hiking, cross-country skiing, sledding, and ice skating. The brochure contains many advertisements, which cover the cost of its printing and distribution.

The Glacier Institute is a nonprofit organization that provides field-based education programs focusing on natural and cultural values of the Crown of the Continent Ecosystem, of which Montana's Glacier National Park is the heart. Figure 10.12 shows the organization's promotional brochure. Programs provided by the institute include adult field courses, youth summer camps, Glacier Naturalists day programs for children, family programs for children aged six to fifteen, and a Discovery School providing K–12 grade school groups with field science lessons (*www.glacierinstitute.org*). The brochure depicted in figure 10.13 is from City of West Des Moines (Iowa) Parks and Recreation. Figure 10.14, from the City of Edmonton (Alberta, Canada) Community Services, shows a brochure presenting the city's children and youth programs. Figure 10.15 shows a brochure for the Mile Hi Council program in Denver, Colorado (*www.girlscoutsmilehi.org*). This brochure contains descriptions of various camp programs, registration forms, health forms, as well as a call for volunteers and financial assistance for girls who, without it, would not be able to go to camp.

Figure 10.11 Brochure, Black Hawk County (Iowa) Conservation Board.

Figure 10.16 shows a brochure containing a map that depicts the areas, facilities, and major transportation links for George Wyth State Park, which is operated by the Iowa Department of Natural Resources (*http://www.state.ia.us/parks*). Maps are often included in brochures that describe an area, facility, or park. They usually present trails, shelters, buildings, and other unique features of interest to visitors.

Fliers

Another widely used form of publicity in leisure service organizations is the flier. Fliers are used as an inexpensive communication tool for mass distribution. They provide the consumer with the vital details of the program designed in such a way as to not only inform but also stimulate interest. Fliers are usually printed on a single sheet of paper and are designed to be read as individual units. The effective flier must be attractive and eye-catching in order to capture the attention and interest of the individual reading it.

The flier can be an elaborately produced item, or it can be relatively simple. A professionally designed and printed flier may be appropriate to promote certain programs within an agency. On the other hand, a handwritten or typed flier produced on an organization's copy machine may be adequate in most cases. Regardless of the method of production, the flier must reflect an effective use of space in terms of layout, design, and color. Fliers should be kept simple and should be constructed around a central theme or idea. The central idea should directly convey the message that the organization wishes to promote. This is usually accomplished by use of an illustration and a headline to draw the reader's attention to the program. Fliers, like brochures, come in many shapes and sizes. Each of these has catchy, bold titles and graphics. They each contain a headline and accompanying illustrations that convey to the reader the nature of the activity and what it is likely to entail. The information presented is uncluttered

Figure 10.12   Brochure, The Glacier Institute, Kalispell, Montana.

Figure 10.13   Brochure, City of West Des Moines (Iowa) Parks and Recreation.

Afterschool & Community Program Opportunities

THE CITY OF Edmonton COMMUNITY SERVICES

Figure 10.14 Afterschool & Community Program Opportunities Brochure, The City of Edmonton (Alberta, Canada) Community Services.

and easy to distinguish. Each flier tells the reader the program to be implemented as well as the location, time, date, and other relevant information. Figure 10.17 shows a U.S. Airforce flyer that promotes trips to Southeast Asia.

Although it is important to include all relevant, accurate information about a given program or activity, this written information is actually secondary in importance to the visual impact of the picture or headline used in a flier. Readers are first attracted to a flier's main thrust, and if it catches their interest and attention, they

will read the details. What should be included in a flier and in what order?

1. *The Name of the Event or Activity*—This might include a brief description of the activities or types of experiences that are to be gained by a customer. This message should be direct, simple, and conveyed in a few words.
2. *Identification of the Target Audience*—For whom is the program designed? One might want to identify the age grouping, sex, geographic location, competence/skill level, and perhaps leisure preference. For example, a flier might designate that a particular activity would especially interest the outdoor enthusiast.
3. *The Location, Date, and Time of the Event*—This might necessitate the inclusion of a map to specify location. When mentioning the date, one might want to further clarify it by mentioning the day of the week. The time should specify not only the time the program starts but also the time the program will end. If the program is to extend over several days, it should be made clear what times the program will be in progress each day.
4. *The Sponsoring Agency*—Include not only the name, telephone number, and address of the agency sponsoring the program, but also the name of a contact person (where appropriate) in the organization.

The distribution of fliers can be carried out in several ways:

1. *Individual Collection*—Individual parties within the distribution area pick up fliers and distribute them or offer them for distribution. For example, the Chamber of Commerce might be involved in the distribution of fliers in this way.
2. *Mailing*—If the budget allows, a leisure service organization can use the postal service to distribute fliers. The mailing of fliers usually targets selected populations. For example, one might mail fliers to given age groupings (such as a flier to senior citizens announcing appropriate trips and activities).
3. *Displaying*—Fliers can be attached to a variety of surfaces. Often the professional will use a window, door, wall, bulletin board, or other surface. In this sense, they become miniposters.

Figure 10.15 Brochure, Girl Scouts—Mile Hi Council, Denver, Colorado.

4. *Personal Distribution*—Perhaps the most frequently used method is personal distribution of fliers. The professional may hand out the fliers himself or herself, or may convince schools, grocery stores, or clubs to distribute the fliers. Selection of the distribution points should complement the program involved. For example, a children's program can be effectively promoted by distributing fliers through the schools. A communitywide event, on the other hand, might be better publicized if fliers are distributed through community grocery stores.

Fliers are useful and efficient tools for promoting leisure services and programs—an inexpensive way for the organization to communicate with prospective customers. Care should be given to choosing both the design and distribution methods. A poorly designed flier or one distributed at the wrong place or the wrong time will not be effective in promotion of programs; however, fliers that are "on target" can serve the promotional efforts of the organization well. In any case, fliers are inexpensive enough that the

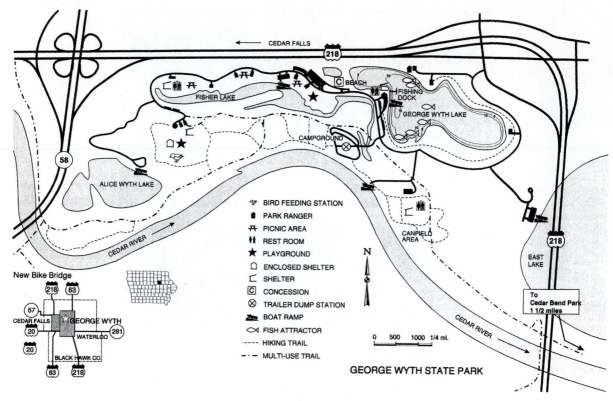

Figure 10.16   Map, George Wyth State Park, Iowa Department of Natural Resources.

organization can afford to experiment with design and distribution points in order to determine their most effective use.

Many leisure service organizations are using computers to design and print high-quality, innovative fliers in-house. The advent of desktop publishing, facilitated by laser printers, provides the necessary tools for developing professional-quality fliers at a reasonable price for distribution. For example, the QuarkXPress software program provides a wide array of options that can be used in designing fliers. Some of the options include creating text, importing text, importing graphics into text, wrapping text around graphics, creating different fonts/type styles, and creating different sizes of text. It is also possible to get clip art software programs for computers, to print in color with a color printer, and to create your own graphics with a graphics software program.

Newsletters

A newsletter is a means of communicating with an organization's membership and constituents. It can be thought of as a tool for providing information in a more concise and brief manner than that of a newspaper or magazine. The newsletter is a direct means of communication. Similar to other tools used to promote a program, its major objectives are to inform individuals and to create a positive image of the organization. Newsletters can represent the viewpoint of the chief executive of the organization or can be indicative of the broader viewpoint of the organization's membership.

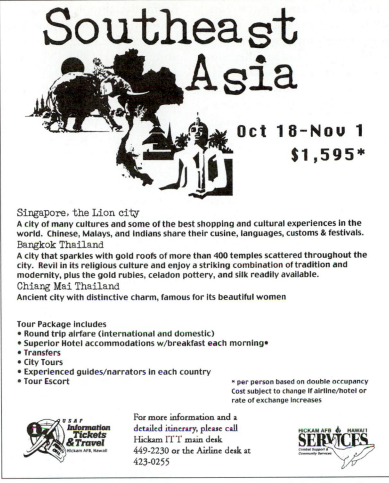

Southeast Asia

Oct 18–Nov 1
$1,595*

Singapore, the Lion city
A city of many cultures and some of the best shopping and cultural experiences in the world. Chinese, Malays, and Indians share their cusine, languages, customs & festivals.
Bangkok Thailand
A city that sparkles with gold roofs of more than 400 temples scattered throughout the city. Revil in its religious culture and enjoy a striking combination of tradition and modernity, plus the gold rubies, celadon pottery, and silk readily available.
Chiang Mai Thailand
Ancient city with distinctive charm, famous for its beautiful women

Tour Package includes
• Round trip airfare (international and domestic)
• Superior Hotel accommodations w/breakfast each morning•
• Transfers
• City Tours
• Experienced guides/narrators in each country
• Tour Escort

* per person based on double occupancy
Cost subject to change if airline/hotel or
rate of exchange increases

USAF Information Tickets & Travel Hickam AFB, Hawaii

For more information and a detailed itinerary, please call Hickam ITT main desk 449-2230 or the Airline desk at 423-0255

HICKAM AFB HAWAII
SERVICES
Combat Support & Community Services

Figure 10.17   Flyer, Hickam AFB Services, Hickam AFB, Honolulu, Hawaii

In developing a newsletter, Logan (1975: 22–25) has suggested five major points of concern. One must consider the *audience* toward which the newsletter is to be directed. Is the newsletter going only to the members of the organization, or will it be distributed to the public as well? If distributed to the public, will it be distributed to a given geographic area or another type of population grouping? The audience that the newsletter is aimed at will dictate the type of news that it will include as well as the way in which the news is written (e.g., newslet-

ters that are designed for an organization's members only may be written more specifically and might have a more personal orientation).

Size and format should also be considered in developing a newsletter. Size and format (and the sophistication of the format) can vary widely. The newsletter can be a mimeographed sheet of paper or an elaborately produced item resembling a magazine. The newsletter should in any case employ a format that is readable and attractive. The type of format that an organization employs will primarily be determined by the funds available to produce it. These funds can be enhanced by selling advertising space in the newsletter to outside business interests.

Central to the development of an effective newsletter is the *organization* of a newsgathering operation. Depending on the complexity and sophistication of the newsletter, this operation may involve an entire staff (e.g., in very large governmental organizations or commercial recreation and leisure organizations) or a single contact individual to whom articles for the newsletter are submitted. This individual may also seek out and report information relevant to the organizational newsletter.

The *type of printing* and *method of distribution* of a newsletter may also vary widely, according to its sophistication and the funds available. Printing involves the use of graphics, selection of type, color, and paper. Often, an organization might combine the printed form with the more economical typed and copied format by having the heading printed commercially and using a copy machine to print the bottom of the front page and the remaining pages of the newsletter. This is a shrewd approach because the heading is bold and eye-catching—encouraging the attention of the reader—but the newsletter is still economical and can be produced on a monthly or bimonthly basis. Newsletters can emphasize a specific program or can be focused more broadly.

Annual Reports

An annual report can be thought of as a year-end, comprehensive summary detailing the financial status, program services, physical developments, and prospective changes in a leisure service organization. The annual report is submitted to a governing body or board of directors, depending on the nature of the organization. It is designed to be graphically informative. An annual report can be a useful component of a leisure service organization's promotional activities. The annual report is a way of indicating the current state of affairs to the organization's present customers. Used as a promotional tool, the annual report can serve to entice potential customers. If done well, it will enhance the image of the organization. Kraus and Curtis (1990: 339–40) have noted that annual reports usually include: (1) organization address and staff/director names; (2) opening messages; (3) table of contents and acknowledgments; (4) organizational chart; (5) financial report; (6) major facility developments; and (7) program information, participation, and so on. The St. Louis (Missouri) County Parks and Recreation Departments takes an interesting approach in presenting its annual report (*www.stlouisco.com*). This annual report, which includes a CD-ROM, provides a thumbnail sketch of the organization's achievements. Alternative formats are available upon request (see Figure 10.18).

Electronic Information

The computer holds great promise as a vehicle for dissemination of information regarding leisure services. As society continues to move through a dramatic information transformation, electronic culture will play an increasingly important role in how individuals access information about leisure opportunities. As noted by Bullaro and Edginton (1986: 323), "We have evolved from a culture solely dependent upon written and oral communication to one in which communication is achieved more and more through the electronic media."

For example, touch-sensitive computers have been available and used in leisure service organizations and tourist programs and facilities for a number of years. Basically, such technology allows a customer to interact with computers by pressing the screen to select various options that provide information. In many airports throughout North America, touch-sensitive videos provide travelers with information about destination attractions, hotels, entertainment, car rentals, travel services, and other relevant information. Touch-sensitive videos are used at interpretive sites to help visitors gain information and knowledge regarding points of interest.

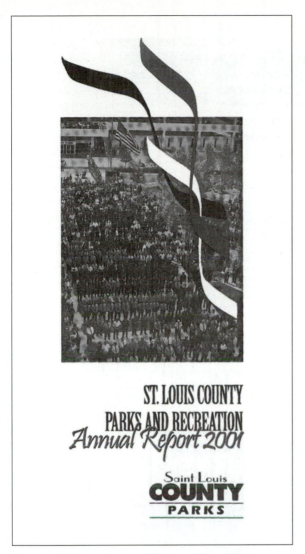

Figure 10.18 Annual Report, St. Louis County (Missouri) Parks.

Perhaps the most significant development in recent years is the advent of the World Wide Web (WWW). The WWW provides opportunities for individuals, organizations, and businesses to establish a home page. A home page can be accessed through the WWW system by other individuals and organizations worldwide and offers the opportunity to provide (and receive) information. A leisure service organization can provide access to all types of program information, including target audiences, types of programs offered, location, costs, and information regarding instructions and leaders. Home pages can be designed to be visually attractive as well as informative. For example, quick-time videos and pictures can provide a more graphic portrayal of the services available from an organization. Home pages can be updated periodically so that they are accurate, providing customers with the most up-to-date information. Figure 10.19 is a sample of the first page of the home page (http://www.uni.edu/campadv) for *Camp Adventure*™ *Youth Services* at the University of Northern Iowa. The computer also provides opportunities for rapid transmission and distribution of information. Electronic mailing lists can be established and information can be disseminated rapidly and at relatively low cost. Further, many individuals prefer to receive information electronically rather than in the more traditional fashion. Electronically transmitted information provides opportunities for program promotion, general information dissemination, and on-line registration, as well as opportunities to answer specific questions through e-mail.

Information and Press Kits

Leisure service organizations should have material available that offers background information about the organization—its staff, programs, and facilities. Such information can be used to provide current and new community members with detailed information about opportunities for leisure participation. The same information may be useful to public officials and individuals who are becoming active volunteers and assuming leadership positions with the leisure service organization. In addition, information packets or press kits can be useful in enhancing a public speech about the organization. Obviously, leisure service organizations should have a press kit on file with local newspapers and radio and television stations. In general, whenever the organization is making professional contacts, the press kit can be an asset.

Welcome!

Camp Adventure™ Youth Services

who we are · alliance · calender · get involved · programs · contract with us · kids zone · FAQs · press room · staff resources · home

- Welcome
- Learn About Us
- History
- Vision
- Mission
- Motto
- Values & Traditions

Catch the Magic!

"We create magic moments for children that last for a life time."

HOME > WHO WE ARE > WELCOME

Welcome!

The University of Northern Iowa's *Camp Adventure™ Youth Services* program provides an extraordinary opportunity for university and college-age students to participate in a worthwhile and valuable service learning experience. We welcome your interest and participation in the *Camp Adventure™ Youth Services* program. We are a not-for-profit, educational organization. The *Camp Adventure™ Youth Services* program professional staff is made up of a number of caring, committed, and competent individuals dedicated in their service to children and youth. The *Camp Adventure™ Youth Services* program provides a wide array of opportunities to serve children and youth, integrate theory with practice, develop new knowledge, skills and competencies, as well as to be a part of a worthwhile endeavor. *Camp Adventure™ Youth Services* program is noted for its dynamism, zest, energy, and enthusiasm, as well as commitment to quality and excellence.

Your participation in the *Camp Adventure™ Youth Services* program can make a difference in the lives of others, and to help you discover your inner talents and abilities.

We hope that you find the opportunity to participate in *Camp Adventure™ Youth Services* a valuable one, and look forward to you involvement!

Best wishes,

Christopher R. Edginton, Ph.D.
Founder
Camp Adventure™ Youth Services

Camp Adventure™ Youth Services
1223 W. 22nd Street,
Cedar Falls, IA 50614-0156
Tel: (319) 273-5960 Fax: (319) 273-2058
Email: *camp.adventure@uni.edu*

Figure 10.19 World Wide Web Homepage, *Camp Adventure™ Youth Services,* University of Northern Iowa, Cedar Falls, Iowa.

It is difficult to compile a comprehensive list of information packet contents that would apply to all leisure service organizations. However, the following list of suggested material should be helpful to the leisure professional:

1. A brief history of the organization;
2. An organizational chart;
3. Biographical sketches of staff members;
4. Organizational programs, services, and facilities;
5. The annual report;
6. Reprints of newspaper articles, editorials, or other media material; and
7. Photographs of activities, services, and facilities.

A press kit can be assembled into a binder, folder, manila envelope, or other organized form. For the sake of expediency and cost, the folder or manila envelope is probably the best method for presenting the press kit. A well-prepared and well-organized press kit can make a positive and lasting impression and can provide an individual with a good deal of insight into an organization. In addition, it is extremely important that an information packet be kept up to date with names of people, current photographs, accurate charts and maps, and so on. Outdated or incorrect information about an organization can have a more negative effect than no available information at all. The packet often carries the name of the organization and the individual providing the information. Figure 10.20 shows an example of an information sheet profiling the staff, mission, and other salient factors of the Lake County (Illinois) Forest Preserves.

Postage Meter Message

One technique that is a useful promotional tool and that can be incorporated into brochure and flier distribution or used on other mailings or organizational correspondence is the postage meter message. An example of a postage meter message used in Dundas, Ontario. The phrase "Your Leisure is Our Business" is affixed to all correspondence sent from this organization.

Logos and Emblems

Through logos and emblems, a leisure service organization can gain the public's awareness. The visual identity of a graphic design is very important to any organization. In essence, the logo or emblem is a communicative device—at a glance, it conveys to the individual viewing it the presence of "the organization." In other words, it is a visual symbol that represents the organization. Some organizations with easily identifiable logos or emblems are the YMCA/YWCA, the Girl Scouts, the 4-H Club, and professional sports teams (e.g., the "Seahawks" for Seattle).

Logos and emblems become representative of the organizations involved; as a result of this association, they are imbued with shades of meaning for the individual who views them. For example, the YMCA/YWCA symbol conveys not only the reality of the organization (in terms of buildings and facilities) but also certain values, such as integrity, dependability, stability, and community service. When a logo or emblem is able to convey such a set of values, it is a valuable asset to any organization. Leisure service organizations have this potential—that is, their logo may come to be identified with values that are considered to be helpful to the organizational image. However, if an organization is involved in or associated with actions that are considered indicative of poor values, the logo or emblem can elicit those same connotations in the minds of individuals viewing it. Logos or emblems can be many things—geometric designs, organic objects, or animate or inanimate objects. Smokey Bear, for example, has long been a symbol for park fire safety and prevention. Ideally, a logo or emblem is simple in form and design. The colors, shapes, and objects employed and the manner in which these are blended and laid out will affect the impact of the logo design.

How and where do leisure service organizations employ logos and emblems? They can be used wherever they can be employed with taste—on stationery, business cards, fliers and brochures, posters, press release forms, annual

Agency Profile

LAKE COUNTY FOREST PRESERVES

spring 2002

Board of Commissioners

PRESIDENT
Al Westerman, *Waukegan*

VICE PRESIDENT
Carol Calabresa, *Libertyville*

TREASURER
Sandy Cole, *Grayslake*

COMMISSIONERS
Mary J. Beattie, *Lake Forest*
Robert M. Buhai, *Highland Park*
Bonnie Thomson Carter, *Ingleside*
Angelo D. Kyle, *Waukegan*
Larry W. Leafblad, *Grayslake*
Martha Marks, *Riverwoods*
Judy Martini, *Antioch*
Loretta McCarley, *Beach Park*
Stevenson Mountsier, *Lake Barrington*
Pamela O. Newton, *Vernon Hills*
Audrey H. Nixon, *North Chicago*
Diana O'Kelly, *Mundelein*
Brent Paxton, *Zion*
Robert G. Sabonjian, *Waukegan*
Suzi M. Schmidt, *Lake Villa*
John E. Schulien, *Libertyville*
Peggy Shorts, *Waukegan*
Carol Spielman, *Highland Park*
David B. Stolman, *Buffalo Grove*
Michael Talbett, *Lake Zurich*

EXECUTIVE DIRECTOR
Steven K. Messerli

SECRETARY TO THE BOARD
Corinne R. McMahon

ASSISTANT SECRETARY
Julie Gragnani

Our Mission

To preserve a dynamic and unique system of diverse natural and cultural resources, and to develop innovative educational, recreational and cultural opportunities of regional value, while exercising environmental and fiscal responsibility.

Your Forest Preserves

Formed in 1958, the Lake County Forest Preserves now emcompasses nearly 24,000 acres. We welcome over 2.5 million visitors each year who enjoy award-winning programs, events and facilities. The District is home to more than 50 endangered species and boasts some of Illinois' finest remaining natural areas.

Governing Board

The state law governing forest preserve districts provides that when a district's boundaries are contiguous with those of the county, the County Board Members also serve as Forest Preserve Commissioners. Your Lake County Forest Preserve District is governed by the same 23 people who serve as your County Board Members. The Forest Preserve Board of Commissioners holds its regular meetings the third Friday of the month, beginning at 9 a.m., at the Independence Grove Visitors Center, 16400 W. Buckley Road (Rt. 137), Libertyville. Committees meet regularly during each month at the Forest Preserve Offices in Libertyville.

General Offices

The Forest Preserve General Offices are located at 2000 North Milwaukee Avenue in Libertyville. Office hours are Monday - Friday, 8 a.m. to 5 p.m., Saturdays, 8 a.m. to 4 p.m., and Sundays, noon to 4 p.m.

For a free Preserve Packet with trail maps, a calendar of events, newsletters and other information, call 847-367-6640, send us an e-mail at forestpreserves@co.lake.il.us, or visit our web site at www.LCFPD.org

Figure 10.20 Information Sheet/Agency Profile, Lake County (Illinois) Forest Preserves.

reports, novelty items (especially T-shirts), organizational vehicles, uniforms, signs, and so on. The use of a logo or emblem on organizational vehicles and uniforms can be especially useful in promoting the organization, since vehicles and uniforms are seen in all areas of a community. A distinctive logo that attracts attention appearing on organization vehicles seen in various parts of town on a frequent basis gives the appearance of a busy organization at work.

Ours is a visually oriented society; hence, the creation of a distinctive, dynamic logo is an important aspect of an organization's overall promotional effort. Examples of designs used to promote leisure service organizations are found in Figures 10.21, 10.22, and 10.23. Figure 10.24 shows the logo of the City of Long Beach (California) Parks, Recreation & Marine. These logos serve as visual symbols for the organizations represented. They suggest that the organizations involve people-oriented services. Although some

Contact:
Metha Sizemore
408.277.2930
metha.sizemore@ci.sj.ca.us
                    December 2001
FOR IMMEDIATE RELEASE   --30 seconds--

Parks, Recreation and
Neighborhood Services

Currently, the City of San José has Master Plans to improve all parks in San José. Some of the improvements are already in place, others have yet to come. Interested in finding out more on improvements at parks in San José? Read the <u>Greenprint,</u> a twenty-year strategy for the improvement of parks, community facilities and programs. It is at your local library in the reference section.

This message is brought to you by the City of San José- Parks, Recreation and Neighborhood Services. *We Connect People.*

Figure 10.21   30-Secong Public Service Announcement, City of San Jose (California) Parks, Recreation and Neighborhood Services.

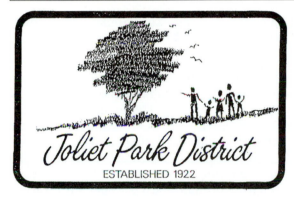

Figure 10.22   Logo, Joliet (Illinois) Park District.

of the designs are more abstract than others, all are effective organizational logos that could become easily recognizable in a community.

Awards and Citations

There are many ways to recognize community organizations and groups for their contributions to leisure service organizations. Awards and citations are one way. They are used primarily as public relations tools. Awards become meaningless if they are given too freely, but they should be presented—when they are deserved—to promote goodwill and support for the organization.

Figure 10.23   Logo, Hennepin (Minnesota) Parks.

Not only are such types of recognition useful in promoting positive relations between the leisure service organization and community groups and individuals, but also the presenta-

Figure 10.24　Logo, Lane County Ice, Eugene, Oregon.

Figure 10.25　Logo, Long Beach (California) Parks, Recreation & Marine.

tions of awards and citations are often newsworthy events and serve to promote organizational efforts. A picture in a newspaper accompanied by a news story serves as publicity for the organization and may arouse interest in the organization's programs and services.

What actions should the leisure organization recognize with awards and citations? Individuals and groups within the community can serve and support a leisure service organization in many different ways that can culminate in their recognition. First, and perhaps most important, is the contribution of time, energy, and creativity toward the promotion of the organization in general or of a specific activity. For example, an organization might want to recognize a local service club that sponsors an activity (such as an annual Easter egg hunt), an individual serving as a member of a policy-making board (e.g., a park board), or a program volunteer. An award for this type of action is especially important in that it formally recognizes a contribution of service. The organization will also want to recognize tangible contributions—represented, for example, by gifts of cash, land, buildings, trees, play equipment, and so on. There are

other meritorious acts, occurring during the daily workings of the organization, that do not fit easily into a category. The leisure services professional should have the insight to recognize such efforts and reward them as they occur.

What types of rewards and citations should the organization distribute? Wall plaques, framed certificates and desk sets are probably most often given as awards. Figure 10.25 shows a Certificate of Participation from the Parks Board and Recreation Commission of the Town of Clarkstown, New York. In special circumstances, the organization may want to be a little more personal—awarding paintings, sculpture, or other items appropriate to the situation. Often, when an individual or group financially supports the building of a park or facility, plants a grove of trees, purchases a significant amount of playground equipment, or generously contributes to refurbishing a room or other leisure space, the organization will name the gift after the major contributor.

The organization should not neglect its own members and customers when they make special contributions or appear to be noteworthy in their efforts. Organizational morale is served well by awarding members of the organization with plaques, citations, and so on. However, as mentioned before, these should be given sincerely, or they lose their meaning to the individual or individuals receiving them.

Individuals participating in organizational programs have come to expect awards (certificates, ribbons, trophies, etc.) for activities in which competition is involved. Many leisure service organizations only give awards to customers for excellence—for winning a baseball tournament, placing first in a swim meet, and so on. Such awards usually take the form of trophies, ribbons, clothing, and certificates. However, an organization that wishes to promote participation may want to consider the distribution of some type of award to all customers. For example, all individuals participating in a cross-country run might receive a patch, T-shirt, or ribbon as recognition of involvement. We feel that this approach should be encouraged more in leisure services. This action does not discourage awards for excellence; rather, it encourages a blend of the two approaches—that is, a form of recognition for all customers as well as a distinctive award for excellence (e.g., first-, second-, and third-place finalists).

Novelty Items

Promotion can be accomplished through the use of novelty items such as buttons, decals, and banners. Individuals are often attracted by and enjoy participating in such forms of promotion; even though the professional may not think to employ such items and methods, they can be very effective in promoting programs, services, and the organization itself. For example, the use of a logo or phrase printed on T-shirts is effective in promoting programs with all customers; bumper stickers might be useful to the professional attempting to promote an upcoming event or project. Novelty items that can be employed by a leisure service organization include:

1. Decals and bumper stickers;
2. Buttons and pins;

3. Imprinted matches, pencils, pens;
4. Banners and flags;
5. Postcards;
6. Toys and sports equipment;
7. Imprinted clothing; and
8. Patches.

Many other novelty items can be utilized in promoting programs and services: key chains, ribbons, blotters, calendars, badges, patches, armbands, hats. Distribution of such items is most easily accomplished when people are massed together (e.g., in a sports activity, at a convention, or at special events). This type of promotion can create a feeling of goodwill; the organization is paired with the act of giving, which is a positive association in the mind of a potential consumer. Often, commercial, profit-oriented organizations will absorb the cost of novelty items if their logo or advertising message is paired with that of the public or nonprofit organization. This can be a mutually beneficial arrangement, both organizations accomplishing their promotional goals. Figures 10.26, 10.27, 10.28, 10.29, and 10.30 show examples of novelty items—a bumper sticker, a pin, a refrigerator magnet, a rotary card, and a bookmarker.

Special Print Promotions

Like novelty items, special print promotions are used to feature events and activities as well as to generate enthusiasm and interest. They can range from a note card to a bookmark to a special coupon or admission ticket. The possibilities for such items are virtually unlimited. Print promotions can be incorporated into the promotional strategies of any program. Figure 10.31 is an example of a special print promotion.

Exhibits, Displays, and Demonstrations

Leisure service organizations can use the exhibit, display, and demonstration methods to highlight their program services and organizational efforts or for purposes of interpretation. The professional can use these methods in two ways—as a part of a program service (e.g., a display in a

Figure 10.26 Recognition Certificate, Parks Board and Recreation Commission, Town of Clarkstown, New York.

Figure 10.27 Bumper Sticker (Novelty item), Virginia Beach (Virginia) Parks and Recreation.

museum) or as a vehicle to facilitate promotional efforts aimed at public involvement or support of a program (e.g., sale of a product like cookies).

Exhibits and displays have the same characteristics. A display is usually two-dimensional; an exhibit often includes three-dimensional objects. They both use inanimate objects and materials only. A demonstration, on the other hand, uses organizational members or customers as "demonstrators." It is a dynamic

Figure 10.28 Promotional Pin (Novelty item). Long Beach (California) Parks, Recreation & Marine.

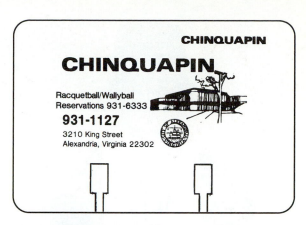

Figure 10.30 Rotary File Card, Chinquapin Park and Recreation Center, Alexandria (Virginia) Department of Recreation, Parks, and Cultural Activities.

NSSRA

NORTHERN SUBURBAN
SPECIAL RECREATION
ASSOCIATION

3105 MacArthur Boulevard
Northbrook, IL 60062
www.nssra.org
Email: info@nssra.org

Voice or TDD:
847 509-9400
Fax:
847 509-1177

*NSSRA provides recreation
opportunities for people with
disabilities of all ages who reside
in our 12 partner communities.*

Figure 10.29 Magnet (Novelty item), North Suburban Special Recreation Association, Northbrook, Illinois.

approach to program promotion, featuring individuals who perhaps have participated in a leisure service organization's activities (e.g., a tumbling, ballet, or swimming demonstration). Although an interpretive exhibit is usually con-

fined to a specific location, displays and demonstrations promoting an organization's services may be conducted in a variety of settings. A gymnastics demonstration during the half-time show of a football game, a mime troop performing on a street corner, and a bear cub from the local zoo at a shopping mall are all demonstrations. Exhibits used to promote the programs of an organization can be placed in a church, school, shopping mall, bank lobby, town square, or department store.

Stationary Advertising
Stationary advertising differs from other forms of advertising in that it is not delivered to the prospective consumer. As a result of this restriction, it is vital that stationary advertising be strategically placed so that it is likely to be viewed by the prospective customer. Although exhibits and displays may also be classified as stationary promotional tools, they are designed to be moved from location to location for specific purposes. The stationary tools described here are generally intended to remain where they are—stationary. Four types of stationary advertising are used by leisure service organizations: bulletin boards, posters, billboards, and signs. Following is brief discussion of each.

Figure 10.31   Bookmarker (Novelty item), Virginia Beach (Virginia) Parks and Recreation.

Bulletin Boards

For the purposes of this discussion, a bulletin board can be thought of as any large, bordered surface used to inform through the display of announcements, schedules, projects, and other informative material. The bulletin board can be fixed or portable—enabling it, for example, to be carried from school to school or to various areas in a hospital. The material presented on a bulletin board should be arranged in a neat and orderly way and should employ the use of color and design to emphasize the information it is presenting. Bulletin boards can also be organized around a theme. For example, an activities center might want to emphasize the seasons of the year in a bulletin board format when promoting programs. Items attached to a bulletin board are usually tem-

porary in nature, so that they may be changed to keep the bulletin board current and stimulating.

Posters

Posters are usually thought of as large advertisements appearing on posterboard (cardboard). The elements that are important in the design of a good flier are also relevant to the design and layout of an effective, dynamic poster. The poster, however, is usually more "finished" than the flier, since it is often professionally printed or silkscreened. The color choices for poster design may also be greater than those available for a flier. Posters can be displayed in store windows, on the top or side of a counter, and on bulletin boards in schools, churches, and recreation centers. It is important to be selective in the placement of posters because they usually represent a greater investment than fliers do. Also, one should be conscientious about placing posters; the posters that are distributed should be retrieved by the organization from the distribution points after they have served their purpose. Posters should not be displayed in places that do not complement the aesthetics of the environment—for example, on telephone poles, wooden fences, and so on. Figure 10.32 shows a poster from the Fort Worth (Texas) Parks and Community Services, Fort Worth Independent School District, and the City of Fort Worth Library System that advertises collaborative summer activities for children and youth.

Billboards

Billboards are large outdoor signs that are usually placed in key, heavily trafficked areas. Although billboards may come in a variety of sizes and shapes, they are usually about 13 feet tall and 40 feet wide. Illustrations and written messages are either pasted or painted on these advertisements. As in other forms of advertising, billboard messages are usually built around a central theme or idea. The copy and illustrated elements must be dynamic in nature, combining use of color and space. The billboard has a very limited amount of time in which to deliver its

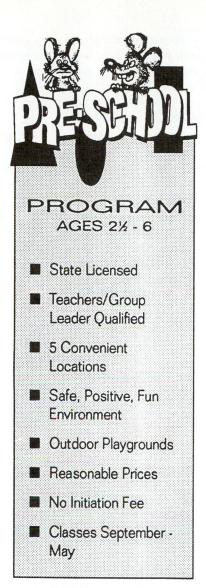

PROGRAM
AGES 2½ - 6

■ State Licensed

■ Teachers/Group
Leader Qualified

■ 5 Convenient
Locations

■ Safe, Positive, Fun
Environment

■ Outdoor Playgrounds

■ Reasonable Prices

■ No Initiation Fee

■ Classes September -
May

CALL TODAY
696-4300

City of Aurora

Figure 10.32 Special Print Promotion, City of Aurora (Colorado) Parks, Recreation, and Open Space.

message. Motorists traveling by a billboard may see it for a few seconds only; thus, it must be extremely pointed and concise in its message. Although this avenue of advertising is used primarily by commercial enterprises, advertising agencies will often dedicate a selected number of billboards for free public use. A large facility (e.g., a public zoo) may erect one or more billboards to promote its services. Many public leisure service organizations are not able to purchase billboard space; however, they can use this same concept on a smaller scale by installing relatively large "billboards" in shopping areas and public parks to publicize special events. For example, the Wooster (Ohio) Parks and Recreation Department designed and displayed two "billboards" (approximately 4 feet by 6 feet) in a downtown shopping square and on a busy street to publicize its annual "Art in the Park."

Signs

Signs can be used in several capacities. First, an identification sign can be used simply to provide individuals with information as to the location of a given building. An identification sign (such as one reading "The City of Denton Parks and Recreation Department") also indirectly acts as a form of advertising each time it is viewed by an individual. This is true as well of identification signs for such areas as parks, golf courses, and ski areas. Consequently, such signs should not be underplayed; they should be nicely designed and maintained. Signs can be used in another capacity—to more specifically inform the consumer as to the proper use of services, facilities, and park areas. For example, symbolic signs in a park area might show silhouettes of individuals engaged in sailing, hiking, hunting, or picnicking. On the other hand, such signs might depict, for example, a picture of a bicycle with a red slash through it, indicating that bicycling is not allowed in the park.

Signs in parks can intrude on the landscape if they are not designed to blend with the surroundings; thus, professionals should give due consideration to the symbols used and the shape of the sign as well as its color, size, and style of lettering.

Radio and Television

Use of television and radio to promote leisure programs and services is becoming increasingly important to a large number of agencies throughout Canada and the United States. Television reaches a large percentage of people nationwide. Radio, on the other hand, is more geographically oriented; in addition, its audiences are more specifically defined for given programs. Radio—perhaps more than any other medium—reaches youth.

Television and radio stations that cover local events are perhaps the best sources through which to promote a leisure service program. In addition to providing news coverage for the local leisure service organization's activities, these stations will often provide air time for free public service announcements to either public or non-profit private community service organizations.

Television and radio are publicity tools that should not be overlooked by leisure service organizations when they do not have the means to purchase advertising. Described here are a number of approaches that can be taken in using these media.

Advertising

Two types of advertising can be purchased—advertising that will sponsor an entire program, and commercial spots. When purchasing advertising, one should consider the desired audience—remembering that television reaches a broad, general audience and radio tends to reach more select, geographically limited audiences.

Television and radio commercials place a proposition before the potential customer. This proposition must be attractively and dynamically introduced to be effective. The commercial might involve employment of actors, artists, producers, directors, some designers, and other personnel. Most radio and television commercials have a duration of sixty seconds or less. Thus, one must get the message across quickly; this

implies extreme selectivity in the amount of information presented. Since radio commercials are not visual, an image must be created in the mind of the consumer.

Public Service Announcements

Public service announcements (PSAs) are similar to commercials; they are created to sell an idea or concept. PSAs can be made for fund-raising or charitable purposes, for educational or informational campaigns, and for sale of non-profit organizational services. Often, the PSA format can be used to promote a special event or convey an idea related to a theme, such as "plant a tree." Most television and radio stations prepare guidelines for organizations and are willing to help organizations produce professional-quality announcements.

Spot announcements can range from ten to sixty seconds. Shorter announcements, in general, stand a better chance of being used on the air. Approximate word counts to apply in preparing announcements are:

10 seconds = 25 words

20 seconds = 40 words

30 seconds = 80 words

60 seconds = 120 words

Whether a PSA is being prepared for radio or television, the "who, what, when, where" questions still apply. The same timing in the length of a PSA applies both to radio and television, but television gives the opportunity to appeal to both ear and eye. Consultation with television professionals is necessary to determine the most effective type, size, and quality of visual materials. Figure 10.32 shows an excellent example of a thirty-second public service announcement by the City of San José (California) Parks, Recreation and Neighborhood Services. An excellent example of a way to provide information for a public service media announcement is found in Figure 10.33. The thirty-second message provided by the City of San José (California) Parks,

Figure 10.33 Poster, Fort Worth (Texas) Parks & Community Services and Ft. Worth (Texas) Library System.

Recreation and Neighborhood Services Department provides information regarding its strategy for improving parks, facilities, and programs.

Talk Shows
One popular concept used in radio and television today is the talk show. Talk shows usually offer an opportunity for a more lengthy promo-

tion of a given idea or service than does a traditional PSA. They are also more casual in their approach. Talk shows usually follow a question and answer format. The person being interviewed is not given a script or set of prepared questions. He or she is interviewed spontaneously—although the producer or script person may ask for some background information prior to the show from which he or she can formulate various questions. Because of the spontaneity of the interview, it is vital for the leisure service professional to keep in mind the points he or she wants to make so that the discussion does not wander too far. The professional should attempt to guide questions that are off the subject back to those items he or she is interested in promoting. The most important thing to remember when involved in a radio or television interview is to be yourself—avoid artificial posturing.

Television and Radio News Releases

News releases can be designed for the community calendar format (strictly program and service information), or they can be intended for release as news items (e.g., to appear on the 5 P.M. news along with other information such as park board decisions). News releases to television and radio should be distinctive and should not merely duplicate corresponding releases to the newspaper.

Public Speaking

One of the most effective ways to promote a program is through public speaking appearances. The only cost involved (at least in terms of local speaking) is transportation and time. How important is effective speaking by professional staff members to an organization? Individuals who have the ability (innate or developed) to present themselves well in a public speaking situation will also reflect well on their organization. They add a personal touch to communications with various individuals, organizations, and groups. Often newspapers cover such speeches and further publicize the organization and its efforts. However, professionals who do not have a gift for public speaking and whose presentations are likely to be weak, ineffectual, and boring will not serve the interests of their organization by inflicting themselves on community groups.

What elements do good speakers incorporate in their speeches? Good speakers should enlighten, inform, and entertain the audience. To accomplish this, speakers must first have a message that they wish to convey. In other words, the speech must have a purpose. It is also vital that speakers be in tune with their audience not only in terms of topic but also in method of presentation. Another important factor to consider is the length of the speech. All people have a limited attention span, and leisure professionals should take this into consideration when determining the length of a speech.

The actual presentation of a speech can range from a spontaneous delivery to one that is read from a manuscript. Ideally, speakers want to give the appearance of speaking extemporaneously—as though communicating conversationally with the audience. Whether in a room of 15 or 500 people, speakers using the extemporaneous approach will appear as though they are speaking individually to each person in the audience. Speakers, whether or not they are using a microphone, must ensure that their voice can be clearly understood by those present. Speakers should put animation and changes of pace in their voice; although the message may be loud enough and excellent in content, the audience will tune it out if it is delivered in a dull monotone.

Speakers can enhance their speech with various materials such as slide and powerpoint presentations, transparencies, flip charts, graphs, and photographs. These aids can be a valuable asset to any presentation, but speakers should not attempt to hide behind such technology—these devices should complement the presentation, not vice versa.

Using the Telephone

The leisure service professional often does not consider using the telephone (telemarketing) to promote a program—probably with good reason. First, time is money and it can take a good deal of time to contact individuals by telephone. Organizational personnel would have to be paid for the time and effort involved in this type of promotion. Second, generally speaking, people do not like telephone solicitation. Consequently, such an approach not only might have limited effectiveness but also might actually engender hostility toward the leisure service organization. When used correctly and appropriately, however, telemarketing is one of the most direct, personal, and effective tools of promotion.

When is it correct to use telephone solicitation? It is appropriate to contact individuals already involved in activities of the organization. Phone use can be simply a form of encouragement or a reminder to individuals who have prior knowledge of activities. For example, phone use is appropriate when the organization is attempting to contact members of a league, club, youth drop-in center, or senior citizens center about a special activity or an upcoming trip.

Once the decision has been made to use the telephone to contact individuals, the caller should employ certain telephone courtesy and protocol. The caller should begin the conversation by personally addressing the individual by name, then identifying himself or herself by name, title, and organizational affiliation. The caller should describe the program or service involved in terms of location, date, time, and activities that will occur. The benefits of participation should also be covered in a subtle way (e.g., "your presence would be greatly appreciated"). Needless to say, the caller should be very courteous—speaking politely, in a calm, inviting tone of voice. Although the caller may be very enthusiastic about his or her program or service, an ebullient approach can appear overbearing; it has been shown that the calm, informative approach is more effective in phone promotion.

Another type of telephone-related service that leisure service organizations can provide is information and facilitation. A customer seeking information might use the telephone as a resource to obtain knowledge about programs, services, current activities, and facility locations. Whether an individual is calling the leisure service organization for specific or general information, the call is obviously an excellent way to promote the agency's services. An organization can formally address the need to provide information over the telephone (via the establishment of an information line, for example) or telephone information dissemination can occur on an ad hoc basis. Either way, staff members must be schooled in the appropriate use of the telephone.

Organizations often take or give information using taped messages. Use of such devices can extend an organization's resources and services to people, especially after regular working hours. Although answering machines may offend some individuals by their impersonal quality, such a service that provides information on an organization's current activities—including special events, facility hours, rates of programs, and especially information that may fluctuate daily (such as the ice safety factor of park ponds)—is indeed valuable.

Computer-Generated, Video, and Slide Presentations

Another effective means of promoting a program is through the use of visual aids. Computer-generated presentations, videotapes, and slides can be used to complement other promotional efforts (e.g., a display or exhibit) or they can stand by themselves. Today, digital cameras and camcorders are frequently used in conjunction with such computer programs as PowerPoint to produce superior presentations that can be stored, edited, and accessed electronically. Professionals, when appearing before civic groups or service clubs, often use a computer-generated presentation or slide show in conjunction with their verbal presentations. This enables the audience to visualize the topics, concepts, programs, and services that the professional is promoting.

Obviously, organizations will want to consider producing their own computer-generated presentation, videotape, and slide shows. However, there are opportunities for the professional to use visual aids that have been approved by various national organizations (available on a rental or purchase basis).

The production of computer-generated presentations, videotapes, and slide shows involve basically the same steps. The first step in the process is to identify the subject matter. What is the story that is to be told? Does the topic concern the organization's entire line of services? Is the organization attempting to promote just one aspect of its services (such as its aquatic program)? Is the organization putting together a presentation in support of an idea or concept, such as ecology? The next step in the process of production is to prepare a script— that is, the specific content of the story, the organization of the content, the narration, and so on. The script should be in tune with the visual presentation, it should be logical, and it should hold the attention of the audience throughout the entire presentation.

The actual gathering of graphics, pictures, or photographs, or the videotaping, should offer a representative and accurate portrayal of the subject matter to be covered. The presentation does not have to be shot in sequence order; scenes that are geographically similar might be taped or photographed at the same time. Material can be collected over a short period of time; photographs and other images for a computer or slide presentation, however, can be taken throughout the year. It is necessary to accumulate a much larger number of computer images, slides, or more tape than actually needed to allow for the best selections. Once the photography, taping, or collecting of computer images has been completed, the presentation must be edited and put together in an effective manner. Editing involves the selection of scenes that best tell the story or convey the concept being promoted. If appropriate, music might also be included as part of the finished presentation. Some presentations are effective with accompanying music only, without narration of any kind.

Summary

This chapter has discussed various channels for promoting recreation and leisure service programs. Promotion involves the ability of the organization to communicate effectively with those it intends to serve. The leisure service organization (the communicator) provides a message through various channels of distribution to an audience or target population. This communication attempts to persuade and stimulate the prospective customer into action (participation in programs or services) that will meet his or her individual needs.

Five channels of communication are used to distribute information—advertising, publicity, sales promotion, personal selling, and public relations. Advertising is a paid message distributed primarily through the mass media in what may sometimes appear to be an impersonal way. Publicity can be thought of as free media coverage generated by a leisure service organization—it is the news that an agency generates.

Sales promotion is a way of creating interest in a program or service by employing special promotional techniques (such as sampling, coupons, contests, and demonstrations). Personal selling uses direct, face-to-face contact with an individual. Public relations is a management function directed toward the cultivation of goodwill between an agency and the public it serves. An organization can employ numerous tools within the five channels of program promotion: newspapers, brochures, fliers, newsletters, annual reports, information and press kits, postage meter messages, logos and emblems, awards and citations, novelty items, exhibits, displays, demonstrations, stationary advertising, radio and television, public speaking, telephones, and video, slide and computer generated presentations. These promotional tools, when well developed and used effectively, can be very influential in communicating with the current and future customers of a leisure service organization.

─── *Discussion Questions and Exercises* ───

1. Discuss the process of communication of information in relation to the promotion of programs in leisure service organizations.

2. Define and identify five channels used by leisure service organizations to promote programs. Discuss how an agency might employ each of these methods in promoting its services.

3. Discuss and apply tools of promotion for the major channels of the program promotion process.

4. Identify the components of a press release. Write a press release describing a leisure activity for a public leisure service organization.

5. Using a computer graphics program, prepare a flier for a leisure service activity.

6. Describe the elements important to effective public speaking.

7. Identify the important elements involved in producing a brochure. Also identify and discuss methods of distributing brochures.

8. How can the use of the telephone be important in promoting a recreation and leisure service program?

9. Prepare a short public service announcement for a local television station promoting a leisure activity. Visit the television station and discuss with representatives the procedures they use in receiving and handling such requests for promotion.

10. Create a resource file of promotional activities. Collect one or more of each of the promotional tools described in the chapter.

─── *References* ───

Bullaro, J. J., and C. R. Edginton. 1986. *Commercial leisure services: Managing for profit, service, and personal satisfaction.* New York: Macmillan.

Edginton, C. R., and J. G. Williams. 1978. *Productive management of leisure service organization.* New York: John Wiley.

Kraus, R. G., and J. E. Curtis. 1990. *Creative management in recreation, parks, and leisure services.* 5th ed. St. Louis: Times Mirror/Mosby College Publishing.

Logan, D. 1975. What's in a newsletter? *Trends*, January/February, 22–25.

Nylen, D. W. 1975. *Advertising.* Cincinnati, OH: Southwestern.

O'Sullivan, E. L. 1991. *Marketing for parks, recreation, and leisure services.* State College, PA: Venture.

Rossman, J. R. 1995. *Recreation programming: Designing leisure experiences.* Champaign: IL: Sagamore.

Rubright, R., and D. MacDonald. 1981. *Marketing health and human services.* Rockville, MD: Aspen Systems Corporation.

Ryan, K. F. 1988. Getting the word out to the media through news releases and news advisories. *Voluntary Action Leadership* (summer): 18–19.

Program Budgeting and Resource Attainment

LEARNING OBJECTIVES

1. To assist the reader in understanding the *importance of budgeting and resource attainment* in the process of leisure service programming.

2. To acquaint the reader with various *trends that have an impact on budgeting and resource attainment* in leisure service organizations.

3. To help the reader understand *how budgets and resource attainment plans assist the leisure service programmer.*

4. To assist the reader in differentiating between *cost (expenditures) and revenues.*

5. To help the reader understand the concept of budgeting and various *types of budgets.*

6. To help the reader analyze *budget worksheets* and other budget planning procedures and methods.

7. To help the reader understand the concept of resource attainment and various *strategies used to acquire resources.*

INTRODUCTION

The success or failure of any leisure service organization is directly connected to its ability to manage its finances successfully. The challenge to be customer driven, as well as performance oriented, is especially evident in the management of a leisure service organization's finances. Developing a financial plan for an activity or event may be as important as the actual creativity that goes into planning the content of the program. Today, leisure service organizations are being challenged to create financial plans that are entrepreneurial and that generate revenue, promote self-sufficiency, maximize the use and effectiveness of resources through collaboration, and are tied to outcomes.

The processes involved in financial management are known generally but not exclusively as budgeting. Budgeting involves the acquisition and distribution of financial resources. Central to the process of budgeting is the recording of financial transactions to ensure integrity, accuracy, and accountability. This chapter focuses on the topic of budgeting as it relates to leisure service programming. The intent here is to provide the reader with information of both a conceptual and practical nature.

Budgets should follow programs, not the reverse. Most leisure service organizations today, however, tend to let the budget be the major controlling factor influencing the design of a program. In reality, a programmer should work to design a program of excellence and then determine appropriate methods to attain the resources required to support the endeavor. Many leisure service organizations are tied to the amount of financial resources that have been allocated to a program in the past. Although historical financial records can be useful as a basis for initiating program activities or developing new events, they should not limit the creativity, innovation, or imagination of the programmer. The secret to successfully developing a program and a financial resource base to support its implementation is to first plan the program and then develop an effective resource attainment plan to ensure that the activity or event can occur.

Drucker (1985: 185) has written that one of the major obstacles to innovation in the public sector is that most agencies are budget based rather than results oriented. Such an orientation reduces the probability that a leisure service organization will be innovative enough to respond to the dynamic changes that are occurring in the marketplace. Programmers must be flexible as well as shrewd in developing strategies to support leisure service program endeavors. Increasingly in leisure service organizations, the ability to manage financial resources is equated with individual and organizational success. Leisure service programmers who can identify and acquire key strategic financial resources will outperform their counterparts who are bound by conventional wisdom and tradition.

This chapter is organized into six major sections dealing with fiscal and other resource management issues as they relate to leisure service programs. The first section covers the topic of trends in budgeting and resource attainment. The second section describes how a budget and resource attainment plan can assist the leisure service programmer. The next section provides background information on cost (expenditures) and revenues. This is followed by a section that defines the concept of budgeting and identifies various budget types available to leisure service programmers. The fifth section of this chapter explains the concept of the resource attainment plan. The final section provides information about the pricing of leisure services.

TRENDS IN BUDGETING AND RESOURCE ATTAINMENT

Over the past several years, a number of trends and issues have emerged that have had an impact on the financing of leisure service programs. These trends and issues affect the scope and nature of the services provided by leisure service programmers. The increased complexity of environments in which leisure services are provided have placed greater demands on programmers to be responsive to fiscal operational concerns.

Several leading authors in the field have discussed some of the emerging changes in financial management that are having an impact on the provision of leisure service programs. Rossman and Schlatter (2000:314), in discussing the work of programmers, have noted that they are no longer simply responsible for designing and producing program services. They must also be concerned with the cost of services and how to generate revenue for them. Crompton (1999), in discussing the role of individuals working in public recreation and parks, notes that the work of the professional has changed from that of being "primarily concerned with the allocation of government funding to that of an entrepreneur who operates in the public sector with minimal tax support." Crompton (1999:10) describes park and recreation entrepreneurs as managers who "seek creative, resourceful ways of using their scarce funds to leverage substantial additional resources through partnering with a wide range of business, nonprofit, and other government entities." Crompton goes on to say that the "service or facility is supported by a 'can-do' positive attitude that managers adopt while pursing an array of possibilities" (11). Some of the trends that leisure service programmers are being challenged to deal with, and need to bring this "can-do" spirit to solve, are listed here.

Mission Driven, Results Oriented, Outcome Focused

Osborne and Gaebler (1992:110) write that organizations are becoming more focused on outcomes and, in fact, are more mission driven and results oriented. Mission-driven organizations are focused on their fundamental purpose rather than on rules and regulations. Such organizations "don't have a thousand rules; we fast forward to the distilled essentials of the deal" (p. 110). Mission-driven organizations lead to results-oriented organizations that focus on outcomes rather than inputs. In the budget process, this translates to "a budget system that focuses on outcomes of the funded activity, e.g., the quality, or effectiveness of services produced" (p. 162). Osborne and Gaebler also note that such budgets are becoming more customer driven; that is, they focus on the needs of customers first.

Agency Effectiveness, Accountability, and Responsiveness

A pervasive theme of the 2000s is a continued focus on organizational accountability and effectiveness. Leisure service organizations will have to focus their attention on fiscal economy and productivity. The desire for greater accountability has been reflected in the use of program and performance budgets over the past several decades.

Equity

Equity issues relate to both social and economic concerns. Equity issues require leisure service programmers to make demanding and difficult decisions regarding the distribution of fiscal resources. At the heart of all equity questions are issues of societal, organizational, and individual values. This complex array of values often makes choices difficult.

Doing More with Less

It seems trite to suggest that organizations will have to do *more* with *less* today. Over the past decade, leisure service organizations have been challenged to become innovative and more entrepreneurial.

Self-Supporting Programs

The idea of self-supporting programs within the leisure services field is not a new one. What is new is the percentage of cost recovery that public park and recreation agencies are attempting to generate from program fees and charges. In fact, the goal of some agencies is 100 percent. The term *target zero* refers to the attempt to produce a completely self-sustaining system and was noted in the literature as early as 1980 by

Howard and Crompton in their text entitled *Financing, Managing, and Marketing Recreation and Park Resources.*

Pricing Philosophy

An unevenness exists in how leisure services have established pricing philosophies. To date, there is no universally accepted system used by leisure service organizations. Pricing will affect accessibility of programs to customers as well as customers' perception of the value of the service. Pricing decisions may well be at the heart of the survival and stability of some leisure service organizations. Successful decisions will enable organizations to return value to their customers, whereas inappropriate decisions may prove to be detrimental to an organization.

Social Cost/Economic Cost

Economic costs of programs are relatively easy to calculate. Social costs are more difficult to calculate. One trend today in viewing fiscal practices in public leisure service organizations is to link social and economic costs together. In the future, stronger consideration will be given to aligning these two variables when determining leisure services. The economic cost of one program may be higher than another, but the lack of a particular program may produce higher social costs. These variables will have to be calculated in making decisions about services.

Risk Management/Liability Concerns

A major factor in the financial management of leisure services is that of risk management. We live in an increasingly litigious society—people are bringing more and more lawsuits against individuals, organizations, and institutions. At the same time, people are demanding more opportunities for risk in their leisure experiences. The result is that while people clamor for more risk, they also are exposing themselves, as well as the agency providing such services, to greater risk. Financial demands occur as a result of the cost of insurance or considerations for the safety of customers.

Technology

The computer is having a dramatic impact on the types and amounts of financial information that can be made available to programmers. The computer allows for the storage and quick retrieval of larger amounts of information. Financial calculations become more routine via the use of the computer, thereby enabling the programmer to react more responsibly and accurately to changes in the marketplace.

These trends and issues provide challenges to leisure service programmers. Further, the rate and speed of change also means that many emerging trends will have to be addressed in the coming years. Economic, political, environmental, and cultural changes will undoubtedly have an impact on the delivery of leisure services and the work of programmers. Careful and thoughtful responses will be required to ensure successful leisure programs in the future.

HOW BUDGETS AND RESOURCE ATTAINMENT PLANS ASSIST THE PROGRAMMER

Budgets and resource attainment plans for leisure service activities and events are valuable tools that the leisure service programmer uses to create leisure service experiences and can provide the leisure service programmer with systematic and analytical information that supports the program in process. Budgets provide information that enables the programmer to determine the size and scale of the endeavor and to evaluate the success of a program in terms of economic costs. Budgets and resource attainment plans also enable the leisure service programmer to link economic costs with broader program goals and objectives. In a sense, the budget and the resource attainment plan provide a basis for equating broader social goals with fiscal resources.

Following are some of the ways that budgets and resource attainment plans can assist the leisure service programmer.

Contributes to the Planning Process

Perhaps first and foremost, budgets and resource attainment plans enable the leisure service professional to engage in the process of proactive planning. They enable individuals to determine how many leaders will be necessary to conduct a program; what types and numbers of supplies and materials will be required; and what other associated services—such as transportation, rental fees, advertising, and so on, that are often used in creating and implementing a leisure experience—will be needed. Detailing a budget requires the leisure service programmer to think about all the resources necessary to ensure that a program is successful.

The budget requires that the resources needed to create and implement a leisure experience are stated in financial terms. In other words, the programmer must translate the actual costs for leaders, materials, supplies, and other services into dollars and cents. This action enables the programmer to understand exactly what is required to organize the program. The budget and the resource attainment plan, if carefully constructed, can serve as an important preimplementation plan, outlining detailed program requirements. The greater attention given to planning an activity or event, the greater the likelihood that it will succeed. Likewise, the more attention given to budgets and resource attainment plans, the greater the probability that the program will be successful.

Supports the Implementation of Leisure Services

Once the budget is in place, the leisure service programmer has the fiscal resources to create a leisure experience. In other words, the budget places at the disposal of the leisure service programmer the resources necessary to "make things happen." The programmer can hire leaders, purchase supplies, and locate other resources to make the leisure experience a reality. As such, programmers working in professional positions are able to expend funds that can result in positive outcomes for participants.

Perhaps one of the most exciting parts of operating as a leisure service programmer is being given the responsibility to develop and implement a program area. With the responsibility comes the opportunity to expend as well as earn fiscal resources. This is the heart of the work of a professional. The budget and the resource attainment plan are the cornerstone of the professional's operations. The program is the budget and the budget is the program. The program is reflected in the budget and it allows the implementation of the desired activities and events.

Provides a Reference Point for Controlling the Expenditure of Fiscal Resources

With the responsibility of developing programs and expending resources comes the responsibility to account for the use of resources. A budget serves as a reference point that allows the leisure service programmer to determine whether funds are being expended in an appropriate fashion. The budget is a benchmark. Wide variations in expenditures or unexplained deviations from budget send a signal to the programmer that there may be problems.

By periodically reviewing expenditures in the budget, the leisure service programmer is able to take corrective action. As a control mechanism, the budget provides the programmer with information on the extent to which resources are being used. Further, the budget provides a measure of the extent to which resources are addressing the goals established by the programmer and the customer. By controlling the use of fiscal resources wisely, the programmer is better able to provide the customer with services of higher quality and greater value. In turn, the organization benefits not only by having a satisfied customer, but also by increasing its profitability or extending its service capabilities.

Translates the Program Concept into Economic Reality

When a program idea is created in the mind of an individual, it is an ideal, a dream, or a vision.

This idea must be translated into economic reality. Simply stated, producing programs requires fiscal resources. Whether the resources are taxpayer funds, user fees, entrepreneurial capital, membership fees, or the volunteer efforts of others, programs require the commitment of a fiscal unit that can be measured or accounted for in some way. The expression of the cost of a program in financial terms occurs through the creation and implementation of a budget. The budget is the management instrument that the leisure service organization uses to turn the ideal, concept, or vision into a tangible expression of value.

One caveat regarding the budget as a management document relates to program development. Because the budget takes the abstract and makes it real, there is a tendency for a budget to be viewed as the source of program inspiration. However, a programmer should guard against seeing only the budget as a source of inspiration. It is important to remember that inspiration, innovation, and insight come from the leisure service programmer. The budget is a tool that helps leisure service programmers translate what they believe can be done and present it in a document that allows for clarity and concreteness and that defines the resources available to a leisure organization.

Establishes Program Priorities

Budgets and resource attainment plans are also very useful tools in helping the leisure service programmer establish program priorities. No organization has an infinite amount of fiscal resources. All organizations are constantly challenged to make decisions concerning the use of their fiscal resources. The budget provides an avenue for comparing the costs and benefits of an individual program with another one. In this way, leisure service programmers are able to make decisions and establish priorities.

One of the important decisions made by public leisure service organizations about the provision of programs has to do with the concept of equity, mentioned in Chapter 1. In par-

ticular, leisure service organizations are required to look at the types of services and programs they are providing in relation to the social and economic status of their customers. Are the services provided being distributed equitably? Are the services financially accessible equally to all groups served by the organization? Should the services be differentiated by income and other variables to enhance their equitability? These questions often involve decisions made within the context of the expenditures of available fiscal resources. The leisure service programmer is often required to make decisions and establish priorities based on the values of the organization and its target audience.

Communicates Program Plans to Various Parties

Budget and resource attainment plans can also help leisure service programmers communicate their intentions. Although most people view budgets and resource attainment plans as collections of uninteresting figures and numbers, these plans can be designed in such a way as to be very appealing graphically. They can be used to communicate the programmer's enthusiasm and excitement for a concept or idea. A budget can also be an effective tool in demonstrating the relationship between the benefits and costs of a leisure service.

Resource attainment plans in particular often require a great deal of creativity in their preparation and presentation. They are often established to encourage a more diversified and creative way of acquiring fiscal resources. They can become important communication devices featuring the unique and appealing parts of a leisure service experience. In a sense, such communication devices are designed with the idea of merging the ideal with the real in an appealing fashion.

Provides a Historical Record

A leisure service organization's previous budgets and resource attainment plans present the programmer with a starting point for the next fiscal cycle. Past budgets and resource attainment plans provide a wealth of information that can help the programmer not only examine the past, but more importantly, prepare for the future. Viewed over an extended period of time (five to ten years), budgets and resource attainment plans can help the programmer identify trends and fads. Such analysis can be useful in projecting future needs based on program demands versus the amount of resources historically available to a program or organization.

With the advent of computers, a considerable amount of financial data can be stored and retrieved instantaneously for comparative purposes. It is possible to integrate information concerning customer needs and levels of satisfaction with financial information in order to determine levels of performance and excellence within an organization. Such trends can be monitored continuously, providing a historical record of the work of an organization and the relative success of its programs. Although we live in a constantly changing environment, it is important for the leisure service programmer to have a clear awareness of previous financial commitments and their impact.

Commits the Organization to a Course of Action

Finally, budgets and resource attainment plans are tangible reflections of the goals and aspirations of individuals and organizations. They symbolize the course of action to which the organization and individuals within it have committed themselves. Budgets and resource attainment plans reflect the hopes and aspirations that individuals hold for the work of the agency. People become committed to these ends. Budgets and resource attainment plans, as a reflection of these goals, serve as a rallying point for action. The budget provides direction to the work of individuals and helps them better understand their work efforts within the context of broader organizational goals.

If budgets and resource attainment plans are to provide direction to leisure service pro-

grammers, there must be mechanisms in place that encourage involvement in the processes that lead to their creation. Leisure service programmers must play an active role in the creation of the budget and in the monitoring of its implementation. The best way for a leisure service manager to instill a sense of ownership in the budget process is to make sure that programmers are a part of its development. Managers must allow leisure service programmers to not only create but also manage their own budgets. Leisure service programmers must become familiar with the process and be prepared to assemble, work with, and monitor their budgets and resource attainment plans.

COSTS (EXPENDITURES) AND REVENUES

The leisure service programmer will be concerned with two budget elements—costs (expenditures) and revenues. Expenditures are the costs involved in running an activity; they reflect those fiscal resources that are spent to create or produce the leisure experience. Revenues are the income that can be earned or generated or that is available to a leisure service organization.

Producing a leisure experience involves costs for the creation and implementation of the activity or event. As mentioned, these costs are called *expenditures* in financial management terms. All organizations expend funds for such items as personnel, materials, and supplies. In an agency's normal course of operation, expenditures for elements that contribute to the creation of a given leisure experience often occur on a regular basis. These types of expenditures or costs are known as *operating costs*. Leisure service organizations also expend funds for larger projects including the development of facilities, the acquisition of equipment, and so forth. Such expenditures are known as *capital expenditures* and usually are not made on a recurring basis.

Different types of leisure service organizations depend on different sources of revenue. For example, in voluntary (nonprofit) organizations, the major sources of revenue are membership fees, program charges, contributions, and grants. In public agencies, revenues for program services come from taxes, fees and charges, contractual fees, and other forms of assistance, such as grants and entitlements. Commercial leisure service organizations will generate their revenue almost exclusively from fees and charges, although there are opportunities for government subsidies in the form of tax breaks and other cooperative relationships.

Costs (Expenditures)

Costs (expenditures) are the resources used by the agency in developing a specific program. Costs include all dollars the agency uses in producing a program regardless of the source of the dollars (Edginton, Hudson, and Lankford, 2001). In other words, cost represents the resources that the organization will use to produce the program. Several different costs must be considered when calculating the total cost of a program. The initial costs are known as *direct* and *indirect*. A brief discussion of each of these follows.

Direct Costs

Direct costs are those *costs that must be made to produce a specific program*. Such costs are not shared with other services and are applied directly to the creation of a given leisure experience. For example, a day camp operated by a leisure service organization must have counselors who meet on a daily basis with the children they are serving. The cost of this leadership is a direct cost associated with producing the program. Without the leaders, there would be no program. Other direct costs might include expenditures made for arts and crafts supplies, swimming pool rental, and transportation.

Indirect Costs

Indirect costs are those *services that are provided or exist within the organization that cannot be directly traced to a specific program*. As Rossman and Schlatter (2000) have written, small, indirect costs are those that the agency incurs regardless of

whether or not it operates a specific program. They are created by two or more objectives and are therefore not traceable to a single cost objective. An example of an indirect cost for a leisure service organization is the expense paid for energy for a multipurpose community center housing several diverse programs. Indirect costs are also sometimes referred to as overhead costs and are charged as part of the general costs that are necessary to maintain an organization.

Calculating the total cost of a program is done by adding direct cost to indirect cost. Indirect costs are difficult to determine. Such costs are usually incurred for the services in support of direct services delivered to customers. Thus, indirect costs are calculated for such support services as clerical work, bookkeeping and accounting, and perhaps building upkeep and maintenance.

Determining Costs

Howard and Crompton (1980) were the first authors to establish the concept of pricing parks and recreation services on the basis of who benefits rather than a "one-fee-fits-all" philosophy. Others in the field (DeGraaf, Jordan, and DeGraaf, 1999; Edginton, Hudson and Lankford, 2001; Rossman and Schlatter, 2000) have embraced this idea. According to Howard and Crompton (1980), there are three categories on which to build a pricing structure: public programs, merit programs, and private programs.

> *Public Programs*—These programs are supported exclusively by tax dollars. Customers pay no additional charges for such programs.
>
> *Merit Programs*—These programs are partially subsidized by tax dollars or donations. However, the customer pays a portion of the cost of the program.
>
> *Private Programs*—These programs are funded entirely through the fees and charges generated from interested and participating customers.

Rossman and Schlatter (2000:327) suggest that program costs can be determined on the basis of the application of a pricing structure and on decisions related to benefits derived from the service. Not all programs have equal benefits to all customers; in fact, no program is equally beneficial. However, some programs are more beneficial to all people than other programs. Therefore, programs that benefit wider populations can be considered as public programs, and those that have a more narrow range of impact would fall in the other two categories. Equity of services is also an important consideration. Some specialty programs that serve smaller numbers of customers may be necessary to ensure equity of access to services—for example, services for the physically challenged.

The Lake County Forest Preserve has established the following fee philosophy for its facilities.

General Premises: Fees should be charged when the service or facility being provided is enjoyed by a limited user group rather than the general public and when significant, identified costs can be directly attributed.

Classification of Services:
a. *Basic services* provide general benefits to the District and all Lake County residents. As such, they are funded through tax revenues and are provided at no additional charge to the user.
b. *Special services* provide direct benefits to limited groups of users and may provide some indirect benefits to the District and the general public. Significant, identifiable costs are incurred to provide the direct to the uses. These services should be funded partially through tax revenues and partially by fees and charges.
c. *Administrative services* such as making copies of documents, blueprints, and aerial photographs for individuals, contractors, and other organizations should be funded through fees and charges designed to recover the cost of labor, overhead, and materials necessary to provide the service.
d. *Enterprise services* funded through fees and charges, and maybe instituted to offset other District expenses. Enterprise services are designed to provide significant direct benefits on a user "pay as you go" basis. The fees for enterprise services should reflect considerations similar to those affecting the pricing of special services, but full recovery of costs will more frequently be appropriate and feasible.

Revenues

Hemphill (1985: 35–36), in discussing sources of revenue for park and recreation systems, has developed an interesting taxonomy outlining various classifications of revenue. He suggests four separate classifications of revenue in leisure service organizations—compulsory resources, earned income, contractual receipts, and financial assistance. The first classification, *compulsory resources,* refers to those cash and noncash revenues that occur, according to Hemphill, as a result of the taxing and regulatory powers of a government agency. Although the general property tax has been the backbone of local government finance for generations, recent taxpayer revolts and swings in the national economy have resulted in significant decrease in allocations to park and recreation departments from this source. According to Crompton (1999:18), "municipalities have shifted to more reliance on sales taxes and various fees and charges."

The next category in Hemphill's classification system is earned income. *Earned income* refers to those cash revenues that are realized through fees and charges. Obviously, this is a very important category of income for leisure service organizations. It is not unusual for some fee or charge to be assessed for nearly every program activity and event operated by a leisure service organization. Fees and charges are the major source of revenue for programming leisure services. Edginton, Hudson, and Lankford (2001), citing earlier literature, have offered the following comprehensive categories for fees and charges:

1. *Entrance Fees*—Fees charged to enter a large park, botanical garden, zoological garden, or other developed recreational area. The areas are usu-

ally well defined but are not necessarily enclosed. The entrance is the patron's first contact with the park. The area may contain additional facilities or activities for which fees are charged.

2. *Admission Fees*—Charges made to enter a building, structure, or natural chamber. These locations usually offer an exhibit, show, ceremony, performance, demonstration, or special equipment. Entry and exit are normally controlled and attendance is regulated.

3. *Rental Fees*—A payment made for the privilege of exclusive use of tangible property of any kind. This fee gives the patron the right to enjoy all the advantages derived from the use of the property without consuming, destroying, or injuring it in any way. Figure 11.1 illustrates rental fees for parks, athletic fields, and community centers in Fort Worth, Texas.

4. *User Fees*—Charges made for the use of a facility, for participation in an activity, or as a fare for a

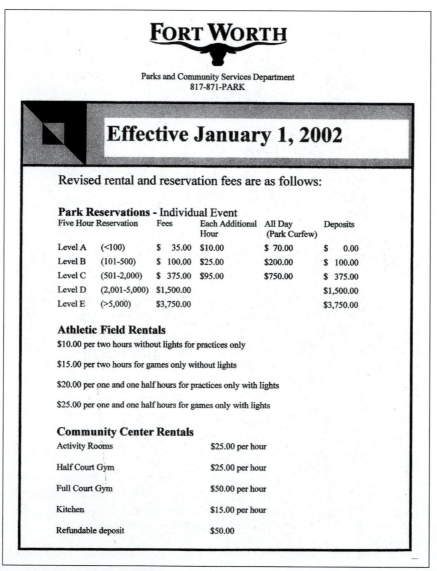

Figure 11.1 Fee Schedule: Fort Worth (Texas).

controlled ride. Patrons usually enjoy the privilege simultaneously with others. They do not have exclusive rights as in the case of the rental fee.

5. *Sales Revenues*—All revenue obtained from the operation of stores, concessions, restaurants, and so on, and from the sale of merchandise or other property. Unconditional ownership of the item must pass from the seller to the buyer with each sale.

6. *License and Permit Fees*—Fees for obtaining a written acknowledgment of consent to do some lawful thing without command. A license or permit grants a liberty or privilege and professes to tolerate all legal actions. It usually involves permission to perform an action. It seldom grants authority to occupy space or use property.

7. *Special Service Fees*—Charges made for extraordinary articles, commodities, or services, or accommodation to the public. Such accommodations must be unusual in character and are not normally considered a required governmental service.

Fees and charges made by organizations are often documented in brochures and made available to the public. Figures 11.2 and 11.3 illustrate fee and membership information for the Crestwood (Missouri) Parks and Recreation Department and Reinstate the Indianapolis (Indiana Parks and the Family YMCA of Lethbridge (Alberta, Canada). The Foothills (Lakewood, Colorado) Park and Recreation District offers a variety of rentals as a fee-generating process (see Figure 11.4). The district encourages rental of its golf course clubhouse and other restaurants for wedding receptions, parties, banquets, rehearsal dinners, and business meetings. Swimming pool time is available for private parties, including birthday parties. Other facilities and services available for rental include picnic shelters, picnic kits, and volleyball kits.

The next classification in Hemphill's taxonomy is known as *contractual receipts*. Contractual receipts are cash revenues that accrue as a result of legal agreements between a park and

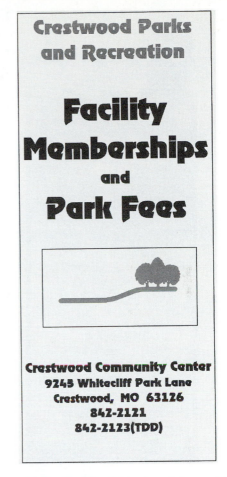

Figure 11.2 Facility Membership and Park Fees, Crestwood (Missouri) Parks and Recreation Department.

recreation agency and other parties. Public/private ventures are an increasingly important way of creating mutually beneficial ways of building cash revenues for both parties. Contracting is valuable because it provides opportunities for producing a specified output at a pre-agreed price. In this way, the contractor bears the burden of producing the service at a fixed cost and the organization benefits by maximizing its revenue generation. In other words, it can provide the organization with money in the bank without great effort.

Figure 11.3   Fee Structure, Indy (Indianapolis, Indiana) Parks and Recreation Department.

Figure 11.4   Rentals, Foothills (Lakewood, Colorado) Parks and Recreation District.

An example of a contracted service enhancing the revenue position of an organization is the relationship that has been established between the University of Northern Iowa and the United States Army. The army has contracted with the University of Northern Iowa for a variety of services for youth. A predetermined fixed price is set between the university and the army. The

army, in turn, is free to establish a fee and charge structure to recover costs as well as to produce profit for the Morale, Welfare, and Recreation Service Organization. The extensive line of youth services under the trademarked name of *Camp Adventure*™ has provided a series of dynamic and innovative youth services. The major benefit of the program to the U.S. armed forces has been access to highly qualified, professionally trained staff members and a program design that can be implemented with great consistency and effectiveness at a variety of locations.

Hemphill's final category is *financial assistance*. This category can be thought of as external funds that come from grant sources, entitlements, donations, or other resources. An example of a gift catalog from the Indianola (Iowa) Parks and Recreation Department is shown in Figure 11.5. This gift catalog outlines different suggestions for donations or gifts that can benefit the park and recreation system and in turn benefit

the citizens of this community. Some suggestions made in the catalog include contributions to parks (shelters, play equipment, trees, etc.), swimming pools, softball complexes, the senior citizen center, the arts and crafts center, or for recreation equipment in general. Another example of a program of financial assistance is the "Hearts Across Your Parks" program, operated by the East Bay (Oakland, California) Regional Park District (see Figure 11.6). This program encourages individuals to make a contribution in honor of their favorite park or trail. Funds are used in maintaining and caring for the park system.

GIFT CATALOG

A guide to community giving

An opportunity to

Give A Gift That Keeps Giving

City of Indianola

Parks & Recreation Department
P.O. Box 299
Indianola, Iowa 50125

Figure 11.5   Gift Catalog, Indianola (Iowa) Parks and Recreation Department.

Figure 11.6   Financial Assistance Program— Hearts Across Your Parks, East Bay (Oakland, California) Regional Park District.

What Is a Budget?

A budget can be thought of as a financial plan. It is a way of estimating the types and amounts of financial resources needed to implement a program for a specific period of time. A budget can be stated in dollars, work hours, units of production, or any other descriptive or measurable unit. It provides information about what resources the organization will acquire, how they will be acquired, how these resources will be spent, and what services will result (Edginton, Hudson, and Lankford, 2001).

The process of budgeting is tied closely to program planning. As Wildavsky (1974: 2) writes, "a budget may be characterized as a series of goals with price tags attached." A budget helps the programmer think ahead and, in fact, develop a blueprint for his or her work in the future. A budget should serve the leisure service programmer. The budget should not drive the program, but rather the program should drive the budget.

Most, if not all, leisure service programmers are required to engage in the budgeting process. Although it is not unusual for a programmer to spend a large block of time developing a budget at one time of the year, budgeting should be viewed as an ongoing, continuous process. Most programmers will be responsible for developing a portion of their organization's budget. These budgetary plans, when integrated with plans from other programmers within the organization, will constitute the beginning of the development of an agency-wide budget. The work of a programmer in this stage of the process of budgeting requires an analysis of the services to be offered and the development of estimates of financial expenditures as well as potential revenues.

As mentioned, budgeting should also be viewed as an ongoing process. The programmer not only is responsible for the initial expenditures and revenues, but also will often be asked to monitor the extent to which these are realized. In other words, the programmer is given the responsibility of making sure that once a budget has been approved, the expenditure of funds does not exceed the authorized amount. Further, the leisure service programmer will be charged with carefully monitoring the amount of revenues generated by a program to ensure that they are satisfactory. Leisure service programmers today are being challenged to ensure that expenditures are made at appropriate levels and that desired levels of revenues are produced. Many programs are self-supporting; that is, the programmer is responsible for generating enough revenue to cover the cost of a program.

Edginton, Hudson, and Lankford (2001: 321) have also noted that the budget process may seem "overwhelming, mysterious and complex." Certainly this may be the case for the novice leisure service programmer. However, with experience, the budgeting process can become simplified and can be viewed as a supportive programming aid. Edginton et. al.(2001) note that budgeting does not need to be complicated or complex. A well-organized budgeting system can be extremely important to the successful operation of any leisure program. The budget, in many respects, is a part of the program development formula. It enables the programmer to express, in financial terms, the elements necessary to create the leisure event or activity.

Budget Types

Leisure service programmers will be exposed to a variety of types of budgets. Although there may be some standardization from agency to agency concerning the types of budgets used (state regulatory laws often require local governments to follow a prescribed set of procedures), in general each individual leisure service organization will develop a unique set of internal budget procedures that will be followed. From a more global perspective, the types of budgets used by organizations have evolved over the last hundred years. This is especially the case in government, which will be the major focus of our discussion in this section. As the need for more diverse types of information has emerged over the past several decades, there has been an evolution in the sophistication of budgets.

When the concept of budgeting was first introduced, the main concern was for improving control of funds. The creation of budgeting systems was basically a product of social reform that occurred during the Progressive Era. As complex organizations grew in government, voluntary, and commercial sectors, so also grew a need to provide more precise information as well as to ensure that fiscal operations were handled with integrity. Discussing the development of budgeting, Deppe (1983) has written that budgeting is primarily a twentieth-century innovation. He notes:

> It was not until 1906 that New York City, under the auspices of the newly established Bureau of Municipal Research, organized a budgeting system that was designed around using an object of expenditure system for budgeting and accounting control. This began the so-called "traditional object of expenditure" type of budget which is still used by cities today. The idea of establishing a budget system spread rapidly to other cities, especially large ones, and by the mid-1920s most cities had adopted budgetary methods (p. 41).

The budget innovations that occurred in the early 1900s set the groundwork for a host of innovations that were to occur over the next several decades. In more recent years, attention has been focused on the development of budgets that link program activities and their resulting outcome with expenditures. Leisure service Organizations can choose from a variety of budget formats. However, in the United States and Canada, formats generally fall into one of four basic designs: line item, program, performance, and zero-base. Each format provides the manager with different types of information. For example, a line-item budget provides a broad perspective of revenues and expenditures but little detail. A program or performance budget provides information about the outputs or benefits that result from a specific aspect of the organization's efforts but does not provide a holistic financial view. The programmer will be well served by having a firm understanding of the particulars of the philosophy and concepts of budgeting used by the organization within which he or she is employed. The following section provides a brief overview of budget types associated with leisure service organizations. A Zero-base budget enables one to closely re-examine budget expenditures each year and determine if the costs are justified.

Line-Item Budgets

This approach to budgeting is also known as *object classification* budgeting. It was developed in the early 1900s as a way of correcting problems that were associated with the mismanagement of funds in government. Prior to that time, the standard process was to pool all funds into one central account. Obviously, it was difficult to determine how funds were being spent.

The line-item budget enables professionals to *identify specific "objects of expenditure" and the cost for each object.* This is the most popular form of budgeting used in government agencies. A number of classifications within the budget are identified, and then the costs are associated with these categories in a standard, systematic, and consistent fashion. Over the years, the line-item approach to budgeting has evolved to include a number of specific, standardized categories:

> *Personnel Services*—This classification includes the direct labor of individuals who are employed within the organization on either a regular or temporary basis and are paid on either an hourly wage basis or a fixed salary.
>
> *Contractual Services*—This classification includes those services that are performed under an expressed or implied contract. The contractual arrangements of a leisure service organization range from postage, telephone, printing, and repairs to the cost of heat, light, and power. A contractual arrangement between a leisure service agency and another organization would not

only involve the use of that organization's equipment, but also the personnel necessary to implement the service.

Supplies—Supplies are commodities that are entirely consumed or show rapid depreciation in a short period of time. Examples would be fuel, office supplies, cleaning supplies, and turf-care products.

Materials—Materials are commodities that have a more permanent and lasting quality than supplies. They may include such things as construction materials and sports equipment.

Current Charges—This type of expenditure includes the cost of clothing allowances, insurance, equipment rental, dues, and any other charges that are contracted at the option of the organization.

Current Obligations—Current obligations consist of fixed charges that have resulted from previous financial transactions entered into by the organization. For example, the payment of the organization's share of social security (United States) or social insurance (Canada) and its contribution to its retirement or pension program would be in this classification. Also included may be the cost of interest on the organization's debts that may result from borrowing money for capital improvements.

Properties—This classification includes the cost of improvements that are made to an organization's physical resources. It also includes the direct purchase cost of any new equipment or other physical resources, in other words, anything that is appreciable and has a calculated period of usefulness. This might include such things as playground equipment, machinery, office equipment, the cost of real estate, and any improvements made to existing properties.

Debt Payment—Debt payments may be distinguished from current obligations in that debt payments refer to the organization's payments on the principal of a given debt, rather than the interest (Edginton, et al., 2001:324–25).

The line-item approach to budgeting is often combined with other types of budgets. The advantage of such a system is that it provides additional ways of producing financial information. Because the line-item approach to budgeting is so widespread, combining it with other types of budgets offers the programmer the opportunity for comparison and standardization. This can be useful when determining the relative cost of one program compared to another.

The drawbacks of using the line-item budget are that it does not link cost with performance measures and it precludes the possibility of clustering all the costs associated with producing a specifically identified event or activity. In other words, costs involved in producing a given activity are scattered throughout the object classification system. Thus, there is no way of formally determining the total cost of the program within the budget structure itself. Despite these disadvantages, the line-item approach to budgeting is a very important and often-used budgetary tool in leisure service organizations today.

Program Budgets

In order to emphasize outcomes rather than costs, more and more agencies have been moving toward a program budget format and away from line-item presentation (Edginton, et al., 2001). The idea behind the program budget is to put more emphasis on dealing with programs that are desirable, and on associating costs with these programs in terms of the resources necessary to carry them out. In this way, a comparative analysis of the costs and, perhaps, the benefits associated with the programs, is possible.

A key to this approach to programming is the establishment of program decision-making packages. A program decision-making package is a budgetary unit wherein the total of all associated costs of that element are identified with that package. In other words, a program decision-making package would include the costs associated with personnel, contractual services, supplies, materials, current charges, current obligations, properties, and debt payment that are necessary to implement a given activity.

Thus, each program decision-making package can be compared with other packages in terms of total costs.

An important part of program budgeting is the analysis and comparison of program decision-making packages. Much of the decision making that takes place concerning program packages will probably occur at management levels. However, a strong trend in leisure service organizations is to encourage the participation of employees in the decision-making process. In developing and presenting program decision-making packages, programmers will want to keep in mind some basic questions regarding the factors that may influence how their ideas are evaluated. In general terms, some of these questions are:

1. What are the goals and objectives of the leisure service organization?
2. What leisure service programs are available or need to be created to move toward goals and objectives?
3. What will each of the leisure service programs cost in human and material resources, and what will each contribute toward accomplishing the desired goals and objectives?
4. Which leisure service programs should be implemented and to what extent?
5. Do we have a feasible plan for implementing them?
6. Can we evaluate at appropriate times the relationship between the proposed and actual accomplishments? (Adapted from Feldman, 1973)

Developing and evaluating program decision-making packages creates an opportunity for a more integrated approach to programming. Budgets can be established in light of organizational goals and objectives as well as programs to be offered. The programs can be compared with one another to determine whether they are effective at fulfilling the goals of the organization and as a result, are meeting real needs. Program budgeting in a sense simplifies the process of budgeting because it enables programmers to review their work (including the budgets that they may propose) in relation to the work of the entire organization. This approach to budgeting enables programmers to understand more specifically how their efforts contribute to the overall achievement of the organization's goals and objectives.

Performance Budgeting

Performance budgeting *links the amount of resources that are consumed in producing a program with its output.* The development of this approach to budgeting is a natural evolution of the need for more information for decision-making purposes. Leisure service programmers need to know what kind of impact their efforts have on the people they are serving and, in turn, whether the investment of resources is an effective one.

The heart of performance budgeting is the identification of performance indicators—the mechanism used by a leisure service organization to identify and measure its output. Crompton (1999: 66–67) has identified three types of performing indicators—workload measures, efficiency measures, and effectiveness measures. These approaches to measuring performance are defined as follows:

1. *Workload Measures*—Workload measures refer to the volume of work that is being completed. Workload measures focus on such questions as: How many hours of service activity are being provided? How many individuals are being served? and so on.
2. *Efficiency Measures*—Efficiency measures refer to how well the resources of the organization are being consumed. Such measures are usually stated as a ratio of the amount of the resources invested and the amount of output produced. So, for example, the leisure service programmer might calculate the total number of hours available in a program and divide it by the program cost. This will provide a measure of the service per hour. An efficiency measure could also be calculated on the basis of individual participation, by measuring the cost of participation for each hour of involvement by each participant.

3. *Effectiveness Measures*—Effectiveness measures refer to the extent to which a program achieves its stated goals and objectives. A program might have skill attainment as its primary goal. Effectiveness measures would then focus on measuring the degree to which an individual has attained the skill. Effectiveness measures are often concerned with customer satisfaction.

Performance budgets can be used in conjunction with line-item budgets. The information derived from budget analysis can be very useful to programmers in determining the relative impact of their efforts. Such knowledge can help guide the programmer in making recommendations and decisions about the types of services to be offered. The most important factor about program budgeting is that it provides a mechanism for leisure service programmers to think about the benefits that they are trying to produce.

Zero-Based Budgeting

First developed in private industry in the late 1960s and then adapted to government in the early 1970s, zero-based budgeting *forces an organization to rejustify its expenditures on a year-to-year basis*. It is not unusual in any organization for funds to be committed to a program or service year in and year out without considering whether that activity or event is actually meeting the needs of the people it is intended to serve.

Zero-based budgeting requires the programmer to focus on two primary concerns. The first asks the question: Are current activities being implemented in an efficient manner? The second asks the programmer: Which current activities could be eliminated or reduced in order to support the development of other, newer activities that might have greater potential of meeting customer needs? These two questions form the basis of the conceptual strategy used to implement the zero-based budgeting concept. They ask: Are we doing things well? and Can some of our activities be changed or eliminated in order to produce more efficient outcomes?

Zero-based budgeting involves four basic steps:

1. *Establish Program Decision-Making Packages*—The establishment of program decision-making packages involves identifying activities to be provided. Program decision-making packages can be built around a set of functions, facilities, or events. They might include the purpose of the activity, the costs and benefits, and the program's performance measures.
2. *Analyze Program Decision-Making Packages*—The next step in the process involves the evaluation and rating of each program decision-making package for the purpose of funding. The task here is to determine which of the program decision-making packages best meets the goals and decisions of the organization. For similar programs, the question would be which program package meets the needs of the organization in the most efficient way possible.
3. *Evaluate and Rank Program Decision-Making Packages*—This is the actual decision-making process. Once all the analytical information has been presented and reviewed, decisions must be made as to which packages are to be funded. These packages are placed in rank order to create the priority system. The most important programs would be funded initially, followed by those of lesser priority.
4. *Prepare a Financial Plan*—The last step in the process is the establishment of a budget for the programs identified within the process. This budget can then be reviewed by decision makers at other levels to determine how much money should be made available to implement proposed programs.

The zero-based approach to budgeting is a useful tool. It provides an opportunity for yearly evaluation and review of activities. It forces the programmer to rethink existing services and rejustify these in light of the goals (which may change) and available resources (which may also change). Conceptually, zero-based budgeting may be one of the most powerful tools available to programmers to help them stay current and up-to-date. Zero-based budgeting may require greater amounts of energy and time in preparing budgeting information, especially as it relates to establishing performance measures.

Budget Worksheets

Most leisure service organizations have developed a system used by programmers to provide financial information concerning activities and events. This system is usually referred to as a budget worksheet. The budget worksheet is prepared in conjunction with the program information worksheet. The purpose of these two documents is to provide both program and financial information for decision-making purposes in a concise standardized fashion. The program worksheet often contains information about the objectives of the program as well as times, dates, and location. From this information, financial estimates can be prepared. The purpose of the budget worksheet is to *help the leisure service programmer project financial estimates.*

The budget worksheet is prepared with a great deal of attention to detail. Detailed consideration must be given to every aspect involved in the construction of the program. Financial costs will be associated with almost every aspect of the program. Leaders must be paid, supplies must be purchased, publicity must be developed, and other costs, such as those associated with transportation, postage, and rentals, must be accounted for on the budget worksheet. Using a budget worksheet allows the programmer to identify in a systematic fashion those costs associated with the elements necessary for creating a leisure experience.

What would be found on a budget worksheet? In general, budget worksheets present three types of information—program description, cost estimates, and potential revenues. First, budget worksheets provide decision makers with a description of the program or an overview of the leisure event or activity. Budget worksheets often detail whom the program serves as well as location, dates, times, and a brief description of the content of the program. Second, a budget worksheet presents information concerning cost estimates. What is included

in cost estimates or expenditures will vary, but in general they will include cost of personnel, supplies and materials, and other miscellaneous expenses. Finally, budget worksheets provide information concerning potential revenues to be earned from the program. This might include revenue generated from fees, the sale of supplies and materials, and other sources.

An example of a budget worksheet is shown in Figure 11.7. The Dallas (Texas) Park and Recreation Department developed this worksheet and uses it for every program offering in its system. The document provides for an analysis comparing last year's budget with this year's proposed budget. Further, the document organizes direct expenses by line item and also presents an opportunity for calculation of indirect cost with a differentiation between different types of services. Last, the worksheet enables identification of the grand totals of expenditures and revenues.

Figure 11.8 presents a recreation program budget worksheet from the Indianapolis (Indiana) Parks and Recreation Department. The worksheet provides opportunities to identify sources of revenue, expenditures (broken out by line-item categories), and the cost of the program. The worksheet breaks down staff expenditures by breaking out the number of sessions per year, number of offerings per session, number of days per session, and number of hours per class. These are calculated against the hourly rate for instructors. Similarly, a breakdown for determining the class fee is also provided on the worksheet.

The budget worksheet is an important tool for the leisure service programmer. It often requires investigative work; that is, the programmer must call businesses or consult trade catalogs to determine the costs of supplies, equipment, and materials. It requires that the programmer understand the organization of the program, event, or activity to be offered in terms of required leadership, facility needs, or other factors that contribute to the success of a program. Creating an idea for a program is the

Program Budget Worksheet For _____

The purpose of the budget worksheet is to help determine appropriate class fees. This will allow Dallas Park and Recreation to offer quality programs and services that are affordable and feasible for the patron as well as the recreation center.

Expense	Formula	Summary
Instructor Cost		
Administration Fee		
Building Use Fee		
Supplies/Materials		
Special Equipment		
Total Expense		

Program Managers and Supervisors will need to estimate the number of paid participants needed in order for the program to break even. If the program does not have the minimum number of registered individuals, it should be canceled and considered for a future program season.

Income	Formula	Summary
Participant Fee		
Minimum # Required		
Break Even		
Participants over Minimum		
Total Registered		
Total Registered x Participant Fee		
Total Income		

Programs should break even or show a positive net balance.

Net (Income–Expense)	

Figure 11.7 Program Budget Worksheet, Dallas (Texas) Parks and Recreation Department. (Source: R. Hurd, "Paths to Leisure" presentation at NRPA Conference, October 2002.)

Recreation Program Budget Worksheet

_____ Budget Year

Fund #   Center #   Activity #   Prepared by   Date

Activity Name

Revenue

Five Digit Acct.#	Class Name	Fee Change Yes/No	# of Sess. per year	# of Offerings per sess.	# of Regist. per class	# of Regist. per year	Class Fee	Revenue
			x	x	=	x	=	
			x	x	=	x	=	
			x	x	=	x	=	
			x	x	=	x	=	
			x	x	=	x	=	
			x	x	=	x	=	
			x	x	=	x	=	

Total Registrants per year

= Total All Revenue $

Total Registrants per Year ___ x $.25 = $ _____ Total Insurance Surcharge
(Do NOT Include In Total All Revenue)

Expenditures

Five Digit Acct.#	Instructor/Staff	# of Sess. per year	# of Offerings per sess.	# of days per session	# of hrs per class (incl. prep time)	Hourly rate	Salaries
50200		x	x	x	x $	= $	
		x	x	x	x $	= $	
		x	x	x	x $	= $	
		x	x	x	x $	= $	
		x	x	x	x $	= $	
		x	x	x	x $	= $	
		x	x	x	x $	= $	
		x	x	x	x $	= $	

TOTAL SALARIES $ _____

PERSONNEL SERVICES

Five Digit #   Rate   x   Total Salaries   **+**

51100	Unemployment	___ x $ _____ = Total Unemployment Insurance $ _____
51110	Worker's Compensation	___ x $ _____ = Total Worker's Compensation $ _____
51200	Social Security	___ x $ _____ = Total Social Security $ _____

PROGRAM SUPPLIES (list item & cost)   **+**

52500 ___ $___ ___ $___ ___ $___
       ___ $___ ___ $___ ___ $___
       ___ $___ ___ $___ ___ $___ Total Program Supplies $ _____

OPERATING SUPPLIES (list item & cost)   **+**

52600 ___ $___ ___ $___ ___ $___
       ___ $___ ___ $___ ___ $___
       ___ $___ ___ $___ ___ $___ Total Operating Supplies $ _____

OTHER EXPENSES (list item & cost)   **+**

       ___ $___ ___ $___ ___ $___
       ___ $___ ___ $___ ___ $___
       ___ $___ ___ $___ ___ $___ Total Other Expenses $ _____

If additional room is needed please use an extra page! DO NOT write on the BACK!!!

= Total All Expenses $

(Revenue minus Expenses) **= Net Program** $

Page ___ of ___

Figure 11.8 Budget Worksheet, Indianapolis (Indiana) Park and Recreation Department.

imaginative, inspirational, and innovative part of the programmer's work. Creating the budget detail for an event or service is the analytical portion of programming. The two cannot be separated. Excellent programmers are not only those individuals who can envision a creative program idea, but also those who can actually organize the event or activity. Developing the budget material to implement a budget program is an important part of the planning process in which successful leisure programmers engage.

RESOURCE ATTAINMENT PLAN

What is a resource attainment plan? In order to plan, organize, and implement a leisure service experience, a variety of resources are required. Discussions of budgeting refer primarily to fiscal resources. However, the programmer must be concerned with not only fiscal resources but other types of resources that have an impact on the creation of an event or activity. The resource attainment plan identifies in a broader sense the resources necessary for program development and implementation. A resource attainment plan is defined as *a process directed toward the identification and procurement of resources other than those found in the budget.*

Edginton et. al. (2001: 302) have written that it is essential that organizations "allocate not only fiscal resources, but all resources within the jurisdiction of the organization . . . [that are necessary for program development] . . . These include equipment, building space, work hours, inventory and all other resources that contribute to the accomplishment of goals and objectives." These authors point out many of the resources that are not contained within the budget proper. These resources can come from within or without the organization. Often the leisure service programmer will be required to utilize many resources outside the budget to produce a program.

The importance of a resource attainment plan is that it focuses the attention of the leisure service programmer on all the details related to program implementation. This plan allows needed resources to be presented in a framework wherein they can be systematically identified and pursued. Many times, programmers' efforts to identify needed resources outside the budget are completed in a spontaneous rather than a systematic fashion. The development of a resource attainment plan requires the programmer to think and plan ahead about the types and numbers of other resources needed. More systematic thinking can create the opportunity for innovative and creative perspectives on resource attainment.

One important feature of a resource attainment plan is that it enables an organization to integrate its efforts with those of other agencies. Leisure service organizations and other agencies often work on a collaborative basis to produce programs. Many contributions are made on an in-kind basis. In other words, services are exchanged without the expenditure of fiscal resources. Often the exchange of such services reduces the charges associated with financial transactions. Locating and developing collaborative relationships often proves to be mutually beneficial to both parties.

What are the uses of a resource attainment plan? First, a resource attainment plan enables the programmer to identify the resources necessary to implement a program. This in turn presents the programmer with an opportunity to prioritize those resources that must be a part of the budget structure and those that can be obtained through alternative sources. A resource attainment plan allows for the identification of alternative sources. In this way, the programmer has an "information bank" that can be tapped for both current and future use. For example, if the resource attainment plan identifies the use of volunteers to implement a program, a list of individuals willing to contribute their time not only becomes available for current use but also for future use. Finally, a resource attainment plan enables the programmer to reconceptualize his or her resource base. The opportunity to acquire resources becomes much broader when viewed in the context of a total community, rather than just the budget of an organization.

Steps in Developing a Resource Attainment Plan

As indicated, the development of a resource attainment plan should be completed in a systematic fashion. Thoughtful attention should be given to the planning of a program and, in turn, the resources necessary to implement that program. A budget is a finite resource, but within any given community an infinite number of resources exist that can be tapped. It is not uncommon for leisure service organizations to be supported generously by the community.

Following are some of the steps that should be addressed in the development of a resource attainment plan:

1. Identify the goals and objectives of a specific activity.
2. Identify and define all the human, physical, fiscal, and technological resources necessary to implement the program.
3. Determine which resources are contained within the organization's budget structure and document.
4. Determine all other resources necessary to implement the program and document.
5. Scan the environment to determine the availability of resources.
6. Coordinate with other agencies, institutions, and businesses to determine the availability of potential resources.
7. Identify which resources can be located on a short-term basis and which require more long-term procurement.
8. Develop strategies for securing resources outside the budget structure of the organization.
9. Locate resources outside the budget structure and secure them.
10. Evaluate the resource attainment plan on a periodic basis to determine its effectiveness in meeting its goals and objectives.

The development of a resource attainment plan follows the procedures used in similar program activities.

Types of Alternative Resources

A number of alternative resources are available to programmers. Although it is impossible to identify all categories of alternative resources, following are several categories that should be considered by leisure service programmers.

Gifts and Donations

A gift or donation is an outright contribution to an organization. Gifts and donations can be made for very specific items related to a particular program. It is not unusual for individuals to contribute a piece of equipment, a game, decorations, food, or other items in support of a program. Gifts and donations can also be made in cash form. They do not have to be offered for any specific service. Gifts and donations can be given by an individual or an organization on a nonspecific basis. That is, funds can be given and used at the discretion of the programmer to develop any portion that he or she sees fit.

The city of Long Beach (California) operates a "Dedicate-a-Tree" program in partnership with "Partners of Parks," a nonprofit corporation dedicated to serving parks, beaches, and recreation in the city of Long Beach (see Figure 11.9). For $55, individuals or groups can purchase a eucalyptus, sycamore, liquid amber, evergreen, Chinese elm, pine, or ash tree to be planted in a city park of their choice. Another example of a donation comes from the city of Crestwood (Missouri) Parks and Recreation Department: the Crestwood Joint-Use Fitness Trail. This facility is operated and sponsored jointly by the city and the Crestwood-Sunset Hills Rotary.

The Oak Lawn (Illinois) Parks Foundation is an umbrella organization that focuses on promoting the "responsible development [and] enhancement of Oak Lawn lands, programs, facilities, and services." The foundation encourages donations, sponsorships, or both, as well as communitywide advocacy for open space, leisure, and environmental preservation. The foundation encourages gifts of all types including cash, commemorative donations, fund-raising activities, last wills and testaments, memorial donations,

Figure 11.9 Dedicate-a-Tree Program, City of Long Beach (California) Parks, Recreation, and Marine Department.

ing of labor, facilities, and/or equipment. For example, a school district might work cooperatively with a leisure service organization by providing a gymnasium at no charge for a particular leisure service event or activity. The school district perceives the sharing of its gymnasium as a contribution to the community's welfare and as a support of its own effort of community service.

Many individuals and organizations contribute in-kind services to support the work of leisure service organizations. The Blackhawk County (Iowa) Conservation Board operates an

Please Join The

ADOPT A PARK

Program

With The

Black Hawk County Conservation Board

3/92

Figure 11.10 Adopt a Park Program, Black Hawk County (Iowa) Conservation Board.

securities, and real property as well as volunteer efforts. The foundation provides opportunities for individuals to become involved in park issues, engage in fund-raising, and become advocates for parks and environmental concerns.

In-Kind Contributions
As previously mentioned, in-kind contributions are those resources that individuals and organizations make available to a program and that require no financial transaction. Although in-kind contributions can include materials and supplies, they more than likely involve the shar-

Figure 11.11 Adopt-a-Beach Program, City of Long Beach (California) Parks, Recreation, and Marine Department.

"Adopt a Park" program. This program encourages clubs, groups, organizations, employee groups, individuals, and families to participate. Activities include painting, picking up litter, pruning, checking for trail passes, and engaging in general maintenance, area security, and sometimes construction projects (see Figure 11.10). Another example is the "Adopt-a-Beach" program operated by the city of Long Beach (California) Parks, Recreation, and Marine Department. Groups, businesses, clubs, or community associations are encouraged to adopt a quarter mile of Long Beach shoreline and clean the litter four times a year for one year (see Figure 11.11).

Sponsorship
It is commonplace among leisure service organizations to seek sponsorship for events and activities. Such sponsorships have historically been made by community service and fraternal organizations. Increasingly, businesses, especially corporations, have engaged in the sponsoring of leisure service events and programs. The Thunder Bay (Ontario) Parks and Recreation Department annually seeks sponsorship of its "Summer in the Parks Concert Series" (see Figure 11.12).

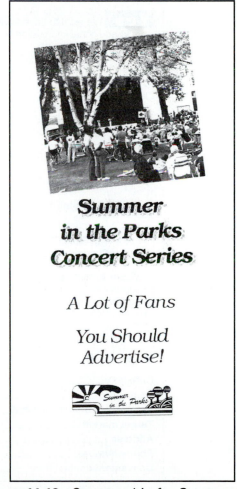

Figure 11.12 Sponsorship for Summer in the Parks Concert Series, Thunder Bay (Ontario) Parks and Recreation Department.

The city of Albany (Oregon) Parks and Recreation Department provides a similar music program. The program receives corporate sponsorship from such corporations as Hewlett-Packard and Weyerhaeuser.

The Morale, Welfare, and Recreation Department in Okinawa, Japan has an active sponsorship program. Its sponsorship program provides for high visibility and increased product recognition for individuals and businesses desiring to make direct contact with its target audience—single, young service members or military families. Within this program, sponsorship activities are not considered a gift or donation; rather, the sponsorship is a contract between the sponsor and the department for cash, products, or in-kind services that provide market recognition and promotional opportunities. Figure 11.13 provides a checklist of some of the sponsorship opportunities available.

● ●

Yes! We want to have a winning season with Marine MWR. Please contact us with additional information on the following sponsorship opportunities:

○ **Golf**
○ Tournaments
○ Tee Markers

○ **Friendship Festivals**
○ Kinser Springfest
○ Hansen Hoedown
○ Futenma Flightline Fair
○ Kuwaefest Carnival
○ Courtney Christmas Fest

○ **Travel & Leisure Expo**

○ **Beach Fun**
○ Oura Wan Beach Bash
○ Super Sunday at Kin Blue

○ **Youth Activities**
○ Islandwide Easter Egg Hunt
○ Family Fun Day
○ Youth Sports Program
○ Summer Day Camps/Learn
   to Swim

○ **Sports**
○ MWR Olympics
○ Pacific-wide Softball Tournaments
○ Islandwide Sports Events
○ Dr. M.L. King, Jr. Basketball
   Tournament
○ Bowling

○ **Commander's Challenge**
○ COMMARFORPAC Tournaments
○ Commanding General (CG) Cup

○ **Races**
○ Habu & Mongoose 5/10K
○ Kinser One-Half Marathon
○ Islandwide 5K Runs
○ Camp Schwab Biathalon

○ **Taste of the World Food Fair**

○ **Marine Corps Birthday Ball**

○ **Other** _____

● ●

Company _____
Name _____ **Title** _____
Product or service provided _____
Target market _____
Address _____
Phone number _____
Convenient contact time _____

Figure 11.13 Sponsorship Opportunities, Morale, Welfare, and Recreation Department, U.S. Marine Corps, Okinawa, Japan. (Source: From Morale, Welfare and Recreation Department, U.S. Marine Corps, Okinawa, Japan.)

The Detroit (Michigan) Recreation Department annually sponsors "Jazz on the Beach." This free concert series begins Memorial Day weekend and continues through Labor Day. This organization has provided an opportunity for businesses and individuals to sponsor the activity. Figure 11.14 shows a flyer that is used to promote the activity; Figure 11.15 presents the costs and benefits associated with cosponsoring the activity.

Scrounging

All programmers, to be successful, must be good at scrounging. Scrounging is the adaptation or recycling of resources that are obtained, usually gratis, through some source. Scrounging requires using imagination and inventiveness to see the potential use for discarded resources. One person's junk is another's treasure. Leisure program staff members are legendary

1995
JAZZ ON THE BEACH SPONSORSHIP OPPORTUNITIES
offered by Detroit Recreation Department

Figure 11.14 Jazz on the Beach, Detroit (Michigan) Recreation Department.

CO-SPONSORSHIP OPPORTUNITY

As a Co-Sponsor of JAZZ ON THE BEACH your company/organization may take advantage of the following co-sponsor benefits. Sponsor signage will receive priority banner placement around Belle Isle Beach and your logo will be included in all promotional materials. The net cost for a Co-Sponsorship package is $20,000.00

SPONSOR BENEFITS

☐ Signage throughout the Belle Isle Beach area (3 Banners)

☐ Limited sampling and/or sales of products at the Beach area

☐ Logo inclusion on promotional material

☐ Inclusion in all press packages

☐ Opportunity to cross promote the Jazz Series in any radio/TV and in-store advertising

☐ Opportunity to place one (1) tent [at sponsor's own expense] and/or table for product distribution at every concert

☐ If product distribution option is selected, workers could wear shirts, caps, etc. with sponsor logo (to be provided by sponsor)

☐ Opportunity to distribute coupons for store purchase of sponsors products throughout the Beach area

☐ Reserved seating/picnic area for twenty-five (25) VIPs at all concerts

☐ Reception opportunity for entertainers and sponsor VIPs at White House at Labor Day Weekend finale

☐ Suggested sponsorship opportunities include, but are not limited to those listed above.

Figure 11.15 Sponsorship Opportunities, Detroit (Michigan) Recreation Department.

scroungers. Program staff may use discarded potato chip containers as decorated "spirit sticks." They may save Styrofoam plastic packing from electronic components and use it for costume decorations in drama productions; they may use discarded soda cans to make "crushed can creatures" for an Earth Day Birthday Recycle Celebration.

Partnerships
When two or more organizations cooperate to provide a program, they have entered into a partnership. Organizations often participate with one another, sharing unique resources to produce programs that are mutually beneficial. Partnerships involve a joint sharing of human, physical, and fiscal resources. Not all partnerships are

equal. In some cases, one organization may share more of its resources. Partnerships usually require a high level of trust between organizations and usually involve a strong commitment to producing a shared program of excellence.

One example of a partnership between two businesses is illustrated in Figure 11.16. In this case, the Seattle Mariners Baseball Club has formed a partnership with Horizon Air to provide a package tour to a baseball game. Customers are invited to fly to Seattle to attend a Mariners baseball game; the package includes round-trip air transportation, overnight accommodations, and box seats to the game. The advantages of this type of arrangement are obvious—the airline benefits from increased travel, the hotel benefits from increased patronage, and the Mariners are able to draw more fans to their games. Partnerships can be formed not only between commercial enterprises but also between public agencies. Partnerships can also be established between commercial and nonprofit organizations.

Volunteers

Volunteers are the backbone of public and voluntary leisure service organizations. Without volunteers, the programs of these organizations would be severely curtailed. The recruitment, training, and recognition of volunteers requires a high level of management sophistication on the part of the programmer. The Thunder Bay (Ontario) Parks and Recreation Department's volunteer development program serves as an example of this excellent resource. This volunteer program, operated in fourteen community centers, equals the work of sixty-three employees, representing a value to the community conservatively estimated at $523,250. More than 570 volunteers in the Department's summer program contributed 4,000 hours of time.

By no means are these the only types of alternative resources. Programmers should recognize that many other sources can be tapped to help in the development and implementation of programs. The development of a resource

PLAY BALL!

Fly to Seattle and catch the exciting *new* Seattle Mariners!

Avoid the long drive and let Horizon fly you to Seattle in minutes for a fun weekend get away, including Mariner baseball. All for a low weekend price.

Mariners Weekend Packages Include:
* Round trip airfare on Horizon Air.
* One night accommodations at the WestCoast Camlin Hotel (downtown).
* Box seat ticket to Mariner weekend game.

$115 to $180
See reverse side for price from your city.

*For information and reservations,
call your travel agent.*

Prices are per person, double occupancy. Valid weekends only. Change and cancellation penalties apply. Extra game tickets, additional nights, single and triple rates available upon request. Prices subject to change without notice. Advance purchase, availability and other restrictions apply. See reverse side for rates from Horizon Air cities.
- Over -

Figure 11.16 Partnership Between Seattle Mariners and Horizon Air.

attainment plan can provide programmers with a systematic approach to identifying resources. The resource attainment plan provides programmers with the opportunity to expand their resource base beyond the structure of a budget.

In a sense, programmers are limited only by their imagination, individual effort, and desire to identify and locate alternative resources.

PRICING

As leisure service programmers have become increasingly responsible for generating revenues to support events and activities, the concept of pricing has become an important dimension to consider when designing the effort. In commercial leisure service organizations, it is often possible for an organization not only to break even but also to generate a profit. In governmental and voluntary organizations, programs are required to, at minimum, make back the direct cost of the event or activity. In either case, pricing has become an important dimension of the program planning process.

Rossman and Schlatter (2000:345) suggest that a program price can be defined as follows: "price is the dollar amount the agency charges . . . [customers] . . . to participate in a specific program." In other words, the price is the cost that the customer must bear in order to participate in the program. The price of a program is usually stated in financial terms (dollars and cents) and is related to the demand for and value of the service. The price that is established for a service not only reflects the costs (both direct and indirect) of the program to the organization, but also often reflects the extent to which individuals seek the service. Usually, the higher the status of the service, the greater the amount individuals are willing to pay. In other words, if an individual customer values the benefits derived from a given leisure service, it is possible that he or she would be willing to pay a higher amount.

Four pricing factors are important in determining the actual price of the program or event—fixed direct, fixed indirect, variable direct, and market demand. Direct and indirect costs were discussed earlier in this chapter in the Costs (Expenditures) section. Fixed costs represent funds charged against a program that do not vary regardless of the number of customers participating. Utility costs are an example of fixed costs. Variable costs are those costs that increase or decrease according to the number of customers participating in a program. Market demand factors are related to the availability of similar services and the actual customer demands for those services. The assumption is that the greater the market demand for services, the higher the price. Another way of looking at the market demand element is to relate it to the value that people place on the benefits they derive from a leisure experience. The amount that individuals are willing to pay for a service may be a reflection of what they value. Sometimes higher-priced services are confirmation of a certain status and reflect the desire for individuals to associate themselves with a quality of program or service.

One pricing strategy that leisure service organizations often use to attract consumers is to vary prices, either to promote volume participation or to attract people to a new service. In the former case, the leisure service organization might create a family pass program. In the latter case, an organization might want to consider providing a free sample or low-cost fee for the first time that a person takes part in a service. Figure 11.17 presents a sample "free individual or family

Figure 11.17 Swimming Pool Coupon, Lively Park Swim Center, Willamalane Park and Recreation District, Springfield, Oregon.

Figure 11.18   Coupon, Aurora (Colorado) Parks and Recreation Department.

admission" to the Lively Park Swim Center, operated by the Willamalane Park and Recreation District in Springfield, Oregon. Another example is the discount coupon offered by the Aurora (Colorado) Parks and Recreation Department. This coupon provides individuals with a $10 reduction of any activity found in this organization's program brochure (see Figure 11.18).

Break-Even Analysis

One approach to determining the price of a program is through the use of a financial tool known as a break-even analysis. This analytical tool can be used to help the programmer determine the point at which the revenues from an activity or event are sufficient to meet the expenditures. Bullaro and Edginton (1986: 278) have noted that a break-even analysis *calculates the point at which revenues generated from the sales of a service can meet expenses.* This analysis provides the programmer with useful financial information to help understand the relationship of direct, indirect, fixed, and variable costs in calculating the price of a program.

Figure 11.19 presents an example of a break-even analysis for a leisure service activity. Fixed direct costs are those costs associated with the actual production of the program. These

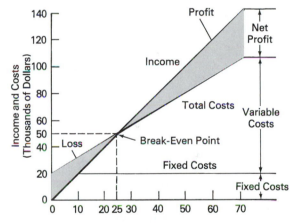

Figure 11.19   Break-Even Chart. (Source: Weston, J. F. and Brigham, E. F. 1978. The *Managerial Finance,* 6th ed. Hinsdale, Il. The Dryden Press.)

expenditures do not change or vary and must be attended to when establishing a program. Fixed direct cost can be considered the minimal cost to produce a program. Fixed direct costs often involve expenditures for a leader, promotion, and an area or facility needed to implement a program. Variable direct costs are those costs that change depending on the volume or number of customers participating. For example, the amount of arts and crafts supplies necessary to implement a program may increase or decrease depending on the number of customers participating. Interestingly, it is the control of variable direct costs that often can produce the profit margins required by an organization. Control of variable direct costs should be a high concern of the leisure service programmer.

Fixed indirect costs in this model result from a variety of expenditures, including salaries paid to administrators and support staff, depreciation on buildings and equipment, and other factors. Fixed indirect costs, as indicated, do not change or vary regardless of the number of customers participating in the program or activity. In other words, in calculating the cost of a program, an additional 20 to 40 percent is added onto the sum of the fixed direct and the variable direct cost of a program.

How do we calculate market demand? Howard and Crompton (1980: 28) notes two basic strategies that can be used to calculate prices when the cost of the program is not solely dependent on the direct or indirect cost. In other words, two general pricing methods are available to leisure service programmers. These are known as *going rate pricing* and *demand-oriented pricing*. Going rate pricing is the amount charged for a service when compared with prices charged by similar leisure service organizations offering similar services. Demand-oriented pricing is built on the assumption that the price should be established by what the customer is willing to pay. The demand-for-services concept in pricing is affected by the availability of services and the perceived quality of services. In other words, demand-oriented pricing can be affected by the number of services available to individuals and their perception of the quality or status of services.

Summary

Budgeting and resource attainment are two important elements that the leisure service programmer must consider in the design and implementation of leisure service programs and activities. It is important to recognize that budgets follow programs, not the reverse. That is, the leisure service programmer should design the program first and then create a budget to support the program's implementation. Today, leisure service programmers are increasingly being held accountable for the financial aspects of service delivery. They are often required not only to produce revenues that meet basic program costs but also to generate revenues for other program services and organizational functions.

A budget and a resource attainment plan can assist the programmer in a number of ways. In particular, these tools help the programmer plan, implement, and control activities and events. Also, the budget and the resource attainment plan are useful in helping the programmer translate program concepts into economic reality, establish program priorities, communicate program plans, establish a historical record, and build commitment to a course of action.

A budget can be thought of as a plan. Stated in financial terms, a budget helps estimate the types of fiscal resources necessary to implement a program. Budgets help the leisure service programmer identify what resources are required and also which methods will be used to locate and secure them. The budget helps the programmer think ahead and establish a blueprint of action for the future. Several types of comprehensive budget systems are available to leisure service programmers. These include line-item budgets, program budgets, performance budgets, and zero-based budgets.

A resource attainment plan identifies in a broader sense the resources necessary to organize and implement a program. A resource attainment plan is concerned not only with fiscal resources but with other resources as well. A key to locating resources is to look for alternative sources outside the leisure service organization. Extraorganizational alternative resources include gifts and donations, in-kind contributions, sponsorships, scrounging, partnerships, and volunteers.

Discussion Questions and Exercises

1. Explain what the statement "budgets follow programs, not the reverse" means.

2. Identify and define eight trends that have an impact on the financial management of leisure service organizations.

3. Identify and define eight ways that a budget and a resource attainment plan can impact on the work of a leisure service programmer.

4. Identify and define seven categories of earned income. Research and provide examples from the leisure service field for each of these categories.

5. Define the concept of budgeting. Identify and define five types of budget systems.

6. Select a leisure service organization of your choice from the commercial, voluntary, or governmental sector and locate a copy of that organization's budget. Analyze the budget in terms of total revenue, expenditures, and type of budget employed, and calculate the percentage of expenditures supported by earned income.

7. Using the budget worksheet shown in Figure 11.8, develop a budget scenario for an arts and crafts class for ten-year-old children. The class should be designed to meet two hours a week for ten weeks.

8. What is a resource attainment plan? How is it different from a budget?

9. Identify and discuss six categories of resources available to leisure service programmers that can be used to support the organization and implementation of leisure service activities and events.

10. Why is pricing important in leisure service programs? How can the break-even analysis be used to calculate the price of a service?

References

Bullaro, J. J., and C. R. Edginton. 1986. *Commercial leisure services*. New York: Macmillan.

Crompton, J. L. 1987. *Doing more with less in the delivery of recreation and park services*. State College, PA: Venture.

Crompton, J. 1999. *Financing and acquiring park and recreation resources*. Champaign, IL. Human Kinetics.

DeGraff, D., D. Jordan, and K. DeGraaf. 1999. *Programming for parks, recreation and leisure services:*

A servant leadership approach. State College, PA: Venture.

Deppe, T. R. 1983. *Management strategies in financing parks and recreation*. New York: John Wiley.

Drucker, P. 1985. *Innovation and entrepreneurship*. New York: Harper and Row.

Edginton C. R., S. D. Hudson, and S. Lankford. 2001. *Managing recreation, parks, and leisure services: An introduction*. Champaign, IL: Sagamore.

Edginton, C. R., and J. G. Williams. 1978. *Productive management of leisure service organizations*. New York: John Wiley.

Feldman, S. 1973. *The administration of mental health services*. Springfield, IL: Thomas.

Hemphill, S. A. 1985. Revenue management: Beginning with basics. *Parks and Recreation* 20(12): 32–38.

Hines, T. I. 1974. *Revenue source management in parks and recreation*. Arlington, VA: National Recreation and Park Association.

Howard, D. R., and J. L. Crompton. 1980. *Financing, managing, and marketing recreation and park resources*. Dubuque, IA: W. C. Brown.

Hurd, R. (October 2002) Paths to Leisure. Presented at National Recreation and Parks Association Congress. Tampa, Florida.

Osborne, D., and T. Gaebler. 1992. *Reinventing government*. New York: Addison–Wesley.

Rossman, J. R. 1989. *Recreation programming: Designing leisure experiences*. Champaign, IL: Sagamore.

Rossman, J., and B. Schlatter 2000. *Recreation programming: Designing leisure experience*. Champaign, IL: Sagamore.

Rossman, J. R. 1995. *Recreation programming: Designing leisure experiences*. 2d ed. Champaign, IL: Sagamore.

Schroth, R. J. 1978. Effects of local government structures on budgetary procedures of municipal park and/or recreation departments. Ph.D. diss., Indiana University.

Wesemann, H. E. 1981. *Contracting for city services*. Pittsburgh, PA: Innovations Press.

Weston, J. F., and E. F. Brigham. 1978. *Managerial finance*. 6th ed. Hinsdale, IL: Dryden Press.

Wildavsky, A. 1974. *The politics of the budgetary process*. 2d ed. Boston: Little, Brown.

Delivering Leisure Programs

LEARNING OBJECTIVES

1. To provide the reader with an overview of the importance of *service quality and the customer/ leader interface.*

2. To help the reader understand components in developing *organizational empowerment.*

3. To help the reader identify and define the *types of interactions* that can be planned, organized, and taught to employees.

4. To identify and define the *hallmarks of excellence in customer/leader interactions.*

5. To provide an overview of the *roles and responsibilities of leisure service programmers* as supervisors.

6. To identify *strategies used in removing barriers* as a supervisory responsibility.

7. To provide an overview of procedures to *manage the flow of a leisure service program.*

INTRODUCTION

Connecting with the customer to provide fulfilling, rewarding leisure experiences is the primary purpose of any leisure service organization. The ability of frontline, direct, face-to-face leaders and leisure service programmers operating as supervisors to effectively deliver leisure experiences is essential to organizational success. Satisfied customers are central to the well-being of an organization. In delivering services, leisure service programmers must be responsive, courteous, and concerned about their customers' welfare.

The leisure service programmer often functions as a supervisor. In this role, he or she is responsible for ensuring that services are delivered effectively and efficiently. The programmer as a supervisor helps clarify and define organizational goals, and to remove the barriers that prevent the successful delivery of leisure services. Supervisors have responsibilities ranging from the production of services to the creation and maintenance of safe work and leisure environments.

Both frontline leisure service leaders and supervisors are involved in managing the flow of programs. Managing a program's flow involves structuring leisure environments to achieve desired goals. It can involve sequencing activities or arranging environmental conditions to produce the desired leisure experiences. In this chapter, the broad concept of delivering leisure programs is presented. First, the customer/leader interface is analyzed, with particular attention paid to the hallmarks of excellence in this area. The topic of managing and supervising leisure service personnel is also presented. Finally, a discussion of the procedures and methods used in managing program flow from both a practical and theoretical perspective is briefly introduced.

SERVICE QUALITY AND THE CUSTOMER/LEADER INTERFACE

Service quality refers to customers' appraisal of the services, the provider, or the entire service organization (Duffy and Ketchand, 1998). According to Wuest (2001), service quality is a continuum, that provides services in three time elements: (1) services experienced before entering a leisure organization; (2) services encountered during the leisure experience; and (3) services experienced after departing a leisure facility.

The services that participants experience before entering a leisure organization include customer information, reservation/registration systems, hours of operation, payment options, and the physical environment surrounding the leisure organizations. For example, Figure 12.1 shows a brochure by the Missouri Department of Natural Resources, that provides customer information on: (1) rules regarding bringing domestic pets to state parks, (2) the harmful effects of domestic pet fecal waste in state parks, and (3) information on fecal waste deposit programs in Missouri state parks. This brochure is provided to customers before they enter most state parks in Missouri. Likewise, the condition of the physical environment surrounding the leisure facility (e.g., landscaping, parking area, adequate lighting, and security) adds to the quality of the impressions generated (Sawyer, 2002).

The services that participants experience before entering a leisure organization have a significant influence on their leisure experiences and satisfaction. In this regard, the way that the leisure service explains and promotes information (see Chapter 10) establishes perceptions and expectations among potential participants. Figure 12.2, adapted from Morgan (1996, as cited in O'Neill, 2001), illustrates how the fit between customer expectations and perceptions can affect service quality. During customer/provider interactions, the customer evaluates whether the provider is able to fulfill his or her expectations and deliver the leisure benefits that generate satisfaction (Reisinger, 2001a). In short, a large gap between participant expectations and perceptions of services leads to a quality gap (O'Neill, 2001).

The services that the participant encounters during the leisure experience include customer assistance and services, condition of the facility, and check-in/check-out procedures. For example, leisure facilities that are clean, maintained, and updated give the participant a feeling of security. Figure 12.3, from the National Program for Playground Safety (located at the University of Northern Iowa), provides important information relevant to developing a comprehensive playground maintenance program that keeps American playgrounds clean and safe (for additional information, see www.uni.edu/playground). Likewise, service quality improves when staff members are friendly, appreciative of the customer, gracious, tactful, courteous, and attentive (Martin, 1987; Reisinger, 2001b). To this end, Saleh and Ryan (1992) have argued that staff appearance (e.g., cleanliness) in leisure organizations, such as in the area of tourism and hospitality, is more important than the range of facilities and programs being offered.

Services that occur after the participant has departed the leisure facility include customer evaluation, complaint resolution, follow-up

PET POLLUTION? A SOLUTION!

To encourage proper disposal of pet waste while visiting our parks and historic sites, the Missouri Department of Natural Resources has initiated a pilot program to dispense fecal waste deposit bags to visitors with pets. Please obtain these bags from park staff when visiting the following Missouri state parks and historic sites:

Arrow Rock State Historic Site

Dr. Edmund A. Babler Memorial State Park

Sam A. Baker State Park

Graham Cave State Park

Lake of the Ozarks State Park

Meramec State Park

Pomme de Terre State Park

Roaring River State Park

Route 66 State Park

Thousand Hills State Park

Watkins Woolen Mill State Park & State Historic Site

Weston Bend State Park

For the purpose of this project, equestrian and service animals are not considered domestic household pets.

BE NICE TO YOUR PET, YOUR PARKS AND OTHER PARK VISITORS.

Your cooperation will be appreciated.

Missouri Department of Natural Resources

Printed on recycled paper.   10/01

PETS AS PARK VISITORS

The Missouri Department of Natural Resources is pleased to allow you the privilege of bringing your domestic household pet to Missouri state parks and historic sites. It is up to you, the pet owner, to act responsibly with your pet and to be courteous of other park users to help ensure that this privilege is always extended.

Figure 12.1 Pets as Visitors in State Parks, Missouri Department of Natural Resources.

THINGS YOU SHOULD KNOW ABOUT ANIMAL WASTE IN MISSOURI STATE PARKS.

More and more visitors are bringing their pets to the park, which is increasing complaints about fecal waste deposits.

Waste deposits are often unknowingly tracked onto carpet and floors of buildings, tents, vehicles, etc. The smell of any feces is offensive and will attract flies or other vermin to the area.

Dog waste can pose health threats to park users and other dogs, including the transmission of Parvovirus to unexposed and unvaccinated dogs. It can also carry waterborne disease organisms such as E. coli, salmonella, and other gastrointestinal organisms and parasites that can cause serious health effects.

Waste deposits can impact lakes and streams used for recreation by increasing fecal bacteria and other fecal organisms to levels unsafe for swimming. It can diminish the water supply's ecological health through increased plant and algae growth. Waste also can increase the spread of nitrogen-loving noxious weeds at the expense of our native plants.

HERE ARE SOME THINGS TO KEEP IN MIND.

🐾 Responsible pet owners will properly remove and dispose of their pet's waste in dumpsters or trash receptacles.

🐾 State law requires pets to be on a secured leash that is no longer than 10 feet. When meeting or passing other users, please reduce the rein to four feet.

🐾 Pets may feel more secure and dogs will be less likely to bark if kept inside your sleeping unit when camping overnight. Barking is disturbing to other park users.

🐾 Never leave your pet unattended in the park.

🐾 Pets are not allowed in public swimming areas (including beaches) or in public buildings. Service animals assisting persons with disabilities are permitted in these areas.

🐾 Wash your pet at home, not in state park showers, streams, rivers or lakes.

🐾 Never allow your pet to dig in any area of the park or historic site.

🐾 Don't leave your pet inside a vehicle (even with the windows slightly open), as seasonal temperatures can quickly reach dangerous levels.

🐾 Make sure your pet has identification tags in case it gets separated from you.

🐾 State law requires owners to report to park personnel any incidents of pet bites or attacks. Be prepared to show proof that your pet's vaccinations are current.

🐾 Park personnel may ask pet owners to leave the park when their pet is being disruptive to other visitors or when pet owners blatantly ignore pet policies of the park.

🐾 Leaving your pet in the comfort of your home with a caregiver could benefit both you and your pet.

Figure 12.1—*Continued.*

correspondence, and guest incentives. For example, follow-up evaluation enables leisure programmers to identify whether appropriate services were provided (see Chapter 13). Further, through follow-up correspondence, participants can become aware of specific services, new programs, and recent developments. The Core, a private, for-profit leisure organization (in Cedar Falls, Iowa) that focuses on comic books and games of fantasy, sends weekly e-mails informing participants of new comic books, materials, and game tournaments.

In regard to service quality, Schlesinger and Heskett (1991) have suggested four approaches to increase quality services to customers. First, organizations should value investments in people (e.g., dealing appropriately with customer complaints) at least as much as they value investments in machines and technological advancements. Second, providers should use technology to support frontline employees, not to monitor or replace them. For example, the computer software RecTrac (see www.vermontsystems.com) can be used to help frontline recreation staff in such

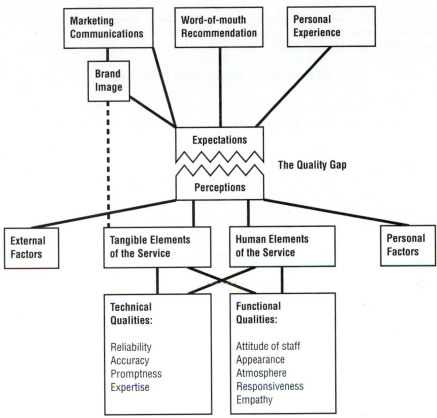

Figure 12.2   Diagrammatic Framework of Service Quality.

areas as scheduling league play, renting equipment, planning trips, and reporting accidents. Third, organizations should hire and recruit energetic employees for positions throughout the leisure organization (e.g., frontline workers, managers, senior executives). Building upon Mack (2000), the following six hiring and recruiting recommendations are suggested (1) hire people who have intrinsic motivation to work in the field of recreation and leisure services; (2) initiate recruitment at the high school level, (3) develop programs at the college level, (4) provide a supportive work environment, (5) develop on-going training throughout employment, and (6) hire people from diverse cultures. Fourth, service providers should link compensation to staff performance at all levels of the organization.

In short, quality services are developed by focusing on both internal and external delivery systems. To this end, Soutar (2001) has suggested the following internal and external strategies to increase service quality, customer satisfaction, and long-term loyalty:

- Compete aggressively to hire employees who have talents and skills in human services.
- Offer a real vision that brings purpose to employees, especially for frontline staff (see Chapter 6).
- Provide training to equip staff to perform service roles.
- Understand that committed teams perform better than uncommitted teams or team members that follow self-agendas.
- Provide real freedom for staff to solve customers' problems.

A comprehensive playground maintenance program must include inspections, upkeep and repair, and documentation. Following are some examples of the types of hazards that an inspector or maintenance personnel would check for. Please note that this is not a complete listing of known hazards.

Playground Inspection Checklist

Name of Playground _____ Date _____

Check the box after each step is completed and note where maintenance is needed.

<u>Needs</u>
<u>Maintenance</u>

General Upkeep
- ☐ Look for miscellaneous debris, broken glass, needles, litter, ropes, etc.   _____
- ☐ Check for missing or full trash containers.   _____
- ☐ Search for damage to the equipment.   _____
- ☐ Check for obstacles in equipment use zones.   _____

Surfacing
- ☐ Check for inadequate levels of surfacing materials.   _____
- ☐ Check for areas of compaction, kick-out, or wear.   _____
- ☐ Look for potential drainage problems.   _____
- ☐ Examine sidewalks, paved surfaces, steps, and platforms for loose surface
  materials and debris.   _____

General Hazards
- ☐ Check for sharp points, corners, and edges.   _____
- ☐ Look for protrusions and projections.   _____
- ☐ Check for missing or damaged protective caps or plugs.
- ☐ Search for potential clothing entanglement hazards such as gaps.   _____
- ☐ Look for pinch or crush points and exposed moving parts.   _____
- ☐ Check for potential trip hazards.   _____
- ☐ Check for low hanging tree branches.   _____

Equipment Deterioration
- ☐ Check wooden equipment for splinters, checking, large cracks, warping, and rot.   _____
- ☐ Look for rust, corrosion, or chipped paint on metal structures.   _____
- ☐ Inspect for holes and cracks in plastic structures.   _____
- ☐ Check for unstable or exposed anchoring.   _____

Hardware Security
- ☐ Check for loose or worn connecting, covering, or fastening devices.   _____
- ☐ Look for open S-hooks.   _____
- ☐ Examine all moving parts for wear.   _____
- ☐ Check for kinked, twisted, or broken chains.   _____

Completed By _____

National Program for Playground Safety 1-800-554-PLAY

Figure 12.3   Playground Inspection Checklist. National Program for Playground Safety. University of Northern Iowa, Cedar Falls, Iowa.

Playground Maintenance Checklist

Name of Playground _____ Date _____

Check the box after each step is completed.

General Upkeep
        ☐ Miscellaneous debris, broken glass, needles, litter, ropes, etc. have been removed.
        ☐ Trash containers are emptied or replaced.
        ☐ Damaged equipment has been repaired or replaced.
        ☐ Obstacles in equipment use zones have been removed.

Surfacing
        ☐ Surfacing materials are of adequate levels (at least 12 inches of loose surfacing such as sand, pea gravel, shredded rubber, wood mulch, or wood fibers **OR** unitary products such as rubber mats/tiles or poured-in-place).
        ☐ Areas of compaction, kick-out, or wear have been leveled or repaired.
        ☐ There are no potential drainage problems.
        ☐ Sidewalks, paved surfaces, steps, and platforms have been swept or cleaned of loose surface materials and debris.

General Hazards
        ☐ There are no sharp points, corners, or edges.
        ☐ There are no protrusions or projections.
        ☐ There are no missing or damaged protective caps or plugs.
        ☐ Potential clothing entanglement hazards have been eliminated.
        ☐ There are no pinch points, crush points, or exposed moving parts.
        ☐ Potential trip hazards have been removed.
        ☐ Hanging tree branches have been trimmed.

Equipment Deterioration
        ☐ Wooden equipment is free of splinters, checking, large cracks, warping, and rot.
        ☐ Metal structures are free of rust, corrosion, and chipped paint.
        ☐ Plastic structures are free of holes and cracks.
        ☐ There are no unstable or exposed anchorings.

Hardware Security
        ☐ There are no loose or worn connecting, covering, or fastening devices.
        ☐ All S-hooks are closed.
        ☐ Moving parts do not show excessive wear.
        ☐ Chains are not kinked, twisted, or broken.

Maintenance Performed By _____

National Program for Playground Safety 1-800-554-PLAY

Figure 12.3—*Continued.*

- Acknowledge achievement publicly.
- Base job design on research with employee consultation.

The Customer/Leader Interface

The most important relationship in the process of programming leisure experiences is that of the customer/leader interface. In fact, the interaction that the leisure professional has with a given customer may well be the pivotal point in the success or failure of the leisure experience. Further, both the short-term and long-term successes of any leisure service organization can be predicted on the goodwill that is established between customers and leaders on a moment-to-moment basis. Reisinger's (2001b) comments underscore the serious nature of the customer/leader interface:

> The [leisure] providers behavior, emotions, skills, knowledge, and the way they perform services, regardless of whether they are backed up by a large amount of equipment, is part of the service experience, which determines consumer evaluation and satisfaction with the service. *The behavior of providers can ruin or enhance the experience* (p. 27, italics added).

Therefore, the interaction that occurs either formally or informally should be carefully thought out and, in fact, planned, organized, and taught to the staff of the leisure service organization.

Albrecht and Zemke (1985: 106) have identified three different service-oriented categories of employees within organizations—primary service staff, secondary service staff, and service support staff. Primary service staff are those individuals who have direct, planned contact with the customer. In other words, primary service staff plan, organize, and implement programs and activities that result in leisure experiences. Secondary service staff are those individuals who have incidental contact with customers. They may conduct registration, provide information, or prepare equipment, supplies, or areas and facilities for primary service staff to conduct programs. Finally, support service staff

are those individuals who provide supervisory or logistical support. For example, the leisure programmer in charge of primary staff members is considered a support staff member. As Albrecht and Zemke note in discussing the support service position, "if you're not serving the customer, you better be serving someone who is."

In many leisure service organizations, programs and services are delivered by seasonal, part-time, or volunteer staff. Finding excellent individuals to occupy such positions is, indeed, a challenging task for any leisure service programmer. These frontline staff members, in all likelihood, make up the vast majority of personnel recruited and hired by leisure service organizations. Little is done to enhance their status within organizations, and as a result, with few exceptions, they do not remain with the organization over an extended period of time. Such individuals are often the lowest paid and receive the least amount of training and development.

The status of frontline staff members in leisure service organizations creates a dilemma. They are the vital link to the customer, and the primary contact point from the organization to those it serves. The first step in establishing a strong customer/leader interaction is to make sure that a leisure service organization's frontline people are its "bottom line." That is to say, the organization must invest in its frontline staff in terms of planning, training, and development. An organization must devote more of its resources to ensuring that its frontline people are knowledgeable and responsive to customer needs.

Frontline staff members should be able to represent the organization as well as the top level managers do. They should be in a position to act independently on behalf of the organization and commit its resources to solving problems. To this end, Chernish (2001) suggested that frontline workers in leisure organization should be empowered—workers should have the authority and resources to accomplish overall organizational goals and objectives. Hodgetts (1993) highlighted that empowerment includes: (1) giving workers authority to make decisions;

(2) maintaining an open communication and decentralized system throughout organizations; (3) solving complex problems through an inter-disciplinary and collaborative manner; and (4) rewarding those employees who assume responsibility and perform well.

Moreover, Blanchard, Carlos, and Randolph (1996) suggested a three-step model to develop organizational empowerment. The first step is to share information with all employees. That is, all employees are given access to information and training so that they can independently make competent decisions. Empowerment is developed because:

- All employees understand the current situations with clarity;
- Open communication begins to build trust throughout the organization;
- Traditional hierarchical thinking and decision-making are broken down;
- Employees become personally responsible; and
- People are encouraged to act like owners of the organization.

The second step is to create autonomy through boundaries. Boundaries define the areas in which employees are free to operate without direct managerial supervision. For example, in a community recreation facility, boundaries might include a variety of program areas such as aquatics, basketball leagues, drama programs, youth summer camps, and so forth. In this second step, empowerment is developed because autonomy through boundaries:

- Develops information sharing throughout different boundaries;
- Clarifies the overall vision and mission with input from all employees;
- Helps translate vision into goals, objectives, strategies, and roles;
- Underscores and helps develop values and rules that underlie desired actions;
- Develops structures and procedures that empower employees; and
- Reminds all employees that empowerment is a journey (not magic).

The third step is to replace hierarchy with self-directed work teams. Self-directed teams consist of employees who have responsibility for an entire service or program. For example, with manager interaction, leaders, and instructors within a dance program (e.g., leaders of ballroom dance, ethnic dance, folk dance, rap dance, and square dance) could work together to take leadership and responsibility for the entire dance program within a community recreation organization (e.g., defining goals and objectives that align to the mission statement). In this step, empowerment is developed because:

- Empowered teams can do more than empowered individuals;
- Employees learn the strengths of being a team member;
- A sense of unity develops as employees are trained in team skills;
- Commitment and support are provided from other areas and management; and
- Teams with information and skills can replace the old hierarchy.

In short, this organizational empowerment model highlights that "empowerment is not magic. It consists of a few simple steps and a lot of persistence" (Blanchard et al., 1996: 115).

Furthermore, Chernish (2001) provides three additional reasons why leisure organizations should develop organizations that empower frontline employees. First, frontline employees provide a large portion of leisure service delivery and are fundamentally responsible for dealing with customers (e.g., questions, complaints). Second, many aspects of a leisure experience are distributed at various locations, making it necessary for employees to operate with a high degree of independence. Third, because leisure service workers frequently interact with participants (e.g., leading youth camps), close supervision is difficult or impractical.

The University of Northern Iowa's *Camp Adventure*™ youth services program makes its front-line leadership a focus for its activities. As indicated in the program's Values and Traditions statement, "Our bottom line is our frontline leaders . . . We promote positive, caring child/leader interactions . . . Sincerity, genuineness, and caring are our hallmarks . . . *Camp Adventure*™ staff are high on life, high on kids." These statements reflect the intention of the program in promoting the value of part-time/seasonal volunteer leaders and the type of interaction desired within the program. The standards established are high, the training provided is thorough and rigorous, and the results that are achieved are extraordinary. In the *Camp Adventure*™ program, all staff members, not just the management team, are trained for a minimum of seventy hours, usually over an eight-week period.

An excellent example of the management of the interactions that take place between customers and professionals is found at Walt Disney World and Disneyland amusement parks. Nearly all forms of interaction are scripted. When an individual customer is greeted at the front gate, the entire process has been scripted, taught, and rehearsed with employees. This scripting is also done with attractions such as the Jungle Boat ride. In fact, even deviations from the script are identified so that there are no ad-libbed activities. In addition, the custodians are taught appropriate strategies for interacting with customers, called "guests," at Disneyland and Walt Disney World theme parks. The results of such a well-planned, well-coordinated effort are obvious. The Disney theme parks provide enjoyable, pleasant, and customer-friendly leisure experiences. One result of the Disney training effort is the consistency of their services across customers. Visitors can expect the same level of hospitality continuously, and the same experience engineered on a consistent basis.

The effects of well-planned, well-organized, and well-taught programs that focus on customer/leader interactions are numerous. First, and perhaps most important, is that they provide opportunities to promote customer satisfaction. The customer's satisfaction with the leisure experience should be the primary goal of any leisure service organization. Satisfied customers, in turn, develop a degree of loyalty and commitment to the organization. Individuals who have been successfully engaged in a leisure experience will more than likely return on a continuous basis to participate in the activities and programs provided by the organization. Well-managed customer/leader interactions also produce a high degree of employee pride. Such pride often results in greater employee productivity, retention, morale, and, ultimately, excellence. In other words, when "good things are happening" between customers and leaders, both parties are affected in positive ways.

What strategies can be employed to select competent, capable individuals who will be effective when interacting with customers? Most leisure service organizations rely on face-to-face, structured, patterned interviews to select individuals for key roles. What is missing in this approach to selection is that individuals are not observed in the type of work or setting in which they will operate (e.g., face-to-face leadership). Edginton and Hanson (1996: 7) have suggested that "lacking in the selection process is a method of appraisal that effectively links desired performance with an individual's ability to engage in skillful professional practice."

An innovative strategy for interviewing potential frontline staff members, known as the Leadership Assessment Center (LAC), has been discussed by Edginton and Hanson (1996: 7–9). LAC is a process wherein individuals are required to demonstrate or carry out activities similar to those required in an on-the-job role (e.g., teamwork, leadership, energy, ability to lead songs or games). Citing the work of the *Camp Adventure*™ youth services program in pioneering this concept, Edginton and Hanson note that the LAC is "highly spirited, well-organized [and]. . . conveys the program's dynamism and energy as well as serves as a means of gathering relevant information about an individual's capability to perform in the expected or designated role [of youth leader]" (9).

What Interactions Can Be Planned?

Many customer/leader interactions can be planned, organized, and taught to employees of a leisure service organization. The interactions presented here are illustrative of the areas that can be identified and managed within leisure service organizations. They are, by and large, interactions that take place between individuals. Our intention is not to diminish the importance of written or electronically communicated information, but our emphasis here is on the people-to-people interaction.

Any interaction that occurs between people within a leisure service organization contains several factors that can be managed. One factor is the acknowledgment and recognition of the impact of body language. Body language, like other forms of communication, sends a message to customers. However, such communication is nonverbal in nature and is influenced by our gestures, body movement, facial expressions, and so on. A frontline staff person can go through the motions of assisting a customer, but negative body language can convey a sense of impatience, hostility, exasperation, and other messages that tell customers that their patronage is not valued.

Another factor that can be managed is that of the actual verbal interaction that takes place between the customer and the leisure service leader. Every customer deserves to be treated as a unique individual; every leisure experience, every occasion, needs to be presented in such a way as to ensure that the customer has a fully satisfactory experience. Often, continuous interaction with customers, or repetition, leads to robotization of the experience. Robotization of experience takes away feelings of freshness, genuineness, sincerity, and concern for the welfare of the individual. The leisure service leader must guard against treating individual customers like numbers to be processed. Even if the same question is asked time and time again, leisure service leaders must respond as though they have not encountered that question before. Each person must

be treated as if his or her concerns are noteworthy and important.

A good example of robotization is the bureaucratic, red-tape responses that individuals give to customers requesting information about a program or activity. For example, staff may defer questions to others even though they could be of assistance if they really wanted to be. Or, they may use the guise of organizational rules, regulations, and procedures to avoid assisting customers when it would be possible to work within the system to solve a problem or help the customer achieve a goal. Leisure service programmers and leaders need to avoid this bureaucratic cop-out—"I can't do it," "I can't respond," "That isn't my area," "That isn't in my job description." The staff within the organization should be willing to bend the rules (but not break them) if it will help customers meet their needs.

Another manageable factor in customer service is how the customer is engaged. Most leisure services require involvement with the leader. The leader has a responsibility for bringing the customer into the experience. This engagement may involve making an individual feel part of a group, teaching a skill that requires feedback, or simply providing information to help a customer make a decision. In each of these cases, customers must be engaged in a way that makes them a part of the experience. Individuals need to feel comfortable and feel that their involvement in the experience is important and desirable. Otherwise, individuals not engaged by the leader may sit on the sidelines and not become involved.

Finally, every act by a leisure service leader is analyzed for its symbolic meaning. Customers look for meaning in the actions of leaders. Careful attention must be given to the behaviors exhibited by the leader to ensure that the intended message and values are being communicated effectively. Casual comments, as well as more formal pronouncements and directives, make a great impact on people. The leader must be careful to sensibly choose words, phrases, and comments directed to customers. This is especially important because many leisure service leaders are viewed as important role models. The youth coach, the teen leader, the after school care leader, the senior citizen specialist, and other individuals in leadership roles have a great impact on those customers with whom they work.

Customer/leader interactions are complex because people from diverse cultures have different communication styles and behaviors (Dieser, 1997; Jordan, 2001). Table 12.1, adapted from Sue and Sue (2002), highlights different verbal and nonverbal communication styles among people from diverse ethnic cultures. It is paramount that leisure service providers realize the many within- and between-group communication differences that occur within ethnic cultures. For example, although many American Indian people have indirect eye gazes when communicating, there still are American Indian people who will make direct eye contact when communicating.

The leisure service programmer should seek to clarify all potential interactions; no interaction is too small or too insignificant to be discounted. All forms of interaction that occur between staff and customers of a leisure service organization can be scripted out and taught to employees. Further, the interactions that occur between customers of a leisure service organiza-tion can also be managed. Some of the interactions that can be planned, organized, and taught are discussed next.

Programs and Activity Interactions

Programs and activity interactions are certainly an area in which leisure service programmers can script the dialogue. How leisure service leaders teach, how they interact with individuals in an instructional program, how they present information, as well as other program services, can be scripted to ensure that consistency and positive interactions with the customer occur.

Telephone Interaction

The manner in which staff interacts with customers while on the telephone can have a great impact on the image and effectiveness of the organization. The initial greeting sets the stage for the interaction that occurs. For example, immediately thanking customers for their interest in the organization sets a positive tone and should be a standard procedure. To this end, although automated telephone messages can provide customers with pertinent information, customers can become annoyed when they have to spend significant time listening to a message that has little relevance to them. Providing an option to bypass an automated message in order to speak to an employee can increase customer satisfaction and service delivery.

TABLE 12.1 Cross-Ethnic Communication Style Differences

American Indian	Asian American	White Euro North American	African American
Speaks softly/slower	Speaks softly	Speaks loud/fast to control listener	Speaks with affect
Indirect gaze when listening and speaking	Avoidance of eye contact when listening or speaking to high-status persons	Greater eye contact when listening	Direct eye contact when speaking, but less when listening
Interjects less and seldom offers encouragement	Interjects less and seldom offers encouragement	Interrupts, uses head nods as nonverbal markers	Interrupts when possible
Delayed auditory (silence)	Mild delayed auditory (silence)	Quick responses	Very quick responses
Low-key and indirect manner of expression	Low-key and indirect manner of expression	Objective and task-oriented manner of expression	Affective and emotional manner of expression

Informational Exchange

It is surprising to note the number of organizations that do not train their staff to disperse information properly. Usually when people want information from an organization, they want it to be accurate so that they will be able to make an informed decision. Leisure service organizations need to make sure that all individuals have full access to pertinent information or knowledge or are able to refer customers appropriately.

Registration Interactions

Registration procedures for programs can be incredibly frustrating for customers. Organizations should review their procedures periodically to make sure that customers are given accurate, timely information, and that the exchange of money is documented and efficient. For example, on-line registration should be reviewed to ensure that registration procedures are user-friendly and secure. Registration interactions can be organized so that the procedures are made as convenient as possible for customers. Figure 12.4 shows the registration form for the Roselle Park District (Illinois). The form provides a phone number to the inclusion manager so that people with special needs can be included in leisure programs in an appropriate manner. People with disabilities can contact the inclusion manager to arrange for program accommodations (e.g., support staff, specialized equipment).

In addition, the organizational staff should anticipate what will happen during the registration process and plan accordingly. For example, a greater volume of registrants at a particular time would require extra staff to handle the registration efficiently. Staff should also anticipate registrants' questions for additional information about the organization and should have materials available. For example, the registration form presented in Figure 12.5 anticipates the needs of customers by noting that they are to bring a painter's smock for Halloween ceramics.

Office Interactions

It is often assumed that the interactions that occur in an office situation are private and not observed by customers. This is far from the truth. Observations by customers of office interaction have a great impact on their perceptions of the leisure service organization. Office or organizational interactions should be carried on in a professional manner, recognizing that there is an audience.

The Hallmarks of Excellence in Customer/Leader Interactions

What are the hallmarks of excellence in customer/leader interactions? What leader behaviors need to be taught, reinforced, and encouraged within leisure service organizations? Can organizations recruit individuals who exemplify desired behaviors? It is important to remember that excellence in customer/leader interactions does not just occur; careful selection and nurturing of professional staff members is required in order to produce desired results. Positive customer/leader interactions do not occur by chance. When such behaviors are planned, organized, and taught to professional staff members, the result is usually superior performance.

Listed here are some of the behaviors desirable in promoting excellence in customer/leader interactions.

Anticipatory Behavior

It is not enough to respond merely to customer needs. Effective leaders should anticipate customer needs and implement strategies to meet these anticipated needs. The leader should put himself or herself in the place of the customer and attempt to determine what service would be desired.

Working Knowledge of Organization

Informed leisure service leaders are better able to serve customers. Working knowledge of the organization implies that each person understands its vision and mission structure, personnel,

Roselle Park District—Registration Form—630-894-4200

Please read the REGISTRATION INFORMATION on page 31
Insert this form, along with your check or money order payable to the Roselle Park District and drop off or mail to:
Clauss Rec Center, 555 W. Bryn Mawr Avenue, Roselle, IL 60172

FAMILY NAME _____   HOME PHONE NUMBER _____

ADDRESS _____   WORK NUMBER _____

CITY, STATE, ZIP _____   E-mail: _____

Participant's Name	Date of Birth	Male/Female	Program Title	Program Code	* 2nd Choice	Fee
Participant Notes/Needs:						
OFFICE USE: initials _____ Pd by CA _____ Ck # _____ CC _____ Rec # _____					**TOTAL**	

*Second choice programs should be indicated in this column with a check (✓). If program fees are not equal, please pay the higher amount; the balance will be immediately refunded if necessary. Participants will automatically be placed in their second choice if the first choice is filled. For additional classes, this form may be duplicated. All registrations are subject to the regular cancellation policy. **Is special assistance required? Please call 894-4200.**

Important! - Registration must be signed and be accompanied with full payment to be processed.

WAIVER AND RELEASE OF ALL CLAIMS

Please read this form carefully and be aware that in registering yourself or your minor child/ward for participation in the above program/programs, you will be waiving and releasing all claims for injuries you or your child/ward might sustain arising out of the above program/programs.

"I recognize and acknowledge that there are certain risks of physical injury to participants in the above program(s) and I agree to assume the full risk of any such injuries, damages or loss regardless of severity which I or my child/ward may have against the Park District and its officers, agents, servants and employees as a result of participating in any of the above program(s). I waive and relinquish all claims I or my children may have against the Park District and its officers, agents, servants and employees from any and all claims from injuries, damage or loss which I or my child/ward may have or which may accrue to me or my child/ward on account of my participation or the participation of my child/ward in any of the above program(s). I further agree to indemnify and hold harmless and defend the Park District and its officers, agents, servants and employees from any and all claims resulting from injuries, damages and losses sustained by me or by my child/ward, and arising out, connected with, or in any way associated with the activities of any of the program(s)."

"I understand that unless specifically stated in writing at the time of registration, photographs of participants may be taken and used for promotional purposes."

Registration will be accepted by mail or fax. You may mail your form to Roselle Park District or send by facsimile transmission to (630) 894-5610. When registering by fax, it is mutually understood that the facsimile registration document (including the **waiver and release of all claims**) shall substitute for and have the same legal effect as the original form.

"I have read and fully understand the above program details and waiver and release of all claims.

_____
Participant (18 years & older or Guardian)

_____
Participant (18 years & older or Guardian)

_____
Date

When registering for an adult program, each adult must sign

CREDIT CARD PAYMENT
Minimum amount if paying by credit card $15.00
Please complete the following:

❏ Visa ❏ MasterCard   Cardholder No ☐☐☐☐☐☐☐☐☐☐☐☐☐☐☐☐☐

Amount _____ Name as it appears on credit card _____

Expiration Date _____ Authorized Signature _____

Figure 12.4 Registration Form, Roselle Park District, Roselle, Illinois.

Willamalane
PARK AND RECREATION DISTRICT

765 North A Street,
Springfield, OR 97477-4770
(503) 746-1669

DO YOU RECALL WHERE YOU FIRST HEARD ABOUT THIS PROGRAM? (Check one)

Quarterly Tabloid ☐	Family Members/Friends ☐
Willamalane Flyer ☐	Newspaper ☐
Radio ☐	Other ______

BRING A PAINTER'S SHIRT/SMOCK.

OFFICE USE ONLY

Dist. $3.50 Non-Dist. $5.25
Date ______ Initial ______
Receipt No. ______
Sig. Card Out ______ Ret'd. ______

Name ______ LAST ______ FIRST ______ (PLEASE PRESS FIRMLY)
Address ______
City ______ Zip Code ______
TLN 30132 Program HALLOWEEN CERAMICS (AGES 3-5)
Date(s) 10/30 START ______ END ______ Day(s) TU Time 3-4P
Doctor ______ Phone ______

Revenue # 00000000000000
Birthdate ______ Age ______
Home Phone ______
Emergency Phone ______
Work Phone ______
Instructor ______
Location YOLANDA ELEMENTARY
Insurance Company ______

Medical Information (Allergies, Asthma, etc.) ______

The undersigned releases Willamalane Park & Recreation District from all liability which may arise from participation of the undersigned in the said program. In the event the participant is under the age of 18, the undersigned agrees to hold the District harmless from any liability it may suffer through the participation of the child in said program. The undersigned hereby requests and permits any hospital emergency department physician, any other physicians he or she may wish to designate and any hospital personnel to render to the above named applicant any medical and/or surgical treatment he/she may require in my absence.

Signature ______ (PARENT OR GUARDIAN SIGNATURE IF APPLICANT UNDER 18) ______ RELATIONSHIP TO APPLICANT

Figure 12.5 Registration Form, Willamalane Park and Recreation District, Springfield, Oregon.

and, most importantly, programs and services. It is surprising how compartmentalized the work of individuals within many organizations is. Working knowledge of an organization can help solve customer problems and create a stronger image of the organization.

Attention to Detail

Little things are what make the difference between a mediocre organizational effort and a superior performance. Attention to detail requires thought, planning, and a creative nature. As Zeithaml, Parasuraman, and Berry (1990: 6) note, "service leaders are interested in the details and nuances of service, seeing opportunities in small actions that competitors might consider trivial. They believe that how an organization handles the little things sets the tone for how it handles the big things. They also believe that the little things add up for the customer and make a big difference."

Competence

The idea of competence is important to the delivery of leisure programs and activities from the standpoint of customer confidence as well as having a leader who is able to perform the function that has been promoted. Zeithaml, Parasuraman, and Berry (1990: 21) have written that competence can be thought of as the possession of the required skills and knowledge to perform a service.

Sincerity

In working with customers, sincere behavior is an important attribute to demonstrate. Sincere individuals operate without deceit, pretense, or hypocrisy. They are individuals who are straightforward in their interactions with the customer.

Friendliness

Friendliness is a characteristic that is manifested in supportive, helping types of behaviors. A friendly person acts in a kindly fashion and is not hostile in his or her behavior toward others. People who promote friendliness have amiable, positive, and supportive relationships with people.

Belief in the Power and Value of What One Does

Perhaps nothing is more powerful than the commitment that a professional makes to pursuing an ideal. For example, belief in the power and value of play is an ideal upon which professional practice is built. Believing in something creates a certain passion and commitment. This passion and commitment is often translated to the customer. Belief in what one does often results in pride. It shows up in details, such as the way that people are dressed, to more important issues, like the way customers are treated.

Empathy

Empathy refers to the caring attitude demonstrated toward individuals as well as to individualized attention (Zeithaml, Parasuraman, and Berry, 1990). In other words, to be empathetic means to understand or be "into" another person's feelings or motives. Empathetic people are generally individuals who are sensitive to others.

Assurance

The customer develops a rapport or an experience with staff or an organization in general that provides a degree of assurance that their needs will be met. In other words, customers develop a sense of trust and confidence in the organization and its staff such that they know that the services they receive will be provided with quality and in a way that will meet or exceed their expectations.

Courtesy

Courtesy is the politeness or generosity demonstrated by the leader in interacting with the customer. Courteous behavior often involves making the customer feel comfortable, being kind, or showing special consideration for the unique needs of an individual.

Problem-Solving Orientation

The ability to help customers solve problems is an important behavior to be exhibited by leisure service leaders. The ability of leaders to help customers overcome barriers to a satisfying leisure experience is essential. Having a problem-solving orientation means being concerned about the welfare of the customer and trying to find ways to resolve issues that stand in the way of successful participation.

High Standards and a Commitment to Excellence

Having high standards suggests a commitment to excellence. "True service leaders aspire to legendary service; they realize that good service may not be good enough to differentiate their organization from other organizations . . . Service leaders are zealous about implementing the service right the first time. They value that goal of zero defects" (Zeithaml, Parasuraman, and Berry, 1990: 6).

Integrity

Integrity refers to an individual's uprightness, honesty, and sincerity. In the discussion of integrity, Zeithaml, Parasuraman, and Berry (1990: 7) have remarked that "one of the essential characteristics of service leaders is personal integrity. The best leaders value doing the right things, even when inconvenient or costly. They place a premium on being fair, consistent, and truthful."

Enthusiasm/Energy

Enthusiasm is an essential element in providing positive customer/leader interactions. People who demonstrate enthusiasm are inspired and eagerly interested in other people and their causes. Enthusiasm, like the commitment that one makes to an ideal, is contagious. Energetic people are often thought of as being very vigorous and dynamic. In the leisure service area, people with energy motivate or energize others to action.

Communications

Effective communications are fundamental to successful customer/leader interactions. As Zeithaml, Parasuraman, and Berry (1990: 22) have suggested, communication involves "keeping customers informed in the language they understand and listening to them."

Generosity

Individuals who are generous are willing to give of themselves or share with others. Generous people are unselfish individuals who are willing to go the extra mile to ensure that the customer has a satisfying leisure experience.

Service Orientation

A service orientation can be thought of as the extent to which an individual focuses his or her attention on the needs of customers. As Rado (1989: 67) has noted, "Customer service includes any activities that demonstrate an attention to customer needs and desires." Having a service orientation means attempting to understand the perception of the customer and placing the needs of the customer foremost.

Access

Access is described as the ability of the customer to approach and interact with the leader; it is the ease of contact that the customer has with the leader (Zeithaml, Parasuraman, and Berry, 1990: 22).

Care and Concern

Of all the qualities that are essential to creating excellence in customer/leader interactions, care and concern are perhaps the most important. Care and concern for other people involve trying to understand their needs and relate to their welfare. A concern for others means a dedication to helping them with compassion and interest.

Freedom from Risk

Most leisure service programs and activities contain an element of risk. Freedom from either psychological or physical risk can influence the success or failure of the leisure experience. Leaders should work to allay customers' fears and enhance customers' competence to participate in leisure events and activities.

Credibility

The credibility of customer/leader interactions refers to the trustworthiness, believability, and honesty of the transaction that takes place (Zeithaml, Parasuraman, and Berry, 1990: 21). Usually the onus for establishing credibility rests on the individual providing the service or is a manifestation of the value of the organization itself.

Striving for Partnerships

The relationship that should emerge between the customer and the leader is one of mutual benefit. Mutually beneficial relationships or partnerships have no losers; rather, the parties strive for a win/win situation. Partners have an equal commitment to the welfare of each other and are able to experience satisfaction from the interaction. The satisfaction for the customer is excellence in the leisure experience, and the leader derives personal satisfaction, organizational profit, or both.

Appearance

The degree to which customers perceive the organization to be competent and well-organized may well be influenced by the physical appearance of the leader. A leader who is disheveled and unkempt will present an unfavorable organizational image. By the same token, the leader who is dressed appropriately for the leisure experience and who takes pride in his or her appearance will convey a more professional and polished image.

Consistency

No matter how many times the leisure service leader has successfully implemented a given service, he or she should approach each new customer and each new situation with the same level of intensity. Once excellence has been achieved, consistency is the next goal. To be consistently excellent in the provision of a service from one situation to the next is a hallmark of outstanding customer/leader interactions.

Reliability

Zeithaml, Parasuraman, and Berry (1990: 21) have written that reliability is the ability to perform the promised service dependably and accurately. Crompton and MacKay (1989) have studied the importance of service quality dimensions in selected public recreation programs. They found that reliability consistently emerged across programs as the most important dimension of service quality (367). Further, MacKay and Crompton (1990) have also reported that perceptions of the importance of various service quality dimensions vary according to type of activity.

Positive Attitude

One's attitude toward the customer can have a great impact on the reception of the program or activity. Upbeat, direct, and encouraging interactions with customers usually reflect a positive attitude. The positiveness in this attitude can be transmitted to other individuals.

Responsiveness

Responsiveness is the desire and willingness to help customers and to be prompt in providing programs and services (Zeithaml, Parasuraman, and Berry, 1990: 21). Individuals like to feel that when they communicate their needs, the leader is attentive. People hate to be ignored and made to feel that their needs are not important. Being responsive is attending to people's needs in such a way that they are made to feel important and special.

Establishing a Positive Physical Climate

Zeithaml, Parasuraman, and Berry (1990: 21) have noted that the appearance of physical facilities, equipment, personnel, and communication materials can influence the extent to which customers view a service as being of high quality. Leisure service organizations can establish a climate that promotes positive customer service. Both the physical environment and the service environment should communicate to customers that their patronage is desired. The physical environment can have an impact on the customers' perceptions of whether the organization is customer friendly. A clean, well-organized, well-ordered, and warm environment communicates the positive intentions of a leisure service organization to its customers better than a disorganized, cluttered, and cold environment does.

Demonstrating Appreciation

Individuals like to feel as if their business is valued and that they are appreciated. Thanking an individual for contributing to your organization's success is good business. The best way to thank individuals is to do it on a day-to-day basis via word of mouth; a word of thanks goes a long way.

Such behaviors must be taught, maintained, and reinforced on a continuous basis. Being customer-oriented means being attentive to those factors that make the leisure experience satisfying to the individual and make leisure areas and facilities hospitable and attractive. No organization should assume that its employees will be oriented toward its customers. Behaviors that lead to positive customer relations should be reinforced and individuals should be given continuous feedback (both positive and corrective) on their performance related to service behaviors. Creating positive customer/leader interactions is no secret; it simply means operating so the customer's "current situation, frame of mind, and needs are addressed" (Albrecht and Zemke, 1985: 32).

Management Strategies for Programming

Several total system designs to promote quality in leisure programming have been identified. In particular, three strategies—Just-in-Time (JIT) Programming, Total Quality Program Planning (TQP), and Agile Leisure Programming—have emerged in the literature and have been successfully employed in professional practice.

Just-in-Time (JIT) Programming

The Just-in-Time Programming concept involves "using only enough effort or investment to obtain the results needed to meet changing market demand while still being consistent with organizational purpose and long-term goals" (Glancy et al., 1984: 2). JIT is borrowed from Japanese corporate management, known as Kanban or just-in-time management. An example of how the JIT concept can be applied to leisure programming is "by allowing the size and nature of the program to be directly proportional to the needs of the customer" (p. 10). One way, according to Glancy (p. 13), that program management functions can be streamlined is to establish "multi-year goal plans, rapid person-to-person communication, assessing needs, and pilot testing and evaluating."

Edginton, Little, and DeGraaf (1992: 69) have suggested that "JIT programming involves creating a system for planning and organizing services." These authors maintain that effort must be taken to minimize the investment of resources prior to implementation. As these authors suggest:

JIT Programming Is NOT
- A rationale for being unprepared
- A way to reduce the number of staff or inventory in order to get a better return on a leisure service system's assets

JIT Programming IS
- An explicit plan
- A process which utilizes experts/professionals

- Discipline
- An investment
- Being organic
- Being prepared to implement stress and coping strategies
- A means of solving problems (pp. 72–73)

Discussing the cost of implementing JIT in the delivery of services as contrasted with the manufacturing of products, Edginton, Little, and DeGraaf (1992: 73) have suggested a number of challenges. First, they observe that "leanness creates intense pressure and large expectations." Further, they suggest that the success of the JIT concept rests on being able to forecast or predict accurately the leisure needs of individuals. Last, they note that a great deal of ambiguity and flexibility is required in the process. Dealing with ambiguity is difficult for large bureaucracies that are unable to flex their resources rapidly to meet changing leisure dynamics.

Total Quality Program Planning (TQP)

Total Quality Program Planning is a concept that was derived from the work of W. Edwards Deming (Edginton and Edginton, 1993b: 40). The concept is based on the idea that quality can be sought within organizations if they are involved first in the creation of benchmarks and then in the continuous measurement of achievement. Total Quality Program Planning empowers employees to be a part of the process of improving leisure services. TQP focuses on several action areas, including the following (p. 42):

1. Leadership that Produces a Commitment to Quality
2. Exceeding Expectations
3. Excellence in Customer Service
4. Knowledge of Leisure Behavior
5. Customer-Centered Planning
6. Setting High-Impact Objectives
7. Quality Assurance
8. Teaming to Problem Solve
9. Using Performance Data

A paramount component of the TQP model is that of exceeding minimum levels of expectations and achievement (Edginton, Hudson, and Lankford, 2001; Jamieson and Wolter, 1999). Whereas a large gap between participant expectations and perceptions of services leads to a quality gap, services that exceed expectations lead to customer satisfaction (O'Neill, 2001—see page 391 of this chapter). The TQP concept of exceeding customer expectations is posited in the following quotation by Edginton, Hudson, and Lankford (2001): "[The TQP model] is directed toward exceeding expectations by constantly improving both the impact and processes used in program planning" (73). In this regard, the TQP model has been successfully adapted to youth organizations (see Edginton and Edginton, 1994). In particular, these authors created a system wherein programs have a core of youth development principles, yet also focus on exceeding levels of achievement and expectations (providing quality).

Agile Leisure Programming

Agile leisure programming is another concept drawn from business and industry. The concept of agility suggests that organizations have the ability to move quickly and rapidly to meet changing market conditions. To respond nimbly to the changing dynamics of the leisure market, organizations must position themselves to move their resources rapidly. Being fluid, responsive, and alert are all hallmarks of agile organizations.

Agile leisure programming is a concept framed by Edginton and Edginton (1993a), adapting information from the Agile Manufacturing Enterprise Forum (EMEF) and Nagle and Dove to the leisure services field. Edginton and Edginton (1993a) suggest that organizations using this concept will transform the way that they do business. Agility in leisure service organizations is "achieved by applying knowledge to leverage the information, skills, and decision-making capabilities of the leisure service organization to produce relevant, current, and meaningful leisure experiences" (p. 1). The characteristics of agile leisure organizations are as follows (p. 8):

1. Coordination of All Functions into an Integrated Whole (Known as Concurrency)
2. Focus on Human Resources
3. Customer Responsiveness
4. Flexible (Re-)Configuration to Accommodate Short Program Life Cycles
5. Open Organizational Architecture
6. Optimum First Time Design
7. Improvement of Quality over Product Life Cycle
8. Technology and Information Sensitivity
9. Vision-Based Management

Application of agile management principles requires anticipatory behaviors on the part of leisure service programmers. It requires that leisure service programmers attempt to look into the future, scrutinize it and apply forward thinking in such a way as to affect program planning and implementation. People in society today are faced with great and continuous change. Being agile allows the leisure service programmer to be flexible, to focus on quality, and to apply technology and information management in a way that structures leisure services to be more meaningful and relevant to the customer.

SUPERVISING LEISURE SERVICE PERSONNEL

Most leisure service activities and events are implemented by seasonal, part-time, or volunteer staff. For example, it is estimated that in the organized camping field, more than 300,000 seasonal staff members are employed to serve as camp counselors, program specialists, and instructors. Such employees are also found in leisure services that are operated by the government, such as municipal parks and recreation departments, by voluntary organizations, such as the YMCA/YWCA, and by commercial organizations, such as theme parks. The supervision of seasonal and part-time employees is a very important part of the work of leisure service programmers.

Most professionals involved in programming positions in the leisure service field are in supervisory positions. They are responsible for developing program ideas; promoting activities and events; recruiting, selecting, and developing staff; and supervising the work efforts of staff. Supervision is the process of helping individuals perform the tasks that they have been assigned. Supervision is often thought of as monitoring or controlling the work of others. However, in reality, the work of a supervisor is one of encouraging the efforts of others and ensuring that leisure service leaders have the opportunity to perform to their fullest capacity.

Supervision: A Working Definition

The term *supervision* has many meanings. Breaking the word into its two component parts—*super* and *vision*—finds that *super* implies over and above, and *vision* means looking over or above or perceiving abstract images. Supervision has also been associated with the terms *leader* and *master*. In most leisure service organizations, the supervisor is the individual who oversees the people involved in the direct delivery of services. A supervisor may also be responsible for overseeing a program area or facility and may be charged with the responsibility of developing and implementing a series of events or activities.

The U.S. government has provided a definition of a supervisor. The Taft-Hartley Act of 1947 defines a supervisor as follows:

> Any individual having authority, in the interest of the employer, to hire, transfer, suspend, lay off, recall, promote, discharge, assign, reward, or discipline other employees, or responsibility to direct them, or to adjust their grievances, or to effectively recommend such action, if in conjunction with the foregoing exercise of such authority is not of a merely routine or clerical nature, but requires the use of independent judgment.

This all-encompassing definition indicates that the work of the supervisor involves a wide variety of managerial functions related to human resources.

Another perspective in defining supervision comes from Terry (1978: 6). He notes that "supervision means achieving desired results through the efforts of others in a manner that provides challenge, interest, and satisfaction in the use of human talents." The emphasis in this definition is on effectively using human resources to achieve desired results. Terry maintains that the supervisor "suggests to the . . . [leisure service leader] . . . how to do it, create and maintain a work environment conducive to a person's personal development, encourage the growth of the person's abilities to their fullest potential, and aid in satisfying both the organizational and individual wants from the job efforts."

Most supervisors not only must have technical knowledge of the program activities or events that they are supervising, but obviously they must be able to work effectively with other people. Most supervisors of leisure service organizations have been in direct service roles and, as a result, often have first-hand knowledge of the problems associated with organizing and implementing leisure services. The work of the leisure service programmer as a supervisor is challenging and complex and is the focal point for the creation of most program efforts within leisure service organizations. Leisure service supervisors are often called on to set standards, create a work agenda, observe behavior, motivate employees, and evaluate the impact of leisure experiences on customers.

Roles and Responsibilities of the Leisure Service Supervisor

Asking 100 leisure service supervisors to identify their specific roles and responsibilities would probably elicit 100 different answers. Each leisure service organization, each job setting that a supervisor works within, and each individual with whom the supervisor works create a great deal of diversity and situation-specific activity. Every supervisory job will be different and uniquely tailor-made for the needs of a given leisure service organization. However, a number of general roles and responsibilities are often associated with the work of leisure service supervisors. According to Boyd (1984: 17–18), some of the roles and responsibilities of the leisure service supervisors are production, quality, cost, methods, morale, training, and safety. Following is a brief description of each of these facets of supervision.

Production

Production, in terms of work within leisure service organizations, refers to the creation of leisure experiences and associated activities (such as the management of concession operations) that contribute to successful programming efforts. The work of the leisure service supervisor in this case is to ensure that leisure events and activities are created in a manner consistent with the vision, mission, goals, and objectives of the organization. It means identifying resources and bringing these resources to bear in a timely, prompt, and meaningful fashion.

Quality

Quality is a perception of excellence that is created or held within the mind of the customer. Today, customers expect high-quality leisure services. The leisure service supervisor can promote high quality by setting high standards, staying in touch with customers, and observing the way in which activities or events are implemented. Quality requires constant attention to the methods and procedures used in delivering services. Higher quality programs are produced when the supervisor and direct-service personnel work in harmony to produce leisure activities and events.

Cost

Boyd (1984: 17) states that cost control and cost reduction are essential in profit, nonprofit, and government organizations. He suggests that supervisors should strive, through cost-control and cost-reduction measures, to enhance the profitability of commercial organizations, and in other types of organizations, the highest quality services should be provided at the lowest possi-

ble expenditure of funds. According to Boyd, "supervisors can help employees understand that they, too, have a responsibility to contribute to cost control and cost reduction." Leisure service supervisors usually contribute to the development and control of budgets and resource attainment plans. In this way, they are able to contribute significantly to the management of finances within leisure service organizations and contribute directly to improving an organization's fiscal well-being.

Methods

The specific methods and procedures used to conduct leisure events and activities usually fall under the direction of the leisure service supervisor. The methods and procedures employed all contribute to cost and quality control. Therefore, careful attention must be given to identifying and continuously reviewing the methods and procedures employed within leisure service organizations. Finding ways to improve work methods and procedures by identifying new technology, by improving patterns of interactions with customers, and by developing new management systems are all part of the leisure service supervisor's roles and responsibilities. A new work method or procedure may very well spell the difference between success or failure within a program. Constant innovation, as well as thoughtful attention and investigation, is required in this area.

Morale

Supervisors also have a responsibility to create and maintain positive morale within the leisure service organization. Morale is the attitude that people have toward their work environment. Morale can be either positive or negative. Positive morale can reflect on the productivity of the organization. Positive morale can create esprit de corps and pride, and can instill a "can do" attitude among employees. Individuals and organizations today often look to their work environments for support. A positive, upbeat, friendly work environment that is conducive to good morale can be an important dimension in creating and maintaining excellent work situations.

Training

There are three types of training that leisure service supervisors organize and implement—orientation, in-service, and developmental. Orientation training helps individuals learn about the organization's values and philosophy. In addition, orientation training often presents information about an organization's structure, roles, and methods and procedures for conducting business. In-service training reinforces previously taught information, upgrades existing skills and knowledge by introducing new technology or methods and procedures for conducting business, and encourages brainstorming for solving existing and emerging organizational problems. Developmental training focuses on the enhancement of the human resources of an organization, with no specific task or job -related function in mind. Developmental training helps individuals develop themselves with the assumption that as people within an organization improve, the organization as a whole is enriched.

Safety Management

Ensuring that leisure experiences are provided and maintained in a safe manner is an important role of the leisure service supervisor. The same can be said about work environments for employees. It is the supervisor's responsibility to ensure that physical work spaces and the procedures that are employed are safe for staff members. The Occupational Safety and Health Act (OSHA) places a strong responsibility on leisure service organizations to maintain safe work environments. OSHA has established guidelines that can be reviewed and used to guide the development of supervisory activities in this area.

Appraising Staff

Supervisors also find themselves involved in the appraisal of direct-service staff. The appraisal function helps individuals understand the criteria used in the evaluation process, establish goals for the future, receive feedback, and discuss ways in which they can change their work procedures or behaviors. The supervisor may occasionally be involved in disciplinary actions. The key to effective handling of disciplinary actions is to keep employees well informed about shortcomings in their performance, to let them know the expectations for their performance, and to allow them the opportunity to correct their performance. If these measures are not effective, more severe measures up to and including dismissal may be necessary.

Removing Barriers: A Supervisory Function of Leisure Service Programmers

One of the most important functions of a leisure service programmer is that of removing barriers that prevent leisure service personnel from implementing programs effectively. To paraphrase Peter Drucker (1985), "the one and only responsibility of . . . [leisure service programmers as supervisors] . . . is to ensure that employees do what they get paid to do." The best way to help individuals do their jobs effectively is to assist in the removal of barriers that prevent them from doing their work successfully.

What are some of the barriers that leisure service programmers can help employees overcome? Numerous specific problems can emerge in any given leisure service setting. In fact, the removal of barriers is probably a day-to-day activity. However, some of the more general ones include the following:

Lack of Knowledge of the Vision and Mission of the Organization

How do individuals fit into an organization? What is the relationship of their effort to the total effort of the organization? What ends or aims is the organization working toward? How can the work of individuals delivering leisure services be integrated with the overarching goals of the leisure service organization? Clarification of these issues can serve to strengthen the work of individuals providing direct services. Lack of knowledge often creates a barrier to achieving the goals of the organization.

Lack of Task and Role Clarity

One barrier to the delivery of services occurs when leaders do not have adequate knowledge of the tasks or roles that they are to perform. In other words, when people don't understand what is expected of them, they can become frustrated, perform poorly, and/or engage in inappropriate work activities. The leisure service programmer must have appropriate technical knowledge to be able to explain to individuals how a task is to be carried out and how the leader's work is related to other functions, people, and resources within the organization.

Fear of Failure

When individuals within organizations are criticized for trying new methods or new procedures, they will usually withdraw from further attempts to be innovative. The lack of such innovation reduces potential gains. One of the most important roles that the leisure service programmer can play is to create an environment in which people are not afraid to try new methods. Such experimentation often leads to greater productivity, innovation, and creativity. People will not risk failure if the consequences of failure are inordinately high. Robert Toalson, general manager of the Champaign (Illinois) Park District, operates his organization using what he calls "the mistake philosophy: that is, if you are not making any mistakes, you are not trying anything new."

Lack of Proper Supplies, Equipment, and Materials

The lack of proper resources—supplies, equipment, and materials—can be a great impediment to implementing successful leisure experiences. One of the great challenges faced by leisure service programmers is to provide the right amount of resources at the right time and at the right place. People need the proper tools to do their jobs. Without adequate resources, employees will find it extremely difficult to successfully implement events and activities. Often, providing supplies, equipment, and materials means that the leisure service programmer will have a working knowledge of the needs of a given program or service and will create a distribution system that ensures the availability of these resources.

Excessive Bureaucracy or Red Tape

Work in most leisure service organizations is organized bureaucratically. This means that the organizations have created rules, policies, and procedures to help achieve their goals. Such bureaucracy often becomes stifling, formidable, and difficult to understand. Most of all, it is frustrating. Leisure service programmers must humanize the rules, policies, and procedures of the organization so that they are reasonable, prudent, and applicable to various situations. Doing things by the book is important, but one of the functions of the leisure service programmer is to use common sense in interpreting rules, policies, and procedures so as to assist individuals in successfully implementing their leisure activities or events.

Lack of Social and Emotional Support

Individuals implementing leisure services are not unlike any other employee. They need support in a variety of forms. People seek approval and praise, as well as empathy, from others in the work environment. They want to be supported in their efforts, socially and emotionally. Providing social and emotional support may involve giving encouragement, cheering the work of individuals, facilitating their efforts, and instilling confidence. Providing social and emotional support to individuals often makes the work environment more humane, less stressful, and more considerate.

Lack of Recognition

The lack of recognition of the efforts of individuals implementing services often produces feelings of apathy and frustration. People develop the notion, "if my leisure service superior doesn't care to recognize me for my efforts, why try harder?" There are many ways to recognize people for their contributions to the work of an organization. Recognition can occur formally or informally. It can be done on a casual basis, or it can be done in such a way as to bring attention and distinction to the work of an individual. Recognition of the efforts of most people is best accomplished by thanking them, showing them that they are appreciated, and reinforcing their own sense of self-worth. The glib, "one-minute manager approach" of methodically, mechanically dishing out praise is not sufficient; praise must be sincere, heartfelt, and genuine to be effective.

Lack of Orientation, In-service, and Developmental Training

Individuals need to be oriented in a formal way to the vision and mission of an organization. These values need to be reinforced and promoted continuously, and new approaches, strategies, and techniques for providing services need to be discussed on an ongoing basis. Leisure service programmers can help direct-service providers by effectively orienting and training them prior to implementation of activities and by helping them acquire new skills and knowledge. Training and development programs can also be established as a way of helping individuals solve problems. These efforts can encourage the creativity of individuals and energize their efforts by providing stimulating challenges and other motivational activities. Often when people are grouped together for training and development programs, synergy occurs, thereby encouraging the formulation of new ideas and new ways of solving problems.

To help individuals implement leisure services effectively, the programmer must ensure that those persons have the autonomy and authority to carry out their assigned tasks. One of the greatest difficulties that direct-service providers face is oversupervision. There is a fine line between offering appropriate supervisory suggestions and recommendations, and stifling the work of individuals. The leisure service programmer has to make sure that values and assigned tasks are carried out, but not at the expense of individuals' creativity, spontaneity, and dignity. Subordinates might not do the job exactly as the supervisor would do it; however, that is often part of the learning process. The leisure service programmer should establish high standards and challenge individuals to meet them, but also create a safety net that is supportive and prevents failure.

MANAGING THE PROGRAM FLOW

One of the most important elements in delivering leisure programs and services is recruiting customers into a leisure experience and then retaining them. How do leisure service programmers create environments that are compelling to individuals, and once they have individuals within these environments, how do they ensure that the anticipated goals for the program will be accomplished? How do leisure service programmers create "magic" for their customers? Magic occurs when the reality of the leisure experience exceeds the customers' expectations. These questions are, indeed, difficult and challenging ones facing leisure service programmers. The questions require programmers to pay attention to customers and to manage the flow of customers while they move through a leisure experience.

In Chapter 2, we discussed the idea that programmers can manage the animation of an event as it moves through time. It is this animation to which we are referring when we speak of the program flow. In other words, *program flow is the movement from one activity to another throughout the life of a given leisure experience.* Activities within a leisure program can be coordinated and integrated with one another to produce an overall experience. Individuals can be encouraged and nurtured; their emotions can be heightened and lowered; their intellects and perceptions can be stimulated in a sequential format that produces the desired program goal or goals. Further, individuals can be given very active roles in shaping their own leisure experiences. Choice can be introduced, control can be reduced, spontaneity and freedom can be encouraged.

The Social Recreation Curve

Probably the earliest recognition of the idea that program flow could be managed was in the formats applied to the management of social recreation activities. A social recreation activity began with icebreakers, followed by mixers, and then more active recreational pursuits. As the program peaked, active activities were reduced and more passive ones introduced. In the literature of the leisure service field, this concept is known as the *social recreation curve.*

Perhaps the most complete discussion of the social recreation curve concept has been developed by Ford (1974: 81–94). Figure 12.6 presents Ford's model of the social recreation curve. In discussing this model, Ford notes that planning programs possess a curve of action to follow. She writes:

In social activities, the pitch of excitement is at a natural quiet or low level as the participants arrive and "start warming up" to the activities and each other. The planner wants the group to leave the event calmly and quietly also. This means that the leader plans through the social

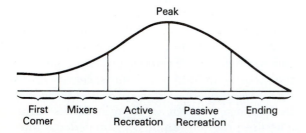

Figure 12.6 Social Recreation Curve. (From Ford, P. M. 1974. *Informal Recreational Activities.* Bradford Woods, IN: American Camping Association.)

events and socialization, that the high pitch of the event will be mid-way through the time of the program (p. 90).

The social recreation curve enables the programmer to engage customers immediately and cut the program at its emotional high. The assumption is that individuals can be guided through a process that will enhance social interaction and create memorable experiences. This approach to managing program flow works and has been successfully applied by leisure service programmers for years. It is a practical, hands-on mechanism for moving from one activity to another; activities are sequenced in relation to one another in a purposeful manner.

Managing the Autotelic Experience

Another example of managing the program flow is more theoretical in nature but suggests the same end. Csikszentmihalyi (1993; 1997) developed a concept known as the *autotelic experience.* An autotelic experience is an activity that a person does for its own sake (intrinsic motivation) because to experience it is the main goal (Csikszentmihalyi, 1997). That is to say, leisure (intrinsic motivation and perceived freedom) occurs when an individual experiences a loss of ego (or individuality) by engaging in an autotelic activity because of sheer enjoyment (Csikszentmihalyi, 1990). In this state, the individual is in control of his or her actions and the environment. The individual has no active awareness of control, but is simply not worried by the possibility of the lack of control or failure. This autotelic state is known as *flow* (see Csikszentmihalyi, 1993, 1997).

Figure 12.7 presents a model of the flow state (Csikszentmihalyi, 1997). In regard to leisure programming, the leisure service provider is to assist individuals in entering the state of flow. Ultimately, the leisure programmer wants to match a challenge from a leisure activity (e.g., chess, dancing, hiking) with the participant's skill level. If the challenge level falls below a participant's skill level, the leisure activity will result in apathy or boredom. If the challenge

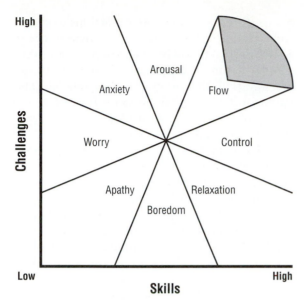

Figure 12.7 A Model of the Flow State. (From Csikszentmihalyi, 1997.)

level is beyond the skill level of the participant, the leisure activity will result in anxiety or worry. In other words, the leisure programmer attempts to match the customer's skill level with a challenge that will produce an experience that is stimulating but not overwhelming.

To this end, Dattilo, Kleiber, and Williams (1998) developed the self-determination and enjoyment enhancement (SDEE) model to help people experience flow and enjoyment. Although their original model was developed to help people with disabilities experience flow, most leisure programmers can implement their suggestions. Four components of this model include self-determination, intrinsic motivation, perception of manageable challenge, and investment of attention. Self-determination involves acting as a primary causal agent in one's life. To encourage the development of self-determination, leisure programmers can provide the following strategies:

- Provide participants with opportunities to express preferences (e.g., providing an option-rich environment).

- Help participants set leisure goals and make choices (leisure education).
- Develop self-awareness (debriefing after an activity).

Intrinsic motivation refers to motivation and decision making that are free from external influences. There is considerable overlap between self-determination and intrinsic motivation—intrinsic motivation energizes behaviors and results in feelings of self-determination. To encourage intrinsic motivation, leisure programmers can provide the following approaches:

- Help participants realize the importance of inherent rewards, as opposed to external awards (e.g., providing positive feedback as opposed to trophies or prizes for successful participation).
- Assist participants in focusing on internal standards of activities, rather than on external standards (e.g., focusing on self-improvement rather than on winning a prize).
- Have clients become aware of their interests (e.g., observing leisure activities).

Perceptions of manageable challenge are oriented toward helping participants improve the likelihood of a good match between challenges and skills. Again, this match is what develops flow and enjoyment. To improve the probability that a good match between challenges and skills occurs, leisure programmers can provide the following actions:

- Assess the participant's skill level (e.g., leisure programmer observes the participant while participating in an activity [e.g., swimming] and makes suggestions regarding appropriate challenge level [swimming lesson level]).
- Help the participant make changes or adaptations associated with a leisure activity (e.g., teaching a participant a different way to grip a golf club).
- Help the participant gain an accurate appraisal of the challenge (e.g., realizing that fear is a normal aspect before a dance competition).
- Assist the participant in developing activity skills (e.g., teaching basketball shooting skills).

Investment of attention refers to helping participants focus attention on the leisure activity or task. Focusing attention on a leisure activity can be enhanced via the following tactics:

- Design a leisure activity in an environment that has few distractions (e.g., facilitating an art program in a room that is away from pedestrian traffic).
- Help participants realize that positive and successful leisure activities are due to their efforts (e.g., verbal persuasion or feedback from recreation leader).

By following the four components of the SDEE model, and the accompanying actions/strategies of each component, customers will have a greater likelihood of experiencing flow (enjoyment).

Managing Program Animation

Program animation is the action of the activity or event. The leisure service programmer puts into motion an event or activity. He or she establishes and controls the animation of the program by ensuring that certain events occur in a timely and sequential pattern. In discussing the idea of program animation, Rossman (1989: 11) has written that the leisure service programmer "anticipates and plans how the action sequences of a program will unfold and then puts in place the elements necessary to guide the interactions." In this approach, the programmer tries to "anticipate and predict the outcomes of the interactions within a program and the order in which the events will unfold."

Managing the action sequences or the animation of a program is analogous to writing and then conducting a symphony. The leisure service programmer plans each of the events and the way in which they are sequenced. As the event is actually implemented, the leisure service programmer will modify the action sequence established in order to produce the desired outcomes. One interesting fact in this approach to programming is that customers actually play a role in shaping the animation of a leisure experience. In other words, their reactions to events and activities can influence the animation of the leisure experience. They can interact with other people or the environment or both to change the way that the program is sequenced. The opportunity for such action provides for a degree of spontaneity, individuality, and personalization in leisure programs.

Rossman (1993) suggests that a program design can include a plan to animate activities or manage program flow. As Rossman notes, "any technique proposed for planning leisure occasions must allow the design to stimulate the interactions needed to facilitate the program and also enable the programmer to predict the outcomes of different plans. Anticipating possible errors by vicariously experiencing a program with imagined interactions will help reduce errors and facilitate error-free operations" (pp. 30–31).

In implementing programs, a reconfiguration of events is often required to meet the needs of the moment. As the design of the program changes, the leisure service programmer must react to emerging needs and conditions. This makes the program process very dynamic, requiring great sensitivity to the way in which customers are responding to various stimuli in the environment. It requires the leisure service programmer to anticipate changes and be prepared to respond with contingent strategies.

Program Life Cycle

In Chapter 2, the concept of the product life cycle was introduced. Programs also have a life cycle. The concept of the *program life cycle* suggests that events and activities have a life span. This life span can be identified, anticipated, and managed. All programs take off, reach their saturation, and then decline. If modifications are not made (increasing the challenge or complexity, perhaps, or enhancing the novelty of the activity for the customer), interest in the program will diminish.

As a program is implemented, the leisure service programmer must know where the activity is in the program life cycle. If the program is a new activity, it may appear very novel to customers. On the other hand, the lack of familiarity with the activity may decrease the customers' level of involvement and commitment to the activity. The programmer will want to make customers familiar with new activities yet promote those program attributes that might be more attractive to them. When a program reaches the saturation point in terms of customers' interest and becomes more or less routine, the leisure service programmer will want to make sure that the conditions that ensure success are held constant. Finally, as interest in the program declines, modifications in the way the program is packaged, priced, and promoted will be necessary in order to sustain interest. In fact, the service itself will have to be modified dramatically to maintain customer interest and involvement.

REGISTRATION

One of the most essential, but often least considered, methods or procedures required in the delivery of leisure service is that of registering customers. Registration involves creating a list or record of customers who wish to participate in a given program or service. Registration can be fraught with problems such as misinformation, long lines, or confusing procedures. The registration process, like other procedures in the delivery of a program, should be managed carefully and with the needs and interests of the customer in mind.

What does the customer expect in a registration process? Individuals want a registration process that is convenient, accessible, easy to understand, orderly, efficient, and well-organized. Customers also will often desire more in-depth, on-the-spot information about programs, activities, and facilities. They often desire written directions and colorful, highly visible graphics to direct them through the registration process. Customers want and demand accountability in terms of cash collection and accounting procedures. These requirements are basic and need to be present or provided.

Rossman and Schlatter (2000) suggested that registration forms should include the following elements of information:

- Date
- The registrant's name, address, day and evening phone numbers
- The program(s) the customer wants to register for
- The fee for each program
- To whom the check should be written
- What to expect after the customer registers (e.g., confirmation, instructions)
- A liability release form
- Information about the method of payment
- Instructions regarding where to send the registration form

A quick scan of the Roselle Park District registration form presented in Figure 12.4 on page 400 highlights all of the elements of information that Rossman and Schlatter suggested.

Furthermore, organizations have an opportunity to present themselves in a favorable light by adding value during the registration process. Adding value includes, for example, refreshments, child care, an information table staffed by a knowledgeable employee, provision of adequate parking, and high-visual-impact brochures about coming events offered by the leisure organization. The organization can also give away at registration inexpensive novelty items imprinted with its logo, motto, or symbols, such as balloons, buttons, key chains, and so on. These actions tell customers that their participation is valued.

Rossman and Schlatter (2000) write about seven basic registration methods used by leisure service organizations. An additional method is electronic mail. These registration methods address the issues of convenience and accessibility, and primarily deal with location of the registration procedure and the processes employed by the organization. They are as follows:

Central Location Method—In this approach to registration, the process is consolidated into a centralized facility. All the information required for registration is contained within this unit, and registration is often advertised in such a way as to focus the registration activities at carefully controlled dates and times.

Program Location Method—This is a more decentralized approach, wherein registration occurs at the actual program site. This approach is more convenient for participants and creates opportunities for the customer to become familiar with the site and the program staff. One problem with this method is that customers have to go to several sites to register for multiple program options.

Mail-In Method—This method of registration involves a completed registration form and payment mailed directly to the leisure service organization. This method is very convenient for the customer, although it does not allow for any personal interaction and feedback.

Telephone Method—The telephone method of registration is gaining in popularity. It can be handled in one of two ways. First, individuals can call in and talk directly with staff members who will take their registration and process necessary information. Second, it can be handled using the telephone and the computer. Computer registration systems using telephone access are becoming more widespread. Although they are costly, computer registration systems will offer more accessibility in the future to leisure service organizations of all sizes.

Fax-In Method—This approach enables individuals to transmit their registration information via facsimile. With this convenient method, individuals may register for programs on a twenty-four-hour basis, which may be more convenient for families who are at work and school during the normal business day.

Internet (World Wide Web)—A number of organizations are organizing home pages on the World Wide Web that not only have information about programs and services, but have registration forms, application forms, and other types of "paperwork" that can be sent in via electronic mail.

Combination of Methods—Many leisure service organizations use a combination of these methods to improve accessibility and convenience to the cus-

tomer and because they recognize that there are multiple ways of meeting people's needs.

The registration procedures used by the Indianola (Iowa) Parks and Recreation Department are found in Figure 12.8. This organization uses a combination of three basic ways to register for programs—mail-in, after hours drop-off, and walk-in. In addition, the form provides a complete discussion of exactly how to sign up for programs so that the customer can easily complete the procedure. Figure 12.9 provides a sample registration form from the Burnaby (British Columbia) Parks and Recreation Department. This mail-in registration procedure provides a simple and direct approach to this process.

MANAGING CUSTOMER CONCERNS

No matter how well planned or organized, any given leisure experience is subject to the interpretation of the customers as to its value, quality, and effectiveness in meeting their needs. Sometimes the organization will make errors that have a negative impact on customers. How should the leisure service programmer deal with frustrated, upset, angry, or disappointed customers? The answer, quite simply, is that the customer is always right.

It is important to remember that the leisure experience is an individually defined one. Customers have different expectations based on previous experiences that can affect their experiences as customers. Further, the demand for higher quality services is ongoing. The demand for excellence in service is greater today than it was ten years ago; ten years from now customers will demand an even higher level of service. Customer complaints or criticism of a leisure service organization can provide valuable information. If organized and managed effectively, such feedback can provide information concerning the quality of customer/leader interaction, the viability of program structures, the appropriateness of areas and facilities, and the administrative procedures used to manage an organization. Customer concerns not only can

REGISTRATION

1 MAIL-IN

Indianola Parks and
Recreation Department
Box 299
Indianola, IA 50125-0299

2 AFTER HOURS DROP-OFF

Place form and payment in a
sealed envelope and drop in
the Drop Box located on the
front of the Parks & Recreation
Office.   301 W. 2nd Avenue

3 WALK-IN

Walk-in Registration
will begin August 28 at
301 W. 2nd Avenue.

HOW TO SIGN UP

Please register early! If a class does not have sufficient numbers of participants registered by two working days prior to the beginning of the class, the class will be cancelled.

COMPLETE REGISTRATION FORM: Be sure all information is correct and the program numbers are included. Registration forms are available on the inside back cover.

ENCLOSE PAYMENT: Total all fees and make check payable to Indianola Recreation or charge the amount to your VISA or MasterCard. Do not send cash. All fees must be paid in full. Registrations with incorrect fees will be notified by telephone and held from processing until the correct fee has been received.

MAIL-IN, DROP-OFF, OR WALK-IN: Mail-in or drop-off registrations will be taken from the time registration information is mailed until the program begins or is filled. **Drop off box is located on the front of the Indianola Parks and Recreation Department Office, 301 W. 2nd.** Indianola Parks and Recreation is not responsible for lost mail.
Walk-in registrations will be taken beginning August 28, 1989, at the Parks and Recreation Office, 301 W. 2nd, until the program begins or is filled. Mail-in and drop-off registrations will have priority before August 28, 1989. Registrations will be processed by random draw on the day they are received up to 5:00 p.m. Those received after 5:00 p.m. will be processed the next day. Only walk-ins will be processed immediately, after August 28, 1989.

CONFIRMATION: Drop-off and mail-in registrations will be sent back a confirmation receipt/verification in the mail.

REGISTRATION INFORMATION: If a class was filled before your registration was processed, you will automatically be placed on a waiting list. We will open additional sections of classes if possible. Our main goal is to meet your needs!
Use current age or grade unless otherwise listed. Use age at beginning of program.
Programs that are taxed are listed as such in the brochure. When entering the fee, please just list the total fee with taxes included.

NON-RESIDENT FEE: Non-residents need to add non-resident fees from each program.
No non-resident registration will be processed until the correct fees have been received.
Non-residents are those that reside outside the CITY LIMITS of Indianola.

REFUNDS: Refunds will only be given if a program is cancelled or a medical excuse from a doctor is presented. We reserve the right to cancel a program due to limited enrollment. A refund will be sent for cancelled programs.

IMPORTANT: By their very nature, many parks and recreation programs involve body contact, substantial physical exertion, emotional stress, and/or use of equipment which represents a certain risk to users. It is recommended that you check with your physician prior to participating in Parks and Recreation activities. Registrants in any program assume responsibility for any risk, implicit or direct, by participation in said activity or facility.

ADDITIONAL REGISTRATION FORMS: Additional Registration forms are available at the Parks and Recreation Office.

Figure 12.8   Registration Procedures, Indianola (Iowa) Parks and Recreation Department.

Registration
I N F O R M A T I O N

Continued from reverse.

Course Name: _____

Activity #: _____ Page #: _____

Location: _____

Day: _____ Time: _____ Start Date: _____

Level: _____ Set: ___ Fee: $ _____

Course Name: _____

Activity #: _____ Page #: _____

Location: _____

Day: _____ Time: _____ Start Date: _____

Level: _____ Set: ___ Fee: $ _____

Course Name: _____

Activity #: _____ Page #: _____

Location: _____

Day: _____ Time: _____ Start Date: _____

Level: _____ Set: ___ Fee: $ _____

The information collected on this form is used for the purposes of course registration only.

Continued from reverse.

Course Name: _____

Activity #: _____ Page #: _____

Location: _____

Day: _____ Time: _____ Start Date: _____

Level: _____ Set: ___ Fee: $ _____

Course Name: _____

Activity #: _____ Page #: _____

Location: _____

Day: _____ Time: _____ Start Date: _____

Level: _____ Set: ___ Fee: $ _____

Course Name: _____

Activity #: _____ Page #: _____

Location: _____

Day: _____ Time: _____ Start Date: _____

Level: _____ Set: ___ Fee: $ _____

The information collected on this form is used for the purposes of course registration only.

Registration Locations

Bonsor Recreation Complex
6550 Bonsor Ave. V5H 3G4
Registration: 430-8851
Fax: 439-5513
Information: 439-1860
Seniors' Office: 439-5513
Registration Hours:
M-F, Su, 9:00am-7:00pm
Sa, 9:00am-4:00pm
Seniors' Registration:
M-F, 9:00am-3:00pm

Burnaby Lake Arena
3676 Kensington Ave.
Phone: 291-1261
Registration Hours:
M-F, 9:00am-3:30pm
(phone for evening hours)
Sa, 6:00-8:00pm
Su, 1:00-3:30pm

C.G. Brown Pool
3702 Kensington Ave.
Phone: 299-9374
Registration Hours:
M-F, 9:00am-8:00pm
Sa, 12:00noon-7:00pm
Su, 10:00am-4:00pm

Cameron Recreation Centre
9523 Cameron St. V3J 1L6
Main Office: 421-5225
Fax: 421-6387
Seniors' Office: 421-1044
Registration Hours:
M-F, 9:00am-7:00pm
Sa, 9:00am-3:00pm

Confederation Community Centre for the Retired
4585 Albert St. V5C 2G6
Phone: 294-1936
Fax: 299-3161
Registration Hours:
M-F, 9:00am-3:00pm

Eastburn Community Centre
7435 Edmonds St. V3N 1B1
Phone: 525-5361
Fax: 540-6983
Registration Hours:
M-F, 9:00am-8:00pm
Sa, 9:00am-3:00pm

Edmonds Community Centre for Older Adults
7282 Kingsway V5E 1G3
Phone: 525-1671
Fax: 540-7936
Registration Hours:
M-F, 9:00am-3:00pm
Sa, 10:00am-3:00pm

Eileen Dailly Leisure Pool & Fitness Centre
240 Willingdon Ave.
Phone: 298-7946
Fax: 298-9036
Registration Hours:
M-F, 9:00am-8:00pm
Sa, Su, 9:00am-6:00pm

Forest Grove Community Office
8525 Forest Grove Dr.
V5A 4H5
Phone: 420-2675
Registration Hours:
M-F (phone for hours)

Kensington Complex
6159 Curtis St. V5B 4X7
Arena Phone: 299-8354
Office Phone: 298-5027
Fax: 294-3245
Registration Hours:
M-F, 9:00am-3:30pm
Su (phone for hours)

Shadbolt Centre for the Arts
6450 Deer Lake Ave.
V5G 2J3
Phone: 291-6864
Fax: 205-3001
Registration Hours:
M-F, 9:00am-7:00pm
Sa, 9:00am-3:00pm
Su, 10:00am-2:00pm

Willingdon Heights Community Centre
1491 Carleton Ave.
V5C 4V5
Phone: 299-1446
Registration Hours:
M-F, 8:30am-7:00pm
Sa, 9:00am-3:00pm

Figure 12.9 Mail-In Registration Form, Burnaby (British Columbia) Parks and Recreation Department.

be a source of information to the organization, but also can paradoxically serve to enhance the organization's relationship with its customers.

Here is an example to emphasize this point. Customer complaint studies conducted for the White House Office for Consumer Affairs by an organization known as Technical Assistance Research Programs, Inc., found that handling dissatisfied customers in a proactive fashion would help in resolving concerns and, in fact, would reflect in a positive fashion on an organization. The organization's findings were as follows:

1. The average business never hears from 96 percent of its unhappy customers. For every complaint received, the average company in fact has twenty-six customers with problems, six of which are serious problems.
2. Complainers are more likely than noncomplainers to do business again with the company that upset them even if the problem isn't satisfactorily resolved.
3. Of the customers who register a complaint, between 54 and 70 percent will do business again with the organization if their complaint is resolved. That figure goes up a staggering 95 percent if the customer feels that the complaint was resolved quickly.
4. The average customer who has had a problem with an organization tells nine or ten people about it. Thirteen percent of people who have a problem with an organization recount the incident to more than twenty people.
5. Customers who have complained to an organization and had their complaints satisfactorily resolved tell an average of five people about the treatment they received (Albrecht and Zemke, 1985: 6).

Immediate and prompt response to customer concerns can have a positive effect on an organization in significant ways. As Wuest (2001) noted, studies suggest that customers who express concerns and have their problems resolved effectively are often more loyal than customers who never faced undesirable experiences. Hence, every attempt should be made to find ways to respond quickly, constructively, and positively to customer complaints and concerns.

Dealing with Individual Complaints

One of the key factors in quickly and satisfactorily responding to expressions of customer concern are the actions and behavior of frontline staff. Frontline staff should be empowered to handle problems. They should be schooled in principles of customer service, including procedures to be used in dealing with negative situations that might arise. Rules for dealing effectively with customers include having a problem-solving orientation, listening and communicating carefully, and responding in a rapid, effective, and direct manner. It is important to remember that the logic of the customer is not always the same as the logic of the organization.

On the other hand, staff members should avoid patronizing, solicitous, nonsupportive behaviors. Very few customers want to complain: in fact, many will avoid complaining and live with the problem. As noted by Plymire (1991, as cited in Wuest, 2001), studies suggest that every complaint that is voiced represents about 2,000 that are left unvoiced. Therefore, a customer must feel very strongly about an issue if he or she takes the time, effort, and emotional energy necessary to confront an organization regarding poor services or products. To this end, leisure organizations should plan and take necessary steps to deal effectively with customer complaints (DeGraaf, Jordan, and DeGraaf, 1999; Wuest, 2001).

Figure 12.10, developed by Sparks (2001), provides an organizational framework oriented toward dealing with customer complaints. The top portion of this framework highlights the many variables involved when leisure service providers recognize a customer is dissatisfied or a service failure has occurred (e.g., customer expectations and actions, organizational factors). Ultimately, the service provider needs to decide on whether he or she will respond to the complaint. If the provider decides to respond to the compliant, recovery is initiated via differing responses, such as compensation, explanation, apology, and so forth. After a recovery strategy is implemented, the customer evaluates the fairness

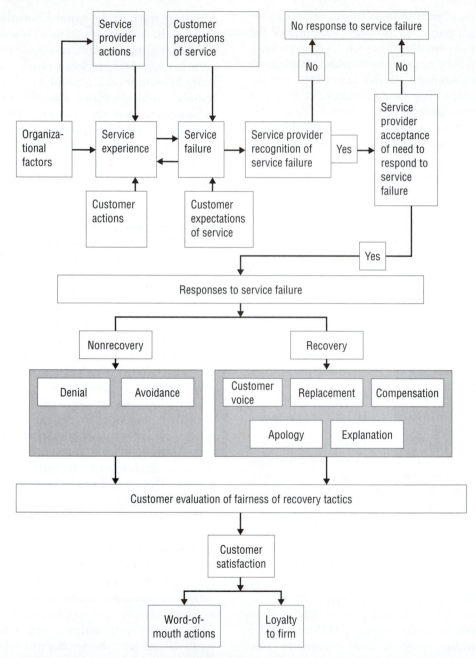

Figure 12.10 Diagrammatic Framework of the Service Failure and Recovery Process.

of the strategy—if the customer feels the strategy is fair, customer satisfaction is maintained or strengthened.

Beyond this organizational framework, leisure service providers can take other actions to deal with customer complaints. Following are actions that leisure service organizations can apply to customer complaints:

1. Acknowledge the importance of the problem immediately.
2. Gather all the relevant information needed to answer the problem quickly. Use open-ended questions that require more than yes or no answers, such as: What is the problem and when did it first occur? What have you done about the problem to date? For more specific answers, use closed questions, such as: Did you push the right button on the vending machine?
3. Once the problem and a plan of action have been determined, the customer should be told precisely what will happen, when, and why. In customer service situations, ignorance is most assuredly not bliss.
4. Review commitments. These commitments should be clearly stated to a customer and confirmed. If a customer expects a call in a week, and is called a month later instead, he or she will feel neglected, even if the problem has been solved.
5. Follow through on commitments. No one should ever make a promise for an organization that cannot be kept. Broken promises lead to irate customers.
6. Listen for nonservice-related cues. Citizens will share a wealth of information when prompted. Your employees can often uncover needs for additional services or problem solutions this way. Employees can alert management to potential problems and opportunities.

Again, responding quickly, maintaining commitments, and understanding the customer's point of view are important elements in answering concerns. The ability of frontline people to effectively manage the expectations of individuals, even when things have gone wrong, can have very dramatic effects on the success or failure of an organization.

Developing a Customer Concern System

Customer concerns should not be handled in a random, haphazard fashion. Leisure service organizations need to develop a system for managing customer concerns. A customer concern system gives an individual the opportunity to provide information to the organization about its services. Such a system, if organized in an effective manner, provides an orderly, organized way not only for the customer to offer meaningful comments but also for the organization to respond.

A customer concern system should meet several criteria. First, the system should provide information to the organization in an organized way that allows for an orderly, well-thought-out response. Second, the system should provide a safety valve, or buffer, for customer complaints, enabling the organization to handle customer concerns at the earliest possible time rather than later, when the situation may be more volatile. Third, the customer concern system should be in writing, making it more accurate and quantifiable. It should provide guidelines for staff behavior and information for decision making.

The Central Oregon Park and Recreation District, located in Redmond, Oregon, has adopted a policy statement entitled "User Concern System" as a guideline for receiving and acting on comments, suggestions, and recommendations from the residents of this area. This policy, shown in Figure 12.11, presents the methods and procedures used by this organization to respond to customer concerns. Written documentation is recorded on a "User Concern" form. The information is distributed to appropriate parties and follow-up procedures are established. All information is analyzed on a biannual basis in order to follow trends.

Figure 12.12 is the Resident Comment Form developed by the Willamalane (Springfield, Oregon) Park and Recreation District. This form is available at the various programs and facilities operated by this organization and can be mailed by customers directly to the superintendent of the district. Every complaint, concern, suggestion, and compliment is reported to the superintendent of

CENTRAL OREGON PARK AND RECREATION DISTRICT

USER CONCERN SYSTEM

Section 1. PURPOSE OF THE USER CONCERN SYSTEM: The comments, suggestions and recommendations of the users of the Central Oregon Park and Recreation District can serve to strengthen, enhance, and identify areas needed for improvement. This policy sets forth, in a systematic fashion, methods and procedures for dealing with comments, suggestions and recommendations made by users. It provides for a structured means of input and review by the professional staff and the Board of Directors. This will encourage responsive action on the part of the professional staff and the Board of Directors as a whole.

Section 2. DEFINITIONS OF USER CONCERNS: A user concern is often framed in a negative sense. That is, it is viewed as a complaint rather than as an opportunity for improvement of the operations, leadership and areas and facilities of the District. Some of the areas that might be commented upon by users could include the following:

A. Areas and Facilities. Suggestions might be made concerningthe cleanliness, design and functional aspects of areas and facilities.

B. Programs. Activities offered by the District can result in expressions of concern.

C. Leadership. The personal interaction that a leader has with a user can be an area of concern.

D. Operational Procedures. Registration, program costs, methods of publicity, as well as others, can all be areas of concern.

E. Other.

Section 3. PROCEDURES TO BE EMPLOYED IN THE USER CONCERN SYSTEM: Often-times, expressions of concern will come to individuals serving as elected or appointed members of the District. The following procedure shall be employed by all individuals, including members of the Board of Directors, the General Manager, full-time permanent employees and temporary employees. Then receiving comments, all individuals are to be courteous and willing to listen to individuals and assist them in completing proper forms.

A. Written Documentation. All expressions of concern shall be recorded on the Central Oregon Park and Recreation District User Concern Form. This form asks for the name, address and telephone number of the individual and a description of the comment, suggestion or recommendation made.

B. Distribution Procedures. All comments shall be recorded by the Administrative Services Coordinator for bi-weekly distribution to the Board of Directors and all permanent full-time staff members.

C. Disposition or Action Procedures. All suggestions that must be acted on immediately because of safety shall be the responsibility of the individual and/or supervisor receiving the user concern. All other routine comments or suggestions shall be acted upon by the appropriate individual within the organization. The resulting action shall be recorded on the user concern form and become a part of the bi-weekly report made to the Board of Directors and all other staff members.

D. Response to User Concerns. An acknowledgement in the form of a letter and/or phone call will be made to all individuals completing a user concern form. This letter will thank the individual for their input and suggest the procedures of review that will be employed. If action is taken on the concern at a later date, an additional follow-up letter shall be written.

E. Bi-Annual Report. On a bi-annual basis, an analysis will be made of all concerns, suggestions and recommendations offered by users to the District. This will be undertaken, in order to determine trends and other areas of concern that may impact upon the operations of the District.

Figure 12.11   User Concern Policy Statement, Central Oregon Park and Recreation District, Redmond, Oregon.

Dear Residents:

The Willamalane Park & Recreation District strives to serve the leisure needs of all its residents. It is the sincere pledge of the staff to provide the best in park and recreation facilities and services to the residents of the District. We value those that we serve. Your comments, suggestions, and input regarding our facilties and services are important to us. If we have not lived up to your expectations, we would appreciate feedback from you. It is our intent to respond to your needs in a timely and responsive fashion; your feedback will help us to better serve you.

Please complete this form and mail it to me or contact our administrative office at (503) 726-4335. Office hours are Monday through Friday, 8:00 a.m. to 5:00 p.m. Thank you.

Daniel R Plaza

Daniel R. Plaza
Superintendent

Tear Here

- -

RESIDENT COMMENT FORM

Your Comments Are Welcome.

	Excellent	Satisfactory	Improvement	Unacceptable
SERVICE QUALITY				
Staff Courtesy	☐	☐	☐	☐
Program	☐	☐	☐	☐
Convenience	☐	☐	☐	☐
Registration	☐	☐	☐	☐
FACILITY QUALITY				
Appearance	☐	☐	☐	☐
Cleanliness	☐	☐	☐	☐

What other facilities or services would you like to see the Willamalane Park & Recreation District provide?

_____

_____

_____

_____

What particular facility/service is this comment directed toward? _____

_____

Date: / /   Time of day: _____

(Optional Information)

Name: _____
Address: _____
City/State/Zip: _____
Telephone: _____

Your Input Helps Us Improve.

Willamalane
Park & Recreation District

RESIDENT COMMENT FORM

Willamalane
Park & Recreation District

FIRST CLASS   PERMIT NO. 40   SPRINGFIELD, OR

BUSINESS REPLY MAIL

POSTAGE WILL BE PAID BY ADDRESSEE:

DANIEL R PLAZA SUPERINTENDENT
ADMINISTRATION BUILDING
WILLAMALANE PARK & RECREATION DISTRICT
151 NORTH FOURTH STREET
SPRINGFIELD OR 97477-5498

NO POSTAGE
NECESSARY
IF MAILED
IN THE
UNITED STATES

Figure 12.12 Resident Comment Form, Willamalane Park and Recreation District, Springfield, Oregon.

the district, the marketing director, and the supervisor of the program or facility affected. Customers making comments are guaranteed a telephone call within two days. Every effort is made to resolve the concern as soon as possible.

Another example is the "Public Complaint Form" provided by the Greeley (Colorado) Parks and Recreation Department (see Figure 12.13). The document provides the name and address of the individual and the nature of the complaint. Further, the form delineates space for the disposition of the complaint and provides a mechanism for routing the complaint to the director of the department.

Extending the concept further, the Morale, Welfare, and Recreation Department of the U.S.

GREELEY PARKS & RECREATION DEPARTMENT

COMPLAINT/SUGGESTION FORM

Date: _____ Time: _____

Name: _____ Daytime Phone: _____

Address: _____

Complaint/Area of Concern/Suggestion: _____

_____

_____

_____

_____

_____

_____

Taken By: _____ Forwarded To: _____

Staff Response/Resolution: _____

_____

_____

_____

_____

_____

_____

Response Completed by: _____ Date: _____

Reviewed by Director: _____ Date: _____

Figure 12.13 Complaint/Suggestion Form, Greeley (Colorado) Parks and Recreation Department.

Marine Corps in Okinawa, Japan, encourages customers to make contact with the organization. This organization is not only concerned about complaints, but also welcomes questions, suggestions, and compliments. It guarantees a response and suggests that it will use the input to improve services (see Figure 12.14).

At a minimum, every leisure service organization should attempt to respond in writing to comments that have been made by customers. While letters of apology cannot rectify problems, they do attempt to extend the goodwill of the organization to the dissatisfied customer.

Observational Program

Another quality control program—in addition to customer complaint/concern forms and routine supervision by leisure service programmers—allows for an organization to implement an observation of its programs and staff. This program places observers appearing as customers in key program settings. These observers evaluate services and staff to provide both positive feedback as well as constructive criticism. Walt Disney World employs this type of observational program within its theme parks, calling it a "shopper program." The focus of this approach

Figure 12.14 Make Contact Form, Morale, Welfare, and Recreation Department, U.S. Marine Corps, Okinawa, Japan. (Continued on Page 426.) (Source: From Morale, Welfare and Recreation Department, U.S. Marine Corps, Okinawa, Japan.)

Date: _____

Name: _____

- ❑ Active Duty ❑ Civilian
- ❑ Spouse ❑ Dependent
- ❑ Accompanied ❑ Unaccompanied
- ❑ Retired ❑ Other

Rank/Organization: _____

Mailing Address: _____

_____

Rotation Date: _____

Housing Area: _____

Phone: (work/home) _____

Are you a club member? ❑ yes ❑ no

How do you hear about Marine MWR activities? Check all that apply:

- ❑ Posters ❑ Friend
- ❑ FEN TV ❑ Other
- ❑ FEN radio _____

Would you like to be on Marine MWR's mailing list?

- ❑ yes ❑ no

Would you be interested in participating in a focus group?

- ❑ yes ❑ no

F004960

Make **CONTACT**

Thank you for taking time to help us improve your Marine MWR. Your comments are greatly appreciated! This is your direct link to Marine MWR – all forms will be addressed and a response is guaranteed! Please fill out this form completely, giving as much detail as possible.

- ❑ Compliment ❑ Complaint/Concern ❑ Suggestion

Marine MWR Facility: _____

Comments: _____

_____

_____

_____

_____

_____

_____

_____

_____

_____

_____

_____

_____

_____

Figure 12.14—*Continued.*

is to provide information about programs and services from the guest's point of view. The quality control program does not attempt to test the staff members through harassment or other difficult behavior, but simply to observe the situation in terms of courtesy and service, employee appearance, cleanliness of facilities and areas, telephone interaction, quality of merchandise and food, and so on.

Observation of staff, services, programs, and other factors should be based on predetermined objectives and criteria. Following are some considerations to implementing an observational program.

1. Define the goal of the shopper program—what is being monitored?
2. Determine who can request the service and for what purpose.
3. Have the normal customer/guest situation.
4. Have the shopper look and act like an average customer.
5. Do *not* have the shopper harass the employee.
6. Note variables of the setting (time of day, day of week, season, attendance—best to shop the person several times).
7. Educate the shopper. List specific procedures or interactions to observe.
8. Use the service for positive feedback to employees as well as suggestions for improvement.
9. Be specific in your observations and suggestions. (Telling someone he or she is not courteous is not specific enough.)
10. Develop a standard form for the shopper to use. (The Disney Approach to People Management, n.d.)

An observational program can be invaluable to a leisure service programmer. It can provide methods for seeing the program or service through the eyes of the customer and thereby provide unique information that may not be obtained in other ways. An observational program can help determine more effective ways to interact with the customer and thereby more effectively anticipate problems.

The city of Indianapolis (Indiana) Parks and Recreation Department operates a "Shopper's Program" to assist in analyzing the quality of programs and services. Shoppers are recruited from an existing volunteer base, although they are reimbursed for their actual costs of participation in the program. Shoppers are instructed to not reveal to other participants the fact that they are analyzing the program and are required to fill out a survey form detailing registration, program, and facility quality issues (see Figure 12.15).

Program Code: _____

Class Title: _____

Location: _____

QUALITY PROGRAMS SHOPPER SURVEY

Date: _____

Instructor's Name: _____

Quality Standards	1	2	3	4	5	Comments
Rate the following on a scale from 1 (poor) to 5 (excellent)						
Registration						
Ease of registering						Date Received:
Timeliness of confirming postcard						
Friendliness of customer service staff						
Knowledgeable customer service staff						
Overall experience with registering						
Program						
Length of program						
Program Content						
Instructor rapport						
Value of program						
Overall experience						
Facility						
Cleanliness						
Restroom cleanliness						
Appropriate program area						
Safe from repairs and construction						
Overall rating of the facility						

	Yes	No	Comments or N/A
Was the instructor identified by a name tag or Indy Parks staff shirt?			
Was attendance taken at the class?			
Did the instructor properly greet and dismiss the class on time?			
Were you notified if changes made to the class (date, time, location)?			
Did the instructor promote other classes or Indy Parks events?			
Did the instructor hand you an evaluation at the end of the class?			
Did the program meet your expectations?			
If not, what expectations were not met?			
Would you enroll in this class again?			
Is this your first time you've enrolled in an Indy Parks program?			
What types of programs would you want to see in the future?			
1			
2			
3			

Your Name _____

Participant's Name _____

Figure 12.15 Quality Programs Shopper Survey Form, Indianapolis (Indiana) Parks and Recreation Department.

Summary

Perhaps one of the most important areas of leisure service programming is the actual delivery of activities or events. This is where the customer and the leader interact, and the leisure experience is created and appreciated. The ability of frontline leisure service leaders and supervisors to deal effectively with customers is an essential element in this phase of program planning. The ability of leisure service organizations to create positive relations and interactions between customers and professional staff members may very well spell the difference between organizational success and failure.

The customer/leader interface is the pivotal point in the delivery of most leisure services. Leisure service organizations employ many primary service professional staff members who have direct contact with customers. In addition, many individuals in leisure service organizations serve in secondary and support roles, in which contact with customers is incidental yet still important.

Customer/leader interactions can be planned and managed. For example, organizations can plan program and activity interactions, telephone interactions, information exchanges, registration interactions, office interactions, and casual conversations. Excellent customer/leader interactions are reflected in attention given by a professional staff member to a variety of behaviors, including but not limited to sincerity, attention to detail, courtesy, integrity, access, generosity, consistency, reliability, and responsiveness.

Because many of the professional staff members delivering leisure services are seasonal or part-time employees, the supervision of such individuals is important. Supervisory activities usually involve the development of program ideas, promotion of programs, recruitment, selection and development of staff, and the control of work efforts. Leisure service supervisors engage in many specific roles and responsibilities. Some of these include attention to production, quality, cost, methods, morale, training, and safety.

An important dimension managed by frontline leaders and supervisors is the flow of an activity or event. Program flow can be thought of as the animation of an event or activity as it moves through time. Leisure programs should be organized and delivered in such a way as to ensure satisfaction with the experience. Events and activities can be organized to produce different emotional states and benefits for customers.

The registration procedure involves placing the names of individuals on lists for programs or services. It can be enhanced dramatically by adding value to the process selected. There are seven basic methods of registration—central location, program location, mail-in, telephone, fax, Internet, and combination. The registration process can set the tone for a person's leisure experience and, therefore, should be managed as a part of the service delivery process.

Responding in a timely fashion to customer concerns is an important activity that can be planned and managed by a leisure service organization. Concerns and complaints that are handled in a timely and prompt fashion can actually work to the advantage of a leisure service organization. A system to manage concerns and complaints often involves the establishment of policies and procedures, forms, and other methods of routing information to ensure a rapid and effective response to expressions of concern.

Discussion Questions and Exercises

1. What is service quality?

2. Explain how service quality is a continuum that provides services in three time elements.

3. Why is customer/leader interface important in the delivery of quality services in leisure organizations?

4. Define *empowerment* and identify three steps in developing organizational empowerment.

5. How does cross-cultural communication highlight the complexity of customer/leader interactions?

6. What are the hallmarks of excellence in customer/leader interactions?

7. Define *supervision* as it applies to the delivery of leisure services

8. What are the roles and responsibilities that leisure service supervisors engage in?

9. What is meant by the phrase "managing the program flow"?

10. Explain four components that leisure programmers can use to help customers experience flow and enjoyment.

11. Identify and discuss five different approaches to program registration.

12. What elements of information should be articulated on registration forms?

References

Albrecht, K., and R. Zemke. 1985. *Service America!* Homewood, IL: Dow Jones-Irwin.

Blanchard, K., J. Carlos, and A. Randolph. 1996. *Empowerment takes more than a minute.* San Francisco, CA: Berrett-Koehler.

Boyd, B. B. 1984. *Management-minded supervision.* New York: McGraw-Hill.

Chernish, W. N. 2001. Empowering service personnel to deliver quality service. In *Service quality management in hospitality, tourism, and leisure,* edited by J. Kandampully, C. Mok, and B. Sparks, (pp. 223–38). New York: Haworth Press.

Crompton, J. L., and K. J. MacKay. 1989. Users' perceptions of the relative importance of service quality dimensions in selected public recreation programs. *Leisure Sciences* 11.

Csikszentmihalyi, M. 1990. *Flow: The psychology of optimal experience.* New York: Harper & Row.

Csikszentmihalyi, M. 1993. *The evolving self: A psychology for the third millennium.* New York: HarperCollins.

Csikszentmihalyi, M. 1997. *Finding flow: The psychology of engagement with everyday life.* New York: Basic Books.

Dattilo, J., D. Kleiber, and R. Williams. 1998. Self-determination and enjoyment enhancement: A psychologically based service model for therapeutic recreation. *Therapeutic Recreation Journal* 32(4): 258–71.

DeGraaf, D. G., D. J. Jordan, and K. H. DeGraaf. 1999. *Programming for parks, recreation, and leisure services: A servant leadership approach.* State College, PA: Venture.

Dieser, R. 1997. Pluralistic leadership in recreation and leisure planning: Understanding minority/ethnic identity development. *Journal of Leisurability* 24(3):33–37.

Disney Approach to People Management. n.d.

Drucker, P. 1985. *Managing in turbulent times.* New York: Harper.

Duffy, J. A., and A. A. Ketchand. 1998. Examining the role of service quality in overall service satisfaction. *Journal of Managerial Issues* 10(2):240–55.

Edginton, C. R., and S. R. Edginton. 1993a. Agile leisure programming. *Management Strategy* 17(3): 1.

Edginton, C. R., and S. R. Edginton. 1993b. Total quality programming planning. *Journal of Physical Education, Recreation, and Dance* 64(8).

Edginton, C. R., and S. R. Edginton. 1994. *Youth programs: Promoting quality services.* Champaign, IL: Sagamore.

Edginton, C. R., and C. J. Hanson. 1996. The Leadership Assessment Center: *Camp Adventure*™— A case study. *Hong Kong Recreation Review* 8.

Edginton, C. R., S. D. Hudson, and S. V. Lankford. 2001. *Managing recreation, park, and leisure services: An introduction.* Champaign, IL: Sagamore.

Edginton, C. R., S. L. Little, and D. G. DeGraaf. 1992. Just-in-time programming: Just for you. *Parks & Recreation* 27(11).

Ford, P. M. 1974. *Informal recreational activities.* Bradford Woods, IN: American Camping Association.

Glancy, M., J. E. Coles, D. Detzel, L. Luck, and B. S. Rupe. 1984. Lessons for managers: Thinking lean with just-in-time management principles. *Journal of Park and Recreation Administration* 2(2).

Hodgetts, R. M. 1993. *Blueprints for continuous improvement: Lessons from the Baldridge winners.* New York: American Management Association.

Jamieson, L. M., and S. A. Wolter. 1999. Management—what is it? In *Management of parks and recreation agencies,* edited by B. van der Smissen, M. Moiseichik, V. J. Hartenburg, and L. F. Twardzik. (pp. 1–18). Ashburn, VA: National Recreation and Park Association.

Jordan, D. J. 2001. *Leadership in leisure services: Making a difference.* 2nd ed., State College, PA: Venture.

Mack, G. H. 2000. Recruit and retain the best: Diversity in youth-serving agencies. In *Diversity and the recreation profession: Organizational perspectives,* edited by M. T. Allison and I. E. Schneider. (pp. 125–30). State College, PA: Venture.

MacKay, K. J., and J. L. Crompton. 1990. Measuring the quality of recreation services. *Journal of Park and Recreation Administration* 8(3).

Martin, W. 1987. A new approach to the understanding and teaching of service behaviors. *Hospitality Education and Research Journal* 11(2): 255–62.

O'Neill, M. 2001. Measuring service quality and customer satisfaction. In *Service quality management in hospitality, tourism, and leisure,* edited by J. Kandampully, C. Mok, and B. Sparks (pp. 159–92). New York: Haworth Press.

Rado, R. 1989. Connecting with the customer. *Training & Development Journal* (7).

Reisinger, Y. 2001a. Concepts in tourism, hospitality and leisure services. In *Service quality management in hospitality, tourism, and leisure,* edited by

J. Kandampully, C. Mok, & B. Sparks (pp. 1–14). New York: Haworth Press.

Reisinger, Y. 2001b. Unique characteristics of tourism, hospitality, and leisure services. In *Service quality management in hospitality, tourism, and leisure,* edited by J. Kandampully, C. Mok, and B. Sparks (pp. 15–50). New York: Haworth Press.

Rossman, J. R. 1989. *Recreation programming: Designing leisure experiences.* Champaign, IL: Sagamore.

Rossman, J. R. 1993. Program design through imagery. *Journal of Physical Education, Recreation, and Dance* 64(8): 34–36, 46.

Rossman, J. R., and B. E. Schlatter. 2000. *Recreation programming: Designing leisure experiences.* 3rd ed. Champaign, IL: Sagamore.

Saleh, F., and C. Ryan. 1992. Client perceptions of Hotels: A multi-attribute approach. *Tourism Management* 13(2):163–68.

Sawyer, T. H. (ed.). 2002. *Facilities planning for health, fitness, physical activity, recreation and sports: Concepts and applications* 10th ed. Champaign, IL: Sagamore.

Schlesinger, L. A., and J. L. Heskett. 1991. The service driven service company. *Harvard Business Review* 69(5):71–81.

Soutar, G. N. 2001. Service quality, customer satisfaction, and value: An examination of their relationship. In *Service quality management in hospitality, tourism, and leisure,* edited by J. Kandampully, C. Mok, and B. Sparks (pp. 97–110). New York: Haworth Press.

Sparks, B. 2001. Managing service failure through recovery. In *Service quality management in hospitality, tourism, and leisure,* edited by J. Kandampully, C. Mok, and B. Sparks (pp. 193–222). New York: Haworth Press.

Sue, D. W., and D. Sue. 2002. *Counseling the culturally different: Theory and practice.* 3rd ed. New York: John Wiley & Sons.

Terry, G. R. 1978. *Supervision.* Homewood, IL: Irwin.

Wuest, B. S. 2001. Service quality concepts and dimensions pertinent to tourism, hospitality, and leisure services. In *Service quality management in hospitality, tourism, and leisure,* edited by J. Kandampully, C. Mok, and B. Sparks (pp. 51–66). New York: Haworth Press.

Zeithaml, V. A., A. Parasuraman, and L. L. Berry. 1990. *Delivering quality service.* New York: Free Press.

Evaluation and Quality Assurance

LEARNING OBJECTIVES

1. To provide the reader with an understanding of the key concepts involved in the *process of evaluation.*
2. To help the reader gain knowledge of key concepts related to *quality assurance.*
3. To assist the reader in understanding the *differences and similarities between evaluation and quality assurance.*

4. To identify and define for the reader *different approaches to the evaluation process.*
5. To provide the reader with an overview of *data collection instruments used in the process of evaluation.*

INTRODUCTION

As accountability in leisure service organizations has grown, so has the importance of evaluation and quality assurance. How do leisure service programmers know they are producing the outcomes that customers desire? What methods are used to determine program efficiency and effectiveness? How is the leisure experience defined? How is customer satisfaction measured? These are challenging yet important questions for leisure service programmers. Noting the importance of evaluation, Farrell and Lundegren (1991: 378) have written that it "is the key to successful program planning, since inherent in it are suggestions for increasing effectiveness." Evaluation processes also may help improve program efficiency.

Most evaluation systems currently operating in the leisure field focus on the measurement of how well organizational resources are used to achieve stated goals. In other words, most evaluation systems are concerned with establishing baseline and reference information about such issues as cost of leadership, supplies, equipment, materials, and utilities. In addition, existing evaluation examines the ratio of the cost of providing a service to the number of customers engaging in a specific activity or using a specific facility. While such evaluation schemes may be useful in effectively and judiciously controlling the use of organizational resources, they often fail to measure customer satisfaction with a given leisure experience.

In this chapter, the similarities and differences between evaluation and quality assurance are discussed. The focus is on defining evaluation and quality assurance, presenting information concerning their respective purposes, and suggesting strategies as to how they may be employed by leisure service organizations. Information concerning the relationship of these two concepts is also presented. In addition, a number of traditional evaluation methodologies, an analysis of more contemporary performance- or productivity-oriented evaluation systems, and, because evaluation involves measurement, some rudimentary information on research strategies and application of statistical procedures are offered as well.

EVALUATION

According to Rossman and Schlatter (2000), "evaluation is judging the worth of programs and services on the basis of an analysis of systematically collected evidence" (p. 356). Farrell and Lundegren (1991) suggest that definitions of evaluation contain two central elements: "ascertainment of the value and assessment whether or not program objectives have been met" (p. 233). These two factors contribute to each other but are important individually as well.

Farrell and Lundegren (1983: 207) indicate that evaluation can be "defined in varying ways . . . with perhaps as many subtly differing nuances as there are authors writing about it." However, in reviewing most authors, we find that *evaluation implies that leisure service programmers attempt to answer some basic questions about what they had hoped to do and what they were able to accomplish* (Fink and Kosecoff, 1978). Evaluation involves making value judgments about the extent to which a customer, a leisure service professional, or a leisure service organization has accomplished a specific set of goals and objectives. Discussing the importance of evaluating program outcomes, Attkisson et al. (1978: 303) have written:

> Businesses must be profitable or in general they are abandoned. In contrast, it is commonly said that [governmental units] resist effective management because they cannot be held accountable for their results. While limited accountability is attained by requiring a program to maintain levels of effort and be accessible to clients, this level of accountability is easily achieved when services are publicly subsidized . . . Beyond this, how can we determine that a program is worth its cost? How can we learn to increase the value and benefits received for expenditures on [government] services?

The issues raised by Attkisson et al. are questions of evaluation that must be addressed by leisure service organizations. Whereas market-oriented (commercial) leisure service organizations have a built-in mechanism for evaluation—profitability—political/governmental (public) and voluntary (private nonprofit) organizations do not have similar methods of accountability.

Why Evaluation?

From a positive perspective, when evaluation programs are planned, organized, and implemented in an appropriate fashion, they can result in great benefit to the recipients of leisure services and the organizations providing them. The importance of evaluation can be viewed from three different orientations. The first orientation is to focus on what happens to the individual customer. Is the individual satisfied as a result of participating or attending a leisure program or facility? Has the customer's leisure behavior been modified or changed in any way? The second orientation is to view evaluation from the perspective of the leisure service programmer. When viewing evaluation in this way, questions arise about the use of program formats, leadership styles, supplies and equipment, and so on. The last orientation is to view evaluation in terms of its value to the leisure service organization as a whole. Certainly information collected in the evaluation process can be used to establish priorities and in turn to distribute organizational resources.

Following are some important reasons for the planning, organization, and implementation of evaluation processes in leisure service organizations in terms of customer orientation, program orientation, and organizational orientation.

Customer Orientation

1. *Evaluation Examines Customer Satisfaction*—Information collected for evaluation provides the leisure programmer with an accurate reading of the extent to which the customer is achieving satisfaction, enjoyment, or other benefits sought from a leisure experience.

2. *Evaluation Helps Measure Change in Customer Leisure Behavior*—Leisure experiences are often organized to produce specific behavioral changes and influence or improve leisure functioning. Leisure service programs frequently are designed to shape specific values, attitudes, and behaviors. Evaluation helps to measure the extent to which these intended behavioral changes have occurred.

3. *Evaluation Provides for Customer Input*—Evaluation systems provide direct mechanisms for customers to give feedback and information to an organization. This feedback increases the probability that an organization can be responsive to the needs, wants, and interests of individual customers. In addition, the customers' sense of control, ownership, or influence regarding their leisure experiences may be enhanced.

4. *Evaluation Encourages Customer Support for the Leisure Service Organization*—By engaging in evaluation, customers actively contribute solutions to their own leisure interests and needs. A form of evaluation directly related to the concept of social action suggests that participatory evaluation is a mechanism for customers to understand their needs and encourage appropriate organizations to take action. This action often results in increased levels of support through ongoing participation in the work of a leisure service organization.

Program Orientation

1. *Evaluation Helps the Programmer Promote Leader/Customer Transactions*—Central to the creation of many leisure experiences, especially in social environments, are the leader/customer interactions or transactions. Evaluation provides feedback to the leisure service programmer concerning the effectiveness of his or her relationship. Measurement in this area provides for a sense of the extent to which a leader is bonding successfully with his or her group.

2. *Evaluation Enables the Programmer to Develop Sensitivity to the Customer*—Greater sensitivity to the customer may develop when evaluation occurs. The evaluation process provides information to the programmer about people's feelings and their reactions to different stimuli as well as their cultural, gender, age, and racial orientations.

3. *Evaluation Allows the Programmer to Determine Program Design Effectiveness*—Evaluation provides input used in changing the elements that can be manipulated in creating programs. These elements, referred to by Rossman (1989: 32), include interacting with people, physical setting, objects, rules, relationships, and animation. Information derived from the evaluation process enables the programmer to modify or change these elements.

4. *Evaluation Indicates the Need for Program Enhancements*—Enhancing program elements can occur via information collected from program evaluation. For example, a physical setting may have to be improved or extended in some fashion to create a successful leisure experience. Program enhancements most often refer to qualitative improvements in service delivery.

Organizational Orientation

1. *Evaluation Links Program Performance to Budgetary Allocations*—One of the important contributions of evaluation is that of linking performance to the distribution of resources. By this we mean that evaluation helps strengthen the relationship between the program desired by the customer and whether the leisure service organization delivers the program in an effective and efficient manner. Thus, the evaluation procedure provides a measure of cost and its relationship to benefits.

2. *Evaluation Focuses on More Specific and Concrete Objectives*—Many leisure service organizations have as their major goal "enhancing, extending, and improving one's quality of life." A global statement such as this is difficult to measure. Evaluation forces an organization to focus on more practical and specifically definable objectives that can be measured.

3. *Evaluation Helps in Determining Program Priorities*—Because evaluation provides information regarding the costs and benefits of programs, prioritizing can occur. Such information is useful in political decision making, in determining acceptable profit margins, and in fund-raising decisions made by voluntary organizations.

4. *Evaluation Aids in Control*—Organizations often set up performance standards and evaluative criteria to gauge their work. Evaluation helps the leisure service programmer recognize whether deviations are occurring and to what extent. Armed with such information, the leisure service professional can take corrective action to ensure acceptable levels of performance.

The leisure service programmer wants the evaluation process to yield positive outcomes. As human beings, we seek confirmation of our professional activities. No one likes to think that his or her work is substandard and fails to meet customers' needs, wants, and desires. However, there is always room for improvement in professional work and in efforts to promote customer satisfaction. Because the information that is derived from evaluation systems can require programmers to change and to modify their efforts, evaluation is often looked at from a negative perspective.

For this reason, evaluation systems in organizations are often de-emphasized, ignored, or even worse, nonexistent. Individuals and organizations do not take time to carefully consider questions such as: What needs to be evaluated? How are programs and services to be evaluated? When should evaluation take place? Further, evaluation efforts are often not clearly linked to goals and objectives, and therefore become meaningless in the overall work of the organization. Evaluation systems also suffer because they do not clearly link organizational reward structures to the implementation of desired changes as identified in evaluation findings. Many evaluation efforts find their way to the shelf in a professional's office because they were ill-timed, poorly conceived, or, worse yet, presented in such a way that the findings were difficult to understand and implement.

Key Concepts of Evaluation

There are a number of key concepts related to evaluation. First and foremost is that evaluation implies that an individual will make a judgment as to whether a program or service is meeting its stated goals and objectives. Goals and objectives established for leisure programs and services often refer to producing some benefit, behavioral change, or level of satisfaction for a customer. Evaluation requires inquiry, appraisal, assessment, and often comparison to established standards. Evaluation helps in decision making, and to be effective, must be continuous and ongoing. Evaluation is a process whereby information is obtained in order to assess the efficiency and effectiveness of a leisure service organization. This information serves as a basis for determining the extent to which movement toward the organization's goals and objectives has occurred. For leisure service organizations, evaluation encourages changes in leisure behavior or functioning in order to increase customer satisfaction.

Following are key terms related to evaluation.

Formative Evaluation—The systematic assessment of each step in the development and implementation of a program is formative evaluation. The focus is on ongoing evaluation using a step-by-step process of decision making, relating to numerous specific aspects of a program rather than to just a single final evaluation (American Institutes for Research, 1970: 14; Mayer, 1975: 44–57).

Summative Evaluation—Summative evaluation is the terminal and overall assessment of a program intended to judge its impact and effectiveness. A decision to continue or discontinue the program is imminent (American Institutes for Research, 1970: 19).

Assessment—Assessment usually is associated with determining the disposition, importance, or value of a program function in relation to the overall leisure delivery system.

Measurement—Measurement refers to precise approaches and procedures to obtain quantitative data, and the use of quantitative measurements (such as cost, time, and test scores) to determine effectiveness, efficiency, and outputs (Farrell and Lundegren, 1978: 208).

Standards—Standards are statements of desirable practice or levels of performance for a given situation. Standards are indirect measurements of effectiveness using the cause-and-effect approach, so that if stated desirable practices are followed, the program should be effective. They allow evaluation by comparison (Van der Smissen, 1972: 4).

Evaluative Research—Evaluative research uses scientific principles and methods involving hypotheses and testing to examine effect or change. It is characterized by the use of clearly delineated protocol in collecting, processing, and analyzing the data.

Figure 13.1 proposes a set of categories for evaluation. The basic purpose of these evaluation questions is to contribute to the measurement of accountability. The categories presented in the figure deal with goals, strategies, program elements, and results. Questions to be answered include: What goals were chosen and met? Which adopted strategies were successful? Which failed? Which program elements that were manipulated led to successful implementation of the service? and finally, What results were achieved? This figure correlates with Figure 5.1 in Chapter 5, Needs Identification and Assessment. Figure 5.1 illustrates the questions that determine need, and Figure 13.1 focuses on evaluative questions that measure results.

The evaluation process is considered a continuous function within the organization. It may be evident as a planned, formal, and didactic effort, but it may also be spontaneous and informal. Obviously, the most desirable approach is the formal and planned effort, because the results are more precise, reliable, and useable. Evaluation is not relegated to an annual or semiannual time slot but is, as noted, continuous.

Evaluation can take place in any given situation in the leisure service organization. All too often, leisure service programmers are convinced that an evaluation must be conducted in a room, building, or other formal setting. On

Purpose	Categories of Evaluative Questions			
	Goals	**Strategies**	**Program Elements**	**Results**
To Aid in Account-ability	What goals were chosen? What goals were considered, then rejected? What alternative goals might have been considered? What evidence exists to justify the goals that were chosen? How defensible is this evidence? How well have the goals been translated into objectives? Overall, what is the merit of the goals that were chosen?	What strategy was chosen? What alternative strategies were considered? What other strategies might have been considered? What evidence exists to justify the strategy that was chosen? How defensible is this evidence? How well was the chosen strategy translated into an operational design? Overall, what is the merit of the chosen strategy?	What was the operational design? To what extent was it implemented? What were the strengths and weaknesses of the design under operating conditions? What was the quality of the effort to implement it? What was the actual design that was implemented? Overall, what is the merit of the process that was actually carried out?	What results were achieved? Were the stated objectives achieved? What were the positive and negative side effects? What impact was made on the target audience? What long-term effects may be predicted? What is the relation of costs to benefits? Overall, how valuable were the results and impacts of this effort?

Figure 13.1 A Matrix for Identifying and Analyzing Evaluative Questions. (From Stufflebeam, D. L. 1974. *Meta-Evaluation.* Kalamazoo, MI. The Evaluation Center.)

the contrary, the evaluation process can take place in any setting in which leisure services are delivered. This encompasses the playground, day camp, business office, park site and its accompanying open space, maintenance shed, or other settings. In essence, evaluation takes place where services are delivered.

Who should conduct the evaluation? Who is best qualified to conduct an evaluation—trained versus untrained personnel, or internal versus external personnel? Usually a "professional" evaluation refers to one that is conducted by someone from outside the organization. Conversely, an "amateur" evaluator is usually identified as someone within the organization designated to conduct the evaluation. Essentially, it is an agency's decision whether to utilize an individual with specialized knowledge of design, data collection, and analysis. In addition, the advantages of using an outside evaluator may be that (1) bias-free judgment is provided, (2) a fresh view of operations is offered, and (3) objectivity regarding the program may be obtained.

Although the inside evaluator (member of program staff) may not have the precise training and expertise of the outside evaluator, he or she may have more firsthand knowledge of the overall program, may be more accepted by the staff, and may function in a less obtrusive manner while conducting the evaluation. An inside evaluator's biases and knowledge of less obvious intervening variables may hinder objectivity. In addition, using an evaluator unskilled in evaluation techniques may render the findings null and void from the outset.

Perhaps a compromise is to provide opportunities for program staff to receive training in evaluation procedures and processes. This training would enable the organization to have a so-called expert on staff with the potential to train additional staff through in-service training efforts. Whoever is selected for the evaluator's role must understand the characteristics of evaluation, including utility, objectivity, judgment, action, and standardization (rather than scholarship, creativity, or pure research).

It is important to delineate which components of the recreation and leisure service delivery system are to be evaluated. Virtually every aspect of the operation is subject to evaluation if the organization is to understand its progress toward goals, objectives, standards, and more efficient decision making. Generally, items for evaluation can be divided into the following "5 Ps" of evaluation (Henderson and Bialeschki, 2002).

1. *Participants*—Those individuals who participate in offerings of the recreation and leisure service delivery system on a regular or intermittent basis; potentially includes full spectrum involvement from individuals representing all age levels and both sexes; a variety of ethnic, religious, and cultural groups; individuals of varying abilities and socioeconomic level.
2. *Personnel*—Direct face-to-face leaders or programmers, supervisory and administrative personnel, and support personnel (maintenance, fiscal, clerical, secretarial); includes the phenomenon of leadership.
3. *Place*—All physical holdings of the agency including the subject buildings; developed and undeveloped areas; land masses and water areas; equipment, materials, and supplies used in the program.
4. *Policies/Administration*—Includes policies, rules, regulations, standards, guidelines, legislative mandates, contracts, fiscal resources, and other dimensions establishing parameters for the organization, its personnel, and customers; the function of administration and supervision of the organization in relation to established standards, goals, or objectives.
5. *Program*—All activity and programmatic efforts including the subcategories of (a) programs, that is, visual arts, new arts, performing arts (drama, dance, and music), social recreation, hobbies and collecting, sports, games and athletics, literary arts, aquatics, volunteer services, aquatic wellness, and outdoor recreation; and (b) operations, that is, fiscal, maintenance, and supportive tasks carried out to support or promote programs, areas, facilities, or administration of the overall delivery system.

The evaluation of programs should include each of the five areas mentioned. These categories are not evaluated entirely independent of each other; there is an interaction among and between each of them. When evaluating customers' outputs, the programmer will undoubtedly examine programs, operations, administration, supervision and leadership, physical and fiscal resources, and the specific personnel who provided the programs.

The comprehensive nature of evaluation is evident. With this in mind, it is important to view the evaluation effort in a holistic sense. In other words, personnel cannot be evaluated in a vacuum. Many other components, variables, or ingredients are necessary before decisions can be made regarding a course of action or before a summative evaluation is provided.

Common Hazards in Evaluation

Any evaluation process may have pitfalls, problems, or hazards. Some may be minute and pass with time or be a timely strategy for eradication. Others, if allowed to go unnoticed, will pose imminent hazards that will affect the success of the overall evaluation effort. The programmer, evaluator, and others engaged in the evaluation process should heed the following warning signs.

Claiming Much, Providing Evidence of Little

Leisure service programmers must be cautious not to overexaggerate what they have really accomplished. A good example is the "turnstile" approach, in which hundreds of people may attend a particular activity or event. The event or activity may be declared a roaring success purely on a quantitative basis. However, the question must be asked, what evidence exists to indicate any qualitative change in attitudes, behavior, or level of need?

Selecting Measurement Instruments Not Logically Related to the Intervention

In some instances, the leisure programmer may choose to upgrade the quality of the instrument being used to assess change. In the zeal to use "standardized instruments," the programmer may overlook the appropriateness of the instrument or its power to draw out the necessary information or data.

Use of Norm-Referenced as Opposed to Criterion-Referenced Scores or Data

Norm-referenced data refers to judging a person's performance in relation to other members of a known group (e.g., all eight-year-olds). Criterion-referenced scores measure the specific performance achieved or level of skill attained (e.g., swam a twelve-minute mile). Although use of norms may be preferred, leisure service programmers rarely have the opportunity to use them in leisure programs and services. The closest approximation is within programs tied to performance in the psychomotor domain. Sometimes using national norms to determine fitness or other life qualities is not desirable. Findings tend to be generalized, which does little to assist the individual in focusing on increasing his or her developmental level. Because few instruments are available, individuals are better evaluated on the basis of where they are in relation to a developmental continuum (criterion referencing).

The Careless Collection of Data

The end result of the evaluation process may mean someone's job, increased costs or waste of money, and inappropriate use of resources. For these reasons, it is imperative that collected data be accurate, organized, and verified. Careless handling and coding of data may have serious repercussions in the future.

Having Limited Skills and Knowledge of Evaluation Procedures and Instrumentation

An evaluator who has limited knowledge and skills in evaluation procedures, methodology, and instrumentation severely hampers the potential contribution evaluation may make to the agency, its program, and its personnel. Anyone assuming the role of evaluator must obtain skills in evaluation protocol, procedures, methods, and data collection so as to ensure high-quality information as a result of the evaluation process.

Allowing Bias, Prejudice, Preconceived Perceptions, or Friendship to Influence the Evaluation Outcomes

Some evaluation situations may appear to require the evaluator to reach a foregone conclusion. This seriously challenges the credibility not only of the evaluator but also of the evaluation process employed. Whatever the situation, the evaluator should not be constrained or otherwise unduly influenced by political situations, innuendo, gossip, friends, or the biases and prejudices common to everyone.

Using Either Internal or External Evaluators Exclusively

It is hazardous to rely solely on either an internal or external evaluator because (1) the internal evaluator may be too close to the situation to be objective (although he or she does have a better grasp of the dynamic interactions and mood of the organization); (2) the external evaluator may not be able to place all the parts of the picture together (perhaps having just arrived or possibly only being assigned to review parts of the entire operation or program). A better approach might be to maintain some semblance of balance by relying on different internal evaluators as well as periodically engaging an outside team of experts to evaluate the program.

Not Planning the Evaluation Effort

If the purpose of a particular evaluation effort is not known, it is difficult at best to forecast what impact or meaning the evaluation will have to those who hold decision-making positions. Additionally, the organization or evaluator must have a detailed evaluation plan to illustrate the purpose of the evaluation, and its scheduled events, approach, requirements, and deliverables or outputs (Nadler, 1969: 125).

Scheduling Evaluation as a Cumulative or Summative Process

Evaluation is an ongoing process, but many individuals perceive it to be what happens *after* a program is completed. Evaluation should not be relegated to a summative position. As programs are planned, developed, and implemented, the process of formative evaluation must take place (Bannon, 1976: 267; Tallmadge, 1977: 61–71).

Ethical Considerations

Whether an individual serves as an internal or external evaluator, he or she must address certain ethical considerations. Although the evaluator may never stoop to the level of payoffs for a favorable evaluation, there is a gray area in which an evaluator may find it difficult to determine ethically whether he or she should "agree or disagree," "accept or refuse," or "call attention to or overlook" a particular situation. Each individual evaluator will enter the evaluation process with a different background and different skills, values, and perceptions of right or wrong. As such, one person's decision may not necessarily be another's.

Anderson and Ball (1978: 148–49) suggest the following positions regarding ethics in evaluation:

1. The evaluator's responsibility transcends simple competence in the work of evaluation. It includes not promising too much at the outset, ensuring that role relationships are proper and secure before work begins, and insisting on appropriate warnings about the limitations of the evaluation in all reports of the results.

2. The evaluator must assume loyalties other than those to the program. These include loyalties to the profession of program evaluation and to the public, which ultimately provides the authority for both program and evaluation. Thus, the evaluator has the responsibility to refuse to perform any evaluation services demanded by a program director or funding agent that the evaluator deems unethical.

3. Evaluations should be as open as possible, within the constraints of the privacy of the participants, the confidentiality of individual data, the contractual obligations, and the smooth working of program and evaluation. When the evaluation is open, germs like suspected evaluator bias and undue program pressure do not thrive as readily. (From S. B. Anderson and S. Ball, *The Profession and Practice of Program Evaluation*, 1978. Copyright 1978 Jossey-Bass, Inc., Publishers.)

The evaluator has specific ethical responsibilities to the individual or agency who commissions the evaluation. Above all, individuals who engage in the evaluation process must consider the ramifications of their work. The slightest deviation, error, or miscalculation in either data collection, observation, recollection, or written or oral communication could have considerable implications for the future of an agency, a program, or an individual employee. The evaluator should respect evaluation but never fear either the process or the outcome.

Is Evaluation Research?

Many practitioners think the terms "evaluation" and "research" are interchangeable. However, while both evaluation and research use the same methods, they have different purposes and outcomes (Henderson and Bialeschki, 2002). These differences are shown in Table 13.1. Both research studies and evaluation projects share common methods of data collection. A good understanding of various methods of data collection and analysis used for evaluation leads to a solid foundation for conducting research. Likewise, a good understanding of various methods of the data collection and analysis used for research leads to a solid foundation for conducting evaluation. In fact, McCormick and Lee (2001) posited that empirical practice, in which leisure professionals use research methods to plan and evaluate programs, should become part of mainstream leisure professions, such as therapeutic recreation practice. Table 13.1 shows how evaluation and research share common methods but have different applications.

QUALITY ASSURANCE

A recently emerging concept, quality assurance, is related to the assessment and evaluation process. Quality assurance can be thought of as a *formal management mechanism that helps regulate services with an eye toward improving procedures that, in turn, result in a higher quality of services for customers.* Although used extensively in the medical profession, quality assurance has historically been directed toward improving health care by improving the quality of care provided. Although applicable in settings that provide therapeutic recreation services (see Burlingame and Blaschko, 2002), quality assurance also has the potential for broader application for other leisure service organizations. For example, the United Kingdom Sports Council developed a quality assurance framework, called QUEST,

designed to evaluate publicly owned sports and leisure facilities, whether operated by the local authority or the private or voluntary sector (Maxwell, Ogden, and Russell, 2001). The primary aim of QUEST is to encourage continuous improvement via setting clear standards (AQS, 1996). QUEST focuses on twenty-four managerial issues listed under four broad categories: facility operations (e.g., service planning, cleanliness, health, and safety management); customer relations (e.g., customer care, customer feedback, promotion); staffing (e.g., supervision, staff planning, management); and service development and review (e.g., objectives, measurement, awards achievement) (see Maxwell et al., 2001).

Quality assurance programs have emerged for a variety of reasons. One of the most important factors influencing the rise of quality assurance programs has been the increase in cost for services. The issue here is to determine ways of maintaining quality while containing or even reducing costs. Another facet influencing the rise of quality assurance programs has been the dramatic change in the demand for leisure services and also in the types of leisure services required in today's society. Because the field is changing rapidly, there is a need to systematically ensure that quality programs and services are provided in the face of rapidly shifting societal leisure preferences. A third reason why qual-

TABLE 13.1 Differences between Evaluation and Research

	Evaluation	Research
Purpose	Focuses on improvement in some area related to the five Ps	Tries to prove or disprove hypotheses
Aim	Concerns problem solving and decision making	Concerns new knowledge that may or may not be applicable immediately
Focus	Problem based; compares the results with objectives to see how well the latter have been met	Theoretically grounded; focuses on outcomes that are related to theory
Motivation	Undertaken when there is a decision to be made and the relative worth of something is not known	Conducted to develop new knowledge
Outcomes	Evaluators are not interested in generalizing results to other situations	Should be generalizable to other situations
Reporting	Information is shared with decision makers only; no wide distribution of results	Widely published; purpose is to add to the body of knowledge

ity assurance has emerged as an important mechanism is the fact that leisure services, in some cases, are perceived to be of poor quality, delivered in a shoddy and unreliable manner. We live in a society that values quality and will accept only those services that produce the highest value and satisfaction; we live in a world where people have high expectations. Increased expectations often lead to dissatisfied, critical, and even litigious customers.

Our society is service oriented. The measurement of services is difficult, challenging, and demanding. Because of the expansion of leisure services in all segments of society, there has also been, in some cases, a deterioration in the quality of services. Those leisure service organizations that address the need to maintain or improve levels of quality are developing uniquely defined niches in society. Quality services occur because of the careful monitoring and management of the routine, day-to-day activities of an organization as well as an awareness of the perceptions of those receiving services. Quality assurance programs demand that organizations manage their programs with excellence, in a cost-effective manner, and with a strong customer orientation.

According to Richards and Rathbun (1983), the essential components of a sound quality assurance program should involve several distinct elements. We have modified their recommendations from the medical profession to apply in a broader sense to the delivery of leisure services. Their recommendations are as follows:

1. *Identification of Problems*—Identification of important or potential problems, or related concerns, in the leisure functioning of customers.
2. *Assessment*—Objective assessment of the cause or scope of problems or concerns. Basically, assessment is determination of the reasons why problems are occurring. It is one thing to identify a problem; it is another matter to know why the situation emerged.
3. *Development of Priorities*—Priorities should be established on the assumption that the resolu-

tion or prevention of problems and enhancements in services will have a positive impact on leisure functioning of customers. Conversely, priorities can be set on the basis of the predicted impact on customers if the problems identified are not resolved.
4. *Implementation*—Implementation of the quality assurance program. In other words, at this point, steps are taken that deal with the quality assurance problems that were identified.
5. *Monitoring*—Keeping track of activities that have been developed to ensure that the desired quality of services has been achieved and then sustained.
6. *Documentation*—Ensuring that appropriate records and other documents related to accountability are maintained.

Quality assurance activities have been mandated for health programs by federal health legislation. Quality assurance activities help ensure accountability to regulatory agencies, funding sources, and consumers of services (Woy, Lund, and Attkisson, 1978). Quality assurance and evaluation activities are clearly linked to each other. Both are concerned with accountability, which has emerged as a mechanism to control the impact and cost of activities. Although this idea is not new in the management of leisure service businesses, it has not been addressed forcefully in the management of political/governmental or voluntary leisure service organizations.

Key Concepts of Quality Assurance

A number of key concepts emerge that are related to the idea of quality assurance. First is the idea that quality assurance activities rely extensively on peer review rather than on internal management analysis. Second, quality assurance programs are focused on the needs and welfare of the customer and not the agency. In other words, they are customer specific rather than organizationally oriented. Next, quality assurance programs are organized in such a way as to identify appropriate and adequate levels of service delivery. Quality assurance programs demand that service levels are compared to costs and, in turn, to appropriate indicators of quality. In other words, a key concept is the cost-quality trade-off; quality should be adequate but not excessive. Finally, quality assurance activities require the development of specific service plans and the planning of the transactions that are to take place between customers and leaders.

Some of the more important definitions and terms associated with the quality assurance concept are as follows:

Quality Assessment—Quality assessment refers to a process directed toward measuring quality. It does not involve any attempt to change or improve levels of leisure functioning or program or service delivery.

Quality Assurance—Quality assurance has a dual purpose. Like quality assessment, quality assurance is concerned with measuring quality. However, quality assurance is also directed toward finding mechanisms that improve the quality of services offered to customers when necessary.

Structural Assessment—Structural assessments in a quality assurance program involve making judgments about whether the conditions that are present provide for excellence. Structural assessments may include the number and size of buildings, ratio of customers to staff, types of equipment, financial support, and staff management.

Process Assessments—Process assessment refers to the need for reviewing what happens to an individual during the course of participation in a leisure experience. In other words, how does the organization interact and handle customers that desire information about its programs, participate in them, or have some other involvement or relationship with the leisure service organization?

Outcome Assessment—Outcome assessment refers to the analysis of the level to which customers exhibit behaviors, attitudes, and skills that are desired or planned as a result of participation in a leisure experience. It can also refer to the level of leisure functioning following participation in a leisure activity.

Efficacy—Efficacy is the degree to which the customer achieves or does not achieve benefit from leisure programs and services under ideal circumstances. Whereas efficiency refers to the benefits derived under average circumstances, efficacy asks the question, What benefits can be obtained when a leisure service is delivered in circumstances that are *most advantageous* to both the customer and the service provider?

Technical Care—Technical care, especially in therapeutic recreation settings, refers to the diagnostic procedures used and methods and treatment techniques applied in terms of their appropriateness.

Art-of-Care—Whereas technical care is concerned with the procedures used in delivering services, art-of-care focuses on the measurement of the quality of interaction between the providers of leisure services and customers. Measurements might include communication patterns, leadership behavior and style, and ethical practices (confidentiality, integrity, honesty, and so on).

In assessing quality within leisure service organizations, two variables can be examined—*program elements* and *desired outcomes*. *Program elements* involve such concerns as the soundness of the physical structures within a leisure service organization, the types of objects present, the rules used to govern interactions, and the process or ordering of the leisure service program or event itself. For example, one key element in ensuring quality is to make sure that the interactions (transactions) taking place between a leader and a customer are positive. Often, this requires that individuals act in a courteous, positive, helpful, competent, and sincere fashion. When referring to *outcomes* as a way of assessing quality, we are referring to what actually happened to the customers in terms of their level of leisure satisfaction, leisure functioning, and so on.

Evaluation and Quality Assurance: Similarities and Differences

Quality assurance and evaluation activities have similarities and differences. However, one thing is clear: Both evaluation and quality assurance are concerned with accountability and control. Perhaps the most significant difference between evaluation and quality assurance is the focus of the analysis. In evaluating leisure programs, there is a tendency to analyze the performance of leisure programs and services in relation to established goals and objectives. In measuring the achievement of goals and objectives, an effort is made to determine the effectiveness and efficiency in meeting these ends. On the other hand, quality assurance activities focus on issues that are customer specific and related to the work of professionals in providing services. For example, Figure 13.2 shows a quality assurance checklist used by the Boy Scouts of America to ensure that Cub Pack units are providing proper

No. 14-220N
2001 Printing

CUB SCOUT PACK
2002 NATIONAL QUALITY UNIT AWARD

- REPORT OF ACHIEVEMENT FOR PAST CHARTER YEAR—(A)
- COMMITMENT FOR THE COMING CHARTER YEAR—(B)

Unit must achieve six of 10 to qualify as a National Quality Pack.
(Four starred [*] items are required, plus two additional items = six total.)

Pack no. _____   Chartered organization _____

City _____   State _____   Recharter month _____

District _____   Council _____

(A) Past Year   **(B)** Coming Year   Mark yes (Y) or no (N) in the box for each item.

*1. ☐ ☐ **Training.** The Cubmaster and at least 50 percent of Cub Scout den leaders and Webelos den leaders will complete Fast Start and Basic Leader Training for their current position.

*2. ☐ ☐ **Two-Deep Leadership.** We will have one or more registered, trained, and active assistant Cubmasters. One registered adult is assigned responsibility for Youth Protection training.

*3. ☐ ☐ **Outdoor Activities.** The Cub Scout pack will participate in one or more of the following experiences: Cub Scout day camp, resident camp, family camp, Webelos den overnighter(s), and/or other activities conducted or approved by the local council.

*4. ☐ ☐ **On-Time Charter Renewal.** The pack will complete its charter renewal before its current charter expires.

5. ☐ ☐ **Pack Meetings.** We will hold a minimum of nine pack meetings a year, and the pack will earn the National Summertime Pack Award.

6. ☐ ☐ **Tiger Cubs.** We will have one or more Tiger Cub dens in our pack.

7. ☐ ☐ **Service Project.** We will conduct a service project annually, preferably for the chartered organization or the community.
_____ Number of hours of community service performed by our youth members last year.

8. ☐ ☐ **Advancement.** Seventy percent or more of our Cub Scouts and Webelos Scouts will advance a rank, or we will have a 10 percent increase over a year ago. Approved rank advancements for this recognition include Bobcat, Wolf Cub Scout, Bear Cub Scout, Webelos Scout, and Arrow of Light.
_____ Number of Cub Scouts and Webelos Scouts at the beginning of the current pack charter year.
_____ Number of these Cub Scouts and Webelos Scouts who will advance rank during the pack charter year.
_____ Percentage of these Cub Scouts and Webelos Scouts who will advance a rank during the pack charter year, or
_____ Percentage increase over a year ago.

9. ☐ ☐ **Boys' Life.** A subscription to *Boys' Life* will go into the homes of all our Tiger Cubs, Cub Scouts, and Webelos Scouts, or we will have a 10 percent increase over a year ago.
_____ Number of Tiger Cub, Cub Scout, and Webelos Scout homes subscribing at the beginning of the current pack charter year.
_____ Number of Tiger Cub, Cub Scout, and Webelos Scout homes subscribing at the beginning of the next pack charter year.
_____ Percentage increase in subscriptions over a year ago, or
_____ Percentage of Tiger Cub, Cub Scout, and Webelos Scout homes subscribing at the beginning of the next charter year.

10. ☐ ☐ **Membership.** We will renew our charter with an equal or greater number of youth registered over a year ago.
_____ Number of youth registered at the beginning of the current charter year.
_____ Number of youth who will register at the beginning of the next charter year.

Achieved National Quality Unit Award past charter year **(A)**   ☐ Yes   ☐ No

_____   _____   _____
Date   Commissioner   Cubmaster

Instructions. Use ballpoint pen.
Top Sheet. Council copy. Attach to Quality Unit Recognition Form, No. 14-238Q, and submit to the local council service center.
Bottom Sheet. Unit copy. Back contains interpretation for Quality Pack Award.

Figure 13.2   A Quality Assurance Cub Pack Checklist from the Boy Scouts of America.

programs and services to Cub Scout participants. Although somewhat simplistic, the Cub Scout Pack 2002 National Quality Unit Award uses evaluation criteria to focus attention on behavioral actions oriented toward improving services (e.g., basic leadership training for den leaders, a minimum of nine Cub Pack meetings per year).

Table 13.2 points out the key differences between program evaluation and quality assurance. Quality assurance programs, especially in medical settings (which would affect many therapeutic recreation programs) have been mandated by legislation. On the other hand, evaluation schemes adopted by leisure service organizations do not emerge because of legal mandates, but often are established as one of the steps in the programming process. Another difference is that quality assurance programs

require extensive peer review, as contrasted with program evaluation, which relies primarily on administrative review. Other notable differences between these two processes are the methods used to gather information and to draw conclusions about service delivery and customer satisfaction.

APPROACHES TO EVALUATION

Although there are numerous approaches to evaluating leisure services and programs, it is important to understand the difference between quantitative and qualitative methods of collecting evaluative data. The following quotation by Henderson and Bialeschki (2002) summarizes the relationship between quantitative and qualitative methods of evaluation:

TABLE 13.2   Contrasting Characteristics between Program Evaluation and Quality Assurance

Key Variables	Program Evaluation	Quality Assurance
Legislative sanctions	Minimal but increasing	Extensive—but only in the past 10 years
Reliance on peer review	Minimal	Extensive
Reliance on administrative review	Extensive	Minimal
Level of analysis	Generalized and program specific, focused on data-based judgments about program (or service modality) effort, efficiency, effectiveness, and relevance	Client-specific and service provider-specific and focused on quality of specific service delivery transactions through reliance on service/client records
Basic objectives	• Maintain high levels of effort relative to program capacity for effort • Assess outcome and select most effective/efficient programs • Assess relevance and impact of total program effort with regard to service needs in a specified community	• Ensure that individual clients receive appropriate care • Detect deficiencies and errors in service provider capacity • Control costs by preventing overutilization and ensuring that needed services are provided in a timely, efficient manner
Principal methods	• Analysis of resource utilization, capacity for effort, and level of effort • Assessment of outcomes and the effectiveness of program effort • Assessment of program efficiency relative to effort and outcomes • Analysis of comparative cost-effectiveness • Analysis of program adequacy relative to needs for services	• Concurrent review —Admissions certification —Continued stay review —Utilization review and "length of stay" analysis • Retrospective review —Medical (clinical) care evaluation —Profile monitoring

From C. C. Atkisson, et al., *Evaluation of Human Service Programs.* Copyright © 1978 Academic Press, Orlando, FL. Reprinted by permission.

In simplest terms, quantitative data are based on collecting and using numerical calculations or statistics. Qualitative data refer to the use of words for data collection and result in patterns ascertained through analyses . . . We believe that different situations may call for a particular type of [evaluative] data. We also believe it is possible to collect and use both qualitative and quantitative data in a single evaluation project if the criteria is such that this combination would be helpful (p. 103).

Generally speaking, quantitative evaluation has the following characteristics (Henderson and Bialeschki, 2002):

- Data collection consists of numbers (quantify values via assigning numerical values)
- Examines one component of a program in isolation from the entirety of the program
- Oriented toward goal attainment
- Uniform in appearance and in data collection (fixed method)
- Typically uses paper- and pencil-techniques as a data collection instrument
- Effective to examine program product (product oriented)
- Preordinate design

Figure 13.3, from the Westerville (Ohio) Parks and Recreation Department, is an example of an evaluation form that uses quantitative methods to collect data. In particular, this evaluation form: (1) examines one component of a program in isolation from the overall recreation experience (e.g., the activity); (2) has a fixed method of collecting data that has preordinate design (e.g., feedback related to the instructor, program, and facility, Likert scale); (3) is oriented toward goal attainment (e.g., fun and enjoyable program); and (4) is product oriented. Although this evaluation form does have some space for general comments, it is specifically oriented toward collecting quantitative data from recreation participants.

Generally speaking, qualitative evaluation has the following characteristics (Henderson and Bialeschki, 2002):

- Data collection consists of words
- Examines a program from a holistic perspective

City of Westerville Parks and Recreation Department
PROGRAM EVALUATION

Dear Participants:
 Thank you for participating in our program. It is our goal to provide you with the best recreation programs and services available. Please help us to do so by telling us what you think.
IF YOU TALK ... WE WILL LISTEN

Activity Title _____

SESSION: ☐ WINTER ☐ SPRING ☐ SUMMER ☐ FALL

	EXCELLENT	GOOD	SATISFACTORY	POOR	UNSATISFACTORY	NOT APPLICABLE
INSTRUCTOR OR COACH (name)_____						
Promptness	☐	☐	☐	☐	☐	☐
Knowledge of Subject	☐	☐	☐	☐	☐	☐
Friendly and Courteous	☐	☐	☐	☐	☐	☐
PROGRAM:						
Met Expectations	☐	☐	☐	☐	☐	☐
Fun & Enjoyment	☐	☐	☐	☐	☐	☐
Skill Development	☐	☐	☐	☐	☐	☐
Cost of Program	☐	☐	☐	☐	☐	☐
FACILITY OR PARK (name)_____						
Appropriateness	☐	☐	☐	☐	☐	☐
Cleanliness	☐	☐	☐	☐	☐	☐
Maintenance	☐	☐	☐	☐	☐	☐
OVERALL RATING	☐	☐	☐	☐	☐	☐

WHAT BENEFITS DID YOU DERIVE FROM THIS PROGRAM?
_____
_____

GENERAL COMMENTS
_____
_____

Name (optional)_____
Address: _____
Telephone: _____
Thank you for your interest
Please return to
Westerville Parks & Recreation
350 N. Cleveland Ave.
Westerville, OH 43082 - Phone (614) 901-6500

Figure 13.3 Quantitative Evaluation Form from the City of Westerville (Ohio) Parks and Recreation Department.

- Evaluative appearance can change based upon sample (flexible appearance)
- Oriented toward a goal-free model
- The evaluator is often (but not always) the data collection instrument

Dear Parks and Recreation Customer:

Our staff members are dedicated to providing you great service. We need the benefit of your observations and impression of the job we are doing. If we fall short in any area, please let us know. If you are pleased with our services, we would like to hear from you. It will encourage us to do even better, and help us to recognize those members responsible for providing you great service.

We value any suggestions or comments you have.

Sincerely,

Sara Hensley
Director
Virginia Beach Parks and Recreation

Dear Sara,

_____

_____

_____

_____

_____

_____

_____

_____

_____

_____

_____

_____

_____

If you would like a response, please complete the following:

Name _____   *Daytime phone* _____

Address _____   *Evening phone* _____

City _____   *Zip code* _____

Facility visited _____   *E-mail address* _____

Figure 13.4 Qualitative Evaluation Form from Virginia Beach (Virginia) Parks and Recreation.

- Effective to examine program effectiveness (process oriented)
- Emerging design

Figure 13.4, from the Virginia Beach (Virginia) Parks and Recreation, is an example of an evaluation form that uses qualitative methods to collect data. In particular, this evaluation form: (1) examines the entire leisure experience from a holistic perspective (not just the activity); (2) allows the recreation participant to have flexibility to write on his/her experiences (opposed to uniformed questions); (3) is more goal-free; and (4) is process oriented.

A number of approaches and models can be used to evaluate the 5 Ps (participants, per-

Experience the Fun!™

Virginia Beach Parks and Recreation

Director
Virginia Beach Parks and Recreation
2408 Courthouse Drive, Building 21
City of Virginia Beach Municipal Center
Virginia Beach, VA 23456

Direct Line to the Director

Your Comments are Important to Us!

Affix postage here

Figure 13.4—*Continued.*

sonnel, place, policies, and programs). This section provides six selected approaches to evaluation, with representative models to illustrate their relationship to recreation programming. These selected approaches are not all-inclusive but do provide the reader with basic tools with which to begin. The value and applicability of any of these models lie in diversity and adaptability, not in uniformity and rigidity (Patton, 1978). Thus, the reader should analyze the underlying premise of how these approaches apply to specific situations rather than try to simply apply the examples to a current problem.

The six selected approaches are: (1) goal/objectives; (2) goal-free; (3) expert judgment; (4) systems designs; (5) policy analysis; and (6) -satisfaction-based.

Goals/Objectives Approach

The goals/objectives approach to evaluation is an example of applying education evaluation techniques to recreation and leisure programs. The basis of this approach is the predetermination of goals and objectives that have measurable outcomes. The more general the goal, the more difficult it is to determine specific outcomes. Thus, this approach focuses on specific objectives in which definite outcomes can be measured.

A goal is a clear, general statement about where the organization and its programs are going and how that relates to its purpose or mission. Some examples of broad goals are:

1. To improve the quality of life
2. To improve leisure wellness
3. To provide leisure for all
4. To help satisfy the leisure needs of customers
5. To contribute to the overall leisure functioning of individuals
6. To provide programs for all community residents

Although these broad goals are admirable, the evaluator is faced with the problem of how to determine whether they are met. Therefore, specific objectives must be set, which if met will contribute to the attainment of the goal in order to provide the mechanism for measurement.

Goal attainment evaluation is based on measuring the congruence between performance and objectives. Objectives can be defined as written or expressed intentions about intended outcomes. This approach requires well-written objectives and good criteria. Writing objectives is time-consuming and exacting work. However, this evaluation approach cannot be done without having measurable objectives that relate to the overall goals of the organization. The essential elements of objectives are: description of a task, who will do it, identifying the action that should be taken and its conditions, and stating the criteria for an acceptable minimal level of performance of the task (Lundegren and Farrell, 1985).

Objectives can be organizational based or performance based. Organizational objectives address the process that is used to achieve the goals of the organization. For example, an organizational objective might be to recruit and train a diversified staff to administer a youth program. Another organizational objective might be to increase program offerings for underserved populations by 10 percent.

Behavior, or performance, objectives are a description of the performance that participants or staff need to be able to exhibit once they have achieved the stated objectives. For instance, a behavioral objective for a basketball class might be that, at the end, a participant is able to shoot ten free throws in a row. A performance objective for a staff member might be that he or she initiated five new interest groups during a specific programming period.

When writing either performance or organizational objectives, it is important to keep in mind the area in which change is desired. Well-written objectives can provide the foundation for collecting data and making judgments about any of the five areas of evaluation (participants, personnel, place, policies, and programs). Written correctly, objectives become the criteria for evaluation.

Goal-Free Approach

An opposite approach to goal-attainment is an approach called goal-free evaluation. This evaluation technique is sometimes referred to as the black box model. Although it has been around for many years, this approach has only recently been adopted for practice by many professionals.

The basis of this approach is the examination of an organization, group of participants, or program irrespective of any goals. In other words, the intent of goal-free evaluation is to discover and judge actual effects, outcomes, or impacts without considering what the effects were supposed to be (Henderson and Bialeschki, 1996). In this approach, the evaluator begins with no preconceived idea about what the outcomes might be. The value of this type of evaluation lies in discovering items that may have unintended side effects. Scriven (1967) states that if the main objective of an evaluation is to assess the worth of outcomes, no distinction at all should be made between those outcomes that were intended as opposed to those that were not.

Realistically, no evaluation approach is goal-free, because the purpose of evaluation is to answer some type of question or to do a comparison. In addition, the evaluator can only select a certain amount of information out of the total information available in order to complete an evaluation. To be useful, data are collected in relation to recognized concerns or guiding questions. These concerns often emerge from issues identified by internal and external publics. The strength of this approach, proponents would argue, is that the evaluator is more responsive to these publics by being free to choose the range of concerns used for an evaluation.

The actual data collection in this model may be either qualitative or quantitative. In this approach, the evaluator usually talks to participants and staff, identifies program elements, discovers purposes and concerns, and conceptualizes issues and problems. Once this is done, the evaluator will identify the qualitative or quantitative data that needs to be collected, select the appropriate data collection methods and techniques to use, match data and the issues of audiences, and prepare and deliver the report.

This approach relies heavily on logical analysis and observation as well as other data collection methods. The major drawback to this approach is that it is very time consuming. In addition, some outcomes may be difficult to measure. However, the advantage of the approach is that it can provide in-depth information about the five Ps of evaluation.

Expert Judgment Approach

Sometimes it is necessary to obtain another opinion regarding the delivery of leisure programs. The use of experts or consultants to evaluate parts of a leisure program, or the entire program, is common practice. Although the expert may choose to use some formal approaches to evaluation, usually the agency seeks the expert's opinions or judgments. For example, due to numerous concerns (e.g., death of animals, uncertainty over state expenditures, financial difficulty), the Utah Legislature hired two expert consultants to provide an extensive evaluation on Hogle Zoo in Salt Lake City (Report to the Utah Legislature, 2002). This government document, which can be viewed at http://www.le.state.ut.us/audit/02_02.rpt.pdf, also includes a response to

the evaluation by the executive director of the Utah Zoological Society.

The positive side of using the expert judgment approach is that the approach and results tend to be specific and void of complicated forms, process, or statistical treatments. In addition, the expert may bring his or her reputation to bear on the outcome of the evaluation. The drawbacks to this approach include: (1) the expert's biases and prejudices; (2) the focus on one portion of the program rather than the entire effort; (3) the lack of a valid and reliable methodology; (4) subjective nature of the effort; and (5) the cost.

Individuals who can provide expert judgment oftentimes bring a fresh point of view to the evaluation process. They may view the program in an entirely different light. Using experts to pass judgments on a portion of a program does appear to be something of a luxury.

A variation of this approach is through the use of standards. This approach is generally used in some type of accreditation process, such as the newly established agency accreditation by the National Recreation and Park Association. This type of expert judgment involves a critical review by an evaluator who is deemed an expert because he or she has had training in judging established predetermined minimum criteria for service delivery.

A standard is a statement of desirable practice or a level of performance for a given situation that has been agreed on by a consensus of professionals. Standards are written as minimal, not maximal, goals of achievement. People adopting professional standards are assuming that if stated desirable practices are followed, the program will be effective. Standards are helpful in that they enable evaluation by comparison through ascertaining what is actually happening within an organization compared with what the accepted standard of desirability is within a given profession.

Because most standards are based on professional judgments about desirability, not scientific evidence, they should be reviewed regularly and revised as conditions change. In order to be effective, standards should:

1. Meet the needs of the population being served
2. Be reasonably attainable
3. Be acceptable and usable to the leisure services professional
4. Reflect the latest information concerning professional practice
5. Stand the test of time (although modification should reflect changing societal conditions)

Organizations using this approach usually do a self-evaluation, make changes and improvements to comply with the minimum expectations or guidelines established by a professional body, and have trained outside experts confirm that the agency is meeting the existing standards. The process of evaluation by standards is well-known in the recreation field. Standards are employed in facility design (National Recreation and Park Association Space Standards) and camps (American Camping Association Standards for Day and Resident Camps), agency operations (National Recreation and Park Association Agency Accreditation), university curricula (National Recreation and Park Association/ American Association for Leisure and Recreation Accreditation), therapeutic recreation programs in hospitals (Joint Commission on Accreditation of Healthcare Organizations), and playgrounds (American Society for Test and Measurement).

The standards used for accreditation are usually criterion referenced. That is, evaluations are based on some standard level of performance. The evaluator assesses whether standard objectives have been met. This type of measurement is not used to compare one organization with another, merely to check if a level of performance has been met.

Norm-referenced standards might also be used in some situations. These measures tell the relative position of a person or thing in reference to another person or thing, using the same measuring tool. The most widely known norm-referencing measurement is the standard IQ test, which has come under considerable fire in recent years. In leisure services, norm-referenced standards are generally used to determine a person's physical fitness in reference to others in the same age group.

Systems Designs and Decision-Oriented Approach

Systems designs, as applied to the provision of leisure services, involve a step-by-step analysis of the procedures and events used in organizing and delivering programs. Subsequently, an analysis of the extent to which these procedural models produce desired outcomes allows for evaluation to occur. Systems designs enable the programmer to gauge the extent to which desired outcomes are produced by a particular preconceived approach to organizing a program. Thus, systems designs guide planning and implementation activities and serve as a basis for review and control of programs.

Three techniques are particularly useful in evaluating leisure services and serve to illustrate the application of systems designs to the evaluation process. These techniques are program evaluation review technique (PERT), critical path method (CPM), and management by objectives (MBO).

PERT is an event-oriented technique that focuses on the planning, scheduling, and controlling of events in a quantitative manner. Its primary analytical device is a network, or flow chart, which illustrates how the programmer moves toward achieving a stated goal or objective. In the PERT chart, major events are noted, with activity linkage between events. Time estimated to complete the event is listed between the events. This estimate of time is expressed in the following manner:

1. *Optimistic Time (to)*—Length of time required without complications or unforeseen difficulties arising in the activity.
2. *Most Likely Time (tm)*—Length of time in which the activity is most likely to be completed; estimated under "normal" conditions.

3. *Pessimistic Time (tp)*—Length of time required if unusual complications or unforeseen difficulties occur (Williams, 1972: 17–18).

A PERT estimate of time, for example, can show that the time needed to complete a particular activity can be estimated optimistically (three hours), realistically or most likely (six hours), and pessimistically (nine hours).

PERT can be used in a variety of ways, including research and development, program planning, construction, maintenance, staff development, and building or area operations. There are six distinct advantages to using PERT:

1. Creation of a realistic, detailed, easy-to-communicate plan, which greatly improves the chances for attainment of project objectives.
2. Prediction of time and uncertainties of performance.
3. Attention focused on parts of a project that are most likely to impede or delay its achievement.
4. Information provided about project resources that are not being fully utilized.
5. Simulation of alternative plans and schedules.
6. Provision of thorough and frequent project status reports.

PERT requires training in order to be used effectively as a technique in parks and recreation. More sophisticated aspects, including computer applications, require additional training in computer programming.

The first step in PERT is to establish the program or project objective. Once the objective is identified, the programmer needs to delineate all tasks or activities necessary to accomplish the objective. The next step is to actually plot the information on a Gantt or bar chart (see Figure 13.5) or on a network.

PERT incorporates the critical path method (CPM) in that each activity is graphically illustrated, so that the least restrictive, most expeditious path is taken to ensure maximum return and efficiency in program delivery. Mittelesteadt and Berger (1972) describe the CPM and its application to program or activity execution. Figure 13.6 illustrates the steps required to produce or sponsor a dramatic show.

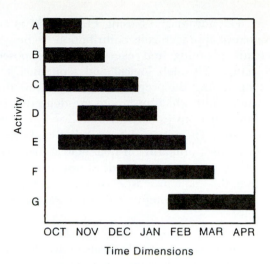

Figure 13.5 Sample Gantt or Bar Chart.

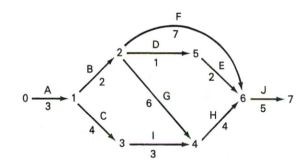

Task	Time
Task A	Choose and obtain play and director
Task B	Cast actors
Task C	Select staff
Task D	Prepare scenery and props
Task E	Install scenery and props
Task F	Advertise play
Task G	Rehearse actors
Task H	Prepare costuming and effects
Task I	Print tickets and programs
Task J	Dress rehearsal

Figure 13.6 CPM for a Drama Presentation. (Mittlesteadt, A. H. & Berger, H. A. 1972. The critical path method: A management tool for recreation. *Parks and Recreation* 8 (7): 14–15.)

The advantage of using PERT/CPM as an evaluative approach is its contribution to the systematic planning and execution of proposed objectives. Through logical and sequential systems planning, the programmer can improve the efficiency with which programs are delivered. In addition, it is an excellent model for formative evaluation. The major drawback is that PERT/CPM focuses primarily on quantitative measurements of performance. It does not attempt to analyze the qualitative aspects of a program.

Additional benefits of PERT/CPM are that it will:

1. Encourage a logical discipline in the planning, scheduling, and control of projects;
2. Encourage more long-range and detailed planning of projects;
3. Provide a standard method of documenting and communicating project plans, schedules, and time and cost performance;
4. Identify the most critical elements in the plan, focusing management attention on the 10 to 20 percent of the project that is most constraining on the schedule; and
5. Illustrate the effects of technical and procedural changes on the overall schedule (Moder and Phillips, 1964: 5–6).

Although there are several key proponents of management by objectives (MBO), there are almost as many definitions as there are proponents. McConkey (1975: 10–11) defines MBO as

A systems approach to managing an organization. . . . It is not a technique, or just another program, or a narrow area of the process of managing . . . it encompasses budgetary (but goes far beyond). First, those accountable for directing the organization determine where they want to take the organization or what they want it to achieve during a particular period. . . . Second, all key managerial, professional, and administrative personnel are required, permitted, and encouraged to contribute their maximum efforts to achieving the overall objectives. Third, the planned achievements (results) of all key personnel are blended and balanced to pro-

mote and realize the greater total results for the organization as a whole. Fourth, a control mechanism is established to monitor progress compared to objectives and feed the results back to those accountable at all levels.

MBO utilizes the systems approach to planning and decision making and is composed of five components: objectives; plan; managerial direction and action; control (monitoring); and feedback.

Policy Analysis Approach

The policy analysis is yet another way to evaluate leisure programs. In order to provide leisure services, organizations, agencies, and businesses promulgate policies, procedures, and practices to guide their work. Analyzing organizational policies prior to their implementation attempts to predict: (1) What effects will be produced if the policy is implemented? or (2) What effects will be produced if the policy is not implemented? The difference between these two courses of action will indicate the predicted effect of the policy. Conversely, analyzing policies after they have been implemented can help the organization determine the degree to which the policy and consequent program have had the intended effect. The policy analysis approach focuses on the examination of agency policies with the intent that thorough examination and evaluation will result in policies being retained, reformulated, or discarded.

Four basic approaches to policy analysis can be employed by leisure service organizations: (1) impact analysis, (2) cost-benefit analysis, (3) implementation analysis, and (4) political analysis. Following is a brief discussion of each of these approaches to policy analysis.

Impact Analysis

Impact analysis attempts to determine what societal changes will occur if a policy is implemented. This analysis constructs a systematic plan to collect and analyze data in order to attempt to predict the impact on society of a given program. A policy can have an economical, political, social, cultural, or environmental impact on individuals, institutions, communities, and social systems.

Cost-Benefit Analysis

Cost-benefit analysis attempts to weigh the resources that will be committed to implement a given policy against the predicted policy outcomes. It is a process for structuring a decision-making framework to evaluate alternatives and select the best course of action. Cost-benefit analysis is particularly useful in trying to decide between two programs or projects that achieve the same objectives.

Implementation Analysis

Implementation analysis focuses on the feasibility of procedures, methods, and practices associated with a given policy. This approach asks the question, Can the agency carry out the policy? Just because a policy is established doesn't guarantee that an organization has the capacity or ability to implement it. Organizations may not produce the desired impact because they lack the resources, not because the policy is faulty.

Political Analysis

Political analysis attempts to determine whether a policy will be acceptable to decision makers. If decision makers are not willing to support a policy, it is not likely to be implemented. Therefore, this is an important aspect of policy analysis.

The examination of policies is an often overlooked practice in the evaluation of programs and services. This approach helps determine the feasibility and desirability of policies that exist within organizations. This approach to evaluation is especially useful in political/governmental organizations and voluntary organizations. However, it is not confined or limited to either of these two sectors.

Satisfaction-Based Approach

The satisfaction-based program approach to evaluation provides specific data concerning participant satisfaction with program services. These data can be used to judge the worth of program services from a client-based perspective. The basic assumption of this approach is that the client is the best judge about whether a specific program has met his or her leisure needs. According to Rossman (1995), participant-reported satisfaction with leisure engagements is a well-accepted measure of leisure outcome.

In this approach, data is gathered by administering an end-of-program questionnaire that relates to identified satisfaction domains. Rossman (1995) has identified ten satisfaction domains, which are shown in Table 13.3. Some or all of these domains may be included in the individual questionnaire administered to the participant. An example of a questionnaire that reflects these domains is shown in Figure 13.7.

Data gathered from a satisfaction-based questionnaire can be helpful to an agency in several ways. First, it can be used to document the outcomes of a specific program from the client's point of view. Although a programmer may observe behavior that he or she interprets as client satisfaction during the course of an activity, this method allows the programmer to document these observations in data form. Thus, the programmer has the facts to back up his or her personal judgment about the value of the activity.

Second, data gathered can help determine if the program goals are being met. As mentioned under the goals/objectives approach, sometimes broad goals are written in too-general terms to provide specific information. This method provides some of the specific information to reinforce the broad goals.

Third, if the same instrumentation is used across program offerings, the data can be used to compare the satisfaction produced in different program areas. For instance, the summarized satisfaction data of cultural arts programs could be compared with the summarized satisfaction data of all leisure wellness programs. This comparison allows programmers to determine the

TABLE 13.3   Satisfaction Domains

Achievement
Provides information concerning mastery of an activity, new skill development, and success at tackling a new experience.

Autonomy
Provides information about participant's sense of control over the situation. Data reveals sense of independence versus dependence.

Environment
Provides information about satisfaction with place including such items as cleanliness, design, and physical attractiveness.

Family Escape
Provides information about participant's feeling that he or she has successfully escaped the cares and worries associated with the interrelationship with family members.

Family Togetherness
Provides information about participant's feeling that the activity has successfully allowed him or her to relate to other family members.

Fun
Provides information concerning the psychological perception of enjoyment and pleasure within an activity.

Physical Fitness
Provides information concerning participant's feeling of becoming physically active and fit.

Relaxation
Provides information about how stress-free an individual feels as a result of participating in an activity.

Risk
Provides information as to the perception of danger (physical, psychological, and emotional) that the individual felt as a result of participation in an activity.

Social Enjoyment
Provides information about companionship and friendship that was experienced during the course of the activity.

strengths and weaknesses of their total program offerings from the client viewpoint.

These six approaches provide a way to frame the evaluation process. They offer a context for assumptions about different methods of determining criteria and collecting data. They can be used in varying degrees by any leisure agency. Prior to engaging in the evaluation process, it is essential to determine which approach best sets the framework for the evaluation. Table 13.4 provides a summary of the strengths and weaknesses of each of the approaches.

Customer satisfaction is of high concern for leisure service organizations. The city of Long Beach (California) provides customer satisfaction survey forms for individuals participating in

programs. The surveys enable individuals to rate the condition of the facilities and the quality of the program and staff as well as provide information about how they learned of the program, service, or facility used (see Figure 13.8).

DATA COLLECTION: AN OVERVIEW OF INSTRUMENTS

Earlier in the chapter, we mentioned the five categories of items to be evaluated (participants, personnel, place, policies, and programs). To evaluate any one or all of these categories, the leisure service programmer selects an appropriate model, or approach. Each of these approaches needs to use some type of instrumentation to collect data. Some of the general

Listed below are statements that may reflect your satisfaction with this program. Please indicate by circling the appropriate number on each scale the degree to which each statement contributed to your satisfaction with this program.

Statement	Very Satisfying	Satisfying	Neutral	Little Satisfaction	No Satisfaction
(Achievement)					
I learned more about the activity	1	2	3	4	5
I was able to develop new skills	1	2	3	4	5
(Autonomy)					
I had control over the activity	1	2	3	4	5
I had a chance to be alone	1	2	3	4	5
(Environment)					
The area was physically attractive	1	2	3	4	5
The design of the facility was appropriate	1	2	3	4	5
(Family Escape)					
I was able to escape my family obligations	1	2	3	4	5
I felt no family obligations during the activity	1	2	3	4	5
(Family Togetherness)					
The activity brought the family together	1	2	3	4	5
Our family could do this together	1	2	3	4	5
(Fun)					
This was a pleasurable activity	1	2	3	4	5
I had fun	1	2	3	4	5
(Physical Fitness)					
The activity helps keep me physically fit	1	2	3	4	5
I enjoyed the physical exercise	1	2	3	4	5
(Relaxation)					
I was able to relax during the activity	1	2	3	4	5
I experienced a sense of tranquility	1	2	3	4	5
(Risk)					
I experienced an element danger	1	2	3	4	5
I like the element of risk in the activity	1	2	3	4	5
(Social Enjoyment)					
I made new friends during the activity	1	2	3	4	5
I enjoyed the social interaction in the activity	1	2	3	4	5

Figure 13.7 Satisfaction-Based Questionnaire. (Adapted from Rossman, J. R. 1995. *Recreation Programming: Designing Leisure Experiences,* 2nd ed. Champaign, IL: Sagamore.)

types of instrumentation used are attitude and rating scales, case and field studies, checklists, importance performance analysis, and questionnaires. However, before data collection can take place, the programmer must first know what is to be evaluated and what technique is to be used in collecting the required information or data.

This section presents an overview of several instruments for data collection. The programmer should be cautious when selecting a

TABLE 13.4 Summary of the Strengths and Weaknesses of Evaluation Approaches

Approach	Strengths	Weaknesses
Goal/Objectives	Most commonly used Uses predetermined goals and objectives Objective viewpoint	Needs good goals and objectives Requires measurement instrument Time-consuming
Goal-free	Allows for qualitative data Examines actual effects Uses logical analysis	Goal-free impossible to attain Possible bias Evaluator driven
Expert judgment	Uses expert opinion Standards based Easy for organization Not time-consuming	Must have trained expert Expensive Does not ensure quality
Systems designs	Process oriented Useful in management	Broad-based Complicated to use
Policy analysis	Provides for alternatives in decision making Determines feasibility of policies Helps determine political consequences to the organization	Policies may be incomplete or nonexistent Time-consuming
Satisfaction-based	Participant-oriented Can provide comparison data	Needs reliable instrumentation

measuring instrument. Farrell and Lundegren (1983: 222–23) suggest twelve attributes of a good measuring instrument:

1. The first attribute and the most important one is that the test should possess reliability, validity, and objectivity. If these qualities are missing, then there is almost no need to judge it further—it is not adequate.
2. The tool should measure the important factors. What these factors are should be determined by the objectives of the program or its subparts.
3. The tool should be appropriate to the participants being evaluated in terms of such things as age, sex, and special factors (e.g., reading level). For example, the Tennessee Self-Concept Scale requires a sixth-grade reading level and is therefore inappropriate for young children.
4. The tool should discriminate between those people, programs, or facilities that possess the trait being measured and those who do not have it, and be sensitive enough to identify a real difference if one exists.
5. The instrument should be given in a reasonable length of time. For example, a questionnaire

that takes one-and-one-half hours to administer would not be the tool of choice at the formative evaluation stage of a new crafts program.
6. A good instrument should be easy to prepare and administer—the less complex the better, providing it still does what it is purported to do.
7. Availability of norms and standards should be considered, as they serve to strengthen interpretation of test results.
8. The tool should have clear, concise directions.
9. The scores should be readily interpretable.
10. The attribute that is being measured should be clearly delineated so as to specify what was lacking and what modification is needed. For example, if a campsite in a state park was rated on a score of one to ten, and it received a score of four, what has the park superintendent learned about modifying the site to receive a score of ten? The person receiving the evaluation should gain some idea of what to change. Feedback should be provided by the instrument.
11. Tested scoring directions should be provided.
12. The tool should measure unique data that have not already been gained in some other way.

Figure 13.8 Customer Survey, City of Long Beach (California) Park, Recreation, and Marine Department.

Attitude and Rating Scales

The *measurement of an individual's attitude* is usually difficult. Several data collection approaches and instruments can be used to obtain quantitative measures. Attitude scales generally attempt to overcome errors obtained from using rating scales. Pelegrino (1979) indicates that two criteria are commonly used in selecting items for inclusion in a scale.

First, the items must elicit responses that are psychologically related to the attitudes being measured. Second, the scale must differentiate among people who are at different points concerning the dimension being measured. To differentiate among such individuals, items that are discriminated at different points on the scale are usually included (Pelegrino, 1979: 158).

The three basic attitude scales are (1) the Likert (summation) scale, (2) equal appearing intervals, and (3) the cumulative scale.

The most popular and widely used attitude scale in recreation is the Likert scale. This data collection technique is a scale of, for example, five items ranging from (5) *strongly agree* to

(1) *strongly disagree*. Other points on the scale would include (4) *agree*, (3) *undecided*, and (2) *disagree*. The ability to assign a numerical value to each category allows for statistical treatment. An example of the Likert scale is provided in Table 13.5.

An additional attitude measurement that is frequently used in leisure studies is the semantic differential technique. The essence of this technique is the establishment of bipolar objective pairs (e.g., leisure-work) and a scale on which the respondent can select a position. Neulinger (1974: 175–76) incorporates this technique in his study of leisure. An example is presented in Table 13.6.

Peterson and Stumbo (2000) provide another type of scale, referred to as a *rating scale*. The intent of the rating scale is to determine the level of performance of an individual during a specific observation period. This is usually done in relation to selected behavioral objectives. Table 13.7 provides information on a therapeutic recreation relaxation program and the performance of each participant.

Each of these measurement tools is appropriate to use in collecting data on personnel, program/operations, policy dimensions/administration, customers, and physical/fiscal resources.

Case and Field Study

Case studies are in-depth investigations of an individual, a unit, an organization, or an agency. The data are organized in a manner that presents not only a historical perspective but also details regarding the individual or unit. Depending on the purpose, the programmer might study a portion of, or the entire life of an individual. For example, Reichwein and Fox's (2001) case study of Margaret Fleming and the Alpine Club of Canada offers historical insights regarding a women's perspective in mountain leisure—this information adds clarity to outdoor recreation and leisure programming (e.g., policies, delivery of services). Case studies are written in a narrative fashion with certain points highlighted or illustrated in the body of the report. For example, Dustin, Schneider, McAvoy, and Frakt (2002) provided a policy analysis, evaluative case study of how the National Park Service and United States Department of the Interior have dealt with recreational conflict among American Indians and traditional rock climbers at Devil's Tower National Monument in

---

TABLE 13.5   Example of Likert Scale

Below are listed a number of free-time activities. Using the scale values given, indicate what in your opinion society's position regarding these activities should be.

This Activity Should Be	Scale Values
Very strongly encouraged	7
Strongly encouraged	6
Encouraged	5
Neither encouraged nor discouraged	4
Discouraged	3
Strongly discouraged	2
Very strongly discouraged	1

Free-Time Activities	Your Position
a—Activities emphasizing mental endeavors such as studying, taking adult education courses, etc.	_____ (1)
b—Activities involving the taking of habit-forming drugs	_____ (2)
c—Activities that consist basically of doing nothing, being idle, "hanging around," etc.	_____ (3)
d—Activities involving active participation in social affairs, such as volunteer work, club activities, etc.	_____ (4)
e—Activities that consist basically of doing nothing or efforts such as writing, painting, or playing an instrument	_____ (5)
f—Activities involving the consumption of alcohol	_____ (6)
g—Activities involving productive efforts, such as certain hobbies like wood-working, leather tooling, sewing, etc.	_____ (7)
h—Activities involving physical exercise, such as sports and calisthenics, hunting and fishing, or just walking	_____ (8)

From J. Neulinger, *The Psychology of Leisure*, 1974. Courtesy of Charles C Thomas, Publisher, Springfield, IL.

TABLE 13.6   Example of Semantic Differential Scale

Below are sixteen 7-point scales, each referring to a word pair. Use these scales to describe what *leisure* means to you. The scale points indicate the following:

1 = Extremely
2 = Quite
3 = Slightly
4 = Neutral or unrelated
5 = Slightly
6 = Quite
7 = Extremely

Put a check mark at that point on the scale that best describes what leisure means to you.

For example, if the word pair is
beautiful   1   2   3   4   5   6   7   ugly

and you feel that leisure is *quite* beautiful, you would check 2 on the scale (as shown in the example); on the other hand, if you feel that leisure is *extremely* ugly, you would check 7 on the scale.

Word Pairs

Leisure Is:

boring	1	2	3	4	5	6	7	interesting	(51)
solitary	1	2	3	4	5	6	7	sociable	(52)
honest	1	2	3	4	5	6	7	dishonest	(53)
empty	1	2	3	4	5	6	7	full	(54)
desirable	1	2	3	4	5	6	7	undesirable	(55)
necessary	1	2	3	4	5	6	7	unnecessary	(56)
powerful	1	2	3	4	5	6	7	powerless	(57)
mature	1	2	3	4	5	6	7	developing	(58)
valuable	1	2	3	4	5	6	7	worthless	(59)
meaningful	1	2	3	4	5	6	7	meaningless	(60)
passive	1	2	3	4	5	6	7	active	(61)
satisfying	1	2	3	4	5	6	7	unsatisfying	(62)
thin	1	2	3	4	5	6	7	thick	(63)
good	1	2	3	4	5	6	7	bad	(64)
refreshing	1	2	3	4	5	6	7	tiring	(65)
pleasant	1	2	3	4	5	6	7	unpleasant	(66)

From J. Neulinger, *The Psychology of Leisure*, 1974. Courtesy of Charles C Thomas, Publisher, Springfield, IL.

Wyoming. Likewise, Dieser (2002) reported an evaluative, narrative-oriented case study that highlighted harmful therapeutic recreation practice when leisure and human service professionals lack cross-cultural competencies.

The data collected in the case study are particularly useful as background information for planning in-depth investigations. Usually because of its intensive nature, the case study will reveal much more than an ordinary investigation or review. The weakness of the case study is in its numbers. Very few statistical treatments are capable of dealing with the small sample size used in this data collection method.

According to Farrell and Lundegren (1983: 239), the general steps in the case study approach are:

1. Identify the focus of the investigation. Is it the behavior of an individual, a study of a community, or a program with a larger structure?
2. Identify the nature of what needs to be studied in regard to this focus. Is it in the affective, the

TABLE 13.7 Example of Likert Scale

Performance Sheet

PROGRAM: _____ Relaxation _____   STAFF: _____
                                                 DATE: _____

ENABLING OBJECTIVES

TPO 1. EO 1. Knowledge of benefits
EO 2. Stress and its sources
EO3. Physical manifestations
TPO 2. EO 1. Diaphragmatic breathing
EO 2. Knowledge of warm-ups
EO 3. Progressive relaxation
EO 4. Centering techniques

NAMES

1. _____
2. _____
3. _____
4. _____
5. _____
6. _____
7. _____
8. _____
9. _____
10. _____
11. _____
12. _____
13. _____
14. _____
15. _____

cognitive, or the psychomotor domain? For example, evaluation of the leader may be in the affective domain, the participant in the psychomotor domain, and the agency in the cognitive domain.

3. Select the measurement tools to collect the appropriate data. The tools used are such things as questionnaires, rating scales, anecdotal records, logs, diaries, attitude scales, life history or biographical forms, and various sociometric instruments.

4. Collect the data in a planned, systematic way (see specifics under the individual methods described earlier in this chapter), optimizing the available evaluators to get the most usable data in a reasonable time frame.

5. Collect and present the data in a logical way.

6. Interpret data in a manner appropriate both to the situation studied and to the audience to whom the report is directed.

7. On the basis of the findings, prepare solutions to problems and make general recommendations.

Case studies as a data collection tool are limited in their application. The primary application would be to personnel and consumers. In some instances, this approach could be used to describe a program or operations, policy dimensions, or administration of a particular effort.

Checklists

Probably one of the most frequently used data collection instruments in recreation and leisure fields is the checklist. This approach is simply *a listing of items to be checked off by a programmer, leader, supervisor, or support personnel.* The varieties of checklists are as abundant as the varieties of processes to collect information.

The use of checklists is somewhat limited in terms of their application to quantitative measurement. The programmer will be able to obtain a frequency indication regarding the particular item being evaluated but the data does not lend itself to higher levels of statistical treatment. Checklists come in many varieties. Table 13.8 provides an example of a checklist used in the maintenance of a program area. The Foothills (Lakewood, Colorado) Metropolitan Recreation and Park District provides customers with a simple checklist for determining whether their expectations have been met or exceeded. This checklist can be placed in a drop box (see Figure 13.9). Another example of a checklist is provided by the city of Aurora (Colorado) Parks and Open Space Department. Figure 13.10 depicts this agency's "Recreation Facility/Program Report Card." This form has an incentive at the bottom of it—that is, a coupon for a drawing.

TABLE 13.8 Maintenance Checklist for Crafts Room

Tudor Recreation Center Daily Maintenance Checklist (Crafts Room) (To be filled out and initialed each day)

M	T	W	Th	F	S	
☐	☐	☐	☐	☐	☐	1. Oven unplugged
☐	☐	☐	☐	☐	☐	2. All water turned off
☐	☐	☐	☐	☐	☐	3. Table tops cleared
☐	☐	☐	☐	☐	☐	4. Storage cabinets locked
☐	☐	☐	☐	☐	☐	5. Tool rack inspected; all tools accounted for
☐	☐	☐	☐	☐	☐	6. Floor swept
☐	☐	☐	☐	☐	☐	7. Trash emptied into large Dumpster outside
☐	☐	☐	☐	☐	☐	8. Floor mopped
☐	☐	☐	☐	☐	☐	9. Lights turned out
☐	☐	☐	☐	☐	☐	10. Windows secured
☐	☐	☐	☐	☐	☐	11. Doors locked
						Thank you.

WEEK OF_____

SIGNED_____

How's our fun factor?

Thanks for making Foothills part of your leisure time! We are committed to providing excellent service at our recreation facilities.

Please give us your candid comments on what we do right and where we need to improve. And thanks in advance for your help!

Bob Bonacci
Executive Director
987-3602

	Exceeded Expectations		Met Expectations		Below Expectations
	5	4	3	2	1
Facility Exterior					
Adequate parking					
Parking lot/entrance lighting					
Appearance					
Signs					
Facility Cleanliness					
Facility overall					
Rest room/locker room					
Facility Staff					
Courtesy					
Knowledge					
Appearance					
Responsiveness					
Registration					
Brochure description					
Registration convenience					

Comments

_____
_____
_____
_____
_____
_____

Was the space appropriate for the activity you participated in? (light, temperature, sound level etc.) ☐ Yes ☐ No

Does the facility schedule meet your needs? ☐ Yes ☐ No
If not, what would you change?

_____
_____

Please leave us your name and comments so we can personally reply to your valuable comments.

Name _____ Phone _____

Address _____

City _____ State _____ Zip _____

Age Group ☐ under 20   ☐ 20–39   ☐ 40–60   ☐ over 60
Do you live ☐ in the Foothills district   ☐ outside of the district
             ☐ in Jefferson County

Figure 13.9 Sample Evaluation Form Using a Checklist, Foothills (Lakewood, Colorado) Metropolitan Recreation and Park District.

Recreation Facility/Program Report Card

Please give us a moment to help us serve you better. Our goal is to make your experience at our facilities and programs an enjoyable one. Completing this survey helps us improve our programs and provide better service. Please be assured your responses will remain confidential.

Completed surveys are entered in a drawing for gift certificates for recreation programs. Please complete and return to the front desk/gate, unless otherwise directed.

1. What recreation facility are you at today? _____

2. What activity/program are you participating in today?
_____

3. How did you hear about the facility/program?
   ☐ Neighbor/Friend   ☐ Leisure Brochure
   ☐ Television Channel 8   ☐ Aurora Sentinel
   ☐ Post/News   ☐ Other (Please specify)
   _____

4. Day of activity
   ☐ Monday ☐ Tuesday ☐ Wednesday ☐ Thursday
         ☐ Friday ☐ Saturday ☐ Sunday

5. Time of activity
   ☐ Morning ☐ Afternoon ☐ Evening

6. Month of activity
   ☐ Jan   ☐ Feb   ☐ Mar   ☐ Apr   ☐ May
        ☐ June   ☐ July   ☐ Aug
   ☐ Sept ☐ Oct   ☐ Nov   ☐ Dec

7. How many years have you lived in the
   Denver/Aurora metro area?_____years

8. How many years have you participated in Aurora Parks and
   Recreation programs?_____years

9. Your age: _____years

10. Please rate this facility:
    Leave answer blank if question is not applicable.

	Below Expectations		Met Expectations		Exceeded Expectations
a. Parking convenience	1	2	3	4	5
b. Lighting (parking lot)	1	2	3	4	5
c. Lighting (entrance)	1	2	3	4	5
d. Directional signs to facility	1	2	3	4	5
e. Facility entrance signs	1	2	3	4	5
f. Exterior visual appearance	1	2	3	4	5
g. Interior visual appearance	1	2	3	4	5
h. Facility interior cleanliness	1	2	3	4	5
i. Rest room/locker room cleanliness	1	2	3	4	5
j. Facility staff courtesy	1	2	3	4	5
k. Facility staff knowledge of programs	1	2	3	4	5
l. Staff appearance	1	2	3	4	5

Please turn survey over to complete.

11. Please rate this activity/program:
    Leave answer blank if question is not applicable.

	Below Expectations		Met Expectations		Exceeded Expectations
a Season of year offered	1	2	3	4	5
b. Day offered	1	2	3	4	5
c. Time of day offered	1	2	3	4	5
d. Condition of equipment/supplies	1	2	3	4	5
e. Instructor/official knowledge	1	2	3	4	5
f. Instructor/official courtesy	1	2	3	4	5
g. Activity content	1	2	3	4	5
h. Size of activity space	1	2	3	4	5
i. Activity space lighting	1	2	3	4	5
j. Activity space noise level	1	2	3	4	5
k. Activity space room temperature	1	2	3	4	5
l. Fees	1	2	3	4	5
m. Brochure description	1	2	3	4	5
n. Registration convenience	1	2	3	4	5

12. Would you recommend this facility to others?
    ☐ Yes   ☐ No

13. Would you recommend this activity/program to others?
    ☐ Yes   ☐ No

We welcome your comments:

_____
_____
_____
_____
_____
_____
_____
_____
_____
_____
_____
_____
_____
_____
_____

Please complete, detach and return both portions to the front desk for drawing.
Name _____
Phone _____
Address _____

Thank you for your assistance!

Figure 13.10 Recreation Facility/Program Report Card, City of Aurora (Colorado) Parks and Open Space Department.

Importance-Performance Analysis Approach

A potentially useful approach that can be applied in this area is known as the importance-performance analysis. This model of evaluation provides *a method for soliciting input from customers* to help a leisure service organization determine how effectively it performed in delivering potential program benefits. The importance-performance analysis involves a pretest and a posttest. Initially, customers are asked to identify those program benefits that they perceive as being most desirable. After they have participated in the program, customers are asked to indicate how effectively the leisure service organization has accomplished the identified program benefits.

The results of these tests (both the pre- and postperceptions of benefits) are graphically displayed on a two-dimensional matrix. As seen in Figure 13.11, the vertical axis on the matrix illustrates responses to pretest inquiries about the importance of various program attributes. The horizontal axis shows the distribution of responses to posttest scores dealing with performance in producing desired program benefits.

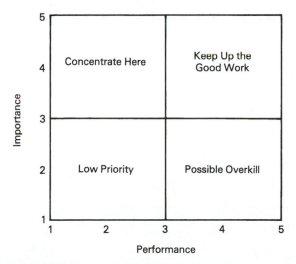

Figure 13.11 Importance-Performance Analysis Matrix.

The importance-performance analysis approach is of value to leisure service organizations because it provides a measure of customer satisfaction. It enables customers to indicate to an organization not only what benefits they desire from a leisure experience but also how effectively the organization has produced those benefits. This approach also enables an organization to focus on those areas that need improvement or should be emphasized more in the design or manipulation of program elements. Rossman (1989: 387) notes that "this technique is particularly useful for formative evaluation of new, developing program services or evaluation of existing services whose attendance may have dwindled." Rossman goes on to note that the importance-performance analysis approach may not be as valuable in the area of summative evaluation.

Questionnaires

The most frequently used method of data collection is the questionnaire—either a paper- and pencil-type in which the respondent fills in the answers, or an interview schedule in which an interviewer asks the questions and the respondent gives oral replies. Questionnaires can *obtain descriptive information about the sample population,* can attempt to assess their attitudes, or can provide data to explain their behavior. The types of questionnaires used may depend on the type of information needed, the time and money available for the survey, and the population to be sampled.

Questions can be phrased in different ways, depending on the amount of information desired and the amount of flexibility the questioner wishes to allow. The most structured questionnaire is the fixed alternative type. The question is asked and the respondent must select an answer from among alternatives offered by the questioner (e.g., yes/no, true/false, multiple choice, checklist, rank order). Because the number of responses is limited, this type of questionnaire is the easiest to administer and process but tends to provide the most superficial responses because there is no avenue by which the respondent can express opinions that differ from the responses offered.

Open-ended questionnaires are the most flexible because the respondent is free to supply whatever answer he or she thinks is appropriate. They are the most effective at getting in-depth responses and true beliefs and may even reveal new possibilities not considered by the questioner. However, because such a wide range of responses is permitted, it is more difficult to process and analyze the results. Persons with poor oral or written communication skills may have difficulty with such a questionnaire. Scale items are a special type of fixed alternative format that presents a statement and asks respondents to express their degree of agreement or disagreement with it. Construction of

Anaheim
Parks, Recreation and Community Services
SUMMER 1993 AQUATICS CLASS EVALUATION

Name of Class [   ]   Class # [   ]   Time [   ]

Location [   ]   Instructor [   ]

The following is a program evaluation designed to assist the Anaheim Parks, Recreation and Community Services Department and the American Red Cross/Orange County Chapter in evaluating our Aquatics program and instructors. Your input will be used to tailor the classes to your needs and to improve class format. We appreciate you taking the time to assist us!!

1. Please indicate the overall evaluation of your class:
   ❑ Excellent   ❑ Good   ❑ Average ❑ Fair   ❑ Poor

2. How did you find out about our program?
   ❑ Dept. Activity Guide ❑ Friend ❑ Newspaper   ❑ Flier Mailed to your Home ❑ TV/Radio
   ❑ Flier Distributed at School ❑ Other _____

3. Was the site, time, and day of the class convenient?
   ❑ Yes   ❑ No   Comment _____

4. Why did you enroll your child in this class?
   ❑ Social Interaction   ❑ Aquatic safety   ❑ He/she has taken prior classes in our program
   ❑ Fitness/physical development ❑ Self-esteem development
   ❑ Other _____
   _____

5. Which method did you use to register?
   ❑ Mail-in Registration   ❑ Walk-in registration on first day of lessons.

6. Was it easy for you to register for your child's class?
   ❑ Yes   ❑ No   Comment _____

7. How would you rate the quality of the aquatics instruction?

	Excellent	Good	Average	Fair	Poor
Instructor's knowledge of subject	❑	❑	❑	❑	❑
Teaching ability	❑	❑	❑	❑	❑
Interaction with students	❑	❑	❑	❑	❑
Course content	❑	❑	❑	❑	❑
Class preparation	❑	❑	❑	❑	❑
Professionalism	❑	❑	❑	❑	❑
Clarity of instruction	❑	❑	❑	❑	❑
Courtesy/helpfulness of staff	❑	❑	❑	❑	❑
Instructor assistance with skills and practice time	❑	❑	❑	❑	❑
Overall evaluation of class	❑	❑	❑	❑	❑

   Comments _____
   _____
   _____

8. Was the equipment in good working order?
   ❑ Yes   ❑ No   Comment _____

Figure 13.12   Sample Evaluation Form, City of Anaheim (California) Parks, Recreation, and Community Services Department.

the questionnaire, whatever its format, will have much to do with its success at securing the desired information. It is advisable to consult a textbook or research technique for guidance in this area.

All leisure service organizations conduct some form of evaluation of their program offerings. Figure 13.12 is an example drawn from the Anaheim (California) Parks, Recreation, and Community Services Department and the American Red Cross/Orange County Chapter. This form is specifically designed to ask questions about the aquatic programs. A general program evaluation form is shown in Figure 13.13, provided by the Elmhurst (Illinois) Park District. This document asks questions regarding the

**ELMHURST PARK DISRICT
RECREATION PROGRAM EVALUATION**

The Elmhurst Park District is interested in your comments in order to improve the recreation programs that are offered. Your responses and comments will be used to improve the quality of the Park District's services.

_____   _____   _____   _____
(Name of Program)   (Program Location)   (Leader/Instructor)   (Season/Year)

For each of the following items, please indicate your current level of satisfaction by circling the number that applies:

		Poor	Below Average	Average	Above Average	Excellent
1.	Quality of program facility	1	2	3	4	5
2.	Length of each class meeting	1	2	3	4	5
3.	Convenience of program time	1	2	3	4	5
4.	Fee charged for the program	1	2	3	4	5
5.	Overall rating of instructor	1	2	3	4	5
6.	Overall management of the program	1	2	3	4	5

7. Did you have enough information about the program, and were your questions answered?

   Before the program started   Yes ____   No ____
   During the program   Yes ____   No ____

   If no, what other information would have been helpful? _____

8. Would you (or your child) register for another program taught by this instructor?
   Yes ____   No ____

9. How did you find out about this program?
   Park District Brochure   ____   From Another Person   ____
   Program Flyer   ____   Other (Please specify)   ____
   Newspaper   ____   _____

10. Why did you (or your child) enroll in this program?
    Broaden my knowledge base   ____   Meet people with similar interests ____
    Develop new skills   ____   Other (Please specify)   ____

11. What would you (or your child) liked to have done that was not offered in this program?
    _____

12. Do you have any suggestions for improving this program?_____
    _____

13. What other programs would you like to see the Park District offer in the future?
    _____

When you have finished answering each item, fold and staple the survey and drop it in the mail. Please make sure that the District's address and stamp are visible before mailing. No stamp is required. Please complete and return the survey by January 23, 1995. Thank you for your help and time.

Figure 13.13 Sample Evaluation Form, Elmhurst (Illinois) Park District.

quality of facilities, length of class, convenience, fee structure, rating of the instructor, and so on.

DATA COLLECTION: AN OVERVIEW OF METHODS

After a leisure programmer chooses the categories of items to be evaluated (participants, personnel, place, policies, and programs) and the instrument (e.g., questionnaire, rating scale), the next task is to decide on the method of collecting data. Although not an exhaustive list, this section outlines commonly used evaluative methods.

Surveys

As stated in Chapter 5, surveys provide a method to gather information about individuals and collective leisure preferences, opinions, and attitudes. According to Henderson and Bialeschki (2002), self-administered questionnaires and interviews are the two major survey approaches used. Self-administered questionnaires can be implemented via mail, call-ahead-and-mail, pickup–drop-off at a facility, group administered, or on the Internet. Interviews are meetings in which leisure professionals gather information that is either written or recorded. Interview strategies include telephone, personal, and groups. Interviews can consist of community forums, focus groups, and a nominal group technique. Table 13.9 underscores the advantages and disadvantages of different survey methods used in evaluation.

Experimental Evaluative Designs

Experimental evaluative design is rooted in experimental research methods. Experimental evaluative designs can take much time and energy to plan and implement, but they are a credible source of demonstrating beneficial outcomes of leisure experiences (Rossman and Schlatter, 2000). Further, advocates of empirical practice, such as McCormick and Lee (2001), argue that leisure professionals should use research methods to plan and evaluate pro-

grams. The chief strengths of experimental approaches are its ability to (1) indicate that a leisure service or program can cause an effect in a human domain (e.g., self-esteem, physical skills); and (2) control and account (but not eliminate) for intervening variables in collection of data (Mitra and Lankford, 1999). Before experimental evaluative designs are explained, basic knowledge about research terminology is needed. As with many research and evaluation books (Campbell and Stanley, 1963; Henderson and Bialeschki, 2002; Mitra and Lankford, 1999), certain symbols are used to explain the evaluative procedure used:

X = Treatment (or in the case of leisure programming, the leisure service or program)

E = Group receiving the experimental treatment (leisure service or program)

C = Control group that receives no treatment (leisure service or program)

R = Randomized sample (randomization refers to the process of assigning people randomly into groups, such as an experimental group or control group)

O = Observation or testing that is done

This section highlights two types of experimental evaluative designs that can be used in evaluation of leisure services and programs. Readers are encouraged to read Henderson and Bialeschki's (2002) book, *Evaluating Leisure Services: Making Enlightened Decisions,* for a thorough and advanced discussion of experimental evaluative design.

The first experimental evaluative design is a *true experimental design.* The method looks like this:

$$R \quad E \quad O1 \quad X \quad O2$$
$$R \quad C \quad O1 \quad \quad O2 \quad X$$

A step-by-step example of this design in a leisure situation might help provide clarity. For example, suppose a one-week summer basket-

TABLE 13.9 Advantages and Disadvantages of Self-Administered and Interview Survey Methods

Technique	
• Advantages	• Disadvantages
Self-administered	
• Ease of presenting questions	• Requires careful wording
• Longer, stage questions can be used	• No chance to clarify misunderstandings
• High degree of anonymity	• Reading skills required
	• Not good for open-ended questions
Mailed Questionnaire	
• Low cost	• Low response rate possible
• Minimal staff/facilities required	• Is right person filling it out
• Widely dispersed samples	• No personal contact
• Time for respondent to respond	• Nonresponse bias
• Easy to administer	• Can't pursue deep answers
• Anonymous and confidential	
• Weather not a factor	
• Good for vested interest groups	
Drop-off/Pickup—*Same as Mailed Questionnaire plus:*	
• Can explain person-to-person	• Costly for staff time and travel
• High response rate	• Access may be a problem
	• Safety of staff
Group Administered	
• High cooperation rates	• Logistics of getting people together
• Low cost	
• Personal contact	
Call-Ahead-and-Mail	
• Usually higher response rate	• More costly with phone calls
• Personal contact	
• Time/money not wasted on nonresponses	
Internet	
• Fast response and data collection	• No population lists available
• Good and easy follow-up	• Restricted to people with access
• Cost savings	• Must use a computer
• User convenience	• Browser incompatibility problems
• Wide geographic coverage	• Respondents are traceable
• No interview bias	• Possibility of multiple submissions
• Flexible use	

From Henderson and Bialeschki, 2002.

ball youth camp is designed for adolescents aged fifteen and sixteen in the month of June. Further, suppose the overall goal of this camp is to improve participants' basketball skills. First, all participants are randomly assigned into one of two groups—an experimental group and a control group. The experimental group receives the basketball skill training camp in the beginning of June and the control group receives the same basketball camp in the latter part of June. Second, observation of basketball skills (e.g., shooting, dribbling, blocking out, defense) among all participants, regardless of which group, will occur. This observation is called a *pretest*. Third, participants in the experimental group will participate in the one-week basketball camp in the early part of June. Fourth, after the experimental group finishes its one-week camp, a second observation of basketball skills will occur for all participants. At this time, the leisure programmer can compare basketball skills between the experimental group and the control group to learn if the experimental group's exposure to the basketball camp caused positive development of basketball skills. Fifth, the control group then participates in a basketball camp at the latter part of June.

The *one-group pretest-posttest*, pre-experimental design is another approach that shares certain characteristics with experimental evaluative design. Pre-experimental methods are more descriptive than true experimental designs and have less control (Henderson and Bialeschki, 2002). The one group pretest-posttest method looks like this:

$$E \quad O1 \quad X \quad O2$$

Again, a step-by-step example of this design in a leisure program might provide clarity. Suppose a community recreation facility develops a leisure education outreach program for elderly people in the community. Furthermore, suppose the overall goal is to help participants experience leisure. First, a group of elderly people is identified. Second, measurement of the groups psychological state of leisure occurs by using the leisure diagnostic battery (pretest). The leisure diagnostic battery is a paper-and-pencil test that measures leisure functioning (see Witt and Ellis, 1989). Third, the leisure education program is implemented. Fourth, upon completion of the leisure education program, the leisure diagnostic battery is given as a posttest to measure leisure functioning. The leisure programmer can then compare scores from the pretest and posttest to see if leisure functioning improved.

Beyond these two experimental evaluative designs, there are numerous other methods. These include the Solomon four-group design, posttest-only control group time series quasi-experimental design, and a static group comparison (see Henderson and Bialeschki, 2002). Which experimental evaluative design is best depends upon the leisure program and what the leisure programmer wants to measure or judge.

Observation

Observation evaluative research is ideal for studying and analyzing commonplace behaviors and entities, such as customer satisfaction, behaviors of participants or staff, and so forth (Mitra and Lankford, 1999). Moreover, there are multiple observational options, such as (Mitra and Lankford, 1999):

- Complete participation (the evaluative role is concealed)
- Observer as participant (the role of evaluation is known)
- Participant as observer (the evaluative observation is a secondary role to the participation role)

Furthermore, observation can be of limited duration (e.g., single observation), long-term duration (e.g., multiple observations), a narrow focus (e.g., a single element), or a broad focus (e.g., multiple elements) (Henderson and Bialeschki, 2002). According to Veal (1996), the basic tasks followed in any observation are the following:

- Decide on a site or program (e.g., aerobic class, puppet show in the park)
- Choose an observational option (e.g., narrow focus, complete observation)
- Establish a time period to cover (e.g., morning, random times)
- Choose a sampling strategy (e.g., number and length of observational periods)
- Determine a behavior or situation to observe (e.g., play behavior)
- Design a recording or observation sheet (e.g., use of frequency counts, qualitative narrative)

To this end, the Scottish Tourism Board (1997, as cited in Maxwell, Ogden, and Russell, 2001) created an observational classification and grading system to judge the worth of tourism-oriented hospitality organizations (e.g., hotels, bed-and-breakfast sites). In particular, evaluative observations were focused on exterior (e.g., appearance of building); bedrooms (e.g., furniture); bathrooms (e.g., fixtures); public areas (e.g., atmosphere); restaurants (e.g., menu presentation); food (e.g., quality); services (e.g., reception); leisure areas (e.g., cleanliness); and other (e.g., appearance of staff). Such observational procedures could be used in many leisure service organizations.

As indicated in Chapter 12, another evaluation procedure premised upon observation is the mystery shopper technique (also known as shoppers' studies or shopper programs). According to Knutson (2001), in a mystery shopper evaluation procedure, a field worker poses as a customer and, following a criterion, interacts with staff in concealment (complete observation). For example, one of the authors of this book experienced the mystery shopper technique when he worked for Famous Players Movie Theaters (Canada) some years ago. In this experience, a concealed employee posed as a customer to observe various service delivery elements, such as cleanliness of the theater, appearance and friendliness of staff, movie and sound quality, and so forth. Some weeks after the mystery shopper interaction, a report was sent to the manager of the local theater and to the central headquarters located in Toronto (Ontario) outlining strengths, weaknesses, and improvements. Based upon the evaluative report, policy and program changes were reviewed, and if needed, changed. A mystery customer procedure could be emulated in many leisure service organizations.

Mixed Methods/Triangulation

Triangulation is a method of collecting data for evaluation by using more than one method, source of data, or evaluator (Henderson and Bialeschki, 2002). The strength of using triangulation is summarized in the following quotation by DeGraaf, Jordan, and DeGraaf (1999):

> Certainly, it makes sense that if participants, leaders, and spectators were asked to evaluate the same program we would receive more detailed and complete information than if just one of those groups were asked the question. Similarity, if two or three program leaders or supervisors were asked to conduct an evaluation of the same program, we would get a more complete picture of that event than if only one person conducted the evaluation. Lastly, if multiple tools were utilized to collect data, we would also enrich our findings. Often, triangulation is constrained by a shortage of resources (e.g., staff, time, money). As much as possible, however, we should try to utilize triangulation in evaluation (pp. 280–81).

To help community recreation organizations provide leisure services for families that have children with developmental disabilities, Mactavish and Schleien (2000a, 2000b) used a mixed method (quantitative surveys and qualitative interviews) community evaluation to understand the leisure attitudes, values, and behaviors among these families. Upon completion of this evaluative study, Mactavish and Schleien (2000a) made the following community recreation programming recommendations: (1) offer a variety of family recreation programs that include a number of activity options (e.g., physical activities, social activities); (2) ensure that programs are designed to accommodate a wide range of families that include members of different age, skill level, and interests; (3) provide staff that are trained and prepared to work with families who have children with developmental disabilities; and (4) partner community recreation service providers with therapeutic recreation specialists to collaboratively plan and implement leisure programs for families that have children with developmental disabilities.

Summary

The leisure service programmer must address the issue of evaluation daily in the delivery of services. In an era of accountability, it is imperative that the programmer is aware of and able to implement various approaches to program evaluation. There is a demand for not only quantitative but also qualitative data to support the continuation of programs.

Evaluation involves making value judgments. The purposes of evaluation are many and can be viewed from three different orientations: customer, program, and organization. Customer-oriented evaluation focuses on customer satisfaction and the leisure behavior of the customer and provides mechanisms that encourage input. Program-oriented evaluation helps in the arrangement of elements related to organizing and implementing a program. Further, it enables the programmer to handle more effectively the transactions that occur between customers and professional staff. Organization-oriented evaluation assists in establishing priorities, objectives, budget allocations, and control of services.

In developing the evaluation, the leisure service programmer will have to determine who will actually conduct the evaluation—an internal or external person. In addition, the evaluator and the agency sponsoring the evaluation must review ethical aspects of the evaluative process before engaging in the actual evaluation. Several components of the leisure service organization can be categorized for evaluation purposes. These include: (1) participants; (2) personnel; (3) place; (4) policy; and (5) programs. Each agency should have a comprehensive evaluation plan that covers all aspects of its operations. The most useful approach is a dynamic system evaluation plan, one that uses feedback loops that route information obtained through evaluation into future planning efforts.

In the past several decades, a new concept known as quality assurance has emerged that is related to evaluation. Quality assurance involves the measuring of services against standards and the development of strategies to improve services in order to ensure that an appropriate level of service delivery is achieved. Quality assurance is related to evaluation in that both are concerned with accountability and control. However, the major difference between the two is that evaluation tends to focus on program components and elements while quality assurance focuses on issues that are customer specific. In other words, quality assurance deals more with customer satisfaction and care and with transactions that occur between customers and leisure service programmers.

Several approaches and models for evaluation provide the recreation and leisure programmer with options that can be applied to selected situations. Six major approaches to evaluation include: (1) goals/objectives approach; (2) goal-free approach; (3) expert judgment approach; (4) systems designs approach; (5) policy analysis; and (6) satisfaction-based approach.

An overview of several data collection instruments and methods has been provided in this chapter. The leisure service programmer should be able to synthesize information and select approaches on a contingency basis. No one approach, instrument, or method will satisfy the demands of all situations. Evaluation should be viewed as an ongoing process that enables the leisure service organization to make better judgments about how to serve its customers and how to use its resources. Unfortunately, evaluation is often undervalued or is not approached in a comprehensive fashion within leisure service organizations.

Discussion Questions and Exercises

1. Define *evaluation*. Discuss how evaluation involves making value judgments within leisure service organizations.

2. Why is evaluation important? Discuss this from three perspectives—that of the customer, the program, and the organization.

3. What is the difference between formative and summative evaluation? What is measurement?

4. Identify five areas in which evaluation can occur within leisure service organizations.

5. What are the hazards in program evaluation? Identify and discuss at least five that have an impact on the work of leisure service organizations.

6. What kinds of ethical responsibilities do leisure service programmers have in the evaluation process?

7. Define *quality assurance*. Discuss how quality assurance programs are customer specific as opposed to program oriented.

8. Identify seven approaches to evaluation. Give an example of each. Locate a leisure service organization and determine which approach is most prevalent in that agency.

9. What are the benefits of policy analysis in evaluating the programs within leisure service organizations? Compare and contrast these benefits with other approaches to evaluation.

10. Develop a program to evaluate a leisure service activity. Include in your plan a discussion of the approach to be used and the instruments that will be necessary to collect relevant information.

References

American Institutes for Research. 1970. *Evaluative research*. Pittsburgh, PA: American Institutes for Research.

Anderson, S. B., and S. Ball. 1978. *The profession and practice of program evaluation*. San Francisco: Jossey-Bass.

AQS. 1996. *QUEST—The quest for quality in sport and leisure*. Sports Council, Ref. No. 0618. London, UK: Sports Council.

Attkisson, C. C., W. A. Hargreaves, N. J. Horowitz, and J. E. Sorensen, eds. 1978. *Evaluation of human service programs*. New York: Academic Press.

Bannon, J. J. 1976. *Leisure resources: Its comprehensive planning*. Englewood Cliffs, NJ: Prentice Hall.

Burlingame, J., and T. M. Blaschko. 2002. *Assessment tools for recreational therapy and related fields*. 3rd ed. Ravensdale, WA: Idyll Arbor, Inc.

Campbell, D., and J. Stanely. 1963. *Experimental and quasi-experimental designs for research*. Chicago: Rand McNally.

DeGraaf, D. G., D. J. Jordan, and K. H. DeGraaf. 1999. *Programming for parks, recreation, and leisure services: A servant leadership approach.* State College, PA: Venture.

Dieser, R. B. 2002. A personal narrative of a cross-cultural experience in therapeutic recreation: Unmasking the masked. *Therapeutic Recreation Journal* 36(1): 84–96.

Dustin, D. L., I. E. Schneider, L. H. McAvoy, and A. N. Frak. 2002. Cross-cultural claims on Devils Tower National Monument: A case study. *Leisure Science* 24(1): 79–88.

Farrell, P., and H. Lundegren. 1978. *The process of recreation programming.* New York: John Wiley.

Farrell, P., and H. Lundegren. 1983. *The process of recreation programming: Theory and technique.* 2d ed. New York: John Wiley.

Farrell, P., and H. Lundegren. 1991. *The process of recreation programming theory and technique.* 3d ed. State College, PA: Venture Publishing.

Fink, A., and J. Kosecoff. 1978. *An evaluation primer.* Beverly Hills, CA: Sage Publications.

Henderson, K., and D. Bialeschki. 1996. *Evaluating leisure services.* State College, PA: Venture. Publishing.

Henderson, K. A., and M. D. Bialeschki. 2002. *Evaluating leisure services: Making enlightened decisions.* 2nd ed. State College, PA: Venture.

Knutson, B. J. 2001. Service quality monitoring and feedback systems. In *Service quality management in hospitality, tourism, and leisure,* edited by J. Kandampully, C. Mok, and B. Sparks (pp. 143–58). New York: Haworth Press.

Lundegren, H. M., and P. Farrell. 1985. *Evaluation for leisure service managers.* Philadelphia, PA: W. B. Saunders.

Mactavish, J. B., and S. J. Schleien. 2000a. Exploring family recreation activities in families that include children with developmental disabilities. *Therapeutic Recreation Journal* 34(2): 132–53.

Mactavish, J. B., and S. J. Schleien. 2000b. Beyond qualitative and quantitative data linking: An example from a mixed method study. *Therapeutic Recreation Journal* 34(2): 154–63.

Maxwell, G., S. Ogden, and V. Russell. 2001. Approaches to enhance service quality orientation in the United Kingdom: The role of the public sector. In *Service quality management in hospitality, tourism, and leisure,* edited by J. Kandampully, C. Mok, and B. Sparks (pp. 123–41). New York: Haworth Press.

Mayer, W. 1975. *Planning curriculum development.* Boulder, CO: Biological Sciences Curriculum Study.

McConkey, D. D. 1975. *MBO for non-profit organizations.* New York: American Management Association.

McCormick, B. P., and Y. Lee. 2001. Research into practice: Building knowledge through empirical practice. In *Professional issues in therapeutic recreation: On competence and outcomes,* edited by N. J. Stumbo (pp. 383–400). Champaign, IL: Sagamore.

Mitra, A., and, S. Lankford. (1999). Research methods in, recreation, and leisure services. Champaign, IL: Sagamore.

Mittelesteadt, A. H., and H. A. Berger. 1972. The critical path method: A management tool for recreation. *Parks and Recreation* 8(7): 14–15.

Moder, J. J., and C. R. Phillips. 1964. *Project management with CPM and PERT.* New York: Reinhold.

Nadler, G. 1969. A universal approach to complex systems design. The Engineering Manager. Montreal: The Engineering Institute of Canada.

Neulinger, J. 1974. *The psychology of leisure.* Springfield, IL: Charles C Thomas.

Patton, M. Q. 1978. *Utilization-focused evaluation.* Newbury Park, CA: Sage Publications.

Pelegrino, D. A. 1979. *Research methods for recreation and leisure: A theoretical and practical guide.* Dubuque, IA: Wm. C. Brown.

Peterson, C. A., and N. J. Stumbo. 2000. *Therapeutic recreation program design: Principles and procedures.* 3rd ed. Boston, MA: Allyn & Bacon.

Reichwein, P. A., and K. Fox. 2001. Margaret Fleming and the Alpine Club of Canada: A woman's place in mountain leisure and literature, 1932–1952. *Journal of Canadian Studies* 36(3): 35–60.

Report to the Utah Legislature. 2002. *A performance audit of Hogle Zoo.* Report No. 2002-02. Salt Lake City, UT: Author.

Richards, E. P. III, and K. C. Rathbun. 1983. *Medical risk management: Preventative legal strategies for health care providers.* Rockville, MD: Aspen Systems.

Rossman, J. R. 1989. *Recreation programming: Designing leisure experiences.* Champaign, IL: Sagamore Publishing.

Rossman, J. R. 1995. *Recreation programming: Designing leisure experiences.* 2d ed. Champaign, IL: Sagamore Publishing.

Rossman, J. R., and B. E. Schlatter. 2000. *Recreation programming: Designing leisure experiences.* 3rd ed. Champaign, IL: Sagamore.

Scriven, M. 1967. The methodology of evaluation. In *Perspectives of curriculum evaluation* by R. W. Tyler, R. M. Gagne, and M. Scriven, 39–83. Chicago, IL: Rand McNally.

Stufflebeam, D. L. 1974. *Meta-evaluation.* Kalamazoo, MI: Evaluation Center.

Tallmadge, G. K. 1977. *The joint dissemination review panel: Ideabook.* Washington, DC: Superintendent of Documents.

Van der Smissen, B. 1972. *Evaluation and self-study of park and recreation agencies: A guide with standards and evaluative criteria.* Arlington, VA: National Recreation and Parks Association.

Veal, A. J. 1996. *Research methods for leisure and tourism: A practical guide.* London: Pitman Publishing.

Williams, J. G. 1972. Try PERT for meeting deadlines. *Park Maintenance* 25(9): 17–18.

Witt, P. A., and G. D. Ellis. 1989. *The leisure diagnostic battery: Users manual.* State College, PA: Venture.

Woy, J. R., D. A. Lund, and C. C. Attkisson. 1978. Quality assurance in human service program evaluation. In *Evaluation of human service programs,* edited by C. C. Attkisson, W. A. Hargreaves, N. J. Horowitz, and V. E. Sorensen. New York: Academic Press.

Leisure Wellness and Education

LEARNING OBJECTIVES

1. To provide the reader with information concerning *barriers and constraints to successful leisure experiences.*

2. To help the reader gain knowledge of various *leisure education models.*

3. To highlight to the reader that leisure education is a *paramount function of leisure programming.*

4. To help the reader understand that leisure education can be a *method for community development*

5. To help the reader understand how *interpretative services can be informal leisure education.*

Introduction

Mahatma Gandhi, the renowned pacifist, once lectured to the British government on behalf of Indian sovereignty for a solid three hours. During this time he not only kept his audience spellbound, he also did not make a single flaw in his eloquent presentation. At the conclusion of his lecture, his press secretary was besieged by members of the British press corps, who wanted to know how Gandhi could lecture so flawlessly without notecards or any other speaking aids.

"It's simple," replied the secretary. "What Gandhi thinks, says, and does are one. You British think one thing, say a second, and do a third. That's why you need notecards to keep track."

The same could be said of the approach to leisure by many people in North America. They tend to think one thing, say another, and do a third when it comes to their leisure lifestyle. Leisure is an area in which customers can profit from greater knowledge of services as well as exploration of attitudes that shape and have impact on their lifestyle. People are seeking more meaningful leisure experiences today and have a desire to develop the appropriate skills, knowledge, and attitudes that are required for successful participation. Leisure service programmers can assist customers in developing a state of leisure wellness by helping them access information, make decisions, and clarify leisure-related values as well as by using traditional strategies such as providing instructional programs and services.

Although leisure is a powerful force because of the multiple benefits it provides, not all people experience leisure or its associated benefits. For example, people with disabilities are often prevented from participating in leisure due to numerous constraints, such as financial and architectural barriers (Dattilo, 2002). Furthermore, numerous scholars (e.g., Ruskin, 2001; Stebbins, 2002) have posited that undeveloped leisure can be a primer for deviant behaviors. For example, Witt (2001) argued that unsupervised free time for youth after school can have problematic consequences, such as illegal drug use. In short, although leisure can provide many benefits, not all people experience leisure. Leisure professionals should understand what prevents people from participating in leisure and develop programs to encourage leisure participation.

Some people avoid leisure involvement because they don't understand what leisure is (e.g., benefits) and do not know how to use free time properly. As Csikszentmihalyi (1997) noted, few people know how to use free time or leisure appropriately:

> The popular assumption is that no skills are involved in enjoying free time, and that anybody can do it. Yet, the evidence suggests the opposite: free time is more difficult to enjoy than work. Having leisure at one's disposal does not improve the quality of life unless one knows how to use it effectively, and it is by no means something one learns automatically . . . All of the evidence points to the fact that the average person is ill equipped to be idle (p. 65).

In this regard, few people understand the complexity, breadth, and beneficial aspects of leisure. As Bregha (1991) suggested, "Many people do not know what they want [during leisure or free time]. Quite practically, they want what they know—or what someone else shows or tells them" (p. 49). In the United States, what most people know about leisure is that it is free time to watch television—numerous studies underscore that watching television is the leading use of free time (see Kelly and Freysinger, 2000; Robinson and Godbey, 1997). The following comments by Dieser (2001) reinforce the centrality of watching television in free time:

> In 1997, while driving through Prince George, British Columbia (Canada) a store named *The World of Leisure* gripped my attention . . . As I entered this store I soon realized it was oriented toward selling satellite TVs. As simple as this experience appears, I have often reflected on how this event is a metaphor for how the masses

perceived leisure—a nonessential service with little value. As so many people have said to me over dinner and supper discussions when I've disclosed that my academic interest lies in leisure theory, education and behavior: "Anyone can experience leisure—I can't believe you have spent 15 years studying it?" Implicit in these statements by others is the notion that leisure, compared to many other aspects of life (e.g. work, family, careers), is not very important. Hence, North-American society has presupposed that people need to be prepared for work, but not prepared for leisure (p. 1).

While watching television can have some benefits (see Csikszentmihalyi, Rathunde, and Whalen, 1993), heavy television watching can have the following harmful effects:

- Development of a sedentary lifestyle that contributes to hypertension, obesity, heart disease, and other illnesses (Kraus, 2001)
- Individual and community isolation (Russell, 2002)
- Erudition of violent behaviors via social learning theory (Grossman, 1996)
- Decrease of quality time or meaningfulness in life (Csikszentmihalyi, 1997; Kubey and Csikszentmihalyi, 1990)
- Erosion of democratic culture and civic involvement (Postman, 1985)

Even if a person has a solid understanding of leisure and knows how to use leisure effectively, there still are barriers or constraints that prevent people from participating in leisure. Although leisure barriers and leisure constraints are often thought of as synonymous, a distinction is sometimes made between the terms. Whereas a leisure barrier presupposes that people have an interest in participating in a leisure activity but are blocked from doing so, a leisure constraint acts to limit interest in a leisure activity itself (Jackson and Scott, 1999; Mannell and Kleiber, 1997). Crawford, Jackson, and Godbey (1991) have described the following three categories of constraints:

- Intrapersonal constraints represent psychological factors that arise internally in an individual (e.g., attitude, personality, moods).
- Interpersonal constraints arise out of interactions with other people or circumstances (e.g., family members, friends, community members).
- Structural constraints are external factors in the environment (e.g., inaccessible buildings, cost of activities, lack of community infrastructure).

The following ten categories of barriers are indicative of the difficulties faced by people in their quest for leisure experiences.

1. *Attitudinal Barriers*—These types of barriers refer to a customer's thoughts about real or imagined factors that hinder participation. An example of an attitudinal barrier is thinking that a person must be athletically gifted to be interested in physical fitness.
2. *Communicative Barriers*—Communicative barriers can be either personal or may exist on a broader organizational level. On an organizational level, communicative barriers relate to the ability of an agency to provide clear, accurate, and meaningful information concerning program offerings. On a personal level, such barriers focus on the individual's ability to receive and send messages clearly.
3. *Consumptive Barriers*—The tendency of individuals to "purchase" experiences based on what is thought to be in vogue rather than what is right for the individual can be a barrier to a meaningful and fulfilling leisure lifestyle. Pursuing leisure needs based on a false agenda can leave the impression that some leisure experiences are not "worth" the expenditure of time and energy.
4. *Economic Barriers*—Lack of access to discretionary income can have an impact on one's ability to develop a leisure lifestyle. This is especially true in a society that has a fully developed commercial leisure service system and continues to reduce accessibility to public and nonpublic leisure services. Also, economics produces perceived barriers because individuals often associate the value and quality of a service with its cost.

5. *Experiential Barriers*—A lack of previous experience with, or orientation to, a leisure activity can be a major barrier. People will participate more often in familiar activities rather than unfamiliar activities. We often avoid what we don't know. This barrier is extremely detrimental to ongoing leisure development.

6. *Health Barriers*—Major traumas, accidents, and illness can impact customers' leisure lifestyle. Current culture places great emphasis on individual physical and mental well-being; people are encouraged to maintain a high level of fitness and social/emotional wellness in order to enjoy life. If circumstances prevent total wellness, health factors can become a barrier to full participation.

7. *Leisure Awareness Barriers*—One of the major barriers that individuals experience today is that of acquiring and maintaining a "leisure ethic." They are unaware of the value of leisure experiences and have been conditioned by the Protestant work ethic. Further, individuals lack knowledge of the leisure skills and leisure resources needed to participate in meaningful leisure programs and services.

8. *Physical Resource Barriers*—Lack of facilities and the overcrowding of others can also be barriers to the development of a person's leisure lifestyle. This is a severe problem with our national parks system because they are being loved to death. It is hard to have a spiritual bond with nature when fifty other people are attempting to do the same thing in a limited space. Many facilities in urban areas are either run down, under funded, or located in places that are not easily accessible for the consumer.

9. *Social Cultural Barriers*—We are in an era of incredible diversity: racial, ethnic, social, economic, political, and cultural. Such pluralism requires an equally diverse approach to providing programs and services. Without attention to diversity, barriers emerge that prevent full development of one's leisure lifestyle.

10. *Temporal Barriers*—Not having enough time or quality time in which to pursue leisure interests can be a barrier in today's society. Today, not only is available leisure time for white-collar workers shrinking, but also the distribution of time (year-round schools, flextime, four-day work weeks) is creating barriers that call for new approaches to address the customer's leisure concerns.

Two noteworthy studies about barriers to participation have been conducted by Godbey (1985) and Searle and Jackson (1985). Godbey has developed a model to measure nonparticipation in public leisure services (see Figure 14.1). Godbey's model focuses on the information level of potential users concerning what leisure services exist. He found that lack of awareness of services was a major factor leading to nonparticipation. However, when viewing the reasons for nonparticipation in specific leisure services, he found that location, lack of interest, lack of time, personal health reasons, and the use of an alternative facility or program were the most highly ranked reasons for nonparticipation. These results are shown in Table 14.1.

TABLE 14.1   Reasons for Nonparticipation in Specific Leisure Services in City A by Rank and Frequency*

Rank	Reason	N
1	Site location inconvenient	47
2	Lack of sufficient interest	43
3	Lack of time	40
4	Personal health reasons	37
5	Use alternative facility or program	32
6	Fear of crime at site	28
7	Lack of skill—don't know how to do activity	18
8	Site too crowded	16
9	Lack of transportation—no car	15
10	Lack of money	12
11	Lack of public transportation	9
11	Fear of crime traveling to and from site	9
13	Site poorly maintained	8
14	Don't know enough about site	7
14	Too old	7
16	Site hours of operation inconvenient	4
17	Site polluted	3
17	Don't know anyone at facility or program	3
17	Don't have other people to do activity with	3
17	Don't like program leader or staff	3
21	Activities not interesting	1

From G. Godbey, *Journal of Parks and Recreation Administration*, 3:1–13, 1985. Journal of Park & Recreation Administration, Bloomington, IN 47405. Reprinted by permission.

*Reasons given by those respondents who knew of the existence of the specific leisure service in question indicated they wished to participate but were prevented from doing so. More than one reason could be given.

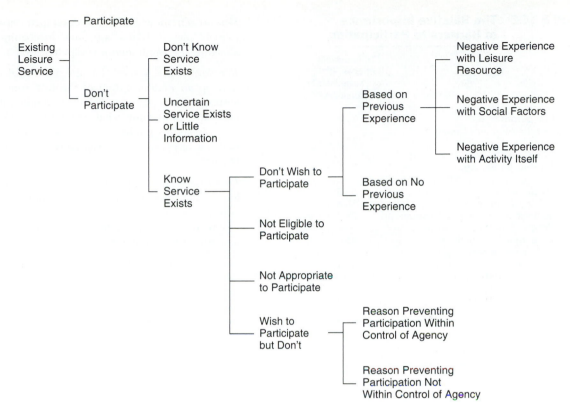

Figure 14.1   A Model of Nonparticipation in Leisure Services. (Godbey, G. *Journal of Park and Recreation Administration* 3: 1–13, 1985.)

Searle and Jackson (1985) studied barriers to participation among 1,240 respondents in the Province of Alberta. Each of the respondents was asked, "Is there any recreation activity that you don't take part in now but would like to start regularly?" Those individuals desiring a new activity were asked to determine whether any of fifteen predetermined reasons were perceived as presenting a barrier. The researchers found that the highest ranked barrier was work commitments followed by overcrowded facilities or areas, problems in locating others to recreate with, lack of opportunity to participate near one's home, and family commitments. Their findings present insight into barriers associated with participation in leisure activities (see Table 14.2).

LEISURE EDUCATION MODELS

Education is important for preparation for leisure. Studies have shown that education level is generally the best predictor of some kinds of leisure participation. People with more years of education are more likely to engage in a variety of sports and cultural activities, have the resources to travel, have access to leisure opportunities, and have interest in such activity (Kelly, 1990).

One of the more articulate proponents of the importance of education for leisure was Charles Brightbill. Brightbill (1961) postulated that "the place of education is everywhere. . . . that freedom, combined with education and leisure, provides the wings upon which mankind

TABLE 14.2   The Relative Importance of Barriers to Participation

Rank	Barrier	% Perceiving Barrier as "Often" or "Sometimes" a Problem
1.	Work commitments	71.3
2.	The recreational facilities or areas are overcrowded	64.4
3.	It is difficult to find others with whom to participate	58.1
4.	There is no opportunity to participate near my home	57.5
5.	Family commitments	55.8
6.	The price of recreational equipment	53.2
7.	Admission fees and charges to use recreational facilities	45.3
8.	I don't know where I can participate in this activity	43.1
9.	I don't know where I can learn the activity	31.8
10.	I am shy about participating in public	29.4
11.	Present price of gasoline	26.7
12.	Not having the physical abilities	21.1
13.	Lack of transportation	17.6
14.	Not having artistic or creative abilities	16.8
15.	I am physically unable to participate	11.2

may soar the highest, that example is the best teacher of all . . . that education is not the exclusive responsibility of any one institution or discipline" (pp. 10–11).

Leisure education is a developmental process through which individuals or groups of people increase their understanding of leisure and the relationships among leisure, lifestyle, and society (Mundy, 1998; Sivan and Ruskin, 2001). As such, leisure education provides education regarding the wholesome use of free time (Sivan, 2001) and teaches various leisure and recreation-related skills, attitudes, and values (Johnson, Bullock, and Ashton-Schaeffer, 1997). Leisure education provides the foundation for a person to achieve leisure. This educational process must contain four elements:

Skills—Each individual must develop a repertoire of play skills that are built on cognitive, affective, and psychomotor competencies.

Knowledge—It is critical for the individual to develop an understanding of the vast array of leisure activity options available; in addition, the individual must know what equipment, materials, supplies are required for a specific activity (as well as where it is located, when it is offered, and so forth).

Experience—The opportunity to experience leisure activities will increase the individual's confidence to explore other dimensions of leisure and to perfect skills that will add to overall leisure fulfillment and wellness.

Attitudes, Values, and Appreciation—The individual must develop a positive perception of leisure. Attitude toward the commodity of leisure plays an important role in determining the value of the leisure experience.

In the past few decades, several leisure education models have emerged. Even though leisure education is often associated with therapeutic recreation practice, the authors of this book agree with Farrell and Lundegren (1991) that leisure education is an important function of leisure programming. The Department of Community Services in the City of Edmonton (Alberta) exemplifies how leisure education is part of leisure programming. The *Priceless Fun* winter guide (2001–2002) highlights numerous free and low-cost recreation opportunities throughout the City of Edmonton (Figure 14.2). Such opportunities include tobogganing areas, major parks, cross-country ski trails, outdoor ice rinks, indoor areas, swimming pools, public libraries, festivals and special events, and a family fun calendar. Figure 14.3 illustrates the city's education guide, which highlights excellent festivals and special events, and explains how to develop a family fun calendar. Further, this leisure education program explains a fee-reduction program for people who have lower incomes (see Figure 14.4). The following section presents an overview of several leisure education models.

TOBOGGANING

Tobogganing Areas

Bring the family, a thermos of hot chocolate and enjoy the fresh air and the thrill of tobogganing!

Emily Murphy Park
Emily Murphy Park Rd.
& Groat Rd.

Whitemud Park
Keillor Rd. & Fox Dr.

Jackie Parker Rec. Area
50 St. & 45 Ave.

Gallagher HIll
95 Ave. & 97 St.

Argyll Park
83 St. & 63 Ave.

Mill Woods Park
23 Ave. & 66 St.

Government House Park
Groat Rd. & River Valley Rd.

Laurier Heights
139 St. & 78 Ave.

Rundle Part
113 Ave. & 29 St.

Figure 14.2 Winter 2001–2002 Priceless Fun Leisure Education Guide, Community Services, Edmonton, Alberta.

Leisure Education Advancement Project (LEAP)

In 1977, the National Recreation and Parks Association (NRPA) developed a leisure education curriculum called the Leisure Education Advancement Project (LEAP) for children and young adults in grades kindergarten through grade twelve. The primary aim of LEAP was to raise the consciousness of public education in the United States toward the value of leisure education. LEAP was significant because the NRPA made a concerted effort for the integration of leisure education into American public schools. LEAP represented a primary effort on the part of NRPA to raise the consciousness of public education toward the value of leisure and leisure education.

The approach taken in the LEAP curriculum model was one of developing positive attitudes toward leisure. In other words, the curriculum materials do more than merely help the teacher develop leisure activity skills; they are directed toward helping people understand leisure phenomena and develop leisure values. The approach of LEAP is based on the central premise that as leisure becomes more important in a person's life, each individual will need to develop skills, abilities, and attitudes in order to have a satisfying leisure experience.

The major purpose of this curriculum model was to assist public schools in instructing students to:

1. Appreciate the use of leisure time (discretionary time) as an avenue for personal satisfaction and enrichment;
2. Understand the array of valuable opportunities available in leisure time;
3. Understand the significant impact that leisure time has, and will have, on society or appreciate natural resources and their relationship to discretionary time and the quality of life; and
4. Make decisions regarding their own leisure behavior (NRPA, 1977: 10).

The LEAP curriculum was designed to be infused into the existing school curriculum. The intent was not to provide an additional content area but to complement and enrich the existing curricular materials toward the achievement of eight basic leisure goals, called targets. Targets, written in terms of objectives to guide curriculum development, were as follows:

1. The student will understand that most life experiences can be leisure experiences. They can be active or passive, alone or with others, physical or mental, planned or spontaneous, anticipatory or reflective.
2. The student will understand that . . . leisure as well as work must be viewed as a very important source of self-worth and dignity. It also influences the quality of life, even actual survival.
3. The student will understand the effect that the dynamic interaction of natural and physical environment, social institutions, and individual lifestyles has on leisure opportunities, choices, and behavior.
4. The student will identify, understand, and evaluate leisure resources available in community,

FESTIVALS AND SPECIAL EVENTS

Festivals and Special Events

Bright Nights Festival
Nov. 23 – Jan. 6
426-4620

New Year's Eve Downtown
Dec. 31
423-2822

Comedy Festival
Jan. 18 – 27
(Free activities on Jan. 19 and 20)
438-8624

Lunar New Year
Feb. 16
423-2628

Family Festival Downtown
Feb.18
424-4085

St. Patrick's Day Parade
Date to be announced
414-6766

FAMILY FUN CALENDAR

Plan to spend some time together with family and friends this month.

How to use: Pick a month (does not need to be a calendar month).

Sit down together and plan some activities that all will enjoy.

Add variety — some indoor, some outdoor, some active, some passive.

For your assistance, we have provided you with some low cost suggestions.

An Evening at Home
• Puzzles
• Board games
• Bake and decorate cookies
• Family movie night
• Card games
• Learn to play a new game — chess, backgammon, etc.
• Listen to different types of music
• Charades

Fun in the Snow
• Go tobogganing
• Build a snow sculpture — go beyond the regular snowman
• Go for a walk in the River Valley
• Plan a winter scavenger hunt — make a list of items found in nature and the first person to find all wins the first cup of hot chocolate

FAMILY FUN CALENDAR

• Create a snow painting in your yard using biodegradable tempera paint or food colouring and water in a spray bottle
• Go snow shoeing or cross country skiing

The "Ice'ing" on the Cake
• Go skating
• Make ice sculptures — freeze water in different sizes of containers and use as building blocks
• Go curling
• Make ice cream

Crafty Creations
• Learn to knit, crochet, woodwork or paint — "Learn To" resources are available at your local public library

• Paint a picture using household items like sponges, string, and fingers
• Various art classes are offered at the City Arts Centre. You may be eligible for the Fee Reduction program
• Make play dough or goop
• Make gelatin gigglers
• Make winter bird feeders out of milk cartons

Season's Greeting
• Send a letter to an old friend
• Make paper snow flakes to decorate your house
• String popcorn
• Take a family photo
• Plan an early (i.e. 9 p.m.) New Year's Eve countdown so the entire family can participate together

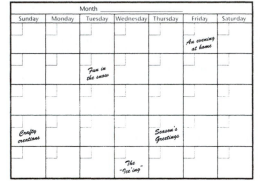

Figure 14.3 Winter 2001–2002 Priceless Fun Leisure Education Guide, Community Services, Edmonton, Alberta.

state, and nation; the student will develop appreciation of various modes that individuals have of utilizing these resources.

5. The student will recognize that leisure experiences are neither good nor bad. The value assigned is a matter of personal and societal judgment. The student will recognize that leisure experiences are chosen because they seem appropriate to the individual, limited by social control.

6. The student will appreciate those intangible qualities of leisure experiences which transcend an individual's physical existence but are experienced on the emotional and spiritual plane.

7. The student will recognize and evaluate the consequences each person's use of leisure has on human, social, constructed, and natural environments. The student will recognize that each person is ultimately responsible for his own leisure as well as for influencing the community to suggest leisure opportunities.

8. The student will understand that leisure, as well as work, family, and other social roles can help develop a life plan to insure personal growth and satisfaction. (NRPA, 1977: 10)

DISCOUNTS

Fee Reduction Program

The Fee Reduction Program:
- is offered by the City of Edmonton Community Services Department
- is for people living in Edmonton
- is for low income individuals and families
- offers a lower price for 12 admissions — you pay only 25% of the cost
- is used at Community Services facilities (swimming pools, Fort Edmonton, Valley Zoo, etc.)
- offers a lower cost on three program registrations — you pay only 25% of the cost
- is good for one year

The Fee Reduction has some restrictions:
- You can take only one lower cost program at a Leisure Centre or City Arts Centre.
- Full-time students at the University of Alberta, NAIT or Grant MacEwan cannot have a Fee Reduction card but family members can.
- People with an ACT membership cannot have a Fee Reduction card.
- Fee Reduction registrations in programs are limited.
- You cannot use Fee Reduction cards for programs that are already low cost.

To apply for a Fee Reduction card, please call

West Service Area 496-7320

East Service Area 496-5860

Central Service Area 496-7275

South Service Area 496-1475

Ask to get the Fee Reduction card. We will ask you questions or give you a form to fill out.

If you qualify for the program, you will receive a Fee Reduction card for yourself and each member of your family.

Figure 14.4 Winter 2001–2002 Priceless Fun Leisure Education Guide, Community Services, Edmonton, Alberta.

Today, leisure and education scholars are recognizing the important role of leisure in learning and are calling upon public schools to develop formal leisure education programs (Mundy, 1998; Shivers, 2001; Sivan, 2001). For example, a study by Csikszentmihalyi, Rathunde, and Whalen (1993) on the development of creativity in adolescents highlights how creative students in schools spend about four more hours a week involved in art and hobbies, than to "average" students. Likewise, Stebbins

(2002) underscored how amateurism and careerism are developed via serious leisure pursuits (e.g., amateur archaeologists, stand-up comics). To this end, Figure 14.5 showcases how leisure activities can provide human development in the intellectual, aesthetic, social, physical, and mental domains (Ruskin, 1995). In short, public schools need to accept some responsibility for developing leisure values and teaching students how to use free time in a wholesome manner (Shivers, 2001).

Mundy and Odum Leisure Education Model

Toward the end of the 1970s, Mundy and Odum (1979) developed a five-component leisure education model. Almost twenty years after this model was first introduced, Mundy (1998) provided an updated version, which is presented in Figure 14.6. The first component, leisure awareness, consists of understanding leisure, the leisure experiences, and the relationship of leisure to one's life, quality of life, lifestyle, and society. The second step, self-awareness, focuses on understanding interests, capabilities, leisure expectations, quality experiences, leisure goals, values, and needs. The third phase, decision-making skills, involves gaining data and alternative skill development, predicting possible outcomes, understanding comparability, and evaluation. The fourth phase, leisure skills, requires process skills, planning skills, and leisure experience skills. The last component, social interaction, consists of verbal communication, nonverbal communication, and interaction patterns in leisure experience. In this model, the individual initially is made aware of leisure and its concomitant properties and is prompted to develop a degree of self-awareness, which culminates in a statement of personal needs and leisure goals. The process continues through an individual's development of leisure skills and subsequently social interaction in which a leisure lifestyle is developed. It is interesting that Mundy and Odum (1979) and Mundy (1998) consider

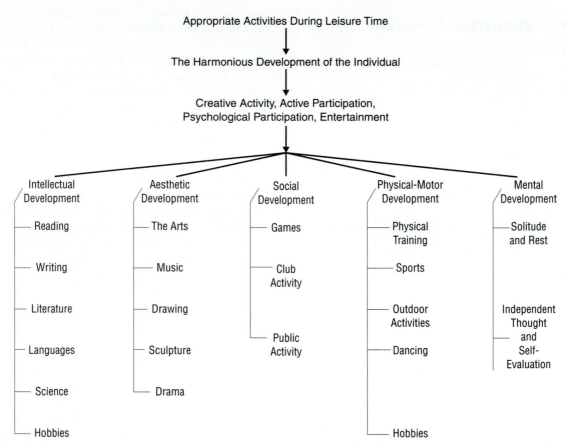

Variety and Balance In Leisure Time Activities

Appropriate Activities During Leisure Time

↓

The Harmonious Development of the Individual

↓

Creative Activity, Active Participation,
Psychological Participation, Entertainment

Intellectual Development	Aesthetic Development	Social Development	Physical-Motor Development	Mental Development
Reading	The Arts	Games	Physical Training	Solitude and Rest
Writing	Music	Club Activity	Sports	
Literature	Drawing		Outdoor Activities	Independent Thought and Self-Evaluation
Languages	Sculpture	Public Activity	Dancing	
Science	Drama			
Hobbies			Hobbies	

Figure 14.5   The Relationships among Leisure, Education, and Human Development.

leisure education from a specific viewpoint. They suggest that leisure education is not:

1. Attempting to replace one set of values with another set of values.
2. A new name for recreation or recreation services.
3. A watered-down, simplified version of a recreational leisure professional preparation program.
4. A focus on the value of recreation or the recreation profession.
5. A focus on getting people to participate more in recreational activities.
6. Imparting standards of what is "good" or "bad" use of leisure.
7. Relating every school subject to leisure.
8. A course or series of courses.
9. Restricted to the educational system.
10. Restricted to what educators should do but not what leisure service personnel do.
11. A program to undermine the work ethic.

On the other hand, according to Mundy and Odum, leisure education can be thought as:

1. A process enabling the individual to identify and clarify his or her own leisure values and goals.

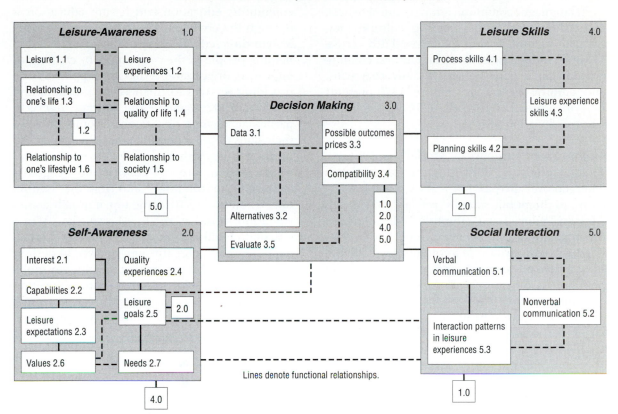

Figure 14.6 Mundy's (1998) Leisure Education Model.

2. An approach enabling an individual to enhance the quality of his or her life during leisure.
3. Deciding for oneself what place leisure has in life.
4. Coming to know oneself in relation to leisure.
5. A lifelong continuous process.
6. Relating one's own needs, values, and capabilities to leisure and leisure experiences.
7. Increasing the individual's options for satisfying, quality experiences in leisure.

The original Mundy and Odum (1979) model appears to be one of the first schematic models that analyzes the component parts of a leisure education process. Its significance may lie in the interactive approach—blending leisure awareness and skill development with self-awareness and social interaction in the quest for improved quality of life.

To this end, Berryman and Lefebvre (1995), building upon the academic work of Mundy and Odum (1979), presented a five-component, cross-cultural leisure education model. First, leisure education focuses on awareness of leisure, self, leisure skills, and leisure resources. Second, cultural self-awareness includes an articulation of a personal history, personal values, and interpersonal awareness. Third, teaching-learning approaches and strategies incorporates the implementation of needs assessments, classroom instruction, field experiences, and guided self-study. Fourth, cultural knowledge concentrates attention on basic cultural concepts, geographic historical perspectives, language/communication, cultural beliefs, and values, and understanding cultural play, recreation, and leisure patterns. Fifth, cross-cultural competencies focus on cultural communication skills, personal services, advocacy skills, and cultural brokerage. Figure 14.7 presents Berryman and Lefebvre's (1995) cross-cultural, leisure education model.

Community Education Model

The community education movement has emerged over the past few years as a viable alternative to the public schools' role as "9:00 A.M. to 3:00 P.M." educators. Community education is a broad philosophical concept, intent on improving the responsiveness of a community to its constituents' needs through optimum utilizing and planning of its resources. Its focus is to bring the citizenry together with its resources and with effective problem solving.

Another way of viewing the link between community education and leisure education is through the concept of system-directed change. System directed changes are strategies aimed at helping people in the community by creating or improving organizations that are supposed to be providing services to them (Dieser, Scholl, and Schilling, 2002; Mandell and Schram, 2003). In particular, change agents are people who use their skills to bring about changes in agencies or social settings, either alone or in concert with others. System-directed change can be generated from the "top down" and from the "bottom up." When it starts from the top, it usually comes via administrative or legislative fiat. When system-directed change starts from the bottom, people force change through the weight of their numbers and the power that weight can mobilize. According to Levy (2001), leisure education should be aimed at changing environmental and social systems, such as families, community orga-

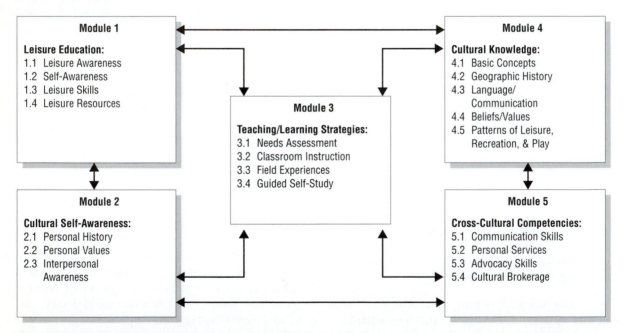

Figure 14.7 Berryman and Lefebvre's (1995) Cross-Cultural Leisure Education Model. Adapted from: Berryman. D. L., and C. B. Lefebvre, 1995. Preparing professionals to conduct cross-cultural leisure education program. In H. Ruskin & A. Sivan (Eds.), *Leisure education: Toward the 21st Century* (pp. 184–200). Provo, UT: Brigham Young University.

nizations, schools, transportation systems, politicians, political shareholders, cultural entities, and ecological management systems. For example, family leisure education should embrace:

- Positive parent-child attachment and interactions
- Effective parenting
- Family expectations regarding family leisure
- Roles and responsibilities for all family members in family recreation
- Participation in community recreation (e.g., volunteer, coach, church service)
- Responsibilities to community recreation organizations (e.g., Boy Scouts, Girl Guides)

Although system-directed leisure education has developed in countries outside of the United States (e.g., Levy, 2001; Sivan, 2001), scant attention has been focused in the United States. Witt (1991), an American advocate for system-directed leisure education, has posited that little attention in leisure education has been given to changing the basic social, economic, and political conditions within the society that affect an individual's ability to undertake meaningful leisure experiences. Further, Witt has added:

> In the case of leisure 'problems,' we tend to overestimate the 'defects' in an individuals values, attitudes, skills, and knowledge regarding leisure without giving proper attention to the service provisions and reinforcements provided by society which influence leisure choices and outcomes. Further, we fail to give proper weight to factors such as unequal distribution of income, social stratification, inequality of power, plus mechanization and urbanization as the source of significant portions of the 'leisure problem' for many individuals (p. 309).

Recent research by Dieser, Fox, and Walker (2002) supports Witt's concern and underscores how leisure education research published in leisure journals has been premised upon individualistic or "blame the victim" approaches. In their research, Dieser and colleagues reviewed

twenty years of research (nineteen studies) concerning learning outcomes of leisure education programs. Their findings are astonishing—only two of 120 learning outcomes considered strategies aimed at helping people experience leisure by improving the community or organizations that are supposed to be providing leisure services. In short, leisure professionals need to use leisure education as a means of community development (Sivan and Ruskin, 2001).

In this regard, Grossman (2001) underscored that leisure professionals are community members who should educate people about the potential value of play, recreation, and leisure in community development. Further, leisure professionals can help community groups and members understand the importance of leisure opportunities, leisure areas and facilities, and how leisure affects community development. Grossman (2001) posited that leisure professionals should take on the roles of advocacy and mobilization in the process of leisure education for community development. As an advocate, leisure professionals should pressure societal power structures for new or improved leisure programs. This includes such endeavors as eliminating barriers to leisure opportunities based upon ethnic, race, and disability discrimination and supporting the right to play or recreate in clean and healthy playgrounds, parks, camps, beaches, swimming pools, and other leisure community structures. Mobilization involves collaboration and support from other organizations regarding leisure opportunities, such as motivating community members to support leisure programs.

An example of leisure education aimed at community collaboration and development is the "From Forest to Ocean: A Voyage of Discovery" community development leisure education program in Halifax, Nova Scotia (Guptill and Howell, 2002). This program had ten students from grade nine who created a 28-foot pulling boat and oars from living trees cut from a forest woodlot located in New Germany (Nova Scotia). Throughout this program, leisure professionals conducted leisure education programs to transfer learning and leisure opportunities into various areas of the students' lives. For example, students learned of the many leisure opportunities in the Halifax community and how leisure endurance is vital for successful leisure experiences. The overall mandate of this program was to provide quality and accessible recreation and leisure programs and services to the citizens of the Halifax Regional Municipality. In particular, goals included: (1) to serve the recreation and leisure needs of children and youth, (2) to serve at-risk populations, and (3) to develop community partnership opportunities. The partnerships in this program include the Parks and Recreation Services from the Halifax Regional Municipality, Nova Scotia Sport and Recreation Commission, Rockingstone Heights School, Dalhousie University (School of Health and Human Performance), and the Nova Scotia Sea School.

Sponsorship of Leisure Education

Although leisure education is commonly associated with public school systems, the responsibility for its existence increasingly transcends the established or formal educational systems. The nature of the leisure experience makes it difficult, if not impossible, to relegate its function to a single agency. Several additional factors support the notion that leisure education is the responsibility of a number of agencies and individuals. These factors include:

1. *Community and Adult Education Movements*—Both of these movements have been based on the concept that learning can take place in the community in a semistructured manner and can address the singular or collective educational needs of the individual. In addition, the multiuse of our community centers and schools during hours outside of traditional school hours is part of an overall cost-effective utilization of public facilities.
2. *Life's Laboratory*—Although skills and simulated situations may be developed in the classroom, their application in everyday life situations is paramount. This necessitates having the indi-

vidual practice leisure skills and develop his or her total leisure environment in the community, in the neighborhood, or at home.
3. *Lifelong Learning*—The learning process does not cease when one graduates from school but continues throughout life.
4. *Semiformal Learning Environment*—The home, community, office, and industry all serve as semiformal centers for learning.
5. *Other Agencies*—Youth-serving agencies (YMCA, YWCA, 4-H, Boy Scouts, CYO, Camp Fire Girls), religious agencies, private enterprises (National Outdoor Leadership School, American Youth Hostels), and federal agencies (U.S. Department of the Interior, U.S. Department of Education, U.S. Department of Health and Human Services, Canadian Ministry of Amateur Sports and Physical Fitness) all provide forms of leisure education.
6. *Public Schools*—For the most part, public schools address only a small segment of our society and only for nine months of the year. After-school hours and summer months are usually spent in some form of leisure pursuit or play experience.

In order to clearly articulate and heighten the opportunities for individuals to develop "leisure literacy," it is the responsibility of the home, school, and community agencies to provide leisure education as well as opportunities for leisure.

The Leisure Education Content Model (developed from the Leisure Ability Model)

The Leisure Education Content Model (LECM) is a conceptual framework rooted within a larger, therapeutic recreation service model known as the Leisure Ability Model (see Peterson and Gunn, 1984; Peterson and Stumbo, 2000). Figure 14.8 displays the LECM within the total Leisure Ability Model. The overall purpose of leisure education is to help participants acquire leisure-related knowledge and skills so that participants can eventually gain an independent leisure lifestyle (Peterson and Stumbo, 2000). This leisure education model consists of the following four components:

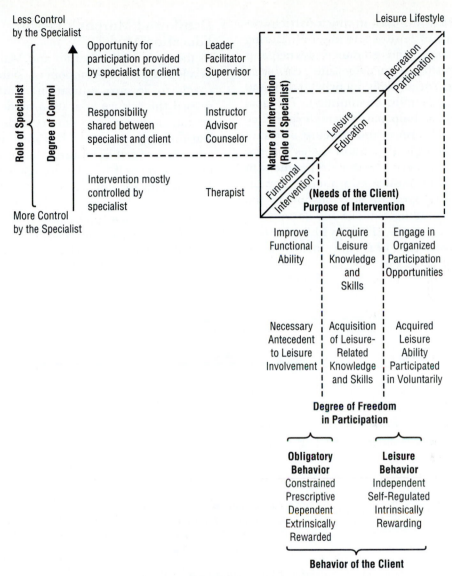

Figure 14.8 Leisure Ability Model. (From Peterson and Stumbo, 2000.)

- *Leisure Awareness*—Knowledge of leisure, self-awareness, leisure and play attitudes, and related participatory and decision-making skills
- *Social Interaction Skills*—Duel, small group and large group
- *Leisure Activity Skills*—Traditional and nontradition activities and skills
- *Leisure Resources*—Activity opportunities, personal resources, family and home resources, community resources, and state and national resources

The Leisure Lifestyle Center (LLC), housed in the Department of Recreation Management and Therapeutic Recreation at the University of Wisconsin-La Crosse (see Ardovino, Todd, and Navar, 2002), is an example of a community-based leisure education program premised upon the Leisure Education Content Model and the Leisure Ability Model (Todd, 2002). This program begins with an individualized assessment in which participants become aware of leisure and the self. During leisure education and guidance, participants learn different leisure activity skills (e.g., decision making, social skills; activity skills) and resources (e.g., family, community). The goal of the LLC is to help participants experience the benefits of leisure and develop a leisure lifestyle. Although the main focus of the Leisure Lifestyle Center is to help people with disabilities, many leisure education programs have been developed to help anyone in the community, including families and community groups (Todd, 2002). Figure 14.9 shows a brochure from the LLC that provides an overview of its program.

Dattilo and Murphy's Leisure Education Model

In the early 1990s, Dattilo and Murphy (1991) developed a seven-component, systematic approach to leisure education. Dattilo (1999) revised this leisure education model by adding greater clarity and precision regarding the seven learning components. The first component, awareness of self in leisure, consists of an exploration of oneself in a leisure context. Learning components include:

- Identify leisure preferences
- Reflect on past participation
- Reflect on current leisure involvement
- Project future leisure

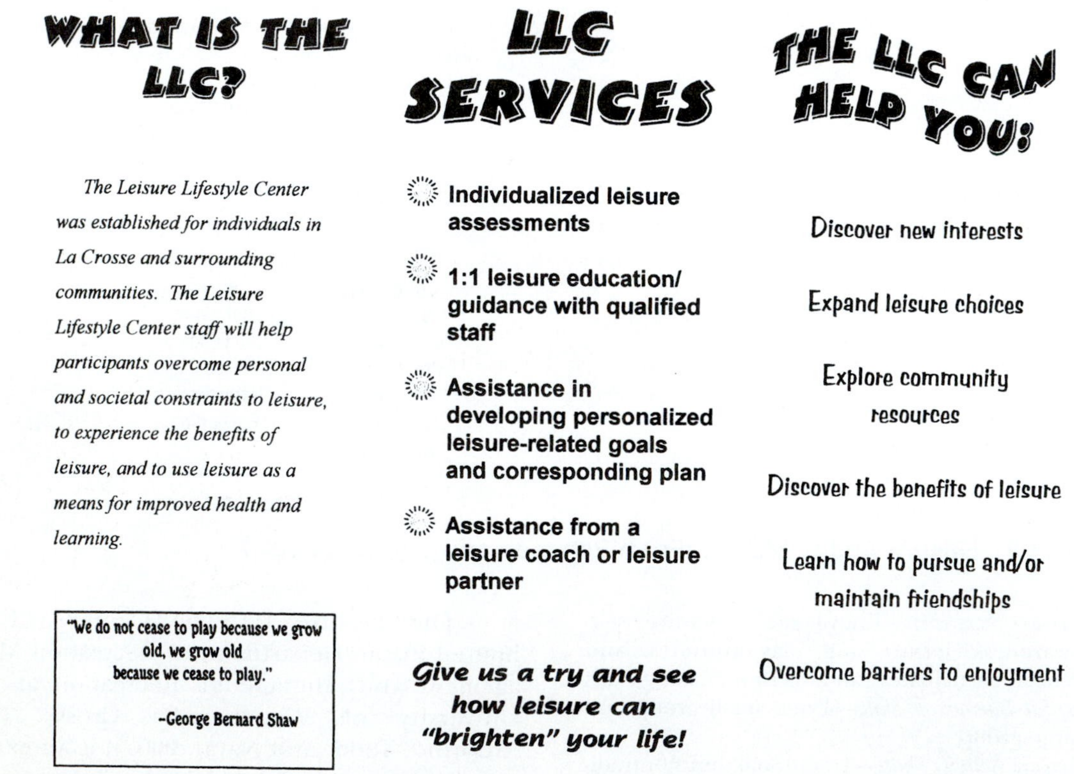

WHAT IS THE LLC?

The Leisure Lifestyle Center was established for individuals in La Crosse and surrounding communities. The Leisure Lifestyle Center staff will help participants overcome personal and societal constraints to leisure, to experience the benefits of leisure, and to use leisure as a means for improved health and learning.

"We do not cease to play because we grow old, we grow old because we cease to play."

-George Bernard Shaw

LLC SERVICES

- **Individualized leisure assessments**
- **1:1 leisure education/ guidance with qualified staff**
- **Assistance in developing personalized leisure-related goals and corresponding plan**
- **Assistance from a leisure coach or leisure partner**

Give us a try and see how leisure can "brighten" your life!

THE LLC CAN HELP YOU:

Discover new interests

Expand leisure choices

Explore community resources

Discover the benefits of leisure

Learn how to pursue and/or maintain friendships

Overcome barriers to enjoyment

Figure 14.9 Brochure from the Leisure Lifestyle Center, Department of Recreation Management and Therapeutic Recreation, University of Wisconsin-La Crosse.

- Understand leisure-related skills
- Examine leisure values and attitudes
- Determine leisure satisfaction

The second component, appreciation of leisure, is oriented toward understanding leisure and the benefits derived from leisure. Learning components include:

- Understand leisure
- Consider leisure benefits
- Realize flexibility of leisure
- Identify context for leisure

Self-determination in leisure is the third component. Its goal is to promote self-initiated, independent use of free time. Subcomponents of this stage include:

- Take responsibility for personal leisure
- Make choices in regard to leisure opportunities
- Learn when to terminate leisure involvement
- Become assertive in relation to leisure needs or opportunities

The next step, leisure decision making, is focused on the identification of leisure barriers and strategies to overcome these barriers. Many of the learning components in this stage are premised upon past components, which include:

- Self-awareness
- Appreciation of leisure
- Development of self-determination
- Ability to identify leisure goals
- Ability to solve problems

The fifth step, utilizing leisure resources, is aimed at acquiring a knowledge base regarding leisure resources. It includes the following actions:

- Identify people as leisure partners
- Locate leisure facilities
- Understand participation requirements
- Match skill to activity requirements
- Obtain answers to questions

The sixth phase, social interaction skills, is oriented toward the development of social skills. Subcomponents of this stage include:

- Learn to use verbal and nonverbal communication appropriately
- Understand social rules of a leisure opportunity
- Acquire social competence
- Develop friendships such as recreation partners

The last step, recreation activity skills, is focused on the selection and development of necessary recreation skills. Learning outcomes include:

- Choose meaningful activities
- Overcome fears

This leisure education model was developed to help people with disabilities experience leisure, but any leisure practitioners can use it to educate individuals or groups for active leisure participation (Dattilo, 1999).

Cross-Cultural, Project-Based Leisure Education

Recently, Dieser and Fox (2002), building upon the academic work of Katz and Chard (2000), articulated a leisure education model that is premised upon a leisure professional working in collaboration with participants from diverse cultures in developing leisure experiences. Project-based leisure education is a comprehensive learning perspective focused on teaching leisure by engaging students in a collaborative process or investigation via an in-depth study of a particular leisure experience. Hence, project-based leisure education is not oriented to individual leisure education; it is premised upon collectivistic culture (Kakakalau, Fox, and Dieser, 2002). Cross-cultural, project-based leisure education moves the learning process away from a leisure expert teaching participants about leisure to a leisure professional learning about and constructing leisure *with* group participants. Using a project-based approach allows the leisure professional to collaboratively explore how leisure can be defined, framed, or operationlized within different cultural groups—that is, cross-cultural, project-based leisure education supports cross-cultural efforts to construct pedagogues consistent with culturally oriented values and beliefs. Tables 14.3, and 14.4, both adapted from Dieser and Fox (2002), present the distinction between traditional and project-based leisure education and explain how to design and implement the model.

Project-based leisure education has three broad stages (Chard, 1998a; Kakakalau et al., 2002). The first stage focuses on designing and planning a leisure project or experience. During this stage, an initial idea is developed and the group plans appropriate actions. Constructing a topic web is one method of developing an initial idea and planning future action. A topic web is a mapping of key ideas, topics, and sub-themes related to the topic (Katz and Chard, 2000). In project-based

TABLE 14.3   Distinction Between Traditional and Project-Based Learning

Traditional Leisure Education	Project-Based Leisure Education
1. Participant's willingness to work for instructor is a source motivation.	1. Participant's interest and involvement promote effort and motivation.
2. Teacher selects learning activities with little or no student involvement.	2. Participants suggest activities and choose from a variety of activities.
3. Teacher is the expert.	3. Participants are experts or quasi-experts.
4. Teacher is accountable for learning.	4. Participants share accountability for learning.

Adapted from: Dieser, R. B., and K. Fox 2002. Cross-Cultural Therapeutic Recreation: A Project Based Leisure Education Approach. *American Journal of Recreation Therapy* 1(1): 21–24.

TABLE 14.4   Design and Implementation of Cross-Cultural, Project-Based Leisure Education

Role Change in Leisure Professionals	Practical Implications
1. Leisure professional moves away from expert and provider of knowledge to that of "student," "listener," "traveler," and "explorer."	1. Leisure professional and participants both learn about culturally appropriate leisure, along with ethnicity, diversity, oppression and power.
2. Leisure professional moves away from programming a leisure experience to being a member of a group that helps create a leisure experience.	2. Leisure professional and participants share roles related to teaching, learning, and demonstrating knowledge and skills about leisure.
3. Leisure professionals discover culturally appropriate awareness, knowledge, and skills relevant to leisure programming within a cultural framework.	3. Leisure professionals may need to use specialized knowledge of leisure to assist participants in assessing the difference between Euro-North American leisure and culturally different leisure.
4. Leisure professionals move away from providing teaching materials for leisure professionals and participants.	4. Leisure resources and information are developed, organized, and evaluated collaboratively.
5. Leisure professionals move away from expert assessment and evaluation to an assess/evaluation process constructed by the leisure professional and participants.	5. Assessment and evaluation include tangible accomplishments such as public display or other demonstrations of leisure-oriented knowledge and skills.

Adapted from: Dieser, R. B., and K. Fox 2002. Cross-Cultural Therapeutic Recreation: A Project Based Leisure Education Approach. *American Journal of Recreation Therapy* 1(1): 21–24.

leisure education, a formal topic is a topic that is directly related to leisure (e.g., trips, basketball, dances) and an informal topic is any idea that may lead to potential leisure experiences. For example, Figure 14.10, adapted from Chard (1998b), shows an example of an informal topic that a family with younger children might use to design potential family leisure experiences. Although "water" (the topic) may seem to have little relevance to leisure, by brainstorming ideas related to water, potential leisure experiences relevant to water can emerge, such as identifying water-based leisure opportunities (e.g., camping, fishing, boating, and sports). Furthermore, learning about fish or birds in local rivers or oceans can develop serious leisure habits (Stebbins, 2002). In this regard, Figure 14.11 shows a home study course in bird biology and behavior by the Cornell Lab of Ornithology in Ithaca (New York). Any group that has a keen interest in birds can enroll in this serious leisure pursuit.

The second stage is oriented toward implementation and further development. A paramount aspect of this stage is discussion among group members. In essence, participants discuss the dimensions of the project work and decide on future actions. Project-based learning requires cognitive, flexible, and interpersonal skills so that participants can (1) provide feedback in a nonthreatening and supportive manner; (2) maintain a focus on group goals; (3) develop a flexible orientation to learning; and (4) sustain mutual trust among diverse people (McKeachie, 1999). Cross-cultural, project-based leisure education helps members of a group learn cross-cultural differences, such as communication and behaviors.

The third stage is concluding the project. In this stage, participants experience the leisure activity. In regard to evaluation, a public display or performance of a leisure experience can occur in a culturally appropriate manner. For example, Kakakalau and colleagues (2002) highlighted

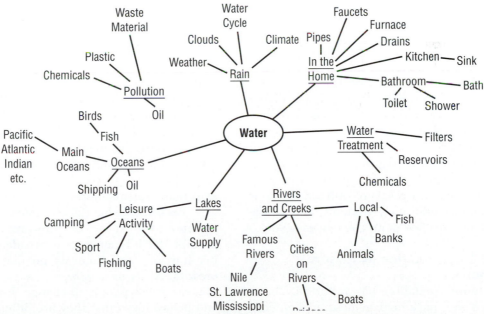

Figure 14.10 Example of an Informal Topic Web that Could Be Used by a Family or Group to Discover Possible Leisure Opportunities.

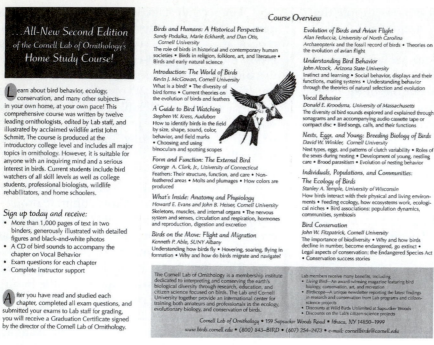

Figure 14.11 Home Study Course in Bird Biology, Cornell Lab of Ornithology, Ithaca, New York.

that at the end of a native Hawaiian youth project-based leisure education program, a large demonstration of the hula dance took place. Figure 14.12 shows a newspaper article (Cairney, 2001) that underscores a cross-cultural, project-based leisure education program of building a First Nation kayak between a Mi'kmaq First Nation leader, University of Alberta outdoor environmental education students, and grade-two students enrolled in an elementary school.

Leisure Interpretation as Leisure Education

Although interpretation has historically been associated with park management, it is an educational process used in various leisure organizations (Knudson, Cable, and Beck, 1995). As Tilden (1967) outlined many years ago, interpretation is an educational activity that aims to reveal meaning and relationships through the use of original objects, by firsthand experience, and by illustrative media, rather than simply to communicate factual information. As Knudson and colleagues (1995) put it, "No doubt should exist that interpretation *is* education" (p. 165).

Beck and Cable (2002) underscored that a paramount purpose of interpretation is to prompt the listener toward broadening his or her horizons and then act on that newfound breadth. At its most powerful level, interpretation can cause people to change their thinking and behaviors so that they live differently, such as finding alternative ways to structure free time (Beck and Cable, 2002). Interpretive service can

Plenty to learn in kayak-building class
By Richard Cairney

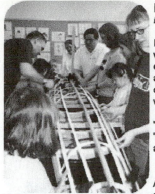

U of A and grade two students build a kayak in the Education Building

February 16, 2001 - Steve Conty is standing over the wooden skeleton of a kayak, explaining to phys-ed. and education students that, in the Far North, you are either an adult or a child. And adults always take time to teach children. The university students take a break from their work on the kayak and listen attentively.

"If a child wants to go off and play, that's fine," said Conty. "And if he comes back five minutes later to ask you another question, you stop and explain what you're doing."

As if on cue, a group of Grade 2 students enter the room and the very traditions Conty is discussing are passed on. Conty's focus shifts from the university students to his younger charges as he explains the next step in building the kayak.

The exercise is part of a teaching experience for both groups of students, says Rod Dieser, a sessional instructor in the faculty of physical education and recreation.

"This shows that you can use outdoor environmental education to teach core curriculum," Dieser said. The Grade 2 students—including his seven-year-old son Chayce—are learning about buoyancy for their science class and about Inuit culture for their social studies class.

"Steve tells them a lot of Inuit and First Nations stories: that the Inuit eat walrus tails for candy—they are learning a lot about native culture," Dieser said.

They certainly are. One young student speaks enthusiastically about mythology surrounding the northern lights; Dieser's son knows how to test seal skin before applying it to a kayak's hull ("you chew it and if tastes like an eraser you can use it, but if your teeth go right through, you can't," he explains).

"The kids remember everything you tell them," says Conty, a Mi'kmaq Indian who teaches traditional kayak building near his home, south of Ottawa. He and his wife, Louise Barker, are on campus at the urging of Dieser and graduate student Chad Clifford, a friend of Conty's.

Dieser says the project, part of an outdoor environmental education class, teaches potential teachers kayak-building skills they can use in schools, gives those students more experience working with children and connects outdoor education with core subject areas.

Cheryl Storie, who teaches the Grade 2 students at the on-campus Child Study Centre, says the project fits in nicely with the school's project-based approach to learning. "We have a boats and buoyancy unit in science and another Canadian communities section in social studies," said Storie. "It's good because it fits the curriculum and gets outdoor ed. students working with kids, learning what a seven-year-old is like."

Fourth-year education student Kendra Eliuk finds the program valuable. "You have an enjoyable time building a kayak, you learn about Inuit culture and you get to work with kids," she said. "That's definitely the best part—you get to see how they learn."

Related link - internal

- The Faculty of Physical Education and Recreation Web site:
  http://www.per.ualberta.ca

Figure 14.12 Newspaper Article Regarding Project-Based Leisure Education, *Express News,* University of Alberta, Edmonton, Alberta.

be so moving and influential via informal leisure education that it can cause an individual or group to become a member of a social movement (e.g., Blue Jay bird restoration), grassroots associations (e.g., dollhouse building, stamp collecting), and community or leisure organization (e.g., becoming a member of the Chicago Historical Society) (Stebbins, 2002). On the other hand, interpretation can be problematic when it lacks accurate and solid understanding of a site or program (Beck and Cable, 2002). For example, Davies (1997) underscored the troubling and superficial educational and interpretative services that Sea World provides, which include: (1) using nature and abusing sea animals as commodities of mass consumption to generate cash; (2) teaching about marine animals, marine habitat, and nature in artificial and contrived settings (e.g., whales follow unnatural scripts of waving to humans due to behavioral manage-

ment techniques); and (3) mixing nature education with selling and marketing beer (Sea World is owned by Anheuser Busch).

The following case study of interpretative services at Little Bighorn Battlefield National Monument (National Park Service, 15 miles north of Hardin, Montana) is a hypothetical example of how leisure interpretation can provide informal leisure education and can cause a person to participate in leisure opportunities. A person can travel to the Little Bighorn Battlefield National Monument to learn about the June 25, 1876 battle between the U.S. Army's seventh cavalry and several American Indian tribes (e.g., Lakota, Cheyenne, Arapaho). Interpretative services include the Custer Battlefield museum (Garryowen, Montana—see Figure 14.13) and a self-guided tour of memorial makers at the Little Bighorn Monument, including such historical sites as Custer's advance, the

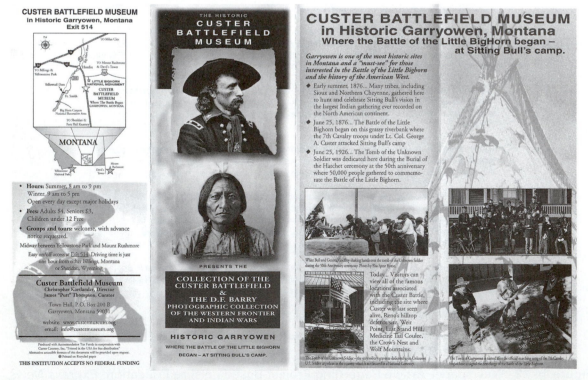

Figure 14.13   Custer Battlefield Museum, Garryowen, Montana.

American-Indian encampment, last stand hill, and the Keogh-Crazy Horse fight. In addition, during the months of June and July, historical, interpretative, and leisure events include Little Bighorn battle re-enactment (which includes American Indian descendents from the Little Bighorn Battle), Crow Native Day celebrations, Little Bighorn Days at Hardin, Cheyenne pow wow, and traditional Crow Indian lifestyle programs and festivals. Participants can travel back to southern Montana annually to learn more about the Battle of Little Bighorn via these many cultural, leisure, and interpretative events. Furthermore, the Friends of the Little Bighorn Battlefield is a volunteer organization designated to promote programs at the Little Bighorn Battlefield National Monument and Little Big Horn College, a tribal community college that pro-

vides educational classes on the Battle of Little Bighorn. Travelers and leisure participants can (1) become volunteer members of the Friends of the Little Bighorn Battlefield, (2) take classes at the Little Big Horn College, and (3) make annual trips to the Little Bighorn Battlefield National Monument and southern Montana to continue life-long learning about this historical event. In this regard, the collective effect of different cultural, leisure, and interpretative events develops an informal leisure education program in which people understand the relationship among themselves, leisure, and society while learning how to structure their free time. Table 14.5, built upon the work of Knudson and colleagues (1995), presents various types of leisure interpretation facilities and services that can lead to informal leisure education.

TABLE 14.5   Types of Leisure Interpretation Services that Can Lead to Informal Leisure Education

Type	Example	Possible Leisure Education Activities
Museums	Jane Addams Hull House Museum, Chicago, Illinois (www.uic.edu/jaddams/hull)	History of Chicago, settlement movement, and famous American women
Villages and farms	Silos and Smoke Stacks National Heritage Area, Waterloo, Iowa (www.siloandsmokestacks.org)	History of American agriculture
Zoos and aquatics	Calgary Zoo, Prehistoric Park and Botanical Garden, Calgary, Alberta, Canada (www.calgaryzoo.ab.ca)	Gardening skills and public education regarding habitat and animals
Camps	Canyon Camp Boy Scouts of America, Stockton, Illinois (www.cayoncamp.com)	Outdoor recreation opportunities, such as rappelling, canoe trips, and woodman camping
Municipal, state, & international parks	Waterton-Glacier International Peace Park World Heritage Site, Southern Alberta and Northern Montana (http://parkscanada.pch.gc.ca/unesco/Water/watere.tmt)	Education regarding the international nature of wilderness and international peace parks
Private sector	Atlantis Submarines, Kona Coast, Hawaii	Underwater eco-system oriented toward underwater eco-systems and coral reef
Heritage sites	Ukrainian Cultural Heritage Site, Edmonton, Alberta, Canada (http://collections.ic.gc.ca/ukrainian/welcome.htm)	History of Ukrainian culture and pioneer settlement in central Alberta
Government	Hill Aerospace Museum, Ogden, Utah (www.hill.af.mil/miseum)	History of United States Air Force and aviation/space technology
Partnerships	Mormon Pioneer National Historical Trail, Church of Jesus Christ of Latter Day Saints and the National Park Service (www.nps.gov/mopi)	American and religious history through Iowa, Illinois, Nebraska, Utah, and Wyoming

--- *Summary* ---

The leisure consumer is often ill-prepared to deal with factors such as an abundance of leisure time, the ever-increasing complexity of choice, and the challenge of living a healthy leisure lifestyle. The increasing interest in leisure means that leisure professionals must take a more proactive role in leisure education. In this era of fiscal conservatism, professionals in the leisure service field must promote the need for leisure education.

To achieve a high level of leisure, a balance must be maintained between the different dimensions of leisure. While recognizing that certain dimensions may take on greater importance at different times throughout a person's life, it is still incumbent upon leisure agencies to provide a balance of activities to help individuals achieve a wholeness in their life.

Leisure education is one way that leisure professionals can build the foundation for leisure wellness. It is the responsibility of many agencies and organizations, not just schools, to provide leisure education throughout the entire life span of the individual. Significant leisure education models such as LEAP should be advocated and implemented, and other leisure education models should also be developed and evaluated.

--- *Discussion Questions and Exercises* ---

1. Why is leisure education an important function of leisure programming?

2. Identify ten barriers to leisure and suggest how leisure education can help people overcome each barrier.

3. Explain three types of leisure constraints. How are leisure constraints different from leisure barriers?

4. Identify and articulate five leisure education models.

5. Provide a rationale for instituting a leisure education curriculum in the public schools.

6. How does leisure education contribute to community development?

7. Identify and explain two types of cross-cultural leisure education models.

8. How is system-directed leisure education different from traditional leisure education models?

9. How are interpretative services considered informal leisure education?

10. What ethical factors should be considered when selecting a given leisure education model or technique?

--- *References* ---

Ardovino, P. S., B. K. Todd, and N. H. Nava. 2002. The leisure lifestyle center: "Its been awesome for me." *Parks and Recreation* 37(5): 40–46.

Beck, L., and T. Cable. 2002. *Interpretation for the 21st century: Fifteen guiding principles for interpreting nature and culture.* Champaign, IL: Sagamore.

Berryman, D. L., and C. B. Lefebvre. 1995. Preparing professionals to conduct cross-cultural leisure education program. In *Leisure education: Toward the 21st century,* edited by H. Ruskin and A. Sivan (pp. 184–200). Provo, UT: Brigham Young University.

Bregha, F. J. 1991. Leisure and freedom re-examined. In *Recreation and leisure: Issues in an era of change* 3rd ed. edited by T. L. Goodale and P. A. Witt (pp. 47–54). State College, PA: Venture.

Brightbill, C. 1961. *Man and leisure; A philosophy of recreation.* Englewood Cliffs, NJ: Prentice Hall.

Cairney, R. (2001, February). Plenty to learn in kayak-building class. University of Alberta *Express News.* Available online http://www.expressnews.ualberta.ca/expressnews/articles/news.cfm?p_ID=289&s=a.

Chard, S. C. 1998a. *The project approach book one: Making curriculum come alive.* New York: Scholastic.

Chard, S. C. 1998b. *The project approach book two: Managing successful projects.* New York: Scholastic.

City of Edmonton, Community Services. 2001–2002. *Priceless fun winter 2001–2002: Your guide to free & low cost recreation opportunities in Edmonton.* Edmonton, Alberta: Author.

Crawford, D. W., E. L. Jackson, and G. C. Godbey. 1991. A hierarchical model of leisure constraints. *Leisure Science* 13:309–20.

Csikszentmihalyi, M. 1997. *Finding flow: The psychology of engagement with everyday life.* New York: Basic Books.

Csikszentmihalyi, M., K. Rathunde, and S. Whalen. 1993. *Talented teenagers: The roots of success and failure.* New York: Cambridge University Press.

Dattilo, J. 1999. *Leisure education program planning: A systematic approach.* 2nd ed. State College, PA: Venture.

Dattilo, J. 2002. *Inclusive leisure services: Responding to the rights of people with disabilities.* 2nd ed. State College, PA: Venture.

Dattilo, J., and W. Murphy. 1991. *Leisure education program planning: A systematic approach* 2nd ed. State College, PA: Venture Publishing.

Davies, S. 1997. *Spectacular nature: Corporate culture and the Sea World experience.* Berkeley, CA: University of California Press.

Davis, L. N. 1974. Planning, conducting, and evaluating workshops. Austin, TX: Learning Concepts.

Dieser, R. B. 2001, December. The importance of leisure. *Utah Turner's Syndrome Society Newsletter:* 3.

Dieser, R. B., and K. Fox. 2002. Cross-cultural therapeutic recreation: A project based leisure education approach. *American Journal of Recreation Therapy* 1(1): 21–24.

Dieser, R. B., K. Fox, and G. Walker. (2002). Recognizing the fundamental attribution error in leisure education research. *Annual of Therapeutic Recreation* 11. 77–96.

Dieser, R. B., K. G. Scholl, and A. Schilling. 2002, April. *Leisure education systems: The Cedar Valley inclusive initiative.* Paper presented at the Midwest Symposium on Therapeutic Recreation, Springfield, IL.

Farrell, P., and H. M. Lundegren. 1991. *The process of recreation programming: Theory and technique.* 3rd ed. State College, PA: Venture.

Godbey, G. 1985. Nonuse of public leisure services: A model. *Journal of Park and Recreation Administration* 3(2).

Grossman, A. H. 2001. Mobility for action: Advocacy and empowerment for the rights of leisure, play and recreation. In *Leisure education, community development, and populations with special needs,* edited by A. Sivan and H. Ruskin (pp 55–64). New York: CABI Publishing.

Grossman, D. 1996. *On killing: The psychological cost of learning to kill in war and society.* New York: Little, Brown and Company.

Guptill, N., and M. Howell. 2002, May. *The benefits approach: Therapeutic recreation at work in the community "From Forest to Oceans: A Voyage of Discovery."* Paper presented at the Canadian Therapeutic Recreation Association Annual Conference, Calgary, Alberta, Canada.

Jackson, E. J., and D. Scott. 1999. Constraints to leisure. In *Leisure studies: Prospects for the twenty-first century,* edited by E. L. Jackson & T. L. Burton (pp. 299–322). State College, PA: Venture.

Johnson, D. E., C. C. Bullock, and C. Ashton-Shaeffer. 1997, November. Families and leisure: A context for learning. *Teaching Exceptional Children:* 30–34.

Kavakulau, K., K. Fox, and R. B. Dieser. 2002, May. *Rethinking the leisure education process.* Paper presented at the Canadian Congress of Leisure Research, Edmonton, Alberta, Canada.

Katz, L. G., and S. Chard, 2000. *Engaging children's minds: The project approach.* 2nd ed. Norwood, NJ: Ablex Publications.

Kelly, J. R. 1990. *Leisure,* 2d ed. Englewood Cliffs, NJ: Prentice Hall.

Kelly, J. R. and V. J. Freysinger. 2000. *21st century leisure: Current issues.* Boston, MA: Allyn & Bacon.

Knudson, D. M., T. T. Cable, and L. Bech. 1995. *Interpretation of cultural and natural resources.* State College, PA: Venture.

Kraus, R. 2001. *Recreation and leisure in modern society.* 6th ed. Boston, MA: Jones and Barflett.

Kubey, R., and M. Csikszentmihalyi. 1990. *Television and the quality of life.* Hillsdale, NJ: Lawrence Erlbaum.

Levy, J. 2001. Leisure education, quality of life and community development: Toward a systematic and holistic copying and resilient model for the third millennium. In *Leisure education, community development, and populations with special needs,* edited by A. Sivan and H. Ruskin (pp 43–54). New York: CABI Publishing.

Mandell, B. R., and B. Schram. 2003. *An introduction to human services: Policy and practice.* 5th ed. Boston, MA: Allyn & Bacon.

Mannell, R. C., and D. A. Kleiber. 1997. *A social psychology of leisure.* State College, PA: Venture.

McKeachie, W. J. 1999. *Teaching tips: Strategies, research, and theory for college and university teachers.* Boston. MA: Houghton Mifflin Company.

Mundy, J. 1998. *Leisure education: theory and practice.* 2nd ed. Champaign, IL: Sagamore.

Mundy, J., and L. Odum. 1979. *Leisure education: Theory and practice.* New York: John Wiley and Sons.

National Recreation and Park Association (NRPA). 1977. *Kangaroo kit: Leisure education curriculum* Vol. 2. Arlington, VA: National Recreation and Park Association.

Peterson, C. A., and S. L. Gunn. 1984. *Therapeutic recreation program design: Principles and procedures.* 2nd ed. Englewood Cliffs, NJ: Prentice-Hall.

Peterson, C. A., and N. J. Stumbo. 2000. *Therapeutic recreation program design: Principles and procedures.* 3rd ed. Boston, MA: Allyn & Bacon.

Postman, N. 1985. *Amusing ourselves to death: Public discourse in the age of show business.* New York: Penguin Books.

Robinson, J., and G. Godbey. 1997. *Time for life: The surprising ways Americans use their time.* University Park, PA: The Pennsylvania University Press.

Ruskin, H. 1995. Conceptual approaches in policy development in leisure education. In *Leisure education: Toward the 21st century,* edited by H. Ruskin and A. Sivan (pp. 137–56). Provo, UT: Brigham Young University Press.

Ruskin, H. 2001. Youth at risk and leisure education. In *Leisure education, community development, and populations with special needs,* edited by A. Sivan & H. Ruskin (pp 153–68). New York: CABI Publishing.

Russell, R. V. 2002. *Pastimes: The context of contemporary leisure.* 2nd ed. Champaign, IL: Sagamore.

Searle, M. S., and E. L. Jackson. 1985. Recreation non-participation and barriers to participation: Considerations for the management of recreation delivery systems. *Journal of Park and Recreation Administration* 3(2).

Shivers, J. 2001. Educating the community for developmental opportunities in leisure. In *Leisure education, community development, and populations with special needs,* edited by A. Sivan and H. Ruskin (pp 13–20). New York: CABI Publishing.

Sivan A. 2001. Community development through leisure education: Conceptual approaches. In *Leisure education, community development, and populations with special needs,* edited by A. Sivan and H. Ruskin (pp 31–42). New York: CABI Publishing.

Sivan. A., and H. Ruskin, eds. 2001. Concluding remarks and recommendations. *Leisure education, community development, and populations with special needs* (pp. 181–189). New York: CABI Publishing.

Southwest Parks and Monument Association. 2000. *Deep Ravine Trail: Little Bighorn Battlefield National Monument.* Tucson, AZ: Author.

Stebbins, R. A. 2002. *The organizational basis of leisure participation: A motivational exploration.* State College, PA: Venture.

Tilden, F. 1967. *Interpreting our heritage.* Rev. ed. Chapel Hill, NC: University of North Carolina Press.

Todd, B. 2002, April. *Innovative leisure education.* Paper presented at the Midwest Symposium on Therapeutic Recreation, Springfield, IL.

Witt, P. A. 1991. Buckpassing, blaming or benevolence: A leisure education/counseling perspective. In *Recreation and leisure: Issues in an era of change,* edited by F. L. Goodale and P. A. Witt (pp. 307–15). State College, PA: Venture Publishing.

Witt, P. A. 2001. Insuring after-school programs meet their intended goals. *Parks and Recreation* 36(9): 32–52.

Future Trends and Professional Issues

LEARNING OBJECTIVES

1. To assist the student in understanding *the role of change in the provision of leisure services.*
2. To help the student identify *factors that are influencing the delivery of leisure services in a changing society.*
3. To acquaint individuals with the strategies and methods that can be employed by the leisure service programmer in *understanding and shaping the future.*
4. To provide information concerning *demographic, technological, economic, and social and cultural trends influencing leisure.*
5. To provide information concerning *professional issues influencing the delivery of leisure services.*

INTRODUCTION

Change will be the most dominant theme of our lives in this century. It is transforming the way that we live, work, and play. Change may create turmoil on one hand and, on the other hand, opportunity for innovation, renewal, and growth. The leisure market is constantly evolving, with people seeking new ways of experiencing leisure. As leisure service professionals we "must be able and willing to identify, analyze, promote and respond to change in society" (Mobley and Toalson, 1992: 11). Our work as a profession depends on our ability to understand that "change is not mysterious" (Conner, 1993: 11), and that we can anticipate and respond to change in a way that is positive and productive.

Leisure service programmers can have two orientations to the change process. One is a passive, noninteractive, reactive approach to change; the other is to be involved proactively as a contributor to activities of the future. The passive, noninteractive, reactive approach to change finds the professional waiting for events to have an impact on his or her organization and then reacting to these events. The leisure service professional assuming this posture does not attempt to anticipate change, but rather scurries to keep pace with the emergence of new patterns of leisure behavior and activity. The question often posed by a professional operating from this perspective is "What *is* occurring?" rather than "What *might* occur?"

The second orientation to the change process is to see oneself as a participator in the creation of the future. As Tindall (1984) has noted, "the ability to understand and keep pace with change, as well as to create innovative responses that can impact its direction, is the one theme most central to prolonged vitality for any profession or business of the future." She further notes that the leisure service professional must become "a master of change and innovation, as opposed to its victim." In the same vein, Brauer (1984) has noted that leisure service organizations must "choose between being

leaders, victims, or survivors" in this era of dramatic and rapid change.

Attempting to predict the future is a challenging task. Weston (1996: 207) notes that "thinking about the future is interesting because it involves prediction." Our ability to accurately and successfully predict the future in the area of leisure is one of our most challenging tasks because of the changing and unpredictable nature of leisure pursuits. As Godbey (1992: 26) has written:

> If history teaches us anything—and it must—it teaches us that one era is connected to another, that the unfolding of the future is not random: It is a reaction to the past, but a reaction that often surpasses our imagination to predict. Predicting anything about leisure is, perhaps, among the most complex exercises in speculation, since one must divine what freedom will mean to people, what they will voluntarily and pleasurably do given a minimum of constraints, the nature and extent of obligation in a society, and other imponderable questions (p. 26).

In this chapter, we explore some of the factors that influence the work of the leisure service professional while leading in an era of change. We explore basic orientations toward change. In addition, a number of tools and strategies that can be used to identify changes are presented. Several future directions—demographic, technological, economic, social, and cultural—are reviewed. Finally, some professional issues are identified.

LIVING IN AN ERA OF CHANGE

It is perhaps trite to suggest that we live in one of the most change-oriented periods in the history of humankind. Changes that have occurred economically, technologically, socially, and politically in the past several decades are staggering, as has been the rate of these changes. There have been more inventions in the last two decades than in the previous 100 years. We have moved in just a short period of time from a society in which the emphasis was on mass production and centralization to one that emphasizes the unique needs of individuals in a decentralized fashion.

Brauer (1984) further suggests that the future will bring more ambiguity and the potential for less understanding and acceptance of basic concepts. This ambiguity will occur because of both the diversity of interests emerging during the present era and the rate of change. In discussing change, Brauer has noted that several different perspectives have emerged. They are as follows:

1. Change will be a constant rather than an exception to long periods of sameness.
2. Change is basic and substantive: New definitions (of family, work, health care); male-female roles/relationships; diminishing resources/increasing toxic wastes; eroding social cements under increased stress.
3. Change is pervasive/persistent/worldwide/self-generated; an interdependent/interconnected world eliminates isolation (p. 58).

These perspectives show that change will be constant, substantial, pervasive, persistent. In other words, change will be with us, and to succeed as leisure service professionals, we will have to understand change, become adept at reading and predicting trends toward change, and provide visionary leadership to meet the challenges of the future.

The Information Era

To develop a foundation for understanding this period of change, it is essential to review history for the past several thousand years. Toffler (1980), in his book *The Third Wave,* has suggested that the history of humankind can be divided into four segments—precivilized society, the agricultural revolution, the industrial revolution, and the technological revolution (or the information era). Each of these changes in the history of humankind represents a major shift influencing the thinking, values, attitudes, and behavior of individuals. Ferguson (1980), author

of *The Aquarian Conspiracy,* calls these changes *paradigm shifts.* They are major changes shaping the way we live all aspects of our lives.

The information era (also known as postindustrial society and the technological revolution) emerged as a result of technological advances and changes in the type and nature of work engaged in by individuals. We are witnessing enormous changes as the industrial society gives way to a new society emphasizing the creation and distribution of information and services. The information era is built on a new set of assumptions and will require new ideas, new concepts, and new strategies in response to the new values that currently exist and will continue to emerge.

Even today, the information era is giving way to the knowledge or learning era. The focus in our current space is not only access to knowledge but, more importantly, production of knowledge or experiences. The paradigm that is emerging is a joined or shared production of experiences in which individuals collaborate with professionals to create meaning. The new emphasis will be on combining action with reflection—a process known as *praxis.* This concept will lead to greater interaction between individuals and professionals.

The information era is challenging leisure service programmers to develop new paradigms, or new ways of solving new problems. The information era is built on a different set of assumptions than the industrial era. For example, in the industrial era, efforts were directed toward standardizing and mass-producing goods and services. This followed the assumption that people were not necessarily unique and that their needs could be met in a systematic, uniform fashion. On the other hand, the information era recognizes the need for uniquely designed and organized services that cater to individual needs, services more specifically suited to individual tastes, values, and behavior.

As we shift from an industrial society to an information society, several factors will have a direct impact on leisure service organizations.

Some of the changes that are impacting both play and work environments are as follows:

- The primary mode of communication has shifted from typography to electronics, thus changing the way people think, converse, and educate themselves.
- Advanced media technology means that a significant shift in one part of the world is almost instantaneously known on the other side of the globe.
- The growth of information is occurring so fast that the "shelf life" of facts and technology has been reduced dramatically.
- The planet's fragile ecosystems will no longer sustain humankind's capacity to reproduce, its increasing demand for natural resources, or its generations of waste.
- Faster modes of transportation are becoming available, creating greater economic opportunities, but with potentially severe psychological and environmental costs.
- The redefinition of traditional male and female, ethnic and racial roles is reshaping the structure of our society (Conner, 1993: 4).

These factors will provide great challenges to leisure service programmers. They will call for a redefinition of the orientation and strategies used by leisure service delivery systems. Not only will leisure service professionals be challenged to cope with change, but they will experience increasing levels of complexity in their professional environments. More variables will need to be considered when planning leisure programs. Not only will individual needs be considered, but also broader social, economic, technical, and political factors will affect the delivery of services.

A New Paradigm for Leisure Service Delivery

The leisure service profession must break new ground. The profession must seek a new paradigm for defining itself, its relationships to those it serves, and the services it provides. It is important to recognize that the information era is built on a different set of assumptions from those of the previous era. Most of our existing leisure service delivery systems are built on assumptions of the past. These assumptions may no longer be relevant or useful in helping define future leisure programs and services.

Designing a new paradigm for the leisure service profession will be challenging. Consider the fact that most leisure service organizations have their historical roots in the industrial era. Municipal parks (ca. 1850s), playgrounds (ca. 1880s), organized camping (ca. 1860s), recreation centers (ca. early 1900s), national parks (ca. 1870s), state parks (ca. 1860s), and youth-serving organizations (ca. late 1800s and early 1900s) all emerged during the Industrial Revolution. Although many of these organizations have continued to evolve, other institutions may need to be created in response to changes in the information era.

Over the past several decades, considerable effort has been made to open the leisure service profession to new and different ways of thinking. For example, a much greater emphasis has been placed on the potential interaction between the public and commercial sectors. New emphasis has been placed not only on defining leisure, but also on assisting leisure service organizations in measuring their impact in terms of economic and social factors.

Perhaps one of the most dramatic changes concerns the way in which social issues and individual values are addressed in the information era. The basic assumptions about the productive capacity of government in particular are being challenged. Lack of public confidence as reflected in referendums directed at reducing property taxes, lack of confidence in government officials, and a decline in the quality of services are forcing a readjustment of our thinking in terms of the ways in which leisure services are delivered.

As we move from a centralized to a decentralized society, a number of fundamental changes have occurred. For example, we have shifted from an era in which political activism was a stronger determinant than the marketplace. In the present era, we are shifting back to a situation in which individual values and social choice may be more fully acted out in the marketplace rather than on a political stage. We have found that government does not have the productive capacity to generate sufficient economic resources for meeting social needs. Heretofore, our political system was capable of evolving internally to accommodate changes and to create new social forms and institutions to meet emerging challenges.

Governmental systems may continue to evolve and be responsive to social needs. However, it appears that the action will be in the marketplace in the future and not in centralized bureaucratic organizations. If this scenario is an accurate one, individuals involved in the creation and delivery of leisure services will need a different set of skills. They will need knowledge of the mechanisms essential in the analysis of a market and of the free enterprise system. In other words, the skills and knowledge of future leisure service programmers must focus on marketing, entrepreneurship, calculated risk-taking, vision, and knowledge of people and their behavior.

In viewing this transformation, it is important to remember that while we search for new, economical ways to meet social needs, our methods must at the same time be ethical and confirm the basic underlying values of the profession—conservation and preservation of natural resources, promotion and protection of human dignity, and the wise use of leisure. The window for innovation is a narrow one; most of the conditions that will serve as a basis for change have already been established. Many new, innovative, and creative concepts have been put in place to meet changing social conditions. The competitive marketplace will sort out those who can meet human needs in the most efficient and effective manner possible. However, there are still opportunities for individuals and organizations to provide fundamental redirection to the movement by creating new strategies to meet newly emerging leisure needs and conditions.

FUTURING: STRATEGIES AND METHODS

A number of strategies and methods can be employed by the leisure service professional in helping understand and shape the future. Tindall (1984) has suggested that the process of *futuring* is both an art and a science. She notes that to be successful, the leisure service professional must develop "one's ability to be both artist and scientist in preparing for the future" (p. 13). Futuring involves not only projecting future trends and issues, but also directing the future by having a vision of a possible, realistic, attainable mission for the leisure service organization.

Data-Based Strategies and Methods

Leisure service professionals can use specific strategies in planning for the future. Most of these strategies involve an understanding of the environment as it evolves. Such strategies usually involve careful analysis of demographic changes, social/cultural trends, economic factors, and environmental changes. As Tindall (1984) notes, statistical analysis can be undertaken to determine changes in "housing, population growth, employment, age groupings, ethnicity, earning and spending patterns, overall economic growth or decline, household or family composition, work and leisure lifestyle patterns, and what people value and how they spend their leisure time." Specific strategies and methods include the following:

1. *Strategic Planning*—Strategic planning focuses on developing a management process that helps establish and maintain a balance between the leisure service organization and the external environment. The function of a strategic plan is to ensure that an organization's resources are brought to bear in a timely fashion to meet opportunities or needs that arise. It is a process directed toward planning that takes into consideration potential changes in the environment.

2. *Market Information System*—A market information system is a strategy directed at gathering information related to customers in an organized and systematic fashion on a regular basis.

A market information system may use both primary and secondary sources of data or use direct interaction with individuals in customer focus groups. Often, a marketing information system involves predicting the demand for a service, a strategy known as forecasting.

3. *Short- and Long-Range Plans*—Most organizations have plans. Short-range plans usually spell out ends desired by the leisure service organization on a one- to three-year basis. Long-range plans spell out goals for a longer period of time, usually ten years or longer. Most leisure service organizations have plans relating to land acquisition and facility development. On the other hand, few leisure service organizations have plans that spell out development activities for leisure programs and services.

In gathering information to plan for the future, a variety of strategies can be used by the leisure service programmer. Secondary sources provide opportunities for the analysis of *demographic characteristics*, usually obtainable from U.S. census data. In addition, leisure service professionals can engage in *environmental scanning*, which involves an analysis of changes in conditions in social, political, economic, cultural, or other elements that can influence the work of an organization. Another mechanism for gathering information is known as *trend or content analysis*. This involves collecting information from various sources, such as newspapers and magazines, to determine the emergence of fads or trends in the environment that might have an impact on the delivery of leisure services. For example, a scan of popular weekly news magazines suggests a rise in interest in physical fitness in the past decade. Finally, *social indices* can be monitored and provide information that can be useful in planning services. For example, changes in discretionary income, employment rate, and so forth can be useful in developing strategies for providing services. The United Way organization regularly gathers information and conducts media scans to identify emerging trends in the nation. It offers several publications that report the results of its efforts.

Artistic Strategies and Methods

Artistic strategies and methods for identifying future directions refer to the use of one's intuitive and creative abilities to build toward the future. As Hitt (1988) notes, there are two kinds of leadership—transactional and transformational. Transactional leaders exchange benefits (money, recognition, status, etc.) for effort. Transformational leaders have the ability to create a vision for the future and inspire individuals to a higher ideal. The principal theme of transformational leadership is lifting people into their better selves. This is done by leaders who have the ability to transform their vision, or the organization's vision, into a significant reality.

In regard to transformational leadership authors such as Peters (1987), Bennis and Nanus (1985), Naisbett and Aburdeen (1985), and Hitt (1988) call for visionary managerial leaders. As Hitt notes:

> Formulating a clear vision of a desired future may be the most important leadership function. Without a clear vision, we might be satisfied that we were doing things right, but we would not know if we were doing the right things. The ability to create a clear vision is the key attribute that separates managers from leaders (pp. 42–43).

Tindall (1984) suggests several strategies to help deal with the complexities of the changing nature of our society. Among the most applicable are the following:

1. *Change-Making*—The term *change-making* is derived from the theme of the book *The Change Masters* (Kanter, 1983). Kanter writes, "the individuals who will succeed and flourish in the times ahead will be masters of change; adept at reorienting their own and others' activities in untried directions to bring about higher levels of achievement" (p. 65). Change-making involves four basic steps: (1) thriving on novelty, (2) inspiring others to a clear vision, (3) working through terms to promote decision making, and (4) promoting self-esteem by encouraging others.

2. *Visionary Leadership*—Providing visionary leadership involves setting a new direction for an organization in times of chaos, turbulence, and uncertainty. Hitt (1988) suggests that it is necessary not only to create the vision, but to determine steps and methods to implement it. A vision without action is useless. Visions empower people. As Bennis and Nanus (1985: 90) note, "when the organization has a clear sense of its purpose, direction, and desired future state, and this image is widely shared, individuals" are empowered.

3. *Entrepreneurship/Intrepreneurship*—We live in a society in which the need for social innovation and change is great. *Entrepreneurship,* according to Drucker (1985), is a process of innovation. It involves the creation of new institutions, programs, or services that meet societal needs. When accomplished within the context of an existing organization, it is known as *intrepreneurship.* Entrepreneurs are individuals who are risk oriented, visionary, inner directed, and often achievement oriented. Entrepreneurship provides a mechanism to bring various resources together to create new programs, services, and organizational structures. Entrepreneurs often have to break with tradition to develop creative and innovative products and services, even though conventional wisdom suggests a more cautious posture. Entrepreneurs are able to analyze and see things in new and bold ways (Bullaro and Edginton, 1986: 21).

These strategies and methods require the leisure service professional to operate in a proactive posture. Their purpose is to encourage leisure service professionals to use their intuitive and managerial abilities to bring about change. The strategies involve creating or managing a vision and, as a result, bringing about change and an ordering of the future. As Drucker (1985) states, successful innovation "consists in the purposeful and organized search for changes and in the systematic analysis of opportunities such changes might offer for economic or social innovation" (p. 35). He notes that the search for change and innovation can be done in a diagnostic and disci-

plined fashion, and can lead to what he calls "innovative opportunity."

Strategic Planning for 2010: A Case Study

In 1997, the City of Edmonton (Alberta) created the Department of Community Services, which combined the former departments of Parks and Recreation, Community and Family Services, and the Office of the Commissioner of Housing. As such, a new strategic plan—*Plan Edmonton*—was outlined to guide service delivery for a ten-year duration (2000–2010) (City of Edmonton, Community Services, 2000). Some of the data collection methods that were used to develop *Plan Edmonton* were public questionnaires, random household surveys, public focus groups, staff focus groups, community service advisory boards, stakeholder roundtables, use of consultants, interviews, public information displays, and open houses. A mixed method, or triangulation evaluative design (see Chapter 13), was used to gather information and make judgments regarding future community service delivery. Figure 15.1 presents the cover of the *Plan Edmonton* document and Figure 15.2 presents a brief list of successful indicators of the group's urban wellness program.

FUTURE LEISURE PROGRAMMING DIRECTIONS AND PROFESSIONAL ISSUES

Making projections for the future or forecasting the future is an exceedingly challenging task. However, a careful review of the professional literature and of social indicators makes it possible to identify and discuss future issues that are emerging and call for the attention of professionals. For example, each year the Research and Planning Department of the YMCA of the USA (2000) publishes a societal trends document to help YMCAs in their future programming. To this end, Table 15.1 presents the YMCA's listing of twelve major societal trends and accompanying programming actions for the beginning of the twenty-first century. Moreover,

Figure 15.1   Future Community/Recreation Planning, the City of Edmonton (Alberta, Canada) Community Services.

Table 15.2 provides an overview of future leisure programming issues that Canadian and American leisure educators and academics have articulated. Although these two tables provide much insight into future issues in leisure programming, they do not rank-order the importance of future programming issues. In a comprehensive study that did rank-order the importance of future pro-

gramming issues, Kraus (2000) reported that recreation, park, and leisure service educators believed that the following twelve issues were most important:

1. Be prepared to serve an increasingly diverse society (e.g., race, age, gender)
2. Emphasize social purpose of recreation (e.g., benefits)

D. Urban Wellness

Overall, Edmontonians enjoy a good quality of life. They have high expectations and support for initiatives that improve quality of life and enhance wellness. On a personal level, Edmontonians want more opportunities for health, fitness and lifestyle support made available closer to home. On a neighbourhood scale, residents want better social interaction and better linkages to parks and recreation facilities and programs. At the city level, support has never been higher for the many festivals, cultural and artistic events that add to the city's cosmopolitan atmosphere. And, across the board, ongoing concerns about safety and security among residents and businesses require our additional attention and resources.

Our view of urban wellness is multi-dimensional and integrated. It includes all the components of a lively urban village: health, fitness, lifestyle, environmental and cultural aspects. We want citizens to take delight and pride in their city's high quality of life. We want to ensure that our essential services and programs help make Edmonton a better place to live, work and play.

TARGETS

- Create Safe and Walkable Neighbourhoods
- Improved Urban Environment
- Active Living Through Recreation and Sport Programs
- Strong Arts, Culture and Heritage Programs

SUCCESS INDICATORS

- Edmontonians believe their neighbourhoods offer safety, walkability, sociability and convenience
- Sustainable and self-reliant communities
- High level of community awareness and understanding of Edmonton's history and different cultures
- Improved community wellness
- Continued support and promotion of arts, culture, recreation, sport and heritage

JULY 2000 – **57**

Figure 15.2 Future Community/Recreation Planning, the City of Edmonton (Alberta, Canada) Community Services.

3. Achieve fuller public understanding of the value of recreation, leisure, and parks
4. Upgrade recreation and park programs and facilities, especially in inner cities
5. Adopt a benefits-based management approach
6. Promote recreation's identity as a health-related field
7. Develop partnerships with environmental organizations to protect the environment
8. Employ marketing approaches to achieve fiscal self-sufficiency and gain public respect
9. Expand family-centered programs and facilities
10. Promote higher values and ethical practices in youth sports competition
11. Strive for fuller mainstreaming of persons with disabilities into community recreation
12. Plan for the long-term role of recreation and leisure in a potentially job-scarce economy.

We are, as professionals, challenged to respond to a number of professional trends that may influence the creation and delivery of services in the future. As such, the following section provides some (but not all) of the future directions or trends that may impact leisure programs.

9/11

The events of September 11 (9/11) 2001, when the World Trade Center and Pentagon were attacked in the United States, changed the world. It is no surprise that recreation and leisure ser-

TABLE 15.1   YMCA Societal Trends and Programming Implications for the Beginning of the Twenty-First Century

Societal Trends	Programming Implications
Changing cultural population	Cross-cultural programming to bring people from different backgrounds together on common ground
Increased demand for resources	Increase collaborative community programs, volunteers, and funding
Greater gap between rich and poor	Bridge this gap by having wealthy people support YMCAs and provide specific programs for the poor
Rapid rate of change	Provide changing and flexible services as societal trends change, such as family programs, after-school programs, and so forth
Lack of time	Provide multiple activities at differing time periods
Increased consumer expectations	Strategic interaction among quality, quantity, and cost of programs and services
For every trend, a counter-trend	YMCAs continue to be examples of common sense and moderation
Search for community	Programs foster a sense of community togetherness
There's got to be something more	Follow the traditional YMCA focus of spirituality by connecting spirit, mind, and body, and by holding to Christian roots while being inclusive to others
More choices, more confusion	Adapt to the needs of communities
Looking for alternatives	YMCAs can be a model of practically and creativity by following moral citizenship (thinking of the needs of the community) opposed to being a traditional business that looks after its own needs first
Everything's a commodity	Treat people in a genuine manner—integrity, opposed to as a commodity

From: YMCA of USA. 2000. *Societal trends and the YMCA movement.* Chicago, IL: Author.

TABLE 15.2   Overview of Future Leisure Programming Issues

Edginton et al. (2002) (USA)	Kelly and Freysinger (2000) (USA)	Searle and Brayley (2000) (Canada)
Population shifts	Gender	Aging
Changes in social roles	Sexuality	Changes in family
Greater equality	Social class	Working mothers
Blurring of public and private sector of leisure services	Race	The poor
Increase in diversity	Combining class and race	Unemployment and under employment
Changes in physical health	World economy	Dependency
Changes in social health	Culture	Crime and violence
Greater sensitivity of environment in development	Technology	Multiculturalism
Natural resource depletion	Urbanization and suburbanization	Environmental protection
Environmental degradation	Family issues	Health
Rethinking of education	Aging	Constitutional reform
Technology	Changes in time	Aboriginal peoples
Economic changes		Rural development
		Fiscal limitations
		Expectations of government
		Planning for the future

vice delivery and leisure behavior have been affected since 9/11. For example, the World Tourism Organization (2002) suggested that the events of 9/11 have restructured travel habits of Americans—tourists are favoring destinations that are closer to home, more familiar, and accessible using means of transportation that are perceived to be safer than mass transportation. To this end, the *Des Moines Register* (Iowa) reported that tourism in Iowa and other midwest states has increased because of terrorism (Crossman, 2001). As such, the authors of this book believe that recreation and leisure professionals ought to examine and expand their roles in the aftermath of 9/11. The question we pose is: What is the future interplay among 9/11, terrorism, and leisure programming? Furthermore, how can recreation and leisure help address the issue of terrorism? These are difficult and complex questions with no easy answers.

An interesting article published in the *Wall Street Journal* (Hallinan, 2002) suggests that Americans are using "serious fun" to help cope with terrorism. In particular, this article suggested that since 9/11, Americans are purchasing recreational vehicles at a significant rate and makers of recreational vehicles are increasing sales:

- Polaris Industries, maker of all-terrain vehicles (ATVs) and watercraft reported a 5 percent increase in ATV sales, a 10 percent increase in jet ski sales, and a 16 percent increase in net income since 9/11.
- Brunswick Corporation, maker of treadmills, pool tables, boats, and motors, reported an 11 percent increase in net income since 9/11.
- Harley-Davison, maker of motorcycles, reported a 25 percent increase in net income since 9/11.
- Winnebago, maker of RVs, reported a 22 percent increase in net income since 9/11.

Hallinan (2002) underscored that many other makers of recreational vehicles and equipment reported similar increases in sales. This article suggests that people are using leisure to escape and deal with 9/11 and the perceived

threat of future terrorism. In this regard, Hamilton (2002) highlighted that during national crises, "people instinctively flock to recreation areas . . ." (p. 45). To exemplify the interplay of leisure during a national crisis, Hamilton provides the following direct quotation from President Franklin Roosevelt in 1942:

> Now that we are at war, we are fortunate in having this rich resource of recreation to give us physical, mental and spiritual power for the titanic task at hand . . . I rejoice in the fact that the strength of the recreation movement in America stems from a feeling of community responsibility" (p. 45).

As reported in Chapter 1, the Freedom Quilt Project is an example of recreation providing a sense of togetherness and community responsibility in the aftermath of 9/11.

Ogah (2002) argued that health and human professionals, which includes leisure professionals, should provide programs to help people cope and deal with the immediate and long-term effects of terrorism. Drawing upon Ogah's treatise, recreation and leisure programs can reduce the conditions that produce violence and acts of terror—programmed activities can help people manage stress and deal with cultural differences (see Chapter 1 regarding the multiple benefits of recreation and leisure). Likewise, leisure education programs can specifically target the importance of leisure during times of crisis (e.g., deal with stress, family bonding). Hamilton (2002) outlined general ideas for how parks, recreation, and leisure facilities can help individuals and communities deal with the aftermath of 9/11 and terrorism: (1) commemorate 9/11 (e.g., provide healing); (2) deal with fears (e.g., art and puppet programs to help children deal with emotions); (3) provide safe havens from stress (e.g., walk in a park); (4) provide opportunities for all people to do a community service project (e.g., community bonding); and (5) dedicate a monument, park, garden, or other public space to remember 9/11 and connect to a national community. For example, Hamilton (2002) reported how the Park and Recreation Department of Middletown Township (New Jersey) will dedicate a park with thirty-six monuments—one for each resident of Middletown who died as a result of 9/11—on September 11, 2003. In short, future leisure programming should be oriented toward remedying symptoms resulting from the trauma of terrorism and as a medium to help people cope and heal during national and global crises.

Upgrading Recreation and Park Programs and Facilities, Especially in Inner Cities

Godbey (1997) underscored that in past eras, parks and recreation organizations were focused on building facilities and that upgrading will be a focus in the future. According to Kraus (2000), many cities are directing an acute focus on upgrading recreation and park programs and facilities. To this end, Daley (2002) provided a case study of how the city of Chicago and numerous leisure services, such as the Chicago Park District, are collaborating to upgrade and rebuild "community anchors" through park and recreation restoration. The following list highlights different restoration projects throughout the city of Chicago.

- Since 1996, the city of Chicago has spent $600 million on capital improvements to city parks, playgrounds, water parks, batting cages, beach improvement, lagoon rehabilitation, and junior golf courses
- Built or fully renovated forty libraries
- Developed streetscapes (decorative painting, paving, and structures), such as a Chinese dragon theme on concrete pillars in Chinatown or gateway structures that resemble Greek temples in Greektown
- Provided rooftop gardens on City Hall and other buildings (the rooftop garden on City Hall has over 20,000 plants)

- Developed community policing programs (neighborhoods working with police departments) to drive gangs out of community parks
- Implemented numerous summer and after-school programs via a partnership among schools, parks, recreation organizations, and libraries
- Opened eleven high school swimming pools to the public
- Developed the Calumet Open Space Reserve, which includes 4,000 acres of prairies, wetlands, and forest areas in Chicago's far southwest side
- Developed neighbor-space areas by converting vacant lots (e.g., abandoned service stations) into small parks and gardens and appointing a community group to manage these neighbor-space areas
- Renovated Soldier Field (home of the NFL Chicago Bears) with an additional 17 acres of new parkland.

Likewise, the Department of Parks and Recreation in New York City is also directing a sharp focus on upgrading recreation and park programs and facilities. According to Salwen (2000), New York City's Department of Parks and Recreation has replaced or refurbished more than 378 parks and playgrounds. For example, Nelson Playground in the Bronx had a twelve-month, $1.17 million upgrade and expansion. Likewise, Paerdegat Park in Brooklyn acquired an additional 3.5 acres of land in its twelve-month reconstruction project. Upgrades and restoration of park and recreation sites are also occurring at the state and federal levels. For example, the National Park Service, in partnership with other organizations, is restoring the physical and biological health of many parks in Florida. In particular, the National Park Service has spent over $67 million on the Southern Florida Restoration Initiative (see http://data2. itc.nps.gov/budget2/documents/south%20flori da%20restoration%20initiative.pdf).

Child Care
The expectations for standards-driven child-care programs will result in new models for service

delivery within leisure service organizations. Although leisure service organizations have historically provided services to young children, there often has been a lack of attentiveness to child-care standards and guidelines. Greater accountability within leisure child-care programs for children and youth is demanded, often by competing commercial providers. Standards such as those offered by the National School-Age Care Alliance (nasca) are having an increasing impact on programs for both children and youth. In addition, a new profession focused on before- and after-school care and latchkey services is emerging. Also emerging are new program development strategies based on principles of constructivist education, an emphasis on choice and other factors.

Children's Rights

An awareness of children's rights stems from the United Nations Convention on the Rights of the Child document, adopted in 1989. As Franklin (1995) notes, "children, too, are equals; as human beings they have the same inherent value as grown-ups. The affirmation of the right to play underlies that childhood is valuable in itself . . . children—especially when they are very young—are vulnerable, and need special support to be able to enjoy their rights in full" (p. iv). A return to an era of "child-saving" has prompted great interest in the protection of children's rights.

Coalition Building/Collaboration

It is important for leisure service programmers to network with other organizations and life units (families) to serve the whole individual. By networking with other community agencies and organizations, fragmentation of services will be diminished and efficiency and effectiveness of services will be enhanced. Fragmentation of services often leads to duplication of services. Collaboration is the coordination and cooperation of two or more organizations toward common goals.

Commodification of Leisure

Kelly (1991: 7) and Wearing and Wearing (1992: 3) discuss the idea of the commodification of leisure. The commodification of leisure concept, according to Kelly, refers to leisure "as a market-mediated instrument of control." In other words, the mass production of leisure has created an "uneasy juxtaposition of freedom of choice in and commodification and conformity in leisure" (Wearing and Wearing, 1992: 3). Using as an illustration the physical activity of running, these authors suggest that this activity "has been transformed by fashion, the organization of commerce, scientific analysis, the media, and the leisure industry into a multimillion dollar industry. The joy of jogging will be enhanced, the advertising suggests, by choosing the best from an array of colored, cushioned, even computerized shoes which tell you how far you have run and what time, at what pace and how many calories you have consumed." Thus, the commodification of leisure may taint or even control the pure form of running for leisure.

Cultural Tourism

Consistent with the emergence of greater global awareness, the desire to reach out to others for understanding, and the wish to experience the ambiance of other cultures has been the growth of cultural tourism. Naisbett (1994: 127) suggests that cultural tourism is one of the rapidly growing segments of the tourism industry. "There is an increasing demand for tourism in which visitors are permitted to observe and participate in the local events and lifestyles in a nonartificial manner" (*World Travel and Tourism Review: 152*).

Culturally Based Programming

North America is becoming more culturally diverse. The U.S. Bureau of the Census (2002) suggested that for the year 2050, demographics are projected to change to: NonHispanic Whites—52.8 percent, African American—13.2 percent, Hispanic—24.3 percent, Asian and

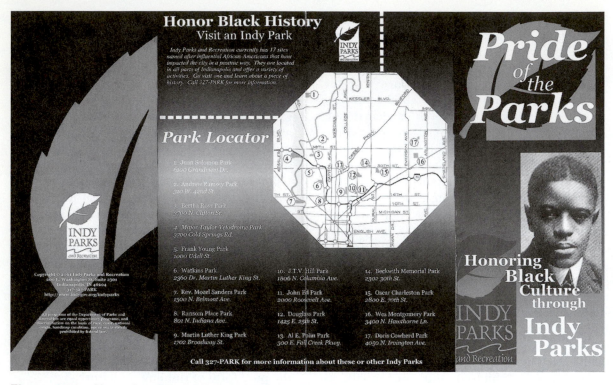

Figure 15.3 Honoring Black History, Visit An Indy Park.

Pacific Islanders—8.9 percent, and American Indians—0.8 percent. In essence, the United States is moving toward greater ethnic diversity with the passing of each day. The result is a need to develop leisure programs and services that meet the needs of different racial, cultural, and ethnic groups. Likewise, leisure professionals need to gain training in cross-cultural competencies. Allison and Schneider (2000) and Dieser and Wilson (2002) provide an overview of cross-cultural competencies and training strategies needed in leisure professionals. Opportunities exist for the creation of programs and services (e.g., festivals, arts, dance, sport) that reflect diverse cultural backgrounds. For example, the *Pride in Parks* program of the Indy Parks and Recreation Department (Indianapolis, Indiana) recognizes the significant impact that African Americans have had on the community by naming parks and recreation facilities in their honor (Figure 15.3 shows a brochure of the *Pride in Parks* program). Likewise, Calgary (Alberta) Parks and Recreation published a multicultural activity guide (1999) so that leisure professionals could include culturally based programming in existing programs and services. Figure 15.4 show one activity explained in its publication.

Elder Care

The aging of our population will continue to result in a greater need for elder care programs by leisure service organizations. It was projected that by the year 2000, 9 million individuals over age sixty-five will require some form of support (Wilkinson, 1989). As the baby boom generation

Figure 15.3 *Continued.*

grays, services for seniors will be even more in demand than they are today.

Environmental Ethics

The leisure service profession maintains a firm commitment to promoting and building a strong environmental ethic. The term *environmental ethic* also refers to *land ethic*. Programs in this area build a strong commitment to the environment. For example, Getchell and Beckman (2000) underscored how golf course construction that minimizes environmental harm can be developed. Moreover, leisure professionals can become environmental stewards and promote programs that respect and help the environment. For example, parks and recreation programs can provide recreation recycling and reuse programs—instead of having people throw away recreation equipment (e.g., skateboards, bicycles, soccer balls, board games), such items can be collected by local parks and recreation departments and given to people who are from a lower socioeconomic status. Likewise, a future leisure education program can be oriented toward educating people on the environmental benefits of biking (e.g., decrease carbon dioxide in the environment).

Family-Oriented Programs

Many leisure service organizations are focusing their energies and efforts on building family-oriented leisure programs. Such programs build family unity and solidarity and promote positive intergenerational links. It should be noted that "families" can be defined in a number of ways. To celebrate families playing together, the American

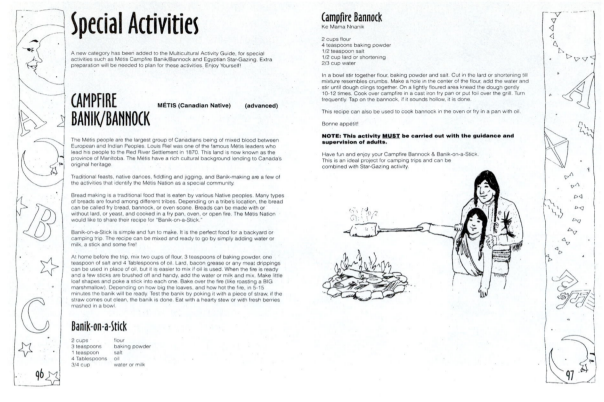

Figure 15.4 Example of Culturally Based Programming, Calgary (Alberta, Canada) Parks and Recreation.

Association for Leisure and Recreation has organized an annual National Family Recreation Day. The idea behind this concept is to promote greater awareness of the many opportunities that are available to families through positive leisure experiences.

Feminization of Leisure

Women's rights have emerged as a growing social and cultural force. For example, a growth in sports programs for women of all ages has occurred as a result of Title IX legislation. The feminization of leisure will continue to occur. Our culture's collective ideas and practices of leisure are likely to be increasingly shaped by females during the 2000s (Godbey, 1992: 31).

Growth of Tourism

As Naisbett (1994: 103) observes, the more we integrate the world, the more we differentiate our experiences. The more exposure we have to other cultures, languages, and landscapes, the stronger our desire is to experience them first-hand. As already mentioned, the events of 9/11 have restructured travel habits of Americans. Although tourism will continue, forecasting suggests that tourists will favor destinations that are closer to home, are more familiar, and are accessible using means of transportation that are perceived to be safer than mass transportation (World Tourism Organization, 2002).

Immediacy and Convenience

North Americans are in a hurry and they value expedience. They desire to have services delivered to them in a timely and convenient fashion. The location and timing of a service is critical to its success. We live in a society that demands that leisure service programmers have programs and activities packaged and organized in such a way that they are easily accessible and delivered when customers desire to have them (usually now).

Technology

Computers, telephones, television, and other forms of technology are influencing leisure and are blending together. For example, during NFL football games, television viewers can log on to websites via the Internet to communicate whether they agree with a referee's penalty call. People use technological advancements for leisure, such as games (e.g., computer games), communication (e.g., e-mail, Internet chat sites), access information (e.g., tourist destinations), and education pursuits. The implications for home entertainment through the use of integrated telecommunication are staggering—electronic entertainment, virtual realities, interactive communication, and fiber optics will become part of the language of leisure service programmers in the future.

Leisure and People with Disabilities

As indicated in Chapter 1, the Americans with Disabilities Act has created greater opportunities for people with disabilities to participate in leisure activities of their choice. Accommodations to make programs accessible are now mandated by law and will continue to have implementations for programming. For example, the Club Car (see *www.clubcar.com*) is a golf cart that is specially made to help people with disabilities participate in golf. The Club Car has a swivel seat that can rotate so that a person with

special needs can swing a golf club from a sitting position (see Figure 15.5). Furthermore, the Club Car has been specially designed to cause no damage to greens, tees, or other sensitive areas of a golf course.

Leisure and Self-Expression

Some people are using their leisure rather than their work as a principal means for self-expression. The work environment today creates some jobs that are repetitive, boring, and routine. As Godbey (1992: 29) writes eloquently, "for a broad cross-section of American workers, the idea that one's job provides both identity and increasing levels of pay will be challenged by the reality." He suggests that individuals will be robbed of their creativity and resourcefulness. "The fragmented, mechanized, automated, bureaucratized, sped-up, and regimented nature of many jobs may be associated with mental and psychological loss." Compensatory leisure will provide opportunities for people to define their self-concept and express themselves.

Leisure Networks

A growing phenomenon is related to increased access to computers and computer networks. E-mail is a tribal maker (Naisbett, 1994: 23). It enables individuals to bond together via electronic linkages around a host of leisure interests. People will use their ability to connect electronically with others to form relationships. This has become a primary form of leisure interaction. In organizations, e-mail creates an instantaneous extension of the informal organization and may have implications for the movement of ideas and concepts and for the ability to influence decision making.

Leisure Popular Culture

America's popular culture is and will continue to be a dominant factor influencing global lifestyles. Leisure service professionals must consider the impact of professional sports, television, popular music, movies, and videos. A visit

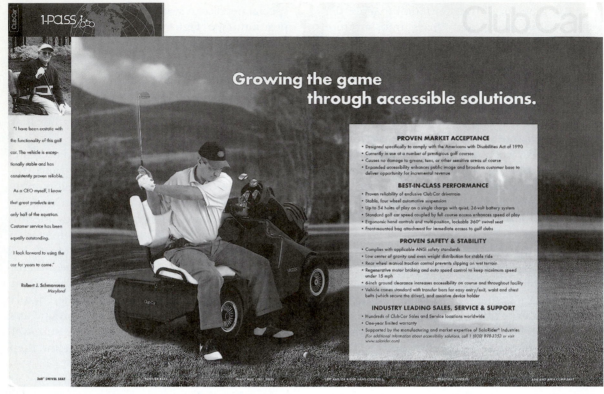

Figure 15.5 Club Car.

to the Guangzhou Grand World Scenic Park in the People's Republic of China reveals a well-developed theme-based amusement park that includes an "American Street," a Grand Canyon–like landscape, a replication of selected features of Yellowstone National Park, a U.S. "southern mansion," and a Hawaiian beach area, as well as features from several other countries. These displays have drawn their inspiration from the popular culture of the United States.

Leisure Time Famine
Americans have less time for leisure than in previous generations. As a result, leisure experiences tend to be of shorter duration (e.g., minivacations consisting of four-day weekends as opposed to traditional two-week family vaca-

tions). There is contradictory information regarding the amount of leisure time available to individuals. Over the past several decades, reports have said that leisure time has increased. However, Robinson (1989) notes that "Americans are facing a time famine and an increasing portion of Americans say that they always feel rushed."

Lifelong Learning
Change is occurring so rapidly that knowledge is becoming quickly obsolete. Leisure service organizations are uniquely positioned to promote lifelong learning. Clearly, people have a desire to continue their intellectual, social, and physical development. Leisure service organizations can play an important role by providing oppor-

tunities that enable individuals to grow and learn throughout their lifespan.

Multicultural Diversity

"People from different cultures bring with them different values, norms, and customs, and that means we will have fewer shared experiences" (Weston, 1996: 197). Our desire to promote multiculturalism is reflected in the delivery of leisure services. According to Fearn and Jarvi (1992: 81), the recreation and park profession should "maintain an all-inclusive attitude about program development [and] . . . increase our understanding of other cultures."

Multiple-Option Programming

Sheffield (1984) has suggested that leisure professionals must engage in multiple-option programming. She notes that various activities can be organized in ways that promote either cooperation, competition, or individualization. The challenge to the leisure service programmer is in creating diverse opportunities that meet a multitude of needs in the marketplace.

New Populations, New Programs

Changing demographic conditions will create opportunities for new leisure services. For example, single-parent households increase opportunities for services for children in latchkey-type activities. Maturity of the baby-boom generation creates opportunities for greater leisure programming for middle-aged adults. The aging of the population presents opportunities for increased programming to older adults.

Outreach Programs

According to Edginton and Edginton (1996), outreach services are increasingly being provided to respond to individual needs that are not met by traditional facility, program, and service strategies or structures—including physical, emotional, social/cultural, cognitive, moral, educational, and employment needs of families and youth. As indicated in Chapter 9, outreach

efforts of community organizations and agencies, including leisure service organizations, are designed to reach out to youth/families who are (1) alienated from services, (2) currently excluded from services, (3) not knowledgeable about services, using vehicles of developmentally sound programs, services, and personal interaction to empower youth to meet their needs (Bannon, 1973).

Packaging or Bundling Services

The concept of packaging or bundling services implies that leisure programmers organize a total service concept. The packaging or bundling concept suggests that as time constraints become a greater factor, there will be a need to cluster services that enable individuals to have a quality leisure experience. A scenario for the future might be one in which the needs of the entire family are met under one roof. The kids swim while the mother engages in aerobic activities and the father jogs. Child care, food concessions, and other services might all be found at one convenient location.

Planned, Deliberate Leisure Programming

Godbey (1986) suggests that conditions of economic restraint as well as the aging of the population and a more highly educated customer will require more planned and deliberate leisure programming. As people become more sophisticated and are required to pay more for services, they will become more selective and demanding in their choices. Thus, greater care will be required in creating and delivering leisure services.

Quality and Value of Services

Quality is a perception of excellence. Quality is often difficult to define, but "you know it when you see it." Value can be thought of as a return on an individual's investment of resources. Quality and value are, and will continue to be, important in the creation and delivery of leisure services. Again, as the population becomes more sophisticated in their selection of leisure experiences, quality and value will be important dimensions that will influence customer decision making. As Godbey (1986) notes, the critical leisure customer will increasingly seek higher quality in both leisure products and the leisure experience.

Reshaping of Work and Leisure

Industry continues its trend of downsizing, right-sizing, and restructuring of how work is organized. Flextime, flexible schedules, job sharing, and home-based work environments all continue to be evident in the workplace. This restructuring has dramatic impact on how leisure time is clustered or integrated with work. Increasingly there is a fusion between work and leisure. The "home does not replace the office—it has become a part of it" (Weston, 1996: 215).

Risk Recreation

Naisbett (1994: 126) observes that risk recreation is a growth area. There is an increase in the desire for leisure services that have an element of perceived risk. At the same time, leisure service organizations are being challenged to determine ways to manage leisure environments in such a way as to reduce risk. In fact, concerns over potentially litigious situations are forcing the closure of some leisure service organizations. One challenge that leisure service professionals face in the future will be to satisfy customers' desire for risk in their leisure experiences while at the same time ensuring safe conditions.

Self-Directed Leisure

The literature suggests that self-directed leisure activities will be a major trend in the future. As Scott (1993: 57) writes, "people may become more self-directed during their leisure time." Most leisure activities occur in casual, social occasions rather than in exotic leisure events. For several decades, it has been suggested that the role of facilitator and enabler are appropriate roles for leisure service professionals.

Self-Sufficiency

Individuals will increasingly control their own destiny, including factors related to their leisure. Personal access to computers, Internet, electronic mail, fax machines, and worldwide information makes us more self-sufficient and less dependent as we attempt to accomplish goals.

Service Orientation

The leisure service field is becoming more service-oriented—recognizing the need to place the customer first. Great leisure service organizations have a strong connection with their customers; being "wedded" to the customer is a mindset that develops within such organizations. "People today expect to be valued as customers" (Osborne and Gaebler, 1992: 167). Toalson (1992: 113) writes, "service to people is our goal . . . we are in the people business . . . we must be service-oriented."

Simpler, More Convenient Services

People will seek simpler, more convenient leisure experiences. The demand for such services is a reflection of an aging society, greater time constraints, less discretionary income, less open space, compacted housing conditions, and increases in energy cost. Interestingly, during the next decade home-based activities will continue to be central leisure activities. More families are spending a larger percentage of time at home aided by their video machines and home entertainment units. Single-parent families will look to leisure as a way of reinforcing values in an inexpensive, simple, and convenient manner.

Social Bonding and Leisure

Through leisure activities, people get and remain in touch with other people. As Naisbett (1994: 23) writes, "the bonding commonality of human beings is our distinctiveness." Festivals, community celebrations, special events, classes, workshops, and other activities all bring people in touch with one another in an age of increasing isolation and alienation. Through leisure, people will seek out other people and seek opportunities to bond and create a sense of community.

Spiritual Development

Leisure can be a major force in assisting individuals in their spiritual development. Naisbett (1994: 99) writes that a "spiritual vacuum is sometimes a by-product of material success." In a society punctuated by rapid change, traditional values and the existing support structure are often undermined. This may lead people to a quest for new meaning in their lives or a return to basic, familiar values. Many leisure environments provide ways in which individuals can enhance their spirituality. Leisure provides an opportunity for reflection, contemplation, and heightened awareness of self and others.

Time Distribution

One of the more interesting emerging trends is that of the reconceptualization or distribution of time. The knowledge era presents new ways of viewing work and leisure. For example, many school districts are considering operating on a twelve-month basis. This means that school-age children will be taking their vacations at times different from the normal nine-month cycle. Further, individuals are working different configurations of hours with the opportunity for extended periods of leisure. Finally, technology such as computers and fax machines are providing individuals with an opportunity to define their own work space and location. In other words, it is no longer necessary to go to a workplace or to follow a schedule. This flexibility opens up opportunities for different ways of approaching leisure. One result has been a loss of quality leisure time. In fact, since the 1970s there has been a reduction in what might be seen as quality leisure as the pace and intensity of daily life has increased. Time constraints mean that leisure programs will have to be provided at accessible and convenient times.

Total Journey Concept

Closely related to tourism is the "total journey" concept, an increasingly popular travel option. The total journey concept caters to customers in that everything is taken care of for them—airline tickets, hotel, end destination attractions, car rental, meals, business connections, and other activities. This form of travel is efficient, saving time for today's busy consumer.

Youth Development

Great concern is being expressed about meeting the needs of children and youth. In the park and recreation field, this concern often has been manifested by identifying youth-at-risk. However, other organizations are using the broader term of *youth development* to focus their program efforts. Edginton and de Oliveira (1995) have written that the concept of youth development is multidimensional and can be viewed from a human growth orientation, a philosophical orientation, or a programmatic perspective. They further suggest that a program framework for youth development include the following: academic enrichment, leisure activities, health promotion programs, peer mentoring, life skill building, volunteer/career programs, leadership development, service learning (community/ civic), outreach services, and clubs/special interest groups (Edginton and de Oliveira, 1996: 22).

Wellness and Fitness Programs

A sustained and continued interest in wellness and fitness programs has existed during the past decade and will continue into the next decade. Leisure service organizations will be provided with opportunities to further develop program concepts in this area. The wellness and fitness area is largely a response by the baby-boom generation to concerns about health, appearance, and aging. The fitness area is likely to see further development of the "machine fitness age," with increased emphasis on use of exercise equipment such as computerized stationary bikes and treadmills. Aerobic programs will find new ways to attract individuals and will continue to emphasize low-impact activities. Swimming, water aerobics, and water workouts will increase. Walking and hiking will gain further popularity with an emphasis on interacting with the environment.

Professional Issues

Leisure service programmers must be responsive to a number of emerging professional issues that have a potential impact on the quality of programs and services. Some of these concerns are moral and ethical whereas others are managerial and administrative in nature. Sensitivity to such professional issues can assist the leisure service programmer in responding in an appropriate manner in an environment of great change. Here are the major professional issues relating to leisure service programming.

Accessibility

Accessibility refers to both physical and social access to leisure services that doesn't prevent individuals from participating in leisure opportunities. Work toward the elimination of physical barriers has progressed in the past several decades, although much still needs to be done. The 1990 Americans with Disabilities Act will impact all areas of leisure service programming and delivery. Social barriers are more complex and hence more difficult to remove. Often, individuals misunderstand or distort information, creating a barrier between the leisure service programmer and the customer.

Equity

Equity, as mentioned in Chapter 1, is concerned with whether leisure services are dispersed in a fair manner. Issues of equity require the leisure service programmer to make political, social, and moral judgments. One serious issue of equity is whether individuals are deprived of the opportunity to participate in a leisure service because of the cost. The question becomes how to make fees and charges to programs reasonable so that their impact as a barrier to participation is minimized.

Ethical Behavior

North Americans demand ethical behavior. Integrity, confidentiality, and community citizenship are hallmarks of ethical professional behavior. Customers expect professionals to operate in an objective and honest manner. They also expect that their interactions with professionals be maintained in a confidential fashion. Further, customers expect that professionals exhibit citizenship by participating in the affairs of the community and by contributing to its economic, social, and environmental development and well-being.

Excellence and Innovation

Leisure service professionals are being challenged to operate with excellence. In today's society, people demand quality and also require that professionals pursue their work with a high degree of productivity. To be excellent means that one's work always meets or exceeds the standards established by the profession. Innovation requires forward thinking that is continually creative and focused on the development of new, novel approaches to leisure service delivery. Innovative programmers are not satisfied to maintain the status quo; they are always trying to find better ways to provide services.

Anticipatory Behavior

Because of the rapid changes in product life cycles and economic cycles in North American culture, the effective leisure service programmer will have to engage in anticipatory behavior. Leisure service professionals cannot merely react to changes; they must lead by creating a vision of the future. Anticipation of needs can refer to the needs of the organization or the needs of customers. This process can be bold and visionary, directing the work of the organization, or it can be the routine interactions with customers to make their leisure experience more satisfying and worthwhile.

Development of Human Resources

The majority of leisure programs are delivered by part-time or seasonal staff. The status of such individuals must be elevated so that they receive appropriate orientation, training, and development. Often the lowest-paid individuals are the ones actually delivering the services to the customer. These workers need to be made full partners in the process of meeting the leisure needs of their constituency. Of critical importance is the transference of organizational values, traditions, and expectations for interacting with customers.

Renewal of Infrastructures

To make the leisure experience meaningful and relevant to individuals, the areas, facilities, and other resources must be maintained in a contemporary and up-to-date manner. Many outdated, poorly maintained, and ineffectively designed areas and facilities need to be updated, rebuilt, or augmented. The public leisure service delivery system, in particular, is in great need of renewal.

Accountability

Leisure service programmers are increasingly being held accountable for the use of organizational resources. As resources have become more limited, organizations are requiring individual programmers to demonstrate the benefits derived from involvement in programs and activities. Accountability requires programmers to be responsive and to provide relevant programs and services that meet real needs. The issue of accountability will increase rather than decrease in the future.

Summary

The future will be challenging to leisure service professionals. We live in a period of time in which change is rapid, constant, and pervasive. In order to succeed, leisure service professionals will need to become adept at anticipating and dealing with change. Currently, we are experiencing a major transformation (known as a paradigm shift) in the thinking and behavior of humankind. This shift from the industrial era to the information era will require new approaches to providing leisure services and new ways of meeting and responding to emerging human needs.

A number of major factors will have an impact on the delivery of leisure services in the future. These factors will require a new paradigm for the delivery of leisure services. For example, the public leisure service arena may need to shift from direct service delivery to an enabling of services. Greater skills in marketing and entrepreneurship will be valued in all sectors in which leisure services are created.

Knowledge of trends will be essential for future success. Significant demographic changes are occurring that will influence the delivery of leisure services. The population is becoming older. The family structure is changing dramatically. Technology is influencing the way we communicate with one another as well as our ability to process complex information rapidly and in great volume. The economic environment, emphasizing more service-oriented occupations, is changing the nature of work with the concomitant effects on the way in which leisure is pursued. Leisure is increasingly valued, but time to pursue leisure is declining.

Leisure service programmers will be faced with challenges that affect not only the nature and types of leisure service programs provided, but also the way in which leisure service programmers operate. The future appears to be dynamic and exciting. The challenges of tomorrow will enrich the work of professionals and will also provide opportunities to significantly influence the lives of North Americans.

Discussion Questions and Exercises
---

1. We live in an era of change. What are some of the factors that have contributed to this change?

2. Change can be perceived from several different perspectives. What are they? Provide examples of change that a local leisure service organization has undergone in the last decade.

3. What current paradigm shift is influencing the work of leisure service programmers in North America?

4. Why is there a need to create new programs, services, and institutions as a result of a paradigm shift?

5. Identify ten factors related to change that have a direct impact on leisure service organizations today.

6. How have the events of September 11, 2001 affected leisure and leisure programming? Further, how can recreation and leisure programming help address the issue of terrorism?

7. Identify six strategies and methods that can be used by leisure service programmers in understanding and shaping the future.

8. Identify twenty or more future directions that have a direct impact on leisure programmers and leisure programming.

9. Identify eight or more professional issues that must be addressed by leisure service programmers.

References

Allison, M. T., and I. E. Schneider, 2000. *Diversity and the recreation profession: Organizational perspectives.* State College, PA: Venture.

Bannon, J. 1973. *Outreach: Extending community service in urban areas.* Springfield, IL: Charles C Thomas.

Bennis, W., and B. Nanus. 1985. *Leaders.* New York: Harper and Row.

Brauer, D. G. 1984. Survival in the information era. *Parks and Recreation* 19(5): 58–59.

Bullaro, J. J., and C. R. Edginton. 1986. *Commercial leisure services.* New York: Macmillan.

Calgary Parks and Recreation. 1999. *Multicultural activities.* Calgary, Alberta: Author.

City of Edmonton, Community Service. 2000. *Toward 2010. New perspectives: An integrated service strategy.* Edmonton, Alberta: Author.

Conner, D. R. 1993. *Managing at the speed of change.* New York: Villard Books.

Crossman, J. 2001. Post-attack shifts in tourism are expected to benefit Iowa. *Des Moines Register,* 17 October, 8C.

Daley, R. M. 2002. Chicago invests in citizens. *Parks and Recreation* 37(1): 40–47.

Dieser, R. B., and J. Wilson. 2002. Learning to listen: Cross-ethnic therapeutic recreation delivery. *Parks and Recreation* 37(5): 54–59.

Drucker, P. 1985. *Innovation and entrepreneurship.* New York: Harper and Row.

Edginton, C. R., and W. de Oliveira. 1995. A model of youthwork orientations. *Humanics: The Journal of Leadership for Youth and Human Service* 4(2).

Edginton, C. R., D. J. Jordan, D. G. DeGraaf, and S. R. Edginton. 2002. *Leisure and life satisfaction: Foundational perspectives.* 3rd ed. Boston, MA: McGraw-Hill.

Edginton, C. R., and W. de Oliveira. 1996. Youth development: A program framework. *PERS Review* 1(2).

Edginton, S. R., and C. R. Edginton. 1996. *Youth outreach and service excellence.* Alexandria, VA: U.S. Army Child and Youth Services.

Fearn, M., and C. K. Jarvi. 1992. The recreation and park profession at a crossroad. In *Parks and recreation in the 21st century,* edited by T. A. Mobley and R. F. Toalson. Arlington, VA: National Recreation and Parks Association.

Ferguson, M. 1980. *The aquarian conspiracy.* Los Angeles: Tarcher.

Franklin, B. 1995. *The handbook of children's rights.* London: Routledge.

Godbey, G. 1986. Some selected societal trends and their impact on recreation and leisure. In *A literature review—the President's Commission on American Outdoors.* Washington, DC: Government Printing Office.

Godbey, G. 1997. *Leisure and leisure services in the 21st century.* State College, PA: Venture.

Getchell F. J., and W. K. Beckman. 2000. Are golf courses a water hazard? Meeting the challenge of golf course development. *Parks and Recreation* 35(6): 72–77.

Hallinan, J. T. 2002. 7. Serious fun: In uncertain time, Americans resort to expensive toys. *Wall Street Journal,* 27 August, A1.

Hamilton, E. S. 2002. 9-11: One year later. *Parks and Recreation* 37(7): 44–50.

Hitt, W. D. 1988. *The leader-manager.* Columbus, OH: Battelle Press.

Kanter, R. M. 1983. *The change masters.* New York: Simon and Schuster.

Kelly, J. R. 1991. Commodification and consciousness: An initial study. *Leisure Studies* 10: 7–18.

Kelly, J. R., and V. J. Freysinger. 2000. *21st century leisure: Current issues.* Boston, MA: Allyn & Bacon.

Kraus, R. 2000. *Leisure in a changing America.* 2nd ed. Needham Heights, MA: Allyn & Bacon.

Mobley, T. A., and R. F. Toalson, eds. 1992. *Parks and recreation in the 21st century.* Arlington, VA: National Recreation and Parks Association.

Naisbett, J. 1994. *Global paradox.* New York: Morrow.

Naisbitt, J., and P. Aburdeen. 1985. *Re-inventing the corporation.* New York: Warner.

Ogah, J. K. 2002. Post-9/11: Implications for public health education. *International Journal of Global Health* 1(2): 4–5.

Osborne, D., and T. Gaebler. 1992. *Reinventing government.* New York: Addison Wesley.

Peters, T. 1987. *Thriving on chaos.* New York: Knopf.

Robinson, J. P. 1989. Time's up. *American Demographics* 33(July).

Salwen, P. 2000. Urban recreation: New York City's parks are revamped and rehabilitated. *Parks and Recreation* 35(4): 68–77.

Scott, D. 1993. Time scarcity and its implications for leisure behavior and leisure service delivery. *Journal of Park and Recreation Administration* 11(3).

Searle, M. S., and R. E. Brayley. 2000. *Leisure services in Canada: An introduction.* State College, PA: Venture.

Sheffield, E. 1984. Are you providing multiple-option programming? *Parks and Recreation* 19(5): 56–57.

Tindall, J. P. 1984. Planning with vision: The art and science of futuring. *California Parks and Recreation* 13.

Toalson, R. F. 1992. Where do we go from here? In *Parks and recreation in the 21st century,* edited by T. A. Mobley and R. F. Toalson. Arlington, VA: National Recreation and Parks Association.

Toffler, A. 1980. *The third wave.* New York: Morrow.

U.S. Bureau of the Census. 2000. *Statistical abstract of the United States: The national data book.* Washington, DC: Author.

Wearing, B., and S. Wearing. 1992. Identity and the commodification of leisure. *Leisure Studies* 11: 3–18.

Weston, S. A. 1996. *Commercial recreation and tourism.* Dubuque, IA: Brown & Benchmark.

Wilkinson, G. W., ed. 1989. *What lies ahead.*

World Tourism Organization. 2002. *A year after 9-11: Climbing toward recovery.* Madrid, Spain: Author.

World Travel and Tourism Review 1991. Vol. 1. Wallingford, United Kingdom: CAB International.

YMCA of the USA. 2000. *Societal trends and the YMCA movement.* Chicago, IL: Author.

APPENDIX

KETTERING DEPARTMENT OF PARKS, RECREATION AND CULTURAL ARTS

1994 Citizen Leisure Survey

Interviewer:_____
Date:_____   Day: Tu   W   Th

****
_____

Phone: politely ask for a parent if a child/adolescent answers.
**GOOD EVENING! MY NAME IS {   } WITH THE CITY'S PARKS, RECREATION
AND CULTURAL ARTS DEPARTMENT. WE ARE PHONING SOME OF OUR CITIZENS
TONIGHT ASKING FOR THEIR RESPONSES/OPINIONS TO A SHORT SIX MINUTE
SURVEY. THIS SURVEY WILL HELP US DO A BETTER JOB WITH THE SERVICES
WE ARE OFFERING YOU. YOUR HELP WILL BE GREATLY APPRECIATED!**

****

1. WHAT WOULD YOU CONSIDER YOUR THREE MOST ENJOYABLE PASTIME
ACTIVITIES {THIS MAY INCLUDE RECREATION, CULTURE, OR ARTS}?

A._____   B._____   C._____

1A. {IF OUTSIDE THE HOME}: NAME OF FACILITY?

A._____   B._____   C._____

2. DO YOU REGULARLY PARTICPATE IN FITNESS/EXERCISE PROGRAMS?

YES_____   NO_____   NR_____

{IF YES} WHERE?
_____ AT HOME
_____ AT HEALTH CLUB
_____ COMBINATION

3. HAS ANY MEMBER OF YOUR HOUSEHOLD PARTICIPATED IN ACTIVITIES AT
THE KETTERING RECREATION COMPLEX?
A. {IF YES} WHAT ACTIVITIES?_____

B. {IF YES} DO YOU GENERALLY REGISTER FOR CLASSES OR DROP IN?
REGISTER_____   DROP IN_____

C. {IF REGISTER} ARE YOU SATISFIED WITH THE REGISTRATION PROCESS?
YES_____   NO_____

D. {IF NO} WHY IS THAT?_____

3A. {**IF YES**} OVERALL, ARE YOU SATISFIED WITH THE PRICING SYSTEM FOR ACTIVITIES OFFERED AT THE RECREATION COMPLEX?
YES_____ NO_____

4. DO YOU RECEIVE OUR DEPARTMENT BROCHURE LISTING ALL PROGRAMS AND SERVICES?

YES_____   NO_____

A. {**IF YES**} DOES ANY MEMBER OF YOUR HOUSEHOLD USE THE BROCHURE?
YES_____   NO_____

B.   {**IF   YES**}   HOW   WOULD   YOU   IMPROVE   THE   BROCHURE?
_____
*IF THEY DO NOT RECEIVE THE BROCHURE OFFER TO SEND THEM ONE

5. HOW,THEN,DO YOU OBTAIN INFORMATION ABOUT THE PROGRAMS AND SERVICES BEING OFFERED BY THE DEPARTMENT?

A. CITY'S NEWSLETTER "CONTACT WITH KETTERING"_____
B. SENIOR ADULT NEWSLETTER "ROSEY NEWS"_____
C. FLYERS AND POSTERS_____
D. DAYTON DAILY NEWS_____
E. K-O TIMES_____
F. RADIO_____
G. CABLE TV_____
H. FRIENDS/NEIGHBORS_____
I. DON'T RECIEVE_____
J. OTHER_____
K. NR_____

6. ARE YOU AWARE OF THE DEPARTMENT'S NON-RESIDENT FAIR SHARE POLICY?
YES_____ NO_____

7. WE CHARGE NON-RESIDENTS 100% MORE FOR DAILY ADMISSIONS, 50% MORE FOR A SEASON PASS, AND 25% MORE FOR CLASSES. DO YOU FEEL THAT THIS IS A FAIR INCREASE?

YES_____ NO_____ DK_____
A. {**IF NO**} WHY?_____

8. HAS ANYONE IN YOUR HOUSEHOLD ATTENDED PROGRAMS AT THE FRAZE PAVILION?

YES_____   NO_____ DK_____

A. HOW OFTEN?
WEEKLY_____ MONTHLY_____ OCCASIONALLY_____ NEVER_____
DK_____ NR_____

B. {**IF NO**} WHY?_____

9. HOW DO YOU OBTAIN INFORMATION ABOUT THE PROGRAMS AT THE FRAZE PAVILION?

A. DAYTON DAILY NEWS
B. RADIO
C. CABLE TV
D. FLYERS AND POSTERS
E. FRIENDS/NEIGHBORS
F. CONTACT WITH KETTERING
G. OTHER
G. NR

10. WHAT FRAZE EVENTS ARE YOU PLANNING ON ATTENDING THIS SUMMER?
_____

11. WHAT TYPES OF ENTERTAINMENT WOULD YOU LIKE TO SEE MORE OF AT THE FRAZE?

A.BIG BAND_____   B. COUNTRY_____   C. JAZZ_____   D. DANCE_____
E. COMEDY_____   F. THEATRE_____

12. DO YOU KNOW WHERE THE ROSEWOOD ARTS CENTER IS LOCATED?

YES_____   NO_____   UNSURE_____

13. WERE YOU AWARE THAT THERE IS A FREE ART GALLERY AT ROSEWOOD, OPEN TO THE PUBLIC?

YES_____   NO_____   UNSURE_____

14.HAVE YOU OR ANY MEMBERS OF YOUR FAMILY TAKEN OR ATTENDED ANY CLASSES AT ROSEWOOD?

YES_____   NO_____   DK_____   NR_____

14A. IF NO, WHY?_____

15. HOW OFTEN DO YOU USE KETTERING'S PARKS?

ALMOST   DAILY_____   ABOUT   WEEKLY_____   ABOUT   MONTHLY_____
OCCASIONALLY_____   NEVER_____   NR_____   DK_____

16. GIVEN A SCALE OF 0-10, HOW IMPORTANT IS PRESERVING DELCO PARK TO YOU AND MEMBERS OF YOUR FAMILY?_____

16A. IF RANKED 0-3, WHY?

17. WERE YOU AWARE THAT GENERAL MOTORS IS SELLING EXCESS PROPERTY WORLDWIDE, INCLUDING DELCO PARK?

YES_____   NO_____   NR_____

18. BASED ON OUR ESTIMATE TO PURCHASE DELCO PARK, IT WOULD COST $5.50 PER YEAR FOR 20 YEARS. WOULD YOU BE WILLING TO SUPPORT THAT? THIS ESTIMATE IS BASED ON A HOUSE VALUE OF $100,000+.

YES_____   NO_____   NR_____   DK_____

19. IF THE CITY HAD A PAVED WALKING/BIKING TRAIL SYSTEM THAT CONNECTED SEVERAL SHOPPING CENTERS, SCHOOLS, AND PARKS; AND PROVIDED NATURAL GREEN CORRIDORS THROUGH THE CITY: HOW OFTEN WOULD ANY MEMBER OF YOUR FAMILY USE SUCH A TRAIL?

ALMOST DAILY_____ ABOUT WEEKLY_____ ABOUT MONTHLY_____ OCCASIONALLY____
NEVER_____   DK_____   NR_____

20. HOW MANY MEMBERS OF YOUR HOUSEHOLD RIDE A BIKE 5 TIMES OR MORE PER YEAR?

0____ 1____ 2_____ 3_____ 4+_____   DK_____   NR_____

21. DO YOU HAVE ANY SUGGESTIONS AS TO HOW WE SHOULD IMPROVE ANY DEPARTMENT SERVICES?_____
21A. ARE THERE ANY FACILITIES THAT YOU WOULD LIKE TO SEE ESTABLISHED FOR FUTURE USE?_____

22. FROM THE FOLLOWING AGE CATEGORIES, PLEASE INDICATE WHICH ONE YOU BELONG TO:

　　24-_____   25-44_____   45-54_____   65+_____

23. HOW MANY CHILDREN UNDER THE AGE OF 18 DO YOU HAVE AT HOME?

1_____   2_____   3_____   4+_____

THAT'S ALL! THANK YOU VERY MUCH FOR YOUR TIME!!
OBSERVED

2   GENDER: M_____ F_____

CREDITS

Chapter 1:

Chapter Opener: © Brand X Pictures
Fig 1.1: Carnaval de Québec, Quebec City, Quebec, Canada
Fig 1.2: Department of Recreation, City of St. John's, Newfoundland, Canada
Fig 1.3: Des Moines Register
Fig 1.4: From J.J. Bullaro and Cr. Edginton, *Commercial Leisure Services.* Copyright 1986 Allyn and Bacon. Reprinted by permission.
Fig. 1.5: Department of Parks and Recreation, Virginia Beach, Virginia
Fig. 1.6: Lake County Forest Preserves, Libertyville, Illinois
Fig. 1.7: From YMCA of the USA, Chicago, IL. Reprinted by permission.
Fig. 1.8: Morale Welfare Recreation Department, U.S. Marine Corps, Okinawa, Japan
Fig. 1.9: Morale Welfare Recreation Department, U.S. Marine Corps, Okinawa, Japan
Fig. 1.10: From Anaheim Community Services Department, Anaheim, CA. Reprinted by permission.

Chapter 2:

Chapter Opener: © Brand X Pictures
Fig. 2.1: From City Park Pueblo Zoo, Pueblo, CO. Illustration by Richard Montano (RM Studios). Reprinted by permission.
Fig. 2.6: From J. R. Murphy and R. F. Dahl, The Right to Leisure Expression in *Parks and Recreation,* September 1991, pp 106–107. National Recreation and Park Association, Arlington, VA. Reprinted by permission.

Chapter 3:

Chapter Opener: Author provided
Fig. 3.1: National Recreation and Parks Association, Reston, Virginia
Fig. 3.2: From Paul Hersey and Kenneth H. Blanchard, *Management of Organizational Behavior,* 3rd edition, 1977. Reprinted with permission from the Center for Leadership Studies. Situational Leadership™ is a registered trademark of the Center for Leadership Studies, Escondido, California.
Fig. 3.4: From Fred E. Fiedler, *A Theory of Leadership Effectiveness,* 1976, McGraw-Hill, Inc. Reprinted by permission of Fred E. Fiedler.
Fig 3.5, 3.6: From Paul Hersey and Kenneth Blanchard, *Management of Organizational Behavior,* 3rd edition, 1977. Reprinted with permission from the Center for Leadership Studies. Situational Leadership™ is a registered trademark of the Center for Leadership Studies, Escondido, California.

Fig. 3.7: From W.D. Hitt, *The Leadership Manager,* 1988. Copyright © Battelle Press, Columbus, OH. Reprinted by permission.

Chapter 4:

Chapter Opener: © Brand X Pictures
Fig. 4.2: From *Human Development: The Span of Life,* 3rd edition, by Kaluger/Kaluger, © 1984. Reprinted by permission of Prentice-Hall, Inc., Upper Saddle River, NJ).
Fig. 4.3: From City of Long Beach, California, Department of Parks, Recreation and Marine. Reprinted by permission.
Fig. 4.4: From Seppo E. Iso-Ahola, *The Social Psychology of Leisure and Recreation.* Copyright © 1980 Times Mirror Higher Education Group, Inc., Dubuque, Iowa. All Rights Reserved. Reprinted by permission.

Chapter 5:

Chapter Opener: © Brand X Pictures
Fig. 5.1: From D. I. Stufflebeam, *Meta-Evaluation,* 1974. The Evaluation Center, Kalamazoo, MI. Reprinted by permission.
Fig. 5.3: From Metropolitan Park and Recreation District, Bend, OR. Reprinted by permission.
Fig. 5.4: Morale Welfare Recreation Department, U.S. Marine Corps, Okinawa, Japan Reprinted by permission.
Exhibit 5.2: The City of Edmonton Community Services, Edmonton, Alberta, Canada Reprinted by permission.
Fig 5.6: From *Working With People: The Helping Process,* 5th Edition by Naomi I. Brill. Copyright © 1995, 1990, 1985, 1978, 1973 by Longman Publishers U.S.A. Reprinted by permission of Addison Wesley Educational Publishers Inc.

Chapter 6:

Chapter Opener: © Brand X Pictures
Fig 6.1: From *Camp Adventure™ Youth Services,* University of Northern Iowa, Cedar Falls, Iowa. Reprinted by permission.
Fig. 6.2: From City of Long Beach, California, Department of Parks, Recreation and Marine. Reprinted by permission.
Fig 6.3: From BCI Burke, Fond du Lac, Wisconsin. Reprinted by permission.
Fig. 6.4: From *Camp Adventure™ Youth Services,* University of Northern Iowa, Cedar Falls, Iowa. Reprinted by permission.
Fig. 6.5: From Cincinnati Recreation Commission, Ohio. Reprinted by permission.
Fig. 6.6: From Cincinnati Recreation Commission, Ohio. Reprinted by permission.

Fig. 9.13: From Morale Welfare Recreation Department, U.S. Marine Corps, Okinawa, Japan. Reprinted by permission.
Fig. 9.14: From the City of Edmonton Community Services, Edmonton, Alberta, Canada. Reprinted by permission.
Fig. 9.15: From Champaign Park District, Champaign, IL. Reprinted by permission.
Fig. 9.16: From Morale Welfare Recreation Department, U.S. Marine Corps, Okinawa, Japan. Reprinted by permission.
Fig. 9.17: From City of Kettering Parks, Recreation and Cultural Arts Department, Kettering, OH. Illustration © Dynamic Graphics, Inc. Reprinted by permission.
Fig. 9.18: From Santa Clara County Parks, California and Silicon Valley Parks Foundation. Reprinted by permission.
Fig. 9.19: From Department of Parks and Recreation, Virginia Beach, Virginia. Reprinted by permission.
Fig. 9.20: From Indy Parks and Recreation, Indianapolis, IN. Reprinted by permission.

Chapter 10:
Chapter Opener: © PhotoDisc/Getty Images
Fig. 10.2: From Katrine Fitzgerald Ryan, "Getting the Word Out to the Media Through News Releases and News Advisories" in *Voluntary Action Leadership,* Summer 1988, published by Points of Light Foundation, Washington, D.C.
Fig. 10.3: From Department of Parks, Recreation and Marine, City of Long Beach, California. Reprinted by permission.
Fig. 10.4: From Lake County Forest Preserves, Libertyville, Illinois. Reprinted by permission.
Fig. 10.5: From Morale Welfare Recreation Department, U.S. Marine Corps, Okinawa, Japan. Reprinted by permission.
Fig. 10.6: From *Eugene Register Guard,* 1990, Eugene, OR. Reprinted by permission.
Fig. 10.7: From *Eugene Register Guard,* 1990, Eugene, OR. Reprinted by permission.
Fig. 10.8: Courtesy of the Waterloo-Cedar Falls Courier, Waterloo, IA.
Fig. 10.9: From Department of Parks, Recreation and Marine, City of Long Beach, California. Reprinted by permission.
Fig. 10.10: From Santa Cruz Beach Boardwalk, Santa Cruz, CA. Reprinted by permission.
Fig. 10.11: From Black Hawk County Conservation, Iowa. Reprinted by permission.
Fig. 10.12: The Glacier Institute, Glacier National Park, Kalispell, Montana. Reprinted by permission.
Fig. 10.13: From The City of West Des Moines Parks and Recreation Department, West Des Moines, Iowa. Reprinted by permission.
Fig. 10.14: From Community Services, Edmonton Alberta, Canada. Reprinted by permission.
Fig. 10.15: From Girl Scouts of the U.S.A.-Mile Hi Council, Denver, Colorado. Reprinted by permission.
Fig. 10.16: Courtesy of Department of Natural Resources, State of Iowa. Reprinted by permission.

Fig. 10.17: From Hickman AFB, Honolulu, Hawaii. Reprinted by permission.
Fig. 10.18: From Parks and Recreation, St. Louis County Parks, Missouri. Reprinted by permission.
Fig. 10.19: From *Camp Adventure™ Youth Services,* University of Northern Iowa, Cedar Falls, Iowa. Reprinted by permission.
Fig. 10.20: From Lake County Forest Preserves, Libertyville, Illinois. Reprinted by permission.
Fig. 10.21: Parks, Recreation and Neighborhood Services, City of San Jose, California. Reprinted by permission.
Fig. 10.22: From Joliet Park District, Joliet, IL. Reprinted by permission.
Fig. 10.23: Courtesy of Hennepin Parks, Plymouth, MN. Reprinted by permission.
Fig. 10.24: From Lane County Ice Arena, Eugene, OR. Reprinted by permission.
Fig. 10.25: From Department of Parks, Recreation and Marine, City of Long Beach, California. Reprinted by permission.
Fig. 10.26: From Parks Board and Recreation Commission, Town of Clarkstown, New York. Reprinted by permission.
Fig. 10.27: From Department of Parks and Recreation, Virginia Beach, Virginia. Reprinted by permission.
Fig. 10.28: From Department of Parks, Recreation and Marine, City of Long Beach, California. Reprinted by permission.
Fig. 10.29: From Northern Suburban Special Recreation Association, Northbrook, Illinois. Reprinted by permission.
Fig. 10.30: From Alexandria Department of Recreation, Parks and Cultural Activities, Alexandria, VA. Reprinted by permission.
Fig. 10.31: From Department of Parks and Recreation, Virginia Beach, Virginia. Reprinted by permission.
Fig. 10.32: From City of Aurora Parks—Library, Recreation and Television Services, Aurora, CO. Reprinted by permission.
Fig. 10.33: Parks and Community Services Department, Ft. Worth, Texas. Reprinted by permission.

Chapter 11:
Chapter Opener: David Frazier, Photo Library
Fig. 11.1: Parks and Community Services Department, Ft. Worth, Texas
Fig. 11.2: From Crestwood Department of Parks and Recreation, Crestwood, MO. Reprinted by permission.
Fig. 11.3: From Indy Parks and Recreation, Indianapolis, IN. Reprinted by permission.
Fig. 11.4: From Foothills Metropolitan Recreation and Park District, Lakewood, CO. Reprinted by permission.
Fig. 11.5: From Indanola Parks & Recreation, Indanola, IA. Reprinted by permission.
Fig. 11.6: From East Bay Regional Park District, Oakland, CA. Reprinted by permission.
Fig. 11.7: From R. Hurd, "Paths to Leisure" presentation at NRPA Conference, October 2002.

Fig. 11.9: From City of Long Beach, California, Department of Parks, Recreation and Marine. Reprinted by permission.
Fig. 11.10: From Black Hawk County Conservation Board, Black Hawk County, IA. Reprinted by permission.
Fig. 11.11: From City of Long Beach, California, Department of Parks, Recreation and Marine. Reprinted by permission.
Fig. 11.12: From City of Thunder Bay Parks & Recreation, Thunder Bay, Ontario, Canada. Reprinted by permission.
Fig. 11.13: From Morale Welfare Recreation Department, U.S. Marine Corps, Okinawa, Japan. Reprinted by permission.
Fig. 11.14: From Detroit Recreation Department, Detroit, MI. Design by Kim Waits. Reprinted by permission.
Fig. 11.15: From Detroit Recreation Department, Detroit, MI. Reprinted by permission.
Fig. 11.16: Reprinted by permission of Horizon Air, Seattle, WA.
Fig. 11.17: From Willamalane Park and Recreation District, Springfield, OR. Reprinted by permission.
Fig. 11.18: From City of Aurora—Library, Recreation and Television Services, Aurora, CO. Reprinted by permission.
Fig. 11.19: Chart from *Managerial Finance*, sixth edition by J. Fred Weston and Eugene F. Brigham, copyright © 1978 by the Dryden Press, reprinted by permission of the publisher.

Chapter 12:
Chapter 12 Opener: Author provided.
Fig. 12.1: Courtesy of Missouri Department of Natural Resources, State of Missouri. Reprinted by permission.
Fig. 12.2: Adapted from Morgan (1996) as cited by O'Neil, M. (2001), Measuring service quality and customer satisfaction. In J. Kandampully, C. Mok, & B. Sparks (eds.), *Service quality management in hospitality, tourism, and leisure* (pp. 159–192). New York: Haworth press.
Fig. 12.3: National Program for Playground Safety, University of Northern Iowa, Cedar Falls, Iowa. Reprinted by permission.
Fig. 12.4: From Roselle Park District, Roselle, Illinois. Reprinted by permission.
Fig. 12.5: From Willamalane Park and Recreation District, Springfield, OR. Reprinted by permission.
Fig. 12.6: From Phyllis M. Ford, *Informal Recreational Activities: A Leader's Guide*, 1974, American Camping Association, Inc. Reprinted by permission of Phyllis M. Ford.
Fig 12.7: Adapted from Csikszenthmihalyi, M. (1997). Finding flow: *The Psychology of engagement with everyday life*, New York; Basic Books.
Fig. 12. 8: From Indianola Parks and Recreation, Indianola, IA. Reprinted by permission.
Fig. 12.9: From Burnaby Parks and Recreation Department, Burnaby, British Columbia, Canada. Reprinted by permission.
Fig. 12.11: From Central Oregon Parks and Recreation District, Redmond, OR. Reprinted by permission.
Fig. 12.12: From Willamalane Park and Recreation District, Springfield, OR, Reprinted by permission.

Fig. 12.13: From Greeley Parks & Recreation Department, Greeley, CO, Reprinted by permission.
Fig. 12.14: Morale Welfare Recreation Department, U.S. Marine Corps, Okinawa, Japan
Fig. 12.15: From Indy Parks and Recreation, Indianapolis, IN. Reprinted by permission.

Chapter 13:
Chapter Opener: © Digital Vision
Fig. 13.1: From D. L. Stufflebeam, *Meta-Evaluation*, 1974. The evaluation Center, Kalamazoo, MI. Reprinted by permission.
Fig. 13.2: From Boy Scouts of America, Irving, Texas. Reprinted by permission.
Fig. 13.3: From Parks & Recreation, City of Westerville, Ohio. Reprinted by permission.
Fig. 13.4: Department of Parks and Recreation, Virginia Beach, Virginia. Reprinted by permission.
Fig. 13.6: From A. H. Mittelestat and H. A. Berger, "The Critical Path Method: A Management Tool for Recreation" in *Parks & Recreation*, 8(7) 14-15. Reprinted from the August 1972 issue of *Parks & Recreation* by special permission of the National Recreation and Parks Association.
Fig. 13.7: From J. R. Rossman, *Recreation Programming: Designing Leisure Experience*, 2nd edition. Copyright © 1995 Sagamore Publishing, Champaign IL. Reprinted by permission.
Fig. 13.8: From City of Long Beach, California, Department of Parks, Recreation and Marine. Reprinted by permission.
Fig. 13.9: From Foothills Metropolitan Recreation and Park District, Lakewood, CO. Reprinted by permission.
Fig. 13.10: From City of Aurora Parks—Library, Recreation and Television Services, Aurora, CO. Reprinted by permission.
Fig. 13.12: From Anaheim Community Services Department, Anaheim, CA. Reprinted by permission.
Fig. 13.13: © 1996 Elmhurst Park District, DuPage County, IL. Reprinted by permission.

Chapter 14:
Chapter Opener: © PhotoDisc/Getty Images
Fig. 14.1: From Godbey, *Journal of Parks and Recreation Administration*, 3:1–13, 1985. Copyright © 1985 Sagamore Publishing, Champaign, IL. Reprinted by permission.
Fig. 14.2: From the City of Edmonton Community Services, Edmonton, Alberta, Canada. Reprinted by permission.
Fig. 14.3: From the City of Edmonton Community Services, Edmonton, Alberta, Canada. Reprinted by permission.
Fig. 14.4: From the City of Edmonton Community Services, Edmonton, Alberta, Canada. Reprinted by permission.
Fig. 14.6: Mundy (1998)
Fig. 14.7: Berryman and Lefebvre (1995)
Fig. 14.8: Peterson & Stumbo, 2000.
Fig. 14.9: From Department of Recreation Management and Therapeutic Recreation, University of Wisconsin-La Crosse. Reprinted by permission.

Name Index

SUBJECT INDEX